CLASSICAL AND CONTEMPORARY ITALIAN COOKING

— FOR — PROFESSIONALS

Crescenza, Gorgonzola,
Grana Lodigiano, Mascarpone,
Pannerone, Quartirolo, Robiola,
Stracchino, Taleggio

Fontina
Toma

Castelmagno
Toma
Tomini
Robiola

Caciotta
Canestrato
Pecorino Toscano
Raveggiolo
Ricotta
Toscanello

Pecorino Umbro

Fiore Molle
Pecorino Romano
Provatura
Ricotta

Burrino
Caciocavallo
Mozzarella
Provolone
Ricotta
Scamorza

Crotonese
Moliterno

Caciotta
Dolce Sardo
Fiore Sardo
Pecorino Romano
Raveggiolo

Montasio

Asiago
Casatella

Casatella
Grana Padano
Grana Piacentino
Parmigiano Reggiano
Raveggiolo

Raveggiolo
Caciotta

Fior di Latte
Scamorza

Burrata, Caciotta
Foggiano
Pecorino Foggiano
Ricotta

Crotonese

Pecorino Siciliano
Ragusano
Ricotta

VALLE
D'AOSTA
TRENTINO-
ALTO ADIGE
FRIULI-
VENEZIA
GIULIA
LOMBARDIA
PIEMONTE
VENETO
LIGURIA
EMILIA-
ROMAGNA
TOSCANA
MARCHE
UMBRIA
LAZIO
ABBRUZZO
AND
MOLISE
PUGLIA
CAMPANIA
BASILICATA
CALABRIA
SARDEGNA
SICILIA

The cheeses of Italy by region. *Courtesy of the Italian Trade Commission.*

CLASSICAL AND CONTEMPORARY ITALIAN COOKING

— FOR — PROFESSIONALS

Bruno H. Ellmer, C.M.C.

VNR VAN NOSTRAND REINHOLD
New York

Copyright © 1990 by Van Nostrand Reinhold

Library of Congress Catalog Card Number 88-33907
ISBN 0-442-20642-9

Printed in the United States of America
Designed by Keano Design Studio

Van Nostrand Reinhold
115 Fifth Avenue
New York, New York 10003

Van Nostrand Reinhold International Company Limited
11 New Fetter Lane
London EC4P 4EE, England

Van Nostrand Reinhold
480 La Trobe Street
Melbourne, Victoria 3000, Australia

Nelson Canada
1120 Birchmount Road
Scarborough, Ontario
Canada M1K 5G4

16 15 14 13 12 11 10 9 8 7 6 5 4 3 2 1

Library of Congress Cataloging in Publication Data

Ellmer, Bruno H., 1929–
  Classical and contemporary Italian cooking for professionals.
  Includes index.
  1. Cookery, Italian. I. Title.
TX723.E44 1990   641.5945
ISBN 0-442-20642-9   88-33907
                                                          CIP

Contents

Recipes

Uova / Eggs   137

Pasta   145

Riso e Risotto, Polenta e Gnocchi /
Rice and Risotto, Polenta and Gnocchi

Foreword

We meet many people throughout our lives, but only rarely are we fortunate enough to come into contact with a particularly extraordinary individual who broadens our consciousness and thus subtly alters the way we think and live. Bruno H. Ellmer is just such a person, and meeting and working with him has been a privilege.

Bruno Ellmer was born near Salzburg, Austria, to parents who owned a general store and wholesale cheese business. He began working with them at an early age, and though the work was hard, it prepared him for a life devoted to the culinary arts.

At the age of fifteen, Bruno Ellmer studied for two terms at an Austrian hotel school and then apprenticed with a woman chef whom he remembers as being very strict but extremely knowledgeable. His subsequent employment included stays at Schloss Hotel Moenchstein and the famous Goldener Hirsch in Salzburg, Austria, as well as some of the finest hotels and restaurants in Europe, Canada, the United States, and the Middle East. His first job at the Ritz–Carlton Hotel in Montreal led to a position as Head Chef at the exclusive Montefiore Club. Later, at Intercontinental Hotels, he was responsible for royal banquets in Amman, Jordan. He also helped prepare a 1976 Bicentennial dinner for Britain's Queen Elizabeth in Boston.

Bruno Ellmer has been a Chef-Instructor at the Culinary Institute of America (C.I.A.) since 1967, where he has continued to refine his culinary prowess. In 1973, he was awarded the Escoffier Chair. In addition to capturing a team gold medal with the U.S. Culinary Olympic Team in 1976, he received two individual gold medals and the coveted silver trophy from the Société Mutualiste des Cuisiniers de Paris, awarded to the chef with the most outstanding platter of the show. In that same year, he also received the Goldene Ehrennadel (Golden Honor Needle) from the Austrian Chefs Association.

Today, Bruno Ellmer still teaches at the C.I.A. as zealously as he has for the past twenty-two years, helping students to understand the flavors, textures, and nutritive values of the food they handle. He relaxes while reading and gardening, but otherwise fully devotes himself to teaching his well-practiced craft.

—DANIEL B. TOOKER

Preface

Italian cuisine, although respectably treated in the past, has never been adequately approached in such a way as to offer concrete material applicable to a professional English-speaking kitchen. The recipes contained herein reflect my desire to make this material available. The culinary arts have been valued throughout history as one of the most befitting aspects of our social nature. Fine dining has always allowed people to bask in their own fortune and intelligence and is much more than a combination of cooked ingredients. The presentation of the food and the anticipation of better things to come also play key roles in the enjoyment of fine cuisine.

Nutrition also is a significant aspect of fine dining today. Despite the security that results from living in a wealthy, technologically advanced society, faulty eating habits and the preponderance of chemically adulterated and refined foods are largely responsible for many of the illnesses that continue to plague mankind. A true diet cannot be based merely on caloric intake but must take into account the natural elements that sustain life. One of the keys to maintaining health is an understanding of the composition of the raw foods we eat, as well as what takes place during cooking. Anyone perceiving the sacred beauty inherent in God's creation will not abuse the natural qualities contained therein.

We are experiencing a culinary rejuvenation in the Western Hemisphere and with it comes more enthusiasm for maintaining a healthy, nutritious cuisine. The changing attitudes of many of Italy's most prominent chefs meet today's diners' desire for balanced, healthy meals. This awareness of healthful cooking, however, will in no way affect the traditional ingredients used in many of Italy's most popular dishes. Changes instead involve the addition of less familiar ingredients as they become more readily available and, on occasion, smaller portion sizes and revised meal structures. Traditional cuisines will always exist, but it is important not to revere tradition at the expense of health. Rather than mindlessly insisting that tradition remain sacrosanct, we must consider its effects and concentrate on improving the quality of the food we consume. Italian cuisine, like every cuisine, has its distinct foundations upon which we can build to achieve desired results. It is an absolute necessity for the professional chef to be aware of modern preparation methods and food preferences, adjusting ingredients and techniques to satisfy the needs of today's diners.

Acknowledgments

This book, of which I am extremely proud, is based on experience and knowledge garnered over the last forty-five years. I hope this comforts rather than intimidates those who choose to use this book. But, ironically, what intimidated me about this project was not the task involved, but rather adequately expressing my knowledge. For assisting me in overcoming this barrier, I must thank Daniel B. Tooker. I have encountered many people in the food industry, and most, like myself, came early to the profession. Daniel's recent decision to embark on a career in the culinary arts (after pursuing a Ph.D. and teaching for eight years) is as responsible for this book as anything. His intelligence, knowledge, and considerable skills have made possible my task of collecting the following ideas into a coherent and workable text. In addition to making this work readable while typing and editing the manuscript, Daniel contributed many of the ideas and comments contained herein. I can only hope that the long hours that we devoted to this work together have rewarded him in some way. He certainly has rewarded me.

I also wish to thank Walter Schreyer, whose pastry contributions were indispensable, as was Hedy Gold's work with the Italian translations. In addition, I thank Fred von Husen for his ideas about *zampone* and Linda T. UpdeGraff for her assistance with the custom photographs.

The Italian Trade Commission in New York City and The Green House of Encinitas, California, most graciously allowed me to use material I requested.

For her patience, understanding, and contributions to some of the hot dessert recipes, I must also thank my lovely wife, Wilhelmine.

Introduction

The peninsula of land now known as Italy, surrounded on three sides by the Mediterranean and bounded on the north by the Alps, has had a long, well-documented history. For centuries this land was composed of individual, mostly autonomous provinces noted for their great cities and cultural contributions. In the mid–nineteenth century, most of the regions of present-day Italy were united into one country for the first time. Other minor political changes since then have given us the Italy recognizable by its bootlike shape.

The beginnings of Italian cuisine preceded this unification by more than twenty centuries, and strong regional differences are still evident today. We tend to think of the original Italians as Romans, when in fact the peninsula's earliest inhabitants settled there over 1,000 years before Rome was founded. These people traded with the Celts to the north and the Phoenicians to the east and south. Later, in about 800 B.C., the Etruscans (from which the province name is derived) settled in the areas around present-day Tuscany, and the Greeks colonized the coastal regions in the south, including Sicily. Both of these peoples arrived in Italy from the east: the Greeks from neighboring mainland Greece and its islands, and the Etruscans from the area described by Herodotus as Lydia in Asia Minor. These people remained essentially separated by language and geographic barriers, though the Etruscans did admire the artistic and cultural facets of Greek civilization. Interestingly, Italy has long experienced a north/south division, usually furthered by waves of occupations and conquerors.

Originally the staple diet consisted of pastelike grain mixtures called *puls* and later *pulmentum*. This porridge today remains a part of Italian cuisine, as polenta. The Greeks introduced viticulture and the olive and extensively farmed the rich coastline. The Romans were content with inheriting the best of these two cultures and did little to alter the Italian diet. (Subsequent occupations also followed this trend of borrowing rather than bequeathing). They did develop a passion for spices, especially pepper, and found new trade routes to the east to obtain them. While the rich were feasting on foods brought from all corners of the empire, the balance of the populace was content with subsidized grain allotments from which their grain pastes were made. Unfortunately for imperial Rome, a satisfactory way of feeding and financing the vast Roman legions was never really instituted, and the great empire eventually succumbed to (or, more accurately, allowed for) the waves of barbarian invasions of the fourth, fifth, and six centuries. The first Western cookbook to survive into our time was written by a Roman named Apicius, and in it frequent reference was made to a Roman general named Lucullus, who was purported to be quite a gourmet in the century before Christ.

Though the barbarians from the north and east had little impact on Italian eating habits, another group of settlers from the east did. Arabs, via Spain, were responsible for introducing rice, sugar, and a vast assortment of spices to Italian cuisine. Arab occupation did not completely end until the eleventh century, and Arab influence continued through the thirteenth century as crusading Italians brought back even more Levantine riches. Throughout the Middle Ages, the regional aspects of Italian cuisine strengthened with the lack of any centralized government. The only stabilizing force of the time was the church, both Orthodox and Roman Catholic, and many of the developments found in the diet of the time can be traced to the monasteries, where advances in bread and wine making as well as vegetable cultivation were being made.

By the time of the celebrated marriage of Caterina de' Medici to Henry II of France in the sixteenth century, Italian cuisine was one of the most developed in the world. Fancy sauces, extensive cooking techniques made possible by technological advances during the Renaissance, and continued development of plant and animal cultivation all made for a rich cuisine. The Italians were cultivating cabbages such as cauliflower, broccoli, and broccoli rabe, showing their great propensity for adapting foodstuffs to their particular needs. This coincided with yet another major impact on Italian cooking. At about this time many of the foods discovered in the Western Hemisphere were reaching the populace of the countries that had discovered them. Italians were becoming familiar with tomatoes, corn (maize), peppers *(Capsicum)*, potatoes, squash, turkey, cocoa, and vanilla. The spices that had so long eluded the average household were more readily available with the discovery of new sea routes to the east and west. The art of cooking was being transformed throughout Europe as more advanced cooking methods and a greater availability of raw materials became the norm. Today Italy has joined in the growing world-wide demand that the best cooking techniques and raw materials be used in food preparation. The most outstanding individual attributes of her traditional regional cuisines are being combined with this recent development.

BASIC INGREDIENTS AND PREPARATIONS

—— *Erbe e Spezie* ——
HERBS AND SPICES

The importance of herbs, as well as fruits and vegetables, has been recognized since prehistoric times. Early man discovered the beneficial properties of these important substances as antibiotics, painkillers, narcotics, and stimulants. These people understood intuitively the preventive and curative natures of various indigenous herbs and spices and became the world's first healers. Herbs are mentioned in almost all surviving ancient written records, including the Bible, testifying to their importance within all societies. The prophet Ezekiel said, "Fruit [of the tree] will be for food, and [the] leaves for healing." Later, the apostle Paul advised the weak to eat herbs. Even Hippocrates, who transformed the art of healing into the discipline of medicine, gave the world an everlasting proclamation on herbal remedies. The struggle for the acquisition of these herbs and spices and their use in trade became a major factor in the development of nations.

Why have we always valued herbs and spices? Is it because of the seemingly magical effects they have on the human system, or is it because we have become addicted to the flavors they contribute to our food? Whatever the reason, herbs have played a significant role in the course of human development.

Italian cuisine also owes a great debt to herbs and spices. During the fifteenth century, the western-regulated spice trade fell into disorder. The Mongols, who controlled many of the specific land routes to the east, were superseded by the expanding Ottoman empire. Turkish rule stretched from Asia Minor to the Middle East, toppling the once great Byzantine empire as well as penetrating southeastern Europe. The trade routes to and from the east were virtually paralyzed.

Consequently the search for new spice routes began, led primarily by the great seafaring powers of Europe. The Portuguese successfully reached Africa and India, and the Spanish (led initially by their Italian captain, Columbus) discovered the New World. Following the conquests of Mexico by Hernando Cortés and Peru by Francisco Pizarro in the sixteenth century, exotic new fruits and vegetables reached the royal courts of Europe, eventually changing the taste preferences of the masses and initiating a major culinary revolution. Such foods as Indian corn (maize), tomatoes, chili peppers, potatoes, pineapples, avocados, peanuts, cocoa, and vanilla changed forever the diets of the

Europeans. It would be difficult to imagine Italian cuisine without tomatoes for rich sauces, corn for polenta, potatoes and various sweet and hot peppers, or chocolate or vanilla in pastries. It was the search for spices that served as the impetus for discovering the New World and expanding European cuisines.

COOKING WITH HERBS AND SPICES

No exact specifications govern the application of seasonings other than individual discrimination and appreciation of taste. There is no harm done by eating unseasoned food. Seasoning with compatible aromatics contributes more than sensual enjoyment: it stimulates the appetite and enhances the nutritive value of the food consumed. The art of seasoning requires skill—and requires the use of only the freshest of herbs. Dried herbs have lost their essential oils and thus much of their flavoring ability. Even the flavors of fresh herbs, if cooked too long, will change. **Any herb called for as an ingredient in this book is intended to be fresh.** Color plate 1 shows the fresh herbs most frequently used in Italian cuisine.

Occasionally dishes are flavored with herbs and spices that must be removed before serving; this is often the case with smooth sauces and clear stocks and broths. To facilitate removing the herbs and spices after their flavors have been infused into the dish, a spice sachet or a *bouquet garni* can be used. A spice sachet is a blend of herbs and spices tied together in a small cheesecloth bag. Parsley stems are usually included to keep the bag open so that liquid can freely pass through the bag and come into contact with the chosen aromatics. A *bouquet garni* is a bouquet of fresh herbs tied together with butcher's twine. Parsley stems, thyme, and bay leaves are usually included, but a variety of aromatics, such as tarragon, rosemary, basil, fennel, garlic, and celery can be added as well. A *bouquet garni* can also be made of vegetables tied together with butcher's twine. Leeks, carrots, celery, onions, and sometimes cabbage are used. A vegetable *bouquet garni* is very often added to braised meats, stews, or soups to enhance their flavor.

FRESH HERBS FOR CULINARY USE

Angelica: A green, stalklike plant related to parsley that grows wild in mountainous regions, angelica is grown in Europe and the United States. Fresh sprigs are often candied and used in cake decoration and preserves.

Basil (*Basilico*): A member of the mint family, basil has large leaves that are sharply pointed, green to olive-green, and very sensitive to cold. Basil has traditionally been associated with royalty; its name stems from the Greek *basileus,* which means "king." It has a pleasant, sweet, pungent aroma. A major herb in Italian cuisine, basil is essential for *pesto* and various minestrone soups. It is compatible with all tomato-based dishes, pasta, lamb, seafood, and egg dishes.

Chervil (*Cerfoglio*): Chervil is a parsleylike herb with small curly leaves. It has a very pungent aroma, similar to licorice. Used in classic French cooking, it is also found in northwestern Italian soups, sauces, dressings, and egg dishes.

Chives (*Porrini*): A perennial, green grasslike plant belonging to the lily (onion and leek) family, chives have a sweet garlic-accented aroma. This sturdy plant grows wild in abundance in early spring. Finely chopped, it is used for garnishing soups, sauces, salads, and egg dishes.

Marjoram (*Maggiorana*): A low-growing, small-leafed shrublike plant that is part of the mint family, marjoram is pleasantly sweet and highly aromatic. It is often used in northeastern Italy, where the Austrian influence on cooking is still strong; it is a must for goulash dishes, lamb, soups, stews, and potato dishes.

Mint (*Menta*): Many varieties of mint are used in cooking, with coloration ranging from very green to purple. Peppermint and spearmint are perhaps the best known. A dominant herb in the cuisines of the Middle East, the Balkans, England, and southern Italy, mint is used in soups, sauces, tomato-based dishes, and beverages. Peppermint is also used in some liqueurs.

Oregano (*Origano*): Called wild marjoram, oregano's taste is similar to that of marjoram but more pungent. It is grown in the Balkans, southern Europe, the United States, and Mexico. A perennial herb with leaves a little larger than those of marjoram, it is a major herb in Italian cuisine. Oregano is very compatible with all tomato-based dishes, stews, roasts, soups, sauces, and pasta.

Parsley (*Prezzemolo*): Hardy biennials, the parsleys used in cooking are of several species. The most widely known are curly parsley and broadleaf Italian parsley. The Hamburg parsley or root parsley is preferred in central Europe. The broadleaf Italian parsley is most useful for soups, sauces, stews, and pastas. Curly parsley is used in Italian cooking primarily chopped or whole as a garnish. The roots of the Hamburg parsley are used for stews, soups, salad, or as a vegetable.

Rosemary (*Rosmarino*): Rosemary is a tall-growing perennial plant with narrow, elongated leaves. The upper sides of the needlelike leaves are dark green while the under sides are grayish silver. The taste is slightly bitter, with a strong aromatic flavor. A major herb in Italian cuisine, rosemary is favored for lamb, poultry, and game dishes, but is also used in stews, sauces, and some styles of minestrone.

Sage (*Salvia*): Many varieties of sage are used in cooking. Sage has sturdy oblong leaves that are somewhat hairy and grayish green in color. The strong aroma is distinct and slightly bitter. The French Provençal sage (*petite sauge de provence*) is smaller, with off-white leaves, and is the most esteemed species. A major herb in Italian cuisine, sage is used to flavor variety meats, soups, stews, sauces, and pasta, and it is essential for *saltimbocca alla romana*.

Savory (*Santoreggia, saturcia*): An herb of the mint family, savory of two varieties is used in cooking. Bushy annual summer savory resembles thyme in flavor. The less popular perennial winter savory has a sharper aroma. Savory is primarily used for baked beans, chowders, lamb, game, and stuffings.

Sorrel (*Acetosella*): Sorrel is a hardy perennial that dates back over 5,000 years. Wild field sorrel has long, narrow leaves and is excellent when harvested in early spring. The cultivated variety has large, robust leaves. The cultivated variety is used widely in soups and sauces and is finely shredded for salads.

Tarragon (*Dragoncello*): Tarragon is considered the aristocrat among culinary herbs. It is a perennial bushy plant with elongated, smooth, shiny leaves. The herb is highly pungent with a slight bittersweet taste. It is *the* major herb in classical French cooking, as well as in northwestern Italy, used for poultry, seafood, salads, and hot and cold sauces.

Thyme (*Timo*): Thyme is a low-growing bushy plant with very small leaves and a pungent aroma. It is primarily used for lamb and game dishes and for marinades therefor, and it is also excellent for flavoring soups and shellfish dishes.

SPICES FOR CULINARY USE

The spices listed below are obtained from various seeds, buds, roots, leaves, barks, flowers, and berries of specific plants. They are marketed either whole or ground.

Aniseeds (*Semi di anice*): Also called sweet cumin, these tiny pointed seeds have ribbed surfaces and are grayish green. They are used primarily in cakes and pastries; sometimes they are added to vegetables.

Bay leaves (*Alloro*): Bay leaves are the small shiny leaves of the laurel tree, which is native to the Mediterranean countries. Bay leaves are one of the most commonly used spices in the Western world, flavoring soups and broths, stews, and sauces. *Note:* Do not break bay leaves into small bits. Use them whole and remove them from a finished dish before serving, as they do not soften in cooking and their sharp edges could cause internal injury.

Caraway seeds (*Cumino dei prati*): A biennial plant, caraway, like dill, fennel, and anise, is a member of the carrot family. Caraway seeds may be one of the world's oldest spices. A major spice in central Europe, caraway seeds are used to flavor breads, roasts (especially pork), soups, salads, cheeses, sauces, and liqueurs.

Cardamom (*Cardomomo*): Cardamom is the dried fruit of a plant belonging to the ginger family that is native to India, Sri Lanka, and Guatemala. A major aromatic for coffee in the Middle East, cardamom is an important spice for the sausage industry and is also used in marinades and pastries.

Capers (*Capperi*): Capers are the flower buds of the caper bush, native to Asia Minor, France, and Algeria. The berries vary in size from tiny to the size of a chick-pea, the smaller being the preferred kind. Capers are primarily used in marinades, sauces, salads, and stuffings.

Cayenne Pepper (*Pepi di Caienna*): Cayenne, the most pungent of all spices, is produced from dried *Capsicum* hot peppers grown primarily in Central America, Africa, India, and the United States. The small African variety is the most pungent. It is excellent in all tomato-based dishes, sauces, pâtés, and in seafood and egg dishes.

Cinnamon (*Cannella*): The cinnamon tree, of which there are several species (varying in size and quality), is native to Sri Lanka, India, Indonesia, Malaysia, Vietnam, and China. The most esteemed cinnamon comes from Sri Lanka. Cinnamon is the rolled bark from this tree, which is very thin, though almost a yard long, and yellowish brown in color. It has a very fine sweet but spicy aroma. Cinnamon sticks are used whole or ground (if bought ground, one very often receives cassia, a less pungent relative), depending on the finished product. Cinnamon is used abundantly in cakes, pastries, sugar glazes, creams, sauces, stuffings, marinades, and beverages. It is especially harmonious with apples and bananas.

Cloves (*Chiodi di garofano*): Native to the Molucca Islands but probably from China originally, today most cloves are harvested in Zanzibar and Madagascar. These nail-shaped, sun-dried buds of a tropical tree in the myrtle family are a dark brown color and extremely pungent and aromatic. Clove buds are sold whole or ground and are very compatible with fruit dishes, pies and compotes, pâtés, cakes, confections, and smoked pork.

Coriander (*Coriandolo*): The round seeds of a plant in the carrot family, coriander is yellow-brown in color. It is related to anise but has a distinct aromatic scent. Coriander was already well known in the days of the Egyptian dynasties and was one of the first spices used by man. Originally from India, it is now cultivated in eastern Europe, the Balkans, Argentina, and Morocco. It is used in breads, soups, sauces, cheeses, salads, pickling, and stews.

Cumin (*Semi di cumino*): The tiny light brown to yellowish cumin seeds, resembling caraway, are five sided, covered with microscopic hairs, and acrid in taste. This distinctive bitterness is regarded as an appetite stimulant. Cumin is native to Egypt and the Mediterranean countries but is also imported from Indonesia, India, and other countries. Cumin, sold as seeds or ground, is a major spice in South American cooking and a key to most exotic cuisines. It is used in curry and chili powders, exotic fish stews, breads, cheeses, sausages, and *couscous.*

Fennel seeds (*Semi di finocchio*): Fennel seeds have a pleasant odor and a sweet aniseedlike taste. The plant is native to Europe but cultivated all over the world. It is one of the ancient spices. The edible part of this plant is a bulbous base with stalks and fernlike leaves and is a very important ingredient in the preparation of various national dishes, including bouillabaisse, borscht, and minestrone. Fennel seeds are used extensively in Italian bread, roll, and pastry making. They are also included in many sausages, tomato-based dishes, stews, and vegetable dishes.

Juniper berries (*Ginepro in bacche*): Juniper is an evergreen bush that grows wild in forests and mountain ravines. The small, lavender-colored berries have a pleasant musty aroma when crushed. A major European spice for all kinds of game cookery and derived sauces, juniper berries are also used in sauerkraut, pickling brines, and marinades. They are perhaps best known as the flavoring for gin.

Mace (*Macis*): Mace is the dried and ground orange-red shell of the nutmeg, native to Indonesia. Mace is actually the seed covering of the nutmeg. The flavor resembles a blend of nutmeg and cinnamon. Mace is mainly used in pies, cakes, cookies, and chocolates, but also for pâtés, sausages, fish sauces, and pickling.

Mustard seeds (*Senape*): Mustard is an annual herb bearing yellow flowers. A native of Asia, mustard is now grown in Europe, Canada, and the United States. There are many species of mustard plants with seeds of different colors, the most common being the white mustard plant with yellow seeds. The seeds are used whole or powdered. These, in turn, are used in pickling, marinades, sauces, relishes, condiments, and salads.

Nutmeg (*Noce moscata*): Nutmeg is the dried, hard, oval-shaped, wrinkled seed of the nutmeg fruit grown in Indonesia. It is highly aromatic. Nutmeg is used in cakes, pies, creams, chocolate desserts, soups, and pâtés.

Peppercorns (*Grani di pepe*): Pepper has been used since ancient times, when it was so costly that its use was restricted to the rich. It was as negotiable as silver and used to pay rent and taxes. Magellan lost his life and most of his fleet in his search for pepper, but the return of just one of his expedition's ships was more than enough to bring a huge profit. Peppercorns are the dried fruit of the Asian vine *Piper nigrum,* and they were one of the first spices to be introduced into Europe. Black peppercorns are obtained from the unripe reddish pepper berries that turn dark when dried. White peppercorns are obtained from ripe pepper berries. The berries are soaked, and the outer hull is removed. The inner core constitutes the white peppercorn, which has somewhat less aroma than the black peppercorn. Pepper, which has preservative and stimulating qualities, is used in almost every culinary preparation.

Poppy seeds (*Semi di papavero*): Poppy seeds come from the same plant that yields opium, but the opiate qualities are lost once the plant is mature. The seeds, which form only in a mature plant, have no narcotic effects. Poppy seeds are used mainly in breads, pastries, and sweet fillings. If used for filling, a special poppy seed grinder should be used to crush the seeds.

Saffron (*Zafferano*): Saffron is made from the dried stigmas of the autumn crocus. The stigmas are hand-picked and sorted by color, a labor-intensive process that makes saffron the world's most expensive aromatic. It is pleasantly bitter and highly potent, used for both its flavor and usually yellow color. Saffron was introduced to Spain by the Arabs. Earlier it had perfumed Roman baths and was valued as an aphrodisiac. In the fifteenth and sixteenth centuries, its cultivation was begun in France and subsequently in Italy. Saffron was so highly prized in Europe that, during the Middle Ages, dealers who adulterated the spice were burned at the stake. Saffron is essential in the preparation of certain national dishes, such as paella valenciana, bouillabaisse, *couscous*, and risotto milanese. Saffron is especially excellent with pasta and butter sauces.

Sesame seeds (*Seme sesamo*): Sesame seeds are from an annual herbaceous tropical plant. They were used in ancient times for food and oil throughout the Middle East. They are a very important ingredient in Oriental and southern European cookery, either raw, toasted, or ground into a paste (*tahini*). Sesame seeds are used today the world over on breadsticks and buns, toasted and sprinkled over spinach or leaf salads, crushed to paste as for *moutabal* or *hummus bi tahini*, or mixed with various dressings and sauces.

Turmeric (*Curcuma*): A member of the ginger family, turmeric is a perennial herb. Its rhizome is deep yellow, making it a useful component in dyeing other food products. Turmeric is used in the preparation of curry powder, mustard, and Oriental sauces. It is also used in pilafs and vegetable and meat cookery.

Vanilla (*Vanigla*): Vanilla is native to Mexico and was held in the highest esteem by the Aztecs. Today vanilla plants are cultivated in various tropical regions, but the Mexican variety is still considered the best. Several kinds of vanilla are sold commercially. The best-quality pods are from 10 to 12 inches long, with a smooth black surface and a slightly frosted appearance. The lesser-quality pods are thicker, reddish brown in color, and about 4 to 8 inches long. Vanilla is the most widely used and favored flavoring in pastry production, including creams and puddings. It is also used in sweet rice dishes, chocolates, and compotes. The vanilla bean may be cooked intact with the substance to be flavored, or the seeds of the pod may be scraped out for an even finer bouquet. The beans are often stored in a jar of sugar, transferring their delicate aroma to the sugar after a short time.

Oli, Grassi, e Aceti
OILS, FATS, AND VINEGARS

Olive oil and the various vinegars play an essential role in Italian cuisine, giving many dishes their distinctive flavors. In addition to olive oil, clarified butter is often used to sauté or pan-fry foods. And a residue from heating certain fats—cracklings—makes a delicious garnish.

Òlio d'Oliva
OLIVE OIL

Virgin olive oil is from the first pressing of the olives from the earliest harvest, and its acidity must be less than 3 percent. Extra-virgin oil is extracted using the same procedures, but all water is removed from the olives. The acidity of extra-virgin oil is less than 1 percent. Olive oil comes in various colors, from pale yellow to pale green. It is perishable and will keep well for between six and nine months only if kept at a temperature of about 60° to 70°F when stored out of direct light. Do not refrigerate olive oil. It is generally recognized that the regions around Tuscany (especially Lucca) produce the finest oils. Olive oil contains monounsaturated fats, making it especially valuable in controlling cholesterol.

Aceto Balsamico
BALSAMIC VINEGAR

Balsamic vinegar is most often associated with the city of Modena. Here it is produced from the boiled-down must of the white Trebbiano grape, to which herbs are added. It is aged in casks of different woods in a manner that resembles the *solera* system of sherry making in Spain. Its acidity is normally around 6 percent or more. It is often used in salad dressings, as well as in marinades and to flavor various dishes.

Burro Chiarificato
CLARIFIED BUTTER

Fresh butter contains approximately 80 percent milk fat and 20 percent miscellaneous components including water, salt, and milk solids. Exposed to high heat, such as that necessary to sauté properly, the milk solids will burn at a relatively low temperature, thus rendering the butter useless. Butter is clarified to eliminate these milk solids. This is easily done by placing whole butter in a narrow container in a hot water bath (*bain-marie*) and heating it to the point where the proteins coagulate and rise to the surface and the solids sink to the bottom. The coagulated proteins are carefully skimmed off the top, and the now clarified butter fat is ladled out, leaving the milk solids behind as sediment in the bottom of the container. The butter will lose much of its flavor when clarified. In another method of removing the clarified butter, the proteins are skimmed from the top and the remaining fat is chilled until hard. The container is dipped in hot water until it loosens, and the chilled mass is inverted over the sink until it slides out. Excess milky solids that cling to the solidified clarified butter are then removed. Clarified butter can be used to sauté almost any food. It can be frozen or refrigerated and used like regular butter.

— *Ciccioli* —
CRACKLINGS

Cracklings are the crisp residue that remains after fat has been rendered. Temperature is important when making cracklings. When making pork cracklings, the crackling may brown while the inside remains greasy if too much heat is used. To prepare cracklings, cut fresh pork or chicken fat or chicken skin into ¼-inch cubes. Heat a little fat or oil in a heavy-bottomed casserole. Add the fat or skin, and render over moderate heat, stirring occasionally to prevent sticking. Cook until the cracklings are very crisp. Strain off all fat (save for another purpose). Drain the cracklings in a colander or sieve until completely dry.

—— *Preparazioni per Verdure* ——
VEGETABLE PREPARATIONS

Tomatoes and peppers are used in numerous ways in Italian dishes. These vegetables, almost synonymous today with Italian food, are relative newcomers to the Italian diet, as they were introduced to Italy from the New World in the sixteenth century. Both are often used as garnishes as well, as their bright colors add to the presentation of many dishes. They sometimes require preliminary treatment, such as peeling and seeding.

If a recipe calls for peeled tomatoes (tomato skins are indigestible), it is necessary to remove the skins without damaging the fruit itself. To do this, have boiling water and very cold water available. Make an inconspicuous incision through the skin of the tomato—do not pierce the pulp—and drop into boiling water for NO MORE than 15 seconds. Remove, and shock in cold water. The skins should slide off easily.

To seed tomatoes, remove the skins, and slice the tomatoes in half crosswise. Grasp the tomato half in your hand, and gently squeeze out the seeds and excess juice.

To peel whole peppers rub them lightly with oil, and lay them on a broiler rack. Grill them as close to a heat source (broiler, grill, stove top) as possible, until the skins start to blister. Place the peppers immediately into a small bowl, and cover with plastic wrap. A small, tightly closed paper bag will also do. This loosens the skins and eases peeling. Do *not* overcook the peppers: they should remain crisp and firm.

TOMATO PETALS

Tomato petals are easily made and make a convenient garnish. Peel a tomato as described above. Cut it in half lengthwise, and then cut each half lengthwise again into three or four sections. Remove the seeds and excess pulp to create the flat shape of a petal.

Pomodori Secchi sott'Olio

OIL-PRESERVED SUN-DRIED TOMATOES

Sun-dried tomatoes have gained exceptional popularity in all major cuisines. They can be found marinated in oil and served plain, mixed with salads, or as spreads. They are most common in conjunction with pasta, seafood, or cheese dishes.

Sun-dried tomatoes are sold dehydrated or marinated in oil and ready to use. If dehydrated tomatoes are used, they must be reconstituted before marinating.

Yield: 6 cups

1 pint	*water*	*2*	*bay leaves*
¾ cup	*lemon juice*	*to taste*	*salt*
¼ cup	*balsamic vinegar*	*2 tablespoons*	*chopped oregano*
4 cloves	*garlic*	*1 pound*	*sun-dried tomatoes*
3	*chili peppers, chopped (or ½ teaspoon dried, crushed hot red pepper)*	*1 cup*	*extra-virgin olive oil*

1.   Combine the water, lemon juice, vinegar, garlic, chili peppers, and bay leaves. Bring to a boil in a small saucepan and simmer over low heat for 5 minutes. Add the salt and oregano.

2.   Place the dried tomatoes in a suitable stainless steel or earthenware container, and pour the hot marinade over them. Cover and let marinate for 12 hours, stirring once or twice in the process. Keep in a cool place.

3.   Add the olive oil, and mix carefully. Cover the container tightly again and store in a cool place. The tomatoes should keep well for several months.

Formaggi
CHEESES

Every region of Italy has been producing fine cheeses for centuries. Today Italy still produces some of the world's finest and best-known cheeses. Like everything else in Italian cuisine, the cheeses are as varied as the landscape, with soft, creamy cheeses as popular as the hard grating varieties. Even the types of milk used to make cheese change from area to area, depending on the presence of cows, sheep, goats, and buffalo and the particular species of these animals living in a certain region.

The basic component of cheese is the solid portion of coagulated milk. This coagulation occurs when heat and (sometimes) rennet are applied to milk. When the milk curdles, the solids, or curds, separate from the liquids, or whey. The solids are then cooked, aged, or processed in almost as many different ways as there are cheeses. Factors directly affecting the types of cheese made are the animal from which the milk is derived; whether that milk is skimmed or whole, pasteurized or unpasteurized; the type and amount of aging the cheese receives; and any special treatments to the finished product, such as brining or cooking. It is also interesting to note that an animal's diet can have a great effect on the milk it produces, thus making it possible for the cheese derived from a single animal to differ from season to season, depending on availability of forage in the animal's diet. This phenomenon is found most often at the local cheese-making level. Much of Italy's cheese making, however, has been taken over by farmers' cooperatives and large processing operations, thus ensuring uniform quality in greater quantity.

TYPES OF CHEESE

Most Italian cheeses fall into several broad categories according to their method of preparation, texture, or ingredients, as described below.

FRESH, UNRIPENED CHEESES

Fresh, unripened cheeses are ready for consumption within days. They are rindless cheeses, moist, soft, and richly creamy in texture. Ricotta and Mascarpone are the two best-known examples of fresh cheese.

SEMISOFT TO SEMIHARD CHEESES

These cheeses are allowed to ripen before consumption. As the cheese ages, bacteria, molds, and other microorganisms or interior molds act on the cheese, helping it to develop a particular flavor and texture. The length of the aging period determines the degree of hardness in the final product. Often these cheeses need a wax coating to retain moisture, but some do develop their own rinds. Examples of these cheeses are Bel Paese, Fontina, and Gorgonzola.

GRANA CHEESES

Grana cheeses are cooked, pressed, and aged for a long period of time, thus giving the cheese a grainy, crumbly, dry texture with a pronounced flavor. When young, these cheeses are excellent as table cheeses. Older cheeses are usually used for grating. Examples include Parmigiano Reggiano and Pecorino Romano.

PASTA FILATA CHEESES

Pasta filata means "spun paste," and that is exactly how these cheeses are made. The curds are bathed in hot whey and spun into threads until they become soft and malleable enough to be shaped. Mozzarella and provolone are two *pasta filata* cheeses.

PECORINO CHEESES

Made from ewes' milk, these cheeses are flavorful and range in texture from soft to hard, depending on how they are produced and how much aging takes place. Also intensely flavored are the *caprini* (goat) cheeses. Both of these types are less abundant than cows' milk cheeses. Because of changing tastes, many of the traditional *pecorino* and *caprini* cheeses are now made with a certain amount of cows' milk.

VARIETIES OF CHEESE

It would be impossible to describe all of Italy's cheeses. The following are some of the best-known varieties, chosen because of their widespread use in Italian cooking. Experimenting with different cheeses while cooking can lead to delicious and satisfying results. Color plates 2 through 5 illustrate some of those listed below.

Asiago: A semifirm to hard cheese made from whole and partially skim cows' milk blended together, from a morning and evening milking. Asiago is straw yellow in color and has many small to medium-size holes. It is a rich, flavorful table cheese when young and a superb grating cheese with age.

Bel Paese: A smooth, mellow dessert cheese.

Burrata: A sweet, compact, creamy cheese made from cows' milk in the Puglia (Apulia) region of Italy. It is shaped like a flask.

Burrini: Similar to Caciocavallo but with hearts of butter. This cheese is often called *burri* or *butirri*.

Caciocavallo: A cheese of the *pasta filata* type, originally from southern Italy, made with cows' milk. It is a mild, sometimes smoky table cheese when young. As it ages, this cheese becomes a sharp, flavorful grating cheese. The shape is usually pearlike with a stubby neck.

Caciota: Produced throughout Italy but usually associated with Tuscany, Sardinia, Apulia, and the Marches. This cheese is made from cows', goats', or sheep's milk or a combination of these. While varying from one area to another, these cheeses are generally semisoft and sweet when young. After aging for several months, they become harder and more flavorful. Caciota usually has a compact interior with many small eyes and an elastic natural rind.

Canestrato: Traditionally made from pasteurized ewes' milk in Tuscany and Sicily. The name comes from the baskets in which the cheese ripens, which leaves a distinctive imprint on the rind.

Caprino: Any cheese made from goats' milk. Most often, these cheeses are fresh, soft, and piquant. They tend to originate in the mountainous regions of Italy, where goats are more common. See color plate 2.

Casatella: A soft, buttery cows' milk cheese with a fresh milk taste. This cheese comes from Emilia-Romagna and Veneto.

Castelmagno: Named for a town in the Piedmont region, this is creamy, herbaceous, green-veined cheese made from cows' milk with a salty, delicate flavor.

Crescenza: A cows' milk cheese resembling Stracchino, produced primarily in Lombardy and other areas in northern Italy.

Crotonese: From the Crotone area in Calabria, this peppery, strong, grana-type cheese is made from a blend of sheep's and goats' milk. It is similar to Foggiano and Moliterno.

Dolce Sardo: A cows' milk cheese from Sardinia that is creamy, soft, white, and slightly sweet.

Fior di Latte: A common cheese in southern Italy that resembles mozzarella and is made from cows' milk fashioned into braids.

Fiore Molle: A soft, aromatic, slightly salty cheese from Latium. Saffron gives this cheese a yellowish tint.

Fiore Sardo: A compact, flavorful cheese from Sardinia made from raw sheep's milk. It is eaten fresh when young (up to three months of age) and used for grating when older. See color plate 2.

Foggiano: A *pasta filata* cheese named for a city in Apulia. It is made from sheep's milk and is a fatty and piquant variety of Crotonese.

Fontina: A semifirm cheese with a slightly nutty flavor produced in the Valle d'Aosta from the raw milk of a breed of cow indigenous to the region. It is creamy smooth when young, becoming drier and more piquant with age. Genuine Fontina has a creamy brown rind imprinted with the seal of the local cooperative. Cheese sold as Fontal can be made elsewhere in Italy (or in another country altogether) and lacks the subtle delicateness of real Fontina. See color plate 3.

Gorgonzola: A blue-type cheese made from cows' milk in the town of the same name in Lombardy. Gorgonzola has been made for over 1,000 years and is renowned for its mild yet savory flavor. Unlike most other blue cheeses, Gorgonzola has a creamy, moist texture. The veins, which are produced by mold, become more pronounced with age, making the flavor somewhat sharper and drying the texture to some extent. See color plate 3.

Grana: Named for its grainy and crumbly texture, this cheese is produced in Emilia-Romagna and Lombardy. It is a hard cows' milk cheese and is known primarily in four types, each named for the specific region of production: Parmigiano Reggiano, Grana Piacentino, Grana Lodigiano, and Grana Padana. These cheeses are excellent table cheeses when young and superb grating cheeses when older, the prototypes for all Italian grana cheese. See color plate 3.

Italico: A group of soft, delicate, ivory-colored cheeses originally from Lombardy. Usually made from whole cows' milk, Italico is increasingly being made with low-fat and skim milks. See color plate 3.

Mascarpone: Another soft, smooth cows' milk cheese from Lombardy, but made with fresh cream only. The cheese is very perishable and blends beautifully with other foods and flavors. It is commonly used in sweet concoctions, but is versatile enough to be used in many other ways and should not be limited to desserts. See color plate 4.

Moliterno: A cheese from Basilicata that resembles a strong, sharp Crotonese or Foggiano.

Montasio: Made in Friuli from partially skimmed cows' milk. After a few months of aging, it is a table cheese. After a year or more, it becomes quite pungent and is used for grating. See color plate 4.

Mozzarella: Originating in southern Italy, this *pasta filata* cheese was originally made from buffalo milk. It is extremely white, firm, and moist. The cheese is best consumed very fresh, when its sweet, delicate flavor is at a peak. Today most mozzarella is made commercially from less rich cows' milk and is not quite as flavorful as the genuine buffalo mozzarella. See color plate 4.

Nostrale: From the area of Cuneo in Piedmont, this cheese is rather rustic, made from cows' milk. It is consumed either fresh or aged. See color plate 4.

Pannerone: Also known as Gorgonzola Bianca or Gorgonzola Dolce, this cheese resembles Gorgonzola without the mold. The Lombardy version has a sweet almond taste and is straw colored with many small holes. The crust is rosy yellow and soft.

Parmigiano Reggiano: A grana cheese, also known as Parmesan, whose production is limited by law to the provinces of Parma, Mantova, Reggio Emilia, Modena, and Bologna. It is still produced in accordance with laws and customs dating back to the eleventh century. Some of these restrictions include that the cheese can only be made between April 1 and November 11, that the milk be obtained from two milkings (one morning and one evening), and that the aging take place only under natural conditions. In Italy, one finds *Parmigiano Reggiano* as a table cheese as well as the preferred grating cheese. It is identifiable by the name, which is always molded into the rind. Always grate this cheese just before using, and never use the so-called Parmesan that is sold already grated.

Pecorino: Any cheese made entirely from ewes' milk may be called *pecorino* in Italy. Amazingly enough, *pecorino* cheeses comprise 15 percent of Italy's total cheese production. It is used much like Parmigiano Reggiano, but is even more used as a grating cheese. There are several outstanding regional varieties. Those made in Tuscany usually carry a local production name or label. The Romano types have been made uninterrupted since the first century. These cheeses were originally produced in the Latium area, but the laws now allow Sardinian production as well. The salty taste of this excellent cheese is a result of salting after production, which retards spoilage and encourages a slight toughening of a natural rind to protect the cheese. The cheese can also be a bit oily.

Pecorino-Umbra, or di Norcia, is a sweeter version of *pecorino* cheese from Umbria. The Sicilian versions are normally referred to as Canestrato, after the wicker baskets in which the cheese is formed; these leave a characteristic imprint on the rind itself. Some of these varieties often contain whole black peppercorns, in which case they are known as Pepato.

Provatura: A very perishable egg-shaped buffalo cheese made in Latium with the *pasta filata* method.

Provola: A spherical cheese that is buttery and sweet, somewhat smaller than provolone.

Provolone: Originally a specialty of Campania in southern Italy, this cheese is now made almost anywhere, using the *pasta filata* method. It is eaten fresh, after two or three months, when it is still sweet, as well as after it becomes piquant with age. Aged provolone is an excellent cooking as well as grating cheese. Like mozzarella, this was a cheese originally made from buffalo milk. Now, like most other cheeses, cows' milk is used.

Quartirolo: A cheese made in Lombardy from whole cows' milk that is similar to Taleggio but is cured in caves, where it acquires a mushroomy flavor.

Ragusano: The name comes from the city of Ragusa in Sicily, where this whole cows' milk cheese is made in the *pasta filata* style. This white or straw yellow cheese is eaten at table when young, up to six months, and it is grated when older.

Raveggiolo: Usually produced in Tuscany or Romagna, this creamy, sweet sheep's cheese resembles Crescenza.

Ricotta: This is a cheese made from cooking the residual whey from other cheese-making processes, originally that of the *pecorino* types (ricotta means "recooked"). Now ricotta cheeses are produced throughout Italy and can vary greatly in texture, flavor, and color, depending on aging and the type of milk used.

Robiola: Originally from the Piedmont and Lombardy areas of northern Italy, this cheese is vaguely reminiscent of the truffles that are so abundant here. This cheese is sold in a crushed round or small square shape and is either pure cows' milk or a mixture of cows' milk with either goats' or sheep's milk. See color plate 5.

Scamorza: These *pasta filata* cheeses can be made purely from cows' milk but are traditionally made from a mixture of cows' and sheep's milk. In Abruzzo and Campania, they are shaped like pears. They are drier than most other *pasta filata* cheeses. See color plate 5.

Stracchino: Traditionally made in Lombardy from cows' milk "still warm from the milking," this cheese is soft with a delicate yet persistent flavor. Usually found in square blocks, it is for immediate consumption and is typified by Crescenza. See color plate 5.

Taleggio: Named for a valley in Lombardy where it has been produced from cows' milk since at least the tenth century, this cheese has an ivory to orange crust and a rectangular shape. Its taste is mild yet piquant, with the body being either soft or more compact, depending on production methods. See color plate 5.

Toma: Made in the north from cows' or ewes' milk, these soft, white cheeses vary in taste and texture but are, for the most part, eaten young.

Tomino: Similar to Toma, but more emphasis is put on low-fat cheese production. It should be eaten fresh and young.

Toscanello: A ewes' milk cheese that is hard and yellow-white. It is also called Maremmano, for the Maremma region in western Italy where it originated. This is a medium-size delicate cheese. See color plate 5.

Many of these above cheeses are not only used as ingredients in Italian dishes but are also enjoyed alone at or near the end of a meal in Italy. They are considered aids to digestion as well as foods to round out the feeling of satisfaction garnered on the palate. More often than not, the finest wine served during a meal is continued during this cheese course.

Vini e Liquori
WINES, LIQUORS, AND LIQUEURS

Italy produces more wine than any other country. Not all of it is great, but it is used in the cuisine of every region, both in cooking and to accompany meals. In this book, both red and white wines are frequently called for in the recipes. Except where otherwise noted below, any imported or domestic wine of decent quality can be used where wine is called for. It is important to remember that the wine affects the flavor of the final product, and therefore should be fairly dry and not too heavy. Some of the liquors and liqueurs discussed are expensive and of limited availability; substitutions are recommended where possible. Since they are used sparingly, however, this is not an argument against having them on hand or making an extra effort to seek them out. The use of good-quality wine combined with strict attention to proper cooking techniques will ensure a satisfactory result.

Amaretto: An Italian liqueur made primarily from bitter almonds.

Barolo: One of Italy's most famous red wines. Named after a town in Piedmont, it is produced from the Nebbiolo grape and has a high alcohol content (a minimum of 13 percent). It is aged at least three years before release and develops an extraordinary depth and finesse with even longer aging. Quality can vary, so it is wise to consult with a knowledgeable person—perhaps the liquor store owner or manager—before purchasing this rather expensive wine. A suitable substitute would be a rich Rhone or Rhone-style wine, of which there are many. Barbaresco, also made in Piedmont, is not as full as Barolo, but may also be substituted.

Cognac: Cognac refers to the brandy produced in the Cognac region of southwest France. A rather nondescript white wine is made primarily from Ugni Blanc grapes, then distilled in an alembic, or pot still. This allows for the "heads" and "tails" (the less attractive, volatile elements released at the beginning and end of the distillation process) to be separated by vaporization from the "*brouilli*," or most desirable elements, which are condensed and then distilled again to make the brandy. Qualities of Cognac vary greatly, depending on which vineyard region of Cognac the wine originates from (the best being from Grande Champagne, the central region). The brandy is aged in oak from Limousin for a legal minimum of three years. Some of the dark color is a result of the addition of caramel, and blending is standard for consistency of quality. For cooking, ignore all terminology (for example, V.S.O.P., X.O.) that alerts the buyer to a Cognac's age; simply purchase a reasonably priced bottle from a respected producer. Although Cognac only comes from a particular region of France, almost all wine-producing countries also produce wine brandies, and those of good quality may readily be substituted in recipes that call for Cognac.

Crème de Cassis: Made primarily in France's Burgundy region from black currants, to which sweetened grape brandy is added.

Frangelico: An Italian liqueur made from hazelnuts and other flavoring ingredients.

Galliano: A golden, intensely aromatic liqueur made from selected herbs and flowers. Galliano is considerably stronger than most other liqueurs.

Grand Marnier: A blend of a sweetened distillate of orange peel and good quality Cognac. Cointreau may be substituted.

Grappa: Grappa is made from the skins, seeds, and pulp remaining after the initial pressing and fermentation of grape juices (pomace). Water is added to the drained pomace to allow the remaining sugar to begin a second fermentation. This liquid is then distilled to make a brandy. Grappa is usually clear and retains some of the special nuances of the grape varieties from which it is made. A good-quality grappa is essential for cooking. Marc, France's equivalent to grappa, is somewhat darker and more refined because it is aged, and is a satisfactory substitute when making darker sauces.

Kirsch: A true fruit brandy, or eau-de-vie (French, literally "water of life"), made from cherries. Although German in name, it is also produced in France, Switzerland, northern Italy, and central Europe. The fruit's natural sugars are used in fermentation; the product is then distilled. These brandies are almost always clear and consumed without additional aging. Cherry brandies, or any other similar types of brandies widely available in the United States, are not suitable when kirsch is called for: kirsch is not sweet and has a much higher alcohol content. Eaux-de-vie are expensive, but, due to their high alcohol content (40 to 50 percent), are used sparingly.

Madeira: A fortified wine, Madeira comes from the small Portuguese island of the same name. Like the ordinary wines used in the manufacture of port, Marsala, and sherry, the white wine produced on Madeira is rather bland. It was found that fortification with brandy and heating over a period of several months gives Madeira its characteristic caramel aroma. The wines are then blended and aged for consistent quality using the solera system developed in Spain for sherry, where the wine is aged in oak barrels and younger wines are blended with older ones to create a superior product. Four types of Madeira, each named for the grapes from which it is produced, are readily available. The sweetest is Malmsey, an excellent, rich brown after-dinner wine. Bual is slightly less sweet. Verdelho is even drier, and is used in much the same way as Marsala (Rainwater is the name of a similar blend which is readily available in the United States). Sercial is the driest style of Madeira, and is mainly used as an aperitif. Madeira is also produced from lesser quality grapes; it is perfectly adequate for making sauces.

Maraschino: A sweet Italian fruit liqueur. Sour marasco cherries (originally those from the Dalmatia region of Yugoslavia) are pounded with their stones. Honey is added to induce fermentation before distillation and the addition of more sugar. Cherry brandy produces a similar result when used for cooking. Some maraschinos are more similar to kirsch, and should not be used when maraschino is called for, but only as substitutes for kirsch.

Marsala: A fortified wine from northwest Sicily. First, an ordinary wine is made from Grillo, Catarratto, and Inzolia grapes. A heated grape concentrate is added to give the desired sweetness, and is then combined with enough brandy to bring the alcohol content to about 18 to 20 percent. Although several types of Marsala are produced, both as aperitifs (including a rather dry version made using the famed Spanish sherry solera system) and as dessert wines, the most commonly available is known as Superiore grade. This is a sweet, amber to brown wine which is the base for Italy's famous zabaglione. Good advice from your wine merchant is best when choosing a Marsala.

Moscato d'Asti: A white wine made in the area around the town of Asti from the Moscato Bianco grape. Moscato d'Asti, unlike some of Italy's other, much sweeter moscati, is drunk young while still fruity. These wines are usually characterized as "*frizzante,*" or mildly effervescent. California muscatel wines, also produced from the Muscat grape, are not recommended. Decent substitutes do exist but most available brands are cloyingly sweet and in some cases fortified. Any medium dry white wine can easily replace Moscato d'Asti if it is unavailable.

Sambuca: An anise-flavored liqueur originally made in the Lazio region of Italy. Other clear, licorice-flavored anisettes can be substituted.

Soave: A white wine produced mainly in the Veneto region of Italy, primarily from the Garganega and Trebbiano grapes. This is a dry, light wine, and many good brands are available in the United States. Soave marked "*classico*" should be of slightly higher quality.

Spumante: In Italian, "*spumante*" means sparkling, and is most often associated with Asti Spumante, or the medium dry sparkling wines made in the area around the town of Asti, in Piedmont. When well made, they are quite pleasant, with a fruity, sweet taste. Asti Spumante is made from the white Muscat, or Moscato Bianco grape, from which some of the finest dessert wines in Italy and the world are made. Unfortunately, there are many inferior Asti wines on the market. If your liquor store owner or manager can't recommend a particular producer, it would probably be best to substitute a quality medium to dry French champagne, or a sparkling wine made by the champagne method; French Crémant (from either Alsace or Burgundy) would be a fine substitute. Italian Prosecco, another sparkling wine, is a little too dry to replace an Asti Spumante. Most Asti Spumante wines lose their bubbles quite rapidly, but these are just as useful in cooking as still wines.

Vermouth: A wine flavored with bitter herbs produced mainly in Italy and France. The name is from the German word for wormwood (*Wermut,* meaning literally "man-courage") which was used to produce absinthe in France. It is essentially made in two styles. More commonly produced in France, the lighter of the two is white to pale yellow. The reddish variety, more typical of the Italian style, is heavier and sweeter, its color a result of caramelized sugars. Exact recipes are carefully protected, but flavorings include various herbs, spices, roots, and barks. The herbs are steeped in neutral spirits to extract the essences before the mixture is added to white wine; in some cases, the herbs are steeped in the wine, to which brandy has already been added. The lighter, drier versions are ideal as aperitifs and for cooking. Many Italian versions contain angostura, or "bitters," to mask the sweetness. When these are used in recipes, an undesirable aftertaste may result.

APPETIZERS

— *Antipasti Freddi* —
COLD APPETIZERS

The preludes to the tradition-rich Italian table are the antipastos. In Italian, *antipasto* means "before meal" and is the first course of a complete meal. Usually selections are listed as *Antipasti Assortiti, Antipasti Misti,* or *Antipasti all'Italiana,* and they may be presented *al carrello,* displayed on a food cart. However, the style of service can vary as much as the offerings.

Antipastos are usually drawn from a rich selection of meats (both smoked and cured), poultry, seafood (fresh or marinated), sausages, vegetables and fruits (fresh, marinated, or oil preserved), salads, and cheeses. As an example of the variation among antipastos, consider the traditional way in which *prosciutto* is served. One finds the familiar thin-sliced meat with fresh fruit, such as melons, figs, or dates, but also with an assortment of highly seasoned, marinated vegetables such as grilled peppers, eggplant, or baby artichokes marinated in the finest extra-virgin olive oil. In addition to *prosciutto di Parma,* which is air-cured in the hills around the city, Parma has given its name to another familiar product often found in antipastos: *Parmigiano Reggiano.* Other cheeses may include mozzarella, buffalo mozzarella, and the various *pecorino* cheeses (traditionally made from ewe's milk), ranging from soft to salty, piquant, and hard. These special delicacies are the product of a climate, terrain, and heritage duplicated nowhere else on earth.

Antipastos would not be complete without a selection of anchovies, sardines, salt cod *(baccalà),* and a variety of shellfish specialties prepared according to regional traditions.

Select these delicacies with contemporary tastes in mind, considering the healthful aspects of each as well. The list of possible antipasto ingredients is as endless as the chef's ingenuity; here are some suggestions:

- paper-thin slices of *prosciutto,* salami, *bresaola,* and *mortadella* (see discussion of Italian meats and sausages, below)
- slices of *zampone,* turkey, capon, and smoked duck or pheasant
- marinated seafood such as squid, shrimp, scallops, scungilli, and mussels

- smoked salmon, sardines, anchovies, and salt cod
- marinated vegetables such as *caponatina,* artichokes, peppers, and onions
- marinated domestic and wild mushrooms
- salads of celeriac, fennel, or *capricciosa*
- sliced cold omelets filled with herbs, mushrooms, or *prosciutto*
- cured olives and hot peppers
- quail eggs stuffed with chicken mousse
- slices of cold squid filled with shrimp mousseline
- assorted cheeses, such as Gorgonzola, Parmesan, and goat cheese

ITALIAN MEATS AND SAUSAGES

Italians prepare meat and sausages from a variety of animals and their by-products. In addition, the same name may be used for quite different products, changing by region. Therefore it is only misleading to list every item and variation. The items below are listed not so much because of their popularity but because of availability to the American consumer. Because it is illegal to import Italian meats into this country, the products called by these names that are available to the American chef are not always of the same character or quality as those in Italy.

All of these meats and sausages are commonly served unadorned (or with freshly ground black pepper and olive oil) on Italian *antipasti carreli,* or appetizer carts.

DRY CURED MEATS AND SAUSAGE

These items are prepared using dry brine cures (usually salts) and then most commonly are air-dried. They are more common in the Alpine regions of Italy, where the dry, cool air allows for moisture loss with less risk of spoilage.

Prosciutto: Whole legs of pork (hams) that are boned and dry cured.
Pancetta: Pork bellies that are rolled into a tight cylinder and dry cured. Less fatty than American-style bacon and usually unsmoked, though available in Italy either cured, smoked, or cooked.
Speck: A German-style slab bacon found in the northern regions, commonly smoked.
Bresaola: Known as *Bündnerfleisch* in neighboring Switzerland, this is an air-dried beef, usually in somewhat of a rectangular form, dark red to brown.
Coppa or **capicollo:** Similar sausages made from different pork parts and dry cured, available in sweet and hot varieties.
Peperoni: A spicy dried pork and beef sausage.

COOKED SAUSAGES

Cooked sausages are made by stuffing meat scraps and spices into casings. They are usually poached or hot smoked to preserve and to add flavor. *Salami* is the general name that is applied to the hundreds of these sausages of different shapes and sizes made throughout Italy and the United States. Common varieties are *mortadella* (a roasted, smooth salami) and *sopressata* (a coarse salami). Salamis available in Italy are often merely cured and cold smoked; this practice is less common in the United States.

RAW SAUSAGES

Also known in the United States as Italian sausages, raw sausages are casings that contain raw pork and spices. These sausages are always cooked before consumption. They are available in sweet and hot variations.

Peperoni Arrostiti, Agrodolce
SWEET AND SOUR ROASTED PEPPERS

Yield: 2 pounds

2 pounds	red or yellow bell peppers	1 tablespoon	salt
		3	bay leaves
		6	garlic cloves, roasted (see chapter 1)
MARINADE:			
2 cups	water	3/4 cup	virgin olive oil
1/2 cup	lemon juice		
1 1/2 teaspoons	sugar		

1.   Rub the peppers lightly with olive oil. Lightly roast the oiled peppers over an open flame or under the broiler until their skins start to blister. Place in a small bowl and immediately cover with plastic wrap. This procedure will loosen the skins and ease the peeling process (see chapter 1).

2.   Halve the peppers lengthwise, seed, and cut into 1-inch-wide strips. Arrange vertically in a glass jar or similar container.

3.   Combine all the ingredients for the marinade except the olive oil in stainless steel saucepan and simmer for 5 minutes. Let cool completely, then add the olive oil.

4.   Adjust the marinade's seasonings as desired. Pour the marinade over the peppers, being sure to cover them entirely.

5.   Cover and refrigerate. Serve cold or at room temperature.

Melanzane e Peperoncini sott'Olio
EGGPLANT AND HOT PEPPERS IN OIL

Yield: 8 to 10 servings

3 pounds	small eggplants, Italian or Oriental	2 tablespoons	chopped oregano
4 tablespoons	salt	1/2 cup	white wine vinegar
6 cloves	garlic	6	small hot chili peppers, chopped
2 tablespoons	chopped mint leaves	3/4 cup	extra-virgin olive oil

1.   Peel the eggplants and cut into 1/4-inch strips.

2.   In a bowl combine the eggplants with the salt. Let rest overnight covered with a light weight (use two china plates).

3.   Squeeze as much liquid as possible from the eggplant, preferably using cheesecloth. Discard the liquid.

4.   Place the eggplant in a mixing bowl; add garlic, mint, oregano, vinegar, and chili peppers. Marinate for 1 hour, then arrange in a ceramic or glass container, pressing down gently with a spoon or ladle to pack the mixture tightly. Add the olive oil, covering the mixture completely.

5.   Cover the container and keep at room temperature. After several hours, check to see if the mixture is totally covered with the oil. If necessary, add more olive oil to cover.

6.   Refrigerate, covered. Stored in this way, the eggplant should keep for several months.

Funghi Assortiti all'Olio e Limone

MUSHROOMS IN OIL AND LEMON JUICE

Yield: 8 servings

2½ pounds	mushrooms (such as porcini, chanterelles, cremini)	to taste	salt and freshly ground black pepper
¾ cup	virgin olive oil	GARNISH:	
1 cup	onions, diced small	8	radicchio leaves
4 cloves	garlic	8 ounces	arugula
1 cup	dry white wine	16	scallions, white part only, trimmed
⅓ cup	lemon juice		
¼ cup	balsamic vinegar	4	tomatoes, peeled and wedged
2	bay leaves		
2	small red chili peppers, chopped	3 tablespoons	chopped Italian parsley

1.   Use either wild or cultivated mushrooms. Trim off the sandy part of the stem ends, then wash quickly in fresh water. If the mushrooms are large, cut in halves, quarters, or thick slices. *Porcino* and *portobello* mushrooms usually must be cut in this way.

2.   In a large stainless steel casserole or *sautoir,* heat 2 ounces of olive oil. Add the onions and garlic and cook until somewhat translucent.

3.   Add the trimmed, cleaned mushrooms. Cook for several minutes.

4.   Add the white wine, lemon juice, vinegar, bay leaves, peppers, salt, and pepper. Cover and cook for about 5 minutes. Remove from heat; cool.

5.   When the mushrooms have cooled completely, mix in the rest of the olive oil. Adjust the seasonings.

6.   Store the marinated mushrooms in a porcelain, glass, or stainless steel container with a tight-fitting cover. Kept in this way, the mushrooms can be stored for several weeks.

7.   To serve, spoon a portion of the marinated mushrooms onto a crisp radicchio leaf and place on each serving plate. Garnish with arugula, scallions, and tomato wedges. Sprinkle freshly chopped Italian parsley over the mushrooms.

— Carciofi —

ARTICHOKES

There are basically two methods for preparing artichokes. In the first, the artichoke is trimmed to the heart, with all the choke removed. Prepared in this way, the artichokes are usually eaten with a knife and fork.

With the second method, only the choke is removed, and the leaves are barely trimmed. Prepared in this way, the artichoke must be eaten with the hands. Each leaf is pulled off and dipped in melted butter or sauce. Only the small portion at the base of each leaf is edible; great care must be taken to avoid the inedible part of the leaf, which is discarded. The heart awaits the patient eater, but must be de-choked before consumption.

Carciofini (baby artichokes) need little trimming and, if very fresh, can be eaten raw.

Regular artichokes need about 15 minutes of cooking time if fresh; otherwise they require more, depending on storage and handling. Dehydration adds to the cooking time here as with any vegetable. Be sure to cook the artichokes in acidulated water.

Carciofini all'Olio e Limone

BABY ARTICHOKES IN OIL AND LEMON JUICE

Yield: 6 servings

¾ cup	virgin olive oil	2	bay leaves
3 cloves	garlic, finely minced	to taste	salt and freshly ground black pepper
1 cup	finely diced onions		
1 cup	dry white wine	to taste	chili peppers, finely diced
2 cups	chicken broth	18	baby artichokes, trimmed completely
½ cup	lemon juice		

1. Heat 2 ounces olive oil in a stainless steel pan. Add the garlic and onions and cook for a few minutes over low heat.

2. Add the wine, chicken broth, lemon juice, bay leaves, salt, pepper, and chili peppers.

3. Cook the artichokes in this marinade for about 10 minutes or until crisp-tender. Remove from heat and cool. Cover the artichokes with the rest of the olive oil and chill in a covered container. The artichokes will keep for 2 weeks when stored this way. They may be served as an appetizer, a garnish, or a salad dish.

Peperoni Arrostiti con Formaggio Caprino e Alici

ROASTED PEPPERS WITH GOAT CHEESE AND ANCHOVIES

Yield: 6 servings

2 heads	garlic	18	cured ripe olives
4 tablespoons	olive oil	6 sprigs	basil
½ cup	meat broth		
2	green peppers	**DRESSING:**	
2	red peppers	⅔ cup	extra-virgin olive oil
2	yellow peppers	¼ cup	lemon juice
4	tomatoes	¼ cup	white wine vinegar
8 ounces	arugula	2 cloves	garlic
6 ounces	mild and creamy goat cheese	2 tablespoons	chopped basil and oregano
12	anchovy fillets	to taste	salt and freshly ground black pepper
12	scallions		
1 tablespoon	capers		

1. Rub the heads of garlic thoroughly with oil. Place in an ovenproof dish and bake at 350°F for 15 minutes. Add ½ cup of meat broth, cover tightly, and continue to cook in the oven for 30 minutes. Make sure garlic stays moist. It may be necessary to add more broth. Remove the garlic from the oven.

2. When garlic has cooled sufficiently, remove the peels. Keep the garlic covered and warm.

3. Rub the peppers with oil. Roast them either over an open flame or under the broiler. In either case, when the skins start to blister, place the peppers in a bowl and cover with plastic wrap. This eases the peeling process. Be careful not to burn the pepper flesh.

4. Peel, halve, and seed the peppers. When completely cool, cut them into uniform wedges or petal shapes.

5. Plunge the tomatoes into boiling water for no more than 15 seconds. After cooling in ice water, peel, halve vertically, and seed the tomatoes. Cut each into 6 petal shapes.

6. To serve, arrange green, red, and yellow peppers and tomato petals on a bed of arugula, creating a floral design.

7. Place a slice of goat cheese (approximately 1 ounce) in the center of each serving.

(continued)

8. Garnish with anchovies, roasted and peeled garlic cloves, scallions, capers, cured ripe olives, and basil sprigs.

9. Combine the dressing ingredients and spoon over the salad.

Bagna Cauda

FRESH RAW VEGETABLES WITH WARM GARLIC-ANCHOVY SAUCE

This is probably a relative of the French crudités. Here a beautiful bouquet of the freshest and most tender raw vegetables are dipped into a heated garlic-anchovy sauce. In our health-conscious society, a dish such as this deserves consideration. Carefully select compatible vegetables, giving particular attention to those that are in season. Allow 8 to 12 ounces of vegetables per serving. The possible combinations are endless; below are listed only some of the vegetables that can be used:

- scallions, trimmed
- *fagiolini* (young green beans)
- sugar snap peas
- miniature carrots, peeled, with 2 inches of stem retained
- asparagus, peeled and trimmed (use thin stalks)
- baby artichokes, well trimmed, with 2 inches of stem retained
- celery hearts
- broccoli florets
- fennel, cut into thin wedges, with the core removed
- red and yellow bell peppers, seeded and cut to finger-sized sticks (bâtons)
- zucchini, small only, cut into finger-sized sticks (bâtons)
- tomatoes, sun-ripened, cut into wedges
- Belgian endive, halved

Yield: 6 servings

SAUCE:

3 ounces	fresh butter
12 cloves	garlic, finely minced
6	anchovy fillets
1 cup	virgin olive oil
¼ cup	lemon juice
to taste	salt and freshly ground black pepper

1.   Heat the butter in a small earthenware dish until it begins to sizzle but not brown. Add the garlic and anchovies, whisking together with a wire whip.

2.   Add the olive oil and lemon juice and remove from heat. Adjust the seasonings. (Heavy cream or reduced heavy cream may be added to the sauce at this time if desired.)

3.   Place the earthenware dish in a napkin folded like an artichoke. Arrange the well-washed, trimmed vegetables around the sauce.

4.   Serve with fresh Italian bread and Fontina cheese.

Verdure Cotte Croccanti con Polpa di Gamberetti e Fegatini

CRISP VEGETABLES WITH SHRIMP AND CHICKEN LIVERS

Yield: 6 servings

6 ounces	shrimp	DRESSING:	
9 ounces	chicken livers	³/₄ cup	extra-virgin olive oil
¼ cup	milk		
3 to 5 ounces	small, young green beans	¼ cup	lemon juice
		¼ cup	balsamic vinegar
3 to 5 ounces	broccoli florets	4 cloves	garlic, finely minced
3 ounces	yellow zucchini, cut into small strips	to taste	salt and freshly ground black pepper
		3 ounces	red bell pepper, cut into small strips
GARLIC TOAST:			
1 head	garlic	12	scallions, white part only, cleaned
¼ cup	water		
1	small red pepper	18	arugula leaves, torn into small pieces
1½ fluid ounces	virgin olive oil		
1 tablespoon	chopped basil		
to taste	salt and cayenne pepper	6	large radicchio leaves
12 slices	Italian bread, ¼ inch thick		

(continued)

1.   Place the shrimp in suitable pot, add just enough cold water to cover completely, and season with salt. Bring to a boil, and immediately remove from heat. Reserve until needed.

2.   Remove the sinews from the chicken livers. Place in a small bowl with ½ cup milk. Reserve until needed.

3.   Cook the green beans in salted water until pleasantly crisp. Remove immediately to ice water, then drain. Cook the broccoli in the same way. Blanch the yellow zucchini for 1 minute, remove to ice water, and drain. Reserve the vegetables until needed.

4.   Coat the head of garlic completely with olive oil, place in an ovenproof dish, and bake in 350°F oven for 10 minutes. Add ¼ cup water to the dish and cover. Cook for another 20 minutes, until the garlic is soft. Cool and peel.

5.   Rub olive oil over the red pepper and hold it over an open flame until the skin blisters (but does not burn). Place it immediately in a bowl and cover tightly with plastic wrap. This eases the peeling process. Peel and seed the pepper.

6.   Put peeled garlic, pepper, basil, and ½ fluid ounce of olive oil in a food processor. Puree until very smooth. Season with salt and cayenne pepper.

7.   Brush the Italian bread slices lightly with the remaining olive oil, and toast both sides under the broiler. Spread a generous amount of the garlic-pepper puree on each slice. Glaze under the broiler just before serving.

8.   Combine the remaining olive oil, lemon juice, vinegar, and garlic.

9.   Peel and devein the cooked shrimp, and cut diagonally into slivers.

10.   Drain the milk from the chicken livers, and pat dry with a paper towel. Cut into small pieces, and sauté quickly in 1 fluid ounce olive oil until medium-well done. Remove to a strainer and season with salt and freshly ground black pepper.

11.   In another skillet, heat half of the dressing to a boil. Add the red pepper strips and scallions, and cook for 20 to 30 seconds. Remove from the heat and add the green beans, broccoli, and yellow zucchini. Mix in the slivered shrimp, sautéed chicken livers, and arugula. Add more dressing if needed.

12.   Serve immediately on radicchio-lined plates, with the garlic toast nearby (see color plate 6).

Insalata di Lenticchie con Pancetta Croccante

LENTIL SALAD WITH CRISP PANCETTA

Yield: 6 servings

1 cup	lentils	1	large red onion, thinly sliced
¼ cup	red wine vinegar		
1 fluid ounce	balsamic vinegar	6	oil-preserved sun-dried tomatoes (see chapter 1)
¾ cup	virgin olive oil		
1 tablespoon	prepared mustard	1 pound	pancetta, diced and fried crisp
2 cloves	garlic, finely minced		
1 tablespoon	capers	2 tablespoons	finely chopped chives
to taste	salt and freshly ground black pepper		

GARNISH:

1 head	romaine lettuce

1. Soak the lentils overnight in water. Drain and cook in fresh water until soft, about 20 minutes. Do not overcook: the lentils should be tender but retain their skins. Drain and place in a bowl.

2. Combine the vinegars, olive oil, mustard, garlic, capers, and salt and pepper.

3. Marinate the lentils with this dressing at room temperature.

4. To serve, arrange hearts of romaine leaves on plates. Spoon the lentils onto the leaves, and garnish with thin slices of red onion and sun-dried tomatoes.

5. Sprinkle crisp *pancetta* bits and finely chopped chives over the lentils.

Mozzarella alla Casalinga

HOMEMADE MOZZARELLA

This homemade mozzarella contains no preservatives and so will not keep very long even when refrigerated. Mozzarella intended as antipastos may be stuffed: rolled with ham, salami, hot peppers, sun-dried tomatoes, *pesto,* or other fillings. It is then sliced and served with various marinades. The cheese can also be shaped into a ball or a log or even smoked.

The following recipe is for a mozzarella roulade. The stuffing is the chef's choice.

(continued)

Yield: 6 servings

1 gallon	water
8 ounces	salt
2 pounds	milk curd (from buffalo milk, if possible)
1 pound	desired filling

1. Place the water in as small a pot as possible, add the salt, and heat to 175°F.

2. Cut the milk curd into small pieces. Place in the heated water, and stir until the curd strings form a solid mass around the spoon.

3. Remove the curd and drain. Knead it by hand to remove as much water as possible.

4. Press and flatten the curd on a sheet pan to a ¼-inch thickness.

5. Spread the filling on cheese and roll up tightly like a jelly roll. Wrap in several layers of plastic wrap, tighten both ends, and secure with string.

6. Place immediately in ice water to shock. Keep refrigerated and use within 5 days.

7. To serve: Cut several ¼-inch slices of mozzarella. Overlap the slices on arugula or radicchio leaves. Sprinkle with virgin olive oil and lemon juice or a marinade (such as the herb dressing in the following recipe). Garnish with roasted peppers, sun-dried tomatoes, stuffed eggs, or any compatible vegetables.

Insalata di Mozzarella all'Erbe
MOZZARELLA WITH PIQUANT HERB DRESSING

Yield: 6 servings

DRESSING:

½ cup	dry white wine	¼ cup	balsamic vinegar
6	sun-dried tomatoes, finely chopped	3 cloves	garlic, finely minced
½ cup	extra-virgin olive oil	1	small chili pepper, finely chopped
1½ fluid ounces	lemon juice	1 tablespoon	chopped Italian parsley

1 tablespoon	*chopped oregano*	*3*	*small tomatoes*
1 tablespoon	*chopped basil*	*1 pound*	*fresh young spinach*
to taste	*salt*		
to taste	*capers (optional)*	*12 ounces*	*red onions*
		to taste	*lemon juice*
		to taste	*salt and pepper*
GARNISH:		*1 pound*	*mozzarella cheese, thinly sliced*
18	*fresh broccoli florets*		
2	*leeks, white part only*		

1. In a small saucepan, bring the wine to a simmer and add the chopped sun-dried tomatoes. Remove from the heat immediately and cool.

2. Combine the remaining ingredients for the dressing. Add the tomatoes and hold at room temperature.

3. Trim the florets from the broccoli and carefully clean the leeks under running water to remove any sand and grit. Cook the broccoli florets and the leeks in salted water until tender-crisp. Chill immediately in cold water, drain, and keep covered and cold.

4. Peel the 3 small tomatoes by plunging them in boiling water for 15 seconds. Chill immediately in ice water and remove the skins. Halve the tomatoes vertically, and re-move the seeds by squeezing. Cut each half into 3 petal-shaped wedges.

5. Remove the stems from the spinach and wash several times in cold water to remove any sand and grit. Drain, cover with a towel, and refrigerate.

6. Cut the red onions into thin slices and sprinkle with a little salt, pepper, and lemon juice. Marinate until needed.

7. To serve, pour a generous amount of dressing on each plate and place a small bouquet of spinach leaves in the center (trim to size if necessary). Overlap thin slices of mozzarella on top.

8. Garnish with the sliced red onions, tomato petals, broccoli florets, and leek whites cut ½-inch thick on the diagonal. See color plate 7.

Caviale d'Olive Nere

BLACK-OLIVE CAVIAR

Black-olive caviar is a convenient relish for any purpose. It may be served by itself in earthenware dishes with raw vegetables or used to fill tomatoes, artichokes, endive leaves, eggs, or mozzarella.

Yield: 1½ cups

2 cups	black olives, pitted and chopped	¼ teaspoon	freshly ground black pepper
4 cloves	garlic, minced	¼ cup	balsamic vinegar
4	anchovy fillets, chopped	¼ cup	virgin olive oil

1.   Place all ingredients in a food processor and chop to the desired texture. Be careful not to puree.

2.   Adjust the seasonings to taste.

Baccalà Mantecato

CHURNED SALT COD WITH CRISP VEGETABLES

This dish was introduced to Italy by the Normans, whose famous sailing exploits were made possible by the preservation of their staple fish, the cod, with salt. In addition to those listed below, other garnishes can be used for this antipasto, including ripe or green olives and hard-cooked egg wedges.

Yield: 6 servings

1 pound	salt-cured cod	½ cup	thinly sliced scallions, white part only
4 cloves	garlic, minced		
¼ to ⅓ cup	lemon juice	to taste	salt
¾ cup	extra virgin olive oil		
1	small chili pepper, finely chopped		

GARNISH:

6	radicchio leaves	1	fennel knob
18	arugula leaves	2 tablespoons	capers
3	small tomatoes	2 tablespoons	chopped parsley
1	small zucchini	¼ cup	Italian salad dressing
1	sweet red onion		

1. In order to de-salt it, soak the salt cod in fresh cold water overnight or for 2 days if necessary, changing the water several times.

2. Place the cod in a pot of cold water and simmer for 10 to 15 minutes. Cool the fish in the poaching liquid for 1 hour before draining. Place it in a mixing bowl and flake with a fork.

3. Stir the flaked fish with a wooden spoon. Add the garlic and lemon juice. Slowly pour in the oil and continue stirring. Mix in the chopped pepper and scallions and adjust seasonings. The churned mixture should keep for 1 week if refrigerated.

4. Clean and wash the radicchio and arugula. Cover with clean towel and keep cold.

5. Peel the tomatoes by plunging them into boiling water for 15 seconds and then immediately shocking them in ice water. Peel, remove the seeds, and cut julienne.

6. Clean but do not peel the zucchini. Cut julienne.

7. Peel the onion, halve it, and cut into thin strips.

8. Clean the fennel knob, and cut across into thin slices.

9. To serve, place some churned cod on a radicchio leaf and set on a platter. Sprinkle with capers and chopped parsley.

10. Decorate with a bouquet of raw julienne of zucchini, onion, fennel, tomatoes, and whole arugula leaves. Dress with salad dressing.

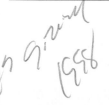

Insalata alla Marinara

SEAFOOD SALAD, MARINER STYLE

Yield: 6 servings

6 ounces	squid	to taste	chopped basil
6 ounces	shrimp, 32 count	to taste	chopped oregano
6 ounces	deep sea scallops		
12	little neck or small cherrystone clams	**GARNISH:**	
12	mussels, debearded and cleaned	3 ounces	celeriac, cut julienne
		12	broccoli florets
		3	small tomatoes
DRESSING:		24	arugula leaves
³/₄ cup	virgin olive oil	6 ounces	red bell pepper, cut julienne
¹/₂ cup	lemon juice		
¹/₄ cup	dry white wine	1	sweet red onion, sliced thinly
4 cloves	garlic, minced		
1 tablespoon	capers	12	black olives, pitted and halved
1 teaspoon	chopped chili pepper		
to taste	salt	12	green olives, pitted and halved
to taste	chopped parsley		

1.   To prepare the squid, remove the tentacles from the body (cutting just ahead of eyes), being sure to remove the beak. Carefully remove the transparent cartilaginous cuttlebone from the body, discard, and rinse the body. Slice into thin rings.

2.   Peel and devein the shrimp, being careful not to remove the fantails.

3.   Bring 1 quart of water to a simmer. Add squid rings and blanch for 15 seconds. Remove and cover. Keep chilled.

4.   Blanch the shrimp and scallops in the same way as the squid. Add to squid.

5.   Steam open the clams and mussels. Discard any that do not open. When cool, add the clams and mussels to the other shellfish.

6.   Combine all the dressing ingredients.

7.   Blanch the julienne of celeriac for 30 seconds, remove to ice water, and drain.

8.   Blanch the broccoli florets for 30 seconds, remove to ice water, and drain.

9.   Place the tomatoes in boiling water for 15 seconds. Remove to ice water. Peel, seed, and halve each tomato vertically. Cut each half into 3 petals.

10.   Arrange 4 arugula leaves on each plate. Place the seafood mixture on the leaves.

11.   Combine the celeriac, broccoli, pepper, onion, and olives. Toss with some of the dressing. Arrange the vegetables around the seafood, and decorate with 3 tomato petals.

12.   Spoon some of the dressing over the seafood before serving (see color plate 8).

Conchiglia di Gamberetti al Profumo d'Arancia

SHRIMP AND CELERIAC WITH ORANGE MAYONNAISE EN COQUILLE

Yield: 6 servings

12	jumbo shrimp (16-per-pound size)	1 teaspoon	prepared mustard
		1½ fluid ounces	orange juice concentrate
1	bouquet garni, small		
		to taste	salt and cayenne pepper
to taste	salt		
1 small	celeriac	**GARNISH:**	
1½ to 2 cups	freshly squeezed orange juice	6	green lettuce leaves
1 small	tart green apple	18	small orange wedges
½	sweet red onion		
		6 sprigs	fresh mint sprigs
DRESSING:		1 tablespoon	red pepper, cut to thin julienne
½ cup	mayonnaise		
¼ cup	Mascarpone		

1.   Add the shrimp and *bouquet garni* to a pot with the salt and enough water to cover. Bring to a boil, remove from the heat, and let the shrimp cool in the liquid. Peel and devein the shrimp. Cover and keep cold.

2.   Clean the celeriac by brushing vigorously under running water. Peel and cut into matchsticks *(allumettes)*, about 1 inch long, ⅛ inch thick. Place the celeriac in a small stainless steel pot and cook, covered, with the orange juice for a few minutes, until tender-crisp. Strain and reduce the liquid into 1½ fluid ounces. Cool and reserve.

(continued)

3. Meanwhile, peel the apple and onion. Cut into matchsticks and combine with the celeriac and reduced orange juice in a mixing bowl.

4. Mix the mayonnaise, Mascarpone, mustard, orange juice concentrate, salt, and cayenne. Adjust the cayenne if desired, then combine with celeriac, apple, and onion.

5. Line 6 *coquilles* with the lettuce leaves.

6. Cut the shrimp in half vertically.

7. Place 2 tablespoons of the dressing in the center of each lettuce-lined scallop shell.

8. Neatly overlap 4 shrimp halves, alternated with 3 orange wedges, fanning them out to the edge of the shell.

9. Decorate with fresh mint sprigs and a few bits of the fine julienne of red pepper.

10. Set the *coquille* in a folded napkin to serve.

Insalata di Cozze alla Salsa Aurora Piccante
STEAMED MUSSELS IN FRESH VEGETABLE AND TOMATO MAYONNAISE

Yield: 6 servings

48	large mussels	3 tablespoons	Mascarpone
1/2 cup	dry white wine	1 tablespoon	capers
2	bay leaves	1 teaspoon	chopped hot red pepper
4 cloves	garlic, minced	to taste	salt and freshly ground black pepper
2 or 3	parsley sprigs		

DRESSING:

GARNISH:

1	large tomato	8 ounces	arugula
1	small red bell pepper, seeded	2	small sweet red onions, cut into rings
1	small green bell pepper, seeded	1 tablespoon	chopped basil
1	fennel knob, peeled	1 tablespoon	chopped parsley
3/4 cup	mayonnaise	as needed	slices of freshly toasted sourdough bread
1 tablespoon	tomato paste		
1 tablespoon	prepared mustard		
1 fluid ounce	lemon juice		

1. Clean the mussels by scrubbing and debearding. Put the mussels in cold water for several minutes, then pick out and discard any that are open. Check for mussels that might be filled with mud by twisting in the hand after soaking: any that can be opened are mud filled and should be discarded.

2. Fill a shallow stainless steel casserole with the white wine, bay leaves, garlic, and parsley. Add the mussels and steam over high heat with a tight-fitting cover until the shells open. The meat should remain plump. Be careful not to overcook, or the meat will shrink and dry out.

3. Remove from the heat and pour off the liquid, straining through cheesecloth. Reserve the liquid. Shell the mussels, place in a container, cover, and keep cold.

4. Reduce steaming liquid to 1 fluid ounce and reserve for the dressing.

5. Peel the tomato by plunging into boiling water for 15 seconds, placing in ice water, and then sliding the skin off. Cut the tomato, bell peppers, and fennel into a 1½-inch-long fine julienne.

6. In a mixing bowl, blend the mayonnaise with the tomato paste, prepared mustard, lemon juice, and reduced steaming liquid. Fold in the Mascarpone, capers, and hot red pepper.

7. Adjust the seasonings. Mix in the julienne vegetables and the mussels. Keep well chilled until ready to serve.

8. To serve, line the center of each plate with arugula and place a mound of the mussel salad (8 mussels per portion) in the center. Garnish with rings of sweet red onion and sprinkle with herbs. Serve with freshly toasted sourdough bread or Italian garlic toast (see Crisp Vegetables with Shrimp and Chicken Livers, earlier in this chapter).

Salmone Affumicato con Salsa Lattuga

SMOKED SALMON WITH GREEN LETTUCE SAUCE

Yield: 6 servings

SAUCE:

4 ounces	lettuce leaves, no stems
¼ ounce	Italian parsley, no stems
½ ounce	scallions
½ cup	virgin olive oil
2 to 3 cloves	garlic, minced
½ fluid ounce	balsamic vinegar
to taste	salt and freshly ground black pepper
18 slices	smoked salmon (about 15 ounces)

GARNISH:

12	arugula leaves
6	tomato wedges, peeled and seeded
12	belgian endive leaves
2 tablespoons	salmon caviar
2 tablespoons	capers
2	sweet red onion, thinly sliced (optional)

1.   Cut the lettuce, parsley, and scallions into small pieces and place in a food processor. Process, gradually adding the oil and the rest of the sauce ingredients. Adjust the seasonings. Process until very smooth.

2.   Neatly overlap three smoked salmon slices near two arugula leaves on each plate. Coat the plate with lettuce sauce.

3.   Decorate with a tomato wedge and two endive leaves filled with salmon caviar.

4.   Sprinkle the capers over the smoked salmon. Add thin slices of sweet red onion if desired.

Filetti di Trota Affumicati con Maionese allo Zafferano
SMOKED TROUT FILLETS WITH SAFFRON MAYONNAISE

Hot-smoked trout is a true delicacy as long as the fish is not overcooked and dry. You will need a heavy-duty aluminum roasting pan with a tight-fitting lid that is 6 to 8 inches deep. To smoke six trout, the pan should be about 12 by 18 inches. You will also need a metal rack to hold the trout. This must fit inside the roasting pan and should rest at least 2½ inches from the base of the pan. Use four metal timbales upside down on the bottom of the pan to keep the rack above the sawdust.

The sawdust is your choice. Do, however, be sure to use a sawdust that is from hardwood (I prefer hickory and apple), and one that is not too fine.

Before smoking, the food is usually marinated in a salted liquid known as a brine. After brining, the food can be either hot- or cold-smoked (the only difference being temperature). Hot-smoking is excellent for poultry and game (especially duck), while colder smoking temperatures are ideal for fish.

Yield: 6 servings

6	fresh trout, 7 to 8 ounces each	6	whole cloves
		1 teaspoon	freshly crushed black pepper
BRINE:			
2 quarts	fresh water	**FOR SMOKING:**	
3 ounces	kosher salt	3 cups	sawdust
4 ounces	sugar		

1.   Clean the trout, leaving the heads on, and place them in a stainless steel or porcelain dish.

2.   Mix the ingredients for the brine well and pour over the fish. Cover and keep chilled for 3 days, turning the fish once a day.

3.   When ready to smoke, remove the trout and pat dry with a towel. Place them on a metal rack, making sure they do not touch.

4.   Sprinkle the sawdust on the bottom of the roasting pan and heat it over a high flame. When the sawdust starts to smoke, place the rack with the trout in the pan, elevated above the sawdust. Cover tightly and smoke for about 10 minutes.

5.   Take the pan from the heat. In a well-ventilated area, remove the cover. Remove the rack with the trout and let cool completely. Wrap the fish in plastic wrap to retain freshness and moisture. Note the exact time and heat used for smoking so that you can repeat or adjust the procedure in the future.

(continued)

6.   To serve, remove the head from each trout. Make an incision along the backbone and carefully remove the fillets from the fish. Watch for and remove any little bones that pull away with the fillets.

7.   Arrange the fillets neatly on a serving platter with saffron mayonnaise (recipe follows) spooned nearby, and sweet red onion slices, tomato wedges, or other compatible garnishes. Green Lettuce Sauce (see Smoked Salmon with Green Lettuce Sauce, earlier in this chapter) is also suitable with smoked trout.

Salsa Maionese allo Zafferano
SAFFRON MAYONNAISE

Yield: 6 portions

pinch	saffron	1	egg yolk
1/4 cup	white wine vinegar	1 cup	olive oil, at room temperature
1 fluid ounce	water		
1 clove	garlic, minced	to taste	salt and lemon juice
1 1/2 teaspoons	prepared mustard	1/4 cup	whipped cream
pinch	cayenne pepper		

1.   Combine the saffron, white wine vinegar, and water in a saucepan. Heat quickly and bring to a boil. Remove to a mixing bowl immediately and let cool.

2.   Add the garlic, mustard, cayenne, and egg yolk. Whisk until thoroughly combined.

3.   Add the olive oil slowly, in fine stream, while mixing. Adjust the seasonings.

4.   Fold in the whipped cream.

Filetto di Trota Marinato al Profumo di Finocchio e Pepe Verde

FILLET OF TROUT IN FENNEL MARINADE WITH GREEN PEPPERCORN DRESSING

This recipe can also be used for bass, salmon, scallops, and other seafood.

Yield: 6 servings

3	fresh river trout, 10 to 12 ounces each
1½ ounces	salt
½ ounce	sugar
½ teaspoon	freshly ground black pepper

MARINADE:

1 cup	fennel tops
½ cup	diced sweet red onions
1 cup	dry vermouth
1 cup	dry white wine
1 cup	water
1	bay leaf

DRESSING:

1 tablespoon	green peppercorns
1 fluid ounce	lemon juice
1 tablespoon	grappa
⅓ cup	virgin olive oil
to taste	salt

GARNISH:

1	whole fresh fennel knob
3	fresh tomatoes
8 ounces	arugula leaves
6	fennel top sprigs

1. Fillet and skin the trout. Use a tweezer to remove any small bones remaining in the flesh.

2. Combine the salt, sugar, and pepper. Rub the fillets gently with this mixture. Place them side by side in flat porcelain or glass dish. Cover with plastic wrap and refrigerate overnight.

3. Place all the marinade ingredients in a nonaluminum saucepan. Heat and reduce by half. Strain, cool, and adjust the seasonings.

4. Turn the trout fillets and cover with the marinade. Cover again with plastic wrap and refrigerate overnight.

5. To make the dressing, press the peppercorns through a fine-mesh sieve into small stainless steel mixing bowl. Whisk in the remaining dressing ingredients. Store at room temperature in small covered container until needed.

(continued)

6. Cut the fennel knob into 6 wedges, being careful to leave the root stem on so the stalks do not detach. Blanch in salted water for 5 minutes and then shock in ice water. Drain and core completely.

7. Peel the tomatoes by immersing them in boiling water for 15 seconds. Remove to ice water and then slide the peels off. Remove the seeds and cut each into 4 wedges.

8. To serve, arrange the arugula leaves on the serving plates. Place bias-cut slices of trout fillet in semicircle on top (see color plate 9).

9. Pour 1 tablespoon green peppercorn dressing inside the semicircle. Decorate each plate with 1 fennel wedge and 2 tomato wedges. Add a sprig of fennel top as well. (The tomato and fennel wedges may be flavored with a light lemon and olive oil dressing.)

Insalata di Pollo e Melone ai Rivoli

CHICKEN AND MELON WITH APPLE-CELERIAC SALAD

Yield: 4 servings

2	chicken breasts, boneless with skin	1 tablespoon	prepared mustard
		1 teaspoon	tomato paste
as needed	salt and pepper	to taste	salt and cayenne pepper
as needed	olive oil		
4 ounces	celeriac	½ cup	whipped cream
1½ cups	fresh orange juice		
4 ounces	tart green apples	GARNISH:	
1 ounce	red bell pepper	4	radicchio leaves
2 ounces	sweet red onion	4	canteloupe wedges, skinned and seeded
DRESSING:		4	mint sprigs
1 cup	mayonnaise		

1. Season the chicken breasts and rub with oil. Place them, skin side up, on rack in preheated 375°F oven and roast until medium-well done (approximately 12 minutes).

2. Remove the breasts to a plate. Cover with another plate and press. Refrigerate.

3. Clean the celeriac. Cut it into matchsticks *(allumettes)*, and blanch in fresh orange juice for several minutes. Drain, reserving the juice, and cool. Reduce the orange juice to ¼ cup and cool.

4. Peel the apple and cut into matchsticks. Cut the pepper and onion into matchsticks.

5. Mix the mayonnaise, mustard, tomato paste, and seasonings. Add the reduced orange juice, and fold in the whipped cream. Adjust the seasonings.

6. Toss the celeriac, apple, pepper, and onion with enough dressing to coat.

7. Arrange a bouquet of salad in radicchio leaves and set on a platter.

8. Cut the melon wedges diagonally and fan into a semicircle.

9. Skin the chicken breast and cut on a bias into thin slices. Arrange this around salad opposite the melon.

10. Spoon some dressing on each side of the chicken. Decorate with mint sprigs.

Vitello Freddo, con Salsa Tonnato e Capperi
SLICED BRAISED VEAL WITH TUNA-CAPER SAUCE

As veal loin is extremely expensive, this dish can also be successfully made with breast of turkey or loin of pork, and should then simply be named as such. For these meats, an internal temperature reading of 145° to 150°F is essential.

Yield: 8 servings

2 pounds	boneless veal loin or top round	1 tablespoon	capers
to taste	salt and pepper	3 cloves	garlic
¼ cup	olive oil	2 tablespoons	tomato paste
2 ounces	onions, thinly sliced	2 to 3	anchovy fillets
2 ounces	carrots, thinly sliced	¼ cup	lemon juice
2 ounces	celery, thinly sliced	1 fluid ounce	reduced braising liquid
½ teaspoon	freshly ground black pepper	1 cup	mayonnaise
1 cup	dry white wine	½ cup	whipped cream
1 cup	meat broth		

TUNA SAUCE:

GARNISH:

½ cup	canned dark tuna meat	2 tablespoons	capers
		as needed	other compatible vegetables

(continued)

1.   Trim the fat and skin from the veal loin. Reserve the trimmings. Tie with butcher twine to maintain uniform shape and rub with salt and pepper.

2.   Sear the meat lightly on all sides in a roasting pan in olive oil. Remove and keep warm.

3.   Add the vegetables to the roasting pan, along with any veal trimmings. Sear lightly, add the black pepper, wine, and meat broth, and bring to a simmer.

4.   Place the seared veal on top of the vegetables, cover, and braise slowly in medium oven (about 350°F) for about 15 to 20 minutes, until the meat reaches an internal temperature of 130° to 135°F. Remove the meat and let cool to room temperature. Place a 1-pound weight on top of the meat and refrigerate.

5.   Strain the braising liquid through a fine-mesh sieve and reduce to 1 fluid ounce. Reserve for the tuna sauce.

6.   Place the tuna, capers, garlic, tomato paste, anchovies, lemon juice, and reduced braising liquid into a blender and puree as fine as possible. Add the mayonnaise and continue to blend until smooth and creamy. Rub through a fine-mesh sieve, adjust the seasonings, and fold in the whipped cream. Cover with plastic wrap and refrigerate.

7.   To serve, coat each serving plate with tuna sauce. Overlap paper-thin slices of veal on the sauce, covering half the space. Sprinkle some capers over the sauce, and garnish as desired (see color plate 10). Anything compatible, such as asparagus spears, scallions, sweet red onion rings, sliced radish, or tomato in any form would enhance the dish.

Anitra Affumicata alla Casalinga
SMOKED DUCK

Duck is an excellent meat for hot-smoking. I have always enjoyed the deep aroma of hickory throughout the kitchen when preparing this dish. The meat itself is very moist, a true delicacy.

Use a heavy cast-iron or aluminum pan with a depth of at least 12 inches for smoking. The diameter of the pan depends on how many items are to be smoked. I have used old army pans with great success.

You will also need a rack on which the duck will rest above the sawdust. Three-inch-deep metal timbales work well in elevating the rack above the sawdust. Place them upside down on the pan's bottom. The rack must remain steady above the smoking sawdust.

For smoking, I use coarse hickory and apple sawdust, but any hardwood sawdust (do *not* use pine) will work well.

Yield: 8 servings

BRINE:

1 gallon	water	1	eviscerated duck, 5 to 6 pounds
6½ ounces	kosher salt		
8 ounces	sugar	4 cups	sawdust
¾ cup	honey	to garnish	fresh fruit, mint sprigs
10	whole cloves		
1 tablespoon	freshly ground black pepper		

1. Combine the brine ingredients in a ceramic or stainless steel bowl. Submerge the duck in the brine. Refrigerate for three days, turning the duck each day.

2. Remove duck and pat dry. Truss the duck to maintain its shape, and place it on smoking rack.

3. Sprinkle sawdust on the bottom of the pan and heat. When the sawdust starts to smoke, place the rack with the duck inside the pan; be sure to elevate it at least 3 inches from the bottom of the pan. To eliminate some of the duck's excess fat, prick the bird through the skin all over, especially the thighs. (This fat is extremely flammable and can start fires. Do not remove the cover from the pan while smoking. Bring the covered pan to a safe area to cool before removing the duck.)

4. Cover tightly and weigh down.

5. Smoke for about 40 minutes over a medium-hot flame. Remove the pan from the heat fire. Open it away from the flame, in a well-ventilated area. Cool, covered.

6. Wrap the duck in plastic wrap. Refrigerate when cool.

7. To serve, bone the duck when cool. Remove the breast and legs. Remove the thigh bones. Slice the breast neatly on a bias and overlap on a serving plate. Slice the thighs similarly. Each serving should have breast and leg meat.

8. Serve with fresh fruit, such as melon, peaches, pears, figs, papaya, currants, or raspberries. Decorate with fresh mint leaves.

Sella di Vitello Farcita con Insalata Capricciosa e Uova Farcite
ROAST STUFFED SADDLE OF VEAL WITH VEGETABLE SALAD AND DEVILED EGGS

Yield: 15 servings

1	saddle of milk-fed veal, 10 to 12 pounds	to taste	salt
¼ cup	brandy	1 ounce	black truffles, diced
to taste	salt and pepper	1 ounce	pistachios, peeled
		1½ ounces	fresh pork fat, finely diced
FORCEMEAT:		2 ounces	cooked ham, diced
8 ounces	veal trimmings (from loin)	6	romaine lettuce leaves, blanched
8 ounces	calf's liver	1 pound	caul fat, soaked in water for 1 hour
4 ounces	pork, cubed small	to taste	salt and freshly ground black pepper
8 ounces	fresh pork fat, cubed small		
2 ounces	flour	**GARNISH:**	
2	egg whites	6 portions	capricciosa (see Cooked and Raw Vegetable Salad in Oil and Vinegar, chapter 13)
pinch	nutmeg		
pinch	thyme		
pinch	marjoram	6	deviled eggs
pinch	cayenne pepper	6	baby squash, blanched
pinch	freshly ground white pepper		

1.   Remove both tenderloins from the veal saddle and reserve.

2.   Completely bone the veal saddle, being sure to leave the side flaps in place while trimming away all fat.

3.   Butterfly the loins by laying skin side down on a cutting board and making an incision lengthwise almost through each loin. Reserve any trimmings for the forcemeat.

4.   Sprinkle the boned saddle with brandy, cover with plastic wrap, and chill.

5.   Remove the silverskin (membrane) from both tenderloins. Season with salt and pepper, and sear quickly on all sides to stiffen. Wrap tightly in plastic wrap to maintain shape, and chill.

6.   To prepare the forcemeat, remove the skin and sinews from the calf's liver, cut into small pieces, and soak for several hours in cold water.

7.   Drain the liver and pat dry. Puree in a food processor, and chill.

8.   Grind veal trimmings and cubed pork through the medium plate of a meat grinder. Put briefly in the freezer until firm.

9.   Grind both meat and the pork fat through same blade with crushed ice.

10.   Place forcemeat in a bowl embedded in crushed ice and fold in the liver puree, flour, egg whites, and all the herbs and spices with a wooden spoon. Cook a tiny portion of the forcemeat and taste to sample the seasoning. Adjust if necessary.

11.   Add the truffles, pistachios, diced pork fat, and diced ham to the forcemeat. Chill.

12.   With boned saddle skin side down, spread some forcemeat along the inside of the butterflied loin. Place the tenderloin on the forcemeat and press firmly. The tenderloin may be wrapped in quickly blanched romaine lettuce leaves before being placed in the loin.

13.   Spread the remaining forcemeat along saddle, in and between the loin.

14.   Fold the side flaps over so they overlap at least 2 inches. Secure every 1½ inches with butcher's twine, and wrap with the caul.

15.   Sprinkle with salt and freshly ground black pepper. Place on a rack in preheated 350°F oven, and roast for about 1½ hours, to an internal temperature of 145°F.

16   After the loin has cooled completely, remove the butcher's twine.

17.   To serve, cut the saddle into uniform slices and shingle on a plate.

18.   Wrap the *capricciosa* in the blanched romaine lettuce leaves, using a log mold. These too should be sliced and fanned opposite the veal.

19.   As additional garnish, place the deviled eggs (yolks deviled with mustard, mayonnaise, and cayenne pepper) on the blanched baby squash (see color plate 11).

Galantina di Cappone di Scozia All'Erbe
GALANTINE OF CAPON WITH GREEN HERB SAUCE

Yield: 10 to 12 servings

4 ounces	lean veal	1 teaspoon	salt
4 ounces	lean pork	1	egg, lightly beaten
8 ounces	fresh pork fat	2 ounces	cooked beef tongue, diced medium
1	small capon, approximately 4 pounds	2 ounces	cooked ham, diced medium
¼ cup	Cognac	2 ounces	fresh pork fat, diced small
1	basil sprig		
1	thyme sprig	2 tablespoons	pistachios, peeled
1	marjoram sprig	1	bouquet garni
pinch	nutmeg	as needed	vegetables to garnish
pinch	cayenne pepper		

1.   Cut the veal, pork, and pork fat into small cubes, and chill.

2.   Bone the capon by first removing the wings at the joints and cutting the skin along the entire length of the backbone. The skin and meat can now be removed carefully from the rib cage. Remove the thigh bones as well. Reserve the bones and trimmings.

3.   Place the boned capon in a bowl, add the Cognac, and marinate for two hours.

4.   Grind the diced veal and pork through the medium plate of a meat grinder, followed by the diced pork fat. Place the meats and the fat in the refrigerator or in the freezer until firm.

5.   Add a little crushed ice to the lean ground meats and fat, and regrind using the fine plate of the meat grinder. Mix forcemeat together in a mixing bowl placed in crushed ice. Add the herbs, spices, and lightly beaten egg. Add the Cognac from the marinade as well.

6.   Fold in the diced beef tongue, ham, pork fat, and pistachios. Cover with plastic wrap, and chill.

7.   Prepare a strong poultry stock with the capon bones and trimmings as well as a *bouquet garni*.

8. Place the boned and marinaded capon skin side down on a damp cloth. Spread the cold forcemeat evenly over the capon, pressing firmly with a spatula to fill all pockets and cavities. Roll the capon very tightly in the cloth and tie both ends as well as loosely around the middle.

9. Place the galantine into simmering stock and cook for about 75 minutes. Do not boil. Remove the pan from the heat and let the galantine cool in the stock. When almost cool, remove the galantine and retie. Place it under a light weight and refrigerate.

10. To serve, spoon about ⅓ cup of herb sauce (recipe follows) on each plate and arrange two slices of galantine over the sauce. Garnish with compatible vegetables such as scallions, asparagus spears, roasted pepper wedges, sweet red onion rings, tomato petals, capers, pickled wild mushrooms, or avocado sections.

Scozia all'Erbe

GREEN HERB SAUCE

Yield: 2 cups

10 ounces	Boston lettuce leaves, stemmed and coarsely chopped	2 cloves	garlic, minced
		1 teaspoon	capers
5 ounces	spinach leaves, stemmed and coarsely chopped	¼ cup	lemon juice
		1 fluid ounce	balsamic vinegar
		1 cup	extra-virgin olive oil
1 ounce	scallions, sliced	1	egg yolk
1 ounce	Italian parsley, chopped	to taste	salt, freshly ground black pepper
2 ounces	fennel knob, grated		
1	small chili pepper, chopped		

1. In a blender (*not* a food processor), puree the lettuce, spinach, scallions, parsley, fennel, pepper, garlic, capers, lemon juice, balsamic vinegar, and half of the olive oil until very smooth.

2. Add the egg yolk and remaining oil and blend on high speed to create an emulsion. Strain through a fine-mesh sieve. Adjust the seasonings and chill.

Piccola Spuma di Fegatini con Frutti Freschi Assortiti

CHICKEN-LIVER MOUSSE WITH ASSORTED FRESH FRUITS

Yield: 8 servings

14 ounces	chicken livers	GARNISH:	
1 cup	milk	8	small fresh figs
5 ounces	butter	3	Bartlett pears
3 ounces	sweet red onions, finely diced	3	peaches
		8 to 10	black grapes
1/3 teaspoon	freshly ground black pepper	8	mint sprigs
1 teaspoon	chopped marjoram	24 slices	crostini (Italian bread croutons)
pinch	ground nutmeg		
1 fluid ounce	brandy		
1/4 to 1/3 cup	heavy cream		

1.   Remove the veins and any green areas from the chicken livers. Wash the cleaned livers in cold water and place in a container. Add milk to cover and soak overnight (this will whiten the livers).

2.   Drain the livers and pat dry with a towel.

3.   Heat 3 ounces of butter in a large frying pan and sauté diced onion and livers until medium-well done. Add the pepper, marjoram, and nutmeg. Cool.

4.   Puree the livers in a food processor with 2 ounces butter and the brandy until very smooth. Remove to mixing bowl and adjust seasonings.

5.   Whip the heavy cream into stiff peaks and fold into the liver puree. Cover with plastic wrap and chill.

6.   To serve, use a large soup spoon to scoop 3 ovals of the liver mousse on one side of each serving plate. Dip the spoon in hot water between scoops.

7.   Decorate with fresh fruits. The peaches should be blanched for 10 seconds, shocked, peeled, and pitted. Cut into fan patterns. The figs can be peeled and cut open to resemble flowers. The idea is to arrange the fresh fruits in compatible color schemes. Garnish each plate with a mint sprig.

8.   Serve with lightly buttered Italian bread croutons on the side, preferably in folded napkins. These croutons should have no garlic on them.

Carpaccio all'Albese

CARPACCIO, ALBA STYLE

Carpaccio was devised by the famous Venetian restaurateur Harry Cipriani. It was named after the sixteenth-century painter Vittore Carpaccio, whose works often included bright red colors.

Essentially *carpaccio* is a cold appetizer of very thinly sliced raw beef tenderloin, white Alba truffles, and *Parmigiano Reggiano*. It is flavored with freshly ground black pepper, lemon juice, and the finest virgin olive oil.

Many new versions of *carpaccio* have emerged lately, served with a variety of raw vegetable *coulis* and purees. But whatever garnish is contemplated, the dish should never be covered with a sauce, as the emphasis is on the red meat.

Carpaccio con Caponatina

THIN-SLICED RAW BEEF TENDERLOIN WITH EGGPLANT-VEGETABLE SALAD

Yield: 6 servings

12 ounces	beef tenderloin	3 tablespoons	extra-virgin olive oil
3 ounces	Parmesan	1 head	curly endive
½ teaspoon	freshly ground black pepper	3 cups	caponatina
		24	cured black olives
2 tablespoons	capers	to garnish	mint leaves

1. Trim the beef tenderloin of all fat and cartilage. Wrap the meat very tightly in plastic wrap and place in the freezer for approximately 1 hour, until semifrozen. This will facilitate slicing.

2. Slice the Parmesan cheese as thinly as possible.

3. Slice the semifrozen tenderloin as thinly as possible and arrange, overlapping, in a half-circle on white serving plates.

4. Put a slice of Parmesan cheese on each beef slice. Sprinkle the black pepper and the capers over the cheese. Drizzle the olive oil on top.

5. Place curly endive leaves on the empty part of each plate and put ½ cup of *caponatina* (recipe follows) in the center of the leaf. Garnish with cured ripe olives and fresh mint leaves (see color plate 12).

Caponatina

EGGPLANT-VEGETABLE SALAD

Yield: 3 cups

1 cup	peeled and sliced eggplant, cut into ¼-inch-thick, 2-inch-long pieces	⅓ cup	virgin olive oil
		8 cloves	garlic, minced
1 tablespoon	salt	½ cup	sliced fennel, cut into ¼-inch-thick, 2-inch-long pieces
½ cup	sliced sweet red onion, cut into ¼-inch-thick, 2-inch-long pieces	1 cup	oil-preserved sun-dried tomatoes (see chapter 1)
½ cup	sliced yellow bell peppers, cut into ¼-inch-thick, 2-inch-long pieces	2	chili peppers, chopped (or crushed red pepper)
1 cup	sliced red bell peppers, cut into ¼-inch-thick, 2-inch-long pieces	¼ cup	toasted pine nuts
		1 tablespoon	chopped basil
		1 tablespoon	chopped oregano
		2 tablespoons	chopped parsley
1 cup	sliced zucchini, cut into ¼-inch-thick, 2-inch-long pieces	to taste	salt
		to taste	lemon juice

1. Place the eggplant pieces in a bowl and add 1 tablespoon salt. Cover and let rest for 1 hour, then squeeze the juices from the eggplant.

2. Sauté the onions, bell peppers, and zucchini quickly in half of the olive oil. Remove the vegetables with a slotted spoon to a colander.

3. Heat the rest of the olive oil and add the garlic, fennel, and eggplant. Cook several minutes. Cut sun-dried tomatoes into small strips and add. Mix in the chopped chili peppers and pine nuts. Remove to a suitable bowl and cool. The vegetables should be crisp.

4. Add the herbs, and flavor with salt and lemon juice. Serve very cold.

Bresaola con Insalata di Riso e Funghi
CURED, DRIED BEEF WITH RICE-MUSHROOM SALAD

Bresaola (or *Bündnerfleisch,* as it is known in Switzerland and Austria) is cured, dried beef with an extremely strong yet delicate taste. Like *prosciutto, bresaola* must be sliced paper thin. Because of its gamy aroma, it is particularly suited to a variety of vegetable and fruit garnishes.

Yield: 6 servings

RICE-MUSHROOM SALAD:

1 fluid ounce	olive oil
1/2 cup	Italian Arborio Rice
1 cup	beef broth, hot (see chapter 3)
8 ounces	porcino or chanterelle mushrooms
1 fluid ounce	virgin olive oil
1	sweet red onion, diced medium
1	red bell pepper, medium diced
1	yellow bell pepper, medium diced
4 ounces	Fontina, medium diced

DRESSING:

1/2 cup	virgin olive oil
1/3 cup	lemon juice
3 cloves	garlic, minced
3	anchovy fillets, chopped
1 tablespoon	chopped chili pepper
1 tablespoon	capers
2 tablespoons	chopped parsley
1 tablespoon	chopped basil
6	small tomatoes
9 ounces	bresaola
8 ounces	young spinach leaves, well washed and drained
1 cup	young green peas, precooked and chilled

1.   Heat the ounce of olive oil in a 1-quart saucepan. Add the rice and, over low heat, coat the rice with the oil. Add the hot meat broth, bring to a boil, cover, and place in preheated 325°F oven for 18 minutes. Do not stir the rice. After 18 minutes, remove and let the rice cool.

2.   Clean the mushrooms of sand and grit, trim the stem ends, and chop the mushrooms into small pieces. Sauté quickly in the olive oil and let cool.

3.   Prepare the dressing by whisking together all the ingredients. Adjust the seasoning.

(continued)

4. Put the cooled rice in a mixing bowl and fluff with a fork. Add the mushrooms, onion, red and yellow peppers, and Fontina. Mix in the dressing and adjust seasoning.

5. Peel the tomatoes by plunging them into boiling water for 15 seconds, shocking them in cold water, and then slipping off the skins. Cut the tomatoes into 4 equal wedges, remove the seeds, and trim to produce petallike shapes.

6. Slice the *bresaola* paper thin. Overlap 1½ ounces of the sliced meat in a semicircle on each serving plate.

7. Place the spinach leaves in an empty spot on the plate.

8. Place a mound of rice-mushroom salad in the center of the spinach.

9. Decorate each serving with 4 tomato petals.

10. Sprinkle the green peas over the rice-mushroom salad.

Prosciutto Crudo con Spuma di Peperoni Rossi con Insalata di Funghi e Spinaci

PROSCIUTTO WITH RED-PEPPER MOUSSE, MUSHROOM SALAD, AND SPINACH

Yield: 8 servings

RED-PEPPER MOUSSE:

1 fluid ounce	virgin olive oil
¼ cup	onions, finely diced
2 cloves	garlic, minced
8 ounces	red bell pepper, diced small
pinch	cayenne pepper
¾ ounce	gelatin
¼ to ⅓ cup	beef broth (see chapter 3) with pinch of saffron
¾ cup	whipped cream

MUSHROOM SALAD:

¼ cup	virgin olive oil
¼ cup	onions, finely diced
2 cloves	garlic, finely minced
12 ounces	porcino or chanterelle mushrooms, sliced
2 tablespoons	lemon juice
2 tablespoons	balsamic vinegar
to taste	salt and freshly ground black pepper
24 ounces	raw prosciutto, trimmed
4 ounces	spinach leaves, washed and drained

1. Heat the fluid ounce of olive oil and sauté the onion, garlic, and red pepper. Add the cayenne.

2. Dissolve the gelatin in the meat broth. Let bloom for 15 minutes.

3. Puree the sautéed vegetables in a blender with the gelatin/meat broth until very smooth. Strain through a sieve into a small saucepan. Reheat (do not bring to a boil), remove from the heat, and adjust the seasonings. Cool to room temperature, stirring occasionally.

4. Fold the whipped cream into the mousse.

5. Line a suitable log mold with plastic wrap. Pour the mousse mixture into the mold and cover with plastic wrap. Refrigerate for at least 2 hours, until well set.

6. Heat the ¼ cup of olive oil and sauté the onions, garlic, and mushrooms. Add the lemon juice, balsamic vinegar, salt, and pepper. Adjust the seasonings. Place in small bowl, cover with plastic wrap, and chill.

7. Slice the *prosciutto* very thin. Arrange overlapping slices in semicircle on each serving plate.

8. Place the spinach leaves on an empty space on each plate. Overlap 3 slices of red-pepper mousse on the spinach leaves.

9. Spoon the mushroom salad near the mousse on the spinach leaves (see color plate 13).

Piccola Tartare di Manzo con Purea d'Aglio e Peperoni Rossi
SMALL STEAK TARTARE WITH GARLIC AND RED-PEPPER PUREE

Yield: 6 servings

3	ripe tomatoes	to taste	freshly ground black pepper
3	eggs		

GARLIC AND RED-PEPPER PUREE:		**GARNISH:**	
2 heads	garlic	*24*	Belgian endive leaves
1 cup	meat broth	*1*	sweet red onion, finely diced
1	red bell pepper		
1 fluid ounce	lemon juice	*3 tablespoons*	capers
¼ cup	virgin olive oil	*3 tablespoons*	chopped Italian parsley
to taste	salt and cayenne pepper	*6*	fresh basil sprigs
12	scallion leaves	*12 slices*	Italian bread
18 ounces	beef sirloin, extra lean		

1.   Peel the tomatoes by immersing in boiling water for 15 seconds and then shocking in ice water. Slide off the skins, remove the seeds, and dice small. Cover and chill.

2.   Boil the eggs for 10 minutes, then shock in cold water. Peel the eggs and press through a sieve. Cover and chill.

3.   Coat the garlic heads with oil. Place them in an ovenproof dish, and bake in preheated 350°F oven for about 10 minutes. Add the meat broth to the garlic, cover, and cook for another 20 minutes, until very soft. Cool and peel. Rub the red pepper with oil, and roast over an open flame or under a broiler until the skin blisters but does not burn. Place the pepper in a small container and cover with plastic wrap to ease peeling. Peel and remove seeds. Put garlic, red pepper, and lemon juice in a food processor. Puree until smooth, adding the remainder of the olive oil as it is processed. Add the salt and cayenne pepper.

4.   Trim scallions to neaten and rinse under fresh water.

5.   Trim the fat and cartilage from the beef. Cut the meat into small cubes. Chop cubes to a medium coarseness either in a food processor or by hand. Season with freshly ground black pepper. Shape the meat into uniform 3-ounce patties using a small ice-cream scoop moistened in fresh water. (You may cut the meat ahead of time, but cover tightly and keep chilled until ready to use.) Do not add salt to the ground meat; it removes moisture.

6.   Spoon garlic-pepper puree into the center of each plate. Place a beef pattie on top. Spoon some of the diced tomatoes in a semicircle on the outer edge of the puree.

7.   Garnish each plate with 4 neat endive leaves filled with diced red onion, capers, chopped parsley, and the chopped eggs.

8.   Place the trimmed scallions near the tomatoes and garnish with fresh basil sprigs.

9.   Lighly toast the slices of Italian bread, butter sparingly, and serve alongside in a folded napkin.

Terrina d'Anitra con Mostarda di Frutti
TERRINE OF DUCK WITH FRUITS IN MUSTARD SYRUP

Terrines are made of the same ingredients as regular meat pies or pâtés, but they are cooked in earthenware dishes called terrines. The terrine molds are lined with some kind of fat and then filled with a forcemeat.

In the case of poultry, the fatty skin of the bird can be used to line the terrine. The accompaniments for a duck terrine can include tart fruit purees or sauces based on wines or liquors. Fruits in mustard syrup or just a simple assortment of fresh fruit sections and berries are also appropriate. The garnish might include a savory component, such as marinated artichoke hearts, eggplant, assorted mushrooms, or peppers.

Yield: 10 to 12 servings

1	duck, 4 to 5 pounds	pinch	ground cloves
½ teaspoon	freshly ground black pepper	pinch	cayenne pepper
		pinch	ground ginger
4 teaspoons	shallots, finely diced	pinch	thyme
¼ to ⅓ cup	brandy	4 ounces	smoked, cooked ham or ox tongue
10 ounces	lean veal, diced small		
15 ounces	fresh pork fat (from shoulder if possible)	4 ounces	fresh pork fat
		1 ounce	pistachio nuts, peeled
2 teaspoons	salt	½ ounce	black truffle, diced small
1 cup	crushed ice		
1	duck liver	3 ounces	pork fatback, sliced thin
1	egg		
pinch	ground nutmeg	1	bay leaf

(continued)

1. Skin the duck, reserving the skin. Bone the duck, starting from the back and removing the breast and leg meat. Trim all fat from the skin and rub the skin with the freshly ground black pepper and shallots. Place it in a suitable dish, add the brandy, cover, and marinate until needed.

2. Dice the duck breast, veal, and 15 ounces of pork fat into small cubes. Chill thoroughly in the freezer, being careful *not* to freeze the meat.

3. Put the chilled meat through the medium plate of a meat grinder, followed by the fat. Chill again in freezer. Add the salt and then regrind, this time through the fine plate of the grinder with the crushed ice. Place the forcemeat in a container and chill.

4. Trim the skin and sinew from the duck liver and puree in a blender. Add the egg and combine thoroughly by turning the blender off and on for 5 minutes. Place in a small container and chill.

5. Add liver/egg mixture to the forcemeat, working with a wooden spoon until the mixture is homogeneous.

6. Add the nutmeg, cloves, cayenne, ginger, and thyme to the forcemeat. Drain the brandy from the duck skin and add. Taste and adjust for salt.

7. Dice the meat from the duck legs, the ham or ox tongue, and 4 ounces of pork fat into small cubes. Add, along with the pistachios and black truffles, to the forcemeat.

8. Line a 3-quart earthenware terrine with the marinated duck skin, outer side down. Fill the terrine with the forcemeat, packing as tightly as possible, especially in the corners. Smooth the top with a spatula, and cover with a layer of thinly sliced pork fatback and the bay leaf. Fold any protruding pieces of skin up over the top to the center. Place a plate on top to keep the skin from curling while cooking.

9. Cover the terrine (with its top or with aluminum foil) and place in a hot water bath. Cook in preheated 325°F oven for about 1¾ hours. The cooking time will depend on the size and shape of the baking dish.

10. To test for doneness, check the fat that rises to the surface. If it appears cloudy and contains bloody juices, the terrine is not yet done. A skewer or needle inserted into the center of the terrine can help in checking the juices. When cooked, remove from oven and cool.

11. Remove the terrine from the mold only when completely chilled. Remove any fat on the sides of the terrine as well. Wrap it in plastic wrap and cover with a piece of board with a weight on top to apply pressure.

12. To serve, set the terrine skin side up. Slice into wedges and turn out on a dish. Serve with fruits in mustard syrup (recipe follows).

Mostarda di Frutti

FRUITS IN MUSTARD SYRUP

Yield: 6 cups

2	Granny Smith apples	1 pint	water
2	Bartlett pears	½ cup	lemon juice
2	peaches	1 pound	granulated sugar
2	nectarines	¼ cup	lemon and orange zests, finely shredded
3	apricots		
2	mandarin oranges	2 tablespoons	grated fresh ginger
6	plums	¼ cup	dry hot mustard
½ cup	pistachios		
1 quart	dry vermouth		

1. Peel and seed the apples, pears, peaches, nectarines, apricots, mandarin oranges, and plums, and cut all into wedges. Peel the pistachios.

2. Bring the vermouth, water, and lemon juice to a boil in a stainless steel or Pyrex glass pan.

3. Blanch each variety of fruit separately for 1 minute, starting with the apples and pears. Remove and reserve the liquid.

4. In a shallow stainless steel saucepan, cook the sugar with the liquid in which the fruit was blanched to a light syrupy consistency. Add the shredded orange and lemon zests and the grated ginger.

5. Place the fruit and nuts in the syrup. Cook for 2 minutes over medium heat. Remove from the heat. Cool, cover, and refrigerate overnight.

6. Bring the syrup with the fruit back to a boil. Simmer for 2 to 3 minutes.

7. Mix the dry mustard and 1 cup of the liquid in which the fruit was blanched in a large bowl. Remove the fruit from the sugar syrup, and add the syrup to this mixture. Bring to a rolling boil and then pour over the fruit.

8. Arrange the fruit in a suitable glass container, being sure that the fruit is covered with syrup. Cover and keep in a cold place. The fruit should keep for several months when prepared in this way.

— *Antipasti Caldi* —
HOT APPETIZERS

Bruschetta

GARLIC TOAST

Bruschetta is toasted or grilled (preferably over charcoal) sliced fresh Italian bread, flavored with garlic and brushed with extra-virgin olive oil. It must be crisp on the outside and soft inside, served immediately when used as a snack or an appetizer. It can also be used as the base for hot canapés, in which case it can have innumerable toppings.

Yield: 12 slices

12 slices	fresh Italian bread, 1/2 inch thick
6 cloves	garlic, mashed into a paste
1/3 cup	extra-virgin olive oil
pinch	freshly ground black pepper

1. Toast or grill the bread slices on both sides.

2. Rub with garlic paste, using a canapé spreader or metal spatula.

3. Season with freshly ground black pepper.

4. Sprinkle or brush with extra-virgin olive oil and serve immediately.

Bruschetta ai Pomodori e Mozzarella
GARLIC TOAST WITH TOMATOES AND MOZZARELLA

The toppings for *bruschetta* can be varied at will with great success. Instead of diced tomatoes, try capers, pickled green peppercorns, anchovies, different herbs, chopped roasted peppers, or chopped olives.

Yield: 12 slices

3	medium tomatoes	3 tablespoons	chopped oregano
12 slices	fresh Italian bread, ½ inch thick	pinch	freshly ground black pepper
6 cloves	garlic, mashed into a paste	3 ounces	mozzarella, coarsely grated
⅓ cup	extra-virgin olive oil		

1.   Peel and seed the tomatoes (see chapter 1) and dice small.

2.   Toast, grill, or broil the bread slices on both sides.

3.   Rub the bread with the garlic paste, using a canapé spreader or metal spatula.

4.   Brush with extra-virgin olive oil.

5.   Top each slice with 1 tablespoon diced tomatoes and some chopped oregano.

6.   Season with freshly ground black pepper (and salt if desired).

7.   Sprinkle with the grated mozzarella and place under broiler for a few seconds to barely melt the cheese. Serve immediately.

Crostini con Fonduta all'Albese

CHEESE FONDUE ON TOAST ROUNDS AND WHITE TRUFFLES

Yield: 4 portions

12 slices	pullman bread
1 pound	Fontina
1 ounce	butter
½ cup	milk or heavy cream
2	egg yolks
to taste	salt and cayenne pepper
1	small white truffle

1. Cut 12 round pieces from the pullman bread and fry until crisp (light brown on both sides). Reserve.

2. Coarsely grate the Fontina or dice small.

3. Place the Fontina, butter, and milk or cream in stainless steel or enamel saucepan or fondue pot, reserving 2 tablespoons of the milk or cream. Melt the cheese, butter, and milk over low heat.

4. Mix the egg yolks with the reserved milk or cream. Whisk it into the melted cheese mixture until very smooth. Season with salt and cayenne.

5. Overlap 3 round toasts per serving in individual ceramic or earthenware dishes.

6. Pour the fondue over the croutons.

7. Shave the white truffle over the fondue and serve immediately.

Crostini di Pane alla Valdostana
GRILLED PROSCIUTTO, TOMATO, AND CHEESE TOASTS

Yield: 6 portions

18 slices	fresh Italian bread, 1/4 inch thick	6 cloves	garlic, finely minced
1/2 cup	virgin olive oil	1/4 teaspoon	cayenne pepper
1/3 cup	dry breadcrumbs, from Italian bread	18 slices	cooked prosciutto, thinly sliced
1/4 cup	chopped Italian parsley	18	peeled tomato wedges (see chapter 1)
1/4 cup	chopped basil	18 slices	Fontina

1. Brush both sides of the Italian bread slices lightly with the olive oil. Cover with plastic wrap and chill.

2. Combine the breadcrumbs, Italian parsley, basil, garlic, and cayenne in a mixing bowl with the remaining olive oil.

3. Trim the *prosciutto,* tomato, and cheese to fit the bread slices.

4. Dip each tomato slice in the herb mixture.

5. Toast the lightly oiled bread on both sides.

6. Arrange 1 slice of *prosciutto,* tomato, and cheese on each toast.

7. Place under the broiler or on the top rack of a very hot oven until the cheese is melted.

8. As an optional garnish, slice sweet red onions and place on a bed of arugula or sautéed scallions alongside.

Soffiato di Pane e Formaggio

BREAD AND CHEESE PUDDING WITH ANCHOVIES

Yield: 4 servings

as needed	butter	4 ounces	mozzarella
1 cup	heavy cream	4 ounces	Fontina
2	eggs	8	anchovy fillets
to taste	salt and cayenne pepper	8 slices	Italian bread, ¼ inch thick
to taste	ground nutmeg	4	basil sprigs

1.   Lightly butter 4 small soufflé dishes or ramekins, each capable of holding 6 to 8 ounces.

2.   Combine the cream, eggs, salt, cayenne, and nutmeg. Mix thoroughly.

3.   Coarsely grate the cheeses.

4.   Place the anchovy fillets on absorbent paper to remove excess oil.

5.   Remove the crusts from the bread. Trim to match diameter of the soufflé dish or ramekin.

6.   Dip 4 slices of bread in the egg/cream mixture and place one in each ramekin. Add half the cheeses over the bread, and top each with 1 anchovy fillet. Repeat the layer with the remaining bread, cheese, and anchovies.

7.   Bake in a 375°F oven for 12 to 15 minutes, until lightly browned.

8.   Garnish with basil sprigs and serve on a folded napkin.

Calzoncelli alla Napoletana

DEEP-FRIED CHEESE AND SAUSAGE TURNOVERS

Turnovers enjoy international popularity. Deep-fried turnovers are known around Naples as *calzoni* or *calzoncelli*. The dough is usually ordinary pizza or bread dough, and the filling may be cheese, meat, or both, spicy or mild depending on the region.

Yield: 6 servings

DOUGH:

12 ounces	bread or all-purpose flour
1 tablespoon	active dry yeast
1/4 cup	olive oil
1 cup	warm water, 110° to 115°F
pinch	salt

FILLING:

1 fluid ounce	olive oil
3 ounces	onions, finely diced
1	medium green bell pepper, chopped
9 ounces	Italian sausage, sweet or hot, coarsely chopped
3	tomatoes, peeled, seeded, and diced (see chapter 1)

1/4 cup	tomato paste
1 tablespoon	chopped basil
2 tablespoons	chopped parsley
12	ripe olives, chopped
1	chili pepper, chopped
pinch	salt
6 ounces	mozzarella, coarsely grated

EGGWASH:

1	large egg
1 tablespoon	water
to deep-fry	oil

1.   Combine the flour, yeast, olive oil, water, and salt in a mixing bowl and beat at low speed until blended. Continue to mix at medium speed, scraping the sides as needed. Add more flour if the dough is too soft.

2.   Remove dough from the mixer and knead by hand on a floured surface until the dough is pliable, firm, and elastic.

3.   Cover the dough and let it rise in a warm place until doubled in volume.

4.   Heat the oil for the filling in a sauté pan, add the onion, and sauté until lightly colored. Add pepper and sausage and cook at high heat for a few minutes.

5.   Add the tomatoes and tomato paste. Cook until the mixture has thickened considerably, remove to a mixing bowl, and cool.

6.   Combine the chopped basil, parsley, olives, chili peppers, salt, and grated mozzarella with the tomato/sausage mixture. Adjust the seasoning.

7.   After the dough has doubled in volume, punch down and divide into 12 pieces. Roll them into smooth balls.

(continued)

8.   With a rolling pin, roll each ball into a thin circle, approximately 5 inches in diameter.

9.   Place a generous amount of filling on one side of each circle. Beat the egg with the water to make the egg wash. Brush the edge of the dough with the egg wash and fold the circle over the filling, forming a turnover shaped like a half moon. Press to seal edges.

10.   Deep-fry the turnovers until golden brown and crisp. Or brush the top of each turnover with egg wash, place on a greased baking sheet, and bake in a preheated 375°F oven until brown and crisp.

Strudel di Verdure, con Salsa Crema ai Pomodori
VEGETABLE STRUDEL WITH TOMATO CREAM SAUCE

Strudel (or *phyllo*) dough may be purchased or homemade. To make your own, see the recipe in chapter 14. If you purchase ready-made *phyllo* dough, use two layers instead of one, gluing the two layers together on top of each other with melted butter.

Yield: 8 to 10 servings

FILLING:

15 ounces	carrots
10 ounces	celeriac
5 ounces	fresh asparagus
5 to 10 ounces	broccoli
5 ounces	porcini
5 ounces	small zucchini, washed
2 ounces	butter
1/2 cup	water
to taste	salt and freshly ground black pepper

VEGETABLE BINDER:

2 ounces	leeks, white part only, cleaned and sliced
4 ounces	onion, sliced
4 ounces	celeriac, diced small
to taste	salt and freshly ground black pepper
1 cup	heavy cream
2	eggs
1/4 cup	chopped Italian parsley
8 ounces	strudel dough
3 ounces	butter, melted
3 cups	tomato cream sauce (see chapter 7)

1.   Clean and peel the carrots, celeriac, asparagus, and broccoli.

2.   Cut off the woody ends of the asparagus and broccoli and discard. Cut the asparagus tips and broccoli florets from the stalks. Reserve.

3.   Cut the mushrooms into thick slices.

4.   Cut the carrots, celeriac, zucchini, and asparagus and broccoli stalks into short strips
¼ inch square and 3 inches long.

5.   Cook each vegetable separately and very quickly in the butter and water. Cook the
vegetables in the following order before removing to a colander with a slotted spoon
and cooling:
   • Cook the carrots and celeriac each for about 5 minutes, covered
   • Cook the broccoli stems and florets for about 3 minutes, uncovered
   • Cook the zucchini and the asparagus stems and tips each for 30 seconds,
     uncovered
   • Cook the *porcini* for about 1 minute
   • Sprinkle vegetables with salt and pepper

After cooking the *porcini,* reduce the cooking liquid almost completely and use it for the
vegetable binder.

6.   Heat up the reduced cooking liquid. Add the leeks and onion, then the celeriac.
Cook slowly, covered, until soft. Season with salt and pepper.

7.   Add the cream and continue to cook until very thick. Cool.

8.   Puree mixture in a food processor. Add the eggs and parsley and mix well.

9.   Combine the cooked vegetables with just enough of this binder to barely hold them
together, *no more*.

10.   Cover the work surface with a clean cloth.

11.   Pull the strudel dough carefully until almost transparent and lay it on the cloth.

12.   Brush the dough with the melted butter. Spread the vegetable mixture onto the
dough, making sure that all the vegetables are pointing in a horizontal direction to avoid
puncturing the dough when rolled. Leave about 2 inches at the top free so that the
dough can be sealed.

13.   To roll up the strudel, hold the cloth at the bottom end (the end toward you)
and lift up evenly. The strudel should roll itself.

14.   Place the strudel, seam side down, on a greased baking sheet, and brush generously with more melted butter. Bake in a preheated 350°F oven for 25 to 30 minutes.
Rest a short time before serving.

15.   To serve, cut the strudel into 2-inch-thick slices. Serve with tomato cream sauce.

Crostata alla Vegetariana

VEGETABLE QUICHE

Yield: 10 to 12 servings

PIECRUST:

6¹/₂ ounces	butter, cut into small pieces
10 ounces	all-purpose flour
1	egg yolk
pinch	salt
pinch	sugar
¹/₄ cup	cold water

FILLING:

4 ounces	leeks, white part only, thinly sliced
2 ounces	porcini, thinly sliced
¹/₂ ounce	butter
4 ounces	spinach leaves
2 ounces	Fontina, grated
2 ounces	Parmesan, grated

1	small chili pepper, chopped
3	eggs, lightly beaten
1 cup	light cream
pinch	freshly ground black pepper
pinch	nutmeg
to taste	salt and cayenne pepper

1	medium-size zucchini
¹/₂ cup	oil-preserved sun-dried tomatoes (see chapter 1)
1 teaspoon	butter
to taste	salt and pepper

1.   Make the piecrust ahead of time. Crumble the butter together with the flour in a mixing bowl. Add the egg yolk, salt, sugar, and cold water. Lightly work the dough with your fingertips until the liquids are just incorporated.

2.   Form dough into a ball and wrap in plastic wrap. Chill in the refrigerator for at least 1 hour.

3.   Remove the dough from the refrigerator and allow it to rest at room temperature until pliable. Roll it out into a circle with a thickness of ¹/₄ inch. Line a greased quiche shell with the dough, trim the edges, and pierce the bottom of the dough several times with a fork to keep the dough from rising and splitting. (If you are using a disposable quiche shell, be careful not to puncture it when piercing the dough.) To ensure that the bottom of the piecrust remains flat while baking, cover it with a circle of oiled parchment or waxed paper, and onto this place about 1 cup of dried beans. Chill thoroughly once more before baking on the lowest rack in a 400°F oven for 10 minutes. Do not let the crust brown. Cool and remove the beans and paper from the partially baked shell. (This is called a partially blind-baked pie shell.) Hold the shell until ready to fill.

4.   Quickly sauté the leeks and *porcini* in the butter. Remove from the heat.

5.   Wash the spinach leaves well, then cut coarsely. Place them in a shallow pan, cover, and steam for a few seconds to extract the excess moisture. Place in a colander to drain and cool.

6.   Sprinkle the Fontina and Parmesan cheeses on the bottom of the half-baked pie shell. Over this arrange the leeks, *porcini,* spinach, and chopped chili pepper.

7.   Mix the eggs, light cream, black pepper, nutmeg, salt, and cayenne. Strain through a sieve and then pour over the vegetables, filling the shell to the rim.

8.   Bake on the lowest rack of a 350°F oven for about 20 minutes, then lower the temperature to 300°F and bake until the mixture sets and is firm. Do not let the mixture swell or rise.

9.   While the quiche is baking, cut the zucchini lengthwise in half, remove the seeds with a melon scoop, and then slice into crescents.

10.   Cut the sun-dried tomatoes into fine strips.

11.   Sauté the zucchini quickly in a little butter. Add the tomatoes, season with a little salt and pepper, and let cool.

12.   Overlap the zucchini and tomato crescents along the border of the cooled quiche.

13.   To serve, cut the quiche into 10 or 12 sections with a thin, sharp knife. Reheat and serve as is or accompanied by compatible sauce or *coulis.*

Suppli alla Fontina con Salsa d'Aglio e Peperoni Rossi

FONTINA-FILLED RICE CROQUETTES WITH GARLIC AND RED-PEPPER SAUCE

Yield: 6 servings

1 ounce	butter	12	Fontina cubes, ½ ounce each
¼ cup	onion, finely diced		
8 ounces	Italian Arborio rice	1	egg
½ cup	dry white wine	½ cup	water
pinch	saffron	1 cup	flour
2 cups	meat broth, well seasoned	2 cups	dry breadcrumbs from Italian or French bread
to taste	salt and freshly ground black pepper	12	whole cloves
to taste	nutmeg	2 cups	garlic and red-pepper sauce (see chapter 7)
1	egg yolk	to garnish	fresh basil leaves
½ cup	heavy cream		
2 ounces	freshly grated Parmesan		

1.   In a 2-quart sauce pot over medium heat, heat the butter and cook the onions until translucent.

2.   Add the rice and stir until well coated with the butter.

3.   Add wine and saffron, stir once, and then add half of the meat broth. Stir again, and cook over low heat for 6 minutes.

4.   Add the remaining broth and season with salt, pepper, and nutmeg. Stir and continue to cook over low heat for another 12 minutes. Remove from the heat and let cool for about 2 minutes.

5.   Combine the egg yolk and cream, whisking well. Fold into the warm rice, followed by the grated Parmesan. Pour the rice into a shallow dish, cover with greased parchment paper, and let cool completely.

6.   When rice is cold and workable, moisten hands with fresh water and shape the rice into 12 equal balls.

7.   Push the Fontina cubes into the rice balls, and then delicately reshape to resemble pears. Refrigerate.

8. Beat the egg with the water until well combined. This is the egg wash. Coat each rice pear first in flour, then the egg wash, and finally in the breadcrumbs. If necessary, reshape the pear.

9. Deep-fry, to order, until golden brown. Drain and insert a whole clove into the top of each for a "stem." Use moderate heat when frying to ensure that the cheese melts thoroughly.

10. To serve, spoon about ¼ to ⅓ cup of garlic and red-pepper sauce into the center of each serving plate. Place two rice croquettes per serving onto the sauce. Garnish with fresh basil leaves.

Crocchette di Polenta alla Valdostana
POLENTA CROQUETTES WITH PROSCIUTTO AND FONTINA

Northern Italians make this dish in a heavy untinned copper bowl called a *paiolo*. To learn more about cooking polenta, see chapter 6.

Yield:　12 servings

5 cups	water	1	egg
8 ounces	yellow cornmeal, coarse-grained	½ cup	water
		1 cup	flour
pinch	nutmeg	2 cups	dry breadcrumbs from Italian or French bread
2 ounces	butter		
2 ounces	Parmesan, grated		
8 ounces	Fontina or mozzarella, thinly sliced	to garnish	scallion leaves, fringed
		to garnish	basil leaves
4 ounces	cooked proscuitto		

1. Bring the water to a boil in a 3-quart saucepan.

2. Very gradually add the cornmeal, stirring constantly with a wire whip to avoid lumps.

3. Stirring frequently with a wooden spoon, cook over low heat for about 1 hour.

4. Remove the polenta from the heat, stir in the nutmeg, butter, and Parmesan, and immediately spread half of the polenta onto an oiled sheet pan, about 6 by 9 inches.

(continued)

5. Layer half the Fontina or mozzarella over the polenta, layer all the *prosciutto* over it, and layer the rest of the cheese on top.

6. Spread the rest of the polenta on top of the cheese. (Polenta is sticky, so it is best to use a spatula frequently dipped in water for this.)

7. Cover with oiled parchment or wax paper and cool completely.

8. Cut into desired shapes. Beat the egg with the water to make an egg wash. Dredge the croquettes in flour, dip in the egg wash, and then dip in the breadcrumbs.

9. Deep-fry at 350°F until nicely browned.

10. To serve, coat each serving plate with an appropriate sauce, tomato or cheese based (see chapter 7 for possibilities).

11. Place 2 croquettes over the sauce on each plate. Garnish with scallion "flowers" and basil leaves.

Gnocchi di Polenta al Ragù di Funghi Assortiti
POLENTA GNOCCHI WITH STEWED MUSHROOMS

To learn more about polenta and *gnocchi*, see chapter 6.

Yield: 6 servings

3½ cups	water	2	small chili peppers, chopped
½ teasoon	salt		
6 ounces	cornmeal	1 cup	oil-preserved sun-dried tomatoes, sliced (see chapter 1)
1½ ounces	butter		
⅓ cup	olive oil		
1 cup	diced red onions	to taste	salt and freshly ground black pepper
6 cloves	garlic, finely minced		
1½ pounds	assorted mushrooms, such as morels, porcini, chanterelles	2 tablespoons	chopped parsley
		1 tablespoon	chopped marjoram
		1 tablespoon	chopped rosemary
1 cup	dry white wine	3 ounces	Parmesan, grated
½ cup	Marsala	1 tablespoon	butter, melted
½ cup	meat glace (see chapter 7)	to garnish	basil leaves

1.   Bring the water to a boil in a 3-quart saucepan. Add salt.

2.   Very gradually add the cornmeal, stirring constantly with a wire whip to avoid lumps.

3.   Stirring frequently with a wooden spoon, cook over low heat for about a ½-hour. Stir in fresh butter.

4.   Spread the polenta onto an oiled sheet pan, ½ inch thick. Cover with plastic wrap and cool.

5.   Heat the olive oil, and sauté the onion, garlic, and mushrooms quickly.

6.   Add the wines and allow to cook several minutes. Remove the mushrooms with slotted spoon and keep warm.

7.   Reduce the wines until all liquid evaporates, and add the meat *glace,* chili peppers, and sun-dried tomatoes. Adjust the seasonings.

8.   Add the stewed mushrooms to the wine sauce. Stir in the parsley, marjoram, and rosemary. Keep hot for service.

9.   Cut the polenta into crescent-shaped *gnocchi,* using a rounded pastry cutter or a clean tin can.

10.   Butter an oval ovenproof dish for each serving and overlap 3 or 4 *gnocchi* in the center of each dish. Sprinkle generously with grated Parmesan and a little melted butter. Brown under a broiler or on the top rack of a very hot oven.

11.   Spoon stewed mushrooms around the polenta *gnocchi,* and decorate with fresh basil leaves.

Gnocchi di Semolina alla Fiorentina Gratinata

SEMOLINA GNOCCHI WITH SAUTÉED SPINACH AND WILD MUSHROOMS

Yield: 8 servings

3 cups	milk	2 cloves	garlic, minced
8 ounces	semolina flour, medium coarse	1½ cups	sliced porcini
pinch	salt	to taste	salt and freshly ground black pepper
½ cup	heavy cream	16	Fontina slices
2	egg yolks	½ cup	fine julienne of red bell pepper
pinch	white pepper	1 teaspoon	butter
pinch	nutmeg	1 cup	fine julienne of prosciutto
2 ounces	grated Parmesan		
2 ounces	mozzarella, coarsely grated	16	mozzarella slices
2 pounds	fresh spinach leaves	2 tablespoons	chopped Italian parsley
2 to 3 ounces	butter	1 tablespoon	chopped basil
1 cup	sliced scallions		

1.   In a heavy-bottomed 3-quart saucepan, bring the milk to a boil. Stir in the semolina with a wire whisk and add a pinch of salt. Cover and cook over low heat for 10 minutes, stirring occasionally. When it forms a thick mass on the whisk as it turns, remove from the heat.

2.   Combine the cream with the egg yolks, white pepper, and nutmeg. Mix well.

3.   Combine the egg yolk/cream mixture with the semolina. Add the cheeses.

4.   Spread mixture on an oiled 6- by 8-inch tray, about ½ inch thick. Cover with plastic wrap, cool completely, and refrigerate.

5.   When completely solid, cut out crescent-shape *gnocchi* with a round cutter. Keep covered. Cut the *gnocchi* in such a way as to minimize waste.

6.   Wash the spinach and break into small pieces.

7.   Heat the butter in a *sautoir* or skillet and quickly sauté the scallions, garlic, and *porcini*. Remove the mushrooms with a slotted spoon and reserve.

8. To the same pan, add the raw spinach and season with salt and pepper. Stir-fry the spinach quickly, 10 to 20 seconds, covered, over high heat. Add the mushrooms and scallions.

9. For each serving, place some spinach/mushroom mixture in the center of an oven-proof dish, preferably an oval au gratin dish.

10. Overlap 3 or 4 *gnocchi* on top and cover with 2 slices of Fontina.

11. Quickly sauté the julienne of red pepper in a little butter. Add the *prosciutto*. Sprinkle over the Fontina.

12. Place 2 slices of mozzarella over the peppers. Bake in a hot oven to melt and lightly brown the cheese.

13. Sprinkle the top with Italian parsley and basil.

Gnocchi di Pollo e Patate alla Genovese
CHICKEN AND POTATO GNOCCHI, GENOA STYLE

This dish is often topped with other sauces, such as *salsa alla pizzaola* or *salsa alla boscaiola,* rather than béchamel.

Yield: 8 servings

8 ounces	diced chicken breast, well chilled	1 gallon	chicken broth
1½ pounds	potatoes, peeled	1 pound	mushrooms, sliced
1 cup	cold water	1 ounce	butter
pinch	salt and white pepper	2	egg yolks
		1 fluid ounce	heavy cream
pinch	nutmeg	3 cups	béchamel sauce (see chapter 7)
1 to 2	egg yolks		
1 ounce	flour	1 cup	Parmesan, grated
1 cup	heavy cream	3 tablespoons	chopped parsley

(continued)

1.   Put the chicken meat through the fine blade of a meat grinder. Keep well chilled in a stainless steel mixing bowl.

2.   Cut the potatoes into small chunks and mix with 1 cup ice-cold water. Liquefy in blender and immediately squeeze out as much liquid as possible, using cheesecloth.

3.   Place the ground chicken in a bowl over crushed ice and add the dry potato pulp. Add the salt, pepper, and nutmeg, and mix with a wooden spoon.

4.   Gradually add the egg yolk and flour.

5.   Mix in the cup of cream, a little at a time, and chill for 1 hour.

6.   Bring the chicken broth to a simmer in a wide, shallow saucepan. Form oblong dumplings from the cold chicken/potato mixture using tablespoons dipped frequently in lukewarm water to prevent sticking. Drop the dumplings carefully into the simmering broth and poach for about 12 minutes or until they float and have almost doubled in size.

7.   Remove the *gnocchi* with a slotted spoon and drain on a towel or absorbent paper.

8.   Butter small individual ovenproof dishes. Place 2 *gnocchi* in each dish.

9.   Sauté the sliced mushrooms quickly in butter, and top the *gnocchi* with them.

10.   Combine the egg yolk with the fluid ounce of cream. Heat the béchamel. Add the béchamel and half of the grated Parmesan to the egg yolk. Spoon this mixture into each dish, covering the *gnocchi* completely. Sprinkle the remaining Parmesan on top and bake in a very hot oven until lightly glazed.

11.   Sprinkle with chopped parsley.

Sformati di Formaggio e Peperoncini
CHEESE SOUFFLÉS WITH HOT PEPPERS

When making soufflés, be sure your oven is properly calibrated, as the correct baking temperature is very important. Many chefs start soufflés at a higher temperature and then reduce the heat when the soufflé starts to rise.

Sometimes soufflé batter sticks to the edges of the mold and will not rise. Careful greasing and dusting of the soufflé mold will prevent this. If this problem is noted early enough (before encrusting), you can cut around the area with the point of a knife.

If the whipped egg whites are not properly incorporated, the soufflé will not rise evenly, may crack, or may even overflow the mold because the air trapped within the beaten whites will not expand uniformly.

Yield: 6 to 8 servings

to coat molds	butter, melted	pinch	nutmeg
to coat molds	flour	1	small chili pepper, minced
2 ounces	butter		
2 ounces	all-purpose flour	1½ ounces	Parmesan, grated
1½ cups	milk, hot	2½ ounces	Fontina, diced small
4	egg yolks	4 or 5	egg whites
pinch	salt		

1. Brush 8-ounce soufflé molds with the melted butter and dust lightly with flour. Set aside.

2. Heat the 2 ounces of butter in a 1-quart saucepan, add the 2 ounces of flour, and cook, stirring, over low heat for a few minutes. Let cool.

3. Stir the hot milk into the cooled roux to make a smooth, thick sauce. Cook over low heat for about 5 minutes, and transfer to a 3-quart mixing bowl. Cover with buttered parchment paper.

4. Just before using, add the egg yolks to the mixture one by one, followed by the salt, nutmeg, chili pepper, and cheeses; be careful not to overwork the mixture when incorporating these ingredients.

5. Beat egg whites to soft peaks and fold half of them into the batter. Then fold in the remaining whites, carefully, until well blended. If the whites are not completely blended, white streaks will be noticeable and the soufflé will not rise evenly. On the other hand, too much folding will cause the mixture to liquefy, also preventing proper rising. Fold only until there are no streaks of egg white or base in the mixture.

6. Fill each soufflé mold with soufflé batter to about ⅛ inch below the rim.

7. Set the dishes on a baking sheet with a little hot water and place in a preheated 375° to 400°F oven on the lowest rack. Bake for about 15 to 20 minutes.

8. Do not overcook the soufflés; they should be a light brown when done, creamy in the middle, almost fonduelike. Serve immediately.

Sformati di Prosciutto Cotti alla Milanese
HAM SOUFFLÉS, MILANESE STYLE

Yield: 6 to 8 servings

to coat molds	butter, melted	pinch	nutmeg
to coat molds	flour	5	egg whites
2 ounces	butter	1 teaspoon	butter
2 ounces	all-purpose flour	½ cup	mushrooms, cut julienne
1½ cups	milk, hot		
4 ounces	cooked prosciutto, finely minced	½ cup	cooked, pickled ox tongue cut in fine julienne ½ inch long
4	egg yolks		
1 ounce	Parmesan, grated		
pinch	salt and cayenne pepper		

1.   Brush 8-ounce soufflé molds with melted butter and dust lightly with flour. Set aside.

2.   Heat the 2 ounces of butter in 1-quart saucepan, add the 2 ounces of flour, and cook, stirring, over low heat for a few minutes. Let cool.

3.   Stir the hot milk into the cooled roux to make a smooth, thick sauce. Cook over low heat for about 5 minutes, and transfer to a 3-quart mixing bowl. Cover with buttered parchment paper.

4.   Place the minced *prosciutto* in a food processor. Add ¼ cup of the cream sauce and puree until smooth. Add the egg yolks to the remaining cream sauce, as well as the cheese, salt, cayenne, and nutmeg. Be careful not to overwork this base mixture. Adjust the seasoning as needed.

5.   Beat the egg whites to soft peaks and fold half into the base mixture, then carefully fold in the rest. Fold only until you see no streaks of either egg white or base mixture.

6.   Fill each soufflé dish halfway with the batter. Quickly sauté the mushrooms, remove from the heat, and add the ox tongue. Place this "Milanese" garnish on top of the batter.

7.   Pour the remaining batter over the garnish to about ⅛ inch below the rim of each dish. Set the dishes on a baking sheet with a little hot water and place in a preheated 375° to 400°F oven on the lowest rack. Bake for 15 to 20 minutes, until light brown. Serve immediately with compatible sauces such as *salsa alla boscaiola* or garlic and red pepper sauce (see chapter 7).

Involtini di Melanzane alla Siciliana

EGGPLANT ROULADES, SICILIAN STYLE

Yield: 6 to 8 servings

2	small eggplants	2	anchovies, minced
to taste	salt and freshly ground black pepper	6	ripe olives, minced
2	eggs	1	hot red pepper, minced
1 tablespoon	milk	1 tablespoon	pine nuts, chopped
1 ounce	Parmesan cheese, grated	4 tablespoons	grated Parmesan
½ cup	flour	2 tablespoons	chopped parsley
to pan-fry	olive oil	1 tablespoon	chopped basil
		1 tablespoon	chopped mint leaves
FILLING:		1	egg
1 fluid ounce	olive oil	3 tablespoons	dry breadcrumbs, from Italian bread
½ cup	finely diced onion		
4 cloves	garlic, minced	18	mozzarella slices, 2½ by 1 inch or smaller
½ cup	diced mixed bell peppers, small		

1.   Peel the eggplants, slice lengthwise ⅛ inch thick, and season with salt and pepper. Beat the eggs with the milk and the Parmesan to make an egg wash. Dredge the eggplant slices in flour, dip in the egg wash, and pan-fry on both sides until lightly browned. Drain on absorbent paper.

2.   Heat the olive oil and sauté the onion, garlic, and mixed peppers for one minute. Place in a mixing bowl.

3.   Add the remaining filling ingredients (not the mozzarella) to the vegetables. Adjust the seasonings.

4.   Spoon the filling onto the eggplant slices. Roll them up tightly, and trim the ends neatly.

5.   Arrange the roulades in an ovenproof tray or dish (not too close together), and top each with a slice of mozzarella. Bake in a hot oven just to heat and melt the cheese. Serve with any tomato-based sauce (see chapter 7 for possibilities).

Peperoni Ripieni alla Napoletana
STUFFED GREEN PEPPERS, NEAPOLITAN STYLE

Yield: 6 servings

6	medium-sized green bell peppers, halved and seeded	12	ripe olives, chopped
		¼ cup	seedless raisins
½ cup	virgin olive oil	6	anchovy fillets
½ cup	toasted breadcrumbs	2 tablespoons	capers
¼ cup	grated Parmesan	1 tablespoon	chopped hot peppers
6 cloves	garlic, minced		
2 tablespoons	chopped parsley	2 tablespoons	chopped pine nuts, toasted
1 tablespoon	chopped mint leaves	12	mozzarella slices
1 tablespoon	chopped oregano		

1. Rub the pepper halves with oil and place, skin side up, on a sheet pan. Place under the broiler, close to the flame, until the skins start to blister. Do *not* cook the peppers. Put the peppers in a closed container and peel when cool.

2. Mix the remaining ingredients well, and fill each pepper cavity. Top each with a slice of mozzarella.

3. Bake in a hot oven about 15 to 20 minutes and serve immediately. Fresh tomato sauce is a good accompaniment (see chapter 7).

Carciofini alla Romana

STEWED BABY ARTICHOKES IN WHITE WINE AND HERBS

Yield: 8 servings

24	baby artichokes	4	anchovy fillets, chopped
4 tablespoons	flour	6 to 8 cloves	garlic, minced
1 quart	water	1/4 cup	chopped fresh mint leaves
1 cup	dry white wine		
1/2 cup	beef broth (see chapter 3)	1/4 cup	Italian parsley
1/2 to 3/4 cup	virgin olive oil	1/4 cup	dry breadcrumbs, from Italian bread
1/4 cup	thinly sliced scallions, white part only	to garnish	tomato petals or wedges of roasted red pepper (see chapter 1)
1 teaspoon	freshly ground black pepper		

1.   Trim the tough outer leaves and stem ends from the artichokes. Mix the flour and water in a bowl and put all trimmed artichokes in this mixture, called a *blanc,* to prevent discoloration.

2.   Combine the remaining ingredients in a mixing bowl.

3.   Dip each artichoke in this mixture, then arrange in an ovenproof baking dish. Pour the rest of the mixture over the artichokes.

4.   Heat the dish over low heat on the top of the stove, then cover and bake in a 350°F oven about 15 to 20 minutes until tender but still somewhat crisp.

5.   Serve the artichokes with the liquid spooned over the top.

6.   Decorate with tomato petals or roasted red pepper wedges.

Crespelle Primavera Gratinate

SPINACH CRÊPES WITH FONTINA AND VEGETABLES

Yield: 12 crêpes (2 per serving)

CRÊPES:

1 cup	washed and chopped spinach
3	eggs
3 ounces	flour
1 cup	milk
to taste	salt and pepper
to taste	nutmeg
1/4 cup	olive oil

FILLING:

2 ounces	butter
2 cups	sliced leeks, white part only
1 1/2 cups	small-diced carrots
3 cups	medium-diced mushrooms

2	egg yolks
1/2 cup	heavy cream
1 1/2 cups	broccoli florets, blanched and cooled
1 cup	green peas, blanched and cooled
1 1/2 cups	grated Fontina
to taste	salt and freshly ground black pepper

TOPPING:

1/2 cup	grated Fontina
1/3 cup	grated Parmesan
1 quart	béchamel sauce (see chapter 7)
to garnish	basil sprigs

1.   Mix the chopped spinach with the eggs. Puree in a blender, then gradually combine with flour and milk in mixing bowl. Eliminate all lumps and season. This crêpe batter should be made ahead of time.

2.   Coat a crêpe pan *(sauteuse)* with oil, heat, and fry thin crêpes approximately 5 inches in diameter. Cool.

3.   Heat the butter in a shallow sauté pan. Add the leeks and cook for 30 seconds. Add the carrots and mushrooms, cover, and stew for about 5 minutes. Uncover and reduce the liquid almost completely.

4.   Mix the egg yolks and cream. Remove the sauté pan from the heat, and quickly stir in the egg/cream mixture to bind the vegetables. Add the broccoli florets and green peas as well as the 1½ cups of Fontina. Adjust the seasonings.

5.   Spoon the vegetable filling onto the spinach crêpes, roll up, and trim the ends. Arrange in an ovenproof dish.

6. Stir the ½ cup of Fontina and the Parmesan into the béchamel sauce. Spoon a generous amount over the crêpes. Place the crêpes on the top rack in a very hot oven until lightly glazed.

7. Garnish with basil sprigs. A small amount of tomato sauce can accompany the crêpes if desired.

Timballo di Lumache e Funghi al Cavolo Verde, con Salsa d'Aglio e Peperoni Rossi

CABBAGE TIMBALES WITH SNAILS AND MUSHROOMS, WITH GARLIC AND RED-PEPPER SAUCE

Yield: 6 servings

1 ounce	dried porcini	1 tablespoon	chopped oregano
1½ fluid ounces	clarified butter (see chapter 1)	1 head	savoy cabbage
		½ fluid ounces	olive oil
3 ounces	onions, finely diced	1 ounce	onions, very finely diced
6 cloves	garlic	to taste	salt and pepper
12	snails, diced small	6 slices	pancetta
¼ teaspoon	freshly ground black pepper	1½ cups	garlic and red pepper sauce (see chapter 7)
6 ounces	mushrooms, diced small	12	scallions, white part only, trimmed
1 cup	dry white wine		
1 fluid ounce	meat glace (see chapter 7)	1 teaspoon	olive oil
½ ounce	stale white bread, diced small	12	arugula leaves
2 tablespoons	chopped parsley		

1. Soak the dried *porcini* in warm water for 15 minutes. Drain and dice small.

2. Heat 1 ounce of the clarified butter in a 7-inch *sauteuse*, sauté the onions, add the garlic and diced snails, and sauté for 1 minute. Season with pepper and remove to a mixing bowl.

3. In the same skillet, heat the remaining butter and sauté the mushrooms and *porcini* until lightly browned. Add to snails.

(continued)

4.   Deglaze the skillet with the wine and reduce until all liquid evaporates. Add the meat *glace* and remove from the heat.

5.   Add the sautéed snails and mushrooms to the skillet and mix with the reduced liquid.

6.   Add the diced white bread, parsley, and oregano to the snail mixture. Adjust the seasonings.

7.   Cut around the core of the savoy cabbage and remove 12 of the most tender leaves.

8.   Blanch the cabbage leaves in boiling, salted water for 3 to 5 minutes, remove with a spider, and shock in ice water. Drain and blot dry.

9.   Line twelve 2-ounce timbales with the trimmed, blanched cabbage leaves. Fill each with 1 ounce of the snail/mushroom mixture and fold the ends of the leaves over the top to seal. Apply pressure to maintain uniform shapes.

10.   Brush an ovenproof baking dish with the olive oil and sprinkle with the very finely diced onions.

11.   Turn out the stuffed cabbages from the timbales. Place in baking dish and brush with olive oil. Season with salt and pepper.

12.   Cut the *pancetta* slices in half and wrap one around each cabbage.

13.   Place in a medium hot oven and bake about 20 to 25 minutes until the *pancetta* is crisp and the timbales are heated through.

14.   To serve, arrange 2 cabbage timbales on each serving plate, with garlic sauce spooned around them.

15.   Sauté the scallions for 10 seconds in a little oil. Place the scallions on the arugula leaves near the cabbage to garnish.

Fiori di Zucchino con Spuma di Frutti di Mare e Fonduta di Pomodoro
ZUCCHINI BLOSSOMS FILLED WITH SEAFOOD MOUSSE, WITH TOMATO FONDUE

Step 6 of the method directs you to blanch the zucchini blossoms before stuffing. This seems to be the standard method. Frankly, I have had far greater success when the blossoms were stuffed without blanching: they retain more flavor and texture after cooking, and they are stuffed more easily. In either case, they should be cleaned very carefully.

Yield: 8 servings

2 tablespoons	chopped shallots	1 cup	dry white wine
½ tablespoon	butter	16	zucchini blossoms
1 cup	dry white wine	¼ cup	melted butter
2 slices	white bread, crust removed and diced	1 tablespoon	fine minced shallots
1½ cups	heavy cream, very cold	8	shrimps, peeled, deveined, with fantail
1 pound	fresh salmon, scallops, and shrimp, peeled (equal amounts)	8	sea scallops
		8	small zucchini halves, cut lengthwise in fan shapes
pinch	salt and white pepper		
pinch	nutmeg	2 cups	tomato fondue (see chapter 7)
pinch	Hungarian paprika		
2	egg whites	8	basil leaves (optional)
1½ to 2 quarts	reduced fish broth (see chapter 3)		

1. Sweat the shallots in the butter. Add the wine and reduce completely until all liquid evaporates. Set aside to cool.

2. Soak bread in ¼ cup heavy cream and refrigerate.

3. Cut the pound of salmon, scallop, and shrimp into small pieces and *chill well*. Grind this through the medium blade of a meat grinder along with the soaked bread and *keep cold*.

4. Place the seafood/bread mixture in the food processor with the shallots, salt, pepper, nutmeg, and paprika. Process very quickly, turning the machine off-on-off-on and adding the egg white a little at a time until a very smooth farce is obtained. The whole process should not take longer than 20 to 30 seconds. Place the seafood farce into a suitable mixing bowl set over crushed ice. Using a wooden spoon, work in the rest of the very cold cream a little at a time. Keep refrigerated until ready to cook. Test the farce by poaching a small amount in the fish broth (see step 5 for heating instructions). It should have a custardlike consistency. If the farce is too firm, add more cream. Adjust the seasonings.

5. Bring the fish broth and wine to a simmer in a shallow saucepan. Using large spoons dipped in lukewarm water, shape the dumplings into 1½-ounce ovals, and poach covered for 8 minutes in the broth, which should be *below simmering* at 185°F. Remove the dumplings with a slotted spoon, and shock in iced water. Drain, wrap, and refrigerate. Reserve the broth.

(continued)

6. Trim the stem ends of the zucchini blossoms as desired, and gently open the blossom to check for dirt and bugs and to remove the pistils in the center. Bring salted water to a boil, and blanch the blossoms for 5 seconds before shocking in ice water. Drain and carefully blot dry.

7. Fill each flower with a seafood dumpling and fold the petals back together. Brush with melted butter.

8. Place the stuffed blossoms in an ovenproof dish that has been well buttered and sprinkled with the finely minced shallots. Add 1 cup of the reserved fish broth and cover with buttered parchment. Cook in a low to medium preheated oven, 300° to 325°F for 10 to 15 minutes until the dumplings are heated through.

9. Meanwhile, reheat the rest of the fish broth in a small saucepan and poach the 8 shrimp, followed by the 8 scallops, until slightly underdone.

10. Blanch the zucchini fans in salted, boiling water for 3 minutes or less. Drain, brush with melted butter, and keep warm.

11. To serve, spoon ¼ cup of hot tomato fondue on each serving plate.

12. Arrange 2 stuffed zucchini blossoms on top of the sauce.

13. Garnish neatly with a poached shrimp, scallop, zucchini fan, and a basil leaf (see color plate 14).

Piccola Spuma di Capesante e Gamberetti con Tagliolini Verdi e Salsa Peperoni Rossi

SCALLOP AND SHRIMP MOUSSELINE WITH SPINACH TAGLIOLINI AND RED-PEPPER SAUCE

Yield: 6 servings

3 ounces	shrimp shells and trimmings, crushed	1 teaspoon	tomato paste
		1 fluid ounce	brandy
1 tablespoon	diced shallots	1 cup	dry white wine
1 clove	garlic, minced	1 cup	chicken stock
½ ounce	clarified butter (see chapter 1)	12 ounces	basic seafood forcemeat, well chilled (see chapter 8)
1 sprig	thyme		
2 leaves	sage		

½ ounce	butter, melted	1½ cups	sweet red-pepper sauce (see chapter 7)
8 ounces	fresh spinach tagliolini (see chapter 5)	6	basil leaves
½ ounce	butter, melted	6	tomato petals (see chapter 1)
1 tablespoon	julienne of black truffle		

1. In a 1-quart saucepan, cook the shrimp trimmings, shallots, and garlic in the clarified butter. After 1 minute add the thyme, sage, and tomato paste, and continue to cook over high heat for 30 seconds.

2. Deglaze the pan with brandy and flambé. Add the wine and chicken stock and simmer over low heat for 10 minutes. Strain through cheesecloth and reduce to 1 fluid ounce. Keep this shrimp reduction refrigerated in a small container until needed.

3. Work 1 tablespoon of shrimp reduction into the seafood forcemeat using a wooden spoon.

4. Brush six 4-ounce molds with the melted butter (demitasse cups work well).

5. Fill each mold with 2 ounces of the seafood forcemeat and place in a hot water bath, cover with parchment paper, and poach for 12 to 15 minutes until firm, like custard. The filling should not rise or overcook. Check frequently.

6. Cook the *tagliolini* by boiling in salted water until *al dente;* drain. Add the melted butter and julienne of black truffle. Adjust the seasoning.

7. Arrange the *tagliolini* in the center of each dinner plate, with an unmolded mousseline nested in the center.

8. Spoon warm sweet red pepper sauce around the *tagliolini.*

9. Decorate with fresh basil leaves and tomato petals (see color plate 15).

— *Calamari* —

SQUID

The squid is a very lean mollusk containing from 18 to 20 percent protein, making it highly nutritious. Squid are naturally tender but become tough and rubbery when overcooked. The best way to prepare squid is therefore by broiling, deep-frying, stir-frying, or quickly poaching.

To clean squid, separate the head and tentacles from the body. The tentacles in turn are separated from the head just ahead of the eyes, and the beak is squeezed out from within. The translucent bone (or "pen") inside the body cavity is also removed. The slippery skin can easily be peeled away from the body and the fins can be pulled off. The ink sac is connected internally to the back of the squid's head. When the head is removed, the sac should be retained and the ink reserved in a cup with a little water in the refrigerator for another use.

Casseruola di Calamari con Risotto

STEWED SQUID WITH RISOTTO

Yield: 6 servings

24 ounces	baby squid, cleaned	1 tablespoon	chopped oregano
1 cup	virgin olive oil	1 tablespoon	chopped basil
4 ounces	onion, sliced	1 tablespoon	chopped parsley
6 cloves	garlic, minced	6 portions	risotto with wine and saffron or white risotto (see chapter 6)
12 ounces	red and green bell peppers, cut in short strips		
2	red chili peppers, chopped	to garnish	basil leaves
2 cups	dry white wine		
12 ounces	plum tomatoes, peeled, seeded, diced (see chapter 1)		

1.   Slice the squid body into ¼-inch-thick rings. Reserve the tentacles. Dry in towels to remove as much moisture as possible.

2.   Heat ¾ cup olive oil in a shallow skillet. Sauté the squid (tentacles and rings) quickly, a bit at a time. Do not overload the skillet. Remove the squid with a slotted spoon before they are completely cooked.

3.   Add the remaining oil to the skillet. Sauté the onions, garlic, bell peppers, and chili peppers for a few minutes. Keep crisp and undercooked. Remove with a slotted spoon and combine with the squid.

4.   Deglaze the pan with the white wine and reduce to about ¼ cup.

5.   Add the tomatoes to the skillet and heat thoroughly. Stir in the squid and peppers. Add the oregano, basil, and parsley.

6.   Place the risotto on the bottom of a china or ceramic casserole. Put the squid on top and decorate with whole basil leaves.

Calamari Ripieni al Solferino
MEAT-STUFFED SQUID WITH WINE AND TOMATOES

Yield: 6 servings

2 ounces	onions, finely diced	SAUCE:	
1 fluid ounce	olive oil	½ cup	onions, diced
18	squid tentacles, finely chopped	4 cloves	garlic
		⅓ cup	virgin olive oil
8 ounces	Italian sausage	2	chili peppers, chopped
2 slices	white bread, chopped		
1	egg	1 pint	dry white wine
2 tablespoons	chopped parsley	1 pound	plum tomatoes, peeled, seeded, and diced
1 tablespoon	chopped oregano		
18	medium-sized squid, cleaned		

1.   Sauté the onions in the olive oil. Add the squid tentacles and cook over low heat for about 15 minutes, covered. Cool.

2.   Grind the Italian sausage through the medium blade of a meat grinder.

3.   Mix the white bread and egg with the sautéed tentacles. Combine with the Italian sausage. Add the parsley and oregano.

4.   Stuff the squid lightly. Secure the openings with toothpicks.

5.   To make the sauce, sauté the onion and garlic in hot olive oil. Add the peppers, wine, and tomatoes. Simmer for 30 minutes.

(continued)

6. Add the stuffed squid to the sauce, and cook over low heat (not quite a simmer) for another 30 minutes. Remove the toothpicks.

7. Serve with grilled or pan-fried polenta or risotto (see chapter 6 for suggestions).

Gamberetti Ripieni Grigliati al Pescatore
BROILED STUFFED SHRIMP, FISHERMAN STYLE

Yield: 6 servings

24	shrimp, 1 ounce each	1 tablespoon	chopped oregano
1 fluid ounce	olive oil	to taste	salt and cayenne pepper
¾ cup	dry breadcrumbs, from Italian bread	to garnish	lemon wedges
1½ cups	melted butter		
3 tablespoons	chopped Italian parsley		

1. Peel the shrimp, leaving the fantail intact. Butterfly the shrimp from the bottom (the leg side), removing the sand vein. Coat with the olive oil.

2. Arrange the butterflied shrimp, cut side down, in an ovenproof dish.

3. Combine the breadcrumbs, ¾ cup melted butter, Italian parsley, oregano, salt, and cayenne.

4. Place approximately 1 teaspoon of this stuffing neatly in the cavity of each shrimp. Coat with the remaining melted butter.

5. Broil quickly under top grill (salamander), or on the upper level of a broiler oven at the highest heat setting. Arrange on a serving dish and drizzle with the butter that ran off during broiling. Serve with lemon wedges.

Frutti di Mare Gratinati
SEAFOOD AU GRATIN

Do not try to store the scallops for this dish too long after purchasing them. They tend to lose their body moisture faster than other bivalves and perish.

Yield: 6 servings

½ pound	pancetta (or bacon), chopped	to taste	salt and freshly ground black pepper
1½ cups	chopped red and green bell peppers	12	oysters, in shell
1	small hot red pepper, chopped	12	cherrystone clams, in shell
10 cloves	garlic, minced	12	large mussels, in shell
¼ cup	chopped parsley	12	scallops, in shell (with roe)
¼ cup	chopped oregano	12	lemon wedges for garnish
1 cup	melted butter		
1½ cups	dry breadcrumbs, from Italian bread		

1. Fry the *pancetta* (or bacon) in a skillet until crisp. Remove all grease from the skillet.

2. Add the chopped peppers and garlic and sauté quickly. Place in a mixing bowl.

3. Add the parsley, oregano, melted butter, breadcrumbs, salt, and pepper. Reserve this gratin.

4. Clean all the shellfish carefully. Scrub off sand and grit and be sure to debeard the mussels.

5. Open all the shellfish (except the mussels) carefully, leaving the inner meats intact and saving the juices.

6. Clean the interiors of the scallops. Remove the tender abductor muscle (the "meat") and the roe (if it is present). Slice the "meat" and return to the deeper shell with the roe.

7. Steam open the mussels in a shallow container with a tight-fitting cover. Steam until just open; do *not* cook. Remove the meats and reserve together with any liquids.

8. Divide gratin evenly and place over the top of each shellfish. If the topping seems dry, add a little melted butter to it.

9. Set up 6 suitable ovenproof cooking dishes with a bed of rock salt in each one.

10. Place 2 of each of the shellfish on the rock salt and broil under the top broiler (salamander) until nicely browned.

11. Set each plate on a folded napkin. Serve with lemon wedges on the side.

Cozze allo Zabaione di Verdure

STEAMED MUSSELS WITH VEGETABLE SABAYON

The whipped cream added to the beaten egg yolks in this dish will loosen up the sauce somewhat, and the *sabayon* will not be as heavy as a dessert *sabayon*. Rather, the sauce should have the consistency of *crème anglaise,* smoothly coating a spoon dipped into it.

Yield: 4 servings

24	fresh large mussels	pinch	saffron
1 ounce	butter	1 cup	dry white wine or dry vermouth
2 ounces	leeks, white part only, cut in julienne	2 or 3	egg yolks
2 ounces	celeriac, cut in julienne	1/2 to 3/4 cup	whipped cream, unsalted
2 ounces	carrots, cut in julienne	1/4 cup	fresh basil, cut in very fine julienne
4 cloves	garlic, minced		
1/4 teaspoon	freshly ground black pepper	24	toast points, preferably sourdough bread
1	bay leaf		

1.   Place the mussels in cold water for several minutes. Discard any that are open.

2.   Clean the mussels thoroughly, removing all sand and beards.

3.   Using a shallow stainless steel or earthenware casserole, melt the butter and place the leeks, celeriac, and carrots on the melted butter. Place the mussels on top of the vegetables with the garlic, pepper, bay leaf, and saffron.

4.   Add the wine and bring to a simmer. Steam the mussels briefly—until they open but remain plump and juicy—using a tight-fitting cover.

5.   Remove the mussels from the shells and arrange 6 mussels per serving in soup plates.

6.   Strain the liquid into a small mixing bowl. Put some of the vegetables over each mussel. The vegetables should still be crisp. The mussels should be kept hot.

7.   Heat water in the bottom of a double boiler until barely simmering. Combine the egg yolks with the strained juices; there should be 3 fluid ounces of liquid for every egg yolk. Set in the double boiler, without touching the water below. Beat vigorously with

a wire whip until an emulsion is achieved. Remove from the heat, fold in the whipped cream, and adjust the seasonings.

8.   Spoon some of the *sabayon* over each mussel and sprinkle generously with the basil julienne.

9.   Serve immediately with toast points, Italian garlic toast, or toasted sourdough bread on the side.

Cozze alla Provenzale

MUSSELS STEAMED IN WHITE WINE, PROVENÇAL STYLE

Yield: 6 servings

60	fresh large mussels	1	small hot pepper, chopped
¼ cup	olive oil		
2 cups	dry white wine	2 tablespoons	chopped Italian parsley
2	bay leaves		
1 sprig	thyme	1 tablespoon	chopped oregano
1 cup	olive oil	1 tablespoon	chopped basil
1 cup	onions, finely diced	to garnish	basil leaves
12 cloves	garlic, minced	to garnish	toasted sourdough or Italian bread
2 cups	peeled and diced tomatoes		

1.   Place the mussels in cold water for several minutes. Discard any that remain open. To test for freshness, press the two shells firmly together. If the shell moves, or opens, the mussel is not fresh.

2.   Clean each mussel with a brush to remove sand and grit, and remove the beard.

3.   Put ¼ cup olive oil, wine, bay leaves, and thyme in a shallow casserole with tight-fitting lid and bring to a simmer. Add the mussels, cover, and steam briefly until the mussels open but the meat remains plump.

4.   Strain the liquid into another pan and reduce to three-quarters the original volume. Keep the mussels covered and warm.

5.   Heat the cup of olive oil in a skillet, add the onions and garlic, and sauté until the onions are somewhat brown.

(continued)

6. Add the tomatoes and heat through. Stir in the hot pepper, Italian parsley, oregano, basil, and reduced mussel liquid. Adjust the seasonings.

7. Arrange 10 mussels per serving (on the half shell) in large, shallow soup plates, and spoon the tomato mixture onto each mussel. Decorate with fresh basil leaves (see color plate 16).

8. Serve very hot with toasted sourdough or fresh Italian bread.

Cosce di Rane alla Diavola con Risotto

DEVILED FROG LEGS WITH RISOTTO

Yield: 6 servings

18	frog legs, boned	¾ cup	dry white wine
to taste	salt, freshly ground black pepper	¾ cup	poultry glace (see chapter 7)
3 tablespoons	flour	2 tablespoons	chopped Italian parsley
⅓ cup	olive oil	1 tablespoon	chopped oregano
¼ cup	brandy	6 cups	Rissotto Milanese (see chapter 6)
¼ cup	olive oil		
¾ cup	finely diced onions	1 cup	julienne of red and green bell peppers
6 cloves	garlic, minced		
2	small hot peppers, chopped	to sauté peppers	olive oil
		to garnish	basil leaves
6	Italian plum tomatoes, peeled and diced		

1. Remove the meat from the frog legs using a sharp utility knife.

2. Season with the salt and pepper and dust with the flour.

3. Heat the olive oil in a sauté pan, and sauté the meat until lightly browned. Add the brandy and flambé. Remove from the pan and keep warm.

4. To make the sauce, add the ¼ cup olive oil to the same pan, and sauté the onions and garlic. Add the hot peppers and tomatoes and reduce a bit. Add the wine and continue to reduce, to half the original volume.

5. Add the poultry *glace* and adjust the seasonings. If the sauce is too liquid, reduce further.

6. Mix the meat, parsley, and oregano into the sauce.

7. The most elegant way to serve this dish is to place risotto in a ring mold, invert, and unmold onto a serving plate. Spoon the deviled frog legs and sauce into the cavity. Sauté the julienne of peppers in olive oil until tender-crisp, and place atop the frog legs. Garnish with fresh basil leaves (see color plate 17).

SOUPS

Today, the creation of soups depends as much on a flavorful base mixture, be it stock or cream or puree, as it does on the garnishes such as rice or meats floating in the soup—indeed these garnishes may be dispensed with entirely, as in a bisque or consommé. However, in medieval times, the garnishes cooked in the liquids were considered most important: soup was a hearty meal consisting of whatever was affordable and available, usually accompanied by dark bread. Because of the virtual nonexistence of eating utensils at that time, the texture of soups was generally thick and chunky, and bread was used as the principal trencher. At the aristocratic table, soups played a different role and assumed different forms, being composed of an abundant variety of luxurious ingredients. Since soups were followed by additional sumptuous courses, their composition did not necessarily match that of soups for poorer people.

During this era, the sequence of menu presentation was more apt to be constructed around fantastic displays, which had become somewhat ritualized. Not until the seventeenth century did the menu begin to revolve around a harmonious blending of ingredients. This reconsideration of the menu framework, combined with the introduction of new ingredients from the newly discovered Western Hemisphere, both increased the Italian fondness for soup and caused recipes to undergo major changes. Loosely defined categories of soups began to evolve.

For soups classified as *minestre* (which means soups), inclusion of flour-based products such as pasta has remained traditional. To this day, a *minestra* or *zuppa* can be a hearty main course or part of the more extended menu framework. More strictly defined are the specialized, usually well-known regional soups. These include *busecca*, a vegetable-tripe soup from Milan (see Tripe Soup, Milanese Style, later in this chapter); *burrida*, a fish soup or stew similar to bouillabaisse, from Genoa; *cacciucco*, a fish and shellfish, from Livorno; *stracciatella* or *mille-fanti*, which are varieties of egg-drop soup; and *zuppa all' pavese*, a broth with whole eggs served with Parmesan and croutons, from Pavia.

Minestrone are usually heavy vegetable soups containing pasta or rice, depending on the particular region. *Minestrina* and *brodo* are clear broths, which can be reduced, doubling their potency, to create *brodo doppio* or *ristretto* ("reduced"). When various types of pasta are added to these broths they become *pasta in brodo*.

Cream soups are also common, mainly in the northern regions, and are usually prepared with vegetables, meat, seafood, or mushrooms before being adjusted with fresh cream and served with an accompanying garnish (or croutons). Italy's *nuova cucina (nouvelle cuisine)* has kept pace with the rest of the gastronomic world by innovatively reinterpreting these soups. Flour is now commonly omitted altogether, and the cooked ingredients are pureed into an emulsion with a blender, finished with fresh cream, and often thickened with an egg yolk–cream liaison. Special wine cream soups are prepared with extremely potent reduced broths that are in turn flavored with aromatics. Sometimes "pure starch"—arrowroot, cornstarch, rice starch—is dissolved in these broths to increase viscosity. The soups are then finished with an egg yolk–cream liaison to achieve the desired velvety consistency, which is the trademark of these remarkable soups.

— *Zuppe Calde* —
HOT SOUPS

Crema di Fagioli con Pancetta Affumicata
CREAMY CRANBERRY-BEAN PUREE WITH SMOKED PANCETTA

This is a contemporary variation of the famous *pasta e fagioli* (a recipe for which appears later in this chapter), pureed to a velvety consistency in a blender. It is one of the many modern soups I encountered in northern Italy. When properly prepared, the soup is delicate, homogeneous, even airy—very pleasant indeed.

Yield: 8 servings

10 ounces	fresh cranberry beans, shelled (or 6 ounces dried beans)	2 ounces	celeriac, finely cut
3 pints	beef or chicken broth (see recipes later in this chapter)	8 ounces	tomatoes, peeled, seeded, and chopped (see chapter 1)
1/4 cup	olive oil	1/2 cup	beef broth (see recipe later in this chapter)
4 ounces	onions, diced small	1	bay leaf
4 cloves	garlic, minced	1 sprig	thyme
3 ounces	prosciutto trimmings, chopped	10	black peppercorns, crushed

1½ ounces	butter	8	small, whole sage leaves
1 ounce	Parmesan, grated		
½ cup	miniature elbow macaroni, cooked		
3 ounces	smoked pancetta (or bacon), cut into ½-inch squares and fried crisp		

1. Place the shelled cranberry beans in a 4-quart soup pot. Add the 3 pints of broth, and simmer slowly for 1 hour, until very soft. Puree the beans through a food mill. (If dried beans are used, first soak them in water overnight. Cook them for 2 hours in the broth before pureeing.)

2. In another 4-quart pot, heat the olive oil, and cook the onions, garlic, and *prosciutto* trimmings over low heat until the onions are soft. Add the celeriac and tomatoes and cook for another 15 minutes.

3. Combine the pureed beans with the onion mixture (add more broth if the consistency seems too thick) and simmer slowly for 30 minutes.

4. In a small sauce pan, bring ½ cup of broth to a boil, add the bay leaf, thyme, and pepper, and remove from the heat. Strain and add to the bean puree, removing that from the heat as well. Let cool slightly and then puree in a blender until velvety and smooth. Strain again through a fine china cap.

5. Return the soup to a simmer. Adjust the seasonings and consistency if necessary.

6. Lower the heat to below a simmer or, preferably, hold the soup in a hot water bath.

7. Stir in the butter and grated Parmesan.

8. Serve with a garnish of cooked miniature elbow macaroni and crisp smoked *pancetta* (or bacon). Place a small whole sage leaf on top of each serving.

Crema al Profumo di Spumante
CHICKEN VELOUTÉ WITH SPUMANTE

Yield: 8 servings

3 cups	chicken broth (see recipe later in this chapter)	1 cup	dry spumante
		1 cup	hot cream
2 tablespoons	arrowroot		
1 cup	dry spumante	**GARNISH:**	
pinch	cinnamon	¾ cup	stale Italian bread, diced very small
pinch	nutmeg	1 ounce	butter
pinch	cayenne pepper	1 cup	whipped cream

LIAISON:

4	egg yolks

1.   Bring the chicken broth to a simmer in a noncorrosive 2-quart pot.

2.   In a mixing bowl, dissolve the arrowroot in 1 cup of *spumante*. Add the cinnamon, nutmeg, and cayenne pepper. Stir this into chicken broth, then remove from the heat.

3.   In a 2-quart stainless steel mixing bowl, combine the egg yolks with the remaining 1 cup of *spumante*. Place the bowl over a pot of boiling water (or use a double boiler), and whisk vigorously until the mixture thickens to a light, creamy consistency. Be careful not to overheat (do not allow the bottom of the mixing bowl to touch the water beneath), or the yolks will coagulate.

4.   Whisk the chicken broth in a *slow stream* into the *spumante* liaison, followed by the cup of hot cream.

5.   Strain and hold in a hot water bath.

6.   Place the diced Italian bread on a sheet pan and let dry in a moderate oven. Heat the butter in a sauté pan and add the dried croutons. Shake the pan until the croutons are lightly browned.

7.   Spoon the *velouté* into cups or soup plates. Place a dollop of whipped cream on top, and sprinkle with croutons.

Crema di Castagne Legate

CHESTNUT VELOUTÉ

Chestnuts have always been synonymous with winter holiday festivities. The recipe that follows demonstrates the versatility of the chestnut in cooking.

Yield: 8 servings

4 to 6 ounces	fresh chestnuts, peeled (or chestnut paste)	pinch	nutmeg
		pinch	cinnamon
8 ounces	leeks, white part only	1 cup	dry spumante
4 ounces	fresh celeriac	**LIAISON:**	
4 ounces	fresh fennel bulb	1 cup	cream
2 ounces	butter	3	egg yolks
1 quart	chicken broth, (see recipe later in this chapter)	**GARNISH:**	
pinch	salt and cayenne pepper	1/2 cup	finely sliced scallion tops

1.   Slit the fresh chestnuts on the flat side through the skin and bake at 375°F until soft (or boil for about 20 minutes until soft). Remove the skin and bitter dark spots between the folds of the nutmeat.

2.   Halve the leeks lengthwise and rinse under running water. Scrub the celeriac under running water and peel. Cut the leeks, fennel, celeriac, and chestnuts into small pieces.

3.   Heat the butter in a 4-quart noncorrosive soup pot, add the vegetables and chestnuts, and cook over low heat for 10 minutes.

4.   Add the chicken broth and simmer over low heat until the vegetables are well cooked.

5.   Add the salt, cayenne, nutmeg, and cinnamon.

6.   Puree the mixture in a blender until completely homogeneous and smooth. Strain through a fine china cap.

(continued)

7.   Return the soup to a simmer, add the *spumante,* and adjust the seasonings.

8.   Combine the cream and egg yolks in a large mixing bowl. Ladle a little of the hot chestnut puree into the liaison slowly while stirring. Then add the liaison to the remaining puree, whisking briskly to prevent cooking the eggs. Do not overheat the soup at this point, or it will curdle.

9.   Serve in soup cups or bowls, garnished with finely cut scallion tops.

Crema di Finocchi con Polpa di Gamberetti e Capesante
CREAM OF FENNEL SOUP WITH SHRIMP AND SCALLOPS

Yield: 8 servings

8	shrimp, peeled and deveined (16 count per pound)	1 cup	dry vermouth
		pinch	saffron
8	sea scallops	pinch	nutmeg
3 ounces	butter	pinch	salt and cayenne pepper
1 quart	chicken broth (see recipe later in this chapter)	1 cup	hot cream
		2	tomatoes, peeled, seeded, and cut in a fine julienne
1 pound	fresh fennel		
2 ounces	sweet red onion, sliced thinly		
4 ounces	leeks, white part only, sliced thinly		

1.   Cook the shrimp and scallops in 1 ounce of butter and a bit of the chicken broth until just underdone. Slice into bite-size pieces and keep warm for later use. Save the cooking liquid.

2.   Discard the green stems from the fennel, saving 8 sprigs of the top leafy part for later use. Peel the outer skin from the fennel knob and slice thinly.

3.   In a noncorrosive 4-quart soup pot cook the fennel, onion, and leeks in the remaining butter over low heat until almost soft. Add the cooking liquid from the shellfish, the dry vermouth, saffron, nutmeg, salt, pepper, and the remaining chicken broth. Simmer over low heat for about 30 minutes.

4.   Puree this mixture in a blender until smooth and homogeneous. Add more chicken stock if necessary.

PRODUCTION SERVICES
KAISER PERMANENTE
1850 CALIFORNIA AV
CORONA CA 91719-3378

Appointment Confirmation

We have made the following appointment for you:

Patient: JAMES S. PEACOCK

Your Medical Record Number is: 1129372

Date / Time : **Wednesday, December 9, 1998, at 9:50 a.m.**
With   **GEORGE MOLLETT, M.D.**
Location :   **ORTHOPEDIC SURGERY CLINIC**
               1425 SO. MAIN ST WALNUT CREEK

CANCELLATION INFORMATION:

To cancel only   : (925) 295-4958   7 days/24 hours

To cancel and reschedule : (925) 295-4130   Mon-Fri 8:00 a.m. to 5:00 p.m.

> NOTE: ORTHOPEDICS IS NOW LOCATED IN MOB2; 1ST FLOOR
> NEXT TO THE LAB.

NOTE

10/26/98

KAISER PERMANENTE
1425 SOUTH MAIN STREET
WALNUT CREEK, CA 94596
ATTN: CENTRAL APPOINTMENTS

KAISER PERMANENTE

RETURN SERVICE REQUESTED

YOUR APPOINTMENT INFORMATION — PLEASE OPEN IMMEDIATELY

Ready for your appointment?
Use the *Ask-the-Doctor Checklist* in your **Healthwise Handbook.** Need a book? Call 1-800-464-4000.

Looking for Health Education services? Send in attached reply card.

JAMES S. PEACOCK
231 LAFAYETTE CIR #203
LAFAYETTE CA 94549-4390

DETACH HERE

REPLY CARD
"PARTNERS IN HEALTH"

☐ Yes, please send me current information about the health education services offered by Kaiser Permanente.

B-11674
**BARCODE ABOVE CONTAINS RETURN ADDRESS DATA
PLEASE DO NOT WRITE ON, DISFIGURE, OR DAMAGE BARCODE**

YOUR APPOINTMENT INFORMATION — PLEASE OPEN IMMEDIATLY

TO OPEN: FOLD AND TEAR AT PERFORATION

5.   Reheat, adjust the seasonings, and add the hot cream. Strain through a fine-mesh sieve.

6.   Serve in bowls with the sliced shellfish. Garnish with the tomato julienne and fennel sprigs.

Thanksgiving 1998

Vellutata di Zucca al Prosciutto e Riso
PUMPKIN VELOUTÉ WITH PROSCIUTTO AND RICE

This soup can also be prepared without the liaison, using just the cream and cheese, no egg yolks.

Yield: 8 servings

2 ounces	fatty prosciutto trimmings	pinch	nutmeg
1 ounce	butter	**LIAISON:**	
4 ounces	sweet red onions, finely diced	³/₄ cup	cream
		2	egg yolks
12 ounces	pumpkin, peeled, seeded, and diced	1 ounce	Parmesan, grated
6 ounces	potatoes	**GARNISH:**	
5 cups	chicken broth (see recipe later in this chapter)	¹/₂ cup	cooked rice
		¹/₄ cup	julienne of prosciutto (preferably cooked)
1	bay leaf		
1	rosemary sprig	8 sprigs	small basil leaves
pinch	salt and cayenne pepper		

1.   Render the *prosciutto* trimmings with the butter in a 3-quart heavy-gauge pot. Add the onions and cook over low heat until translucent.

2.   Add the pumpkin, potatoes, and broth. Wrap the bay leaf and rosemary in cheese-cloth and add. Simmer until the pumpkin and potatoes are completely cooked, about 30 to 45 minutes.

3.   Season with salt, cayenne pepper, and nutmeg. Remove the herb sachet. Puree in a blender until velvety smooth. Strain through a fine-mesh sieve and reheat.

(continued)

4. Combine the cream, egg yolks, and Parmesan in a 4-quart stainless steel mixing bowl. Slowly add the hot pumpkin puree. Stir briskly with a wire whisk to achieve a proper emulsion. Adjust the seasonings.

5. Keep the pumpkin *velouté* warm in a hot water bath (below 165°F) until ready to serve to prevent coagulation of the egg yolks.

6. Serve in earthenware bowls if available, with a garnish of boiled rice and fine julienne of *prosciutto*. Top with basil leaf sprigs.

Crema al Profumo d'Aglio con Crostini e Prosciutto

GARLIC VELOUTÉ WITH CROUTONS AND PROSCIUTTO

Yield: 8 servings

1 ounce	butter		**LIAISON:**	
8 ounces	leeks, white part only		2	egg yolks
12 ounces	onions, sliced		¼ cup	cream
4 ounces	celeriac, diced small			
10 cloves	garlic, minced		**GARNISH:**	
1 quart	chicken broth (see recipe later in this chapter)		¾ cup	diced stale Italian bread, without crust, small
pinch	salt and cayenne pepper		1 ounce	butter
pinch	nutmeg		½ cup	fine julienne of prosciutto
1 cup	hot cream			

1. Heat the butter in a 4-quart noncorrosive pot. Cook the leek whites, onions, and celeriac over low heat. Add the garlic and continue to cook a few more minutes. Do not brown the onions.

2. Add the chicken broth and simmer slowly for another 30 minutes. Add the salt, cayenne, and nutmeg.

3. Puree in a blender until smooth. Reheat and add the hot cream. Adjust the seasonings.

4. Combine the egg yolks and cream in a 2-quart stainless steel mixing bowl. Add slowly to the cream soup while whisking to achieve a proper emulsion. Add more broth if needed. The *velouté* should be velvety in texture.

5. Sauté the small-diced Italian bread in butter until crisp.

6. Serve the soup topped with the croutons and fine julienne of *prosciutto*.

Purea di Ceci Secchi e Porcini

CHICK-PEA AND PORCINI PUREE

Yield: 8 servings

5 ounces	dried chick-peas	INFUSION:	
5 pints	beef or chicken broth (see recipes later in this chapter)	1 cup	beef broth (see recipe later in this chapter)
3 ounces	pancetta, chopped	1	bay leaf
3 ounces	onions, diced small	1	rosemary sprig
3 cloves	garlic, minced	1	thyme sprig
2 ounces	carrots, cut small	1½ ounces	butter
2 ounces	celeriac or parsnips, cut small	1 ounce	Parmesan, grated
3 ounces	potatoes, cut small	GARNISH:	
1	chili pepper, finely chopped	¾ cup	diced stale Italian bread, very small
½ ounce	dried porcini, soaked in ¼ cup broth	1 ounce	butter
to taste	salt	¼ cup	finely sliced scallion tops

1. Soak the chick-peas overnight in water.

2. Place the soaked chick-peas in a 3-quart soup pot with the 5 pints of broth and simmer slowly for approximately 1½ hours.

3. Render the *pancetta* in a 4-quart soup pot. Add the onions and garlic and cook over low heat for several minutes. Add remaining vegetables, the hot pepper, and *porcini* and cook for 5 more minutes.

(continued)

4.   Combine the cooked chick-peas and broth with the vegetables and simmer until all ingredients are soft.

5.   Prepare the infusion (which can be done ahead of time) by bringing the cup of broth to a boil in a small container and adding the bay leaf, thyme, and rosemary. Remove from the heat and let steep until needed (or for about 15 minutes). Strain.

6.   Incorporate the infusion into the pea soup and adjust the seasonings. Remove from the heat.

7.   Puree the soup in a blender until very smooth and velvety. Strain through a fine-mesh sieve.

8.   Reheat the soup without boiling. Stir in the butter and grated Parmesan.

9.   Sauté the diced Italian bread in butter until crisp.

10.   Serve the puree topped with the fine croutons and sliced scallions.

Crema di Zucchini e Porri all'Erbe
ZUCCHINI AND LEEK VELOUTÉ WITH HERBS

Yield: 8 servings

3 ounces	*pancetta, chopped*	**LIAISON:**	
8 to 10 ounces	*leeks, white part only, thinly sliced*	*2*	*egg yolks*
1½ pounds	*zucchini, seeded and sliced*	*¼ cup*	*cream*
		1 ounce	*Parmesan, grated*
6 cloves	*garlic, minced*		
2 quarts	*chicken broth (see recipe later in this chapter)*	**GARNISH:**	
		1 cup	*julienne of raw zucchini, with skin*
pinch	*cayenne pepper*	*2 tablespoons*	*chopped parsley*
pinch	*nutmeg*	*1 tablespoon*	*chopped basil*
to taste	*salt*		
1 cup	*cream*		

1.   Render the *pancetta* in a 3-quart soup pot. Add the leeks, zucchini, and garlic, and cook over low heat for 5 minutes. Add the chicken broth, cayenne, nutmeg, and salt, and continue to cook for another 10 minutes, until the vegetables are soft.

2.   Puree the mixture in a blender until smooth.

3.   Reheat, add the cream, and adjust the seasonings.

4.   Combine the egg yolks, cream, and Parmesan in a 2-quart stainless steel mixing bowl. Slowly add the cream soup while whisking briskly to achieve a good emulsion. Thin with extra broth if too heavy.

5.   Serve topped with the julienne of raw zucchini and sprinkled with chopped basil and parsley.

Vellutata di Cozze al Pesto con Crostini

LEEK VELOUTÉ WITH MUSSELS, PESTO, AND CROUTONS

Yield: 8 servings

32	*fresh mussels, cleaned and debearded*	LIAISON:	
		2	*egg yolks*
3 ounces	*butter*	*¼ cup*	*cream*
1	*thyme sprig*	*½ cup*	*pesto (see chapter 7)*
1	*parsley sprig*		
1	*basil sprig*	GARNISH:	
1 cup	*dry white wine*	*¼ cup*	*clarified butter (see chapter 1)*
10 ounces	*leeks, white part only, thinly sliced*	*½ cup*	*julienne of red bell pepper*
6 ounces	*onions, thinly sliced*	*½ cup*	*julienne of fennel knob*
4 ounces	*celeriac, thinly sliced*	*¾ cup*	*finely diced stale Italian bread*
4 ounces	*fennel knob, thinly sliced*	*8*	*sage leaves*
3 cups	*chicken broth (see recipe later in this chapter)*		
1 cup	*hot cream*		

1.   Place the mussels, 1 ounce of butter, thyme, parsley, basil, and dry white wine in a shallow casserole. Bring to a boil, cover tightly, and steam quickly until the mussel shells open completely. Do *not* overcook. The mussel "meats" should be plump. Remove the shells, strain the liquid through cheesecloth, and reserve. Keep the mussel meats warm.

(continued)

2. Heat the remaining butter in a 3-quart noncorrosive soup pot, and cook the leeks, onions, celeriac, and fennel over low heat until soft. Do not brown the vegetables.

3. Add the reserved mussel liquid to the chicken broth, add to the cooked vegetables, and simmer for about 30 minutes. Remove from the heat and puree in a blender until smooth. Reheat and add the hot cream. Strain through a fine-mesh sieve.

4. Combine the egg yolks, cream, and *pesto* in a 2-quart stainless steel bowl. Slowly add the cream soup while whipping with a whisk to achieve a proper emulsion. Thin with a little heated broth if necessary. The consistency should be velvety. Keep the soup warm in a hot water bath, but do not heat above 180° F or the eggs will curdle.

5. Sauté the red pepper and fennel quickly in the clarified butter. Keep warm.

6. Sauté the diced Italian bread in a little butter until crisp and light brown.

7. Arrange 4 mussel meats in each soup cup or bowl (if they are not warm, reheat in a little broth). Fill with the *velouté* and garnish with the sautéed julienne of vegetables, croutons, and a sage leaf.

Zuppa di Coda di Bue al Veneto
OXTAIL SOUP, VENETIAN STYLE

Yield: 8 to 10 servings

2 pounds	lean oxtails
2 quarts	beef broth (see recipe later in this chapter)
2 ounces	barley
2 ounces	pancetta, chopped
2 ounces	onions, diced small
2 ounces	carrots, diced small
2 ounces	fennel, diced small
2 ounces	celeriac, diced small
6 cloves	garlic, minced
2	chili peppers, chopped
4	tomatoes, peeled, seeded, and diced (see chapter 1)

INFUSION:

1/2 cup	beef broth (see recipe later in this chapter)
1	thyme sprig
1	marjoram sprig
1	rosemary sprig
2	bay leaves

GARNISH:

10	basil leaves, cut in chiffonade (fine strips)

1. Trim all fat from the oxtails. Cut into sections at the natural seams and place into a heated, slightly oiled *rondeau*. Brown in a hot oven on all sides.

2. Place the browned oxtails in a soup pot with the 2 quarts of beef broth and simmer for approximately 3 to 3½ hours. Occasionally skim off the fat.

3. Remove the oxtails and reserve. Strain the broth.

4. Cook barley in the strained broth for about 1½ hours.

5. Render the *pancetta* in a 3-quart soup pot and add the onions, carrots, fennel, celeriac, garlic, and hot peppers. Cook over low heat for 10 minutes. Add the diced tomatoes.

6. Bring the ½ cup of broth to a simmer and add the thyme, marjoram, rosemary, and bay leaves. Remove from the heat and steep for 5 to 10 minutes. Strain and add the liquid to the vegetables. Adjust the seasonings.

7. Remove the meat from the cooked oxtails and dice into small pieces. Add to the soup. Check the consistency and add more broth if needed.

8. Serve in bowls or cups garnished with a chiffonade of fresh basil. Freshly grated Parmesan can be passed with the soup.

Zuppa di Orzo Perlato alla Trentina
VEGETABLE BARLEY SOUP, TRENTINA STYLE

Yield: 8 to 10 servings

2½ ounces	*pearl barley*	1	*marjoram sprig*
3 pints	*beef broth (see recipe later in this chapter)*	1	*rosemary sprig*
		1	*bay leaf*
4 ounces	*pancetta, chopped*	10	*black peppercorns, crushed*
3 ounces	*onions, diced small*		
2 ounces	*carrots, diced small*	pinch	*nutmeg*
2 ounces	*celeriac, diced small*	**GARNISH:**	
2 ounces	*fennel, diced small*	¼ cup	*grated Parmesan*
6 cloves	*garlic, minced*	¼ bunch	*Italian parsley, chopped*
2 ounces	*savoy cabbage, diced small*		
4 ounces	*potatoes, diced small*	1½ fluid ounces	*extra-virgin olive oil*

INFUSION:

1 cup	*beef broth (see recipe later in this chapter)*

1. Cook the barley in 3 pints of broth over very low heat for about 1½ hours, until soft.

2. Render the *pancetta* in a 3-quart soup pot. Add the onions, carrots, celeriac, and fennel, and smother for 5 minutes.

3. When the vegetables are almost tender, add the garlic, cabbage, and potatoes, and continue to cook very slowly for a few more minutes.

4. Prepare the infusion by bringing 1 cup of broth to a boil in a small container. Add the marjoram, rosemary, bay leaf, peppercorns, and nutmeg, and set the pan aside to steep for at least 15 minutes. Strain.

5. Combine the cooked barley (with its broth), the stewed vegetables, and the infusion, and bring to a simmer. If the consistency is too heavy, add more broth.

6. Pour the soup into serving bowls or cups and sprinkle with grated Parmesan, chopped Italian parsley, and olive oil.

Zuppa al Genovese con Pesto

VEGETABLE SOUP WITH PESTO, GENOA STYLE

The *pesto* for this soup may be prepared ahead of time and stored, covered, in the refrigerator until needed, but is best if made daily as needed.

Yield: 8 to 10 servings

¼ cup	olive oil	PESTO:	
2 ounces	onions, diced small	¼ cup	olive oil
2 ounces	leeks, diced small	6 cloves	garlic, minced
2 ounces	carrots, diced small	1 ounce	pine nuts, lightly toasted
2 ounces	turnips, diced small		
2 ounces	potatoes, diced small	1 ounce	pecorino cheese, grated
1 cup	fresh fava beans (shelled broad beans)	1 ounce	Parmesan, grated
2 ounces	savoy or green cabbage, cut small	10	large basil leaves
3 pints	beef broth (see recipe later in this chapter)	GARNISH:	
½ cup	peeled and diced tomatoes (see chapter 1)	½ to ¾ cup	cooked tagliolini, cut short
		½ cup	thinly sliced scallions
2 ounces	zucchini, diced small	to pass	grated Parmesan

1. Heat the olive oil in a 3-quart soup pot and cook the onions, leeks, carrots, turnips, potatoes, fava beans, and cabbage over low heat for 5 minutes. Add hot beef broth and simmer for another 5 minutes before adding the tomatoes and zucchini.

2. Puree all the ingredients for the *pesto* in a blender. Add to the vegetable soup. Adjust the seasonings.

3. Add the cooked pasta before serving and garnish with thinly sliced scallions. Pass grated Parmesan cheese along with the soup.

Pasta e Fagioli al Veneto

PASTA AND BEAN SOUP, VENETIAN STYLE

Yield: 8 to 10 servings

2 quarts	beef broth (see recipe later in this chapter)	1	rosemary sprig
		1	marjoram sprig
10 ounces	borlotti or white kidney beans, fresh (or 5 ounces dried beans)	2	bay leaves
		15	black peppercorns, crushed
3 ounces	fatty prosciutto trimmings	GARNISH:	
1 fluid ounce	olive oil	1 cup	cooked tagliatelle, cut short
3 ounces	onions, diced small	½ cup	grated Parmesan
2 ounces	celeriac, diced small	¼ cup	extra-virgin olive oil
2 ounces	carrots, diced small	¼ cup	chopped Italian parsley
6 ounces	potatoes, diced small		
6 cloves	garlic, minced		

INFUSION:

1 cup	beef broth (see recipe later in this chapter)

1.   Cook the beans in the 2 quarts of broth until soft.

2.   Render the *prosciutto* trimmings in a 3-quart soup pot with the olive oil. Add the onions, celeriac, carrots, potatoes, and garlic; cook in the rendered fat over low heat until soft.

3.   Add the cooked beans with broth to the vegetables.

4.   Prepare the infusion by bringing the cup of broth to a simmer in a small container. Add the rosemary, marjoram, bay leaves, and pepper, remove from the heat, and let steep 5 to 10 minutes. Strain and add the liquid to the soup. Check the consistency and add more broth if needed.

5.   Add the cooked *tagliatelle* to the soup.

6.   Serve in soup bowls or cups, sprinkled with Parmesan, olive oil, and chopped Italian parsley.

Zuppa di Trippa alla Milanese
TRIPE SOUP, MILANESE STYLE

This is a variation on the traditionally thick *busecca*.

Yield: 8 to 10 servings

2½ pounds	beef tripe	**INFUSION:**	
2 quarts	beef broth (see recipe later in this chapter)	1 cup	beef broth (see recipe later in this chapter)
3 ounces	dried white kidney or navy beans, presoaked overnight	1	rosemary sprig
		2	bay leaves
		6	sage leaves
3 ounces	pancetta, chopped		
4 ounces	onions, diced small		
2 ounces	carrots, diced small	**GARNISH:**	
2 ounces	celery, diced small	2 tablespoons	olive oil
2 ounces	green cabbage, cut into small squares	½ cup	fine julienne of red bell peppers
6 ounces	garlic, minced	½ cup	fine julienne of green bell peppers
2	chili peppers, chopped	¼ cup	chopped Italian parsley
4	tomatoes, peeled, seeded, and diced (see chapter 1)	½ cup	grated Parmesan
pinch	saffron		

1.   Blanch the tripe in water for 15 minutes, shock in ice water, and drain. Remove any fatty tissue from the tripe and discard. Cut the tripe into small strips and place in a heavy-duty 4-quart soup pot. Add the 2 quarts of broth, and cook for 6 to 8 hours, until tender.

2.   Cook the presoaked beans in a separate pot with a little broth. Add to the tripe when soft.

3.   Render the *pancetta* and add the onions, carrots, celery, cabbage, garlic, and hot peppers. Cook over low heat for several minutes before mixing in the tomatoes and saffron. Add to tripe and beans.

(continued)

4.   Prepare the infusion by bringing the cup of broth to a boil in a small pan and adding the rosemary, bay leaves, and sage. Remove from the heat and steep for 5 to 10 minutes. Strain and add the liquid to the soup.

5.   Adjust the seasonings. Check the consistency and add broth if necessary.

6.   Quickly sauté the peppers in a little oil until tender-crisp.

7.   Serve the soup in bowls topped with the sautéed peppers in the center. Sprinkle with the chopped Italian parsley and grated Parmesan.

Zuppa di Lenticchie ai Verdure e Prosciutto
LENTIL SOUP WITH VEGETABLES AND PROSCIUTTO

Yield: 8 to 10 servings

5 ounces	lentils, presoaked for several hours	1	thyme sprig
		1	marjoram sprig
2 quarts	beef broth (see recipe later in this chapter)	2	bay leaves
3 ounces	pancetta, chopped	1/2 cup	peeled, seeded, and diced tomatoes (see chapter 1)
4 ounces	onions, diced small		
2 ounces	carrots, diced small		
2 ounces	celeriac, diced small	1/4 cup	balsamic vinegar
4 cloves	garlic	1/4 teaspoon	freshly ground black pepper
1/2 ounce	flour		
4 ounces	potatoes, diced small		
		GARNISH:	
INFUSION:		1/2 cup	finely sliced scallions
		1/4 cup	julienne of prosciutto
1 cup	beef broth (see recipe later in this chapter)		

1.   Slowly cook the presoaked lentils in the 2 quarts of beef broth for about 30 minutes, until soft but still whole. Remove from the heat and strain, reserving both broth and lentils.

2.   Render the *pancetta* in a 3-quart soup pot and add the onions, carrots, celeriac, and garlic. Stir in the flour. Bring the broth from the lentils to a boil and add to the vegetables. Add the potatoes and simmer slowly for 10 minutes. Add the lentils.

3.   Prepare the infusion by bringing the cup of broth to a boil and adding the thyme, marjoram, and bay leaves. Remove from the heat, steep 5 to 10 minutes, and strain, reserving the liquid.

4.   Add the strained liquid, tomatoes, balsamic vinegar, and pepper to the soup.

5.   Check the consistency; if too thick, add more broth.

6.   Serve the soup in bowls or cups topped with sliced scallions and julienne of *prosciutto.*

Zuppa di Fagioli alla Toscana

BEAN SOUP, TUSCAN STYLE

Yield: 8 to 10 servings

6 ounces	dry white kidney or navy beans, presoaked overnight	to taste	salt and freshly ground black pepper
2 quarts	beef broth (see recipe later in this chapter)	**INFUSION:**	
¼ cup	olive oil	1 cup	beef broth (see recipe later in this chapter)
3 ounces	prosciutto trimmings, diced small	1	rosemary sprig
		1	thyme sprig
8 ounces	onions, diced small	2	bay leaves
4 cloves	garlic, minced		
4 ounces	leeks, finely sliced	**GARNISH:**	
4 ounces	celeriac, finely diced	10 small slices	sourdough or rye bread
4	tomatoes, peeled, seeded, and diced (see chapter 1)	1 ounce	butter, softened
		1 clove	garlic, finely minced
		½ cup	grated Parmesan
6 ounces	savoy cabbage, cut in small squares		

1.   Cook the presoaked beans in the beef broth until soft. Remove half of the cooked beans and puree in a food processor.

(continued)

2.   Heat the olive oil, and cook the *prosciutto* trimmings, onions, garlic, leeks, and celeriac over medium heat for about 10 minutes.

3.   Combine the bean soup, the bean puree, and *prosciutto*/vegetable mixture. Add the tomatoes, cabbage, and seasonings, and simmer for 10 minutes. Remove from the heat.

4.   Prepare infusion by bringing the cup of beef broth to a boil in a small pan and adding the rosemary, thyme, and bay leaves. Remove from the heat and steep for 5 to 10 minutes. Strain and add the liquid to the bean soup. Adjust the seasonings.

5.   Prepare croutons by spreading the 10 slices of sourdough or rye bread with garlic butter (combine 1 ounce of softened butter with 1 clove of minced garlic). Sprinkle generously with grated Parmesan and brown under the broiler.

6.   Serve the soup in cups or bowls topped with the croutons.

Pappa coi Pomodori Freschi alla Toscana
FRESH TOMATO SOUP, TUSCAN STYLE

Yield: 8 to 10 servings

⅓ cup	virgin olive oil	1½ ounces	sun-dried tomatoes
2 ounces	Italian bread, sliced	1 quart	beef broth (see recipe later in this chapter)
8 ounces	red onions, finely diced		
6 cloves	garlic, minced	8	basil leaves
⅓ cup	tomato paste	to taste	salt and freshly ground black pepper
2 pounds	tomatoes, peeled, seeded, and diced (see chapter 1)	¼ cup	extra-virgin olive oil
		to garnish	basil sprigs

1.   Heat the ⅓ cup of olive oil in a 3-quart saucepan and fry the Italian bread slices until light brown and crisp. Drain on absorbent paper.

2.   Cook the onions and garlic in the same oil until translucent.

3.   Add the tomato paste and cook for a few minutes with the onions, then add the fresh diced tomatoes and the sun-dried tomatoes and simmer slowly for 30 minutes.

4.   In another 3-quart pot, bring the beef broth to a simmer, remove from the heat, and place the fried Italian bread into the broth to soak for 5 minutes.

5. Combine tomatoes with bread/broth mixture. Add the basil leaves and seasonings.

6. Puree through the fine plate of a food mill.

7. Serve in soup bowls or cups topped with the extra-virgin olive oil and basil sprigs.

Minestrone alla Milanese

MINESTRONE, MILANESE STYLE

If using dry cranberry beans instead of fresh in this recipe, soak overnight and pre-cook for 1½ hours in beef broth or water. Drain the broth and use in the recipe.

Yield: 8 to 10 servings

2 ounces	rice	2 ounces	zucchini, diced small
2 quarts	beef broth (see recipe later in this chapter)	2 tablespoons	chopped parsley
		1 tablespoon	chopped sage
		1 tablespoon	chopped basil
3 ounces	pancetta, chopped	to taste	salt and freshly ground black pepper
1 fluid ounce	olive oil		
2 ounces	onions, diced small	to taste	nutmeg
2 ounces	leeks, diced small		
2 ounces	carrots, diced small	**GARNISH:**	
2 ounces	celery, diced small	½ cup	precooked green peas (cooked, shocked in ice water, and kept cold for good color)
6 cloves	garlic, minced		
3 ounces	fresh cranberry beans, shelled		
2 ounces	savoy cabbage, cut in squares		
		½ cup	grated Parmesan
2 ounces	potatoes, diced small	¼ cup	extra-virgin olive oil
		8 to 10	basil leaves
4	tomatoes, peeled, seeded, and diced (see chapter 1)		

1. Cook the rice, covered, in the beef broth for about 18 minutes. Drain off the broth, and reserve both. Place the cooked rice in a small container mixed with a little olive oil to prevent sticking. Reserve.

(continued)

2. Render the *pancetta* in the olive oil. Add the onions, leeks, carrots, celery, and garlic, and cook over medium heat. Add the reserved beef broth and simmer for a few minutes before adding the shelled cranberry beans, cabbage, and potatoes. Continue simmering for 6 to 8 minutes. Add the diced tomatoes, zucchini, and chopped herbs, and cook for another 5 minutes.

3. Add salt, pepper, and nutmeg. Add the rice.

4. Serve in soup bowls or cups garnished with the green peas, grated Parmesan, and extra-virgin olive oil. Decorate immediately before service with a fresh basil leaf.

Zuppa di Frutti di Mare con Funghi e Riso
SEAFOOD SOUP WITH MUSHROOMS AND RICE

This soup can be prepared in advance up to the last step, when the shrimp and fish are added. If you choose to do this, bring the soup to a simmer before adding the shrimp and fish.

Yield: 8 servings

16	mussels	2	bay leaves
8	baby squid (calamaretti)	2	oregano sprigs
		pinch	saffron
8 ounces	shrimp (½ ounce each)	3 pints	chicken broth (see recipe later in this chapter)
8 ounces	red mullet or red snapper fillet		
½ cup	olive oil	4 ounces	fennel knob, diced small
4 ounces	onions, diced medium		
8 cloves	garlic, minced		
2	chili peppers, chopped	**GARNISH:**	
¼ cup	tomato paste	1 cup	cooked rice
6	tomatoes, peeled, seeded, and diced (see chapter 1)	1 teaspoon	butter
		1 cup	julienne of red and green bell peppers
1 ounce	dried porcini, reconstituted in broth	⅓ cup	finely sliced scallions
		8	oregano sprigs
1 cup	dry white wine		

1.   Soak the mussels in cold water; any that stay open should be discarded. Scrub the shells and remove any beards attached to the shells.

2.   Pull out the head with the tentacles from the bodies of the squid and cut away and discard the heads. Pull and remove the "pens" (the transparent cartilage) and the skin from the bodies and discard. Cut the bodies into 1-inch rings.

3.   Peel and devein the shrimp.

4.   Cut the fish fillets into ½-ounce pieces.

5.   Heat 1 fluid ounce of olive oil in a 3-quart casserole and sauté the onions and garlic for a few minutes. Add the hot peppers and tomato paste, followed by the diced tomatoes, reconstituted *porcini,* and squid rings. Cook slowly over very low heat for about 15 minutes.

6.   Place the clean mussels together with the dry white wine, remaining olive oil, bay leaves, and oregano in a shallow, covered 2-quart casserole. Steam quickly only until the shells open. Mussels should be plump and not overcooked.

7.   Remove the mussel meats from their shells. Strain and reserve the cooking liquid. Cover and reserve the meats.

8.   When the squid has simmered for 15 minutes, add the strained liquid from the mussels, saffron, chicken broth, and diced fennel to the casserole. Continue to simmer for another 15 minutes. Adjust the seasonings.

9.   Add the shrimp and fish to the soup and simmer for a minute. Remove from the heat and add the steamed mussels. Spoon a little rice into each soup bowl and fill with the soup. Garnish with the sautéed julienne of red and green peppers, thinly sliced scallions, and a sprig of oregano.

Stracciatella alla Romana

EGG-DROP SOUP, ROMAN STYLE

This soup is highly nutritious and can be quickly prepared if one has a good, hearty broth on hand. The simplicity of its preparation belies the nutritional complexity of its contents. The soup may be garnished with shredded raw spinach, arugula, or scallions.

Other versions of *stracciatella* include *mille-fanti,* which uses white breadcrumbs in place of semolina, and *stracciata,* which adds boiled rice, finely shredded spinach, and small-diced tomatoes.

(continued)

Yield: 6 servings

3	eggs	1 quart	beef or chicken broth (see recipes later in this chapter)
1½ ounces	Parmesan, grated		
½ ounce	semolina or all-purpose flour	2 tablespoons	finely chopped chives or parsley
pinch	nutmeg		
pinch	salt and white pepper		

1.   Combine the eggs, Parmesan, semolina or flour, nutmeg, salt, and pepper in a mixing bowl. Beat lightly.

2.   Bring the broth to a simmer.

3.   In a slow stream, pour the egg mixture into the simmering broth, stirring to break up lumps of the mixture. Do not stir too briskly.

4.   Let the soup simmer for 30 seconds and remove from the heat. Serve sprinkled with chopped chives or parsley.

Involtini di Frittatine Farcite in Brodo
SLICED, STUFFED CRÊPE ROULADES IN BROTH

Yield: 8 servings

1 ounce	flour	1 clove	garlic, minced
pinch	salt	pinch	salt and freshly ground black pepper
pinch	white pepper		
½ cup	milk	1 tablespoon	chopped parsley
1	egg	1 tablespoon	chopped marjoram
1 fluid ounce	olive oil	1	egg yolk
1½ ounces	calf, pork, chicken, or game liver	½ ounce	dry white breadcrumbs
1 ounce	dried porcini	1 quart	beef or chicken stock
½ fluid ounce	olive oil	3 pints	beef or chicken broth (see recipes later in this chapter)
1 ounce	onions, finely diced		
1½ ounces	lean veal, pork, chicken, or game meat, finely diced	to garnish	finely chopped chives

1.   Prepare the crêpe batter about 1 hour ahead of time. Sift the flour into a mixing bowl. Add the salt and white pepper.

2.   Whisk milk vigorously into the flour until smooth.

3.   Beat in the egg, then let rest 30 minutes.

4.   Heat a 6-inch crêpe pan and coat it with olive oil. Pour enough batter to coat the surface thinly. Cook over medium to high heat.

5.   As each crêpe loosens at the edges of the pan, turn with a spatula and cook a few seconds more, until lightly browned.

6.   Stack the crêpes on a tray lined with parchment paper. Let cool and cover with plastic wrap until ready to use. (Unused crêpes may be wrapped in plastic bags and frozen.)

7.   Trim the liver of sinews and skin. Soak in a bowl of cold water for 2 hours to remove the red pigment. Drain and blot dry. Cut into small pieces.

8.   Soak the *porcini* in warm water for 30 minutes, drain, and chop coarsely.

9.   Heat the olive oil in a 5-inch *sauteuse*. Sauté the onions and diced meat until lightly browned.

10.   Add garlic, *porcini,* and liver, and cook until the liver is medium done. Remove from the heat, and add salt, pepper, parsley, and marjoram.

11.   Put this mixture into a food processor and puree until smooth. Add the egg yolk and breadcrumbs and blend for another 5 seconds. Remove and refrigerate.

12.   Spread this chilled mixture evenly over 4 crêpes and roll up. Place each roulade on a sheet of plastic wrap and roll up firmly. Twist the ends to achieve uniform cylindrical shapes.

13.   Place the meat stock in a pan wide enough to fit the roulades, and bring to a simmer. Poach the roulades for 10 minutes. Remove to ice water, and drain. Keep chilled.

14.   When ready to serve, unwrap the roulades and slice thinly. Place 3 slices in each soup cup or bowl, and add very hot beef or chicken broth. Garnish with finely chopped chives.

Frittatine di Spinaci in Brodo
SPINACH CRÊPES IN BEEF BROTH

Yield: 8 to 10 servings

1	egg	pinch	grated nutmeg
1/3 cup	chopped raw spinach	1/2 fluid ounce	oil
1/4 cup	milk	3 pints	hot beef broth (see recipe later in this chapter)
3/4 ounce	flour		
pinch	salt and freshly ground black pepper	3	scallions, very finely sliced

1.   Make the crêpe batter 1 hour ahead of time. Puree the egg with the chopped spinach in a blender. Combine with the milk, and gradually whisk into the flour in a mixing bowl. Eliminate lumps. Add the salt, pepper, and nutmeg, and let rest for 1 hour.

2.   Lightly coat a heated crêpe pan with the oil. Make thin 5-inch crêpes, and place on absorbent paper to cool.

3.   Roll up the crêpes and cut crosswise to create fine vermicelli-like strips.

4.   Float the crêpe strips in the hot beef broth with the sliced scallions and serve.

Canederli di Semolina in Brodo
SEMOLINA DUMPLINGS IN BEEF BROTH

This recipe is undeniably of Austrian origins and is ubiquitous in the Alto Adige and Veneto regions.

Yield: 8 servings

2 ounces	butter, at room temperature	3 pints	hot beef broth (see recipe later in this chapter)
1	egg, beaten		
pinch	nutmeg	6	chives, very finely chopped
4 1/2 ounces	coarse semolina		

1.   Cream the butter in a 1-quart noncorrosive bowl with a wire whisk.

2.   Slowly beat in the egg and nutmeg a little at a time.

3.   Stir in the semolina, mixing thoroughly. Allow the mixture to rest at room temperature for at least 30 minutes.

4.   Using a teaspoon dipped in tepid water, shape small, oval dumplings. (You can use water-moistened hands to form round dumplings as well.)

5.   Poach the dumplings in salted, simmering water or broth, covered, for about 12 to 15 minutes. They should double in size.

6.   Place 2 dumplings in each serving cup or bowl and cover with hot beef broth. Sprinkle with finely chopped chives.

Zuppa alla Pavese

EGGS IN BEEF BROTH, PAVESE STYLE

Yield: **8 servings**

8 slices	*French bread, ¼ inch thick*
2 ounces	*butter, melted*
8	*eggs*
½ cup	*grated Parmesan*
3 pints	*hot beef broth (see recipe later in this chapter)*
3	*scallions, very finely sliced*

1.   Prepare French bread croutons by brushing the bread slices with melted butter and toasting in a hot oven until nicely browned. Do not dice.

2.   Place 1 crouton in each soup cup. Top with a raw egg (shelled) and 1 teaspoon of freshly grated Parmesan. Be careful not to break the egg yolk. (If eggs are very large, use only the yolk.)

3.   Pour the hot broth into the cup without breaking the egg.

4.   Place in a hot oven for 1 minute. Sprinkle with the finely sliced scallions before serving.

Crostini di Fegato in Brodo

FRIED LIVER CROUTONS IN BROTH

This soup is usually served in soup plates or bowls. If using cups, use very small rounds of French bread and cut the amount of liver spread in half.

Yield: 8 servings

1 ounce	onions, finely diced	1 to 2 tablespoons	white breadcrumbs
½ ounce	butter	1	egg, beaten
1 tablespoon	chopped parsley	pinch	salt
1 teaspoon	chopped marjoram	8 slices	French bread, ¼ inch thick
3 ounces	beef or chicken liver, trimmed of sinews and diced	½ cup	oil
		3 pints	hot beef or chicken broth (see recipes later in this chapter)
pinch	salt and freshly ground black pepper		
pinch	freshly ground nutmeg	3	scallions, very thinly sliced
2 ounces	butter, at room temperature		

1.   Cook the onions in the ½ ounce of butter in a small pan until lightly browned. Remove from the heat, add the parsley and marjoram, and cool.

2.   Combine onion, diced liver, salt, pepper, and nutmeg and puree in a blender.

3.   Cream the 2 ounces of butter in a mixing bowl with a wire whisk. Gradually add the breadcrumbs and the egg, followed by the liver puree. Add pinch of salt.

4.   Spread the sliced French bread with this mixture.

5.   Fry the coated bread slices in hot oil, spread side first, until crisp.

6.   Cut the liver croutons in half and float in hot broth in soup cups or bowls. Sprinkle with the scallions.

Passatelli in Brodo

PASSATELLI IN BROTH

Yield: 8 servings

½ cup	fresh breadcrumbs from Italian bread, no crusts	pinch	nutmeg
		1 tablespoon	chopped parsley
½ ounce	Parmesan, grated	3 pints	beef broth (see recipe later in this chapter)
1	egg		
½ ounce	butter, softened	2 tablespoons	very finely chopped chives
pinch	salt and freshly ground black pepper		

1.   Combine the breadcrumbs, Parmesan, and egg in a mixing bowl. Add the softened butter, stirring briskly. Add the salt, pepper, nutmeg, and parsley. Let rest for 30 minutes.

2.   Bring the beef broth to a simmer in a 4-quart saucepan.

3.   Place the *passatelli* dough in a large-holed colander or perforated pan. Press the dough through the holes into the simmering broth with a plastic scraper. Let the dough simmer in the broth for 2 minutes before removing from heat.

4.   Serve in soup bowls or cups. Sprinkle with chopped chives.

Strudel di Lumache e Funghi Assortiti in Brodo
SNAIL AND MUSHROOM STRUDEL IN BROTH

The following recipe exemplifies the Austrian influence on the cuisine of the Alto Adige region. The strudel should be added to the broth just before serving, or served on the side.

Yield: 8 to 10 servings

8 ounces	strudel dough (see chapter 14)	6	snails, finely diced
1 ounce	dried porcini	6 ounces	mushrooms, finely diced
1 ounce	clarified butter (see chapter 1)	2	egg yolks, beaten
3 ounces	onions, finely diced	1 ounce	dry white breadcrumbs
4 cloves	garlic, finely minced	¼ cup	chopped parsley
6	juniper berries, crushed	3 ounces	butter, melted
¼ teaspoon	freshly ground black pepper	3 pints	hot beef broth (see later in this chapter)
1	thyme sprig, leaves only, chopped	2 tablespoons	finely chopped chives

1. Prepare the strudel dough 1 hour ahead of time and let it rest for 1 hour.

2. Soak the dried *porcini* in warm water for 30 minutes. Drain and dice small.

3. Heat the clarified butter in a 7-inch *sauteuse* and sauté the onions over until lightly browned.

4. Add the garlic, juniper berries, pepper, thyme, snails, *porcini,* and mushrooms. Cook over high heat until the mixture is almost dry and starts to sear. Remove from the heat.

5. Gradually stir in the egg yolks to bind the mixture.

6. Add the breadcrumbs and parsley and adjust the seasonings. If mixture seems too wet, add more breadcrumbs. The consistency should be firm, not runny. Refrigerate until needed.

7. Cover the work surface with a clean cloth.

8.   Pull the strudel dough until almost transparent.

9.   Brush the dough immediately with the melted butter. Spread the snail/mushroom mixture carefully and evenly over the dough. The dough is fragile and tears easily, so work gently.

10.   The mixture should cover a 4- by 12-inch area of dough. Leave about 2 inches at of the top end free of the mixture to ensure a proper seal when rolling the dough.

11.   To roll, grasp the edge of cloth closest to you on both ends and pull up. The dough will roll itself. The strudel should have the shape of a large cigar.

12.   Place the rolled dough on a sheet pan and brush again with melted butter. Bake in a preheated 350°F oven for about 20 minutes. Cool.

13.   Cut the strudel into ¾-inch slices.

14.   Place 2 strudel pieces in each serving bowl or cup and cover with hot beef broth. Sprinkle with finely chopped chives.

Budino di Pollo in Brodo Bolognese
CHICKEN CUSTARD IN BROTH, BOLOGNA STYLE

The custard for this recipe can be prepared with game instead of chicken and served in an appropriate broth.

Yield: 8 to 10 servings

3 ounces	cooked chicken meat	3 pints	hot chicken broth (see recipe later in this chapter)
½ cup	cold chicken broth		
pinch	salt and white pepper	3 tablespoons	finely chopped chives
pinch	nutmeg		
2 or 3	egg yolks		

1.   Chop the chicken meat into pieces and combine with the cold broth. Liquefy in a blender. Add the salt, pepper, nutmeg, and egg yolks, and blend for another 5 seconds. Strain the liquid through a fine-mesh sieve.

(continued)

2.   Pour the liquid into oiled 12-ounce molds or ramekins. Place the molds into a hot water bath and cover with oiled parchment paper. Poach in a preheated 300°F oven until the custard is firm. Cool.

3.   Remove the custard from the molds and cut into small cubes or sticks.

4.   Float the custard in the hot broth and top with the chopped chives.

Brodo Doppio di Pollo alle Uova di Quaglie
DOUBLE CHICKEN BROTH WITH QUAIL EGGS

Yield: 8 servings

1 cup	*cooked angel hair pasta (capelli d'angelo), from spinach pasta*
3 pints	*hot double chicken broth (see recipe for chicken broth later in this chapter)*
8	*fresh quail eggs*
3	*scallions, finely sliced*

1.   Have all ingredients ready to serve; the pasta should be cooked *al dente*.

2.   Place approximately 1 tablespoon of the cooked pasta in each soup cup and add 4½ fluid ounces of boiling hot broth.

3.   Separate the quail egg yolks and add them to the hot broth.

4.   Sprinkle with the sliced scallions.

— *Pasta in Brodo* —
PASTA IN BROTH

Pasta in brodo consists of pasta or *pastina* (small, shaped pasta) served in either hot beef broth *(brodo di manza)* or hot chicken broth *(brodo di pollo)*. The recipes for these broths are on the following pages. Many types of pasta can be served *in brodo*, such as *capelli d'angelo, capellini, vermicellini,* vermicelli, *stelline, quadrucci, ditalini,* tortellini, *cappelletti,* and *anolini.* See chapter 5 for further descriptions of and recipes for the pasta.

Brodo di Manzo
BEEF BROTH

If frozen beef bones must be used in place of fresh in this recipe, place them in cold water and quickly bring to a boil. Drain the blanching liquid and then prepare as directed.

Yield: 4 quarts

6 pounds	fresh beef bones	1 clove	garlic
3 pounds	beef shin meat	1/2	onion, with skin
7 quarts	cold water	10	peppercorns
6 ounces	carrots, coarsely cut	2	cloves
4 ounces	celeriac, coarsely cut	3	bay leaves
4 ounces	parsnips, coarsely cut	1	thyme sprig
4 ounces	leeks, white part only	pinch	nutmeg
5	parsley stems	to taste	salt
3 ounces	turnips or cabbage		

1.   Select beef bones from the neck and rib areas if possible, as they contain more meat after trimming. Cut the bones into small pieces and wash in fresh cold water before placing in a 6-gallon soup pot with the shin meat and cold water. Bring to a simmer, and cook over very low heat for about 2 hours, skimming occasionally.

2.   Remove the meat from the broth and reserve for another use. Continue to simmer the liquid over low heat another 2 hours.

(continued)

3. Tie the carrots, celeriac, parsnips, leeks, parsley stems, turnips or cabbage, and garlic with butcher's twine to make a *bouquet garni.*

4. Sear onion in a hot pan (no oil) until it is light brown.

5. Wrap the peppercorns, cloves, bay leaves, and thyme in cheesecloth to make a spice sachet.

6. Add the *bouquet garni,* onion, and spice sachet to the broth, and simmer for another hour. Add nutmeg and salt.

7. Strain the broth through several layers of cheesecloth or through coffee filters.

8. Remove the fat that rises to the top with blotting paper or paper towels.

Brodo Ristretto di Bue

DOUBLE BEEF BROTH

Double beef broth is a concentrated, crystal-clear beef broth that is usually clarified.

The vegetables added to the broth serve a dual purpose: to bolster the flavor and to help remove the impurities, thus achieving the clearest end product possible. This clarification works when the coagulating albumens (proteins) from the egg whites and the lean beef attract the impurities. Albumen starts to coagulate at 138°F and rises to the surface with the trapped, undesirable particles. The continuous pressure exerted by the heat from below causes all of these particles to float upward and form a so-called raft shortly after the simmering begins.

Preparing the broth to be clarified in a large pot with a base spigot, if available, is helpful, as the clear broth can be drained from the pot without agitating the raft and thereby risking clouding of the final broth. If done correctly, the finished product is not only nutritious but crystal clear.

Yield: 4 quarts

2	onion slices, ½ inch thick	4 ounces	parsnips, cut into strips
		4 ounces	celeriac, cut into strips
2 pounds	lean beef, coarsely ground (shank meat is best)	4 ounces	carrots, cut into strips
		3	fresh tomatoes, cut into small pieces
8 to 10	egg whites, lightly beaten	10	black peppercorns, freshly ground
4 ounces	leeks, cut into strips		

3	bay leaves	pinch	grated nutmeg
3	cloves	5 quarts	cold, clear beef broth
1	thyme sprig		(see previous recipe)

1. Place the thick-sliced onions in a heated cast-iron skillet and burn on both sides until black. Do *not* use any fat. Cool.

2. Mix well all ingredients except the broth. Add this mixture to the cold broth in a soup pot.

3. Heat the broth over high heat, stirring frequently to keep the albumen suspended in the broth. This keeps it from burning on the bottom of the pot. Stirring must continue until the coagulation of the proteins begins; otherwise, the albumen may burn and the broth will acquire an irreversible burnt taste. As soon as the coagulated proteins begin to rise to the surface, stop stirring to allow the formation of the raft, a most important feature in clarification.

4. Let the broth simmer over low heat for 1 hour. Strain the broth through several layers of cheesecloth or coffee filters.

5. Remove any fat that rises to the top of the broth with blotting paper or paper towels.

Brodo di Pollo

CHICKEN BROTH

Double chicken broth can be made with this recipe in the same way that double beef broth is made from beef broth. Substitute chicken stock for beef stock and chopped chicken meat for the ground beef. See the previous recipe for instructions. Do not chop onion for double chicken broth. The broth color should be a pale yellow rather than a dark gold.

Yield: 4 quarts

10 pounds	fowl necks, wings, and carcasses	8 to 12	whole black peppercorns
7 quarts	cold water	3	bay leaves
4 ounces	celery	2	whole cloves
4 ounces	parsnips	1	thyme sprig
4 ounces	carrots	pinch	nutmeg
4 ounces	leeks, white part only	to taste	salt
4 ounces	onions		
2 ounces	white turnips		

1.   Wash the chicken pieces in cold running water and place in a 6-gallon soup pot with the cold water. Bring to a simmer and cook over low heat for 3 hours, skimming occasionally.

2.   Tie the celery, parsnips, carrots, leeks, onions, and turnips together with butcher's twine to make a *bouquet garni*.

3.   Wrap the peppercorns, bay leaves, cloves, thyme, nutmeg, and salt in cheesecloth to make a spice sachet. Add both the sachet and the *bouquet garni* to the broth. Simmer for another hour.

4.   Strain the broth through several layers of cheesecloth or coffee filters. Adjust the salt.

5.   Remove any fat that rises to the top with blotting paper or paper towels.

Brodo Bianco di Pesce

WHITE FISH BROTH

Yield: 4 quarts

14 pounds	fish trimmings and bones, preferably from turbot, pike, bass, and/or sole (lean fish)	3	bay leaves
		1	thyme sprig
		6	parsley stems
½ cup	olive oil	10	white peppercorns
4 ounces	leeks, white part only, sliced	3	cloves
		1 cup	dry white wine
4 ounces	onions, sliced	6 quarts	cold water
4 ounces	celery, sliced	to taste	salt
4 ounces	parsnips, sliced		

1.   Wash the fish trimmings and bones under cold tap water and cut into small pieces.

2.   Heat the olive oil in a 6-gallon soup pot and sweat the leeks, onions, celery, and parsnips over moderate heat for 5 minutes. Add the fish bones, bay leaves, thyme, parsley, peppercorns, and cloves, and continue smothering for several minutes.

3.   Add the wine and reduce completely, until all liquid evaporates.

4.   Add the 6 quarts of water and bring to a simmer. Cook over low heat for 20 to 30 minutes. Skim off any impurities and fat as they rise.

5.   Strain the broth through several layers of cheesecloth. Salt to taste. Remove any fat that rises to the top with blotting paper or paper towels.

6.   Return the fish broth to the stove, and continue to reduce to 4 quarts. Strain again.

Brodo Ristretto di Pesce
CONCENTRATED, CLARIFIED FISH BROTH

Clarification of fish or seafood broth is recommended for the production of high-quality clear *zuppa di pesce* or *essenza di pesce* (fish *fumet*). The process for clarifying fish broth is the same as for other broths, but the ingredients are different and the cooking time is significantly shorter.

Yield: 4 quarts

1½ pounds	boneless seafood trimmings from halibut, bass, pike, sole, or scallops, coarsely ground	5	parsley stems
		10	white peppercorns, crushed
8	egg whites, slightly beaten	1	thyme sprig
		3	bay leaves
8 ounces	leeks, white part only, cut in strips	3	cloves
		pinch	saffron
4 ounces	celeriac, cut in strips	pinch	nutmeg
4 ounces	parsnips, cut in strips	to taste	salt
2 ounces	fresh fennel, cut in strips	4½ quarts	fish broth (see previous recipe)

1.   Mix all the ingredients except the broth in a suitable container. Combine in a 6-quart soup pot with the fish broth.

2.   Heat the mixture over high heat. Stir frequently to keep the albumen in the whites suspended in the broth until they start to coagulate. As soon as the whites coagulate and float to the top of the broth, stop stirring.

3.   Simmer over low heat for about 30 minutes. Strain through several layers of cheese-cloth or through coffee filters.

4.   Adjust the salt.

—— Zuppe Fredde ——
COLD SOUPS

Zuppa Fredda di Pomodori Freschi e Peperoni Rossi
CHILLED FRESH TOMATO SOUP WITH RED PEPPERS

Yield: 8 servings

1 pound	fresh, sun-ripened plum tomatoes, peeled (see chapter 1)	1	egg yolk (optional)
		5 fluid ounces	extra-virgin olive oil
		1 fluid ounce	lemon juice
8 ounces	red bell peppers, roasted and peeled (see chapter 1)	1 fluid ounce	balsamic vinegar
4 ounces	cucumbers, peeled	**GARNISH:**	
3 cloves	garlic, minced	1 tablespoon	finely chopped scallions
1	chili pepper	1 tablespoon	finely chopped basil
3 cups	cold beef broth (see recipe earlier in this chapter)	1 tablespoon	finely chopped arugula
pinch	salt and freshly ground black pepper	2 tablespoons	extra-virgin olive oil

1.   Seed the tomatoes, peppers, and cucumbers.

2.   Cut 1 cup of tomatoes and roasted red peppers in a fine julienne, to be used as a garnish. Use the trimmings for the body of the soup.

3.   Slice the tomatoes, peppers, and cucumbers into small pieces and blend in a blender with the garlic, chili pepper, beef broth, and seasonings until liquid. If a light emulsion is desired, add the egg yolk and olive oil in a stream while blending. If you prefer a more liquid soup, do not use the egg yolk and add the olive oil in the next step. Strain through a fine-mesh sieve into a noncorrosive container.

4.   Add the lemon juice and balsamic vinegar. Adjust the salt and pepper to taste. Mix in the olive oil if not already added. Hold on ice or in a cold place.

5.   Serve in well-chilled cups or bowls. Top with 1 tablespoon of the julienne of tomatoes and peppers. Sprinkle with the chopped scallions, basil, and arugula. Drizzle a little olive oil over the top before serving.

Zuppa Fredda di Cetrioli e Lattuga
COLD CUCUMBER AND LETTUCE SOUP

This soup is extremely healthful, particularly because none of the vegetables is cooked and therefore none of the nutrients is lost. The addition of an egg yolk (and therefore cholesterol) is optional but enhances the velvety texture of the finished product. A dab of sour cream or even fresh cream as a final touch can vary the presentation of the soup.

Yield: 8 servings

8 ounces	cucumbers, peeled and seeded	¼ cup	lemon juice
8 ounces	crisp lettuce, leaves only	pinch	salt and cayenne pepper
6 ounces	Granny Smith apples, peeled and seeded	5 fluid ounces	extra-virgin olive oil
		1	egg yolk (optional)
6 ounces	sweet red onions	1 cup	julienne of seeded cucumbers
2 cloves	garlic, minced		
½ cup	arugula, chopped (no stems or ribs)	8	mint sprigs
1 quart	cold chicken broth (see recipe earlier in this chapter)		

1. Cut the cucumbers, lettuce, apples, and onions into small pieces.

2. Blend in a blender (not a food processor) with the garlic, arugula, chicken broth, lemon juice, and seasonings.

3. Puree until liquid. If a light emulsion is desired, add an egg yolk while blending. Add the olive oil in a stream.

4. Remove to a noncorrosive container and keep chilled.

5. Pour the well-chilled soup into cold bowls or cups. Garnish with the julienne of cucumber and a mint sprig.

4 *Uova*

EGGS

Unlike Americans, Italians do not eat eggs for breakfast. Egg dishes occasionally appear on Italian menus as first courses or sometimes as light main course. The most traditional method of preparing eggs is the *frittata,* or pancake-style omelet.

Eggs are almost a perfect food. They are economical, nutritious, and easy to prepare. Like milk, eggs contain valuable vitamins. The yolks, though high in cholesterol, are abundant sources of fat and iron, while the whites are high in protein.

The digestibility of eggs depends to a large extent on the method of preparation, as cooking changes the classical structure of the egg as well as the flavor. Raw egg whites, for example, are very difficult to digest.

The quality of an egg, as well as the egg's composition, depends on the breed of the hen and its diet. The shell color of the egg has nothing to do with quality. Fresh eggs are preferable for the preparation of a high-quality products. Eggs are considered fresh for up to 4 weeks if stored between 45° and 50°F and kept isolated from foodstuffs such as onions and cheese, the odors of which can easily penetrate the porous shell. A fresh egg has a firm, tightly congealed yolk and a rather small air pocket. As it ages, the egg becomes flaccid and runny and the air space increases in size as moisture is lost through the shell. Eggs are graded for quality, with AA being the finest quality; A, the next-best grade, and B and C grades, generally reserved for baking. Grades are not an indication of freshness.

Uova Sode e Uova Mollette
HARD-COOKED EGGS AND SOFT-COOKED EGGS

Eggs should never be boiled vigorously but should be simmered instead. Prolonged cooking at high temperatures and improper cooling result in the formation of a green film around the outside of the yolk. This discoloration is caused by the combination of the sulfur in the whites and the iron in the yolks. This reaction can be prevented by plunging the just-boiled eggs into very cold water, thereby releasing the pressure on the outside of the egg white and allowing the gases that cause discoloration to escape.

Soft-cooked eggs *(uova mollette)* are simmered for 3 to 5 minutes, whereas hard-cooked eggs *(uova sode)* require 10 to 14 minutes.

—— Uova Affogate ——
POACHED EGGS

Eggs are often poached in acidulated water (1 tablespoon distilled vinegar to 1 quart liquid) to toughen the albumen, which helps to set the white around the yolk. Only the freshest eggs should be used for poaching, because runny whites present a problem in poaching. The distilled vinegar will not affect the egg's flavor and will help to solidify the egg. To poach eggs:

1. Fill a shallow pan with water and the appropriate amount of vinegar and bring to a simmer.
2. Break the egg into a small bowl and slide it gently into the water.
3. Poach for 3 minutes for a soft, tender egg.
4. Remove with a slotted spoon and let drain.

Eggs can also be "poached" in special double-boiler inserts. These actually steam the eggs, but they give comparable, satisfactory results.

Uova Affogate con Fonduta all'Albese
POACHED EGGS WITH CHEESE FONDUE, ALBA STYLE

Yield: 4 servings

8	Italian bread slices, 1/4 inch thick	8 ounces	Fontina, grated
		pinch	salt and white pepper
2 ounces	butter, softened	pinch	freshly grated nutmeg
1 clove	garlic, peeled	8	large eggs
1/2 cup	milk	1	fresh white truffle, brushed and washed
2	egg yolks		

1.   Brush the Italian bread slices with the softened butter. Toast both sides under a salamander or broiler.

2.   Rub top part of a double boiler with the garlic and bring water to a simmer in the lower part. Mix the milk and egg yolks in the garlic-rubbed upper part of the double boiler, stirring with a wooden spoon or wire whisk until the mixture starts to thicken slightly. Add the grated Fontina.

3.   Cook over low heat, stirring constantly to prevent the eggs from separating and giving the mixture a grainy texture.

4.   Remove the double boiler from direct heat, keep warm, and add the salt, pepper, and nutmeg.

5.   Poach the eggs.

6.   Place 2 toasted bread slices in each shallow porcelain serving dish (a shirred egg dish or coddler).

7.   Place a poached egg on each slice and cover with the cheese fondue mixture.

8.   Shave or finely slice the truffle over the eggs and serve immediately.

Uova Affogate Fiorentine

POACHED EGGS, FLORENTINE STYLE

Yield: **4 servings**

1 pound	*fresh spinach leaves*	*2 ounces*	*pancetta, diced small*
4	*ripe tomatoes, peeled and seeded (see chapter 1)*	*2 cloves*	*garlic, peeled, finely minced*
1½ fluid ounces	*olive oil*	*1 ounce*	*red onion, finely diced*
to taste	*salt and freshly ground black pepper*	*to taste*	*nutmeg*
		6 ounces	*mozzarella, coarsely grated*
2 tablespoons	*chopped basil*	*2 ounces*	*Parmesan, coarsely grated*
16	*scallions*		
8	*large eggs*		

1.   Remove the stems from twice washed and drained spinach leaves.

2.   Cut the tomatoes into a small dice, and sauté quickly in half of the olive oil. Season to taste with salt and pepper; add the chopped basil. Do not cook the tomatoes completely. Remove from the heat.

3.   Trim the scallions, cutting off the root ends and green tops, retaining the white parts only, about 3 inches in length. Sauté the scallions in a bit of olive oil for 5 seconds and remove from the skillet.

(continued)

4.   Poach the eggs.

5.   Heat the remaining olive oil with the *pancetta* in a 10-inch skillet. Add the garlic, sauté for 30 seconds, remove from heat, and add onions and spinach leaves. Season to taste with salt, pepper, and nutmeg. Quickly stir-fry for a few seconds; the spinach should remain crunchy. Place the spinach in a colander to drain.

6.   Arrange the spinach neatly in each shallow round or oval serving dish (shirred egg dish or coddler). Place 2 tablespoons of the sautéed tomatoes on top of each, making two nests.

7.   Place a poached egg in each nest.

8.   Cover the eggs completely with the grated cheese and place in a 350°F oven until cheese is completely melted. Garnish with the sautéed scallions.

Uova Affogate in Purgatorio
POACHED EGGS WITH SHRIMP MARINARA SAUCE

Yield: 4 servings

8	Italian bread slices, ¼ inch thick	4	tomatoes, peeled and seeded (see chapter 1)
2 ounces	butter, softened		
¼ cup	olive oil	2	chili peppers, chopped
8 ounces	shrimp, peeled, cleaned, and diced small	½ teaspoon	whole green peppercorns
2 ounces	red onions, finely diced	1 tablespoon	chopped parsley
		8	eggs
4 cloves	garlic, minced	1 tablespoon	chopped marjoram
1 ounce	red bell pepper, diced small	1 tablespoon	chopped basil
		to garnish	basil leaves
1 cup	dry white wine		

1.   Brush each slice of Italian bread with the softened butter and toast under the broiler on both sides.

2.   Heat 1 fluid ounce of olive oil in a skillet. Quickly sauté the shrimp pieces, but do not cook through. Remove with a slotted spoon and reserve.

3.   Add the remaining oil to the same skillet. Cook the onions, garlic, and red pepper for 1 minute, until softened.

4.   Add the wine and reduce completely, until all liquid evaporates.

5.   Coarsely chop the tomatoes. Add, along with the chili pepper and whole green peppercorns, to the skillet. Reduce to a thick consistency.

6.   Add the shrimp, parsley, marjoram, and basil, and remove from the heat.

7.   Poach the eggs.

8.   Place the poached eggs in round porcelain serving dishes (shirred egg cups). Spoon the shrimp marinara sauce over the eggs and arrange the bread nearby. Decorate with fresh basil leaves.

—— *Uova in Padella* ——
FRIED EGGS

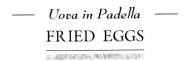

Use fresh eggs and a nonstick pan for best results when frying eggs. The butter in which the eggs are fried must be hot enough to set the whites, but not so hot that the edges begin to brown, or the egg will be rubbery. Avoid too low a temperature, or the egg will spread too much in the pan before setting. Also watch the amount of fat used, as too much fat will result in a greasy end product.

—— *Uova Strapazzate* ——
SCRAMBLED EGGS

The freshest eggs should be used for scrambling eggs, together with a nonstick pan. Beat the eggs slightly with a little water or milk (approximately 1 tablespoon of liquid for every 2 eggs). Pour eggs into a buttered and appropriately heated pan. The eggs should begin to coagulate on contact, but the edges should not foam and brown. Stir gently with a spoon until the desired consistency is achieved. The eggs should be fluffy and soft. The eggs will continue to cook after being removed from the heat; keep this in mind when judging consistency. To avoid the formation of a film on the eggs, remove to a serving plate immediately.

— *Frittate* —

OMELETS

One usually thinks of a smooth, swelling golden oval, moist on the inside, when an omelet is mentioned. This is the justly famous French version of this popular egg dish. The Italian-style omelet, the *frittata,* is similar to the American pancake-style or Western omelet. An omelet can be prepared in minutes and can contain whatever the chef desires.

A nonstick omelet pan should always be used, preferably Teflon coated. Professionals usually use the sloped-sided iron *sauteuse.* These must be seasoned when new: rub the pan generously with oil and heat gently for several minutes. Clean with a paper towel and store until ready to use. After using the pan, do *not* clean with water; just wipe with a clean, dry paper towel and store again.

Preparation of *frittate* varies. Some recipes call for the *frittata* to be browned on both sides, and some call for the eggs to be covered, finished in the oven, and cut into wedges like a quiche. There are countless ways to serve the *frittata,* with fillings including vegetables, herbs, meats, mushrooms, or seafood. Just enough eggs are used to hold the mixture together.

Because a professional kitchen is bound by constraints of time and cost, a set production sequence is outlined below. Use a well-seasoned 3½-inch bottom-diameter skillet for an appetizer *frittata.* Use a well-seasoned 5-inch bottom-diameter skillet for an entrée *frittata.* Because the eggs are not stirred as for French omelet, a smaller-diameter pan produces a quichelike *frittata* without a crust.

Appetizer

FRITTATA

Yield: 1 appetizer-sized *frittata*

1 teaspoon	clarified butter or oil
1	egg, beaten
1 teaspoon	milk or light cream
pinch	salt and freshly ground black pepper
2 ounces	filling (see recipes below)
1 teaspoon	chopped herbs

Entrée

FRITTATA

Yield: 1 entrée-sized *frittata*

1 tablespoon	*clarified butter or oil*	*4 ounces*	*filling (see recipes below)*
3	*eggs, beaten*	*1 tablespoon*	*chopped herbs*
1 to 2 tablespoons	*milk or light cream*		
pinch	*salt and freshly ground black pepper*		

1.   Beat the eggs in a mixing bowl with the milk, salt, and pepper.

2.   Heat the oil or clarified butter in an omelet pan. Add the egg mixture and the filling. Stir just enough to incorporate.

3.   Cook over low to moderate heat until the bottom sets and the *frittata* slides easily.

4.   Flip the *frittata* over and cook until it puffs up. Slide onto a preheated serving plate. The *frittata* can also be finished quickly under the broiler, after the bottom sets, without flipping. This too causes it to swell. If you want to fold the *frittata,* be sure to undercook it slightly so that the edge will not split.

5.   Sprinkle with freshly chopped herbs and any sauce that might be desired.

Riempimenti per Frittate

OMELET FILLINGS

All of the following recipes will fill one entrée-sized *frittata*.

Frittata con fegatini di pollo e funghi (**Chicken-liver and mushroom omelet**): Sauté 3 ounces diced chicken livers (with sinews removed) in 1 fluid ounce olive oil until medium-cooked. Remove with a slotted spoon. In the same pan, sauté 1 ounce finely diced onion, 1½ ounces fresh mushrooms, such as *porcini* or chanterelles, and ½ clove garlic finely minced, until tender. Add a pinch of salt and of freshly ground black pepper, 1 tablespoon chopped arugula, and 1 tablespoon marjoram. Combine the vegetable mixture with the chicken livers and use as *frittata* filling. A Marsala sauce often accompanies this *frittata,* served separately (see chapter 7).

(continued)

Frittata con formaggi e porrino (**Cheese and chive omelet**): Combine 3 ounces of diced cheeses (such as mozzarella, Fontina, and Parmesan), 2 tablespoons finely chopped chives, and a pinch of salt, of freshly ground black pepper, and of nutmeg; use as a *frittata* filling.

Frittata con prosciutto cotto e spinaci (**Cooked *prosciutto* and spinach omelet**): Sauté 3 finely chopped scallions and 2 ounces cooked *prosciutto* cut in fine julienne in ½ ounce butter until heated through. Remove with a slotted spoon to a small bowl. In the same pan, sauté 2 ounces coarsely shredded fresh spinach until wilted. Add spinach to the ham mixture; season to taste with salt, freshly ground black pepper, and nutmeg; and sprinkle with 1 tablespoon grated Parmesan cheese. Use as a *frittata* filling.

Frittata con verdure fresche (**Omelet with fresh vegetables**): Separately blanch 3 ounces broccoli florets and 3 ounces fresh green peas; shock in ice water and drain. Peel and seed tomatoes to make 1 ounce (see chapter 1); cut the tomato into strips. Dice 3 ounces zucchini and 1 ounce red onion small. Heat 1 ounce butter in a skillet. Add the onions and sauté for 10 seconds. Add the zucchini, broccoli, peas, and finally the tomato strips. Stir in 2 tablespoons chopped herbs (such as parsley, basil, or oregano), and a pinch of salt, of freshly ground black pepper, and of nutmeg. Sauté until heated through and use as a *frittata* filling. This omelet is also known as *tortino di verdure*.

Frittata con carciofini freschi (**Omelet with fresh baby artichokes**): Heat ½ fluid ounce olive oil in a skillet. Add 4 thinly sliced scallions and 3 ounces trimmed, thinly sliced baby artichokes, plus a couple of tablespoons of water. Cover and cook over medium heat for a few minutes, until the artichokes are cooked through but still crisp. Add ½ teaspoon chopped chili pepper, 1½ tablespoons chopped arugula, 1½ tablespoons chopped parsley, and a pinch of salt and of freshly ground black pepper. Place this mixture in a small bowl, add 1 tablespoon grated Parmesan, adjust the seasonings, and use as a *frittata* filling. This omelet is also known as *tortino di carciofi alla toscana*.

Frittata con ciccioli di pollo e porcini (**Omelet with chicken cracklings and mushrooms**): Heat ½ ounce butter in a skillet. Sauté 3 sliced scallions and 3 ounces sliced *porcini* quickly. Remove from the heat and add a pinch of salt and of freshly ground black pepper. Place this mixture in a small mixing bowl and add 1 ounce chicken cracklings (see chapter 1), 1 tablespoon grated Parmesan, and 2 tablespoons chopped parsley. Use as a *frittata* filling. A light marinara or other tomato-based sauce is often served alongside this omelet (see chapter 7 for a selection of sauces).

Frittata ai frutti di mare all'erbe (**Seafood and herb omelet**): Heat ½ ounce butter in a skillet. Sauté 1 ounce *each* of small-diced red onion and of coarsely diced scallops, shrimp, and lobster meat until half cooked. Remove to a small mixing bowl with a slotted spoon. Add ¼ cup dry white wine to the skillet and reduce completely, until the liquid evaporates. Add ¼ cup heavy cream and reduce to ½ fluid ounce (reduce by three-quarters). Remove the skillet from the heat and add the onions and shellfish. Add a pinch of freshly ground black pepper or cayenne pepper, 1½ tablespoons chopped parsley, 1½ tablespoons chopped basil, and 1 ounce cooked green peas. Use as a *frittata* filling.

PASTA

So much has been written about the history of pasta that it would be foolish for me to try to sort out the avalanche of material pertaining to this subject that has come crashing down upon us. My main objective here is to deal with the culinary aspects and the methods of preparing pasta, and I will therefore forgo any discussion of the fascinating history.

Pasta is the main staple throughout Europe and in some areas of Asia. The distinctive types of pasta arise through the variety of grains used to make the dough and through the quality of the flour used. The desired quality is achieved by particular ingredients in any given pasta recipe and also by the myriad shapes and colors into which the various doughs are cut or shaped.

Good-quality pasta flours are derived from the inner kernels of hard, or durum, wheat. This same wheat can also be milled into different textures and may range from very fine to very coarse. In the United States, many chefs use semolina, which is by definition ground from hard wheat. Pastas may in fact be prepared from various flour mixtures, including bread and all-purpose flours. Essential to good pasta texture is the elasticity of hard wheat flour, which comes from its high gluten content.

It is almost impossible to find a group of chefs who agree on a specific pasta recipe. Arguments can center on the type of flour or combination of flours used. Some years ago I spent time in Italy observing world-famous master chefs with the intention of gaining firsthand knowledge about the growing Italian trend toward *nuova cucina (nouvelle cuisine)* and, in particular, about the preparation of pasta and risottos. The arguments concerning flour preferences or flour ratios are very real. Generally speaking, however, one can say that the dough for stuffed pasta preparations, such as ravioli, *anolini, cappelletti, tortelloni,* or *cannelloni,* should be somewhat lighter than the dough for straight, or flat, pasta such as spaghetti, fettuccine, and lasagne. Controversy also surrounds the addition of expensive ingredients to the doughs. The argument seems legitimate when one considers water-soluble ingredients, especially saffron, the aromas and subtle flavors of which easily leach out during the cooking process. I believe one should concentrate more heavily on the sauces, garnishes, and fillings, rather than the dough, when considering expensive ingredients for a dish. This provides greater nuance of flavor and greater nutritive value.

The worldwide concepts of pasta dishes have changed everywhere except within the regional family traditions. The growing awareness of nutritional concepts has had much to do with these changes. In addition, the greater variety and availability of ingredients have caused the emergence of new pasta combinations and have redefined pasta sizes, shapes, and textures. These new ideas, together with traditional discrepancies, have helped to make one of the world's most important foodstuffs one of our most interesting and unique menu items.

Pasta, a high-energy food, may be prepared in one of three ways:

- *Pasta in brodo* (pasta in broth): suitable sizes and shapes of filled or flat pasta, such as *cappelletti*, tortellini, *farfalle, ditalini, capelli d'angelo,* vermicelli, and *quadrucci,* simmered in broth. See chapter 3 for recipes.
- *Pasta asciutta* (dry pasta): pasta cooked in lots of salted water and served with fresh butter and grated cheese or with any special garnish or sauce.
- *Pasta al forno* (baked pasta): pasta prepared in the oven, such as lasagne, *cannelloni,* manicotti, or any gratinated pasta.

The principal cheeses that complement pasta are freshly grated *Parmigiano Reggiano* or *pecorino.*

PASTA DOUGHS

The composition of pasta dough most often consists of high-gluten durum flour for straight pasta such as macaroni, spaghetti, vermicelli, and linguine and unbleached all-purpose flour mixed with durum flour for stuffed pasta. These flours are combined with eggs or sometimes water or oil.

Unbleached all-purpose flour (sometimes called "family flour") is made from hard (winter) and soft (spring) wheats. In the United States, the market determines the types of flour most readily available. In the north, hard wheat is more common because it is better suited to the various regional yeast products produced in these parts. In the south, where quick breads are so common, more soft wheat is found.

The flour and liquid compositions of pastas change with every region that produces Italian cuisine and are also heavily influenced by production techniques. Pasta made with all-purpose flour is easier to knead and is often preferred when making homemade pasta. Variations also abound from chef to chef. My personal observations while traveling in Italy have led me to the conclusion that the ideal combination lies in the mixing of Canadian durum, or Manitoba, flour with all-purpose flour.

The methods for mixing pasta dough are almost as numerous as the recipes. Usually a well is made in the dry ingredients and the eggs and/or liquid is poured into the well and gradually incorporated. It is easier, however, and just as effective to put the flour in a mixing bowl, add the eggs and/or other liquids, and stir with a fork or spatula until the flour has absorbed the other ingredients. In either case, once the dough is a homogeneous mass, it must be kneaded on a floured board with the palm of your hand until it takes on a satiny texture. Add more flour if the consistency is soft or moist—this will keep your hands cleaner as well. (It is wise to reserve some of the measured flour from the recipe while mixing the dough, adding the reserved flour gradually as needed once all the ingredients are mixed together. It is always easier to add flour to too soft a dough than it is to try to incorporate liquid into too dry a dough.) When done, wrap the dough airtight and let rest for at least 30 minutes.

The ratio of the dough ingredients is traditionally 1 pound flour to 11 ounces whole eggs (approximately 6 large eggs). My personal preference for straight pasta is 80 percent Manitoba flour to 20 percent all-purpose flour (about 13 ounces to 3 ounces). For pasta destined to be filled, I like to use equal amounts of Manitoba and all-purpose, adding 1 ounce of water before mixing the dough.

The following are some standard recipes for some of the more common pasta doughs. All are prepared according to the basic guidelines outlined above. Where the ingredient *flour* is listed, the ratios above should be considered.

Pasta verde (**Spinach pasta**): Stem 4 ounces fresh spinach and wash thoroughly. Chop coarsely. In a blender, puree the spinach with 4 eggs. Prepare the pasta dough with the spinach/egg puree and 1 pound flour. This dough should be very firm.

Pasta al pomodoro (**Tomato pasta**): Prepare the pasta using 1 pound flour, 3 eggs, and 6 to 7 ounces tomato paste.

Pasta all'erbe (**Herb pasta**): Clean 2 ounces mixed fresh herbs, such as parsley, sage, sorrel, and thyme. Combine with 5 eggs in a blender and puree. Prepare the pasta dough with the herb/egg puree and 1 pound flour.

Pasta con zucca (**Pumpkin pasta**): Puree 6 to 7 ounces cooked pumpkin with 3 eggs in a blender. Prepare the pasta dough with the pumpkin/egg puree and 1 pound flour.

Pasta alla barbabietola rossa (**Beet pasta**): Puree 8 ounces peeled and grated young beets, 1 tablespoon lemon juice, and 3 eggs in a blender. Strain, and add ½ ounce olive oil. Prepare the pasta dough with the beet/egg puree and 1 pound flour.

Bigoli (**Whole-wheat pasta**): Whole-wheat flour (or graham flour) is a product milled from the whole kernel of wheat, including the germ and the bran. The resulting dough is somewhat softer and brownish, with a pleasant, nutty flavor. Whole-wheat pasta is native to northeastern Italy (influenced by Austrian cuisine). Prepare the dough by mixing 5 eggs with 1 ounce olive oil and adding to 1 pound whole-wheat flour.

ROLLING OUT THE PASTA DOUGH

By hand: Dust the work surface (usually a board) with flour. Use a rolling pin to push down and stretch the dough. When an area has been flattened, continue to roll, applying pressure from the center outward. This direction is important; if the dough is simply rolled up and down, it will contract rather than stretch. Roll to the desired thickness, let the dough dry a bit, and then cut as desired. Be sure to sprinkle the dough sheet with a little semolina to prevent it from sticking.

With hand-cranked steel rollers: These machines are usually equipped with two cutting blades, one for *tagliatelle,* which is a bit broader than fettucine, and another for *tagliolini,* which is a bit broader than linguine. Take a small amount of the dough and flatten it a bit by hand. Set the rollers to their widest setting and feed the dough between the rollers with one hand while turning the crank with the other. Fold the dough in half and repeat this process several times until the dough feels smooth. Now the rollers can gradually be moved closer together after each roll to thin the dough, until the desired thickness is reached. The surface area naturally increases while the dough is thinned between the rollers. If the dough sheet becomes too wide, just cut it in half lengthwise and continue. Store any dough you are not rolling airtight.

The thinned sheets must be dried somewhat before cutting. The sheets can be hung from a homemade miniature rack (such as a towel rack) or on a wire-mesh screen. It is important that air circulates around the dough to remove any excess moisture before cutting. When the dough is no longer sticky (the time required will depend on humidity, atmospheric pressure, room conditions, and the like) it is ready to cut. Do *not* overdry the dough, or the pasta will crack or break when cut. After cutting, curl the strands of noodles on a tray, and if not using immediately, let dry *completely* before storing. This whole procedure takes little time to learn and greatly enhances the flavor of your finished product.

With professional motor-driven steel rollers: This apparatus has two sets of rollers to flatten and stretch the dough. This machine can be equipped with a number of cutting attachments as well. The advantage to such a device is that the dough need not be worked by hand as much before rolling. Knead to incorporate the ingredients, then proceed as for rolling with hand-cranked rollers.

With extruders: These machines mix the dough and then force it through a plate much as a meat grinder does. The mix cannot be too moist; it must remain somewhat granular in order to fall into the tube to be extruded. Using this machine, a ratio of 1 pound flour to 4 eggs is effective. This machine is also made with many different attachments and is very often found in kitchens that make great volumes of pasta.

CUTTING AND SHAPING PASTA

Once the pasta has been rolled out, it can be cut or shaped into a wide variety of forms. These can, however, be classified to some extent, first based on whether they are to be stuffed or not, and then according to their places of origin. An ordinary kitchen knife or pastry wheel can be used to cut a variety of homemade pasta. Some of the pastas discussed below are shown in color plates 18 and 19.

STRAIGHT PASTA

The following list includes the most common straight (nonstuffed) shapes and sizes, which are cut from rolled-out pasta sheets.

Capelli d'angelo (angel hair): the finest-cut pasta, less than $\frac{1}{16}$ inch wide—very difficult to cut by hand.

Vermicelli (little worms): very thin, spaghettilike noodles, originally from Campania.

Linguine (little tongues): spaghettilike noodles cut about $\frac{1}{8}$-inch wide.

Tagliolini (little cuts): thin, ribbon-like pasta cut a bit wider than linguine, a Florentine specialty.

Fettuccine (little slices): another ribbon pasta, about $\frac{1}{3}$ inch wide, a Roman specialty.

Trenette: ribbon pasta, the same as fettuccine, which may be rippled, a specialty of Genoa.

Tagliatelle (noodles): ribbon pasta similar to but slightly wider and thinner than fettuccine, a Florentine and Bolognese specialty.

Pappardelle: rectangles or rhombuses cut 1 by $2\frac{1}{2}$ inches.

Farfalle (butterflies): rectangular strips cut 1 by $2\frac{1}{2}$ inches and pinched together in the center to make butterflies or bow ties.

Lasagne: pasta sheets, about 4 inches wide, usually used for layering between cheese, meat, vegetables, or seafood fillings, a specialty of Campania.

Quadrucci (**little squares**): 1½ by 1½ inch squares.

Orecchiette (**little ears**): small olive-sized pieces of pasta pressed with the thumb into the shape of ears, a specialty of Apulia.

STUFFED PASTA

Most of the stuffed pasta mentioned below can be made in small quantities by hand without the aid of sophisticated equipment. Some pasta machines do come with ravioli-making attachments, and a variety of ravioli boards and presses are on the market. They are very easy to use for quick, limited production. Ravioli is the most recognizable form of stuffed pasta, but there are many others, though sometimes nothing really changes from region to region but the name.

Ravioli: stuffed, square, pillow-shaped pasta.

Raviolini: the same as ravioli but smaller.

Casonsei di Bergamo: rectangular, parcel-shaped pasta in the Bergamo style.

Tortelloni: stuffed, cushion-shaped pasta, usually with scalloped edges.

Tortelli: the same as *tortelloni* but smaller.

Anolini: stuffed, semicircular pasta.

Agnolotti: stuffed pasta, either semicircular or square, depending on the region.

Panzarotti: like *anolini* but breaded and deep-fried.

Tortellini: stuffed hat-shaped pasta with curled-up edges. Circles of thinly rolled pasta 3 inches in diameter are filled with cheese, spinach, meat, nuts, or seafood. The circle is then folded over in half, the edges are moistened, and they are pinched to seal, as for the *anolini* and *agnolotti*. The characteristic hat shape is achieved by grasping both ends of the semicircle, pulling them together, and sealing with pressure. The outer edge of the semicircle is then bent over to shape the traditional "collar."

Cappelletti: similar to tortellini but cut into squares instead of disks. They are usually served in broths. Two-inch squares are filled and shaped as for tortellini but without the collar.

COMMERCIAL MACHINE-MADE PASTA

Originally pasta was made in lengths as long as 18 to 24 inches. Now commercially sold pasta averages about 8 inches. The term *macaroni* was applied to all commercially made pasta products outside of Italy. Recently this has changed.

Commercially made pasta is available in a wide variety of shapes; the following list defines some of the types. Many of the handmade pastas listed previously are also available in this form.

Spaghetti: long, round pasta without holes, available in various thicknesses.

Spaghettini: very thin spaghetti.

Fusilli: long, spiral-shaped pasta.

Bucatini: long, thin, smooth pasta tubes.

Perciatelli: long, medium-thick pasta tubes.

Ziti: long, thick pasta tubes.

Mafaldine: long, rippled pasta strips, narrower than *mafalde.*

Maccheroni, macaroni: tubular pasta, either smooth or ribbed, available in short or medium lengths, a specialty of Naples.

Rigatoni: large-ribbed macaroni that are cut short.

Penne: short to medium-long macaroni cut diagonally at both ends.

Maccheroni rigati: any macaroni that has ribs.

Tubetti: short-cut tubular macaroni, mostly used in pasta salads in the United States.

Conchiglie: fluted, shell-shaped pasta for stuffing.

Lumache: snail-shaped pasta for stuffing.

Zitoni: long, very thick pasta tubes.

Mafalde: long, rippled pasta strips, similar to but thinner than fettucine.

COOKING PASTA

The general standard for cooking pasta for professional kitchens is to use one part pasta to five parts salted water. The water must come to a rolling boil before the pasta is added, pushed down, and stirred at once. The water should come to a second boil as soon as possible, and the pasta is then cooked until *al dente*—firm to the bite, not mushy. Drain well and serve, or rinse with fresh boiling water and serve.

When cooking pasta, several factors affect the cooking time:

- personal taste preference, either *al dente* or well cooked
- different sizes, shapes, and thicknesses of the pasta
- freshness of the pasta
- altitude at which the pasta is cooked

Monitor the degree of doneness continually by removing and tasting.

AUTOMATIC SPAGHETTI COOKERS

For continuous pasta production, the automatic spaghetti cooker is essential. This piece of equipment has two sections, one for cooking and reconstituting, the other for rinsing and storage. The storage capacity can be modified to meet individual requirements. The cooking section is equipped with a stainless steel cook pot, a movable water spout, an automatic (timed) basket lifter, stainless electric heaters, and a quick-opening drain valve. The basket is automatically lifted from the cooking liquid when the desired time has elapsed.

The storage section consists of a stainless steel storage sink where the starch is rinsed from the cooked pasta. When orders are received, the desired (premeasured) amount of pasta is lowered into the cooking section and finished to the desired doneness. Reconstitution takes a mere 30 seconds.

SAVING COOKED PASTA

If pasta is to be saved for reheating some time after it is cooked, rinse it in cold water, drain, and arrange in portion sizes on a suitable tray. The pasta should be covered airtight with plastic wrap. If the pasta is to be used for a salad, coat it lightly with oil to prevent sticking.

Linguine con Ragù di Trippa alla Trentina
LINGUINE WITH STEWED TRIPE, TRENTINA STYLE

This dish is quite simple to prepare, but the tripe requires a rather lengthy cooking time, so it is wise to prepare part of the recipe ahead of time.

Yield: 6 servings

3 pounds	fresh beef tripe	1/2 cup	grappa
3 quarts	beef broth (see chapter 3)	1/4 cup	chopped parsley
		1/4 cup	chopped oregano
3 ounces	pancetta, chopped	1/4 cup	chopped rosemary
1/4 cup	olive oil	1 fluid ounce	olive oil
1 pound	onions, sliced medium fine	1	green bell pepper, cut julienne
6 cloves	garlic, minced	1	red bell pepper, cut julienne
2	chili peppers, chopped	2 cups	sliced scallions, 1/2 inch, diagonally cut
1/2 cup	tomato paste	1/2 cup	halved black olives
6	tomatoes, peeled, seeded, and chopped (see chapter 1)	1 1/4 pounds	linguine
		1 cup	grated Parmesan
1/4 cup	balsamic vinegar		
2 cups	dry white wine		
to taste	salt and freshly ground black pepper		

1.   Wash the tripe, and blanch it for about 15 minutes. Drain and shock in cold water. Trim off any excess fat, and cut into 1/4-inch strips.

2.   Place the tripe strips in a 4-quart saucepan with the beef broth. Cover and simmer very slowly for 5 to 6 hours, until tender. Keep adding water to the pot if necessary. The tripe is extremely gelatinous and may scorch if there is not enough liquid.

3.   Drain the tripe, reserving both tripe and broth.

4.   Render the *pancetta* with oil in a heavy-bottomed 4-quart casserole. Sauté the onions and garlic until light brown.

5.   Add the chili peppers and tomato paste. Cook for about 5 minutes over medium heat.

(continued)

6. Add the chopped tomatoes, balsamic vinegar, and wine. Simmer until the mixture reduces by half.

7. Mix in the precooked tripe with some of the broth, and continue to cook for 1 hour, until the sauce has a thick consistency.

8. Adjust the seasonings, and add the grappa. Cook another 5 minutes. Mix in the parsley, oregano, and rosemary.

9. To serve, heat the 1 fluid ounce olive oil in a large skillet and quickly sauté the red and green peppers, scallions, and olives. Mix with the tripe.

10. Cook the linguine *al dente*, drain, and arrange on a serving plate with the tripe ragout on top. Sprinkle with the Parmesan. An additional garnish of tomato petals (see chapter 1) and oregano sprigs enhances the presentation (see color plate 20).

Linguine alla Pescatore
LINGUINE, FISHERMAN STYLE

Yield: 6 servings

24	fresh mussels	1	chili pepper, chopped
9 ounces	squid bodies (preferably baby squid)	6	sun-ripened tomatoes, peeled, seeded, and cut into strips (see chapter 1)
9 ounces	shrimp, 25-to-30-per-pound size		
6 ounces	sea scallops		
1 cup	dry white wine	1½ pounds	linguine
2	bay leaves	¼ cup	parsley, coarsely chopped
1	thyme sprig		
¼ cup	onions, finely diced	1 tablespoon	chopped oregano
6 fluid ounces	olive oil	1 tablespoon	chopped basil
1 cup	sliced scallions, white part only, cut diagonally	⅓ cup	finely chopped scallions, green tops only, cut on the bias
6 to 9 cloves	garlic, minced		
1	red bell pepper, cut into matchsticks (allumettes)		

1.   Soak the mussels in cold water for 5 minutes. Discard any that remain open. Scrub thoroughly, removing the beards and any sand. Cover with a wet towel and keep cool.

2.   Clean the squid by pulling the tentacles from the bodies. Cut off the tentacles just below the eyes and squeeze out the beak, which is the hard lump where the mouth is. Carefully remove the transparent pen from each, and rinse the inner body cavity. Peel off the skin and cut the bodies into ¼-inch rings. Dry with a towel.

3.   Peel and devein the shrimp. Refrigerate.

4.   Cut the scallops into thick slices. Refrigerate.

5.   Steam the mussels by placing them in a shallow casserole with the wine, bay leaves, thyme, and onions. Cover and steam over high heat just until the shells open. Do *not* oversteam; mussels should be plump and moist. Strain the liquid through cheesecloth or a fine-mesh sieve. Reserve the mussels and juices.

6.   Heat ¼ cup olive oil in a large skillet. Sauté the squid for about 15 seconds, until they just stiffen slightly. Remove with a slotted spoon and reserve with the mussels.

7.   Reduce the liquid in the skillet completely, and add 1 fluid ounce olive oil. Quickly sauté the shrimp, again keeping them slightly underdone. Add to the mussels and squid.

8.   Reduce the liquid in the skillet completely, add 1 fluid ounce olive oil, and sauté the scallops for about 15 seconds. Add to the other shellfish.

9.   Reduce the liquid in the skillet completely. Pour in the remaining olive oil and sauté the scallion whites, garlic, red pepper, chili pepper, and tomato strips for a couple of minutes. Add the reserved mussel broth and reduce by half.

10.   Cook the linguine *al dente*.

11.   Add the seafood to the vegetable mixture and adjust the seasonings. Keep in mind that the seafood already has a high sodium content.

12.   Reheat the mixture, and add the pasta, parsley, oregano, and basil. Toss well. Arrange neatly on serving plates; sprinkle liberally with the chopped scallion tops (see color plate 21).

Linguine alla Viareggina

LINGUINE WITH CLAMS, WHITE WINE, AND TOMATOES

Yield: 6 servings

72	littleneck clams	1/4 cup	chopped Italian parsley
2 cups	dry white wine	1 tablespoon	chopped oregano
1 cup	virgin olive oil	to taste	salt and freshly ground black pepper
6 cloves	garlic, minced		
1 cup	onion, diced small	1 1/2 pounds	linguine
6	tomatoes, peeled, seeded, and diced (see chapter 1)	1/3 cup	finely chopped scallions, green tops only
2	chili peppers, chopped		

1.   Scrub the clams briskly and thoroughly in cold water.

2.   Place the clams and 1 cup white wine in a large, shallow casserole. Add 1/4 cup olive oil and 2 minced cloves of garlic. Cover tightly and steam over high heat until the clamshells open, but the clams remain firm and plump. Strain, reserving the liquid.

3.   Remove the clams from the shells and reserve, covered, in a suitable dish.

4.   Heat 1/4 cup olive oil in a 3-quart casserole. Sauté the onions until light brown. Add the diced tomatoes and remaining garlic and cook over medium heat for a few minutes.

5.   Deglaze the casserole with remaining cup of white wine and add the reserved clam juice. Reduce by half.

6.   Simmer until consistency is glossy, and add the remaining olive oil, chili peppers, Italian parsley, and oregano. Adjust the seasonings.

7.   Cook the linguine *al dente* and drain.

8.   Add the cooked clams to the sauce and serve over the hot linguine. Sprinkle with the finely chopped scallion tops.

Linguine alla Carbonara

LINGUINE WITH PANCETTA CREAM SAUCE

Yield: 6 servings

1¼ to 1½ pound	linguine	1½ cups	hot heavy cream
2 ounces	butter	½ teaspoon	freshly ground black pepper
4 cloves	garlic, minced	to taste	salt
9 ounces	pancetta, diced medium and rendered until just crisp with fat drained off (smoked pancetta is best)	2	egg yolks
		½ cup	heavy cream
		6 ounces	Parmesan, grated

1.   Cook the linguine *al dente* and drain.

2.   Heat the butter with the garlic and rendered *pancetta* in a large skillet. Do not overheat.

3.   Add the 1½ cups hot cream and heat thoroughly. Season with the black pepper and salt and remove from the heat.

4.   Combine the egg yolks and ½ cup cream to make a liaison, and add to the skillet. Combine the sauce with the linguine. Toss well—all the pasta should be amply covered with the sauce.

5.   Add the Parmesan, toss well again, and serve at once. Offer additional pepper and cheese alongside.

Tagliolini di Spinaci al Gorgonzola
SPINACH TAGLIOLINI WITH GORGONZOLA CREAM SAUCE

Yield: 6 servings

1½ pounds	spinach tagliolini	to taste	freshly ground black pepper
1 cup	heavy cream, reduced by half	to taste	grated nutmeg
3 ounces	Gorgonzola, coarsely grated	¼ cup	chopped parsley
4 ounces	Parmesan, grated	1 tablespoon	chopped basil

1.   Prepare the *tagliolini al dente* and drain.

2.   Heat the ½ cup reduced cream in a stainless steel or enamel skillet. Remove from the heat and add two-thirds of the cheeses, plus the pepper, nutmeg, parsley, and basil.

3.   Add the hot *tagliolini*. Toss well.

4.   Arrange the pasta on serving plates and sprinkle with the remaining cheeses. For additional appeal, serve small-diced tomatoes, sautéed in butter, around the pasta.

Tagliolini alla Panna e Salmone Affumicato
TAGLIOLINI WITH SMOKED SALMON IN CREAM

Yield: 6 servings

6	shallots, finely diced	⅓ teaspoon	freshly ground black pepper
3 cloves	garlic, finely minced	2	tomatoes, peeled, seeded, and cut into short strips (see chapter 1)
6 ounces	mushrooms, cut in julienne		
1 ounce	butter		
1 cup	dry white wine	1½ pounds	egg tagliolini
½	chili pepper, chopped	3 ounces	smoked salmon, finely slivered
1¼ cups	heavy cream		
to taste	salt	½ cup	basil chiffonade

1.   In a large skillet, sauté the shallots, garlic, and mushrooms in the butter for 10 seconds.

2.   Add the white wine and reduce completely.

3.   Add the chili pepper and cream, and reduce by half, or to light coating consistency. Add the salt and pepper, and remove from the heat.

4.   Mix in the tomato strips.

5.   Prepare the *tagliolini al dente,* drain (do not rinse), and toss with the cream sauce.

6.   Place the pasta in the center of each serving plate and sprinkle the slivered salmon and basil chiffonade over the top. The salmon should not be overheated.

Tagliolini Freschi al Mascarpone e Limone
TAGLIOLINI WITH MASCARPONE AND LEMON

Yield: 6 servings

1½ pounds	*tagliolini flavored with lemon zest*
18 ounces	*Mascarpone*
½ cup	*grated Parmesan*
1 teaspoon	*grated lemon zest*
to taste	*salt and freshly ground black pepper*
¼ cup	*finely chopped mint leaves*
to garnish	*mint sprigs*

1.   Prepare the *tagliolini al dente* and drain.

2.   Heat the Mascarpone and add the Parmesan, lemon zest, salt, pepper, and chopped mint. Adjust the seasonings.

3.   Combine the *tagliolini* with the cheese sauce. Arrange neatly on serving plates and garnish with sprigs of mint.

Tagliatelle alla Trasteverina

TAGLIATELLE WITH STEAMED CLAMS AND SHRIMP

Yield: 6 servings

24	littleneck or small cherrystone clams	1	chili pepper, chopped
		1 tablespoon	capers
1 cup	dry white wine	to taste	salt and freshly ground black pepper
2	bay leaves		
½ teaspoon	fennel seeds	½ cup	chopped parsley
1½ pounds	shrimp, ½ ounce each	1 tablespoon	chopped oregano
		2 ounces	butter
¼ cup	olive oil	1½ pounds	tagliatelle
4 ounces	red onions, diced small	to garnish	basil leaves
6 cloves	garlic, minced		
6	tomatoes, peeled and seeded (see chapter 1)		

1.   Scrub the clams and place in a shallow 3-quart saucepan. Add wine, bay leaves, and fennel seed, and steam, covered, over high heat until the clams open but remain slightly underdone.

2.   Strain the clam juices through cheesecloth. Reserve the clams and juices.

3.   Shell and devein the shrimp. Refrigerate.

4.   Heat the olive oil in a skillet, and sauté onions and garlic until translucent. Add the reserved clam juice and reduce by one-third.

5.   Cut the tomatoes into ¼-inch strips and add to the skillet.

6.   Add the chili pepper, capers, salt and pepper, and shrimp. Simmer for 1 minute, and remove from the heat.

7.   Add the clams, parsley, and oregano. Mix in the butter.

8.   Cook the *tagliatelle al dente* and drain.

9.   Toss the *tagliatelle* with the seafood and decorate with fresh basil leaves. The seafood can also be spooned over the noodles on serving plates.

Spaghetti al Sugo di Vongole Bianche
SPAGHETTI IN WHITE CLAM SAUCE

Yield: 6 servings

60	littleneck or small cherrystone clams	to taste	salt
1 to 1¼ cups	olive oil	1½ pounds	spaghetti
1½ cups	dry white wine	¼ cup	chopped parsley
1 cup	onions, finely diced	1 tablespoon	chopped oregano
6 cloves	garlic, finely minced	½ cup	chopped scallions, green tops only, cut on a bias
1	chili pepper, chopped		
¼ teaspoon	freshly ground black pepper		

1. Scrub the clams well and place in shallow 6-quart casserole. Add 1 fluid ounce olive oil and ½ cup white wine. Steam clams over high heat, tightly covered, until the shells open, but clams remain moist and plump.

2. Strain the cooking liquid through cheesecloth or a fine-mesh sieve. Remove the clams from the shells, discard the shells, and reserve the clams along with the strained liquid.

3. Heat the remaining olive oil in a large skillet and sauté the onions and garlic. Add the remaining wine and reserved clam juices, and reduce by half, to a light coating consistency. Adjust with the chili pepper, black pepper, and salt.

4. Prepare the spaghetti *al dente* and drain.

5. Combine the clams with the sauce and bring to a simmer. Mix in the parsley and oregano, and toss with the pasta.

6. Arrange neatly on serving plates and sprinkle with the finely chopped scallion tops.

Spaghetti Aromatici

SPAGHETTI WITH OLIVES AND ANCHOVIES

At the core of this recipe are anchovies. Several varieties are native to American waters, but most are used only as bait fish. Anchovies are most often encountered flat-packed in oil, in cans. Anchovy paste is also available. If the canned variety is used, you may want to wash the fillets in water and blot dry, to remove excess salt.

Yield: 6 servings

³/₄ to 1 cup	olive oil	18	pickled black olives, chopped
1 cup	thinly sliced scallions, white part only	1 tablespoon	capers
		¹/₄ cup	chopped parsley
6 cloves	garlic, minced	¹/₄ cup	chopped mint leaves
6	anchovy fillets, diced	1¹/₂ pounds	spaghetti
1	red bell pepper, diced small	¹/₃ cup	finely chopped scallions, green tops only
1	chili pepper, chopped		

1.   Heat the olive oil in a large skillet, and sauté the scallion whites, garlic, anchovies, and red pepper for 1 minute.

2.   Add the chili pepper, olives, capers, parsley, and mint.

3.   Prepare the spaghetti *al dente* and drain. Toss with the sauce.

4.   Arrange neatly on serving plates, and sprinkle with the chopped scallion tops.

Spaghetti con Capperi e Olive Nere

SPAGHETTI WITH CAPERS AND BLACK OLIVES

Yield: 6 servings

¾ cup	*olive oil*	*30*	*black olives, pitted and sliced*
1	*red onion, sliced*		
4 cloves	*garlic, minced*	*2 tablespoons*	*chopped parsley*
2 tablespoons	*tomato paste*	*2 tablespoons*	*chopped basil*
4	*tomatoes, peeled, seeded, and diced small (see chapter 1)*	*to taste*	*salt and freshly ground black pepper*
1 tablespoon	*capers*	*1½ pounds*	*spaghetti*
2	*chili peppers, chopped*	*to pass*	*pecorino cheese*

1. Heat 3 fluid ounces of olive oil in a skillet. Sauté the onions and garlic over moderate heat. Do *not* brown.

2. Add the tomato paste, and cook for a few minutes. Add the diced tomatoes, and cook over very low heat for about 15 minutes.

3. Press the liquids from the capers, and chop them coarsely.

4. Mix the chili peppers, black olives, capers, parsley, and basil into the tomato sauce. Add the salt and pepper.

5. Prepare the spaghetti *al dente* and drain. Arrange it on serving plates and drizzle the remaining olive oil over it.

6. Spoon the sauce over the spaghetti. Serve grated *pecorino* cheese alongside.

Spaghetti alla Bolognese

SPAGHETTI WITH MEAT SAUCE

Yield: 6 servings

1 ounce	butter	½ to ¾ cup	tomato paste
3 fluid ounces	olive oil (or 3 ounces chopped bacon, optional)	6	sun-ripened tomatoes, peeled, seeded, and chopped (see chapter 1)
6 ounces	onions, finely diced		
2 cloves	garlic, minced	1 cup	dry red wine
1	carrot, coarsely grated	to taste	salt and freshly ground black pepper
1	celery stalk, coarsely grated		
8 ounces	beef, coarsely ground	1½ pounds	spaghetti
		¼ cup	chopped parsley
8 ounces	pork, coarsely ground	¼ cup	chopped basil
8 ounces	veal, coarsely ground	1 cup	grated Parmesan

1.   Heat the butter and oil. Add onions and garlic and cook over medium heat in a heavy-bottomed, 3-quart saucepan until lightly browned. Add the grated carrot and celery and the ground meat. Cook over high heat for 5 minutes.

2.   Add the tomato paste, chopped tomatoes, and red wine. Simmer over low heat for about 45 minutes, adding a little broth or water if the sauce thickens too much. Add the salt and pepper.

3.   Prepare the spaghetti *al dente* and drain.

4.   Arrange the spaghetti in soup (or flat) plates and top with the sauce, parsley, basil, and Parmesan.

Paglia e Fieno alle Tre Formaggi
PASTA WITH THREE CHEESES

Paglia e fieno literally means "straw and hay." The pasta usually consists of spinach noodles and egg noodles *(tagliatelle)* served with a light sauce.

Yield: 6 servings

10 ounces	spinach tagliatelle		to taste	nutmeg
10 ounces	egg tagliatelle		2 ounces	Parmesan, grated
1 ounce	butter		2 ounces	Gorgonzola, coarsely grated
4 cloves	garlic			
1	chili pepper, finely chopped		4 ounces	Fontina, coarsely grated
1 cup	hot heavy cream		1/2 cup	finely chopped scallions, green tops only, cut on a bias
to taste	salt and freshly ground black pepper			

1.   Cook the spinach and egg *tagliatelle al dente* and drain.

2.   Heat the butter in a large skillet and add the garlic and chopped chili pepper. Cook over low heat for 30 seconds.

3.   Add the hot cream to skillet, along with the salt, pepper, and nutmeg.

4.   Toss the pasta with the cream. Reheat thoroughly and then remove from the heat.

5.   Add the cheeses and mix completely.

6.   Arrange neatly on serving plates and sprinkle with the chopped scallion tops.

Fettuccine all'Amatricana

FETTUCCINE, AMATRICE STYLE

This style of preparation, using bacon, garlic, and tomatoes, originated in the small town of Amatrice in Latium, near Rome.

Yield: 6 servings

1 pound	pancetta (preferably smoked)	to taste	salt
1 fluid ounce	olive oil	1/4 teaspoon	freshly ground black pepper
6 ounces	onion, diced small	2 ounces	butter
1	red bell pepper, diced small	1 1/2 pounds	fettuccine
1	chili pepper, chopped	1/4 cup	coarsely chopped basil
3 cloves	garlic, minced	1/4 cup	chopped parsley
3/4 cup	dry red wine	3 ounces	Parmesan, grated
6	sun-ripened tomatoes, peeled, seeded, and cut into strips (see chapter 1)		

1.   Cut the *pancetta* into strips. Heat the olive oil in a large skillet. Add the *pancetta*, onion, red pepper, chili pepper, and garlic, and sauté quickly. Do *not* brown.

2.   Add the red wine and reduce completely.

3.   Add the tomatoes and continue cooking for several minutes.

4.   Add the salt and pepper and adjust to taste.

5.   Add the butter.

6.   Prepare the fettuccine *al dente* and drain. Toss with the sauce.

7.   Arrange neatly on serving plates and sprinkle with the basil, parsley, and grated Parmesan.

Trenette alla Genovese

TRENETTE WITH BASIL PUREE

Originally the basil for this sauce was pounded with a mortar and pestle; hence its popular name, *pesto*. The wonderful green color of *pesto* is further enhanced in this recipe by the addition of chopped, fresh spinach leaves; the spinach is optional.

Yield: 6 servings

2 ounces	pine nuts, lightly toasted (and walnuts if available)	2 ounces	Parmesan, grated
		1 ounce	pecorino cheese, grated
3 cloves	garlic, minced	1½ pounds	trenette
¾ cup	extra-virgin olive oil	to pass	Parmesan, grated
24 to 30	basil leaves, no stems		
½ cup	chopped fresh spinach leaves (optional)		

1.   Puree the nuts and garlic in a blender. Add the olive oil, basil, and spinach, and continue to puree until a smooth emulsion is achieved. Add cheeses and blend well.

2.   Remove the *pesto* to a suitable container (noncorrosive) and reserve until needed.

3.   Prepare the *trenette al dente* and drain. Toss the pasta with the *pesto* or arrange the pasta neatly on serving plates and spoon the *pesto* over it (see color plate 22).

4.   Serve extra grated Parmesan alongside.

Fusilli con Salsa di Melanzane e Pancetta Affumicata
FUSILLI WITH EGGPLANT AND SMOKED PANCETTA

Yield: 6 servings

1½ pounds	eggplant, peeled and diced small	6	sun-ripened tomatoes, peeled and seeded (see chapter 1)
1 ounce	salt		
¾ cup	olive oil	to taste	salt and freshly ground black pepper
3 ounces	onion, finely diced		
6 cloves	garlic, minced	1¼ pounds	fusilli
1	red bell pepper, diced small	1 pound	smoked pancetta, diced or cut in julienne
1	green bell pepper, diced small	¼ cup	chopped parsley
2	chili peppers, chopped	¼ cup	chopped basil
1 cup	dry white wine	¼ cup	chopped oregano
		1 cup	grated Parmesan

1. Combine the eggplant with the ounce of salt. Place in a colander and drain for 1 hour. Pat dry with paper towels.

2. Heat half the olive oil in a large skillet, and sauté the eggplant, a bit at a time, until nicely browned. Remove with a slotted spoon and reserve.

3. Add the remaining oil to the skillet, and sauté the onions, garlic, and peppers quickly. Do not brown.

4. Deglaze the pan with the white wine and reduce a bit.

5. Dice the tomatoes small, and add them, along with the sautéed eggplant, to the skillet. Let simmer slowly until the desired texture is achieved. Add the salt and pepper.

6. Prepare the *fusilli al dente* and drain.

7. Fry the *pancetta* until slightly crisp. Drain and reserve.

8. When the sauce reaches the desired consistency, add half the parsley, basil, and oregano. Toss with pasta.

9. Arrange the pasta neatly on serving plates, and sprinkle with crumbled *pancetta*, grated Parmesan, and the remaining herbs.

Fusilli con Gamberetti e Peperoni Misti alla Panna
FUSILLI WITH SHRIMP AND MIXED PEPPERS IN CREAM

Yield: 6 servings

2 ounces	butter, clarified (see chapter 1)	1	green bell pepper, cut into matchsticks
18 ounces	shrimp, 35-to-the-pound size, peeled and deveined	1	chili pepper, chopped
		1 cup	dry white wine
1 cup	sliced scallions, 1 inch long, cut on a bias	3 cups	heavy cream
		to taste	freshly ground black pepper
4 cloves	garlic, finely minced	12	sage leaves, coarsely chopped
1	red bell pepper, cut into matchsticks (allumettes)	1¼ to 1½ pounds	fusilli
		½ cup	chopped Italian parsley
1	yellow bell pepper, cut into matchsticks		

1. Heat half the clarified butter in a large skillet. Sauté the shrimp quickly and remove. (Leave the shrimp slightly underdone.)

2. Add the remaining butter to the same skillet, and quickly sauté the scallions, garlic, and peppers. The vegetables should be underdone. Add to the shrimp.

3. Deglaze the skillet with the white wine. Reduce completely.

4. Add the cream. Bring to a simmer, and reduce by half. Add the pepper and sage.

5. Prepare the *fusilli al dente* and drain.

6. Toss the cooked *fusilli* with the cream sauce. Let the pasta absorb some of the cream.

7. Combine the shrimp and vegetables with the pasta. Serve immediately: neatly arrange on serving plates and sprinkle with chopped Italian parsley (see color plate 23).

Fusilli alla Romana

FUSILLI WITH SPINACH, PROSCIUTTO, AND GARLIC

Yield: 6 servings

1 fluid ounce	olive oil	to taste	grated nutmeg
1 ounce	butter	1	chili pepper, chopped
2 ounces	pancetta, chopped		
3 ounces	onion, finely diced	pinch	salt
6 cloves	garlic, minced	1 pound	fusilli
1 pound	fresh spinach, no stems, very coarsely chopped	12	sage leaves, coarsely chopped
1½ cups	fresh cream, reduced by half	8 ounces	prosciutto, cooked, cut in short julienne
to taste	freshly ground black pepper	½ cup	grated Parmesan

1. Heat the oil and butter in a skillet. Cook the *pancetta* until lightly crisp over high heat. Add the onions and garlic, and cook until soft.

2. Add the spinach and stir-fry over high heat for a few seconds.

3. Add the ¾ cup of cream and remove from the heat. Add the pepper, nutmeg, chili pepper, and salt.

4. Prepare the *fusilli al dente* and drain.

5. Combine the cooked *fusilli* with the spinach cream, and arrange on serving plates.

6. Sprinkle sage, *prosciutto,* and Parmesan over the pasta. Serve additional Parmesan on the side.

Penne alle Verdure di Stagione
PENNE WITH SEASONAL VEGETABLES

Yield: 6 servings

1	red bell pepper, peeled (see chapter 1)	1 cup	dry white wine
		3 fluid ounces	chicken glace (see chapter 7)
4 ounces	scallions, white parts only	to taste	salt and freshly ground black pepper
4 ounces	small mushrooms		
4 ounces	zucchini	3 ounces	butter
4 ounces	pea pods	1¼ pounds	penne
6 ounces	broccoli	¼ cup	chopped Italian parsley
2	fresh artichokes, thinly sliced	2 tablespoons	chopped basil
3	tomatoes, peeled and seeded (see chapter 1)	⅓ cup	finely chopped scallions, green tops only
3 fluid ounces	clarified butter (see chapter 1)	1 cup	grated Parmesan
3 cloves	garlic, minced		

1. Prepare all vegetables in the following order and keep separate:

- Cut the peeled red pepper into thin short strips
- Cut the scallion whites into 1-inch-long diagonals
- Cut the small mushrooms in half (if large, thickly slice)
- Cut the zucchini into short strips
- Cut the pea pods lengthwise into small strips
- Cut tiny florets from the broccoli; peel the stem and cut it into short strips, blanch it for 2 minutes, shock in ice water, and drain
- Trim the artichokes of all nonedible parts; hold in lemon-acidulated water until needed
- Cut the peeled tomatoes into strips

2. Heat 2 fluid ounces of clarified butter in a large skillet, and sauté the pepper, scallions, mushrooms, zucchini, pea pods, and blanched broccoli until tender-crisp. Drain the vegetables in a small colander placed over a small container to collect all liquids and keep warm.

3. Add the remaining clarified butter to the skillet. Add the artichokes and garlic and cook over medium heat for 3 to 5 minutes. Remove with a slotted spoon and add to the vegetables. Deglaze the pan with white wine, and reduce the liquids by half.

(continued)

4. Add the chicken *glace* and liquids from the sautéed vegetables and the salt and pepper. Add the tomato strips. Bring to a short simmer. Adjust the seasonings.

5. Stir in the 3 ounces of butter to create an emulsion.

6. Prepare the *penne al dente* and drain.

7. Combine all the vegetables with the sauce. Toss with the pasta.

8. Serve neatly arranged on serving plates topped with the chopped parsley, basil, and scallion greens (see color plate 24). Serve the grated Parmesan alongside.

Penne alla Boscaiola

PENNE WITH MUSHROOMS AND TOMATOES, WOODSMAN STYLE

Yield: 6 servings

8 ounces	porcini	¼ teaspoon	freshly ground black pepper
8 ounces	chanterelles		
6	tomatoes, peeled and seeded (see chapter 1)	3 fluid ounces	meat glace (see chapter 7)
		2 tablespoons	chopped parsley
1 pound	pancetta	2 tablespoons	chopped basil
¼ cup	olive oil	2 tablespoons	chopped oregano
1 cup	sliced red onions, in short strips	2 ounces	butter
		1½ pounds	penne
6 cloves	garlic, minced	2 tablespoons	chopped parsley, to garnish
½ cup	Marsala		
1 cup	dry white wine	1 cup	grated Parmesan
1	chili pepper, chopped		

1. Clean the *porcini* and chanterelles. Cut off the sandy bottoms, wash quickly, and pat dry with a towel. Cut into thick slices. (If the chanterelles are small, leave them whole.)

2. Cut the tomatoes into strips.

3. Cut the *pancetta* into strips and pan-fry until very crisp. Drain and set aside.

4.   Heat the olive oil in a large skillet and sauté the onions, garlic, and mushrooms for 1 minute. Add the wines, and reduce the liquid by three-quarters.

5.   Add the chili pepper, black pepper, meat *glace,* and tomatoes, followed by the parsley, basil, oregano, and butter. Create an emulsion with the butter.

6.   Prepare the *penne al dente* and drain.

7.   Toss the pasta with the sauce. Arrange neatly on serving plates, and sprinkle with the crisp *pancetta* and some chopped parsley. Serve the grated Parmesan on the side.

Maccheroni Gratinati alla Napoletana
RIBBED ELBOW MACARONI BAKED WITH MOZZARELLA

Yield: 6 servings

¼ *cup*	*olive oil*	¼ *cup*	*chopped parsley*
2 ounces	*pancetta, chopped*	*2 tablespoons*	*chopped oregano*
1 cup	*small-diced onions*	*1*	*chili pepper, chopped*
⅓ *cup*	*small-diced celery*		
⅓ *cup*	*small-diced fennel*	*to taste*	*salt and freshly ground black pepper*
⅓ *cup*	*small diced carrots*		
4 cloves	*garlic, minced*	*1½ pounds*	*ribbed elbow macaroni*
½ *cup*	*tomato paste*		
1½ cups	*dry white wine*	*1 pound*	*mozzarella, diced small*
6	*tomatoes, peeled, seeded, and chopped (see chapter 1)*	½ *cup*	*grated pecorino cheese*

1.   Heat the olive oil in a heavy-bottomed saucepan, and render the *pancetta.* Add the onions, celery, fennel, carrots, and garlic, and cook over medium heat for 5 minutes.

2.   Add the tomato paste, and cook for another 5 minutes.

3.   Add the wine, and reduce until thick.

4.   Add the chopped tomatoes, and simmer again until thick.

(continued)

5.   Add parsley, oregano, chili pepper, salt, and pepper.

6.   Prepare the macaroni *al dente* and drain.

7.   Toss the pasta with the sauce. Add half the mozzarella and half the *pecorino* cheese.

8.   Divide into 6 au gratin dishes, and top with the remaining cheeses. Bake on the upper rack of a preheated 450°F oven until lightly browned.

Pappardelle all'Arretina con Carciofini

PAPPARDELLE WITH DUCKLING AND BABY ARTICHOKES

This dish is traditionally made with a rich duck stock that you will probably want to make ahead of time.

Yield: 6 servings

1	duckling, approximately 3 pounds	1/4 cup	grappa
1/2 cup	small-diced carrots	1 cup	dry white wine
1/3 cup	small-diced celery	to taste	salt
1/3 cup	small-diced onions	12	baby artichokes, trimmed (see chapter 2)
1 tablespoon	tomato paste	2 tablespoons	lemon juice
5 cups	chicken broth (see chapter 3)	1 1/2 pounds	pappardelle
2 ounces	prosciutto trimmings	2 ounces	butter
1/2 cup	small-diced onions	1 1/2 cups	sliced scallions, white part only, 1 inch long, cut on a bias
1	fennel stalk, diced small		
1	carrot, diced small	1	red bell pepper, cut in fine julienne
1 tablespoon	green peppercorns	1	chili pepper, chopped
1	thyme sprig		
1	rosemary sprig	to taste	salt
1	bay leaf	2 tablespoons	chopped parsley
2	tomatoes, diced small	2 tablespoons	chopped oregano

1. Bone the duckling, reserving breast meat, leg meat, bones, liver and fat.

2. Render some of the duck fat in a heavy-bottomed 4-quart casserole, and add the chopped duck carcass, neck, and wings. Brown these together with the cup of diced carrots, celery, and onions. Add the tomato paste and continue to cook until the paste begins to caramelize. Add the chicken broth and simmer very slowly for 2 to 3 hours. Strain through a fine-mesh sieve, and reduce to about 2 cups. Reserve this stock.

3. Render a bit more of the duck fat in a small casserole. Sear the duck meat and liver on all sides. Remove the meat and liver and most of the fat, and reserve the meat and liver.

4. Add the *prosciutto* trimmings and render. Add the ½ cup of onions and lightly caramelize. Add the fennel stalk and small-diced carrot, green peppercorns, thyme, rosemary, bay leaf, tomatoes, grappa, and dry white wine. Reduce to ½ cup. Adjust salt to taste.

5. Return the duck meat to the casserole, and braise, covered, over low heat until tender but still firm, about 30 to 40 minutes. Remove the meat to a suitable dish, cover, and cool.

6. Add the prepared duck stock to the casserole and reduce the liquid to 2 cups. Strain through a fine-mesh sieve, pressing out as much of the solids as possible (including the liver, which is not returned to the duck meat). Keep the sauce warm. It should have a heavy coating consistency.

7. Cut the duck meat into thin strips.

8. Cut the trimmed artichokes into paper-thin slices and sprinkle with lemon juice.

9. Prepare the *pappardelle al dente* and drain.

10. Heat the butter in a large saucepan. Cook the sliced artichokes, scallions, red pepper, and chopped chili pepper over moderate heat until tender-crisp. Add salt to taste.

11. Add the sliced duck.

12. Toss the cooked *pappardelle* with the sauce, and add the duck/vegetable mixture. Arrange neatly on warmed serving plates and garnish with fresh chopped herbs.

Pappardelle Tre Colori all'Italiana

TRICOLORED PAPPARDELLE, ITALIAN STYLE

Yield: 6 servings

1 pound	pancetta, preferably smoked	8 ounces	egg pappardelle
		8 ounces	spinach pappardelle
1/4 cup	dry white wine	8 ounces	tomato pappardelle
6	sun-dried tomatoes	1/3 teaspoon	freshly ground black pepper
1 1/2 ounces	butter		
3 ounces	red onions, finely diced	10	sage leaves, coarsely cut
3 cloves	garlic, minced	to taste	salt
8 ounces	sliced mushrooms	5 ounces	Parmesan, grated
1 1/4 cups	heavy cream		

1.   Render the *pancetta* over medium heat until very crisp but not too brown. Drain the fat.

2.   Heat the white wine in a small saucepan and add the sun-dried tomatoes. Cover and steam for 30 seconds. Remove the pan from the heat, cover, and let the tomatoes absorb the liquid. When cool, cut the tomatoes into strips and reserve.

3.   Heat the butter in a large skillet, and sauté the onions, garlic, and mushrooms for 3 minutes.

4.   Add the heavy cream, and reduce to a light coating consistency. Remove from the heat.

5.   Prepare the *pappardelle al dente* and drain.

6.   Stir the black pepper, sage leaves, and salt into the cream sauce. Mix in the tomato strips.

7.   Add 3 ounces of grated Parmesan and the crisp *pancetta* to the sauce. Toss the pasta with the sauce.

8.   Arrange the pasta neatly on warmed serving plates. Serve the remaining grated Parmesan alongside.

Pappardelle all'Aragosta
PAPPARDELLE WITH LOBSTER AND FENNEL

Yield: 6 servings

2	live lobsters, 1½ pounds each, preferably female	1 quart	chicken stock
		1	bay leaf
1½ fluid ounces	olive oil	1	chili pepper, chopped
½ cup	finely diced red onions	pinch	saffron
1 clove	garlic, minced	1 ounce	butter
¼ cup	finely diced carrots	1 cup	sliced fennel knob, in short, thin strips
¼ cup	finely diced celery	1 cup	sliced mushrooms
1 tablespoon	tomato paste	1½ pounds	egg pappardelle
⅓ cup	grappa	1 pint	heavy cream
1½ cups	dry white wine	6	sage leaves
2	tomatoes, peeled, seeded, and chopped (see chapter 1)		

1.   Plunge the lobsters (heads only) into boiling water to kill. Place in a preheated 450°F oven for about 8 minutes. Remove and cool.

2.   Separate the tail and claws from the body of each lobster. Remove all flesh and, if lobsters are female, any coral as well as tomalley. Reserve the shells.

3.   Crush the lobster shells into small pieces.

4.   Heat the olive oil in a heavy-bottomed 4-quart saucepan. Add the lobster shells and cook for approximately 30 seconds over high heat. Add the onions, garlic, carrots, and celery, and cook over moderate heat for 5 minutes.

5.   Add the tomato paste. Stir well.

6.   Add the grappa and flambé. Deglaze with wine.

7.   Add the chopped tomatoes, chicken stock, bay leaf, chili pepper, and saffron. Reduce to 2 cups. Strain through a fine-mesh sieve and press out as much of the solids as possible.

(continued)

8. Reduce the strained liquid to 1 cup and remove from heat. In a small bowl, mash the lobster coral with tomale and mix with the reduced liquid. Strain the sauce again through a fine sieve. Keep warm.

9. Heat the butter in a small skillet and cook the fennel strips with the mushrooms until tender.

10. Cut the lobster meat into small strips.

11. Prepare the *pappardelle al dente* and drain.

12. Reduce the cream to 1 cup. Add 1 cup of the lobster sauce and remove from the heat. Add lobster meat and cooked fennel and mushrooms. Adjust the seasonings.

13. Arrange the pasta neatly on serving dishes. Spoon lobster sauce over it, and garnish with sage leaves.

Orecchiette con Fegatini di Pollo e Ciccioli

ORECCHIETTE WITH CHICKEN LIVERS AND CRACKLINGS

Yield: 6 servings

1½ ounces	chicken livers, sinews removed	1 cup	beef broth, seasoned (see chapter 3)
⅓ teaspoon	freshly ground black pepper	½ cup	chopped oil-preserved sun-dried tomatoes (see chapter 1)
1½ ounces	flour		
3 to 4 ounces	clarified butter (see chapter 1)	¼ cup	chopped parsley
6 ounces	red onions, diced small	2 tablespoons	chopped marjoram
		1¼ pounds	orecchiette
3 cloves	garlic, minced	⅓ cup	finely sliced scallions, green tops only
1	small chili pepper, chopped		
6 ounces	porcini	1 cup	chicken cracklings (see chapter 1)
1½ cups	dry red wine		
¼ cup	grappa	1 cup	grated Parmesan

1.   Cut the chicken livers into small pieces. Season with the black pepper and sprinkle with the flour.

2.   Heat the clarified butter in a large skillet and quickly sauté the livers, underdone. Remove with a slotted spoon and keep warm.

3.   In the same skillet, sauté the onions, garlic, chili pepper, and *porcini*. Caramelize slightly.

4.   Add the red wine and grappa and reduce by half.

5.   Add the beef broth and again reduce by half.

6.   Add the chopped tomatoes, parsley, and marjoram. Combine sautéed livers with the sauce. Keep warm.

7.   Prepare the *orecchiette al dente* and drain.

8.   Toss the pasta with the liver mixture.

9.   Arrange the pasta neatly on serving plates. Sprinkle with the finely sliced scallion tops and chicken cracklings. Serve the Parmesan on the side.

Bigoli al Ragù di Polpi

WHOLE-WHEAT SPAGHETTI WITH A RAGOUT OF BABY OCTOPUS

Fresh octopus and squid are unfortunately not readily available in most U.S. markets. Regions with large ethnic populations are more apt to have these wonderfully nutritious items fresh. They are also available frozen in many places, and these are for the most part very satisfactory.

Yield: 6 servings

18	baby octopuses	pinch	saffron
1½ ounces	dried porcini	6	tomatoes, peeled, seeded, and chopped (see chapter 1)
1 cup	dry white wine		
¾ cup	olive oil		
6 ounces	onions, diced	1¼ pounds	whole-wheat spaghetti
4 cloves	garlic, minced		
1	red bell pepper, chopped	¼ cup	chopped parsley
		2 tablespoons	chopped basil
1	green bell pepper, chopped	1 tablespoon	chopped fennel, tops only
1	chili pepper, chopped	to taste	salt and freshly ground black pepper
½ cup	Marsala		

1.   Clean the octopuses. The bodies should be turned inside out and rinsed. Cut off the mouth (with the hard beak) from each, and cut the body and tentacles into smaller pieces. The skin can remain intact.

2.   Soak the dried *porcini* in the white wine to reconstitute.

3.   Heat ½ cup olive oil in a heavy-duty 4-quart casserole and sauté the octopuses over high heat for several minutes. Add the onions, garlic, and peppers, cover, and simmer over low heat for 15 minutes.

4.   Add the soaked *porcini*, white and Marsala wines, saffron, and chopped tomatoes. Simmer for 20 minutes or until octopus is tender.

5.   Prepare the whole-wheat spaghetti *al dente*, and drain.

6.   Add the remaining ¼ cup olive oil and half the parsley, basil, and fennel to the sauce.

7.   Arrange the pasta on serving plates and top with the sauce. Sprinkle the remaining parsley, basil, and fennel and some freshly ground black pepper on top. Do *not* serve grated cheese alongside.

Quadrucci all'Erbe
HERB-INLAID PASTA SQUARES

Quadrucci are pasta squares that, when rolled out, have fresh herbs, usually Italian parsley, pressed between the layers of dough. This pasta is sometimes served with melted butter and freshly grated Parmesan, seasoned with freshly ground black pepper. More commonly, *quadrucci* are served in a double broth, a *brodo doppio* (see chapter 3 for recipes for these broths).

Yield: 4 servings

1 pound   *egg pasta dough*
32   *Italian parsley leaves*

1.   Roll the pasta dough into 2 very thin sheets, each about 4 inches wide, and 8 inches long. Do not let sheets get too dry, or the parsley will not be sufficiently sealed and the dough will separate when cooked.

2.   Imagine one dough sheet as consisting of thirty-two 1-inch squares. Place 1 parsley leaf at the center of each of these squares. Cover the dough and parsley with the second dough sheet, and roll the whole "sandwich" again to seal.

3.   Use a pizza or pastry cutter to cut 32 even squares. Cook to order.

Cannelloni di Ricotta e Spinaci Gratinati

CANNELLONI WITH RICOTTA AND SPINACH

Yield: 6 servings

12	4- by 5-inch egg pasta sheets	to taste	salt and freshly ground black pepper
1½ pounds	fresh spinach, well cleaned and drained	to taste	nutmeg
2 ounces	pancetta, chopped	2 cups	béchamel sauce (see chapter 7)
½ ounce	butter	3 ounces	mozzarella cheese, coarsely grated
2 ounces	onions, finely diced		
2 cloves	garlic, minced	3 ounces	Parmesan, grated
9 ounces	ricotta	2 cups	tomato-mushroom sauce, woodsman's style (see chapter 7)
3 ounces	Parmesan, grated		
2	eggs	6	basil sprigs
¼ cup	chopped parsley	2	tomatoes, peeled, seeded, and wedged (see chapter 1)
1 cup	fresh white breadcrumbs		

1.   Cook the pasta sheets in a generous amount of salted water *al dente*, drain, and shock in cold water. Drain again. Arrange side by side on a tray lined with moistened towels and cover with plastic wrap.

2.   Plunge the spinach leaves into boiling water for 5 seconds. Drain and shock in ice water. Drain again in a colander and press out all moisture. Chop.

3.   Cook the *pancetta* in the butter until translucent. Add the onions and garlic and cook 5 minutes over medium heat. Remove from the heat and cool.

4.   Combine the spinach, fried *pancetta*, onions, and garlic, plus the ricotta, Parmesan, eggs, parsley, breadcrumbs, salt, pepper, and nutmeg.

5.   Spread each pasta sheet with approximately ½ cup of the filling and roll into tubes. Place the *cannelloni* in a greased ovenproof baking dish. Cover each with 2 tablespoons of béchamel sauce, and sprinkle with the grated mozzarella and Parmesan.

6.   Bake in a hot (450°F) oven or brown under a top broiler until nicely browned.

7.   Place 2 *cannelloni* on each serving plate with ⅓ cup of the tomato-mushroom sauce on the side. (Other tomato-based sauces are also appropriate; see chapter 7 for suggestions.) Garnish each with a basil sprig and small tomato wedges on either side.

Tortelloni di Porri e Zucca alla Salsa di Burro all'Erbe

TORTELLONI WITH LEEKS, PUMPKIN, AND PROSCIUTTO IN HERBED BUTTER SAUCE

Yield: 6 servings

2 pounds	peeled and seeded pumpkin	3 cloves	garlic, very finely minced
1½ pounds	leeks	3 fluid ounces	chicken glace (see chapter 7)
8 ounces	prosciutto	1½ cups	heavy cream
3 ounces	butter	6 ounces	butter, cut into small pieces
½ cup	ricotta	to taste	salt
2 or 3	egg yolks	¼ cup	chopped parsley
½ teaspoon	freshly ground black pepper	2 tablespoons	chopped basil
pinch	salt	1 tablespoon	chopped sage
pinch	nutmeg	to taste	freshly ground black pepper
1½ to 2 pounds	egg pasta dough		
1	egg		
1 tablespoon	water		

GARNISH:

as needed	whole basil leaves
½ cup	grated Parmesan

SAUCE:

½ ounce	butter
½ cup	very finely diced red onion

1.   Dice the pumpkin small.

2.   Trim the roots from the leeks and cut off most of the green tops. Slice crosswise and rinse thoroughly under cold running water to clean. Drain.

3.   Chop the *prosciutto* very finely (or grind in a meat grinder).

4.   Heat the butter in a large saucepan and add the leeks. Cook over high heat for 5 minutes. Add the pumpkin, cover, and steam until soft. Remove the cover and cook off the liquid. Place the pumpkin and leeks in a mixing bowl and cool. This mixture should be very dry.

5.   Combine the *prosciutto*, ricotta, egg yolks, pepper, salt, and nutmeg with the pumpkin and leeks. Mix well. Refrigerate in a covered container.

(continued)

6.   Roll out a strip of pasta 6 inches wide. Beat the egg with the water to make an egg wash. Brush the egg wash on the pasta strip. Place a teaspoon of the pumpkin mixture every 1¾ to 2 inches along the strip in straight rows. Cover with another, identically sized pasta strip. Press out the air pockets and trim to 2-inch squares with a ravoli or pastry cutter. Press all edges of each square to seal. Cook *al dente* in a generous amount of salted water.

7.   Heat the ½ ounce of butter for the sauce in a shallow saucepan *(sautoir)*, and cook the onion and garlic over low heat for several minutes.

8.   Add the poultry *glace* and cream and reduce by half. Remove from the heat.

9.   Vigorously stir in the 6 ounces of butter, in small pieces, to achieve an emulsion. Adjust the salt to taste.

10.   Add the parsley, basil, sage, and freshly ground black pepper.

11.   Arrange 6 or 7 *tortelloni* on each serving dish. Top with the sauce, and garnish with whole fresh basil leaves. Serve the grated Parmesan cheese alongside.

Tortellini alla Bolognese
MEAT-FILLED TORTELLINI, BOLOGNESE STYLE

Yield: 6 servings

2 pounds	egg pasta dough	4 tablespoons	fresh breadcrumbs
½ cup	diced onions	1½ cups	grated Parmesan
2 ounces	butter	to taste	salt and freshly ground black pepper
4 ounces	veal, diced		
4 ounces	chicken, diced		
2 ounces	raw prosciutto, diced small	to taste	nutmeg
		4 tablespoons	chopped parsley
4 ounces	mortadella, diced	2 quarts	chicken broth (see chapter 3)
1	egg		
¼ cup	cold chicken broth (see chapter 3)	¾ to 1 cup	melted butter
		to garnish	chopped parsley

1.   After preparing the pasta dough, let it rest, tightly covered, for at least 30 minutes.

2.   Sauté the onions in the butter until translucent. Add the diced meats to the onions, and cook over medium heat until well done. Remove and cool.

3.   Grind the cooked meat mixture through the medium blade of a meat grinder. Mix with the egg, cold chicken broth, breadcrumbs, ½ cup grated Parmesan, salt, pepper, nutmeg, and parsley.

4.   Prepare the tortellini with the dough and meat filling. (See instructions at the beginning of this chapter.) Cook *al dente* in the 2 quarts of chicken broth.

5.   Arrange the pasta neatly on each serving plate, and coat with the melted butter and the remaining grated Parmesan. Sprinkle with the chopped parsley.

Pasticcio di Tortellini alla Valdostana
BAKED TORTELLINI, VALLE D'AOSTA STYLE

Yield: 6 servings

3 ounces	butter	9 ounces	Fontina, coarsely grated
60	tortellini, varying colors	3 ounces	Parmesan, grated
4 ounces	onions, finely diced	to taste	salt and freshly ground black pepper
1 pound	mushrooms, cleaned and diced large	to taste	nutmeg
8 ounces	cooked prosciutto	¼ cup	chopped parsley
2 ounces	red bell pepper, diced	1 tablespoon	chopped rosemary
		½ cup	light cream
2 ounces	green bell pepper, diced	3	eggs
2 ounces	carrots, cut in matchsticks (allumettes)	1½ cups	tomato sauce (see chapter 7)

1.   Coat a 6- by 9-inch ovenproof baking dish with butter. If using ramekins, line the bottoms of 6 individual 8-ounce ramekins with a circle of parchment paper brushed with melted butter.

2.   Prepare the tortellini *al dente* and drain. Shock in cold water and drain again.

3.   Heat the remaining butter in a skillet and sauté the onions for 1 minute. Add the mushrooms, and continue to cook over high heat to evaporate most of the moisture. Add the *prosciutto* and peppers. Remove from the heat and reserve.

4.   Blanch or steam the carrots until tender-crisp. Reserve.

(continued)

5. Combine the cooked tortellini, onions, mushrooms, peppers, carrots, and two-thirds of the grated cheeses in a large mixing bowl. Add the salt, black pepper, and nutmeg. Mix in the parsley and rosemary and blend all ingredients well.

6. Arrange the mixture in the buttered baking dish or ramekins. Combine the light cream with the eggs and season to taste. Pour the egg/cream mixture over the pasta and let settle.

7. Sprinkle the remaining grated cheeses over the pasta and bake at 350°F until heated through but not dry. Ramekins should not take longer than 15 minutes. One large baking dish with all the pasta will take about 25 minutes. Let rest at least 10 minutes after baking, before serving. If using one large pan, cut into 3- by 3-inch sections to serve. Surround with the tomato sauce and decorate as desired with fresh greens. If using ramekins, unmold, surround with tomato sauce, and decorate as desired with fresh greens.

Pasticcio alla Panna con Funghi Assortiti
LASAGNE BAKED IN CREAM WITH MUSHROOMS

Yield: 9 servings

1 pound	egg pasta dough	pinch	ground nutmeg
1½ pounds	assorted mushrooms (domestic and wild)	2	chili peppers, chopped
2 ounces	butter	½ cup	chopped basil
2 cups	finely diced onions	½ cup	chopped parsley
1 quart	heavy cream	8 ounces	Parmesan, grated
pinch	salt and black pepper	24 ounces	mozzarella, coarsely grated

1. Roll out the pasta dough fairly thick, and cut 9 pieces of 3 by 12 inches, making lasagne.

2. Cook the lasagne *al dente,* drain, shock in cold water, and drain again.

3. Clean the mushrooms thoroughly (remove sandy ends). Slice and sauté in the butter for several minutes. Drain in a colander and reserve.

4. Blanch the onions for 15 seconds in lightly salted boiling water. Drain.

5. Bring the cream to a simmer in a large casserole. Add the blanched onions, and reduce by half. Add the salt, freshly ground black pepper, and nutmeg. Remove to a suitable bowl.

6.   Spread a few tablespoons of the onion/cream reduction on the bottom of a 9- by 12-inch ovenproof baking dish, and place 3 lasagne on top. Layer on one-third of the onion/cream mixture; half of the sautéed mushrooms, the chili peppers, the basil, and the parsley; and one-third of the Parmesan and mozzarella.

7.   Top with another 3 lasagne and repeat the procedure. Arrange the final 3 lasagne on top, and cover with the remaining cream and cheeses.

8.   Bake in a preheated 350° to 375°F oven for about 20 minutes.

9.   Let rest for at least 15 minutes after removing from the oven. Cut into 9 sections. Garnish as desired with fresh herb sprigs.

Lasagne Verde al Forno Bolognese
OVEN-BAKED SPINACH LASAGNE, BOLOGNA STYLE

Yield: 9 servings

1 pound	*spinach pasta dough*	*½ cup*	*finely diced carrots*
SAUCE:		*½ cup*	*finely diced celery*
¼ cup	*olive oil*		
9 ounces	*Italian (pork) sausage*	FILLING:	
1½ cups	*diced onions*	*1 pint*	*ricotta*
3 cloves	*garlic, minced*	*2*	*egg yolks*
9 ounces	*beef chuck, coarsely ground*	*2 ounces*	*Parmesan, grated*
9 ounces	*pork shoulder, coarsely ground*	*2 ounces*	*mozzarella, coarsely grated*
1 cup	*dry red wine*	*¼ cup*	*chopped parsley and basil*
½ teaspoon	*fennel seed*	*¼ teaspoon*	*freshly ground black pepper*
3 to 4 tablespoons	*tomato paste*	TOPPING:	
4	*tomatoes, peeled, seeded, and chopped (see chapter 1)*	*1 pint*	*béchamel sauce (see chapter 7)*
		3 ounces	*Parmesan, grated*
1	*chili pepper, chopped*	*6 ounces*	*mozzarella, coarsely grated*
to taste	*freshly ground black pepper*	*9*	*basil sprigs*

(continued)

1.   After preparing the spinach pasta dough, let it rest for at least 30 minutes, tightly covered.

2.   Roll the dough into a fairly thick sheet and cut 9 strips of 3 by 12 inches with a pastry or pizza cutter, making lasagne.

3.   Cook the lasagne *al dente,* drain, shock in cold water, and drain again. Store layered on a tray with plastic wrap between layers.

4.   Heat the olive oil in a heavy-bottomed casserole and sauté the Italian sausage on all sides. Remove, drain, and cut into thin slices.

5.   Add the onions and garlic to the casserole and sauté for a few minutes.

6.   Add the ground beef and pork and cook over medium heat for 10 minutes.

7.   Stir in the wine, fennel seed, tomato paste, and chopped tomatoes, and cook for 45 minutes or until thick. Add the chili pepper, black pepper, carrots, and celery and cook an additional 5 minutes. Remove from the heat. Mix in the sliced sausage.

8.   Combine all the ingredients for the filling.

9.   Spread a couple of tablespoons of the meat sauce on the bottom of a 9- by 12-inch ovenproof baking dish.

10.   Arrange 3 lasagne over the sauce, and spread with half the filling and half the sauce.

11.   Repeat with 3 lasagne, the remaining filling, and the remaining sauce. Top with the remaining 3 lasagne and cover with the béchamel, Parmesan, and mozzarella topping.

12.   Bake in a preheated 350°F oven for 30 minutes, until lightly browned on top. The cheese topping should not be too crusty or dry.

13.   Remove from the oven and rest for at least 15 minutes before cutting into 9 sections. Garnish with basil sprigs.

Lasagne con Animelle e Gamberetti
INDIVIDUAL LASAGNE WITH SWEETBREADS AND SHRIMP

Yield: 6 servings

2 pounds	spinach pasta dough	12 ounces	small shrimp, peeled and deveined
1½ pounds	calf's sweetbreads		
3 ounces	butter	2	tomatoes, peeled and seeded (see chapter 1)
2 cups	finely sliced leeks, white part only		
½ cup	grated fennel knob	1	red bell pepper, peeled (see chapter 1)
2	bay leaves		
pinch	salt	1 tablespoon	whole green peppercorns, rinsed
pinch	nutmeg		
18 ounces	mushrooms, cleaned and thickly sliced	1 cup	ricotta
		2¼ cups	heavy cream
1 cup	beef broth (see chapter 3)	6	basil sprigs
1 cup	dry white wine		

1.   Roll out the spinach dough thinly and cut into 18 pieces, each 3 by 4 inches. Cook this lasagne *al dente*, drain, shock in cold water, and drain again. Store layered on a tray, with plastic wrap between the layers.

2.   Soak the sweetbreads in fresh water for 2 hours. Remove the membranes and impurities, and cut into small pieces of about ½ ounce each.

3.   Heat 2 ounces of butter in a shallow 2-quart casserole. Add the leeks and fennel and cook over medium heat for several minutes. Add the bay leaves, salt, nutmeg, mushrooms, sweetbreads, broth, and wine, and cook over very low heat for 8 to 10 minutes. Place the mixture in a colander to drain.

4.   Cook the shrimp in the remaining butter in another skillet. Keep underdone, and add to the sweetbread mixture.

5.   Chop the tomatoes and the red pepper very finely and add to the skillet. Cook over high heat, add the liquid drained from the cooked sweetbreads, and add the green peppercorns. Reduce completely, until all liquid evaporates.

6.   Add the ricotta to the vegetables, and stir in the cream. Bring to a simmer and adjust the seasonings. Simmer until the sauce has a creamy consistency. Set aside 1½ cups of the sauce for topping.

(continued)

7.   Combine the cream sauce with the sweetbread/shrimp mixture.

8.   Spoon some of the sauce onto the bottom of 6 individual-size ovenproof baking dishes, and line each with a sheet of the cooked lasagne. Spoon some of the sweetbread/ shrimp mixture onto the pasta. Cover each with another layer of lasagne, top with sweetbread/shrimp mixture, and finish with the remaining lasagne.

9.   Coat the top layer of each dish with the cream sauce only, and bake in a preheated 375°F oven for 10 to 12 minutes to heat thoroughly and glaze the top of the lasagne. Garnish with fresh basil sprigs.

Timballo di Maccheroni alla Spuma di Gamberetti Aurora

MACARONI TIMBALE WITH SHRIMP MOUSSELINE AND SAUCE AURORA

Prepare the shrimp mousseline for this dish ahead of time, and keep well chilled.

Yield: 8 servings

6 ounces	shrimp, peeled, deveined, chopped, and chilled	2 ounces	red pepper, peeled and diced small (see chapter 1)
6 ounces	sea scallops, chopped and chilled	1 tablespoon	coarsely chopped arugula
1 ounce	fresh white bread, no crust	1 tablespoon	coarsely chopped basil
pinch	white or cayenne pepper	1 tablespoon	coarsely chopped parsley
pinch	nutmeg	1 pound	long, tubular macaroni, such as bocatini, perciatelli, mezzani, or ziti
½ teaspoon	salt		
2	egg whites, lightly beaten and chilled		
1 to 1¼ cups	heavy cream, well chilled	2 ounces	butter, softened
		2 cups	sauce aurora (see chapter 7, Light Hollandaise Sauce with Shrimp Coulis)
4 ounces	shrimp, peeled, deveined, diced small		
4 ounces	sea scallops, diced small		

1. Place the 6 ounces of shrimp and of scallops in a blender. Add the white bread, pepper, nutmeg, and salt, and blend until almost smooth. Add the egg whites in a stream while continuing to blend. Remove the puree to a stainless steel mixing bowl, and hold over crushed ice in the refrigerator.

2. When the seafood puree is extremely cold, add the very cold cream (inside a walk-in refrigerator, if possible) by slowly working it into the puree with a spatula or wooden spoon. Poach a small tasting sample and adjust the seasonings. Mix in the 4 ounces of shrimp and of scallops and the red pepper, arugula, basil, and parsley.

3. Prepare the macaroni *al dente,* drain, shock in cold water, and drain again. Hold the macaroni, wrapped in plastic wrap, on a tray until needed.

4. Generously brush 8- or 10-ounce metal or porcelain timbale molds with the softened butter. Refrigerate to harden the butter.

5. Line the timbales with the macaroni by coiling the cooked pasta in one overlapping layer. Do not leave any gaps. Refrigerate.

6. Fill the lined timbales with the mousseline and cover each with aluminum foil.

7. Place the timbales in deep pan filled with boiling water so that the molds are three-quarters submerged. Poach in a preheated 325°F oven for about 12 minutes. (If using a single 3-quart mold, allow 30 to 35 minutes.) Be sure to check for doneness: the mousseline should be firm.

8. Remove the timbales from the oven, and let rest for 5 minutes before inverting onto serving plates.

9. Serve with the sauce aurora around the timbale bases. Decorate with fresh basil sprigs (see color plate 25). Each timbale can have a small diagonal cross cut through it at service time for more eye appeal.

Cappelletti con Salsa di Rognoni e Peperoni

CAPPELLETTI WITH VEAL KIDNEYS AND PEPPERS

Yield: 6 servings

2 pounds	egg pasta dough	1	chili pepper, chopped
1 pound	ricotta		
2 ounces	Parmesan, grated	1 cup	dry red wine
4 ounces	mozzarella, grated	1 fluid ounce	balsamic vinegar
2	eggs	1½ cups	brown veal stock (see chapter 7)
½ cup	chopped parsley		
1	egg	2 tablespoons	chopped marjoram
1 tablespoon	water	1 ounce	butter
1½ pounds	veal kidneys	1	red bell pepper, cut in julienne
¼ cup	olive oil		
1 ounce	flour	1	green bell pepper, cut in julienne
1½ ounces	butter		
1 cup	finely diced onions	1	scallion, cut in ½-inch diagonal slices
4 cloves	garlic, finely minced		
2 tablespoons	tomato paste	1 cup	grated Parmesan
3	tomatoes, peeled, seeded, and finely chopped (see chapter 1)		

1.   After preparing the dough, let it rest for at least 30 minutes, covered.

2.   Combine the ricotta, Parmesan, mozzarella, 2 eggs, and parsley for the filling.

3.   Roll out the pasta dough very thin. Lightly beat the egg and water, and brush onto the dough.

4.   Using a pastry bag with a straight tip, pipe teaspoons of the filling in straight, even rows, 2½ inches apart, onto the pasta.

5.   With a pizza or pastry cutter, cut the rows into straight-edged strips and then cut the strips into equal squares, with a teaspoon of filling centered in each square. Fold each square into a triangle, pressing the edges together to seal. Wrap each triangle around a finger and press the two ends that meet to make the characteristic cap shape.

6.   To prepare the ragout, remove the fat and gristle from each kidney. Cut into very small, thin slices.

7.   Heat the olive oil in a large skillet, and dust the kidneys with the flour. Sauté quickly and remove with a slotted spoon (keep underdone).

8.   Heat the butter in the same skillet, and brown the onions. Add the garlic, tomato paste, chopped tomatoes, chili pepper, red wine, balsamic vinegar, and brown veal stock. Simmer, reducing to a light coating consistency. Adjust the seasonings.

9.   Add the marjoram and sautéed kidneys. Heat but do not simmer.

10.   Cook the *cappelletti al dente,* drain, shock in cold water, and drain again. Arrange 8 *cappelletti* in a circle on each serving plate and spoon the kidney ragout in the center of plate.

11.   Sauté pepper garnish and scallions in butter for just 15 seconds, then spoon over the kidney. Sprinkle grated Parmesan on top.

Anolini al Ragù di Lumache e Prosciutto
ANOLINI WITH SNAILS AND PROSCIUTTO

Chopped spinach is very often added to the filling for this dish.

Yield: 6 servings

1½ to 2 pounds	egg pasta dough
1	egg
1 tablespoon	water

FILLING:

2 ounces	onions, finely diced and sautéed in a little butter
2 ounces	prosciutto trimmings, finely chopped
8	sage leaves, chopped
8 ounces	ricotta
3 ounces	Parmesan, grated
¼ cup	chopped fresh white bread, no crusts
1 to 2	egg yolks
to taste	salt and freshly ground black pepper

SAUCE:

1 fluid ounce	clarified butter (see chapter 1)
3 ounces	onions, finely diced
6 cloves	garlic, minced
18	snails, halved
2 ounces	cooked prosciutto, cut in julienne
½ ounce	dried porcini, reconstituted in water
1 cup	dry white wine
1 pint	heavy cream
2	tomatoes, peeled, seeded, and cut in julienne (see chapter 1)
1	chili pepper, chopped
to taste	salt and freshly ground black pepper
3 tablespoons	chopped parsley
1 tablespoon	chopped sage

1. After preparing the pasta dough, allow it to rest for 30 minutes.

2. Combine the sautéed onions, *prosciutto* trimmings, sage, ricotta, Parmesan, bread, egg yolks, salt, and pepper to make the *anolini* filling.

3.   Roll out the pasta dough fairly thinly. Lightly beat the egg with the water, and brush the pasta sheet. Using a 3½-inch circle cutter, cut circles from the dough. Place a teaspoon of filling in the center of each circle, fold the circle over to create a half-circle, and press the edges to seal.

4.   Cook the *anolini al dente,* drain, shock in cold water, and drain again.

5.   Heat the butter in a skillet and quickly sauté the onions, garlic, snails, *prosciutto,* and *porcini.* Remove with a slotted spoon and reserve.

6.   Add the wine to the skillet and reduce completely.

7.   In another saucepan, reduce the pint of cream to 1 cup. Add the cream to the skillet, along with the tomatoes, chili pepper, salt, and pepper.

8.   Combine the sautéed mixture with the cream sauce, which should be of coating consistency.

9.   Arrange the *anolini* in a circle on each serving plate. Spoon sauce in the center of the circle, and sprinkle with the chopped parsley and sage.

Ravioli di Coniglio in Salsa Funghi e Pepe Verde
RAVIOLI WITH SAUTÉED RABBIT IN MUSHROOM–GREEN PEPPERCORN SAUCE

Yield: 6 servings

2 pounds	egg pasta dough

FILLING:

1 pound	fresh spinach leaves, no stems
2 ounces	pancetta, chopped
1 ounce	butter
2 ounces	onions, finely diced
2 cloves	garlic, minced
2	egg yolks
8 ounces	ricotta
1/4 cup	white breadcrumbs
to taste	salt, freshly ground black pepper
to taste	nutmeg

SAUCE:

6 ounces	loin of rabbit, boned and skinless
6 ounces	porcini
2 fluid ounces	clarified butter (see chapter 1)
1/2 cup	small-diced red onions
8 cloves	garlic, finely minced
1/2 cup	Marsala
1 cup	dry red wine
1/2 cup	meat glace (see chapter 7)
1 tablespoon	pickled green peppercorns
1/2 cup	small-diced red and green bell peppers
2 ounces	butter, cut in small pieces
1/4 cup	chopped Italian parsley
1	rosemary sprig, chopped
to taste	salt
6	basil sprigs

1. After preparing the pasta dough, allow it to rest for at least 30 minutes.

2. Wash the spinach leaves several times in deep cold water. Quickly steam the spinach in a little water, then shock in ice water. Drain in a colander and squeeze dry. Chop finely and reserve.

3. Render the *pancetta* in butter. Add the onions and garlic, and cook soft over medium heat. Cool.

4. Combine the spinach, *pancetta,* onions, garlic, egg yolks, ricotta, breadcrumbs, salt, pepper, and nutmeg. Chill.

5.   Roll out the pasta dough into 2 rectangles. Place a teaspoon of filling at regular intervals in straight even rows along one sheet of dough. Cover with the second sheet, and press with your finger between the mounds, marking squares. Cut out the squares with a pastry or pizza cutter, and press to seal all the way around. (A variety of ravioli-making equipment can also be used to mark the dough before and after adding the filling.) Place the ravioli in layers on a tray, with plastic wrap between the layers, and chill till needed.

6.   Remove all sinews from the rabbit loin and cut into strips. Reserve. Clean the *porcini* and cut into thick slices.

7.   Heat 1 fluid ounce clarified butter in a large skillet and quickly sauté the sliced rabbit for about 10 seconds. Remove with a slotted spoon and keep warm. The meat should be cooked medium at best.

8.   Sauté the mushrooms in ½ fluid ounce of clarified butter for 2 minutes and remove with a slotted spoon. Add to the rabbit.

9.   Sauté the onions and garlic 1 minute in the remaining clarified butter. Add the Marsala and red wine, and reduce by half.

10.   Add the meat *glace* and green peppercorns and continue to reduce until the liquid has a light coating consistency.

11.   Add the diced peppers, and remove from the heat.

12.   Vigorously mix the butter pieces into the sauce to achieve an emulsion. Add the parsley, rosemary, and salt.

13.   Cook the ravioli *al dente,* drain, shock in cold water, and drain again.

14.   Reheat the sauce, and add the mushrooms and rabbit. Do *not* boil the sauce.

15.   Arrange 6 to 8 ravioli on each serving plate with the sauce spooned over. Garnish with basil sprigs (see color plate 26).

Ravioli alla Panna con Tartufi Neri
RAVIOLI IN BLACK-TRUFFLE CREAM SAUCE

Yield: 6 servings

2 pounds	egg pasta dough	2	egg yolks
3 ounces	black truffles	1/4 cup	grated Parmesan
1/2 cup	Marsala	to taste	salt and freshly ground black pepper
3 cups	dry white wine		
pinch	salt and freshly ground black pepper	to taste	nutmeg
		1/4 cup	fresh white breadcrumbs
1/4 cup	olive oil		
3 ounces	prosciutto, diced small	1/3 cup	finely diced celery
		1/3 cup	finely diced carrots
6 ounces	lean veal, diced small	1/3 cup	finely diced fennel
		2 ounces	butter
6 ounces	lean pork, diced small	3 cups	heavy cream
		3 fluid ounces	chicken or meat glace (see chapter 7)
2 cloves	garlic, minced		
2 tablespoons	chopped parsley		
1 tablespoon	chopped oregano		

1.   After preparing the pasta dough, allow it to rest for at least 30 minutes.

2.   Brush the truffles, and scrape off the skin, but do *not* wash.

3.   Place the truffles, Marsala, and 2 cups white wine in a noncorrosive saucepan, season with salt and pepper, and simmer over low heat for about 10 minutes. Remove from the heat and let the truffles steep in the wine. Cover and reserve. (This step can be done well in advance.)

4.   Heat the olive oil in a skillet. Sauté the *prosciutto,* veal, and pork for 3 minutes. Add the garlic and remaining cup of white wine, and reduce completely. Remove from the heat and let cool.

5.   Grind the cooked meats through the fine blade of a meat grinder, and combine with the parsley, oregano, egg yolks, Parmesan, salt, pepper, nutmeg, and breadcrumbs. Adjust the seasonings, and chill.

6.   Roll out the pasta dough into 2 rectangles. Place a teaspoon of filling at regular intervals in straight, even rows along one rectangle. Cover with the second rectangle, and press with your finger between the mounds of filling to mark squares. Cut out the

squares with a pastry or pizza cutter, and press the edges all the way around to seal. (A variety of ravioli-making tools may also be used to mark the dough before and after adding the filling.) Layer the ravioli on a tray, with plastic wrap between the layers, and chill till needed.

7. Cook the diced fennel, celery, and carrots in 1 ounce of butter in a noncorrosive saucepan over low heat for 5 minutes.

8. Drain the truffles, reserving the marinade and setting the truffles aside. Add the marinade to the vegetables and reduce almost completely.

9. Reduce the cream by half, to 1½ cups.

10. Add the meat *glace* and cream and adjust the seasonings.

11. Cut the truffles into a small dice, and add to the cream sauce. Keep hot but do not boil. Mix in the remaining ounce of butter just before service.

12. Prepare the ravioli *al dente,* drain, shock in cold water, and drain again. Arrange neatly on warm serving plates and top with the truffle cream sauce.

Ravioli di Melanzane e Pomodori
RAVIOLI WITH EGGPLANT AND TOMATOES

Yield: 6 servings

2 pounds	egg pasta dough	¼ cup	chopped parsley
		to taste	salt and freshly ground black pepper
FILLING:			
1½ pounds	Italian or Oriental eggplant	**SAUCE:**	
½ ounce	salt	¾ cup	olive oil
¼ cup	olive oil	6 cloves	garlic, finely minced
1½ cups	finely diced onions	1	chili pepper, chopped
4 cloves	garlic, finely minced	¼ cup	chopped basil
4	ripe tomatoes, peeled and seeded (see chapter 1)	¼ cup	chopped parsley
½ cup	chopped sun-dried tomatoes	to garnish	basil sprigs
		1 cup	grated Parmesan
½ cup	grated Parmesan		

(continued)

1.   After preparing the pasta dough, allow it to rest for at least 30 minutes.

2.   Peel the eggplant and dice coarsely. Sprinkle with salt and place in a strainer or colander to drain for 30 to 60 minutes.

3.   Rinse the eggplant in fresh water and blot dry.

4.   Heat the olive oil in a large skillet. Sauté the onions until lightly browned.

5.   Add the garlic and diced eggplant. Fry over high heat for 5 minutes.

6.   Dice the peeled, seeded tomatoes. Add both the fresh and sun-dried tomatoes to the eggplant mixture. Continue to cook over low heat until the mixture thickens to a pasty consistency. Remove from the heat and place in a noncorrosive bowl.

7.   Add the Parmesan, parsley, and pepper. Adjust the seasonings.

8.   Roll out the pasta dough into 2 rectangles. Place teaspoons of the eggplant/tomato filling at regular intervals in straight, even rows on one rectangle. Cover with the second rectangle of dough, and press with your finger between the mounds of filling to mark squares. Cut out the squares with a pizza or pastry cutter, and press the edges all the way around to seal. (A variety of ravioli-making tools can be used to mark the dough before and after adding the filling.)

9.   Cook the ravioli *al dente,* drain, shock in cold water, and drain again.

10.   Heat the olive oil in a skillet and add the garlic. Remove from the heat immediately—do *not* let the garlic brown. Add the chili pepper, basil, and parsley.

11.   Arrange the ravioli on warm serving plates. Spoon the garlic sauce over the ravioli. Garnish with basil sprigs or other fresh herbs. Serve the Parmesan on the side.

RICE AND RISOTTO, POLENTA AND GNOCCHI

—— *Riso e Risotto* ——
RICE AND RISOTTO

Although rice has been eaten in Asia since the beginning of time, it only reached Western Europe around A.D. 700, when it was introduced to Spain by the Moors. In Italy rice did not become popular until the mid-sixteenth century.

Four categories of rice are generally recognized in Italy. They are: *Commune* (short grain), *semi-fino* (medium grain), *fino* (long grain), and *super-fino* (extra-long grain). The long-grain and extra-long-grain varieties are most commonly used for risotto because the grains absorb great amounts of liquid without losing their shapes. Piedmont is the most abundant source of northern Italy's rice, but the method of preparation in Lombardy has become the standard. The result lies somewhere between risotto and pilaf. The technique calls for an uncovered pot at all times, and very often the rice is constantly stirred until the liquid is absorbed. On the other hand, in Piedmont, Valle d'Aosta, and Alto Adige, the risotto may be covered and is more frequently left unstirred. In Venice the style is distinctively creamy, of an almost flowing consistency known locally as *all'onda*, meaning "like a wave."

There is a major difference between *riso* and risotto that is easily overlooked. *Riso* is boiled rice, used primarily in salads and moistened most often with virgin olive oil or served hot with melted butter or a variety of sauces. Risotto is made by cooking in liquids only after the rice has been sweated, or quickly fried in oil.

The cooking time of either style of rice and the ratio of liquids used depend on the desired texture, the type of rice being prepared, and the type of utensil being used. *Short-grain rice* generally takes less cooking time. It is soft and has a distinctive round grain that is rich in starch. This type of rice is most often used in desserts (such as puddings) and soups. The cooking time is 14 to 16 minutes. *Medium-grain rice* is used like short-grain rice but is also used in some risottos. Cooking time is 16 to 18 minutes. *Long-grain rice*, an excellent rice for risotto, is cooked for 18 to 20 minutes. *Extra-long-grain rice* is the most expensive of the rices from Italy, with long, sturdy kernels containing less starch than the others and most suitable for boiled rice preparations. It is also commonly used in the preparation of *risotto milanese* (risotto with wine and saffron). Cooking time is 20 to 22 minutes.

Unlike Asians, Italians usually forgo the washing of rice before cooking. The rice is, however, checked for foreign debris and bad kernels. Perhaps the reason for less scrutiny of the rice lies in the improvement of storage and shipping techniques. The old loosely woven burlap bags used to transport the rice have almost disappeared, replaced by materials that allow less penetration of undesirable substances.

Riso in Bianco

BOILED RICE

Yield: 1 appetizer portion

2 ounces	long-grain rice (use 4 ounces for an entrée portion)
	boiling water, slightly salted

1. Stir the rice into the boiling water. Simmer, uncovered, for 20 minutes (rice, like pasta, should be cooked *al dente*). Stir occasionally.

2. If rice is to be used cold or served later, drain, shock in cold water, and drain again before covering in a suitable container and storing. Some chefs lightly coat the rice in extra-virgin olive oil. If the rice is to be served immediately, drain completely and serve with fresh butter, grated Parmesan, and herbs, or any compatible sauce, as for pasta.

Risotto Bianco

WHITE RISOTTO

Bianco refers to risotto cooked in white wine and water, rather than broth. Below are outlined the major steps in risotto preparation.

- Select a heavy-bottomed, noncorrosive casserole or straight-sided saucepan, preferably stainless steel or stainless steel lined.
- Use Arborio rice, classified "fine–super fine," the most popular rice in Italy.
- Cook the rice in oil or butter, with or without finely diced onions, stirring often with wooden spoon until well glazed and translucent. This is an important step in making risotto and should be carried out carefully.
- Add the liquid gradually, stirring each time it is added. The total amount of liquid will depend on the type of rice being used.

- When cooked to the desired texture, remove from the heat and let rest, covered, to allow for any additional cooking. Finally add the fresh butter and grated cheese. Italians do *not* use Parmesan with their fish and seafood risottos.

Yield: 6 servings

6 ounces	butter
1/2 cup	very finely diced onions
3 cups	Arborio rice
1 cup	dry white wine
8 cups	water, hot and salted
to taste	white pepper
to taste	nutmeg
to taste	bay leaf
1 cup	grated Parmesan

1. Heat half of the butter in a 3-quart, straight-sided casserole.

2. Add the onions and cook until transparent.

3. Add the rice and stir with a wooden spoon until well glazed and translucent.

4. Add the wine and cook, stirring until the wine evaporates.

5. Add 3 cups of salted hot water. Stirring occasionally, cook over low heat for 5 minutes. Add 3 more cups of hot water, along with the white pepper, nutmeg, and bay leaf. Follow this with 2 more cups of hot water. Stir whenever the liquid is added to the rice. Total cooking time of the rice should be 18 to 20 minutes.

6. Remove the risotto from the heat. Cover and let rest for 2 minutes.

7. Add the remaining butter and half the Parmesan. Stir with a wooden spoon to achieve creamy texture, known as *alla mantecato*.

8. Serve in soup plates, sprinkled with the remaining cheese.

Risotto alla Milanese

RISOTTO WITH WINE AND SAFFRON

This is a classic recipe of Lombardy. Make sure that you use an excellent quality beef broth, one that is rich and absolutely clear.

Yield: 6 servings

2 ounces	veal or beef marrow	½ cup	finely diced onions
pinch	saffron	3 cups	Arborio rice
8 cups	hot, clear beef broth, well-seasoned (see chapter 3)	1 cup	dry white wine
		pinch	white pepper
6 ounces	butter	1 cup	grated Parmesan

1.   Soak the marrow in salted, cold water for about 2 hours to extract the red pigment.

2.   Cut the marrow into small pieces and reserve.

3.   Dissolve the saffron in ½ cup hot beef broth and reserve.

4.   Heat half of the butter in a 3-quart, straight-sided casserole. Cook the onions until transparent.

5.   Add the marrow and rice and stir with a wooden spoon until the rice is well glazed.

6.   Stir in the wine and cook until it evaporates.

7.   Add 3 cups of hot beef broth and, stirring occasionally, cook over low heat for 5 minutes. Add 3 more cups of the hot broth, stir, and simmer for another 5 minutes. Add the remaining hot broth (including that with the saffron) and simmer for 8 to 10 minutes. Total cooking time will be from 18 to 20 minutes. Add the pepper.

8.   Remove the casserole from the heat and let rest, covered, for 2 minutes.

9.   Stir in the remaining butter and half of the grated Parmesan. Serve in a deep dish sprinkled with the remaining Parmesan.

Risotto con Calamari Napoletano
RISOTTO WITH SQUID AND TOMATOES

Yield: 6 servings

3 pounds	*squid*	*3 cups*	*Arborio rice*
4½ fluid ounces	*virgin olive oil*	*8 cups*	*hot chicken stock, well seasoned*
1½ cups	*diced onions*		
6 cloves	*garlic, minced*	*2 ounces*	*butter*
1½ cups	*dry white wine*	*1 cup*	*sliced red and green bell peppers, cut in small julienne*
4	*tomatoes, peeled, seeded, and sliced into strips (see chapter 1)*		
		1½ cups	*finely sliced scallions*
2	*chili peppers, chopped*		
30	*black olives, pitted and quartered*		

1.   Prepare the squid by separating the tentacles from the body (cutting just above the eyes) and removing the hard beak from the mouth area. Save the tentacles, and carefully remove and discard the transparent cartilaginous bone, or pen, from the body cavity. Rinse the body and slice into 1-inch rings.

2.   Heat ¼ cup of olive oil in a shallow, heavy-bottomed 4-quart casserole. Sauté the onion for several minutes.

3.   Add the garlic, squid rings, and tentacles and cook for about 5 minutes. Add the wine and cover. Simmer for 20 minutes, then add the tomatoes, chili peppers, and black olives. Simmer for 5 more minutes. (This part of the recipe may be done in advance.)

4.   Heat 1½ fluid ounces of olive oil in another 3-quart casserole and add the rice. Stir and cook over low heat until well glazed.

5.   Add 4 cups of hot chicken stock, stir, and simmer over low heat for 10 minutes. Add the remaining hot stock and adjust the seasonings. Simmer an additional 8 minutes. Remove from the heat and keep covered.

(continued)

6.   Combine the squid mixture with the risotto and mix in the butter.

7.   Heat the remaining olive oil, and sauté the julienne of red and green peppers quickly, until tender-crisp.

8.   Serve the risotto in a deep dish or soup plate. Garnish with the sautéed red and green peppers. Sprinkle with the finely cut scallions.

Risotto ai Paesano

RISOTTO WITH BACON, SAUSAGE, AND GREEN BEANS

Yield: 6 servings

1 pound	*small green beans*	*3 cups*	*Arborio rice*
8 cups	*beef broth (see chapter 3)*	*to taste*	*salt and freshly ground black pepper*
6 ounces	*lean bacon, diced small*	*2 ounces*	*butter*
12 ounces	*Italian sausage (hot or sweet)*	*1 cup*	*grated Parmesan*
1 cup	*diced onions*	*¼ cup*	*chopped parsley*
6 ounces	*cooked salami, diced small*	*½ cup*	*finely sliced scallions*

1.   Clean the green beans and cut in 1-inch diagonal lengths. Cook quickly in the beef broth and drain, reserving the liquid. Shock the beans in iced water. Reserve.

2.   Render the bacon in a 4-quart casserole. Add the sausage and fry over moderate heat until well done on all sides. Let cool, and slice the sausage into thick pieces.

3.   Add the onions to the bacon fat and cook until transparent. Add the salami and rice and stir until well glazed. Mix in 4 cups of hot broth, and simmer slowly for 10 minutes. Add 4 more cups of hot broth, and cook an additional 8 to 10 minutes. Remove from the heat, cover, and let rest for several minutes. Adjust the seasonings.

4.   Stir in the butter and half of the Parmesan, as well as the cooked sausage and green beans.

5.   Serve in a deep dish, sprinkled with the remaining Parmesan, parsley, and the sliced scallions.

Risotto con Quaglie e Rigaglie

RISOTTO WITH QUAIL AND GIBLETS

Yield: 8 servings

12	quail, including giblets	3 cups	Arborio rice
4 ounces	clarified butter (see chapter 1)	pinch	saffron
		1 cup	dry white wine
1/3 cup	diced onions	2 ounces	butter
1/3 cup	diced celery	1/2 cup	grated Parmesan
1/3 cup	diced carrots	1/4 cup	meat glace (see chapter 7)
3 quarts	cold water		
1	thyme sprig	1 teaspoon	chopped rosemary
1	bay leaf	1/3 teaspoon	freshly ground black pepper
2 cups	diced leeks, white part only	1/3 cup	finely sliced scallions
1/4 cup	dried porcini, reconstituted in water and drained	1/3 teaspoon	chopped parsley

1.   Reserving the giblets, debone the quail completely. Remove the skin. Save the bones and skin for the broth.

2.   Remove the leg sinews, and cut the breasts and legs into thin strips. Reserve.

3.   Slice giblets and reserve.

4.   Chop all bones and skins. Reserve.

5.   Heat 1 fluid ounce of clarified butter in a shallow, heavy-bottomed casserole and sear the quail bones with the diced onions, celery, and carrots. Add 3 quarts of cold water, the thyme, and bay leaf; simmer for 1 hour. Strain and reserve this broth. Keep hot.

6.   Heat 1½ fluid ounces of clarified butter in a heavy-bottomed 3-quart casserole. Add the leeks and reconstituted *porcini,* plus the sliced quail giblets, and sauté for 2 minutes.

7.   Add the rice and stir with a wooden spoon until well glazed. Dissolve the saffron in the wine and stir in. Simmer until the wine evaporates.

8.   Add 4 cups of quail broth and, stirring occasionally, simmer for 10 minutes. Add another 4 cups of quail broth and continue to simmer for 8 minutes. Remove from the heat and let rest 4 minutes.

(continued)

9. Mix in the 2 ounces butter and the Parmesan.

10. Heat the remaining clarified butter in a large skillet. Sauté the sliced quail meat quickly until slightly underdone. Remove the skillet from the heat and mix in the meat *glace*, rosemary, black pepper, and scallions.

11. Arrange the risotto in a deep dish or soup plate. Spoon the sautéed quail into the center, and garnish with chopped parsley. More color can be added by using sautéed julienne of red pepper or whole chili peppers and black olives as a garnish.

Risotto alla Certosina con Cosce di Rane

RISOTTO WITH CLAMS, MUSSELS, SHRIMP, AND FROG LEGS

Most seafood is high in protein and will immediately toughen if overcooked, producing an unappetizing dish. For this recipe, cook all the seafood separately to avoid overcooking any one item. Any liquids that you collect from the cooking or steaming of the seafood should be added to the risotto as well.

Yield: 6 servings

18	mussels	1 cup	diced onion
18	littleneck clams	3 cups	Arborio rice
12	shrimp, medium size	8 cups	hot chicken broth, well seasoned (see chapter 3)
12 pairs	frog legs		
1 cup	dry white wine	to taste	freshly ground black pepper
3 fluid ounces	olive oil		
2	bay leaves	2 ounces	butter
1	thyme sprig	1/3 cup	chopped parsley
4 cloves	garlic, minced	1 cup	very finely sliced scallions
2	chili peppers, chopped	6	basil sprigs
6	tomatoes, peeled, seeded, and diced (see chapter 1)		

1.   Scrub and clean the mussels and clams. Set aside.

2.   Peel and devein the shrimp. Set aside.

3.   Bone the frog legs. Set the meat aside.

4.   Heat ½ cup of white wine with ½ fluid ounce of olive oil in a shallow 4-quart casserole. Add the bay leaves, thyme, and clams. Cover tightly, and steam until the clams open but remain tender. Remove with a slotted spoon and place in a colander to drain.

5.   Repeat with the mussels, using the same casserole and liquid. Again, cover tightly and steam, but do not overcook. Remove the mussels with a slotted spoon to the colander with the clams. Strain all liquid through cheesecloth and reserve. Pick the clams and mussels from their shells; discard the shells.

6.   Quickly sauté the frog leg meat in ½ fluid ounce of olive oil in a large skillet. Reserve.

7.   Add another ½ fluid ounce of olive oil to skillet and sauté the shrimp, underdone. Add to the frog legs.

8.   In the same skillet, heat the garlic and chili peppers. Add the diced tomatoes, and cook for several minutes. Remove from the heat.

9.   Combine the seafood with the tomatoes. Keep warm. (The dish may be prepared ahead of time up to this point.)

10.   Heat 1½ fluid ounces olive oil in a 4-quart, heavy-bottomed casserole, add the onions, and cook until transparent.

11.   Add the rice and stir until well glazed. Add ½ cup of white wine and simmer until it evaporates. Add 4 cups of hot chicken broth and, stirring occasionally, simmer for 10 minutes. Add 4 more cups of the hot chicken broth and the reserved (reheated) shellfish juices. Stir and cook slowly for another 8 to 10 minutes. Remove from the heat.

12.   Combine the seafood and tomatoes with the risotto. Add the pepper.

13.   Mix in the butter and parsley.

14.   Serve in deep bowls or soup plates. Sprinkle with the sliced scallions, and garnish with basil sprigs.

Risotto con Fegatini di Pollo e Ciccioli
RISOTTO WITH CHICKEN LIVERS AND CHICKEN CRACKLINGS

Yield: 6 appetizer servings

12	chicken livers, sinews removed	1	rosemary sprig, chopped
2 ounces	pancetta, chopped	1	parsley sprig, chopped
1/2 cup	diced onions	1/2 teaspoon	freshly ground black pepper
1 1/2 cups	Arborio rice	1 1/2 ounces	butter
2 cloves	garlic, minced	1/2 cup	grated Parmesan
1 cup	white or red wine	1/2 cup	finely sliced scallions
4 cups	hot, clear chicken broth, well seasoned (see chapter 3)	1 cup	chicken cracklings (see chapter 1)
1/4 cup	olive oil		
1	marjoram sprig, chopped		

1.   Trim the chicken livers and cut into small pieces. Reserve.

2.   Render the *pancetta* in a 2-quart casserole. Cook the onions in the fat until lightly browned.

3.   Add the rice and garlic, and stir until the rice is well glazed.

4.   Add the wine and simmer until it evaporates.

5.   Stir in 3 cups of chicken broth and, stirring occasionally, simmer over low heat for 10 minutes.

6.   Add the remaining broth, stir, and simmer for an additional 8 minutes.

7.   Remove from the heat, cover, and let rest for 2 minutes.

8.   Heat the olive oil in a skillet and quickly sauté the chicken livers until done medium well. Season with the chopped herbs and black pepper.

9.   Stir in the butter and half of the Parmesan. Mix in the sautéed livers.

10.   Serve in deep dishes, sprinkled with the scallions, cracklings, and remaining Parmesan (see color plate 27).

Risotto con Pancetta e Radicchio Rosso
RISOTTO WITH PANCETTA AND RED RADICCHIO

Yield: 6 appetizer servings

8 ounces	pancetta, sliced into thin strips	1 cup	red wine
½ cup	diced red onions	4 cups	hot beef broth, well seasoned (see chapter 3)
1½ pounds	red radicchio, cleaned and coarsely shredded		
1	chili pepper, chopped	to taste	freshly ground black pepper
to taste	salt	to taste	nutmeg
2½ ounces	butter	½ cup	grated Parmesan
1½ cups	Arborio rice	¼ cup	chopped parsley

1. Render the *pancetta* until crisp. Drain off the grease, reserving both the meat and grease.

2. Heat ¼ cup of the *pancetta* grease in a 2-quart casserole. Cook half the onions in the grease for 2 minutes. Add the shredded radicchio, chili pepper, and salt, cover, and braise slowly until tender, about 20 minutes.

3. In another 2-quart casserole, heat 1½ ounces of butter and cook the remaining red onions for 2 minutes. Add the rice and stir until well glazed. Add the red wine and stir again. Simmer until the wine evaporates.

4. Add 3 cups of beef broth. Stirring occasionally, simmer over low heat for 10 minutes. Add the remaining broth, stir, and simmer for another 8 minutes. Remove from the heat. Add the pepper and nutmeg.

5. Add the radicchio, remaining butter, and half of the Parmesan.

6. Serve in deep dishes, sprinkled with crumbled *pancetta,* grated Parmesan, and chopped parsley.

Risotto di Rognoni e Peperoni Misti

RISOTTO WITH VEAL KIDNEYS AND MIXED PEPPERS

Yield: 6 appetizer servings

2 ounces	butter	1	chili pepper, chopped
½ cup	diced onions		
1½ cups	Arborio rice	½ cup	Marsala
½ cup	white wine	to taste	marjoram, chopped
4 cups	beef broth (see chapter 3)	2 cloves	garlic, minced
12 ounces	veal kidneys	to taste	salt and freshly ground black pepper
¼ cup	olive oil		
1 cup	diced red and green peppers	½ cup	grated Parmesan
		1 cup	julienne of red and green peppers
1 cup	sliced mushrooms		
to taste	black pepper	1 tablespoon	olive oil
3	tomatoes, peeled, seeded, and diced (see chapter 1)	3 tablespoons	chopped parsley

1. Heat 1 ounce of butter in a 2-quart casserole. Cook the onions until lightly browned. Add the rice and stir until well glazed. Add the wine and stir again. Simmer until the wine evaporates.

2. Add 3 cups of beef broth. Stirring occasionally, simmer over low heat for 10 minutes. Add the remaining broth, and stirring occasionally, cook for 8 more minutes. Remove from the heat.

3. Cut the veal kidneys in half. Remove all fat and gristle and cut into thin slices.

4. Heat the olive oil in a large skillet and quickly sauté the veal kidneys until medium done. Remove to a suitable dish and keep warm. Add the red and green peppers to the same skillet. Cook briefly and add to the kidneys. If necessary, add more fat to the skillet, then quickly sauté the mushrooms. Season with black pepper, and add the diced tomatoes, chili pepper, Marsala, marjoram, and garlic. Cook for 1 minute only.

5. Mix the sautéed veal kidneys and peppers with the mushroom mixture. Add the salt and pepper.

6. Combine this mixture with the risotto. Add 1 ounce of butter and half of the Parmesan.

7.   Serve in deep dishes. To garnish, quickly sauté the julienne of red and green peppers in a little oil. Sprinkle over the risotto with the remaining Parmesan and chopped parsley.

Risotto ai Porcini

RISOTTO WITH WILD PORCINI

Of the many edible wild mushroom varieties, *porcini (Boletus edulis)*, also known as *cèpes*, are among the most sought after in Europe. Very few other varieties can match the *porcino*'s superb, delicate, musty fragrance. Even when dehydrated, much of the aroma and subtleties of taste survive.

Yield: 6 appetizer servings

1 pound	fresh porcini	4 cups	hot beef broth, well seasoned (see chapter 7)
2 ounces	pancetta, chopped	to taste	freshly ground black pepper
2 ounces	butter		
½ cup	diced onions	to taste	nutmeg
3 cloves	garlic, minced	½ cup	grated Parmesan
1½ cups	Arborio rice	½ cup	chopped Italian parsley
1 cup	dry white wine		

1.   Clean the *porcini* of grit and sand, and cut off the stem ends. Slice into thick pieces.

2.   Render the *pancetta* with 1 ounce of the butter in a heavy-bottomed 3-quart casserole.

3.   Sauté the *porcini* for several minutes before removing with a slotted spoon. Let the mushrooms drain while catching the drippings. Reserve both.

4.   Reheat the casserole and evaporate the liquid. Add the onions and cook over moderate heat for several minutes until translucent.

5.   Stir in the garlic and rice and cook until the rice is well glazed. Add the wine and stir again. Simmer until the wine evaporates.

6.   Add 3 cups of hot beef broth and simmer for 10 minutes, stirring occasionally. Add the *porcini* liquid and the remaining beef broth and cook another 8 minutes. Remove from the heat. Add the pepper and nutmeg.

7.   Combine the *porcini* with the risotto and 1 ounce of butter. Add half of the Parmesan.

8.   Serve in deep dishes, sprinkled with the remaining Parmesan and chopped Italian parsley.

Risotto con Zucca e Prosciutto

RISOTTO WITH PUMPKIN AND PROSCIUTTO

If fresh pumpkin flowers *(fiori di zucca)* are available, remove the pistils from the blossoms, cut into small pieces, and stew in butter for a few minutes. Add to the finished risotto just before serving.

Yield: 6 servings

3½ ounces	butter	3 cups	Arborio rice
2 ounces	prosciutto, chopped	1	chili pepper, chopped
1 cup	diced onions	1 cup	grated Parmesan
1 pound	pumpkin, peeled, seeded, and diced small	6	pumpkin flowers, if available
9 cups	hot, clear chicken broth, well seasoned (see chapter 3)	½ cup	very finely sliced scallions
		6	basil sprigs
to taste	salt and freshly ground black pepper		

1. Heat 1 ounce of butter in a 2-quart saucepan and add the *prosciutto* and half of the onions. Cook over moderate heat for 5 minutes.

2. Add the diced pumpkin, cover, and cook over low heat for another 5 minutes.

3. Add 1 cup of hot chicken broth and continue to cook until the pumpkin is soft. Season with salt and pepper.

4. In another pot, heat 1½ ounces of butter and add the remaining onions. Cook until translucent.

5. Add the rice. Stirring frequently, cook over moderate heat until well glazed.

6. Add 4 cups of hot chicken broth. Stirring occasionally, cook over low heat for 10 minutes.

7. Add another 4 cups of hot chicken broth. Stir and cook for 8 more minutes over low heat. Remove from the heat and add the chopped chili pepper.

8. Combine the cooked pumpkin mixture with the risotto and adjust the seasonings.

9. Stir in the remaining butter and half of the Parmesan. Add the stewed pumpkin flowers if available.

10. Serve in deep dishes, sprinkled with the remaining Parmesan and the sliced scallions. Garnish with fresh basil sprigs (see color plate 28).

Risotto con Tartufi Neri

RISOTTO WITH BLACK TRUFFLES

When working with the prized delicacy of the truffle, the real challenge to the chef lies in the perfect blending of the various ingredients so as not to dominate the truffle's subtle aroma in the following dish.

Yield: 6 appetizer servings

1	black truffle	pinch	cayenne pepper
1/2 cup	white wine	to taste	salt
2 1/2 ounces	butter	3 tablespoons	grated Parmesan
1/2 cup	diced leeks, white part only	1/2 cup	hot cream
1 1/2 cups	Arborio rice		
4 cups	hot white veal stock, preferably clarified (see chapter 7)		

1. Clean the truffle by brushing off any grit. Poach in the white wine for about 6 to 8 minutes. Cool in the wine. When cool, remove the truffle and reserve the wine as well.

2. Heat 2 ounces of butter in a 2-quart casserole and add the leeks. Cook for a few minutes before adding the rice. Stir with a wooden spoon until the rice is well glazed. Add the wine and simmer until it evaporates.

3. Stir in 3 cups of hot well-seasoned veal stock. Simmer over low heat for 10 minutes, stirring occasionally. Add the remaining stock and continue simmering for another 8 minutes.

4. Remove from the heat, cover, and let rest for 2 minutes. Add the cayenne and salt.

5. Mix in the grated Parmesan cheese and hot cream.

6. Arrange in deep dishes, shave the truffle over the risotto, and serve.

Risotto in Bianco alla Valdostana

WHITE RISOTTO WITH FONTINA

Yield: 6 appetizer servings

3 ounces	butter	to taste	nutmeg
1/2 cup	diced onions	1/4 cup	grated Parmesan
1 1/2 cups	Arborio rice	1/2 cup	coarsely grated Fontina
4 1/2 cups	clarified chicken broth (see chapter 3)	1/3 cup	very finely chopped chives
to taste	salt and white pepper		

1.   Heat 1½ ounces of butter in a 2-quart straight-sided casserole.

2.   Add the onions, and cook until translucent.

3.   Add the rice, and stir with a wooden spoon until well glazed. Add 2 cups of the broth. Stirring occasionally, simmer for 10 minutes. Add the remaining broth, and stir and simmer for another 8 to 10 minutes. Remove from the heat, cover, and let rest for several minutes. Add the salt, pepper, and nutmeg.

4.   Mix in 1½ ounces of butter and the cheeses. The Fontina will make a very creamy risotto.

5.   Serve in deep dishes, sprinkled with the chopped chives.

Risotto con Carciofi e Pancetta Croccante

RISOTTO WITH ARTICHOKES AND CRISP PANCETTA

Yield: 6 appetizer servings

6	small, fresh artichokes	1 pound	smoked pancetta, cut in julienne
1 fluid ounce	lemon juice	3 ounces	fresh butter
4 1/2 cups	hot, clear beef broth, well seasoned (see chapter 3)	1/4 cup	finely diced onions
		1 1/2 cups	Arborio rice
1 cup	sliced leeks		

to taste	*freshly ground black*	¹/₂ cup	*grated Parmesan*
	pepper	¹/₄ cup	*chopped parsley*
to taste	*nutmeg*		

1. Remove the inedible parts of the artichokes and discard. Cut the artichokes into small pieces, sprinkle with the lemon juice, and cook *al dente* in the simmering beef broth. Drain, reserving the broth, and shock the artichokes in ice water. Drain and reserve. Keep the beef broth hot.

2. Clean the leeks in cold, running water. Slice into thin rings and reserve.

3. Fry the thinly sliced *pancetta* slowly until crisp. Drain.

4. Heat half the butter in a 2-quart casserole and cook the onions until translucent.

5. Add the rice to the onions, and stir with a wooden spoon until the rice is well glazed.

6. Add 3 cups of hot beef broth. Stirring occasionally, simmer for 10 minutes.

7. Add the remaining hot broth, leeks, and artichokes, and cook over low heat for another 8 minutes, stirring occasionally. Remove from the heat, cover, and let rest for 2 minutes.

8. Mix in the remaining butter, pepper, and nutmeg. Stir in half of the Parmesan.

9. Serve in deep dishes, sprinkled with crumbled *pancetta,* the remaining cheese, and the chopped parsley (see color plate 29).

- *Polenta* -
POLENTA

For centuries the staple of the Roman population was a grain paste or porridge mixture called *puls,* and later, *pulmentum*. Water was mixed with a grain and simply eaten as such.

In the sixteenth century, maize (corn) was introduced to the European continent from the New World, and it quickly became the mainstay of the middle classes in Europe, especially in the Balkan region and northeastern Italy. This staple was not significantly different from the *puls* of Roman times, but it was made with cornmeal rather than wheat or barley.

Corn is native to the Western Hemisphere. In the United States, corn ranks second to wheat as the grain most used as a foodstuff in one form or another. It is especially popular in the South for all sorts of bread making.

As a grain, corn is an excellent source of nourishment and one of the cheapest and most generous suppliers of starches and fats. Yellow corn also contains significant amounts of carotenes, which the body converts into vitamin A.

Cornmeal is available in fine, medium, and coarse grinds. The selection of a particular grind is, as always, dependent on the region. For polenta, the preferred cooking vessel in an untinned copper bowl or pot, called a *paiolo*. Brass pots are also used. Another excellent—and more practical—utensil is a copper-bottomed stainless steel pot.

The cornmeal used in polenta should always be added carefully to the simmering salted liquid to avoid lumps. The easiest way to achieve a smooth-textured product is by allowing the cornmeal to flow in a stream into the liquid while stirring vigorously with a whip until the meal has absorbed all of the liquid. At this point, the whip is put aside, and a long-handled wooden spoon is used to stir the polenta occasionally until cooked to the desired doneness (usually when it pulls away from the side of the pot. At the very end, mix with fresh butter.

Cooking time depends on regional preferences (as does the above procedure to some extent), and as for pasta, one opinion has no place in Italy. It is generally agreed that 30 to 60 minutes are sufficient when preparing polenta. When cooking the polenta, it is most advisable to use the lowest heat possible and to be on the lookout for grains that literally explode out of the pot. I have witnessed severe burning of the face and hands when the meal was being hurriedly cooked over high heat. Polenta is delicious, so do not let this sound discouraging. Cooking over low heat generally avoids these problems. It is also possible to partially cover the pot while cooking. Many chefs let the mixed polenta finish cooking, covered, in the oven, stirring occasionally. When done, the polenta is usually finished with fat, butter, or hard cheeses to increase palatability. Polenta is also commonly prepared as a savory and, when sweetened, makes an excellent dessert.

The ratio of cornmeal to liquid will, like rice, depend on the recipe. The average is approximately one part cornmeal to four to five parts liquid (in pounds).

Polenta may be prepared grilled, pan-fried, deep-fried, rolled, as *gnocchi*, or as a plain mush.

GRILLED AND PAN-FRIED POLENTA

Less liquid is usually used when preparing polenta in this fashion. Prepare the polenta with 1 pound of cornmeal and 4 pints of salted water. Mix 4 ounces of butter into the cooked polenta. Roll into large logs and cool until firm. Slice the logs to the desired thickness. Grill on a very hot well-conditioned grill or pan-fry in a hot skillet.

DEEP-FRIED POLENTA

Very often, cheeses, ham, sausage, or meats are sandwiched between thin polenta layers. When cool, the polenta is cut into squares, rectangles, or finger-sized strips, breaded, and deep-fried. The product should be fried to order and served with a tomato-based sauce (see chapter 7).

BAKED POLENTA

Use individual-size au gratin dishes or a large ovenproof baking dish. Line with sliced polenta and various fillings. Top with cheese and bake in an oven. This preparation is similar to lasagne.

ROLLED POLENTA

To roll polenta, the cooled polenta is flattened between two sheets of plastic wrap, and a rolling pin is used to roll out the polenta to the desired thickness. To trim the sheet to its proper size, the top sheet of plastic is removed and the edges are cut off.

Any filling or garnish of sausage, meats, seafood, or cheeses can now be rolled into the polenta sheet. There is a marked similarity making rolled polenta and making a jelly roll. But it is also possible to make very small rolls, similar to *cannelloni*. Wrap the rolled polenta tightly in plastic wrap, and refrigerate until needed.

To use small rolls, cut 3- to 4-inch lengths of the stuffed polenta rolls and place two or three in a buttered, individual-size au gratin dish. Top with cheese and bake in a preheated 375°F oven until lightly glazed.

To use very small rolls, fill the polenta sheet with any fine ragout, such as rabbit, snail, or seafood, roll, and cut into 1½-inch lengths. Top with cheese or reduced cream, and glaze in a hot oven. These make excellent side or appetizer dishes as well.

To use large rolls, cut the stuffed polenta rolls into ½-inch slices and overlap in individual-size au gratin dishes. Top with cheese and glaze in a hot oven. Usually a tomato-based sauce is spooned around slices before serving.

POLENTA GNOCCHI

A sheet of ½-inch-thick polenta is cut into crescent shapes, topped with cheese and baked in individual-size au gratin dishes for appetizers or starchy side dishes. These *gnocchi* are baked in a tomato or cream-based sauce and are often flavored with Gorgonzola cheese and a variety of herbs.

POLENTA MUSH

Mush simply means the polenta is served as is, from the pot. In this form, the polenta may also be placed in timbales (and kept warm in a water bath until serving) and turned out onto plates when needed.

Polenta Grigliata di Coniglio e Peperoni
GRILLED POLENTA WITH RABBIT AND PEPPERS

Yield: 6 servings

24 ounces	rabbit meat (preferably young), boneless	1 cup	sliced scallions, 1½ inches, diagonal cuts
to taste	salt and freshly ground black pepper	1 cup	diced red onions
		6 cloves	garlic, minced
1 ounce	flour	1 tablespoon	tomato paste
1 ounce	dry porcini	3	tomatoes, peeled, seeded, and diced (see chapter 1)
½ cup	Marsala		
12 ounces	yellow cornmeal	½ cup	dry white wine
6 cups	water	½ cup	meat glace, veal (see chapter 7)
1 teaspoon	salt		
3 fluid ounces	olive oil	¼ cup	chopped parsley
1	red bell pepper, cut in julienne	1 tablespoon	chopped rosemary
		2½ ounces	butter
1	green bell pepper, cut in julienne		

1. Remove all sinews from the rabbit meat and cut into thin slices. Season with salt and pepper and sprinkle with the flour.

2. Reconstitute the dry *porcini* in the Marsala.

3. Prepare the polenta with the cornmeal and salted water.

4. Roll the polenta between two sheets of plastic wrap with a rolling pin until about ¾ inch thick. Cool completely.

5. Heat ¼ cup olive oil in a large skillet, and quickly sauté the rabbit meat; keep underdone. Remove with a slotted spoon to a suitable dish.

6. Sauté the peppers and scallions in the same skillet, adding more oil if needed. Keep the vegetables crisp. Add to the rabbit.

7. Add the onions to the skillet (again, use more oil if necessary), and lightly brown. Add the garlic and tomato paste and caramelize slightly. Add the tomatoes, *porcini* with Marsala, and dry white wine. Reduce until thick.

8. Add the veal *glace* and adjust the seasonings. Combine the cooked rabbit and vegetables with the sauce. Add the chopped parsley and rosemary.

9. Cut the polenta sheet into the desired shapes (strips or rectangles, for example), and brush with oil or butter. Cook on a conditioned hot grill.

10. To serve, place overlapping grilled polenta slices on each plate and arrange the rabbit-pepper mixture neatly along one edge. Decorate, if desired, with fresh herb sprigs.

Involtini di Polenta con Lumache alla Romana
ROLLED POLENTA WITH SNAILS AND MUSHROOMS

Yield: 6 servings

4 ounces	onions, finely diced	4 ounces	mozzarella
4 ounces	butter	1/4 cup	chopped parsley
6 cloves	garlic, minced	2 tablespoons	chopped mint leaves
18 ounces	mushrooms, diced small	12 ounces	yellow cornmeal
		7 1/2 cups	water
24	snails, cut into small pieces	1 teaspoon	salt
4	anchovy fillets, chopped	2 1/4 cups	fresh tomato sauce with red peppers and pancetta (see chapter 7)
2	chili peppers, chopped		
3 fluid ounces	meat glace (see chapter 7)	1 1/2 cups	julienne of roasted, peeled, and seeded red and green bell peppers (see chapter 1)
to taste	salt and freshly ground black pepper		
2 ounces	Pecorino Romano	6	basil sprigs

1.   Sauté the onions in 2 ounces of butter in a large skillet for 1 minute.

2.   Add the garlic and mushrooms and continue to cook over high heat until the mushrooms are dry and start to caramelize.

3.   Add the snails, anchovies, and chili peppers, and cook until all moisture has evaporated.

4.   Add the meat *glace* and remove from the heat. Add the salt and pepper.

5.   Place this snail filling into a suitable bowl and mix in 2 ounces of Pecorino Romano and 4 ounces of mozzarella. Add the parsley and mint and let cool.

6.   Prepare the polenta with the cornmeal and salted water.

7.   Line a large sheet pan with plastic wrap (or use smaller pans to make separate, smaller sheets).

8.   Spread the cooked polenta on the plastic wrap, using a metal spatula dipped in hot water. Cover with another layer of plastic wrap. Roll with a rolling pin to 1/8-inch uniform sheets.

9. Cut 4½-inch-wide strips from the polenta sheets. Spread the filling over half of each strip and roll up the entire length from one side to the other, like a jelly roll, using the plastic to support the roll. Refrigerate until completely cold.

10. Cut each roll into 3½-inch pieces, similar in size and shape to *cannelloni*.

11. Place each of the rolls in an oval individual-size au gratin dish.

12. Bake in a hot oven 375°F, until well glazed.

13. Serve with Amatricana sauce spooned around the rolls with the sautéed peppers neatly arranged on one side and a basil sprig on the other (see color plate 30).

Pasticcio di Polenta ai Funghi e Prosciutto

POLENTA PIE WITH MUSHROOMS AND PROSCIUTTO

The pie may be set up in individual-size ovenproof, shallow au gratin dishes or layered in a 6- by 9-inch baking pan.

Yield: 6 entrée servings or 18 side dishes

12 ounces	yellow cornmeal, medium coarse	6 ounces	cooked prosciutto, cut in julienne
7½ cups	water	2	chili peppers, chopped
½ teaspoon	salt	½ cup	finely chopped parsley
3½ ounces	butter	3 ounces	Parmesan, finely grated
12 ounces	onions, diced		
1½ cups	heavy cream	6 ounces	mozzarella, coarsely grated
to taste	salt and freshly ground black pepper	6 ounces	Fontina, coarsely grated
1 pound	mushrooms (porcini, chanterelles, and the like)	3 cups	tomato-based sauce

1. Prepare polenta with the cornmeal, water, and salt. Mix in 1½ ounces of butter and pour into an oiled, 3-inch-wide loaf pan. Cover with plastic wrap and cool completely.

2. Heat 1 ounce of butter in a large, noncorrosive skillet, preferably stainless steel or enamel, and add the onions. Cook slowly until very soft, but do not brown.

(continued)

3.   Add the cream to the onions and reduce to a heavy pulp. Remove from the heat, and add salt and pepper to taste.

4.   Clean and slice the assorted mushrooms. Heat 1 ounce of butter in a large skillet, and sauté the mushrooms until lightly caramelized. Add the julienne of *prosciutto* and adjust the seasonings. Remove from the heat and cool.

5.   Turn out the cooled polenta from the loaf mold and cut into ¼-inch-thick slices (like bread).

6.   Brush the baking dishes with the onion mixture and arrange a slice of the polenta on the bottom of each.

7.   Spread the polenta with more onion mixture, the sautéed mushrooms, chopped chili peppers, chopped parsley, and half of the cheeses.

8.   Cover each with another polenta slice.

9.   Spread the tops with more onion mixture, and sprinkle with the cheeses.

10.   Bake in a preheated 350°F oven for 15 to 20 minutes.

11.   Serve with any tomato-based sauce (see chapter 7 for suggestions) on the side or around the polenta. Garnish with fresh herb sprigs if desired.

Gnocchi di Polenta alla Gorgonzola

POLENTA GNOCCHI WITH GORGONZOLA

Yield: 6 servings

12 ounces	*yellow cornmeal*	6 ounces	*Fontina, coarsely grated*
7 cups	*water*		
1 teaspoon	*salt*	6 ounces	*Gorgonzola, coarsely grated*
2 ounces	*butter*		
1 cup	*béchamel sauce (see chapter 7)*	to taste	*freshly ground black pepper, cayenne pepper*
½ cup	*heavy cream*		

1.   Prepare the polenta with the cornmeal, salted water, and butter.

2.   Spread the polenta immediately on a small sheet pan in a ½-inch-thick layer. Cool completely.

3.   With a 3-inch round cutter, cut crescent-shape *gnocchi*. Cut contiguously, and there will be little or no waste of polenta.

4.   Overlap 5 *gnocchi* in each oval au gratin serving dish.

5.   Heat the béchamel sauce with the cream; remove from the heat. Add the cheeses and peppers.

6.   Spoon the cheese sauce over polenta *gnocchi* and bake in a hot (400°F) oven until well glazed.

Polenta alla Napoletana
POLENTA PIE WITH PORK CRACKLINGS, SAUSAGE, AND MOZZARELLA

Yield: 12 servings

8 ounces	pork fatback	6 ounces	pecorino cheese, finely grated
18 ounces	Italian sausage, hot (spicy)	18 ounces	mozzarella, coarsely grated
5 pints	water	3 cups	tomato sauce (see chapter 7)
1 pound	yellow cornmeal		
1½ teaspoons	salt		

1.   Prepare the pork cracklings with the pork fatback (see chapter 1). Strain and reserve the fat remaining.

2.   Bake or broil the Italian sausage until well done and cool. Peel off the casings and cut the meat into thin slices.

3.   Brush a 9- by 12-inch deep baking dish with some of the strained crackling fat.

4.   Bring the water to a boil in a 3-quart, heavy-duty pot and prepare the polenta with the cornmeal and salt. When the polenta is cooked, remove from the heat, and mix in the cracklings, 3 ounces of *pecorino* cheese, and 3 ounces of mozzarella.

5.   Pour half of the polenta mixture into the greased baking dish. Use a metal spatula to smooth it out. When the cornmeal starts to stick to the spatula, dip it in hot water and continue to smooth.

6.   Arrange the sliced sausage and half of the remaining cheeses over the polenta.

(continued)

7. Spread the remaining cornmeal on top, smooth, and cover with the last of the cheeses. (This recipe may be prepared ahead of time up to this point.)

8. Bake in a preheated 350°F oven for 25 to 30 minutes. Let rest for 10 minutes.

9. Slice neatly into 12 sections. Serve with tomato sauce.

— Gnocchi —

GNOCCHI

When dealing with such terms as *original* or *classic* in connection with world-renowned dishes, it is often difficult to isolate the concept behind the dish. Every country has, at one time or another, borrowed a name or idea for a particular dish whose origins over time have become clouded with traditional and regional variations.

A good example of this distortion is *gnocchi* (singular, *gnocco*). Here again one encounters endless dispute. In English we have the term *dumpling,* which applies to almost any starch-based lump of dough. Dumplings may be poached, steamed, fried, or even baked. But in most areas, separate names have evolved to accompany the various shapes, cooking methods, and serving techniques for the different types of dumplings.

Gnocchi are a specialty of northern Italy, and they are known throughout Europe. The French call them *noques;* the Austrians, *Nockerl.* The Austrian influence is very much evident in the Trentino–Alto Adige, particularly in Bolzano and Merano, and in Friuli and Venetia. These *gnocchi* are generally made from cooked potatoes, but other starch products, such as semolina, farina, cornmeal, *choux* paste, or breadcrumbs, are used as well. (See the recipes for *gnocchi* in chapter 2 for examples.)

Mature potatoes are the best to use for potato *gnocchi.* European cooks use the ubiquitous yellow potato common to central Europe. These potatoes tend to produce a light-textured product. Red potatoes and potatoes with a high moisture content are less satisfactory. Ideal would be a potato well suited to both baking and boiling. In any case the potatoes used in Europe are usually of a local variety, with unique growing conditions that affect the quality of the end product. In addition to the type of potato used, each chef usually has a personal preference for using either whole eggs or egg yolks exclusively and for deciding whether semolina is mixed with the potato dough.

Gnocchetti is a term used for a variety of small potato dumplings, or dumplings with ingredients other than potato, usually served with melted butter and grated cheese.

COOKING GNOCCHI

The key to making good *gnocchi* is to have the cooked potatoes as dry as possible. The dough should be firm and pliable. Too much moisture will necessitate a greater amount of flour, resulting in rubbery, heavy *gnocchi.*

1. Halve the washed and peeled potatoes and set them in lightly salted cold water. Heat, and cook slowly until soft. When done, drain the potatoes and

place them in a moderately hot oven to evaporate as much of the water as possible. (Some chefs cook the potatoes in their skins.)

2. With a ricer or potato press, puree the potatoes quickly when dry. If the pulp is too moist, return them briefly to the oven to dry, stirring frequently. Cool the potatoes completely and mix in the recipe ingredients. Combine quickly.

3. Roll the dough into finger-thick cylinders and cut crosswise into 1½-inch-long pieces.

4. Press each *gnocchi* into the curve of a flour-dusted dinner fork or press against the smooth side of a coarse grater. In either case the outside surface should be ridged and the form should be curved, making the gnocchi centers thinner.

5. Cook in a big pot of lightly salted boiling water. When the *gnocchi* start to rise to the surface, remove them with a wire skimmer or spider. Do *not* overcook, or the *gnocchi* will be waterlogged and glassy looking. Drain in a perforated hotel pan or shallow colander.

6. Potato *gnocchi* are usually arranged in au gratin dishes with tomato or cream sauce, topped with cheese, and glazed in a hot oven. It is not uncommon simply to cook the *gnocchi* and serve them in a compatible sauce with a garnish.

Gnocchi di Patate con Salsa di Carciofi
POTATO GNOCCHI WITH STEWED ARTICHOKES

Yield: 6 servings

1 pound	mature yellow or russet potatoes	2	bay leaves
1 ounce	butter, melted	6	sun-ripened tomatoes, peeled, seeded, and diced small (see chapter 1)
2	egg yolks		
2½ ounces	bread flour		
2 ounces	semolina	¼ cup	coarsely chopped parsley
pinch	salt and white pepper		
pinch	nutmeg	2 tablespoons	chopped basil
6	artichokes	to taste	salt and freshly ground black pepper
½ cup	virgin olive oil		
1	onion, sliced	as needed	olive oil
4 cloves	garlic, minced	1 cup	finely chopped scallions
1 cup	dry white wine	1 pound	pancetta, fried crisp
1	chili pepper, chopped	1 cup	grated Parmesan

(continued)

1. Cook the potatoes with the skins on. When cooked, peel and mash while still hot, using a ricer.

2. Add the butter, egg yolks, flour, semolina, salt, white pepper, and nutmeg. Mix the ingredients quickly. Add more flour if necessary to make the dough thick enough to work.

3. Roll and shape the *gnocchi.*

4. Cook the *gnocchi* in a large pot of lightly salted boiling water for 6 to 8 minutes over low heat. Remove with a slotted spoon.

5. Trim the artichokes of all inedible parts.

6. Cut the trimmed artichokes into thin pieces.

7. Heat the olive oil in a casserole and cook the sliced artichokes over moderate heat for 2 minutes. Add the onions and garlic, and cook for several more minutes.

8. Add the wine and reduce by half. Add chili peppers, bay leaves, and tomatoes and simmer for 15 minutes. Add the parsley, basil, salt, and pepper.

9. Coat the cooked *gnocchi* with a little olive oil. Spoon the artichoke sauce on each serving plate and arrange the *gnocchi* neatly in the center of the sauce. Sprinkle with the chopped scallion and crumbled *pancetta.* Sprinkle with the Parmesan cheese.

Gnocchi al Pesto alla Genovese
GNOCCHI WITH BASIL SAUCE, GENOA STYLE

Yield: 6 servings

1 pound	mature yellow or russet potatoes	1/2 cup	melted butter
2	egg yolks	6 cloves	garlic, minced
2 tablespoons	melted butter	6	anchovy fillets
5 to 6 ounces	bread flour	2	chili peppers, chopped
pinch	salt and white pepper		
pinch	nutmeg	1 ounce	pine nuts, lightly toasted
		1 ounce	walnuts, lightly toasted
BASIL SAUCE:		36	basil leaves
1/2 cup	extra-virgin olive oil		

2 ounces	pecorino cheese, finely grated	to garnish	basil sprigs
1	egg yolk	12	tomato petals (see chapter 1)
as needed	melted butter		
¾ cup	finely grated Parmesan		

1. Cook the unpeeled potatoes until soft. Peel and puree with a ricer while still hot. Cool.

2. Add the egg yolks, 2 tablespoons of butter, flour, salt, pepper, and nutmeg to the potatoes. Knead quickly, adding more flour if necessary to work the dough.

3. Roll and shape the *gnocchi*.

4. Cook the *gnocchi* in a large pot of lightly salted boiling water for about 5 minutes. Remove and drain.

5. Puree the olive oil, ½ cup of butter, garlic, anchovies, chili peppers, pine nuts, walnuts, basil, and *pecorino* cheese in a blender (not a food processor) until smooth. Add the egg yolk, and blend for another 20 seconds to achieve a homogeneous sauce. Keep warm (not hot).

6. Spoon the sauce on each serving plate. Coat the *gnocchi* with a little melted butter and arrange in the center of the sauce. Sprinkle with the Parmesan. Decorate with basil sprigs and 2 tomato petals each.

Gnocchi alla Piemontese Gratinati
GNOCCHI AU GRATIN WITH TOMATO SAUCE

Yield: 6 servings

1 pound	mature russet potatoes	6 tablespoons	melted butter
1	egg yolk	6 ounces	Fontina, coarsely grated
2 tablespoons	melted butter	6 ounces	Parmesan, finely grated
5 ounces	bread flour		
pinch	salt and white pepper	2½ cups	tomato sauce (see chapter 7)
pinch	nutmeg	6	basil sprigs

(continued)

1.   Cook the unpeeled potatoes until soft. While still hot, peel and puree with a ricer.

2.   Add the egg yolk, melted butter, flour, salt, pepper, and nutmeg. Mix quickly, adding more flour if necessary to work the dough.

3.   Roll and shape the *gnocchi*.

4.   Cook the *gnocchi* in a large pot of lightly salted boiling water for a few minutes. Remove and drain.

5.   Place the *gnocchi* in individual-size au gratin dishes. Sprinkle with the melted butter and cheese.

6.   Bake in a very hot oven or broil under a top broiler until well glazed.

7.   Spoon the tomato sauce around the *gnocchi*. Garnish each with a sprig of basil.

Gnocchi di Semolina alla Romana
SEMOLINA GNOCCHI AU GRATIN WITH TOMATO SAUCE

Yield: 6 servings

1 quart	milk	6 ounces	Parmesan, grated
8 ounces	semolina	4 ounces	mozzarella, coarsely grated
pinch	salt and white pepper	2¼ cups	tomato sauce (see chapter 7)
pinch	nutmeg		
2	egg yolks	6	basil sprigs
¼ cup	heavy cream		

1.   Scald the milk in a 3-quart saucepan, stirring frequently with a wooden spoon to prevent scorching.

2.   Stir in the semolina carefully in a small stream while whisking to avoid lumps. Keep stirring with a wooden spoon and add the salt, pepper, and nutmeg.

3.   Place a lid partly over the pot to avoid spattering, and cook for about 10 minutes.

4.   Remove from the heat. Combine the egg yolks with the cream and mix into hot semolina. Add half of the Parmesan.

5. Spread the semolina mixture in a ½-inch-thick layer on a moistened small sheet pan. Cool, then cover with plastic wrap. Refrigerate until completely firm.

6. Using a 3-inch round cutter, stamp out crescent-shaped *gnocchi*. Cut contiguously to limit waste.

7. Overlap 6 *gnocchi* in each individual-size au gratin dish. Sprinkle with the mozzarella and remaining Parmesan. Broil under a top broiler or bake on the top rack of a very hot oven until lightly browned and glazed.

8. Spoon tomato sauce around the *gnocchi*. Garnish with the basil sprigs.

Gnocchetti di Spinaci ai Pomodori Secchi
SMALL SPINACH GNOCCHI WITH SUN-DRIED TOMATOES

Yield: 6 servings

1 pound	mature yellow or russet potatoes	1 ounce	dry porcini, reconstituted
4 ounces	fresh spinach, no stems	1 cup	dry white wine
3	egg yolks	1 cup	sun-dried tomatoes, marinated (as purchased)
2 ounces	semolina		
2½ ounces	bread flour	9 fluid ounces	heavy cream
1 ounce	dry white breadcrumbs	¼ teaspoon	freshly ground black pepper
2 tablespoons	melted butter	1 tablespoon	chopped marjoram
pinch	salt and freshly ground black pepper	2 tablespoons	chopped parsley
		to taste	salt
pinch	nutmeg	1 cup	sliced scallions, 1 inch long, diagonally sliced
2 ounces	butter		
½ cup	finely diced onions	¾ cup	grated Parmesan
4 cloves	garlic, minced		

1. Cook the unpeeled potatoes until soft. Peel and puree with a ricer while still hot.

2. Wash the spinach several times in deep, cold water. Drain. Place in a shallow casserole, cover, and quickly steam in their own moisture. Shock in ice water and drain again. Squeeze out all liquid and chop. Place in a food processor, add the egg yolks, and puree.

(continued)

3. Combine the potatoes, spinach/egg puree, semolina, flour, breadcrumbs, melted butter, salt, pepper, and nutmeg. Mix quickly, adding more flour if necessary to work the dough.

4. Roll the dough into finger-thick cylinders, and cut into 1-inch pieces. Roll each piece again with the palm of your hand on a flour-dusted board into a small oval, pointed on both ends. These are the *gnocchetti*.

5. Cook the *gnocchetti* in a large pot of lightly salted boiling water. Remove as soon as they float to the top.

6. Heat the 2 ounces of butter in a large skillet, and sauté the onions for 1 minute. Do *not* caramelize. Add the garlic and reconstituted *porcini*, and cook over moderate heat for several minutes.

7. Deglaze the skillet with the wine, and reduce almost completely.

8. Cut the marinated tomatoes into smaller pieces and add to the skillet. Simmer until well heated.

9. Add the cream, pepper, marjoram, parsley, and salt. Bring to a simmer.

10. Toss the cooked *gnocchetti* with the sauce, and arrange neatly on each serving plate. Sprinkle with the sliced scallions and Parmesan.

Gnocchetti di Ricotta con Salsa di Fegatini e Noci

SMALL RICOTTA GNOCCHI WITH CHICKEN LIVERS AND WALNUTS

Yield: 6 servings

16 ounces	ricotta, very dry	18 ounces	chicken livers, sinews removed
3	egg yolks	1/2 teaspoon	freshly ground black pepper
2 1/2 ounces	semolina		
2 ounces	all-purpose flour	1 tablespoon	flour
pinch	salt and white pepper	1/2 cup	olive oil
pinch	nutmeg	1 1/2 cups	sliced scallion, white parts only, cut 1 inch long, diagonally
1 1/2 ounces	dry white breadcrumbs		
1 fluid ounce	olive oil		

1 cup	julienne of red bell peppers	12 cloves	garlic, roasted (see chapter 1, garlic puree)
1 cup	julienne of green bell peppers		
½ cup	Marsala	½ cup	halved walnuts, toasted
1 cup	dry red wine	½ cup	coarsely chopped basil leaves
6 tablespoons	meat glace (see chapter 7)	as needed	melted butter
1 cup	strained tomato sauce (see chapter 7)	1 cup	finely chopped scallions, green tops only
2	chili peppers, chopped	1 cup	grated Parmesan

1. Make sure the ricotta is very dry. Puree it. Mix the ricotta, egg yolks, semolina, 2 ounces of flour, salt, white pepper, nutmeg, and breadcrumbs in a suitable bowl. Add more flour if needed to make a firm, pliable dough. Let the dough rest for at least 30 minutes.

2. Roll the dough into finger-width cylinders and cut into 1-inch segments. Roll each segment over a flour-dusted board into a tiny oval pointed on both ends. These are the *gnocchetti*.

3. Condition a large skillet by letting some olive oil gradually heat to a moderate temperature. Remove the skillet from the heat.

4. Trim the livers and cut into smaller pieces. Sprinkle with the black pepper and flour.

5. Heat 6 tablespoons of olive oil in a skillet and pan-fry the livers a little at a time over high heat until crisp on the outside but pink on the inside. Remove with a slotted spoon and keep warm.

6. In the same skillet, heat the remaining 2 tablespoons of olive oil, and sauté the scallion whites and red and green peppers quickly. Keep them crisp. Add to the chicken livers.

7. Deglaze the skillet with the wines, and reduce to ½ cup. Add the meat *glace* and strained tomato sauce, and adjust the seasonings.

8. Mix in the chopped chili peppers, roasted garlic cloves, and toasted walnuts.

9. Cook the *gnocchetti* in a large pot of lightly salted boiling water. Remove as soon as they float to the top, and drain.

10. Combine the chicken livers and vegetables with the sauce. Keep hot. Add the chopped basil.

(continued)

11.   Spoon sauce onto each serving plate. Coat the cooked *gnocchetti* with a little melted butter and arrange 10 to 12 in the center of each plate. Sprinkle with the chopped scallion tops and Parmesan.

Gnocchi di Zucca

PUMPKIN GNOCCHI

These *gnocchi* are very often served with a meat sauce or a nut-flavored cream sauce. They make excellent side dishes to accompany an entrée as well.

Yield: 6 servings

1½ pounds	*pumpkin, peeled*
7 ounces	*bread flour*
3 tablespoons	*melted butter*
pinch	*salt and white pepper*
pinch	*nutmeg*
½ cup	*melted butter*
¾ cup	*grated Parmesan*

1.   Remove the seeds from the peeled pumpkin and cut into small pieces. Steam in a double-boiler or cook in a little salted water until almost soft. Drain and place in a 300°F oven to evaporate the excess moisture.

2.   Pass the dry pumpkin through a food mill or ricer. Let cool completely. Mix the flour, 3 tablespoons of melted butter, salt, pepper, and nutmeg with the pumpkin. Knead into a smooth dough.

3.   Roll and shape the *gnocchi.*

4.   Cook the *gnocchi* in a large pot of lightly salted boiling water for about 5 minutes.

5.   Remove the *gnocchi* as they float to the surface with a wire skimmer or spider and drain. Toss with the melted butter and Parmesan and serve.

STOCKS AND SAUCES

Italian sauces are of natural ingredients, usually either vegetable or tomato based, and in many cases are thickened with pureed nuts, cheeses, eggs, or fruits. Flour-based sauces are found mainly in the northern regions, where the influences of French, Austrian, and Swiss cooking are the strongest. In fact, even tomato-based sauces in these regions are often flour based. But in the rest of Italy, reductions and puree-based sauces are more frequently encountered.

It is most important to realize that refined and flavorful sauces are a fundamental part of any good cuisine and should complement the taste and appearance of the foods with which they are served. There should exist a logic behind the marrying of a certain sauce with a particular food.

For stock-based sauces, it is necessary to understand the fundamentals of preparing high-quality white and brown stocks to be used as the backbone of these sauces or to be further altered on their own to achieve a desired viscosity or glaze. These are detailed first in this chapter.

Fondo Bruno di Vitello

BROWN VEAL STOCK

Yield: 2 quarts

1¼ cups	vegetable oil	2 cups	dry white wine
10 pounds	fresh veal bones (not frozen)	2 cloves	garlic
		2	thyme sprigs
2 pounds	veal trimmings	1	rosemary sprig
11 quarts	cold water	3	bay leaves
1 pound	onions, coarsely cut	2	whole cloves
4 ounces	carrots, coarsely cut	15	black peppercorns, crushed
4 ounces	celeriac, coarsely cut		
4 ounces	parsnips, coarsely cut	1 cup	mushroom trimmings
¾ cup	tomato paste	to taste	salt

1. Condition a large roasting pan by coating with half the oil and heating in a 300°F oven for 15 to 20 minutes. Raise the temperature to 500°F, and heat until oil is just below the smoking point.

2. Cut the veal bones into about 2-inch pieces. Add to the hot roasting pan. Do not stir.

3. Roast bones at 500°F until they begin to brown and give off a distinct aroma. Stir, add the veal trimmings, and lower the heat to 450°F. Continue to roast, stirring occasionally, until thoroughly browned.

4. Remove the bones to an 8-gallon stock pot, add 10 quarts of water, and bring to a boil. Reduce the heat, and simmer for about 6 hours.

5. Pour off the fat from the roasting pan, and deglaze with 1 quart of cold water. Heat over the stove to dissolve all the meat drippings. Add to the stock pot.

6. Heat the remaining oil in a large skillet, and add the onions. Let them brown, stirring only as needed to prevent burning. When the onions begin to brown, add the carrots and continue to caramelize. Mix in the celeriac and parsnips.

7. Add the tomato paste and cook over moderate heat until the paste begins to turn brown as well. Stir occasionally.

8. Add the dry white wine, garlic, thyme, rosemary, bay leaves, cloves, black peppercorns, mushroom trimmings, and salt. Add to the stock pot, and simmer for another 2 hours. Strain through fine cheesecloth.

9. Return the liquid to the stove, and simmer until reduced to 2 quarts. Skim off any impurities and fat from the top of the stock as they form.

10. Strain again through a fine-mesh sieve and cool quickly in an ice-water bath. Store in a suitable container, well covered, in the refrigerator after the stock has cooled sufficiently.

Fondo Bianco di Vitello

WHITE VEAL STOCK

White veal stock is considered a neutral stock and is therefore useful in the preparation of vegetable cream soups or as an addition to cream sauces. It is also excellent as a *glace* to be added to reduction sauces with a vegetable *coulis*.

Yield: 4 quarts

6 pounds	fresh veal bones	10	white peppercorns, crushed
3 pounds	veal trimmings		
7 quarts	cold water	3	bay leaves
3 ounces	celeriac	3	cloves
3 ounces	parsnips	5	parsley stems
4 ounces	leeks, white parts only	1	thyme sprig
6 ounces	onions	pinch	grated nutmeg
2 ounces	white turnips	to taste	salt

1. Select veal bones from the neck, back, and rib area. It is important that only fresh bones, not frozen, are used. Chop the veal bones into 2-inch pieces and place in a 6-gallon stock pot with just enough cold water to cover them. Bring to a quick boil and blanch for about 1 minute. Drain off the water, wash the bones and the veal trimmings with fresh water, and drain.

2. Add the 7 quarts of cold water to the bones and bring to a boil.

3. Reduce the heat and simmer for approximately 5 hours over very low heat, skimming constantly to remove any impurities and fat that float to the top.

4. Prepare a *bouquet garni* with the celeriac, parsnips, leeks, onions, and turnips (see chapter 1).

(continued)

5. Prepare a spice sachet with the peppercorns, bay leaves, cloves, parsley, thyme, nutmeg, and salt (see chapter 1).

6. Add the *bouquet garni* and spice sachet to the veal and stock, and simmer for another hour. Adjust the seasonings.

7. Strain through several layers of cheesecloth or a large coffee filter.

8. Cool the stock immediately in an ice-water bath. Store, covered, in a suitable container in the refrigerator after the stock has cooled.

Fondo Bruno di Cacciagione e Selvaggina

BROWN GAME STOCK

The proportion of bones of the different game varieties used in this stock depends largely on the taste of the stock desired. If the stock is to be used in conjunction with a game fowl entrée, use only game fowl bones for the preparation of the stock. If furred game is to be used as an entrée, then use the corresponding bones.

Yield: 2 quarts

1¼ cups	vegetable oil	6 tablespoons	tomato paste
6 pounds	venison bones, cut small	2 cups	dry white wine
		10	juniper berries, crushed
4 pounds	pheasant, partridge, or wild rabbit scraps	15	black peppercorns, crushed
9 quarts	cold water		
12 ounces	onions, coarsely cut	3	bay leaves
4 ounces	carrots, coarsely cut	1	thyme sprig
4 ounces	celeriac, coarsely cut	3	sage sprigs
2 ounces	parsnips, coarsely cut	to taste	salt

1. Condition a large roasting pan by coating with half of the oil and heating in a 300°F oven for 15 to 20 minutes. Raise the temperature to 500°F, and heat until the oil is just below the smoking point.

2. Add the bones and game scraps to the pan. Do not stir.

3. Lower the heat to 450°F and roast, stirring occasionally, until all the bones are thoroughly browned.

4. Remove the bones from the pan and place in a 6-gallon stock pot. Add 8 quarts of cold water, and bring to a boil. Reduce the heat and simmer for 3 hours.

5. Pour off the fat from the roasting pan, and deglaze the drippings with 1 quart of fresh water. Heat on the stove to dissolve the meat drippings. Add to stock pot.

6. Heat the remaining oil in a large skillet and add the onions. Brown, stirring only as needed to prevent burning. When the onions start to brown, add the carrots, celeriac, and parsnips, and continue to caramelize. Add the tomato paste, and cook over moderate heat until brown.

7. Add the white wine, juniper berries, peppercorns, bay leaves, thyme, sage, and salt. Add to the stock pot, and simmer for another 60 to 90 minutes. Strain through cheesecloth.

8. Return the game stock to the stove, and reduce to 2 quarts. Skim off any impurities and fat while reducing.

9. Strain a second time and cool quickly in an ice-water bath. Store in a suitable container, tightly covered, in the refrigerator after cooling.

Fondo di Crostacei

SHELLFISH FOND

Shellfish fonds are always in demand, especially for certain classic seafood sauces and for the preparation of seafood *blanquettes* and ragouts.

When reduced to a gelatinous *glace*, the product should keep successfully for several weeks if stored properly in a noncorrosive, tightly covered container in the refrigerator. The fond can be frozen indefinitely.

Yield: 2 quarts

4 to 5 pounds	*fresh shellfish trimmings and shells from lobster, shrimp, crayfish, and the like*	2 cups	*Moscato d'Asti (sparkling muscatel)*
1 pound	*butter*	4 quarts	*clear chicken broth (see chapter 3)*
4 ounces	*shallots, minced*	10	*black peppercorns, crushed*
4 ounces	*leeks, white parts only, cut small*	1/2 teaspoon	*hot red pepper, crushed*
4 ounces	*fresh fennel, cut small*	3	*bay leaves*
4 ounces	*celeriac, cut small*	1	*tarragon sprig*
1/4 cup	*tomato paste*	pinch	*saffron*
2 cups	*dry white wine (such as Soave)*		

1.   Crush and chop the shellfish shells and trimmings.

2.   Heat the butter in a wide 3-gallon heavy-duty pan, and add the crushed shells and trimmings.

3.   Add the shallots, leeks, fennel, and celeriac, and cook for 5 minutes.

4.   Add the tomato paste, and cook for another 5 minutes. Deglaze with the white wine and sparkling muscatel. Reduce completely.

5.   Add the chicken broth, peppercorns, hot red pepper, bay leaves, tarragon, and saffron, and simmer slowly for about 20 to 30 minutes.

6.   Strain through fine cheesecloth and cool before refrigerating.

7.   When chilled, remove the top layer of solidified butter from the stock. Reserve, wrapped in plastic wrap, in the refrigerator or freezer. (This butter is very useful in the preparation of many classic seafood sauces, ragouts, risottos, and soups.)

8.   Put the strained stock back on the stove and bring to a boil. Simmer and reduce to 2 quarts. Strain again through fine cheesecloth and cool quickly in an ice-water bath. Store in a tightly covered, noncorrosive container in the refrigerator.

—— *Essenze* ——
GLACES

Glaces are reductions of excellent-quality broths or stocks to a semihard gelatinous viscosity. They are practically indispensable in the preparation of classic reduced sauces and in the reinforcement of the flavor of many culinary preparations. When using fish or chicken, start with a broth or stock that is absolutely clear (clarify if necessary) before reducing to make the *glace* (follow the instructions for clarifying broths in chapter 3).

To make a *glace*, reduce the appropriate stock or broth in a large saucepan by half.

- For game *glace (essenza di cacciagione)*, use brown game stock.
- For chicken *glace (essenza di pollo)*, use clear chicken stock.
- For fish *glace (essenza di pesce)*, use clear fish broth.
- For crustacean or seafood *glace (essenza di crostacei)*, use crustacean fond.

Strain into a smaller pot and reduce until the desired viscosity is achieved (usually a heavy, syrupy consistency). While reducing, be sure to skim away any impurities and fats that rise to the surface. Strain a second time before using or storing. Covered tightly, the *glace* will keep for many weeks in the refrigerator. One can freeze a *glace* almost indefinitely.

Salsa Besciamella
BÉCHAMEL SAUCE

Yield: 1 quart

¼ cup	clarified butter (see chapter 1)	pinch	salt and white pepper
1 tablespoon	finely diced onion	pinch	nutmeg
2½ ounces	all-purpose flour	1 tablespoon	butter
5 cups	hot milk		

(continued)

1. Heat the clarified butter in a 2-quart noncorrosive saucepan. Add the onion and cook gently until translucent.

2. Add the flour, and cook over low heat, stirring frequently, for about 8 minutes (do *not* brown the onions or flour). Cool.

3. Pour the hot milk into the roux while whisking vigorously with a wire whip.

4. Simmer for approximately 45 minutes, and add the salt, pepper, and nutmeg. Strain through a fine-mesh sieve.

5. Brush the tablespoon of butter on top of the sauce to prevent a skin from forming, or cover with well-buttered parchment paper until needed.

Salsa Olandese

HOLLANDAISE SAUCE

Classic hollandaise sauce is always made with a reduction as outlined below. Very often, because of convenience or preference, the reduction is omitted, the emulsion made with egg yolks, lemon juice, and water (½ ounce of liquid per yolk), and the finished sauce is flavored with lemon juice and cayenne pepper. According to national health standards, the hollandaise sauce must be served within 2 hours or discarded in order to prevent salmonella food poisoning.

Yield: 2 cups

1 teaspoon	finely minced shallots	3	egg yolks
2 tablespoons	white vinegar	1 cup	butter, melted, hot, but not above 160°F
1	bay leaf		
5	whole black peppercorns, freshly ground	1 tablespoon	lemon juice
		to taste	salt
¼ cup	water		

1. Bring all ingredients to room temperature.

2. Reduce almost completely the shallots, vinegar, bay leaf, and ground peppercorns in a small saucepan. Add the water and bring to a boil. Strain through cheesecloth.

3. Combine the egg yolks with the reduced liquid in a 2-quart stainless steel bowl. Place over a hot water bath and beat vigorously with a fine wire whisk to achieve an emulsion. (The amount of whipping and amount of heat is a fairly delicate balance, and this process may take some practice before becoming second nature.)

4. When the mixture resembles a soft custard, begin to beat in the hot butter very gradually. Add a few drops of water now and then to keep the sauce light.

5. Add the lemon juice and season to taste.

6. Strain through cheesecloth or a fine-mesh sieve if sauce is not perfectly smooth.

7. Keep the hollandaise sauce warm (at about 140°F).

Salsa Maionese

MAYONNAISE

Italian mayonnaise is made primarily with olive oil, which makes it a good deal heavier than the mayonnaise most Americans know. Nowadays olive oil is mixed with sunflower or vegetable oil to lighten the final product. Any oil may be used, mixed with other oils or alone.

Yield: 2 cups

2	*egg yolks*	*³⁄₄ cup*	*sunflower oil (or other preferred oil)*
1 tablespoon	*lemon juice*		
pinch	*salt and white or cayenne pepper*	*1 tablespoon*	*hot white vinegar*
		1 tablespoon	*hot water*
³⁄₄ cup	*olive oil*		

1. Bring all ingredients to room temperature, except the vinegar and water, which should be hot.

2. Whisk the egg yolks with the lemon juice, salt, and pepper in a stainless steel bowl.

3. Beat in the oil gradually, drop by drop at the onset, then in a light stream, until the sauce begins to thicken.

4. Adjust the consistency if desired, by adding more lemon juice, white vinegar, or warm water, depending on taste.

5. Add the hot white vinegar mixed with the hot water to maintain the emulsion.

Coulis di Gamberetti
SHRIMP COULIS

Shellfish *coulis* is a useful addition to reduced sauces and soups. It can also be added to reduced cream for various seafood/pasta dishes. The same formula as that outlined below for shrimp *coulis* can be used to make *coulis d'aragosta* (lobster *coulis*) if you substitute lobster meat for the shrimp.

Yield: 6 to 7 cups

4 ounces	butter	1½ pounds	ripe tomatoes, peeled, seeded, and chopped (see chapter 1)
2 pounds	small shrimp, peeled and deveined		
4 ounces	finely diced shallots	2 quarts	shellfish fond (see recipe earlier in this chapter)
¼ cup	brandy		
2 cups	dry white wine		

1.   Heat the butter in a wide 1-gallon saucepan and add the shrimp. Cook very quickly, and remove the shrimp while they are still underdone. Reserve.

2.   Add the shallots to the same pan, and cook over moderate heat until translucent.

3.   Deglaze the pan with the brandy and flambé (carefully). Add the wine, and reduce by half.

4.   Add the chopped tomatoes, and cook slowly until the mixture has a pureelike consistency.

5.   Add the shellfish fond, and reduce again to 1 quart.

6.   Mix the cooked shrimp into the reduction and bring to a boil. Remove immediately from the heat and puree in a food blender (not a food processor). Strain through a fine-mesh sieve.

7.   Cool quickly in an ice-water bath, and store in a suitable noncorrosive container. Keep refrigerated and tightly covered. Use the *coulis* within 3 days.

Pesto alla Genovese

BASIL SAUCE, GENOA STYLE

Originally the basil was pounded with a mortar and pestle for this sauce, hence the word *pesto*. The wonderful green color of this sauce can be further enhanced with the addition of ½ cup of chopped, raw spinach leaves.

Although most often served with pasta dishes, pesto is also very compatible with poached fish and shellfish.

Yield: 2 cups

2 ounces	pine nuts or walnuts, lightly toasted	to taste	freshly ground black pepper or crushed red pepper
6 cloves	garlic, minced		
1 cup	extra-virgin olive oil	2 ounces	Parmigiano Reggiano, grated
30	basil leaves, no stems		
½ cup	fresh spinach leaves (optional)	1 ounce	Pecorino Romano, grated

1.   Puree the nuts and garlic with the oil in a blender.

2.   Add the basil, spinach, and pepper. Continue to puree until a smooth emulsion is achieved. Add the cheeses and puree for another few seconds.

3.   Reserve in a suitable noncorrosive container, chilled and covered until needed. The pesto should be used within 3 days.

— *Salsa Pomodori Freschi* —
FRESH TOMATO SAUCE

It is impossible to imagine Italian cuisine without its ubiquitous tomatoes and peppers. It is remarkable how recently these foodstuffs were added to the Italian chef's repertoire, for it was not until the discovery of the Americas that they became available to European kitchens.

Botanically, the tomato is what is known as a berry fruit, being pulpy and containing one or more seeds that are not stones (as in a peach, for example). Tomatoes are native to tropical climates and therefore do not tolerate cold storage temperatures. A cool place, about 50°F, is ideal.

While Italian cuisine clearly has never been based solely on the tomato, somehow more arguments concerning Italy's tomato-based products (sauces included) have arisen than debates on other aspects of its cuisine. It may be the ease with which tomatoes are grown and stored or their nutritional wealth, rich in vitamins A and C (in addition to supplying potassium and phosphorus, among other minerals), that have made them so popular. A fresh, sun-ripened tomato is packed with goodness while containing only 30 calories. It is important to note that, like other fruits, tomatoes should not be eaten raw if unripe. Unripe fruits tend to be starchy (the sugars have yet to develop) and difficult to digest.

When considering tomatoes for sauce, use only sun-ripened tomatoes (be careful with the term *vine-ripened*) from local, trusted sources. The tomatoes that are harvested commercially are picked for convenience and economy when still green or pink. They lack flavor, color, and finesse.

Plum tomatoes are often preferred for sauces because of their higher sugar levels, lower moisture content (they are meatier), and bright red pigmentation.

When fresh tomatoes are unavailable, use canned whole plum tomatoes in conjunction with tomato puree and/or paste (paste usually contains sugar). For the ultimate Italian tomato sauce, the best-quality tomatoes, most excellent virgin olive oils, and freshest herbs are imperative.

Salsa di Pomodoro
TOMATO SAUCE

This recipe yields a simple tomato sauce with the typically correct proportion of ingredients. This sauce can be modified with countless additions.

Yield: approximately 2 quarts

3 pints	whole plum tomatoes with liquid (canned)	¾ cup	virgin olive oil
		4 ounces	onions, finely diced

2 cloves	garlic, finely minced	to taste	salt and freshly ground black pepper
2 ounces	green bell pepper, finely diced		
¾ cup	tomato paste	10	basil leaves, chopped
1 pint	tomato puree		
2 tablespoons	lemon juice		

1.   Puree the whole plum tomatoes through the coarse blade of a food mill.

2.   Heat the olive oil in a 4-quart heavy-bottomed saucepan, and add the onions, garlic, and green peppers. Cook over low heat until the onions are translucent.

3.   Stir in the tomato paste, followed by all the tomato puree and the lemon juice.

4.   Simmer the sauce over moderate heat until the desired consistency is achieved (about 1 hour).

5.   Remove from the heat, and add the salt, pepper, and chopped basil.

Fonduta di Pomodoro
TOMATO FONDUE

Tomato fondue is excellent served with seafood, mousseline, or pasta.

Yield: approximately 1 quart

½ cup	virgin olive oil	1 tablespoon	lemon juice
4 ounces	red onions, finely diced	pinch	crushed hot red pepper
2 cloves	garlic, finely minced	to taste	salt and freshly ground black pepper
2 pounds	sun-ripened plum tomatoes, peeled, seeded, and chopped (see chapter 1)	8	basil leaves, coarsely chopped
		2 to 3 ounces	butter

1.   Heat the olive oil in a saucepan and add the onion and garlic. Cook over low heat for 10 minutes until the onions are soft (do not brown).

(continued)

2.   Add the chopped tomatoes and lemon juice. Simmer over low heat until slightly thickened, approximately 20 minutes.

3.   Season with the hot red pepper, salt, and black pepper.

4.   Puree through a food mill and return to the stove. Continue to cook until the desired consistency is achieved. Remove from the heat. Add the chopped basil.

5.   Stir in the butter a little at a time to create an emulsion.

Salsa alla Pizzaiola

PIZZA-STYLE TOMATO SAUCE

Though traditionally used on pizza and pizzalike dishes, this sauce may also accompany broiled beef filets and steaks.

Yield: 5 to 6 cups

INFUSION:		1	chili pepper, chopped
½ cup	dry white wine		
2 tablespoons	virgin olive oil	¾ cup	tomato paste
2	oregano sprigs	2 pounds	sun-ripened tomatoes, peeled, seeded, and diced (see chapter 1)
2	bay leaves		
2	basil sprigs		
1	Italian parsley sprig	1½ cups	dry white wine
		to taste	salt and freshly ground black pepper
½ cup	virgin olive oil		
4 cloves	garlic, finely minced		
4 ounces	onions, finely diced		

1.   Bring the wine and oil for the infusion to a boil. Add the oregano, bay leaves, basil, and parsley. Steep for 30 minutes and strain, reserving the infused liquid.

2.   Heat the ½ cup of olive oil in a 3-quart saucepan, add the garlic and onions, and cook over low heat for several minutes.

3.   Add chopped chili pepper and tomato paste and stir until well combined. Add the diced tomatoes and 1½ cups white wine, and cook over moderate heat to the desired consistency.

4.   Add the salt, pepper, and the herb-infused liquid.

5.   Strain through a fine-mesh sieve.

6.   Additional olive oil may be added at the end.

Salsa alla Marinara

MARINARA SAUCE

This is a quick, no-nonsense Neapolitan sauce of fresh, sun-ripened tomatoes, olive oil, and basil. In some areas, black olives and capers are included. The name *alla marinara,* though usually associated with seafood dishes, means simply "in the sailor's style" and probably referred originally to a meatless sauce.

Yield: 1 quart

3 pounds	*sun-ripened fresh tomatoes*	*¼ cup*	*chopped basil*
¾ cup	*extra-virgin olive oil*	*2 tablespoons*	*chopped parsley*
4 cloves	*garlic, finely minced*		
to taste	*salt and freshly ground black pepper*		

1.   Peel the tomatoes (see chapter 1) and halve. Squeeze out the seeds into a small sieve, and save all juices surrounding them. Strain the juice. Dice the tomatoes small.

2.   Heat the olive oil in a skillet and add the garlic. Cook over moderate heat for a minute or so, but do *not* brown. Add the strained tomato juice.

3.   Add the diced tomatoes, and cook over moderate heat until the sauce starts to thicken.

4.   Add the salt and pepper, and remove from the heat.

5.   Add the basil and parsley.

Salsa all'Amatricana

FRESH TOMATO SAUCE WITH RED PEPPERS AND PANCETTA

Yield: 5 cups

¼ cup	virgin olive oil	to taste	salt and freshly ground black pepper
3 ounces	pancetta, chopped		
6 ounces	onions, finely diced	1 tablespoon	chopped basil
4 cloves	garlic, finely minced	2 tablespoons	chopped parsley
4 ounces	red bell pepper, finely minced	1 ounce	butter
1	chili pepper, chopped	1 ounce	Pecorino Romano, grated
1 cup	dry red wine		
2 pounds	sun-ripened tomatoes, peeled and seeded (see chapter 1)		

1.   Heat the olive oil in a 4-quart saucepan and add the chopped *pancetta*. Render over low heat.

2.   Add the onions, garlic, red pepper, and chili pepper. Cook over low heat until soft.

3.   Add the red wine and reduce completely.

4.   Dice the peeled and seeded tomatoes small, and add to the saucepan. Strain the liquid from the squeezed-out seeds and add as well. Simmer the sauce over moderate heat until thickened to the desired consistency.

5.   Season with salt and pepper and remove from the heat.

6.   Mix in the chopped basil and parsley, butter, and grated cheese. Do not simmer again after adding the cheese.

Salsa alla Bolognese

MEAT SAUCE, BOLOGNA STYLE

This excellent (and frequently used) sauce is especially good for lasagne, tortellini, and spaghetti.

Yield: 2 quarts

2 ounces	pancetta, chopped	4 to 5 cups	hot tomato sauce (see recipe earlier in this chapter)
2 ounces	butter		
6 ounces	onions, diced small	4	tomatoes, peeled, seeded, and diced (see chapter 1)
3 ounces	carrots, diced small		
3 ounces	celery, diced small		
3 cloves	garlic, finely minced	6 tablespoons	meat glace
6 ounces	beef chuck, coarsely ground	to taste	salt and freshly ground black pepper
6 ounces	veal shoulder, coarsely ground		
6 ounces	pork shoulder, coarsely ground	1/4 cup	chopped basil
		2 tablespoons	chopped parsley
2 cups	dry red wine		

1.   Render the *pancetta* in the butter in a wide, heavy-bottomed 4-quart saucepan.

2.   Add the onions, carrots, celery, and garlic, and cook over moderate heat for about 5 minutes.

3.   Add the ground meats, and stew for 10 minutes.

4.   Add the wine and reduce by half.

5.   Add the tomato sauce and diced tomatoes and continue to simmer slowly for 1 hour.

6.   Add the meat *glace,* salt, and pepper, and remove from the heat. Stir in the basil and parsley.

Salsa alla Boscaiola

TOMATO-MUSHROOM SAUCE, WOODSMAN'S STYLE

Yield: 3 to 4 cups

1/4 cup	clarified butter (see chapter 1)	3/4 cup	meat glace
4 ounces	onions, medium-diced	6	tomatoes, peeled, seeded, and diced small (see chapter 1)
4 cloves	garlic, minced		
1	chili pepper, chopped	to taste	salt and freshly ground black pepper
8 ounces	porcini, sliced		
1/2 cup	Marsala	2 tablespoons	chopped Italian parsley
2 cups	dry white wine	1 tablespoon	chopped oregano
3/4 cup	tomato sauce (see recipe earlier in this chapter)	2 ounces	butter (optional)

1.   Heat the clarified butter in a large skillet, and sauté the onions until they are lightly browned. Add the garlic, chili pepper, and *porcini*, and sear. Remove only the mushrooms with a slotted spoon.

2.   Deglaze the pan with the wines, and reduce to approximately ½ cup.

3.   Add the tomato sauce and meat *glace*, and continue to simmer until the sauce has a light coating consistency.

4.   Add the diced tomatoes and simmer to the desired consistency.

5.   Return the mushrooms to the sauce and adjust the seasonings.

6.   Mix in the Italian parsley and oregano and the butter if desired.

Salsa d'Aglio e Peperoni Rossi

GARLIC AND RED-PEPPER SAUCE

This sauce may be made more pungent by adding more chili peppers, green pepper-corns, chopped capers, chopped olives, or mustard. It is excellent with pork, poultry, or seafood.

Yield: 1 quart

2 ounces	butter	GARNISH:	
1 cup	finely diced onions	1/2 cup	small-diced red and green bell peppers
10 cloves	garlic, minced		
2 cups	dry white wine	1/2 cup	peeled, seeded, and diced tomatoes (see chapter 1)
1/2 cup	Marsala		
2	roasted red bell peppers (see chapter 1)		
		1 tablespoon	butter
		4 ounces	bacon, diced
1 cup	brown veal stock (see recipe earlier in this chapter)	2 tablespoons	chopped oregano
		2 tablespoons	chopped parsley
1	chili pepper, chopped		
to taste	salt and freshly ground black pepper		

1.   Heat the butter in a saucepan, and sauté the onions until lightly browned. Add the garlic and cook for a few more minutes.

2.   Deglaze the pan with the wines, and reduce to 1 cup.

3.   Seed the red peppers, cut into small pieces, and puree in a blender. Add the red pepper puree, veal stock, and chili peppers to the wine reduction and bring to a simmer. Adjust seasonings and keep warm.

4.   Prepare the garnish by sautéing the diced peppers and tomatoes quickly in a little butter. Cut the bacon into squares and pan-fry until crisp. Drain off the fat and place on absorbent paper.

5.   Combine the garnish and herbs with the sauce.

Salsa Crema al Pomodoro
TOMATO CREAM SAUCE

This too is a versatile sauce. If using for fish or seafood dishes (such as a mousse-line), add ½ cup fish *fumet* when adding the wine. Garnish with a chiffonade of basil.

Yield: 4 cups

2 pounds	butter	1	chili pepper, chopped
2 ounces	onions, finely diced	1	bay leaf
2 ounces	leeks, white parts only, finely sliced	1 cup	dry white wine
		1½ cups	heavy cream, reduced to ¾ cup
2 cloves	garlic, minced		
2 ounces	fennel, thinly sliced	to taste	salt and cayenne pepper
2 pounds	sun-ripened tomatoes, peeled, seeded, and finely chopped (see chapter 1)		

1. In a large skillet, heat the butter and cook the onions, leeks, garlic, and fennel over moderate heat until soft but not brown.

2. Add tomatoes, chili pepper, bay leaf, and white wine, and simmer over low to moderate heat until sauce resembles a thick puree.

3. Add the reduced cream and heat to a simmer. Strain through a fine-mesh sieve, and add the salt and cayenne.

Salsa di Peperoni Rossi, Dolce
SWEET RED-PEPPER SAUCE

Sweet red peppers have always been appreciated for their pungent flavor. They have been enjoyed the world over since being introduced from the New World in the six-teenth century. Spain and Hungary both dry and grind red peppers of various kinds into paprika. Around the Mediterranean and in the Middle East, red peppers are often scorched, peeled, and marinated, to be served as appetizers or in salads. Naturally they are ubiquitous in the cuisines of South and Central America, their place of origin. When scorched, peeled, and pureed with an emulsifying ingredient, red peppers make an excellent sauce, the application of which is modern but is derived from an age-old concern for taste and nutrition.

Yield: 1 quart

2 cups	chicken broth (see chapter 3)	3 cloves	garlic, minced
2 cups	dry white wine	2 ounces	carrots, finely sliced
1	thyme sprig	2 ounces	celeriac, finely sliced
3	bay leaves	6 tablespoons	tomato paste
10	black peppercorns, crushed	1 pound	red peppers, roasted and peeled (see chapter 1)
5 ounces	butter	to taste	salt and cayenne pepper
2 ounces	red onions, finely sliced	1/2 cup	chicken glace
2 ounces	leeks, white parts only, finely sliced		

1.   Prepare an infusion by combining 1 cup of the chicken broth with the white wine. Reduce to 1 cup and add the thyme, bay leaves, and peppercorns. Remove from the heat, and steep 30 minutes. Strain through cheesecloth and reserve.

2.   Heat 2 ounces of butter in a 1-quart saucepan. Add the onions, leeks, garlic, carrots, and celeriac. Smother, tightly covered, over low heat. Do not brown.

3.   Add the tomato paste and continue to cook over low heat. Add the remaining cup of chicken broth and the herb infusion.

4.   Seed the roasted peppers. Cut into small pieces and add to the saucepan.

5.   Puree the sauce in a blender (not a food processor) until very smooth.

6.   Reheat in a suitable saucepan. Add the salt and cayenne. Reduce the sauce if it seems too thin; add some more broth if too thick.

7.   Stir in the chicken *glace*, which intensifies the sauce's flavor.

8.   Just before serving, stir in the remaining 3 ounces of butter to achieve an emulsion. If the sauce is not to be served immediately, do *not* mix in the remaining butter. The sauce should keep for up to 1 week if refrigerated properly.

Salsa Alle Verdure
VEGETABLE SAUCE

This sauce is excellent with poached meats or fish.

Yield: 5 cups

2 cups	dry white wine	2 ounces	fresh fennel, thinly sliced
1/4 cup	balsamic vinegar		
1/2 cup	virgin olive oil	1 quart	beef broth (see chapter 3)
4 cloves	garlic, minced		
4 ounces	leeks, white parts only, thinly sliced	to taste	salt and freshly ground black pepper
2 ounces	onions, thinly sliced	2 tablespoons	chopped parsley
3 ounces	carrots, thinly sliced	1 tablespoon	chopped tarragon
2 ounces	celeriac, thinly sliced	4 ounces	butter
2 ounces	parsnips, thinly sliced		

1.   Combine the white wine and balsamic vinegar in a noncorrosive saucepan, and reduce to ½ cup; reserve.

2.   Heat the olive oil in a 3-quart noncorrosive saucepan and add the garlic, leeks, onions, carrots, celeriac, parsnips, and fennel. Cover and cook over moderate heat for 10 minutes, stirring frequently.

3.   Add 2 cups of beef broth, and continue to cook over low heat until the vegetables are completely soft. Add the salt and pepper.

4.   Mix in the parsley and tarragon. Puree in a blender (not a food processor) until smooth. Add more broth to achieve a light coating consistency. Reserve.

5.   Just before serving, reheat the sauce. Add the reduction of wine and vinegar to taste. Stir in the butter to create an emulsion. This sauce should be used soon after preparing.

Salsa Crema all'Erbe

HERB CREAM SAUCE

A variety of green vegetables and herbs can be used in making this sauce, including spinach, watercress, arugula, and fennel. When making green, or herbal, sauces, a number of points should be remembered:

- All greens must be kept cold while working with them in order to retain their natural color.
- Always use noncorrosive cooking utensils.
- Use no acid, unless it is added immediately before serving.
- Herbs and tender leaf vegetables (such as spinach, sorrel, basil, parsley, asparagus, watercress, arugula, or fennel) are quickly precooked: steamed or sweated in a little water and butter, then cooled, pressed, and pureed.
- Stalk vegetables should be peeled, chopped, and quickly smothered with some finely cut leek whites, shallots, or onions in butter until soft, immediately cooled, and then pureed with just enough liquid (nonacid!) in a blender (do not use a food processor).
- Reduced white stocks or *glaces* can be added to increase potency.
- Use reduced cream and/or butter to improve texture and body.
- Season with a pinch of nutmeg, freshly ground black pepper, or cayenne pepper.
- Do not subject cream sauces with herbs or leaf vegetables to prolonged high heat. It is best to prepare them *à la minute;* that is, quickly cooked and served.

Yield: 3 cups

4 ounces	*greens*	*to taste*	*salt and freshly ground black pepper*
1 ounce	*butter*		
2 ounces	*leeks, white parts only, finely sliced*	*to taste*	*nutmeg*
		2 cups	*heavy cream*
2 ounces	*celery hearts, finely sliced*		
4 cups	*white veal stock (see recipe earlier in this chapter) or chicken broth (see chapter 3)*		

1.   Trim and wash all greens carefully. Quickly blanch or steam them in a bit of water, drain, shock in cold water, and drain again. Chop and refrigerate.

2.   Heat the butter in a small, noncorrosive saucepan. Smother the leeks and celery over low heat. Add the stock or broth, and simmer until soft.

(continued)

3.   Add the salt, pepper, and nutmeg. Remove from the heat and cool.

4.   Place the chilled greens and softened, cooled leeks and celery in a blender; blend at high speed to achieve an emulsion. Strain through a fine-mesh sieve into a suitable noncorrosive container. Cover and refrigerate this *coulis* until needed.

5.   Reduce the cream by half, and add the *coulis*. Heat and adjust the seasonings. Serve immediately.

Salsa Crema al Pepe Verde

CREAM SAUCE WITH GREEN PEPPERCORNS

This sauce is excellent with poached sweetbreads, sautéed fowl, or veal or pork *médaillons*. It can be kept, tightly covered and refrigerated, for a week or more if the cream is not added; after storing in this way, reheat the sauce and add the cream just before serving.

Yield: 2½ cups

1 ounce	butter	2 cups	heavy cream, reduced to 1 cup
½ cup	diced scallions, white parts only	to taste	salt and freshly ground black pepper
4 cloves	garlic, minced		
½ cup	Marsala	½	red pepper, cut in brunoise and quickly sautéed
1½ cups	dry white wine		
½ cup	poultry glace		
2 tablespoons	green peppercorns, drained	3	whole scallions, finely sliced

1.   Heat the butter in a saucepan. Add the ½ cup of scallions and the garlic and cook, without browning, for 1 minute.

2.   Add the wines and reduce to ½ cup.

3.   Add the poultry *glace* and green peppercorns.

4.   Add the reduced cream, salt, and pepper. Stir in the sautéed *brunoise* of red pepper and sliced scallions.

Salsa Crema di Porrino

CREAM SAUCE WITH CHIVES

This sauce is delicious with poached white meats as well as red meats, smoked ox tongue, and sweetbreads. If using with poached fish or seafood, replace the meat *glace* with fish *glace*.

Yield: 2½ cups

½ ounce	butter	2 cups	heavy cream, reduced to 1 cup
1 ounce	shallots, finely diced		
1 ounce	mushroom trimmings (clean and fresh)	to taste	salt and white or cayenne pepper
		to taste	nutmeg
1 cup	Moscato d'Asti (sparkling muscatel)	2 tablespoons	grated fresh horseradish
2 cups	dry white wine	¼ cup	chives, finely chopped
2 tablespoons	lemon juice		
½ cup	chicken glace	¼ cup	whipped cream

1.   Heat the butter in a 2-quart noncorrosive saucepan. Add the shallots and mushrooms, and cook, covered, until the shallots are translucent.

2.   Add the wines and lemon juice and reduce to ½ cup.

3.   Add the chicken *glace,* and continue to simmer until the sauce has a light coating consistency.

4.   Stir in the reduced cream, and add the salt, pepper, and nutmeg. Strain through a fine-mesh sieve or cheesecloth.

5.   Add the horseradish and chives just before serving. Fold in the whipped cream to achieve an emulsion, and serve.

Salsa Crema alla Mostarda
MUSTARD CREAM SAUCE

This sauce is suitable for *à la minute* (quickly cooked) items such as pork *médaillons,* poultry breasts, sweetbreads, or calf's liver.

Yield: 2½ cups

½ ounce	butter	¾ cup	veal glace
½ cup	diced scallions, white parts only	2 cups	heavy cream, reduced to 1 cup
1 cup	dry vermouth	2 to 3 tablespoons	prepared mustard
2 cups	dry white wine		
2	bay leaves	to taste	salt and freshly ground black pepper
10	black peppercorns, crushed	¼ cup	whipped cream
1	thyme sprig		
1 stalk	fresh fennel, chopped		

1. Heat the butter in a 2-quart noncorrosive saucepan. Add the scallions, and cook over low heat for 1 minute.

2. Add the wines, bay leaves, peppercorns, thyme, and fennel. Reduce to about ¾ cup.

3. Add the veal *glace,* and simmer until the sauce has a light coating consistency.

4. Add the reduced cream, and return to simmer. Mix about ¼ cup of this mixture with the mustard, then stir the mustard into the saucepan. Add salt and pepper, and strain through a fine-mesh sieve or cheesecloth.

5. Fold in the whipped cream just before serving.

Salsa Crema al Profumo di Zafferano

CREAM SAUCE WITH SAFFRON

This sauce is suggested for poached fish. If adding the optional hollandaise, remove the finished saffron sauce from the heat before whisking in the hollandaise to create a heavier sauce.

Yield: 2 cups

1 ounce	butter	2¼ cups	heavy cream, reduced (by half) to 9 fluid ounces
2 tablespoons	finely chopped shallots		
1 ounce	mushroom trimmings	to taste	cayenne pepper
1½ cups	dry white wine	2 tablespoons	hollandaise sauce, optional (see recipe earlier in this chapter)
pinch	saffron		
¾ cup	fish glace		

1. Heat the butter in a 2-quart saucepan. Sweat the shallots and mushroom trimmings.

2. Add the wine and saffron; reduce to about ¼ cup.

3. Add the fish *glace*, and bring to a simmer.

4. Add the reduced cream and cayenne. Strain through a fine-mesh sieve.

5. If desired, remove the sauce from the heat, and whisk in the hollandaise sauce, creating an emulsion.

Salsa Crema ai Carciofi
ARTICHOKE CREAM SAUCE

Because of the acid in this sauce, do not attempt to keep it for a prolonged period of time.

Yield: 3 cups

6 ounces	artichoke bottoms, cooked (see chapter 12)	to taste	white or cayenne pepper
		to taste	nutmeg
1 ounce	spinach, quickly blanched, drained, and chopped	1 ounce	shallots, minced
		4 cups	dry white wine
1	parsley sprig, leaves only	2	bay leaves
1	basil sprig, leaves only	1 cup	fish glace
1 cup	chicken broth (see chapter 3)	2 cups	heavy cream, reduced to 1 cup

1.   Combine the artichoke bottoms, spinach, parsley, and basil in a blender (do not use a food processor). Add the chicken broth, and puree until an emulsion is formed. Add the pepper and nutmeg, and strain this *coulis* through a fine-mesh sieve. Keep refrigerated in a noncorrosive container, covered tightly. It should keep well like this for approximately 3 days.

2.   Combine the shallots, white wine, and bay leaves in a small saucepan. Reduce to about ½ cup, and add the fish *glace*. Bring to a boil, and strain through cheesecloth. Cover tightly and reserve in the refrigerator. This should keep for up to 1 week.

3.   To finish the sauce just before serving, for *each* serving, heat 2 tablespoons of the *glace* reduction, 2 tablespoons of reduced cream, and 1 tablespoon of the artichoke *coulis*. Bring to a simmer and serve immediately.

Scozia di Gamberi Aurora
LIGHT HOLLANDAISE SAUCE WITH SHRIMP COULIS

This is a great sauce with steamed lobster, shrimp, or scallops. The sauce can also be prepared with mayonnaise, rather than hollandaise sauce, and served lukewarm if desired.

Yield: 2 cups

1 cup	*hollandaise sauce (see recipe earlier in this chapter)*	*2 tablespoons*	*dry sherry (Manzanilla or fino is best)*
¼ cup	*shrimp coulis (see recipe earlier in this chapter)*	*½ cup*	*whipped cream*

1.   Heat the shrimp *coulis* and combine with the hollandaise in a small saucepan. Add the sherry and heat to 140°F.

2.   Fold in the whipped cream and serve immediately.

Zabaione alle Verdure e Pepe Verde

VEGETABLE SABAYON WITH GREEN PEPPERCORNS

This sauce is an excellent accompaniment to poached or steamed salmon, scallops, or other seafood. It is equally good with poached sweetbreads, ox tongue, and poultry *suprêmes*. If the *sabayon* is to be used with fish, use a fish broth in preparation; if it accompanies meat, use beef broth; if it accompanies poultry, use chicken broth.

Yield: 2 cups

1 tablespoon	*brunoise of carrots*	*2*	*egg yolks*
1 tablespoon	*brunoise of celeriac*	*to taste*	*salt and cayenne pepper*
1 tablespoon	*brunoise of fennel*		
1 tablespoon	*brunoise of leeks*	*1 teaspoon*	*green peppercorns, drained*
¾ cup	*fish, beef, or chicken broth (see chapter 3)*	*1 tablespoon*	*finely chopped chives*
1 cup	*dry white wine*	*½ cup*	*whipped cream*
¼ cup	*Moscato d'Asti (sparkling muscatel)*		

1.   Cook the carrots, celeriac, fennel, and leeks in the broth until soft. Strain the liquid and reserve both.

2.   Combine the wines and the vegetable broth, and reduce to ½ cup.

(continued)

3.   Combine the egg yolks and the wine/broth reduction in a 2-quart stainless steel bowl. Beat over a hot water bath until the yolks begin to thicken, and a cooked emulsion is formed. Season with salt and cayenne pepper.

4.   Add the green peppercorns, chives, and the cooked vegetable *brunoise*.

5.   Fold in the whipped cream, and serve immediately.

Zabaione al Caviale Rosa
SABAYON WITH SALMON CAVIAR

This is another sauce that is excellent with poached or steamed salmon or scallops.

Yield: 2 cups

2	egg yolks	to taste	salt and cayenne pepper
¼ cup	shrimp coulis (see recipe earlier in this chapter)	2 tablespoons	salmon roe
¼ cup	dry white wine	½ cup	whipped cream

1.   Combine the egg yolks with the shrimp *coulis* and white wine in a 2-quart stainless steel bowl. Place over a hot water bath, and whip vigorously with a fine wire whip until the yolks begin to thicken. Season with salt and pepper.

2.   Fold in the salmon roe and whipped cream. Serve immediately.

Burro al Vino Rosso

RED-WINE BUTTER SAUCE

This sauce frequently accompanies poached salmon, red snapper, or shellfish. It can be adapted for meats and poultry by substituting the appropriate *glace*.

Yield: ½ cup (approximately 2 servings)

1 teaspoon	finely diced shallots	2 tablespoons	fish glace
1 tablespoon	red wine vinegar	to taste	salt and freshly ground black pepper
½ cup	Barolo		
¼ teaspoon	chopped chili pepper	2 ounces	butter

1.   Combine the shallots, vinegar, wine, and chili pepper in a small saucepan. Reduce to about 2 tablespoons, and strain into a small skillet.

2.   Add the fish *glace*, and bring to a simmer. Remove from the heat, and add the salt and pepper.

3.   Whisk in a little butter at a time until a creamy consistency is achieved.

Burro Bianco all'Erbe

WHITE-WINE BUTTER SAUCE WITH HERBS

This sauce is usually served with *suprêmes* of chicken or partridge, as well as with sweetbreads. If used for seafood, replace the chicken *glace* with fish *fumet*.

Yield: ¾ cup (3 servings)

1 teaspoon	finely diced shallots	2 ounces	butter
1 tablespoon	white vinegar	1 tablespoon	chopped parsley
½ cup	dry white wine	1 tablespoon	chopped tarragon
2 tablespoons	chicken glace	1 tablespoon	minced chives
to taste	salt and freshly ground black pepper	¼ cup	whipped cream

(continued)

1.   Combine the shallots, vinegar, and white wine in a small saucepan. Reduce to about 2 tablespoons, and strain into a small skillet.

2.   Add the chicken *glace,* and bring to a simmer. Remove from the heat, and add the salt and pepper.

3.   Whisk in a little butter at a time until the sauce has a creamy consistency. Add the parsley, tarragon, and chives.

4.   Just before serving, fold in the whipped cream.

Maionese Tiepida al Profumo d'Aragosta
WARM LOBSTER MAYONNAISE

This sauce may be served with steamed or poached lobster, crayfish, shrimp, and scallops.

Yield: 2 cups

¼ *cup*	*lobster coulis (see shrimp coulis, earlier in this chapter)*	*2 tablespoons*	*warm dry sherry wine*
2 tablespoons	*fish glace*	½ *cup*	*whipped cream*
1 cup	*mayonnaise (see recipe earlier in this chapter)*	*to taste*	*salt and cayenne pepper*

1.   Heat the lobster *coulis* and fish *glace.* Stir into the mayonnaise. Keep warm.

2.   Add the lightly heated sherry, and fold in the whipped cream. Add the salt and pepper and serve immediately.

FISH AND SHELLFISH

World fish consumption has increased significantly over the last fifteen years (much to the despair of environmentalists, who abhor the overharvesting techniques frequently used, and chefs, who more and more see the quality of fish handling declining because of increased yields). The reason for this increased popularity is simple: today's diners want not only fresh foods, but lighter foods, with less fat. Seafood is generally an excellent source of protein, vitamins, and minerals, while being low in fat.

In Italy almost every region is bound to the sea. Her entire coastline is blessed with many fishes, and this abundance has fortunately always been at the pinnacle of her culinary tradition.

Seafood can be classified into two categories: fin fish and shellfish. Fin fish include all edible freshwater and saltwater fishes, whereas shellfish are the crustaceans, including crayfish, shrimp, lobsters, and crabs, and the mollusks, which include mussels, clams, oysters, scallops, snails, and *scungilli* (whelks).

To maintain purchased seafood in the best possible condition, always make sure the fish was gutted immediately after it was caught. An additional precaution is to remove, at the same time, the intestines and gills, both being major sources of bacterial contamination. Digestive enzymes, like our own, are very powerful, and if not cleaned out quickly, will attack the walls of the cavities in which they are present.

To discern acceptable quality when buying fish, follow these guidelines:

- All seafood should have a clean, even sweetish odor.
- The eyes of the fish should be clear, not milky. In addition, the eyes should not have sunk into their cavities. This is a sign of dehydration and age.
- The inside of the gills should be bright red with a touch of the same sweetish odor. They should not be grayish or sticky.
- When pressed with the finger, the flesh should be firm and elastic to the touch, almost resistant to the finger's pressure. If scales fall off easily, the fish is old.

COOKING FISH

Most fish require far less cooking time than meat does because the flesh contains much less connective tissue than that of other animals. Overcooking fish, either for too long a time or at too high a temperature, will cause the proteins in the flesh to contract and toughen. Cooking methods depend on the composition and structure of the fish being prepared. Therefore, the fat content of the fish is also important. Fatty fish are best suited for broiling, baking, or poaching, whereas lean fish are more suitable for sautéing or deep-frying. Cooking methods should, in any case, coincide with the preference for leaner foods with higher protein content but less fat. Although traditional cooking techniques sometimes favor or even demand the deep-frying of a particular item or the accompaniment of a reduction or cream sauce, in choosing preparation techniques, the chef must consider the question more and more diners ask today: "How will it affect my health?"

Since most seafood is low in fat and high in protein, it is ideal for weight reduction diets. In addition, seafood contains no more sodium than a like portion of meat. The fat content of fish may vary from 1 to 25 percent. Fish such as cod, haddock, and sole may be even less than 1 percent fat, while mackerel, lake trout, and some salmon may actually contain more that 25 percent. The protein content is more consistent, usually around 20 percent. The mineral content is from 1.5 to 2 percent and will vary according to fat content. But it is important to remember that the fatty fish are an excellent source of vitamin A. Even caviar, as expensive and fatty as it is, is a potent source of minerals.

POACHING

Poaching can be defined as cooking in liquid just below the simmering point, at 140° to 185°F. There are several categories of poaching.

Deep-liquid poaching (submerged): The item is slowly cooked on top of the stove in a large amount of water, court bouillon, or stock. The cooking liquid is not usually reserved, and a separate sauce is made.

Items for deep-poaching may be either large or small, whole fish or single servings. If whole fish are poached, the deep-poaching method must be used, and in order not to lose all of the flavor of the fish in the poaching liquid, a highly flavored cooking medium is used. If deep-poaching a large piece or a whole fish, always start it in cold water so that skin and flesh do not contract and distort the shape of the fish or rupture (an exception to this rule is the famous *truite au bleu*). Starting in hot water may also cause the outside to be overdone long before the inside is cooked at all.

Shallow-poaching: This technique is usually reserved for small whole fish, or individual fillets. It resembles braising in many ways, except for the shorter cooking time. The fish is placed on a bed of chopped shallots or aromatics in a well-buttered shallow dish. A small amount of liquid, usually fish stock or white wine, is then added, never enough to fully cover the fish. The fish is then covered with buttered or oiled parchment paper that is vented (also known as a *cartouche*).

The most important thing to remember when shallow-poaching is never to boil the liquid. The best results occur at temperatures between 145° and 185°F. This produces moist, tender flesh with the least amount of protein loss. After the liquid, with the fish in it, has reached this temperature (heated on the stove), place in a 300° to 325°F oven until cooked to the desired degree of doneness.

Remember that small fish have a different fiber, fat, and protein structure than large fish do, and therefore take proportionately less time to cook. For example, a fillet of sole needs only a few minutes to reach an internal temperature of 160°F, whereas a whole, boneless, stuffed small fish may take from 8 to 10 minutes or longer. Lower temperatures are important in any case when cooking fish.

When the fish is cooked, remove from the pan and keep warm and covered. The remaining liquid from the cooking process becomes the key ingredient in the sauce for the finished product. Much of a shallow-poached fish's flavor goes into the liquid, and this makes an excellent sauce base. The liquid may be finished by

- the addition of fresh butter (emulsification)
- the addition of reduced cream and herbs
- the addition of a cream/egg yolk liaison
- any of the above plus aromatics and *coulis*
- the addition of vegetables, *coulis,* or olive oil (no cream or butter)

Poaching in encasement: This process involves complex preparation of mousselines, custards, timbales, and other specialties. This is actually a technique whereby the fish is partially poached and partially steamed. Items to be cooked are placed in a special timbale or mold and set in a *bain-marie* filled with boiling water, which should reach about two-thirds of the way up the mold. If the item is prepared on the stove-top, it is best to insert a wire mesh rack under the *bain-marie* to prevent scorching from the heat source. Cover the *bain-marie* loosely and cook over low heat.

If cooked in the oven, cover the timbale or mold completely with buttered parchment paper or foil. Place the water bath with the timbale or mold in it in a low oven, 300° to 325°F or below. Never allow the water to boil.

If these procedures are followed, the temperature surrounding the mold will never exceed 212°F. The fish preparation will cook thoroughly yet evenly and have a smooth, velvety texture.

COURT BOUILLON

Court bouillon is acidulated water that sometimes contains sliced carrots, onions, and celery along with bay leaves, whole peppercorns, salt, and herbs. Seafood is often poached in it; it is also used to poach variety meats.

STEAMING

Low-pressure steam cooking has become a much used method for the cooking of fish and other seafood. When properly executed, there is less loss of nutrients, a more natural flavor, and less shrinkage.

The most obvious danger here is applying excessive heat pressure. This decreases the cooking time considerably. In fact, an increase of 5 pounds of pressure equals a 228°F increase in temperature.

The amount of pressure used depends on the type of equipment being used. A steam pressure cooker that is sealed and builds up incredible amounts of steam pressure is not suitable for tender and delicate fish flesh. The product will self-destruct. To steam fish, the steam must be under no pressure and must be able to surround the food it is cooking. This is accomplished by venting. The best and simplest way to accomplish this is to use a deep hotel pan with a perforated insert, or steaming basket.

Anguilla con Salsa Verde

BRAISED EEL IN WHITE WINE AND HERBS

If you purchase live eels, the easiest way to kill them is to place them in a container of coarse salt. This also serves to deslime the fish. To remove the skin, knot a strong cord around the neck, just below the animal's gills, leaving a small loop at one end. Secure this loop around a nail that has been driven into a board; the cord will keep the slimy eel in place. With a sharp blade, cut the skin of the eel just below and around the neck, then grasp the loosened skin with both hands and peel it off with a quick pull (pliers will help if you are having difficulties). Cut off the head and carefully cut open the soft underbelly just beneath the head to remove the gall bladder.

If using baby eels, it is entirely unnecessary to skin them. If fillets are desired, cut the flesh on both sides from the backbone. This flesh is firm and fattier than that of most fish. Therefore, a longer cooking time than normal is required.

Yield: 6 servings

1½ ounces	butter	to taste	freshly ground black pepper
4 ounces	leeks, white parts only, sliced	to taste	nutmeg
4 ounces	celeriac, cut in julienne	to taste	bay leaves
4 ounces	fennel, cut in julienne	3	egg yolks
4 ounces	carrots, cut in julienne	1½ cups	heated cream
6 cloves	garlic, finely minced	¼ cup	finely chopped parsley
3 pounds	baby eels	1 tablespoon	chopped oregano
1½ cups	dry white wine	1 tablespoon	chopped basil
1½ cups	chicken broth (see chapter 3)	24	large potato balls, steamed (use a melon scoop to size)
to taste	salt		

1.   Heat the butter in a shallow 6-quart casserole. Add the leeks, celeriac, fennel, carrots, and garlic, cover, and smother for a couple of minutes.

2.   Cut the eels into 1-inch pieces. Add to the pan on top of the vegetables.

3.   Add the wine, cover, and cook for a few minutes.

4.   Add the chicken broth, salt, pepper, nutmeg, and bay leaves, and continue to cook, uncovered, for several minutes.

5.   Mix the 3 egg yolks with 6 tablespoons of the warm cream to make a liaison.

6.   Add 1 cup of the hot cream to the eel mixture, and bring to a simmer. Remove from the heat, and mix in the egg/cream liaison carefully, to create an emulsion.

7.   Adjust the seasonings, and add the chopped parsley, oregano, and basil.

8.   Serve in earthenware bowls or soup plates with neatly turned, boiled potato balls.

Anguilla in Salsa di Barolo
EEL IN BAROLO SAUCE

Yield: 6 servings

1/4 cup	virgin olive oil	2	thyme sprigs
3 ounces	onions, diced small	2	bay leaves
		4 pounds	baby eels
2 ounces	carrots, cut small	2 1/2 to 3 ounces	butter
2 ounces	fennel, cut small	1 cup	small, trimmed mushrooms with stems
2 ounces	celeriac, cut small		
3 cloves	garlic, minced		
2	chili peppers, chopped	1 cup	small round carrots, steamed
6	sun-ripened tomatoes, peeled, seeded, and chopped (see chapter 1)	1 cup	small pearl onions, steamed
		1/2 cup	pitted small black olives
2 cups	chicken broth (see chapter 3)	1/2 cup	coarsely sliced scallions, tops only
3 to 4 cups	Barolo		

1.   Heat the olive oil in a 4-quart saucepan, and add the diced onions, carrots, fennel, celeriac, and garlic. Stirring frequently, brown slightly.

2.   Add the chili peppers, tomatoes, chicken broth, Barolo, thyme, and bay leaves and reduce to about 3 cups.

3.   Remove the bay leaves, and puree the sauce in a blender. (Up to this point, this sauce can be made ahead of time.)

(continued)

4.   Skin and dress the eels (see the previous recipe for directions). If using baby eels, the skin need not be removed.

5.   Steam the eels until almost tender.

6.   Reheat the Barolo sauce in a shallow saucepan, and add the eels. Simmer together for a few minutes, and adjust seasonings.

7.   Swirl in 1½ to 2 ounces of butter in small pieces.

8.   Melt the remaining butter in a skillet, and heat the mushrooms, carrots, onions, and black olives (remember, the carrots and onions are presteamed).

9.   Arrange the cooked eel on each serving plate, and spoon the sauce over. Top with the heated vegetables, and sprinkle with the scallion tops.

Filetti di Branzino in Salsa di Riccio di Mare
FILLETS OF SEA BASS WITH CREAMED SEA URCHINS

Yield: 6 servings

1 ounce	butter	pinch	saffron
3 tablespoons	finely diced shallots	6	fresh sea urchins
6	fillets of sea bass, 5 ounces each	1 tablespoon	fresh green (Madagascar) peppercorns
1 cup	dry white wine		
1 cup	dry vermouth	6 tablespoon	fish glace (see chapter 7)
1½ cups	fish broth (see chapter 3)	2 cups	cream, reduced to 1 cup
to taste	salt and white pepper		

1.   Butter a large skillet. Sprinkle the finely diced shallots in the bottom of the pan. Arrange the bass fillets over the shallots without overcrowding.

2.   Combine the wines, fish broth, salt, pepper, and saffron, and bring to a simmer.

3.   Cover the bass fillets with buttered parchment paper, and pour the hot wine and broth over the parchment.

4. Place the skillet into a preheated 325°F oven for about 3 to 5 minutes. Do not let the fish boil in the liquid. The skillet should be removed while the fillets are still somewhat undercooked.

5. Place the fish on a suitable platter, and cover with the same parchment paper to keep warm.

6. Cut the urchins around the concave side (mouthside) with a scissor, and remove the top section of the shell. Drain out the liquid, strain through a cheesecloth, and reserve for the sauce. Shake out the viscera (which may be a little messy). Scoop out the roe and keep well chilled. Sea urchin roe may also be purchased without the shell and frozen.

7. Strain all the poaching liquid into a noncorrosive shallow saucepan, and add the liquid from the sea urchins. Reduce to ¼ cup.

8. Add the green peppercorns and fish *glace*, and continue to reduce to the desired consistency. The sauce should be somewhat syrupy.

9. Add the reduced cream and remove from the heat if the sauce is the desired consistency. Add the sea urchin roe to the sauce.

10. Arrange the hot fish fillets on serving plates, and top with the sauce (see color plate 31).

Filetti di Branzino ai Profumi di Stagione in Cartoccio
FILLETS OF SEA BASS WITH SEASONAL VEGETABLES, BAKED IN PARCHMENT

Yield: 6 servings

6	fillets of sea bass, 5 ounces each	3 ounces	leeks, white parts only, cut in julienne
1½ ounces	butter	3 ounces	fennel knob, cut in julienne
1 ounce	shallots, finely diced		
1 cup	dry white wine	3 ounces	carrots, cut in julienne
1 cup	dry vermouth		
2	bay leaves	2 tablespoons	water
½ cup	fish glace	6 ounces	tomatoes, peeled, seeded, and cut in julienne (see chapter 1)
2 cups	cream, reduced to 1 cup		
1 tablespoon	green (Madagascar) peppercorns	9	basil leaves, finely shredded
to taste	salt	2 tablespoons	coarsely chopped parsley
3 ounces	celeriac, cut in julienne		

1.   Fold 6 pieces of 10- by 12-inch parchment paper in half. Cut out half a heart shape from each so that unfolded, each resembles a Valentine heart.

2.   Cut each fillet diagonally into 3 pieces and keep refrigerated.

3.   Heat ½ ounce of butter in a 2-quart saucepan. Add the shallots, wines, and bay leaves. Reduce over high heat to ¼ cup and add the fish *glace*. Continue to reduce, to a syrupy consistency. Stir in the reduced cream and the green peppercorns. Add salt. Strain out the bay leaves, and reserve the sauce in a suitable bowl.

4.   Heat the remaining ounce of butter in a large skillet. Add the celeriac, leeks, fennel, carrots, water, and a bit of salt. Cover and cook over high heat for 2 minutes. Remove the vegetables when they are still crisp, slightly undercooked, and cool.

5.   Arrange the vegetable strips on the left half of each parchment paper "heart."

6   Spoon 2 tablespoons of the sauce on top of the vegetables.

7.   Cover with 3 overlapping slices of bass fillet.

8.   Spoon the tomatoes on top of fish, and sprinkle with the basil and parsley. Pour the remaining sauce over the tomatoes.

9.   Fold the empty, right half of the parchment over the fish. Crimp the edges of the parchment together, sealing the packets completely.

10.   Place the packets on a metal tray, and bake in a preheated, 375°F oven for about 10 to 12 minutes. When ready, the packets will be slightly brown and puffed. They should be served in this way and opened at the table.

Baccalà all'Agliata

SALT COD WITH GARLIC SAUCE

Salt cod is a legacy from the Norsemen (Vikings) who, after devastating much of the coast of Europe in the early Middle Ages, successfully made their way to Sicily. Without salt cod (and a fierce spirit), the Norsemen would not have been able to sail wherever they pleased. Salt cod is now a familiar food in many of the countries the Norsemen raided.

Yield: 6 servings

6	fillets of salt cod, 6 ounces each	6 cloves	garlic, minced
		1/4 cup	chopped parsley
1 cup	milk	2 tablespoons	chopped basil
1 cup	flour	1/3 teaspoon	freshly ground black pepper
1/3 teaspoon	freshly ground black pepper	to taste	salt
1/2 to 3/4 cup	olive oil	1 1/4 cups	extra-virgin olive oil
1 to 2 tablespoons	white vinegar		
1/2 cup	fresh white breadcrumbs		

1.   Soak the cod in fresh water for 1 to 2 days, changing the water several times.

2.   Drain the fillets, pat dry, and place in a small dish with the milk until needed.

3.   Dredge the fillets in the flour, and season with the black pepper.

(continued)

4. Heat the olive oil, and pan-fry the fillets in medium to hot oil until both sides are crisp and lightly browned. It is best to finish the cooking in a 325°F oven, rather than trying to cook the fish through on the stove. Keep warm.

5. Mix the vinegar with the breadcrumbs. Squeeze out any excess vinegar.

6. Combine the garlic, parsley, basil, pepper, and salt with ½ cup of extra-virgin olive oil, add the soaked breadcrumbs, and work until smooth.

7. Place the bread mixture in a food processor and process, adding the remaining olive oil gradually to achieve an emulsion.

8. Serve the sauce alongside the pan-fried cod. Steamed potatoes and green vegetables are good accompaniments.

Baccalà alla Panna
SALT COD IN CREAM

Yield: 6 servings

6	fillets of salt cod, 4 ounces each	2 ounces	Parmesan, grated
3 ounces	flour	¼ teaspoon	freshly ground black pepper
6 tablespoons	virgin olive oil	to taste	salt
2 cups	dry white wine	1½ cups	cream
3 cloves	garlic, minced		
12	basil leaves, coarsely chopped		

1. Soak the salt cod in fresh water for 1 to 2 days. Change the water at least once while soaking.

2. Drain the cod, pat dry, and dredge in the flour.

3. Heat the oil in a large skillet, and pan-fry the cod on both sides until lightly browned. Deglaze the pan with the white wine, and cover the skillet. Cook over low heat until all the wine has evaporated.

4. Arrange the fillets in individual-size oval-shaped ovenproof casseroles.

5. Mix the garlic, basil, Parmesan, pepper, salt, and cream.

6. Spoon the cream mixture over each fish fillet, and bake in a 350°F oven on the top rack for about 15 to 20 minutes, until the cream has lightly browned. Steamed potatoes and fennel stalks make good accompaniments to this dish.

Baccalà in Purgatorio con Polenta
SALT COD IN DEVILED TOMATO SAUCE WITH POLENTA

Yield: 6 servings

6	fillets of salt cod, 5 ounces each	2 tablespoons	lemon juice
½ cup	flour	to taste	salt and freshly ground black pepper
1 cup	virgin olive oil	18	black olives, pitted and halved
6 ounces	red onions, diced		
4 cloves	garlic, minced	¼ cup	chopped parsley
3	hot red chili peppers	1 tablespoon	chopped oregano
¼ cup	tomato paste	½ cup	grated Parmesan
8	ripe tomatoes, peeled, seeded, and chopped (see chapter 1)	6 servings	polenta, pan-fried, grilled, or mush (see chapter 6)

1. Soak the cod in fresh water for 1 to 2 days, changing the water several times.

2. Drain the cod and pat dry. Dredge it in the flour. Heat the olive oil, and pan-fry the cod on both sides until lightly browned. Remove to individual-size ovenproof dishes.

3. In the same oil, sauté the onions, garlic, and chili peppers for several minutes.

4. Add the tomato paste, chopped tomatoes, and lemon juice, and simmer over low heat for about 15 minutes. Add the salt, pepper, olives, and half of the oregano and parsley.

5. Spoon the sauce over the cod, and sprinkle with the Parmesan. Bake in a moderately hot oven for 12 to 15 minutes.

6. Sprinkle with the remaining herbs.

7. Serve with the polenta alongside.

Bollito Misto di Pesce alla Giardiniera
POACHED SEAFOOD MEDLEY WITH BABY VEGETABLES

This highly nutritious seafood potpourri is best made in a shallow, noncorrosive casserole or a deep hotel pan with a perforated insert, or steaming basket, and tight-fitting cover. The fish should be placed in the insert, submerged in good-quality fish broth, and poached to between 165° and 185°F. The vegetables may be cooked in salted water or steamed.

Yield: 6 servings

3 pints	fish broth (see chapter 3)	6	fillets of sea bass, 1½ ounces each
½ cup	dry white wine		
¼ cup	dry sherry, Manzanilla or fino	3	scampi (langoustines)
		1	bay leaf
12	baby carrots, with green tops	6	parsley stems
		4 ounces	cold butter
12	baby turnips with green tops	to taste	salt and freshly ground black pepper
12	baby leeks	12	tomato petals (see chapter 1)
12	baby zucchini		
12	baby artichokes	6	basil sprigs
6	fillets of red snapper, 1½ ounces each	¼ cup	chopped parsley
6	fillets of John Dory, 1½ ounces each		

1.   Combine the fish broth and wines in a poaching vessel.

2.   Peel the carrots and turnips, leaving about ½ inch of their green tops intact. Clean the leeks and zucchini. Trim and cut the artichokes in half. Cook all vegetables separately in salted water, or steam, until tender-crisp. Keep warm.

3.   Place all the fish pieces on a perforated tray, and poach, covered, in 185°F fish broth for approximately 5 minutes.

4.   Cook the *scampi* in simmering salted water along with the bay leaf and parsley stems for 3 to 5 minutes. Drain, and keep the *scampi* warm.

5.   Strain the fish broth into a shallow saucepan, and reduce over high heat to 2 cups. Remove from the heat and gradually whisk in the cold butter, one small piece at a time. Add salt and pepper.

6.   Arrange the seafood and vegetables neatly on large soup plates. Coat the seafood with the reduced broth. Garnish each plate with 2 heated tomato petals and a sprig of fresh basil. Sprinkle the chopped parsley over the entire dish.

— *Calamari* —
SQUID

Calamari, or squid, are mollusks that, though always well liked in Italy, are just beginning to enjoy popularity in the United States. Like most seafood, squid is rich in protein and other nutrients. Unlike other seafood, however, a high percentage of the squid is usable. Squid is naturally tender but toughens when cooked over high heat or for a prolonged period of time. Cook either quickly over moderate to high heat or very slowly over low heat. The possibilities include cooking quickly by broiling, stir-frying, or deep-frying; poaching, for only a few seconds; or braising slowly, especially suitable if the squid is stuffed with ricotta or other custardlike fillings. When braising, cook just below the simmering point, right in the sauce.

To clean squid, separate the head and tentacles from the body. The tentacles are then separated from the head just above the eyes, and the beak is squeezed out. The translucent bone, or pen, can be easily slipped out of the body cavity. The slippery skin is readily peeled from the body, and the fins detached from the sides. The ink sac is connected internally to the back of the head and should come out when the head is separated. It may be stored, refrigerated, in a cup (add a touch of water), and used in sauces as desired.

Calamaretti Ripieni alla Napoletana
SQUID STUFFED WITH RICOTTA IN MARINARA SAUCE

Yield: 6 servings

1 pound	ricotta, very dry	1 stalk	fennel, chopped
3	egg yolks	2 cups	dry white wine
3 ounces	white breadcrumbs	2	chili peppers, chopped
2 tablespoons	chopped parsley		
2 tablespoons	chopped basil	8	ripe tomatoes, peeled, seeded, and diced (see chapter 1)
1/3 teaspoon	freshly ground black pepper		
1/2 teaspoon	salt	to taste	salt and fresh ground black pepper
30	small squid bodies, cleaned		
3/4 cup	virgin olive oil	2 tablespoons	chopped parsley
1 cup	finely diced onions	2 tablespoons	chopped basil
4 cloves	garlic, minced	2 tablespoons	chopped mint leaves

(continued)

1.   Combine the ricotta, egg yolks, breadcrumbs, parsley, basil, pepper, and salt. Using a pastry bag with a plain tip, stuff the cleaned squid bodies with this filling.

2.   Heat the olive oil in a heavy-bottomed shallow 6-quart casserole. Sauté the onions until translucent. Add the garlic and fennel, and cook over low heat for several minutes.

3.   Add the wine, and reduce to 1 cup.

4.   Add the chili peppers and tomatoes, and simmer for 5 minutes.

5.   Season with salt and pepper, and remove from the heat.

6.   Add stuffed squid to the sauce, and braise *very* slowly, below the simmering point, for about 20 minutes or until tender.

7.   Add the chopped parsley, basil, and mint, and adjust the seasonings. Polenta or risotto make good accompaniments to this dish (see color plate 32).

Calamaretti Arrabbiati di Spiedini
GRILLED SQUID KABOBS WITH TOMATOES AND HOT PEPPERS

Yield: 6 servings

30	small squid	8	ripe tomatoes, peeled, seeded, and diced large (see chapter 1)
1¼ to 1½ cups	virgin olive oil		
6 tablespoons	lemon juice		
14 cloves	garlic, minced	3	hot chili peppers, chopped
2 tablespoons	chopped oregano		
2 tablespoons	chopped parsley	to taste	salt
¼ teaspoon	freshly ground black pepper	2 tablespoons	chopped mint leaves
30	pearl onions, peeled and blanched for 2 minutes	2 tablespoons	chopped parsley
		1 cup	pine nuts, toasted
½ cup	thinly sliced scallions, white parts only		

1.   Clean the squid.

2.   Combine ¾ cup of olive oil, 4 tablespoons of lemon juice, 10 garlic cloves, oregano, parsley, and pepper in a stainless steel bowl. Add the squid bodies and tentacles and the pearl onions, and stir together. Steep for 1 hour or more. Keep well chilled.

3.   To assemble the kabobs, place one pearl onion in each squid body. Thread the bodies and tentacles alternately on metal skewers. (Spike the skewer through the onion within the body cavity to keep the squid stationary on the skewer.) Keep covered and chill until ready to broil.

4.   Bring the marinade to a simmer and keep warm.

5.   Heat ½ cup of olive oil in a skillet, and sauté the 4 garlic cloves, the scallions, and the tomatoes over high heat for a few minutes. Add the chili peppers, 2 tablespoons of lemon juice, and the salt. Keep warm.

6.   Broil the skewered squids quickly over (or under) high heat, being sure to keep the squid undercooked to avoid excessive shrinkage.

7.   Heat the reduced marinade. Stir the chopped mint and parsley into the tomato mixture. Remove the squid from the skewers, and arrange the bodies with the tentacles in a neat row on each serving plate. Spoon the tomato garnish alongside the squid, and sprinkle the garnish with toasted pine nuts. Pour the heated marinade over the squid.

Calamari Fritti con Maionese Tiepida al Profumo d'Aragosta
BATTER-FRIED SQUID WITH WARM LOBSTER MAYONNAISE

The batter for this dish is simple but provides a crisp, nongreasy coating. The secret is to keep all the batter ingredients ice cold before and during incorporation.

Yield: 6 servings

30	small squid, cleaned and halved lengthwise	to taste	freshly ground black pepper
		to dredge	flour
6 tablespoons	lemon juice	to deep fry	oil
½ cups	ice-cold beer	2¼ cups	warm lobster mayonnaise (see chapter 7)
6 to 7 ounces	cold bread flour		
½ teaspoon	salt		
pinch	cayenne pepper	to garnish	lemon wedges

(continued)

1.   Marinate the squid in the lemon juice until needed. Keep well chilled.

2.   Combine the beer, bread flour, salt, and peppers. Keep cold, especially if not using immediately. For a heavier coating, increase the amount of flour in the batter.

3.   Dredge the squid pieces lightly in the flour, then dip into and coat with the cold batter.

4.   Heat the oil to 360° to 375°F, and deep-fry the squid until golden brown.

5.   Arrange the squid in neatly folded napkins. Serve the warm lobster mayonnaise in ramekins, along with the lemon wedges, on the side.

Calamari con Spuma di Scampi in Salsa Crema al Pomodoro
SQUID STUFFED WITH SCAMPI MOUSSELINE IN TOMATO CREAM SAUCE

Yield: 6 servings

30	small squid	1 cup	ice-cold cream
12 ounces	scampo meat (or red Spanish shrimp)	3 quarts	chicken broth, well seasoned (see chapter 3)
1/2 teaspoon	salt		
pinch	cayenne pepper	2 1/4 cups	tomato cream sauce (see chapter 7)
pinch	nutmeg	18	tomato petals (see chapter 1)
1	ice-cold egg white		
1 ounce	white bread, no crusts, finely chopped	6	basil sprigs

1.   Clean the squid.

2.   Chop or grind the *scampi,* and add the salt, cayenne, and nutmeg. Place in the freezer for 15 minutes, or refrigerate for 1 hour. The *scampi* must be cold.

3.   Combine the egg white with white breadcrumbs by adding just a bit of the egg white to the breadcrumbs to form a paste and then gradually adding the remaining egg white. Keep chilled.

4.   Puree the *scampi* in a well-chilled food processor, and slowly add the egg white/bread mixture. The whole process should take no longer than 30 seconds.

5. Remove the *scampo* farce to a 2-quart stainless steel mixing bowl, and place on ice. Refrigerate for 15 minutes.

6. Slowly work the cream into the farce with a wooden spoon or pestle. Make a test sample of the farce by dropping a teaspoon of the mixture into a little chicken broth that has been treated to 180°F. Poach the sample for 6 minutes. If too firm, add a bit more cold cream.

7. Using a pastry bag with a straight tip, stuff the squid bodies with the farce, half full.

8. Heat chicken broth to 180°F in a shallow casserole, and add the stuffed squid. Poach at 170°F for about 12 minutes.

9. To serve, pour some tomato cream sauce on each serving plate and arrange 5 poached squid neatly on top. Garnish each plate with 3 heated tomato petals and a basil sprig (see color plate 33).

— *Capesante* —
SCALLOPS

The sea scallop, which is taken from deep waters, is more available to the professional chef than the smaller bay scallop is. Sea scallops are taken from shells approximately 5 inches in diameter; the part of the scallop that we eat is the adductor muscle of the animal, which allows it to open and close its shell. This muscle is more evident in scallops than in other shelled mollusks because the scallop opens and closes its shell to propel itself around in the water, whereas most other shelled mollusks are primarily sedentary. The smaller scallops, with shells that are 2 to 3 inches in diameter, are dredged from shallow coastal waters. Because off-shore pollution has destroyed or ruined many of their beds, they have become a delicacy.

Since scallops cannot keep their shells closed for a great length of time, once removed from water, they dehydrate quickly and die. For this reason, the fisherman removes the valuable muscle when the scallop is harvested and keeps it on ice. This unfortunately makes the orange-colored coral, the scallop's roe, hard to come by because it is usually discarded, even though it is a gourmet delight. An expert harvester can remove the roe along with the muscle and thus preserve both parts intact.

When exposed to prolonged heat, a scallop will lose most of its moisture and flavor. When sautéing scallops, it is important, therefore, to dry them completely and to cook them briefly (underdone) over high heat. Overcooking shrinks and toughens the meat. When deep-frying, be sure to serve immediately, as cooking continues after they are removed from the hot fat.

Capesante al Vapore con Zabaione alle Verdure

STEAMED SCALLOPS WITH VEGETABLE SABAYON

Yield: 6 servings

2 tablespoons	finely diced carrots	1 tablespoon	whole green (Madagascar) peppercorns
2 tablespoons	finely diced fennel		
2 tablespoons	finely diced leek, white part only	to taste	salt and cayenne pepper
2 tablespoons	finely diced celeriac	1½ pounds	sea scallops
1 cup	fish broth (see chapter 3)	6 tablespoons	whipped cream
½ cup	dry vermouth	1 tablespoon	finely chopped chives
½ cup	dry white wine	1 tablespoon	chopped parsley
3	egg yolks		

1.   Cook the carrots, fennel, leek, and celeriac in the fish broth for 3 to 4 minutes. Strain the liquid and reserve.

2.   Combine the strained liquid with the wines, and reduce in a small saucepan to ¾ cup. Reserve.

3.   In a 2-quart mixing bowl, beat the egg yolks with the reduction over boiling water (as in a double boiler) to make a smooth, emulsified sauce. Add the peppercorns, cooked vegetables, salt, and pepper.

4.   Steam the scallops; they should remain underdone.

5.   Fold the whipped cream into the vegetable sauce.

6.   Pour the vegetable sauce onto preheated serving plates, arrange the steamed scallops over sauce, and sprinkle with the chives and parsley.

Capesante ai Porcini e Pomodori Venezia

SCALLOPS WITH PORCINI AND TOMATOES

Yield: 6 servings

³/₄ cup	extra-virgin olive oil	12	basil leaves, cut in chiffonade (fine strips)
1½ pounds	sea scallops with coral	to taste	salt and freshly ground black pepper
12 ounces	fresh porcini		
6	ripe tomatoes, peeled and seeded (see chapter 1)	¼ cup	chopped Italian parsley
6 cloves	garlic, minced		
2	hot chili peppers, chopped		

1.   Heat the olive oil in a large skillet, and sauté the scallops over high heat; keep undercooked. Remove the scallops from the pan with a slotted spoon, and keep warm.

2.   Cut the *porcini* and tomatoes into thick slices.

3.   Reheat the oil in the same skillet, and sauté the garlic and *porcini* over high heat. Add the tomatoes and chili peppers.

4.   Add the basil, salt, pepper, and parsley, and combine with the cooked scallops (see color plate 34). Risotto goes well with this dish.

Farcia di Pesce

FISH FARCE

If this mixture is to be used for a seafood terrine or sausage, combine an equal amount of small-diced fresh shellfish to the ready-to-use fish farce.

Yield: 1½ pounds

1 tablespoon	finely diced shallots	pinch	nutmeg
1½ cups	dry white wine	⅓ teaspoon	white pepper
1	bay leaf	to taste	salt
1¼ cups	heavy cream	3	egg whites
1½ ounces	white breadcrumbs, no crusts		
1 pound	fresh fillets of sole, pike, and/or halibut (not frozen)		

1.   Chill all ingredients well.

2.   Combine the shallots, wine, and bay leaf in a small saucepan. Reduce completely, and remove the bay leaf. Chill the shallots.

3.   Mix ¼ cup cream with the breadcrumbs, and chill well.

4.   Cut the fish into small pieces, and chill well.

5.   Place the fish in a prechilled food processor. Add the chilled shallots, nutmeg, pepper, and salt, and process quickly to a smooth farce.

6.   Add and process the egg white a bit at a time, followed by the bread/cream panada a bit at a time. The complete process should require no more than 30 seconds.

7.   Remove the fish farce to a 4-quart stainless steel bowl set on crushed ice. Refrigerate.

8.   Using a pestle or wooden spoon, work in the rest of the cold cream gradually. Keep cold.

9.   Make a sample of the farce by poaching a spoon-sized dumpling in seasoned fish broth (or chicken broth) at 175°F for about 8 minutes. If it is too firm, add more cream. Adjust the seasonings.

10.   Keep the farce refrigerated and use within 2 days.

Farcia di Frutti di Mare

SEAFOOD FARCE

Because such seafood as turbot, lobster, and shrimp contain high amounts of protein, fewer egg whites are required when they are included in this farce.

Yield: 2½ pounds

1 teaspoon	butter	8 ounces	fresh shrimp, peeled and deveined
2 tablespoons	finely diced shallots	8 ounces	fresh sea scallops
2 cups	dry white wine	½ teaspoon	salt
2	bay leaves	pinch	nutmeg
2½ cups	heavy cream	pinch	cayenne pepper
1½ ounces	white bread, no crusts, diced small	3	egg whites, lightly beaten
8 ounces	fresh (not frozen) fillets of white-fleshed fish—pike, sole, and halibut are best		

1.   Chill all ingredients well.

2.   Heat the butter in a small saucepan, and smother the shallots. Add the wine and bay leaves, and reduce completely. Remove the bay leaves, and chill well.

3.   Mix ¼ cup cream with the white breadcrumbs. Keep cold.

4.   Cut the fish, shrimp, and scallops into small pieces. Keep cold.

5.   Place the chilled seafood in a well-chilled food processor, and add the cold shallots, salt, nutmeg, and cayenne. Process on and off very quickly until smooth. Add the egg whites a bit at a time, followed by the bread/cream panada a bit at a time. The whole process should take 20 to 30 seconds or less.

6.   When smooth, place the farce in a 4-quart stainless steel mixing bowl in crushed ice. Refrigerate.

7.   Using a pestle or wooden spoon, work the remaining cold cream into the farce. Refrigerate.

8.   Make a sample of the farce by poaching a tablespoon of it in seasoned fish broth at 175°F for about 8 minutes. If too firm, add more cold cream.

9.   Keep the farce refrigerated and use within 2 days.

Gamberi
SHRIMPS AND PRAWNS

Many fish and shellfish are known by more than one name in English, and Italian too has its quirks. Perhaps the best example is the famous Venetian dish *scampi,* often translated as shrimp or prawns. The term actually refers to a Dublin Bay prawn, or Norway lobster, which are neither prawns nor shrimp. The *scampo* is a small crayfish that is abundant in the Mediterranean region, especially in the Adriatic, and along northern European coasts. It is more correctly called a *langoustine.* The spiny lobster is also common and is properly referred to as a *langouste.* The common lobster, which is not common in the Mediterranean, is known in Italy as *aragosta.*

Shrimp, on the other hand (and prawns, for that matter), are a matter for even greater confusion and are taken from both freshwater and saltwater sources. They are classified in Italian according to size: *gamberi* are medium to large shrimp; *gamberelli* are small shrimp; and *gamberetti* are tiny shrimp.

Gamberi all'Aromi
SHRIMP WITH HERBS AND VEGETABLES

Yield: 6 servings
---

³⁄₄ to 1 cup	extra-virgin olive oil	3 ounces	fennel, peeled and cut julienne
36	shrimp, 16-to-20-per-pound size, peeled and deveined	3 ounces	scallions, cut in diagonal 1½-inch lengths
3 ounces	flour		
10 cloves	garlic, minced	3	tomatoes, peeled, seeded, and cut into fine strips (see chapter 1)
3	hot chili peppers, minced		
2 cups	dry white wine	to taste	salt and freshly ground black pepper
3 ounces	onions, cut into fine strips		
3 ounces	pea pods, cut into fine strips	¼ cup	chopped parsley
		1 tablespoon	chopped oregano
3 ounces	red bell pepper, cut into fine strips	1 tablespoon	chopped basil

1.   Heat 5 fluid ounces of olive oil in a large skillet. Dredge the shrimp in the flour, and sauté, a small amount at a time, until crisp on the outside but still undercooked within. Remove with a slotted spoon to a suitable bowl. Keep warm.

2.   Add the garlic and hot chili pepppers to the skillet. Deglaze the pan with the white wine and reduce by half. Add the shrimp, and keep warm.

3.   Heat the remaining oil in another skillet, and quickly sauté the onions, pea pods, peppers, fennel, and scallions. Cover, and steam for 1 minute.

4.   Mix in the tomatoes, salt, pepper, parsley, oregano, and basil.

5.   Combine the vegetables with the shrimp. Adjust the seasonings, and serve immediately. Rice goes very well with this dish (see color plate 35).

Gamberi alla Provenzale
SHRIMP, PROVENÇAL STYLE

Yield: 6 servings

³/₄ to 1 cup	virgin olive oil	3	sun-dried, marinated tomatoes (commercially available)
36	shrimp, 18-to-the-pound size, peeled and deveined		
12 ounces	onions, sliced	¹/₄ cup	chopped Italian parsley
8 cloves	garlic, finely minced		
4 ounces	fennel, cut into fine strips	1 tablespoon	chopped oregano
		to taste	salt and freshly ground black pepper
1	hot chili pepper, chopped		
1¹/₂ cups	dry white wine	¹/₂ cup	finely sliced scallions
6	tomatoes, peeled, seeded, and cut into strips (see chapter 1)	6	basil sprigs

1.   Heat ½ cup of olive oil in a large sauté pan. Sauté the shrimp in small batches; keep undercooked. Remove with a slotted spoon to a strainer or colander.

2.   Add the remaining oil to the skillet and reheat. Sauté the onions, garlic, and fennel for about 1 minute. Add the chili pepper.

3.   Deglaze the pan with the wine, and reduce by half.

4.   Add the tomato strips and sun-dried tomatoes, and cook for a few minutes.

5.   Add the parsley, oregano, salt, and pepper, and combine with the cooked shrimp. Sprinkle the scallions over the shrimp, and garnish with fresh sprigs of basil. Serve immediately.

Gamberi al Vapore con Salsa di Pompelmo e Semi di Melagrana
STEAMED PRAWNS WITH PINK-GRAPEFRUIT AND POMEGRANATE-SEED SAUCE

Yield: 6 servings

2 to 3	large pink grapefruit	to taste	salt and cayenne pepper
1	pomegranate	24	jumbo shrimp, 1 to 1½ ounces each, peeled and deveined
6½ ounces	butter		
2 tablespoons	finely diced shallots		
1 cup	dry vermouth	6 tablespoons	whipped cream
1 cup	dry white wine	1 ounce	melted butter
½ cup	fish glace (see chapter 7)	6	mint leaf sprigs

1. Peel the grapefruit, and set aside 12 sections. Squeeze the juice from the remaining grapefruit to produce ¾ cup.

2. Remove the seeds from the pomegranate by cutting around the stem end, scoring the skin vertically in several places. Remove the stem end, and soak the pomegranate in cold water for 10 minutes. Then simply break the fruit apart with your fingers and separate the seeds. Strain the seeds through a sieve, and set aside 3 tablespoons. Liquefy the remaining seeds in a blender, strain through cheesecloth, and reserve ¼ cup.

3. Heat ½ ounce of butter in a large, noncorrosive *sautoir*. Add the shallots, cover, and sweat them. Add the wines, and reduce completely.

4. Add the grapefruit and pomegranate juices, and reduce to ¾ cup. Strain into a smaller saucepan.

5. Add the fish *glace* and season with salt and cayenne pepper. (The sauce may be prepared ahead of time up to this point.)

6. Steam the shrimp; be sure to keep undercooked.

7. Reheat the sauce if necessary, and reduce further as necessary to coat properly. Swirl in the 6 ounces of butter, piece by piece, to achieve a good emulsion. Fold in the whipped cream.

8. Pour the sauce onto preheated plates, and neatly arrange 4 shrimp on each plate over the sauce. Sprinkle the pomegranate seeds over the sauce.

9. Brush the grapefruit sections with melted butter, and heat in the oven or under a top broiler for a minute or so.

10. Decorate with the grapefruit sections and mint sprigs.

Bianchetti di Langoustino e Capesante con Carciofini e Funghi

LANGOUSTINE AND SCALLOPS BLANQUETTE WITH ARTICHOKES AND MUSHROOMS

Yield: 6 servings

2 quarts	chicken broth (see chapter 3)	18	langoustine tails or red Spanish shrimp, 1 to 1¼ ounces each
2 tablespoons	lemon juice		
12	baby artichokes, halved	12	sea scallops
		2	egg yolks
12	large mushrooms, thickly sliced	1 ounce	butter
4 ounces	fennel knob, peeled and cut into fine strips	**GARNISH:**	
		3 small	ripe tomatoes, peeled, seeded, and cut into strips (see chapter 1)
1 tablespoon	clarified butter (see chapter 1)		
¼ cup	finely diced shallots		
2 cups	dry white wine or dry vermouth	½ cup	scallions, finely sliced
1¼ cups	heated heavy cream	6	basil crowns
to taste	salt and cayenne pepper		

1. Heat the chicken broth with the lemon juice, and cook the halved baby artichokes until cooked through but still firm.

2. Add the mushrooms and fennel strips, and cook a few more minutes before removing from the heat.

3. Drain the vegetables, reserving the liquid. Hold the vegetables in a suitable container, tightly covered, until needed. Keep warm.

4. Heat the clarified butter in a noncorrosive 4-quart saucepan, and sweat the shallots. Add the wine, and reduce completely.

(continued)

5. Add the reserved broth from the vegetables, and reduce to 4 cups. Add 1 cup of warm cream, and simmer for a few more minutes. Season to taste.

6. If using *langoustines*, steam them for 4 to 5 minutes, then shock them in ice water, remove the tails from the shells, and set aside. If using Spanish shrimp, peel and devein, and arrange in a buttered *sautoir*. Add the scallops, and sprinkle with a little white wine. Cover with buttered parchment paper or foil, and place in a 325°F oven until the shrimp and scallops are somewhat undercooked. Drain the liquids from the pan and add to the creamed chicken broth. Keep the shellfish warm and covered.

7. Lightly beat the egg yolks with ¼ cup of cream in a 2-quart stainless steel bowl.

8. Slowly stir the creamed chicken broth into the yolks, creating an emulsion. Strain through a sieve and keep hot (do not bring to a boil).

9. Arrange 3 *langoustine* tails (or shrimp), 2 scallops, 4 artichoke halves, and some sliced mushroom and fennel in each of 6 deep soup plates. Add about ¾ to 1 cup of creamed chicken broth to each, and garnish on top with tomato strips, sliced scallions, and basil crown. Serve with fresh sourdough bread (see color plate 36).

Molecche fra Diavola
SAUTÉED SOFT-SHELL CRAB WITH DEVIL SAUCE

The blue crab is commonly found along the eastern seaboard of the United States, as well as the northern coastal areas of Europe and in the Mediterranean. During the summer months, the crabs remain close to shore and in shallow waters, where they spawn from May to October. In the process of growth, the crabs shed their shells. While their new shells are growing, they are soft, and crabs caught at this stage are the much sought delicacy, the soft-shell crab.

Once the crab is properly dressed, the entire animal, including body and legs, can be eaten. To dress the crab:

- Lift up the bottom rear part, or apron, and remove completely.
- Lift up both side flaps and remove the spongy tissue material.
- Cut the eyes from the body with scissors.
- Press above the legs to remove the bile sac.

The two most popular methods of cooking soft-shell crab are deep-frying and sautéing. Both methods result in a crisp outer body, the most desirable characteristic of the soft-shell crab.

Yield: 6 servings

18	soft-shell crabs, dressed	6	ripe tomatoes, peeled, seeded, and diced (see chapter 1)
1/2 teaspoon	freshly ground black pepper	1/4 cup	chopped parsley
1 teaspoon	salt	2 tablespoons	chopped oregano
1 cup	flour		
3/4 cup	olive oil		
1/4 cup	brandy or grappa	**GARNISH:**	
		18	scallions, cut diagonally in 1 1/2-inch lengths
SAUCE:			
6 tablespoons	extra-virgin olive oil	1	red bell pepper, cut in fine strips
3 ounces	onions, finely diced		
6 cloves	garlic, minced	1	green bell pepper, cut in fine strips
1 cup	dry white wine		
1/2 cup	poultry glace (see chapter 7)	1 tablespoon	olive oil
2	hot chili peppers, chopped	to taste	salt and freshly ground black pepper

1. Season the dressed crabs with the salt and pepper, and dredge in the flour.

2. Heat 3/4 cup of olive oil in a large skillet, and sauté the crabs on both sides until crisp. Deglaze the pan with the brandy, and flambé. Remove the crabs from the skillet, and keep warm.

3. Wipe the skillet clean with a paper towel. Heat 6 tablespoons of olive oil in it.

4. Add the onions, and sauté for 1 minute. Add the garlic, and stir. Add the wine and reduce almost completely.

5. Add the poultry glace, hot chili pepppers, and tomatoes. Cook until thick, and add the parsley and oregano.

6. To serve, spoon the sauce onto each serving plate, and arrange the crabs neatly over the sauce. Quickly sauté the scallions and peppers in a little oil, season with salt and pepper, and spoon over the crabs.

Polipo alla Solferina

BABY OCTOPUS IN OLIVE OIL, WHITE WINE, AND TOMATOES

During my tour of Italy several years ago, a trip undertaken to explore new gastronomic trends in various regions of the country, I focused my attention primarily on the excellent variety and quality of fresh fish and shellfish. Foremost in my memory is a jaunt from the city of Mestre, on the outskirts of Venice (where, one evening, I sampled at least fifteen different seafood dishes) south along the coast, one week later, to Lucca. There I was blessed to witness the delivery of the fresh catch at the Ristorante Solferino. For several days I had the pleasure of observing the Gemignani brothers in their establishment, and I will never forget the great quality and quantity of the squids and octopuses they presented so simply, yet so sumptuously on our dinner table.

Yield: 6 servings

30	baby octopuses, 2 ounces each	6	tomatoes, peeled, seeded, and diced (see chapter 1)
¾ to 1 cup	virgin olive oil		
12 ounces	red onions, diced small	to taste	salt and freshly ground black pepper
9 cloves	garlic, finely minced	2 teaspoons	chopped basil
2 cups	dry white wine	2 teaspoons	chopped oregano
2	hot chili peppers, chopped	2 teaspoons	chopped parsley

1.   Wash the octopuses, and turn the bodies inside out to clean thoroughly. Remove and discard the eyes. Small octopuses need not be peeled.

2.   Heat the olive oil in a 4-quart, heavy-bottomed casserole, and cook the onions until translucent. Add the garlic, and continue to cook for a few minutes over medium heat.

3.   Add the wine and the chili peppers.

4.   Add the tomatoes, and bring to a simmer. Add the octopuses, and cook over very low heat until tender, about 30 to 40 minutes.

5.   Add the salt and pepper.

6.   Stir in the basil, oregano, and parsley just before serving. Rice or polenta goes well with this dish.

Spuma di Rane in Salsa Crema di Porrino
MOUSSE OF FROG LEGS IN CREAM SAUCE WITH CHIVES

Prepare this mousse with fresh frog legs only, as the frozen product is very water-logged and will result in a granular farce. If frozen frog legs are the only alternative, then be sure to mix the frog legs with shrimp. This will produce a decent emulsion.

Yield: 6 servings

2 tablespoons	finely diced shallots	2	eggs, lightly beaten and chilled
1 cup	dry white wine		
1	bay leaf	1½ cups	cold heavy fresh cream
1 cup	chicken broth (see chapter 3)	6 ounces	spinach tagliolini (see chapter 5)
30 ounces	boned frog legs, trimmed of gristle	2¼ cups	cream sauce with chives (see chapter 7)
1½ ounces	white bread, no crusts, chopped		
to taste	salt and white pepper	18	tomato petals (see chapter 1)
to taste	nutmeg	6	basil sprigs

1. Heat the shallots, wine, bay leaf, and chicken broth in a shallow saucepan.

2. Add 10 ounces (one-third) of the frog legs, and poach over low heat for about 8 minutes. Remove the pan from the heat, and cool the frog legs quickly in the liquid. When cool, remove with a slotted spoon and reserve in a suitable bowl, covered and refrigerated.

3. Reduce the liquid completely, until the shallots are dry but not brown. Remove the bay leaf, and keep the shallots well chilled.

4. Put the remaining frog legs and the shallots through the medium blade of a meat grinder. Mix with the chopped white bread, salt, pepper, and nutmeg, and refrigerate until well chilled.

5. Place the chilled farce in the bowl of an ice-cold food processor, and process quickly until smooth. Gradually add the beaten eggs. The whole procedure should take no more than 20 to 30 seconds. Place the farce in a 3-quart mixing bowl set over crushed ice, and refrigerate for 30 minutes.

6. Work the cold cream into the farce with a wooden spoon, a bit at a time, and refrigerate again until ready to cook. Be sure to make a sample of the farce.

(continued)

7.   Coat six 6- to 8-ounce ramekins or timbales with softened butter. Fill almost completely (about 90 percent full) with the farce, being sure to press the mixture well to squeeze out excess air.

8.   Place the molds in a hotel pan. Add enough hot water to reach halfway up the sides of the molds. Cover with a sheet of oiled parchment paper.

9.   Cook gently in a 300° to 325°F oven until firm or custardlike in texture.

10.   Cook the spinach *tagliolini,* drain, shock in cold water, and drain again. Toss with a little butter in a mixing bowl. Reheat the poached frog legs in a little broth and butter. Arrange the *tagliolini* in a semicircle on each serving plate, and unmold the mousse inside the circle. Spoon the poached frog legs opposite, and cover with the cream sauce with chives. Decorate with 3 heated tomato petals and a basil sprig.

Cosce di Rane Fritte con Salsa Tirolese

DEEP-FRIED FROG LEGS WITH TYROLEAN SAUCE

The taste and succulence of freshly caught frog legs is lost in freezing. Breading and deep-frying seals in these flavorful juices while also giving the frog legs a wonderful crispness.

Yield: 6 servings

24 pairs	*frog legs, medium size*	*¼ cup*	*tomato paste*
to taste	*salt and freshly ground black pepper*	*2*	*ripe tomatoes, peeled, seeded, and diced small (see chapter 1)*
1 cup	*flour*		
2	*eggs*	*2 tablespoons*	*lemon juice*
½ cup	*water*	*pinch*	*cayenne pepper*
3 cups	*fine breadcrumbs, from stale Italian bread*	*¼ cup*	*heavy cream*
		2	*lemons, sliced into wedges*
1½ cups	*mayonnaise (see chapter 7)*	*1 bunch*	*fresh parsley*

1.   Divide the frog leg pairs into single pieces, and trim off the ends close to the joints. Season with salt and pepper.

2.   Dredge the frog legs in the flour.

3.   Beat the eggs with the water. Dip the frog legs into the egg mixture, then coat with the breadcrumbs.

4.   Combine the mayonnaise, tomato paste, diced tomatoes, lemon juice, and cayenne in a 2-quart stainless steel bowl. Whip the cream lightly, until foamy, and fold into the sauce. Add salt and black pepper to taste.

5.   Deep-fry the breaded frog legs until golden brown. Arrange on folded napkins with the lemon wedges and parsley sprigs. Serve the sauce separately.

—— *Rombo* ——
TURBOT

Rombo, or turbot, is a general name used for various flatfish. The two most interesting species from a culinary standpoint are *Rombo chiodato,* or the eastern Atlantic turbot, which is the larger of the two, weighing from about 2 pounds (turbotin) to over 30 pounds, and the smaller brill, or *Rombo liscio,* which ranges from about 2 pounds to over 15 pounds.

Most people will agree to the superiority of the turbot. It has a delicate flavor and a high gelatin and protein content. For this reason, turbot should never be cooked at high temperatures or for too long, as the protein then toughens and the fish becomes dry.

The turbot is easily recognizable by its diamond shape and characteristic scalelike tubercles on the dark-skinned side. Unfortunately, the exquisite quality of this fish has led to a phenomenal demand, making turbot almost unaffordable for the average consumer.

Filetti di Rombo alla Ligure
FILLETS OF TURBOT, LIGURIAN STYLE

Yield: 6 servings

2 ounces	spinach leaves, blanched, shocked, and drained	to taste	salt and cayenne pepper
6 ounces	cooked artichoke bottoms (see chapter 12)	1/2 cup	flour
		6 tablespoons	olive oil
4 tablespoons	chopped parsley	1 cup	dry white wine
1 cup	cold chicken broth (see chapter 3)	6 tablespoons	fish glace (see chapter 7)
to taste	nutmeg	2 cups	heavy cream, reduced to 1 cup
to taste	salt and cayenne pepper	2	eggs, hard-cooked whites and yolks chopped separately
6	fillets of turbot or brill, 5 to 6 ounces each	6	basil sprigs

1.   Squeeze all moisture from the blanched spinach, and chop with the cooked artichoke bottoms. Combine with 1 tablespoon of chopped parsley, the chicken broth, nutmeg, salt, and cayenne. Puree in a blender. Store in a small noncorrosive container, covered and well chilled. (This puree may be prepared ahead of time.)

2.   Season the fish fillets with salt and cayenne, and dredge lightly in the flour.

3.   Heat the olive oil in a large skillet, and pan-fry the fish on both sides over moderate heat until crisp on the outside. Remove to a suitable dish and keep warm.

4.   Drain the oil from the skillet and wipe clean with a paper towel. Add the wine, and reduce quickly over high heat to about 3 fluid ounces. Add the fish *glace* and bring to a simmer.

5.   Stir in the reduced cream and reheat.

6.   Whisk ¾ cup of the cold artichoke puree into the sauce.

7.   Spoon the artichoke cream sauce onto each hot dinner plate, and neatly arrange a fillet over the sauce. Garnish with the chopped egg yolk, egg whites, and 3 tablespoons chopped parsley in alternating lines on top. Decorate with a basil sprig.

Coda di Rospa alla Salvia
POACHED MONKFISH WITH SAGE BUTTER SAUCE

Yield: 6 servings

5 ounces	*butter, cut into knobs*	*to taste*	*cayenne pepper*
1 cup	*thinly sliced scallions, white parts only*	*6*	*fillets of monkfish, cut into 3-ounce slices*
3 cloves	*garlic, minced*	*6*	*ripe tomatoes, peeled, seeded, and cut into strips (see chapter 1)*
1 cup	*dry white wine*		
½ cup	*dry vermouth*	*12*	*sage leaves*
2 cups	*strong fish broth (see chapter 3)*		
to taste	*salt and freshly ground black pepper*		

1.   Heat 1 ounce of butter in a large skillet, and cook the scallions and garlic over low heat for about 2 minutes.

2.   Add the wines, fish broth, salt, pepper, and cayenne. Bring to a boil.

3.   Add the fish fillets, and cover with buttered parchment paper. Poach in a preheated 300°F oven for 6 minutes, until the fish is still slightly undercooked. Do not let the liquid boil.

4.   Remove the fillets to a suitable dish, and cover with the same parchment paper. Keep warm.

5.   Reduce the liquid in the skillet to 3 fluid ounces (6 tablespoons).

6.   Add the tomato strips, and heat thoroughly.

7.   Add the butter knobs, and mix carefully with the tomatoes, shaking the pan gently to achieve an emulsion. Adjust the seasonings.

8.   Cut the sage into chiffonade (very thin strips), and add to the sauce.

9.   Arrange a fish fillet on each serving plate, and spoon the sauce over the fish.

San Pietro in Bianco

JOHN DORY IN WHITE-WINE SAUCE

The American John Dory (or English St. Peter's fish) is easily recognized by the large round black spot on its side. The fish is plentiful in most oceans of the world, as well as in the Mediterranean.

The flesh of John Dory is white, and the fillets resemble those of flatfish and can be prepared accordingly. John Dory is also an excellent addition to seafood stews and soups.

Yield: 6 servings

1½ ounces	butter	1½ ounces	carrots, cut in julienne
3 tablespoons	chopped shallots		
12	fillets of John Dory, 1½ to 3 ounces each	1½ ounces	celeriac, cut in julienne
to taste	salt and cayenne pepper	6 tablespoons	fish glace (see chapter 7)
1	bay leaf	2 cups	heavy cream, reduced to 1 cup
½ cup	dry white wine		
1 cup	dry sherry (Manzanilla or fino)	1½ ounces	small pearl onions, blanched
1½ cups	strong fish broth (see chapter 3)	3 tablespoons	finely chopped chives
1½ ounces	fennel, cut in julienne	2 tablespoons	finely chopped parsley

1.   Butter a large, shallow skillet, and sprinkle the bottom with the chopped shallots. Arrange the fillets overlapping slightly on the narrow ends, on top of the shallots. Add salt, cayenne, and bay leaf.

2.   Combine the wines with the fish broth, and bring to a simmer.

3.   Steam or cook the fennel, carrots, and celeriac in a little salted water until they are tender-crisp. Drain, reserving the liquid. Keep the vegetables warm.

4.   Cover the fillets with buttered parchment paper, and pour the hot wine/broth mixture over the paper but *not* on top of the fillets.

5.   Place the skillet in a preheated 325°F oven for about 3 to 5 minutes. Do not let the fish boil in the liquid.

6. Place the fish in a suitable container, and cover with the same paper to keep warm. Strain the liquid from the fish and from the vegetables into a noncorrosive shallow saucepan, and reduce to ¼ cup.

7. Add the fish *glace* and the reduced cream. Adjust the seasonings.

8. Arrange the fillets on serving plates, and spoon the sauce over them. Garnish with the cooked vegetables and pearl onions. Sprinkle with chives and parsley.

Trance di Salmone al Vapore con Zabaione al Caviale
STEAMED SALMON STEAKS WITH CAVIAR SABAYON

Yield: 6 servings

2 tablespoons	finely diced leeks	3 tablespoons	salmon caviar
2 tablespoons	finely diced carrots	½ cup	whipped cream
2 tablespoons	finely diced celeriac	to taste	salt and freshly ground black pepper
1 cup	dry white wine		
1 cup	dry vermouth	6	salmon steaks, 6 ounces each
2	bay leaves		
¼ teaspoon	hot crushed red pepper	12	tomato petals (see chapter 1)
6 tablespoons	shellfish glace (see chapter 7)	6	basil sprigs
3	egg yolks		

1. In a small saucepan, combine the leeks, carrots, celeriac, wines, bay leaves, and crushed red pepper. Reduce to about ¾ cup. Strain through cheesecloth.

2. Mix the reduction with the shellfish *glace* and egg yolks in a 3-quart stainless steel mixing bowl. Beat over a double boiler to achieve an emulsion.

3. Fold in the salmon caviar and whipped cream, and adjust the seasonings.

4. Steam the salmon steaks.

5. Pour the *sabayon* on each warm serving plate, and arrange the steamed salmon over the sauce. Garnish with tomato petals and basil sprigs (see color plate 37).

Scungilli
WHELKS

These gastropods are more in demand in Greece, Italy, and Spain than in the United States. But whelks have been considered delicacies since the days of ancient Rome, and today, like their relative, the land snail, these marine snails are often associated with strong aromatics and the deep scent of garlic.

The whelk eaten as *scungilli* is the common, white, or waved whelk *(Buccinum undatum)*. These creatures are found from the Arctic to New Jersey, most abundantly in New England. Whelks are sold under the name *scungilli* in most food stores and are usually shelled and frozen; defrost in the refrigerator. If fresh whelks are used, they must always be blanched and removed from the shells. They can be cooked like snails and served with polenta, *gnocchi,* risotto, or pasta.

Scungilli Trifolati all'Aglio e Peperone
WHELKS IN GARLIC, TOMATO, AND PEPPER SAUCE

Yield: 6 servings

¾ cup	virgin olive oil	2 pounds	sun-ripened tomatoes, peeled, seeded, and chopped (see chapter 1)
1½ pounds	shelled whelks, thinly sliced		
6 ounces	onions, diced small		
8 cloves	garlic minced	to taste	salt and freshly ground black pepper
3	hot red chili peppers		
1	red bell pepper, seeded and diced small	3 tablespoons	chopped parsley
		2 tablespoons	chopped oregano
1 cup	dry red wine	⅓ cup	grated Parmesan

1.   Heat half the olive oil in a large skillet, and quickly sauté the sliced whelk for several minutes. Remove with a slotted spoon, and reserve.

2.   Add the remaining oil to the same skillet, and sauté the onions, garlic, and peppers for 1 minute.

3.   Add the red wine, and reduce by half.

4. Add the tomatoes, and simmer over medium heat for about 10 minutes.

5. Add the sautéed whelks and continue to cook over low heat for 15 minutes. Add salt and pepper.

6. Stir in the parsley, oregano, and Parmesan, and serve.

Filetti di Sogliola Ripieno alla Salsa di Bottarea

POACHED FILLETS OF SOLE STUFFED WITH SEAFOOD MOUSSE IN CAVIAR WINE SAUCE

Yield: 6 servings

12	fillets of sole, 2 ounces each	1½ cups	dry white wine
12 ounces	seafood farce (see recipe earlier in this chapter)	6 tablespoons	fish glace (see chapter 3)
		2 cups	heavy cream, reduced to 1 cup
1 ounce	butter, melted	1 tablespoon	green peppercorns
2 tablespoons	finely diced shallots		
2	bay leaves	3 tablespoons	salmon caviar
1 pint	fish broth (see chapter 3)	4 to 6 tablespoons	whipped cream

1. Trim the sole fillets so that they are somewhat even in size. Remove as much of the thin white membrane as possible. This may cause shrinkage if left intact.

2. Spread each fillet with 1 ounce of seafood farce, and roll into roulades. Spread the farce smoothly on both side-ends.

3. Brush a deep 6- by 9-inch pan with the melted butter, and sprinkle with the shallots and bay leaves.

4. Arrange the stuffed sole fillets neatly in the dish, seam side down and not too close to one another. Brush with a little melted butter, and cover with oiled parchment paper.

5. Bring the fish broth and wine to a boil, and pour over the parchment paper (not directly over the fish).

(continued)

6. Place in a 325°F oven, and poach for about 8 minutes. The fish must never boil in the liquid.

7. When the fillets are cooked, remove them from the pan, and hold, covered, in a warm place. Strain the liquid into a wide-bottomed skillet, and reduce to ½ cup.

8. Add the fish *glace* to the reduction; continue to reduce if necessary until syrupy.

9. Add the reduced cream and green peppercorns. Keep warm.

10. Place 2 stuffed fillets on each serving plate. Add salmon caviar to the sauce, and fold in the whipped cream. Coat the stuffed fillets evenly with the sauce, and serve immediately. Steamed turned potatoes, angel hair pasta, or *fleurons* of puff pastry go well with this dish.

Trance di Pesce Spada ai Ferri alla Palermitana
GRILLED SWORDFISH STEAKS, SICILIAN STYLE

Yield: 6 servings

6 tablespoons	virgin olive oil	to taste	salt and freshly ground black pepper
3 ounces	onions, finely diced		
3 cloves	garlic, minced		
3	anchovy fillets	¼ cup	chopped mint leaves
2	chili peppers, chopped	6	swordfish steaks, 6 ounces each
3	ripe tomatoes, peeled, seeded, and diced (see chapter 1)	¼ teaspoon	freshly ground black pepper
		1 clove	garlic, minced with salt
6	green olives, pitted	¼ cup	olive oil
1 tablespoon	capers		

1. Heat the 6 tablespoons of olive oil in a 2-quart saucepan, and cook the onions over medium heat until translucent. Add the 3 cloves of garlic, anchovies, and chili peppers, and cook slowly for 5 minutes.

2. Add the tomatoes, olives, and capers, and cook for an additional 5 minutes over low heat. Season with salt and pepper; add the mint leaves. Puree in a blender until completely smooth. Adjust the seasonings, and keep warm.

3. Rub the swordfish steaks with the pepper, clove of garlic, and ¼ cup of olive oil, and broil under high heat until slightly undercooked.

4. Pour the sauce on each serving plate, and arrange the swordfish steaks neatly on top of the sauce.

— *Tonno* —
TUNA

There are various species of tuna, which are available for consumption fresh, frozen, or canned. Each species differs in size, texture, flavor, and color, the white flesh being of superior quality and most delicate in flavor.

The albacore, or white tuna, is found on both sides of the Atlantic. The yellow-fin tuna is somewhat darker and is found almost everywhere. The blue-fin tuna is the largest of the tunas and yields mostly dark meat.

Tuna today is cooked quickly over very high heat. It is ideal for grilling or sautéing. Tuna may also be cut into thin slices and served with highly aromatic or garlicky sauces.

The idea of serving tuna in chunks or thinly sliced with a variety of sauces and garnishes comes to us from the Far East. Raw tuna marinated in citrus juice, similar to a *seviche,* with a garnish of scallions, peppers, tomatoes, avocados, and hot chili peppers, originated in South America.

Trance di Tonno alla Crema Alici e Olive
GRILLED TUNA STEAKS WITH ANCHOVY OLIVE SAUCE

Yield: 6 servings

6	tuna steaks, 6 to 7 ounces each	6	anchovy fillets
3 tablespoons	olive oil	10 cloves	roasted garlic (see garlic puree, chapter 1)
6 ounces	butter		
6 ounces	onions, finely diced	to taste	salt and freshly ground black pepper
2	hot red chili peppers, chopped		
12	olives, pitted	½ cup	basil chiffonade
1 cup	dry white wine		
1 cup	fish or chicken broth (see chapter 3)		

(continued)

1.   Brush the tuna steaks with olive oil. Set aside.

2.   Heat 2 ounces of butter in a skillet, and add the onions and hot chili peppers. Cook over moderate heat until the onions are translucent. Add the olives.

3.   Add the wine, and reduce completely.

4.   Add the broth, and reduce to ¾ cup. Remove from the heat.

5.   Combine the sauce with the anchovies and roasted garlic in a blender, and puree until smooth.

6.   Reheat the sauce in a 1-quart saucepan, and add salt and pepper. Remove the sauce from the heat, and vigorously whip in the remaining cold butter, a little at a time.

7.   Season the tuna, and cross-grill (so that the grill leaves perpendicular marks) over high heat as quickly as possible on both sides. Spoon the sauce onto each serving plate, and arrange the grilled tuna on top. Garnish with basil chiffonade.

— *Triglia* —
RED MULLET

Triglia, or mullet, is not a true mullet at all, but rather a member of the Mullidae, or goatfish, family. The true mullet, the gray mullet, belongs to the family Mugilidae and is only distantly related.

Red mullet live mainly in tropical and subtropical waters, but are oddly found as far north as Norway. All are golden to orange to red in color. They were already greatly prized in ancient Rome, and to this day, the *triglia* holds an esteemed position among Mediterranean fish.

Red mullet is required for the preparation of a great many famous regional dishes, such as *cacciucco* and bouillabaisse. It has no counterpart in northern waters. It resembles our red snapper, though the two are in no way related.

Filetti di Triglie ai Ferri al Profumo di Finocchio
GRILLED RED-MULLET FILLETS WITH SAUTÉED FENNEL

Yield: 6 servings

6 tablespoons	virgin olive oil	to taste	salt and freshly ground black pepper
3 tablespoons	lemon juice		
1 tablespoon	capers	¼ cup	virgin olive oil
2 tablespoons	chopped oregano	3 ounces	red onions, sliced
¼ teaspoon	crushed hot red pepper	2 cloves	garlic, minced
9	fillets of red mullet	to taste	salt and freshly ground black pepper
GARNISH:		18	fennel tips
2	fennel knobs		

1.   Combine the 6 tablespoons of olive oil, lemon juice, capers, oregano, and red pepper. Place the fish fillets in a noncorrosive pan, and pour the marinade over the fillets. Marinate for several hours. Remove the fillets, and reserve the liquid.

2.   Split the fennel bulbs and stalks lengthwise, and remove the cores. Cut into very thin strips and season with salt and pepper. Rest for a few minutes.

3.   Heat the ¼ cup of oil in a large skillet, and sauté the onions, garlic, and sliced fennel quickly, without browning.

4.   Add the marinade, and cook for a few minutes. Remove from the heat, and add the salt and pepper.

5.   Grill the fillets, turning only once.

6.   Arrange 3 fillets neatly on each serving plate, skin side up, and spoon the fennel garnish along the fillet near the rim of the plate. Decorate with the small tips of fennel.

Filetti di Trota con Olive Nere

SAUTÉED FILLETS OF TROUT WITH BLACK OLIVES

Yield: 6 servings

6	fresh trout, 7 to 9 ounces each	4	anchovy fillets, chopped
to taste	salt and cayenne pepper	3/4 cup	pitted and quartered black olives
2 tablespoons	lemon juice		
1/2 cup	flour	6	ripe tomatoes, peeled, seeded, and cut into strips (see chapter 1)
1 cup	virgin olive oil		
2 cups	sliced scallion, white parts only, cut diagonally in 1-inch lengths	1/2 cup	finely sliced scallions, tops only
4 cloves	garlic, minced	6	basil crowns
2	hot red chili peppers, chopped		

1. Fillet and skin the trout. Sprinkle with salt, cayenne pepper, and lemon juice. Dredge in the flour.

2. Heat ½ cup of olive oil in a large skillet, and pan-fry the trout fillets over medium-high heat until brown and crisp. Remove from the pan, and keep warm.

3. Add the remaining oil to the same skillet, and quickly sauté the scallions, garlic, chili peppers, and anchovies. Add the olives and tomatoes, and adjust the seasonings.

4. Arrange 2 trout fillets neatly on each serving plate, and top with the vegetable garnish. Sprinkle with the chopped scallion tops and garnish with the basil crowns.

Piccola Zuppa di Pesce allo Zafferano e Finocchio

SEAFOOD STEW WITH SAFFRON AND FENNEL

This is a modern version of a classic *zuppa di pesce*, which is high in nutrients and low in fats and cholesterol. The fish is completely boneless and steamed for quick service. A deep hotel pan with a perforated insert will work well for low-pressure steaming, which produces more satisfying results than pressure steaming does.

Yield: 6 servings

6	*fillets of salmon, 2 ounces each*	*4 ounces*	*fennel, cut in julienne*
6 ounces	*baby squid bodies, cleaned and thinly sliced into rings*	*4 ounces*	*leek whites, cut in thin rings*
6 ounces	*sea scallops, thickly sliced*	*2 quarts*	*hot clarified fish broth (see chapter 3)*
12	*langoustine tails or Spanish shrimp*	*pinch*	*saffron, infused in 2 ounces of hot fish broth*
18	*mussels, thoroughly cleaned*	*¼ cup*	*chopped Italian parsley*
4 ounces	*celeriac julienne*	*12*	*tomato petals (see chapter 1)*
4 ounces	*carrots, cut in julienne*	*6*	*basil sprigs*

1.   Steam all seafood until just underdone in the following sequence.

   • salmon fillets, squid rings, and scallops for a few minutes.
   • *langoustine* tails 4 to 5 minutes, and shell after steaming.
   • mussels, until they open; shell after cooked firm and plump.

   Keep all seafood warm, covered by a bit of hot fish broth.

2.   Cook the celeriac, carrots, fennel, and leeks in the fish broth until tender-crisp.

3.   Arrange the seafood neatly on each serving plate or in a large soup bowl.

4.   Add the saffron infusion into the fish broth and add about 1 cup of hot fish broth to each bowl. Gently place some of the cooked vegetables on top, in the center of each bowl. Sprinkle with parsley, and arrange the tomato petals with a basil sprig on the outer edge. Garlic toast or toasted sourdough bread goes well alongside (see color plate 38).

MEATS AND VARIETY MEATS

— *Vitello/Vitella* —
VEAL

Veal is the flesh of bovine animals no older than one year of age. The U.S. commercial ratings officially designate veal as a twelve-week-old calf. The highest-quality veal available is known as milk-fed veal, or *vitelluccia da latte*. The word *vitella* is the Tuscan term for veal and refers to the meat from animals slaughtered around four weeks old, which is of premium quality. *Vitello,* on the other hand, can refer to milk- or grass-fed veal.

Milk-fed veal gets its color (or, rather, lack of it) from its diet. The animal is actually anemic, lacking most minerals, especially iron. With iron depletion, the red pigments normally present in the animal's blood and flesh cannot be produced, leaving the flesh rather pale. As soon as the animal is given grass and other food rich in iron, the flesh reddens as the pigments are once again produced.

Veal is perhaps appreciated more in Italy than anywhere else. This might explain the ambiguities often encountered in the terminology of various veal dishes. What follows is an attempt to sort out the multitude of terms used when Italian chefs refer to veal.

A chop or a cutlet with the bone in could be termed *costa, costola, costata, costatella, costellata, costoletta,* or *costolettina.* A boneless veal cutlet is referred to as a *scaloppa, scaloppina,* or *cotoletta.* A veal steak (large cutlet taken from the knuckle) is called a *cotoletta.* A small cutlet (approximately 1½ to 2 ounces) is a *piccata;* usually three *piccate* make up one serving. Veal cutlets that have been pounded very thin are known as *battuta di vitello.* A *blanquette* of veal is a *bianchette di vitello.* Small stuffed veal roulades are *braciolette di vitello ripiene* or *rollatine di vitello.* If these roulades are small and cooked on skewers, they become *involtini di vitello.* A regular stuffed veal cutlet is a *portafoglio di vitello,* and a stuffed breast of veal, *cima di vitello.* Veal stew is *spezzatino di vitello,* whereas *polpettino, polpettone,* and *polpetta* all apply to a ground veal in various forms. Small *scaloppine* flavored with sage and garlic, then rolled and sautéed, grilled, or braised, are known as *vitello all'uccelletto,* or "in the style of wild birds." The well-known *saltimbocca* (literally, "to jump into the mouth") is *scaloppine* topped with sage leaves and *prosciutto.* If the number of terms in Italian for veal and veal dishes is any indication, the Italians clearly consider veal an integral part of their cuisine.

Ossobuco alla Milanese
BRAISED VEAL SHANK, MILANESE STYLE

Yield: 6 servings

6	1-inch veal-shank pieces with bone (for a 6-ounce meat yield)	
½ cup	flour	
½ cup	clarified butter (see chapter 1)	
6 ounces	onions, finely diced	
3 cloves	garlic, crushed	
¼ cup	tomato paste	
6	ripe tomatoes, peeled, seeded, and chopped (see chapter 1)	
2 cups	dry white wine	
1 quart	brown veal stock (see chapter 7)	
to taste	salt and freshly ground black pepper	
to taste	thyme	
to taste	bay leaves	

SPECIAL GARNISH:

1 tablespoon	finely grated lemon rind
1 tablespoon	chopped rosemary leaves
3 tablespoons	chopped Italian parsley
3	anchovy fillets, chopped

GARNISH:

1 cup	sliced mushrooms, in strips
½ cup	julienne of cooked pickled ox tongue
½ cup	julienne of cooked prosciutto
1 tablespoon	butter

1.   Dredge the veal shank pieces in the flour.

2.   Heat the clarified butter in a shallow 6-quart *rondeau,* and brown the veal shanks on all sides over medium heat. Remove and keep warm.

3.   Add the onions to the same *rondeau,* and cook until lightly browned. Add the garlic and tomato paste, and continue to cook over moderate heat until the tomato paste has lightly browned. Add the chopped tomatoes and white wine, and reduce by half.

4.   Add the brown veal stock, salt, pepper, thyme, and bay leaves, and bring to a simmer. Add the browned veal shanks, and braise slowly for 1 hour, until the meat is fork tender.

5.   Remove the cooked veal shanks to a suitable container, and cover to keep warm.

6. Strain the remaining sauce through a fine china cap, pressing on the solids that remain behind to extract all liquid. Bring the sauce to a boil again, and reduce as necessary to obtain a coating consistency. Degrease the sauce while reducing. Adjust the seasonings, and pour over the veal shanks. Cover again to keep warm.

7. Combine the lemon rind, rosemary, Italian parsley, and anchovies for the special garnish, known as *gremolada*.

8. Sauté the mushrooms, ox tongue, and *prosciutto* in butter until heated through—do not actually cook.

9. Arrange the veal shanks on a serving platter. Add the *gremolada* to the sauce, and pour over the shanks. Top with the mushrooms, ox tongue, and *prosciutto*. This dish is traditionally served with *risotta alla milanese* (risotto with wine and saffron), the recipe for which is in chapter 6.

Ossobuco alle Verdure
BRAISED VEAL SHANKS WITH FRESH VEGETABLES

Yield: 6 servings

6	1-inch veal shank pieces, with bone (for a 6-ounce meat yield)	to taste	salt
		to taste	bay leaves
		to taste	thyme
½ cup	flour	to taste	rosemary
½ cup	olive oil	to taste	grated lemon rind
6 ounces	onions, finely diced		
4 cloves	garlic, minced	**GARNISH:**	
½ cup	coarsely grated carrot	2	scallions, white parts only
¼ cup	grated fennel	1	fennel, cored and cut into 6 wedges
¼ cup	grated celeriac		
6 tablespoons	tomato paste	8 ounces	young zucchini, cut into 2-inch sticks
6	tomatoes, peeled, seeded, and chopped (see chapter 1)	6 ounces	snow peas
		6 ounces	carrots, cut into 2-inch sticks
2 cups	dry white wine	12	tomato petals (see chapter 1)
1 quart	brown veal stock (see chapter 7)	2 tablespoons	melted butter

(continued)

1.   Dredge the veal shank pieces in the flour.

2.   Heat the olive oil in a shallow 6-quart *rondeau*, and brown the veal shanks on all sides over medium heat. Remove and keep warm.

3.   Add the onions to the same *rondeau*, and cook until lightly browned. Add the garlic and the grated carrots, fennel, and celeriac, and cook for 5 minutes over moderate heat.

4.   Add the tomato paste, tomatoes, and wine. Reduce by half.

5.   Add the brown veal stock, salt, bay leaves, thyme, rosemary, and lemon rind. Bring to a simmer. Add the browned veal shanks, shaking the *rondeau* to distribute the starch (from the *flour*) from the shanks. Cover the *rondeau*, and cook over low heat for 1 hour, until the meat is fork tender.

6.   Remove the cooked veal shanks to a suitable container, and cover to keep warm.

7.   Strain the remaining sauce through a fine china cap, pressing on the solids that remain to extract all liquid. Bring the sauce to a boil again, and reduce as necessary to obtain a coating consistency. Degrease the sauce while reducing. Adjust the seasonings, and pour over the veal shanks. Cover again to keep warm.

8.   Steam the scallions, fennel, zucchini, snow peas, and carrots for the garnish until just done. Brush the tomato petals with butter and place in a 350°F oven to heat through.

9.   Arrange the braised veal shanks on a serving platter, and pour the sauce over the meat. Arrange the steamed vegetables neatly around the shanks. Decorate with tomato petals. White risotto (chapter 6) or *tagliolini* (chapter 5) go well with this dish.

Ossobuco alla Merana
BRAISED VEAL SHANKS, MERANESE STYLE

The method here is somewhat unusual, because the shank is boned, the meat is roasted, and the marrow bone is cut into 1-inch pieces and cooked separately in a potent broth. But despite the extra effort involved, this recipe offers better portion control and no waste. Never cook marrow at too high a temperature, or it will contract and slip from the bone.

Yield: 6 servings

2	veal shanks from milk-fed veal, 2½ pounds each	¼ cup	tomato paste
		4	ripe tomatoes, peeled, seeded, and chopped (see chapter 1)
½ tablespoon	chopped or grated lemon rind		
½ tablespoon	chopped or grated orange rind	3 cups	dry white wine
		1 quart	brown veal stock (see chapter 7)
2 tablespoons	chopped Italian parsley		
		2	bay leaves
2 to 3 cloves	garlic, minced	1	rosemary sprig
6 tablespoons	olive oil	⅓ teaspoon	freshly ground black pepper
8 ounces	onions, finely diced		
2 ounces	carrots, diced	½ teaspoon	salt
2 ounces	fennel, diced	1 pint	double beef broth (see chapter 3)
4 ounces	celeriac, diced		

1.   Bone the veal shanks, keeping the meat in one piece if possible.

2.   Cut the marrow bones into six 1- to 1½-inch pieces with a meat saw or hacksaw. Place the cut pieces in a container with salted water for several hours to whiten the marrow. Use any end trimmings from the bones for the sauce.

3.   Combine the lemon and orange rind, Italian parsley, and garlic. This mixture is called the *gremolada*.

4.   Spread three-quarters of the *gremolada* into the cavities of the boned shank meat. Roll the meat tightly, and secure with butcher's twine.

5.   Heat the olive oil in a 6-quart *rondeau*. Sear the veal rolls on all sides over moderate heat. Remove and keep warm.

(continued)

6.   Add the onions, carrots, fennel, and celeriac, and brown slightly. Add the tomato paste and continue to brown. Stir in the chopped tomatoes and wine, and reduce by half. Add the brown veal stock, bay leaves, rosemary, pepper, and salt.

7.   Add the seared veal rolls, and braise slowly, covered, for about 1¼ hours, until the meat is fork tender. Remove the veal, and keep warm.

8.   Strain the remaining sauce through a fine china cap, pressing on the solids to extract all liquid. Bring the sauce back to a boil, and reduce further as necessary to obtain a coating consistency. Degrease the sauce while reducing. Keep sauce hot in a small saucepan.

9.   Arrange the marrow bones in a small dish, and poach them in very strong beef broth over low heat until just underdone. The marrow should remain slightly pink in the middle and very plump.

10.   Remove the twine from the veal rolls, and cut into 2 slices per serving. Spoon the hot sauce over each heated serving plate, and arrange the veal neatly on top. Place the poached marrow, topped with the remaining *gremolada*, between the slices. Risotto (see chapter 6), *tagliolini* (see chapter 5), or *gnocchi* (see chapter 6) go well with this dish.

Rognonata di Vitello al Forno

ROAST VEAL LOIN AND KIDNEY

Yield: 8 servings

8 ounces	pork caul	2 ounces	carrots, diced small
3 pounds	veal loin, with 2-inch flank intact	2 ounces	celery, diced small
		4 ounces	onions, diced small
1	veal kidney, with suet covering intact	1 teaspoon	tomato paste
½ teaspoon	freshly ground black pepper	1 quart	brown veal stock (see chapter 7)
½ teaspoon	salt	to taste	bay leaves
1 tablespoon	chopped rosemary	to taste	cloves
1 tablespoon	chopped marjoram	to taste	black peppercorns
¼ cup	chopped parsley	to taste	salt
3 tablespoons	dried egg white (if available)		

1.   Place the pork caul in water to cover, and soak for 1 hour.

2.   Cut the veal loin twice lengthwise to butterfly. Keep any trimmings for the sauce.

3.   Trim most of the fat from the veal kidney, and cut the kidney lengthwise in half.

4.   Combine the pepper, salt, rosemary, marjoram, and parsley, and spread onto the butterflied loin.

5.   Sprinkle the seam with the dried egg white.

6.   Place halved veal kidney lengthwise along the cut side of the loin, and roll the loin up tightly. Tie every 2 inches with butcher's twine to secure.

7.   Remove the pork caul from the water, and blot dry with paper towels. Spread the caul out on a table, and completely wrap the stuffed loin in it. Season with additional black pepper and salt.

8.   Place the loin on a rack in a roasting pan; add any leftover veal trimmings to the pan. Place in a preheated 400°F oven; after 10 minutes lower the temperature to 350°F. Roast the loin for about 1¼ to 1½ hours.

9.   Remove the roast from the oven; leave the veal trimmings. Degrease the pan, add the carrots, celery, and onions, and brown lightly. Add the tomato paste, and continue to cook over moderate heat until the paste begins to turn brown.

10.   Add the brown veal stock, bay leaves, cloves, peppercorns, and salt. Reduce to 2 cups. Strain, and keep hot in a hot water bath.

11.   Remove the twine from the veal loin, and cut into 1 thick piece (rather than 2 thinner pieces) per serving. Arrange on hot serving plates, and spoon the sauce around the meat. White risotto (see chapter 6) or a steamed medley of vegetables, such as carrots, zucchini, green beans, leeks, and fennel, goes well with this dish.

Cima di Vitello alla Tirolese
STUFFED VEAL BREAST, TYROLEAN STYLE

Milk-fed veal breast from the youngest animals are best for this recipe. The quality of this meat is so succulent that even the cartilage is soft enough to be cut with a knife after roasting.

If veal from older, heavier animals is the only meat available, bone the breast when butterflying it. The meat can then be stuffed and secured with butcher's twine.

When rolling meat that is to be sliced later, use dried egg whites along the seams if possible, to ensure easy slicing.

(continued)

Yield: 6 servings

½ cup	olive oil	4½ pounds	breast of milk-fed veal, bone in
3 ounces	onions, finely diced		
3 ounces	lean smoked bacon, diced small	4 ounces	onions, coarsely chopped
¼ cup	chopped parsley	2 ounces	carrots, coarsely chopped
12 ounces	stale Italian or French bread	2 ounces	celery, coarsely chopped
1	egg	1	thyme sprig
¼ cup	milk	1	rosemary sprig
¼ teaspoon	freshly ground black pepper	1	bay leaf
pinch	salt	3 cups	brown veal stock (see chapter 7)
pinch	nutmeg		

1. Heat 3 tablespoons of oil in a skillet, and sauté onions until lightly browned. Add the bacon and parsley (both uncooked), and remove from the heat.

2. Cut the stale bread into ¼-inch cubes, and combine with onions, bacon, and parsley in a 4-quart mixing bowl.

3. Beat the egg lightly with the milk, stir in the pepper, salt, and nutmeg, and pour over the bread mixture. Mix carefully so as not to crush the bread. Let rest for 1 hour.

4. Remove the rib bones from the breast without cutting into the meat itself. Save the bones and trimmings.

5. Separate the upper and lower parts of the breast along the membrane with your fingers (and perhaps a small knife), making a pouch between the two layers of meat.

6. Fill the pouch with the stuffing. It is important not to overstuff the pouch, as the meat contracts when cooking. If overstuffed, the stuffing will be forced out or the meat will split.

7. Secure the opening with wooden or bamboo skewers.

8. Brush the veal breast with the remaining oil, and season with salt and pepper.

9. Place the stuffed breast on a rack in a roasting pan with the bones and trimmings. Roast in a preheated 350°F oven for about 1½ hours, until fork tender. Baste frequently while roasting. Remove and keep warm.

10. Add the onions, carrots, and celery to the bones and trimmings still in the pan and brown slightly. Add the thyme, rosemary, bay leaf, and brown veal stock, and reduce to 2 cups. Degrease the pan while reducing the liquid. Strain through cheese-cloth. (A bit of tomato paste may also be added before the stock.)

11.   Cut the veal into 1 thick slice per serving. Spoon the sauce onto each plate, and place the meat on top. Sautéed chanterelles and glazed carrots and fennel go well with this dish.

Tenneroni di Vitello Farcito al Cavolo Verde con Salsa d'Aglio e Pepe Verde
STUFFED VEAL TENDERLOIN WRAPPED IN SAVOY CABBAGE WITH GARLIC AND GREEN-PEPPERCORN SAUCE

Yield: 6 servings

8 ounces	pork caul	2 tablespoons	chopped marjoram
2	large veal tenderloins, 1½ pounds each	2 tablespoons	chopped parsley
		to taste	salt
		1½ ounces	white breadcrumbs
2 tablespoons	olive oil	8	savoy cabbage leaves
1 ounce	pancetta, diced		
1 ounce	butter		
2 ounces	onions, diced small	**SAUCE:**	
2 cloves	garlic, minced		
9 ounces	mushrooms, diced small	1½ ounces	butter
		12 cloves	garlic
½ cup	dry white wine	1 cup	dry white wine
2 tablespoons	meat glace (see chapter 7)	½ cup	Marsala
		6 tablespoons	meat glace (see chapter 7)
¼ teaspoon	freshly ground black pepper	1 cup	tomato sauce (see chapter 7)
1	egg yolk, beaten	2 tablespoons	green peppercorns
1	roasted red pepper, diced small (see chapter 1)		

1.   Soak the pork caul in water for 1 hour.

2.   Trim any fat and cartilage from the veal tenderloins, and cut away the very narrow (tail) end. Discard the fat; use the meat trimmings and cartilage for other recipes, as for brown veal stock.

(continued)

3. Sear the tenderloins quickly in the oil on all sides until medium-rare. Remove and cool.

4. Render the *pancetta* in a large skillet and drain the fat.

5. Add the butter to the *pancetta,* and reheat. Add the onions, garlic, and mushrooms, and sauté until lightly caramelized.

6. Deglaze the pan with the wine, and reduce completely. Add the meat *glace.* Remove from the heat, and stir in the black pepper, egg yolk, red pepper, marjoram, and parsley. Add the salt, and cool.

7. Mix in the breadcrumbs, and refrigerate.

8. Blanch the cabbage leaves in salted water for 20 to 30 seconds. Drain, refresh with a little cold water, and blot dry with a towel. Cut out the ribs.

9. For the sauce, melt ½ ounce of butter in a 1-quart saucepan. Add the garlic cloves, cover, and stew in a moderate oven for 10 minutes. Add the wines, and simmer on the stove over low heat for 10 minutes. Remove the garlic cloves and reserve.

10. Add the meat *glace* and reduce to the desired consistency if necessary. Add the tomato sauce, and bring to a simmer. Strain the sauce through a fine-mesh sieve, and adjust the seasonings.

11. Reheat the sauce, and add the green peppercorns and reserved cooked garlic cloves.

12. Spread the pork caul on a work table and blot dry with a towel.

13. Arrange 2 sets of 4 cabbage leaves on the table in a layer. Spread the filling over the leaves. Set each veal tenderloin in the center of the cabbage leaves, and roll tightly. Place the rolls on the caul, and wrap tightly again, being sure that the fat goes around twice. Tuck under the ends, and refrigerate until ready to cook.

14. Place the stuffed veal tenderloin on a roasting rack set on a sheet pan in a preheated 350°F oven. Bake for about 20 minutes. Rest for 10 minutes before serving.

15. Slice the tenderloins into 3 slices per serving, and arrange neatly on hot serving plates. Swirl the remaining butter into the hot sauce, and spoon the sauce around the veal. Potatoes Anna (see chapter 12), grilled zucchini and leeks, and tomatoes go well with this dish.

Basil

Chervil

Chives

Italian parsley

Marjoram

Mint

Oregano

Rosemary

Sage

Savory

Sorrel

Tarragon

Thyme

1. Fresh herbs most frequently used in Italian cooking. *Courtesy of The Green House, Encinitas, CA.*

2. Caprino, Caprino with herbs and spices, and Fiore Sardo. *Courtesy of the Italian Trade Commission.*

3. Fontina, Gorgonzola, Grana, and Italico. *Courtesy of the Italian Trade Commission.*

4. Mascarpone, Montasio, Mozzarella, Nostrale, and Torta mascarpone. *Courtesy of the Italian Trade Commission.*

5. Robiola, Scamorza, Stracchino, Taleggio, and Toscanello. *Courtesy of the Italian Trade Commission.*

6. *Verdure Cotte Croccanti con Polpa di Gamberetti e Fegatini*
Crisp vegetables with shrimp and chicken livers
Page 27

7. *Insalata di Mozzarella all'Erbe*
Mozzarella with piquant herb dressing
Page 30

8. *Insalata alla Marinara*
Seafood salad, mariner style
Page 34

9. *Filetto di Trota Marinato al*
Profumo di Finocchio e Pepe Verde
Fillet of trout in fennel marinade with
green peppercorn dressing
Page 41

10. *Vitello Freddo, con Salsa*
Tonnato e Capperi
Sliced braised veal with tuna-caper sauce
Page 43

11. *Sella di Vitello Farcita con*
Insalata Capricciosa e Uova Farcite
Roast stuffed saddle of veal with
vegetable salad and deviled eggs
Page 46

12. *Carpaccio con Caponatina*
Thin-sliced raw beef tenderloin with
eggplant-vegetable salad
Page 51

13. *Prosciutto Crudo con Spuma di
Peperoni Rossi con Insalata di
Funghi e Spinaci*
Prosciutto with red-pepper mousse,
mushroom salad, and spinach
Page 54

14. *Fiori di Zucchino con Spuma di
Frutti di Mare e Fonduta di
Pomodoro*
Zucchini blossoms filled with seafood
mousse, with tomato fondue
Page 84

15. *Piccola Spuma di Capesante e Gamberetti con Tagliolini Verdi e Salsa di Peperoni Rossi*
Scallop and shrimp mousseline with spinach *tagliolini* and red-pepper sauce
Page 86

16. *Cozze alla Provenzale*
Mussels steamed in white wine, Provençal style
Page 93

17. *Cosce di Rane alla Diavola con Risotto*
Deviled frog legs with risotto
Page 94

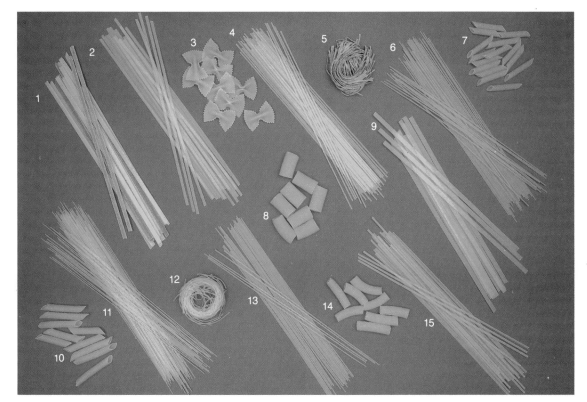

18. Examples of straight (nonstuffed) and machine-made pastas: 1 Paglia e fieno; 2 Fettuccine; 3 Farfalle; 4 Linguine fino; 5 Tagliolini verde; 6 Spaghettini; 7 Penne rigate; 8 Rigatoni; 9 Fettuce; 10 Penne lisce; 11 Capellini; 12 Capelli d'angelo; 13 Spaghetti; 14 Mezze rigatoni; 15 Linguine.

19. Examples of stuffed pastas, and other straight and machine-made pastas: 1 Conchiglie and conchigliette; 2 Lasagne; 3 Tortelloni; 4 Iolanda; 5 Maccheroncelli; 6 Perciatti; 7 Manicotti; 8 Tubettini; 9 Tortellini; 10 Mafalde; 11 Bucatini; 12 Ravioli; 13 Linguine di passero (bigoli); 14 Mezzani; 15 Tubetti; 16 Fusilli bucati; 17 Cavatelli.

20. *Linguine con Ragù di Trippa
alla Trentina*
Linguine with stewed tripe,
Trentina style
Page 151

21. *Linguine alla Pescatore*
Linguine, fisherman style
Page 152

22. *Trenette alla Genovese*
Trenette with basil puree
Page 165

23. *Fusilli con Gamberetti e Peperoni Misti alla Panna*
Fusilli with shrimp and mixed peppers in cream
Page 167

24. *Penne alle Verdure di Stagione*
Penne with seasonal vegetables
Page 169

25. *Timballo di Maccheroni alla Spuma di Gamberetti Aurora*
Macaroni timbale with shrimp mousseline and sauce aurora
Page 188

26. *Ravioli di Coniglio in Salsa Funghi e Pepe Verde*
Ravioli with sautéed rabbit in mushroom–green peppercorn sauce
Page 194

27. *Risotto con Fegatini di Pollo e Ciccioli*
Risotto with chicken livers and chicken cracklings
Page 208

28. *Risotto con Zucca e Prosciutto*
Risotto with pumpkin and *prosciutto*
Page 212

29. *Risotto con Carciofi e Pancetta Croccante*
Risotto with artichokes and crisp *pancetta*
Page 214

30. *Involtini di Polenta con Lumache alla Romana*
Rolled polenta with snails and mushrooms
Page 220

31. *Filetti di Branzino in Salsa di Riccio di Mare*
Fillets of sea bass with creamed sea urchins
Page 270

32. *Calamaretti Ripieni alla Napoletana*
Squid stuffed with ricotta in *marinara* sauce
Page 277

33. *Calamari con Spuma di Scampi in Salsa Crema al Pomodoro*
Squid stuffed with *scampi* mousseline in tomato cream sauce
Page 280

34. *Capesante ai Porcini e Pomodori Venezia*
Scallops with *porcini* and tomatoes
Page 283

35. *Gamberi all'Aromi*
Shrimp with herbs and vegetables
Page 286

36. *Bianchetti di Langoustino e Capesante con Carciofini e Funghi*
Langoustine and scallops *blanquette* with artichokes and mushrooms
Page 289

37. *Trance di Salmone al Vapore con Zabaione al Caviale*
Steamed salmon steaks with caviar *sabayon*
Page 299

38. *Piccola Zuppa di Pesce allo Zafferano e Finocchio*
Seafood stew with saffron and fennel
Page 307

39. *Scaloppine al Sorrentino*
Veal *scaloppine* with tomatoes, peppers, and Fontina
Page 320

40. *Nodini di Vitello alle Noci*
Veal loin steaks with walnut cream sauce
Page 327

41. *Rognoni di Vitello Farciti ai Funghi in Salsa Marsala*
Roast veal kidneys stuffed with mushrooms in Marsala sauce
Page 334

42. *Medaglione di Animelle di Vitello alla Crema Basilico*
Broiled *médaillons* of veal sweetbreads with basil cream sauce
Page 336

43. *Costate d'Agnello ai Funghi in Mille-Foglie con Salsa d'Aglio e Peperoni Rossi*
Lamb chops with mushrooms in puff pastry with garlic and red-pepper sauce
Page 350

44. *Zampone*
Stuffed pig's trotter
Page 358

45. *Medaglione di Bue alla Castellana*
Sautéed beef *médaillons* with artichokes and tomatoes
Page 374

46. *Spezzatino di Filetto di Bue alle Verdure Fresche in Bordura di Riso*
Sautéed beef strips with fresh vegetables in a rice ring
Page 378

47. *Trippa di Bue alla Veneto*
Braised beef tripe with tomatoes and grappa
Page 386

48. *Petti di Pollo Ripieni con Prosciutto e Porri in Salsa Crema all'Erbe*
Chicken breasts stuffed with *prosciutto* and leeks in herb cream sauce
Page 390

49. *Pulcini Ripieni in Tecia agli Spugnole*
Baby chickens stuffed with morels, baked in earthenware
Page 396

50. *Giambonette di Pollo Farcite alla Boscaiola*
Stuffed chicken legs with wild mushroom and garlic sauce
Page 398

51. *Noci di Capriolo in Salsa Crema di Ginepro con Castagne e Cipolline Glassate*
Noisettes of venison in juniper cream sauce with glazed chestnuts and pearl onions
Page 428

52. *Medaglioni di Capriolo in Salsa d'Arancia e Mirtilli Rossi*
Venison *médaillons* in orange sauce with cranberries
Page 429

53. *Sella di Coniglio Selvaggio Farcita di Cavolo Verde e Funghi con Salsa Marsala e Peperoni Rossi*
Roast saddle of wild rabbit stuffed with savoy cabbage and mushrooms in Marsala sauce with red peppers
Page 432

54. *Cosciotti di Coniglio alla Cacciatora*
Rabbit legs braised in white wine, tomatoes, and mushrooms
Page 434

55. *Quaglia Arrosta Ripiena al Sugo d'Aglio*
Stuffed roast quail with garlic sauce
Page 437

56. *Suprema di Quaglie Affogate alle Verdure Fresche*
Poached quail breasts with fresh vegetables
Page 442

57. *Suprema di Fagiano in Salsa Crema di Porcini e Pepe Verde*
Sautéed pheasant breasts in *porcini* and green-peppercorn cream sauce
Page 450

58. *Fagianelle Grigliate con Burro alla Diavola*
Grilled baby pheasants with deviled butter sauce
Page 451

59. *Soufflé Dolce al Frangelico*
Frozen soufflé with hazelnut liqueur
Page 518

60. *Cassata Napoletana*
Neapolitan bombe
Page 523

61. *Baverese alla Vaniglia con Purea di Lamponi*
Vanilla bavarian cream with raspberry puree
Page 530

62. *Baverese alla Cioccolata con Fonduta di Cioccolata*
Chocolate bavarian cream with chocolate fondue
Page 532

63. *Bavarese tricolori con Purea di Lamponi e Ribes*
Chocolate, vanilla, and strawberry bavarian creams with raspberry and red-currant puree
Page 533

64. *Torta allo Zabaione di Cioccolata*
Chocolate *sabayon* cake
Page 540

65. *Zabaione al Cioccolato in Tazzette con Fonduta alla Cioccolata*
Chocolate *sabayon* timbales with chocolate fondue
Page 544

66. *Bomba di Marzipane*
Marzipan bombe
Page 545

67. *Savoiardi, Amaretti, e Biscotti alla Fiorentina*
Ladyfingers, macaroons, and Florentine cookies
Pages 548–549

68. *Crespelle con Frutte Fresche al Galliano*
Crêpes with fresh fruit in Galliano
Page 565

69. *Gnocchetti di Patate di Papaneri con Composta di Susine, Purea di Lamponi e Ribes Rosse*
Small potato *gnocchi* in buttered poppy seeds with plum compote and raspberry and red-currant puree
Page 566

70. *Canederli di Patate con Susine alla Tirolese*
Potato dumplings filled with plums, Tyrolean style
Page 568

Polpettini di Vitello con Salsa d'Aglio e Peperoni
VEAL PATTIES WITH GARLIC AND RED-PEPPER SAUCE

Yield: 6 servings

PATTIES:

24 ounces	lean veal, finely ground
½ cups	finely diced onions, sautéed in butter
2	eggs
to taste	salt and freshly ground black pepper
to taste	nutmeg
¾ cup	coarse breadcrumbs from Italian bread
½ cup	heavy cream
to pan-fry	oil

SAUCE:

5 tablespoons	virgin olive oil
½ cup	finely diced onions
12 cloves	garlic, peeled
1 cup	dry white wine
1½ cups	brown veal stock (see chapter 7)
1 cup	puree of roasted red bell peppers (see chapter 1)
2	chili peppers, chopped
to taste	salt and freshly ground black pepper

GARNISH:

2 tablespoons	olive oil
1 cup	medium-diced red and green bell peppers
1 cup	peeled, seeded, and diced tomatoes (see chapter 1)
¼ cup	coarsely chopped parsley
2 tablespoons	coarsely chopped oregano
6	basil sprigs

1.   Chill all the patty ingredients except the oil until very cold.

2.   Mix the ground veal with the onions, eggs, salt, pepper, nutmeg, breadcrumbs, and cream. Chill for 1 hour.

3.   Use a serving spoon, dipped frequently in water to prevent sticking, to shape the veal mixture into 12 oval patties. The surfaces of all the patties must be smooth and free of cracks and crevices.

4.   Arrange the patties on a tray that has been lightly sprinkled with dry breadcrumbs. Refrigerate until ready to cook.

5.   Heat 5 tablespoons of olive oil in a 3-quart saucepan, and sauté the onions until slightly brown. Add whole peeled garlic cloves, and cook for another few minutes.

(continued)

6. Deglaze the pan with the wine, and reduce completely.

7. Add the brown veal stock, and reduce to 1 cup.

8. Add the puree of roasted red peppers, chopped chili peppers, salt, and pepper. Remove from the heat, and keep hot in a suitable dish.

9. Heat the oil for pan-frying in a large skillet, and pan-fry the patties over moderate heat on both sides, turning once. Remove and drain. Keep warm.

10. Heat 2 tablespoons of olive oil in the skillet, and quickly sauté the diced peppers. Stir in the tomatoes, parsley, and oregano, and remove from the heat. Add to the sauce.

11. Spoon sauce onto hot plates, and arrange 2 veal patties neatly on each. Garnish with fresh basil sprigs.

Scaloppine al Sorrentino
VEAL SCALOPPINE WITH TOMATOES, PEPPERS, AND FONTINA

Yield: 6 servings

1 ounce	pancetta, chopped	to taste	salt
1 ounce	butter	12	veal scaloppine, 2 ounces each
3 ounces	red onions, diced medium		
2 cloves	garlic, minced	to taste	salt and freshly ground black pepper
2	hot chili peppers, chopped		
		1/3 ounce	flour
3 ounces	red bell peppers, cut in short julienne	6 tablespoons	clarified butter (see chapter 1)
2 cups	julienne of peeled and seeded tomatoes (see chapter 1)	2 cups	brown veal stock (see chapter 7)
		12	Fontina slices, 1 1/2 by 2 1/2 inches
6	basil leaves, coarsely chopped		

1. Render the *pancetta* with the ounce of butter in a large skillet. Quickly sauté the onions, garlic, chili peppers, and red peppers until tender-crisp. Add the tomatoes, basil, and salt, and remove from the heat. Cool.

2. Season the *scaloppine* with salt and pepper, and dredge in the flour.

3. Heat the clarified butter in a large skillet, and quickly sauté the *scaloppine* on both sides, turning once. Keep them undercooked. Remove to an ovenproof dish.

4. Degrease the skillet, and add the brown veal stock. Reduce to 1 cup, strain, and keep hot.

5. Place 1 tablespoon of sautéed vegetables on each *scaloppina,* and top with a slice of Fontina. Place in a preheated hot oven just long enough to melt cheese. Place 2 *scaloppine* on each heated serving plate, and spoon the sauce around the meat (see color plate 39).

Scaloppe di Vitello alla Valdostana
VEAL CUTLETS WITH FONTINA AND PROSCIUTTO

This is one of two Valdostana-style preparations; the other calls for white truffles instead of *prosciutto.* It is also possible to secure the folded cutlet edges with dried egg white. Just sprinkle the inside edge with the powder, fold, and pound the edge lightly with the pointed side of a mallet.

Yield: 6 servings

6	thin veal cutlets, 5 to 6 ounces each	1 cup	dry vermouth
6	Fontina slices, 3 by 2 inches	2 cups	brown veal stock (see chapter 7)
12	cooked prosciutto slices, 3 by 2 inches	³/₄ to 1 cup	heavy cream
¹/₂ cup	flour	to taste	salt and freshly ground black pepper
6 tablespoons	clarified butter (see chapter 1)	3 tablespoons	finely chopped chives

1. Flatten the veal cutlets with a meat cleaver between sheets of plastic wrap until approximately 6 by 6 inches.

2. Sandwich the slices of Fontina between the slices of cooked *prosciutto.*

3. Place the sandwiched ham and cheese on half of the flattened cutlet, and fold the other half over. Secure the three open sides with toothpicks.

(continued)

4.   Dredge the stuffed cutlets in flour.

5.   Heat the clarified butter in a large skillet, and fry the cutlets on both sides over moderate heat, turning once, for about 2 minutes each side. Remove and keep warm.

6.   Degrease the pan, deglaze with the vermouth, and reduce by half.

7.   Add the brown veal stock to the skillet, and again reduce by half.

8.   Add the cream and continue to reduce until the desired coating consistency is reached. Add the salt and pepper.

9.   Add the cutlets to the sauce, and bring just to a simmer to allow the flour from the cutlets to thicken the sauce a bit more. Remove the skillet from the heat. Remove the cutlets from the sauce and remove the toothpicks.

10.   Place a cutlet on each serving plate, and spoon the sauce over the top. Sprinkle with the chopped chives. Rice, pasta, or polenta go well with this dish.

Saltimbocca alla Romana

VEAL SCALOPPINE WITH SAGE AND PROSCIUTTO

Yield: 6 servings

12	veal scaloppine, 1½ to 2 ounces each	6 tablespoons	clarified butter (see chapter 1)
12	sage leaves	¼ cup	dry Marsala
½ teaspoon	freshly ground black pepper	1 cup	dry white wine
		2 cups	brown veal stock (see chapter 7)
12	thin cooked prosciutto slices, 2 by 3 inches	1 ounce	butter
½ cup	flour		

1.   Flatten the veal *scaloppine* fairly thin with the flat side of a mallet. Place a leaf of fresh sage on top of each, and season with black pepper. Top each with a thin slice of *prosciutto.*

2.   Place the meat between layers of plastic wrap, ham side up, and gently pound the top with an edged mallet. This will keep the ham in place during cooking.

3.   Carefully remove the plastic, and dredge the *scaloppine* in the flour. Shake off any excess.

4.   Heat the clarified butter in a large skillet, and sauté the *scaloppine* for about 30 seconds on each side, turning once, starting with the ham side down. Keep the *scaloppine* undercooked. Remove from the pan, and keep warm.

5.   Degrease the skillet, and deglaze the pan with the wines. Reduce slightly, add the brown veal stock, and reduce again to 1½ cups. Strain into a small saucepan, and swirl in the butter to create an emulsion.

6.   Arrange a *scaloppina* on each heated serving plate, and spoon the sauce over the top. Spinach fettuccine go well with this dish.

Frittura di Piccata

SMALL VEAL CUTLETS WITH LEMON SAUCE

Although the name *piccata* implies small veal cutlets that are fried, this dish can greatly vary in presentation and composition. The *piccata* is often sautéed plain, coated in egg batter, or sometimes even breaded. One most often encounters one of the first two presentations, but the sauce is always seasoned with lemon.

Yield: 6 servings

12	small veal cutlets, 2 ounces each	1 cup	brown veal stock (see chapter 7)
to taste	salt and freshly ground black pepper	2 tablespoons	lemon juice
		1½ ounces	cold butter
¼ cup	flour	1 tablespoon	chopped parsley
1	egg, lightly beaten	to taste	salt and freshly ground black pepper
6 tablespoons	clarified butter (see chapter 1)		

SAUCE:

1 cup	dry white wine

1.   Season the veal cutlets with the salt and pepper, and dredge first in flour, shaking off any excess, and then in the beaten egg.

(continued)

2.   Heat the clarified butter in a large skillet, and pan-fry the cutlets until nicely browned. Remove to a hot plate.

3.   Degrease the skillet, and deglaze with the white wine. Reduce by half, then add the brown veal stock. Reduce again by half.

4.   Add the lemon juice, and swirl in pieces of cold butter to create an emulsion. Add the chopped parsley, and adjust the seasonings.

5.   Arrange 2 pieces of veal on each hot serving plate, and spoon the sauce over the top.

Scaloppe di Vitello alla Bolognese
VEAL CUTLETS WITH PROSCIUTTO AND GRUYÈRE, BOLOGNESE STYLE

Yield: 6 servings

12	small veal cutlets, 2 ounces each	1½ cups	dry white wine
to taste	salt and freshly ground black pepper	1½ cups	brown veal stock (see chapter 7)
¼ cup	flour	12	thin cooked prosciutto slices, the size of the veal
6 tablespoons	clarified butter (see chapter 1)	12	thin Gruyère slices, the size of the veal
½ cup	dry sherry (fino)	1½ ounces	butter

1.   Flatten the veal cutlets to the desired thickness, and season with salt and pepper. Dredge lightly in the flour.

2.   Heat the clarified butter in a large skillet, and sauté the veal quickly, until medium done. Remove to an ovenproof pan.

3.   Degrease the skillet, deglaze with the wines, and reduce to ¼ cup.

4.   Add the brown veal stock, and reduce over high heat to ¾ cup. Adjust the seasonings, and strain into a small saucepan. Keep hot.

5.   Place a slice of *prosciutto* topped with a slice of Gruyère on each cutlet.

6. Place the veal in a preheated hot oven, just long enough to melt the cheese.

7. Swirl the butter into the sauce to create an emulsion. Arrange 2 pieces of veal on each hot serving plate, and spoon the sauce neatly over the cheese topping. Grilled polenta (see chapter 6) and sautéed sliced zucchini with olive oil, garlic, and oregano or grilled radicchio (see chapter 12) go well with this dish.

Costate di Vitello alle Senape con Funghi di Bosco
SAUTÉED VEAL CHOPS IN MUSTARD CREAM SAUCE WITH WILD MUSHROOMS

Yield: 6 servings

6	veal chops, well trimmed, with bone, 6 to 7 ounces each	1½ cups	dry white wine
to taste	salt and freshly ground black pepper	6 tablespoons	veal glace (see chapter 7)
6 tablespoons	clarified butter (see chapter 1)	1 pint	heavy cream, reduced to 1 cup
1 ounce	shallots, finely diced	1 tablespoon	prepared mustard
12 ounces	fresh porcini, thickly sliced	1 tablespoon	fresh lemon juice
		2 tablespoons	finely chopped chives

1. Season the veal chops with salt and pepper. Heat the clarified butter in a large skillet, and fry the chops over moderate heat on both sides, turning once, until slightly underdone (pink in the middle). Remove from the skillet, and place in a warm oven.

2. Reheat the skillet, and sauté the shallots and *porcini*. Do not let the mushrooms lose their shape by overcooking—they should be somewhat stiff. Remove the mushrooms from the skillet and keep warm.

3. Deglaze the skillet with the wine, and reduce to ¼ cup.

4. Add the veal *glace*.

5. Add the reduced cream, and whisk in the mustard and the lemon juice. Adjust the seasonings, and add the cooked mushrooms. Add the chives.

6. Spoon some sauce onto each hot serving plate. Place the cooked veal chops on top of the sauce. Steamed leeks, broccoli, and baby carrots go well with this dish.

Involtini di Vitello con Prosciutto e Mozzarella all'Erbe e Aromatiche
VEAL ROULADES WITH PROSCIUTTO, MOZZARELLA, AND HERBS

Involtini are small veal roulades layered with ham and sage or other herbs. They are threaded on skewers, and most often cooked in butter, though they can also be broiled or grilled. To ensure uniformity in size, cut all the veal, *prosciutto,* and mozzarella to the same size.

Yield: 6 servings

FILLING:

1½ ounces	butter
½ cup	finely diced onions
4 cloves	garlic, finely minced
1	red bell pepper, finely diced (brunoise)
2	hot chili peppers, chopped
½ cup	finely diced mushrooms
½ cup	finely diced porcini
1	egg yolk, lightly beaten
3 tablespoons	dry Italian breadcrumbs
to taste	salt and freshly ground black pepper
¼ cup	chopped parsley

1 tablespoon	chopped sage
2 tablespoons	chopped basil
18	thin veal cutlets, 1 ounce each
18	very thin cooked prosciutto slices
18	thin mozzarella slices
6 tablespoons	clarified butter (see chapter 1)
to taste	salt and freshly ground black pepper
6 tablespoons	dry Marsala
¾ cup	dry red wine
2 cups	brown veal stock (see chapter 7)
1 ounce	butter

1.   Heat the butter in a large skillet, and sauté the onions for 1 minute. Add the garlic, red and chili peppers, mushrooms, and *porcini,* and continue to cook over high heat, stirring frequently, until almost no liquid remains in the skillet. Remove the skillet from the heat, and stir in the lightly beaten egg yolk, breadcrumbs, salt, pepper, parsley, sage, and basil. Put the filling in a suitable bowl, and let cool completely.

2.   Flatten the veal cutlets carefully between sheets of parchment paper or plastic wrap to a uniform size, using the dull side of a meat cleaver. Carefully remove the flattened cutlets from the paper, and place 1 slice of cooked *prosciutto* and of mozzarella on each cutlet. The *prosciutto* should be paper thin.

3.   Spread 1 teaspoon of filling over the cheese on each cutlet, and roll the cutlet up tightly.

4.   Thread 2 bamboo skewers through the rolls, as close to the seam as possible to secure them (using only 1 skewer makes the roulades more difficult to handle).

5.   Heat the clarified butter in a large skillet. Season the roulades to taste with salt and pepper, and cook them over moderate heat on both sides. Keep the roulades underdone. Remove from the pan and keep warm in the oven.

6.   Degrease the skillet, add the wines, and reduce by half. Add the brown veal stock, and reduce to about ¾ cup. Strain the sauce into a small saucepan and whisk in the butter to create an emulsion.

7.   Slide the roulades from the skewers, and place 3 on each serving plate. Spoon the sauce over the top. Risotto with wine and saffron (see chapter 6) and stewed baby artichokes in white wine and herbs (see chapter 2) go well with this dish.

Nodini di Vitello alle Noci

VEAL LOIN STEAKS WITH WALNUT CREAM SAUCE

Yield: 6 servings

¼ cup	clarified butter (see chapter 1)	1½ cups	brown veal stock (see chapter 7)
12	veal loin steaks, well trimmed, 2 ounces each	1½ cups	heavy cream, reduced to ¾ cup
2½ ounces	walnuts, blanched and peeled	to taste	salt and freshly ground black pepper
½ cup	dry sherry (Manzanilla)	1 tablespoon	lemon juice
1 cup	dry white wine	2 tablespoons	whipped cream

1.   Heat the clarified butter in a large skillet, and cook the veal steaks (*noisettes*) over moderate heat for about 2 minutes on each side, until just underdone.

2.   Remove the veal from the skillet to a suitable dish, and keep warm. Drain all grease from the pan.

(continued)

3. Add the walnuts to the same skillet, and deglaze with the wines. Reduce almost completely before removing the walnuts with a slotted spoon. Reserve the walnuts.

4. Add the brown veal stock to the skillet, and reduce again, to a light coating consistency.

5. Add the reduced cream, salt, pepper, and lemon juice.

6. Return the walnuts to the sauce.

7. Fold the whipped cream into the sauce to make it more velvety.

8. Arrange 2 veal steaks on each hot serving plate, and spoon the walnut sauce over the top. Steamed broccoli, carrots, and leeks go well with this dish (see color plate 40).

Spezzatino di Vitello alla Chipolata
VEAL STEW WITH CHIPOLATA SAUSAGES

Yield: 6 servings

6 tablespoons	olive oil
3 pounds	veal shoulder, cut in 1-inch cubes
3 tablespoons	flour
4 ounces	onions, finely diced
4 cloves	garlic, minced
6 tablespoons	tomato paste
6	ripe tomatoes, peeled, seeded, and chopped (see chapter 1)
1 cup	dry white wine
2 cups	brown veal stock (see chapter 7)
2	hot chili peppers, chopped
2 tablespoons	chopped parsley
1 tablespoon	chopped marjoram
to taste	salt and freshly ground black pepper

GARNISH:

6 ounces	small pearl onions
12	chestnuts
1 tablespoon	olive oil
18	chipolata sausages (miniature pork sausages)
1	red bell pepper, cut into strips
24	pitted black olives
2 tablespoons	chopped parsley

1. Heat the 6 tablespoons of olive oil in a heavy-bottomed 4-quart casserole. Dredge the veal in the flour, and sear it quickly in the hot oil. Remove the meat with a slotted spoon, and keep warm.

2. Add the onions to the same casserole, and brown. Stir in the garlic and tomato paste, and continue to cook for a few more minutes.

3. Add the chopped fresh tomatoes, wine, brown veal stock, chili peppers, parsley, marjoram, salt, and pepper. Reduce until lightly thickened.

4. Add the seared veal cubes, and braise covered, over low heat for 1 to 1¼ hours, until tender.

5. Peel and steam the pearl onions. Make a cross cut into the flat ends of the chestnut shells with a paring knife, and steam until soft. Remove the shells and skins.

6. Heat the tablespoon of olive oil in a large skillet. Add the chipolata sausages, and sauté until lightly colored. Add the onions and red peppers, and continue to sauté for another minute. Mix in the olives and chestnuts, and remove from the heat. Add the parsley.

7. Combine the stewed veal with the garnish when ready to serve. An alternative is to arrange the stew neatly in ceramic bowls or on dinner plates with the garnish placed on top. Polenta mush, molded or scooped, goes well with this dish (see chapter 6). (An ordinary ice-cream scoop, first dipped in hot water, is the most convenient way to serve this kind of polenta.)

Spezzatino di Vitello e Gamberetti con Peperoni Misti in Bordura di Riso
SAUTÉED VEAL AND SHRIMP WITH MIXED PEPPERS IN A SAFFRON RICE RING

Yield: 6 servings

12 ounces	veal loin, cut into 2½-inch strips	to taste	salt and freshly ground black pepper
18	medium shrimp, peeled and deveined, with fantails	3	hot chili peppers, chopped
½ cup	flour	18	black olives, pitted and quartered
1 cup	olive oil	4	tomatoes, peeled, seeded, and cut into strips (see chapter 1)
6 ounces	scallions, cut diagonally into 1½-inch lengths	½ cup	basil and oregano, coarsely chopped
12 ounces	red, green, and yellow bell peppers, cut into strips	6 to 7 cups	risotto with wine and saffron (see chapter 6)
8 cloves	garlic, minced	1 cup	grated Parmesan
6 ounces	porcini, cut into thick strips	6	basil sprigs
6 tablespoons	grappa		
1½ cups	dry white wine		
½ cup	veal or poultry glace (see chapter 7)		

1.   Dust the veal and shrimp with flour.

2.   Heat ¼ cup of olive oil in a large skillet for about 5 minutes to condition the pan and prevent the sticking.

3.   Add the veal strips, and sauté very quickly, until only partially done. Remove with a slotted spoon to a small colander placed over a dish to collect the juices.

4.   Heat another ¼ cup of olive oil in the skillet, and quickly sauté the shrimp, again until underdone. Remove with a slotted spoon to a strainer, and recover the juices as for the veal.

5.   Add additional oil to the skillet, and sauté the scallions and peppers until tender-crisp. Remove with a slotted spoon and add to veal, again, saving the drained juices. Sauté the garlic and mushrooms quickly, just until heated through, and add to the veal.

6. Degrease the skillet, and deglaze with the grappa. Add the wine, and reduce to ½ cup. Add the drippings from the sautéed shrimp, veal, and vegetables, and the *glace*. Adjust the seasonings.

7. Combine the shrimp, veal, and vegetables with the sauce, and heat thoroughly. *Do not simmer.* Mix in the chili peppers, olives, tomato strips, chopped basil, and oregano. Keep hot.

8. Mold the risotto in 1-cup ring molds. Turn the molds onto the serving plates.

9. Arrange the veal and shrimp mixture neatly in the center of each rice ring. Sprinkle with grated Parmesan and decorate with basil sprigs.

Fricassea di Vitello e Funghi alla Toscana
VEAL FRICASSEE WITH PORCINI, TUSCAN STYLE

This fricassee is rich, and so it is best served with plain vegetables, such as steamed asparagus, broccoli, leeks, zucchini, carrots, and fennel.

Yield: 6 servings

½ cup	clarified butter (see chapter 1)	to taste	salt and white pepper
3 pounds	veal shank or shoulder meat, cut in 1-inch cubes	to taste	nutmeg
		¾ pound	porcini, cleaned and thickly sliced
3 ounces	flour	1 cup	hot heavy cream
4 cups	hot white veal stock (see chapter 7)	2	egg yolks
1 cup	dry white wine	¼ cup	heavy cream
1	bouquet garni of celery, leek, and carrots (see chapter 1)	¼ cup	chopped parsley

1. Heat the butter in a heavy-bottomed 6-quart casserole. Add the cubed veal, and cook until the meat stiffens but does not color.

2. Stir in the flour, and cook for 3 to 4 minutes. Remove the pot from the heat and cool.

(continued)

3.   Add the hot white veal stock and wine, and stir carefully to avoid forming lumps. Bring to a simmer.

4.   Add the *bouquet garni*, salt, pepper, and nutmeg, and simmer over very low heat for 45 minutes.

5.   Add the *porcini*, and continue to cook over low heat for 10 minutes. Remove the *bouquet garni*.

6.   Mix in the hot cream and adjust the seasonings. Remove from the heat and keep covered.

7.   Whisk together the egg yolks and ¼ cup heavy cream. Spoon a cup of sauce into this yolk/cream mixture and stir well. Combine this carefully back into the sauce. Be careful: if the sauce is too hot, the egg yolks may coagulate. Garnish with chopped parsley. Spinach *tagliolini* (see chapter 5) or boiled rice (see chapter 6) mixed with sautéed bacon, green peas, and grated Parmesan, known as *risi e bisi*, goes well with this dish.

Cuori di Vitello Farciti coi Fagioli alla Toscana

STUFFED, BRAISED VEAL HEARTS WITH WHITE KIDNEY BEANS

Yield: 6 servings

2	veal hearts, from youngest milk-fed veal	1½ cups	fresh tomatoes, peeled, seeded, and chopped (see chapter 1)
6 to 8 ounces	hot Italian sausage	3	hot red chili peppers, chopped
¼ cup	olive oil		
2 ounces	pancetta, chopped	2	bay leaves
6 ounces	onions, diced small	¼ cup	chopped parsley
4 cloves	garlic, minced	to taste	salt and freshly ground black pepper
9 ounces	white kidney beans (cannellini), soaked overnight		
1½ quarts	beef broth (see chapter 3)	1 tablespoon	chopped rosemary
		1 tablespoon	chopped marjoram
6 tablespoons	tomato paste		
1 cup	dry white wine (optional)	**GARNISH:**	
		2 tablespoons	olive oil

1½ cups	sliced scallions, cut diagonally in 1-inch lengths	to taste	salt and freshly ground black pepper
1½ cups	sliced porcini		
3 to 4	fresh tomatoes, peeled, seeded, and cut into strips (see chapter 1)		

1.   Cut open the veal hearts and wash out the insides to rid them of coagulated blood. Blot dry with a towel.

2.   Remove the casings from the Italian sausage, fill the hearts with the sausage, and sew up the openings.

3.   Heat the olive oil in a 3-quart saucepan, and add the *pancetta*, onions, and garlic. Cook over medium heat until the onions are translucent.

4.   Place the stuffed hearts on the onions, and cook over moderate heat until all sides are lightly colored. Remove the hearts to a suitable dish and keep warm. Hold the onions in the pan.

5.   Place the white kidney beans in a noncorrosive 2-quart saucepan. Add the beef broth and cook over low heat for about 1¼ to 1½ hours.

6.   Add the tomato paste to the onions, and cook for several minutes. Stir in the wine, chopped tomatoes, chili peppers, bay leaves, parsley, rosemary, marjoram, salt, and pepper. Bring to a simmer, and return the veal hearts to the pan. Cover and cook over low heat for 1½ hours maximum. If extra liquid is needed, add some of the liquid in which the beans are cooking. The cooking time here will depend largely on the quality of the veal hearts, especially the age of the animal from which the hearts came. The hearts are cooked when they yield to finger pressure and feel soft. Remove them from the pan, and keep covered and warm.

7.   Reduce the cooking liquid until thick, and add the cooked, drained white kidney beans.

8.   Heat the 2 tablespoons of olive oil in a large skillet. Quickly sauté the scallions and sliced *porcini* in the olive oil for no longer than 10 seconds. Add the tomato strips, and remove from the heat. Season with salt and pepper.

9.   Spoon the beans onto hot serving plates. Slice the veal heart, and overlap 2 slices on each plate of beans. Garnish with the sautéed vegetables in a semicircle around the heart slices. Crisp potato cakes go well with this dish (see chapter 12).

Rognoni di Vitello Farciti ai Funghi in Salsa Marsala
ROAST VEAL KIDNEYS STUFFED WITH MUSHROOMS IN MARSALA SAUCE

For this dish to be successful, it is essential to procure dried egg whites from a specialty store dealing with charcuterie products (sausage and related items). Otherwise, slicing the roasted stuffed kidneys will be very difficult.

Yield: 6 servings

1 pound	pork caul	1 tablespoon	white breadcrumbs
1 tablespoon	clarified butter (see chapter 1)	2 ounces	butter
		1 ounce	shallots, finely diced
1 ounce	onions, very finely diced	3 cloves	garlic, minced
6 ounces	mushrooms, very finely diced	1/2 cup	Marsala
		1 cup	dry red wine
3 ounces	porcini, very finely diced	2 cups	brown veal stock (see chapter 7)
1/4 cup	dry white wine	1	thyme sprig
1	egg yolk, beaten	3	veal kidneys, fat removed
1 tablespoon	chopped marjoram		
1 tablespoon	chopped parsley	5 tablespoons	dried egg white
to taste	salt and freshly ground black pepper	6	bacon strips

1.   Soak the pork caul in fresh water for an hour. Drain thoroughly.

2.   Heat the clarified butter in a 7-inch skillet, and quickly sauté the onions and all mushrooms. Add the white wine, and reduce almost completely. Remove the skillet from the heat, and stir in the egg yolk, marjoram, parsley, salt, pepper, and breadcrumbs. Let cool in a suitable dish. (This stuffing can be prepared days in advance if desired.)

3.   Heat 1/2 ounce of butter in a 3-quart saucepan, and lightly sauté the shallots and garlic. Add the Marsala and red wine and reduce to 1/2 cup. Add the brown veal stock, and reduce to 1 1/2 cups, being sure to skim off any impurities that rise to the surface. Add the thyme, and add salt and pepper to taste. Strain through cheesecloth, and keep hot in a small hot water bath.

4.   Butterfly the veal kidneys, and remove the fat and nerves from the interior. Spread the mushroom filling on the insides, and fold the kidneys back together tightly. Sprinkle the dried egg white along the seams and in the crevices. Wrap 2 strips of bacon around each kidney. Spread a 9- by 9-inch piece of caul on a work table, and place the stuffed kidneys in the middle. Wrap tightly in the caul.

5.   Place the stuffed veal kidneys on a roasting rack with a drip pan underneath, and roast in a preheated 400°F oven for about 12 to 15 minutes, depending on desired doneness. Let rest at least 5 minutes before slicing. Do *not* cook the kidneys until well-done, as the meat will be dry and tough.

6.   Slice the kidneys with a sharp knife, and overlap 3 slices on each heated serving plate. Swirl the remaining 1½ ounces of butter into the sauce, creating an emulsion. Spoon the sauce around the kidneys (see color plate 41).

Rognoni di Vitello Trifolati all'Aceto Balsamico
SAUTÉED VEAL KIDNEYS WITH BALSAMIC VINEGAR

Yield: 6 servings

3 pounds	veal kidneys	1 tablespoon	chopped marjoram
6 ounces	porcini	½ teaspoon	chopped rosemary
2 ounces	butter	to taste	salt and freshly ground black pepper
6 ounces	onions, finely diced		
3 cloves	garlic, minced		
1	hot chili pepper, sliced	½ cup	flour
¼ cup	balsamic vinegar	6 tablespoons	clarified butter (see chapter 1)
½ cup	dry white wine		
2½ cups	brown veal stock (see chapter 7)		

1.   Remove all fat and connective tissue from the veal kidneys, and cut into fairly thin slices. Keep chilled.

2.   Wipe the *porcini* clean, and slice into thick pieces.

3.   Heat the butter in a shallow 3-quart saucepan. Sauté the onions until light brown. Add the garlic, chili pepper, balsamic vinegar, and wine, and reduce almost completely. Add the brown veal stock, and reduce to 2 cups. Add the marjoram, rosemary, salt, and pepper. Keep warm in a hot water bath until needed.

(continued)

4.   Dredge the kidney slices in the flour, shaking off any excess.

5.   Heat the clarified butter in a skillet, and sauté the kidneys until just underdone. Remove with a slotted spoon to a suitable dish to keep warm. Do not try to cook too many kidney slices at one time.

6.   Quickly sauté the *porcini* for 1 minute in the same skillet.

7.   Add the sauce to the *porcini,* and bring to a simmer. Add the kidneys to the sauce, bring to a simmer again, and immediately remove from the heat. The sauce should now have a light coating consistency. Serve immediately. Molded polenta mush goes well with this dish (see chapter 6).

— *Animelle di Vitello* —
VEAL SWEETBREADS

The hardest thing to control with sweetbreads is portion size. To serve the most uniform portions with minimal waste is the goal of every chef. When purchased, this fine delicacy should be as white as possible and free of blood spots and bruises.

Veal sweetbreads, the thymus glands of calves, are of two types; the most desirable is called the heart and is plump and round. Less desirable is the throat, recognizable by its elongated, uneven appearance.

Years ago I devised a poaching method that helps to overcome the problem of nonuniformity and low yield. The trick is to marry the heart and the throat together, thus distributing both within each portion.

1.   Trim the sweetbreads of all gristle and connective tissue and soak in cold water for 1 hour.

2.   Place the sweetbreads in a colander to drain, and pat dry with a towel.

3.   Put the sweetbreads in a mixing bowl and dust liberally with dried egg white.

4.   Place the sweetbreads on a large sheet of plastic wrap and sprinkle with more dried egg white, working it into the crevices especially.

5.   Wrap tightly in the plastic wrap in a thick sausagelike roll, about four to five layers total. Twist both ends, and tie with butcher's twine at both ends and around the center.

6.   Carefully puncture the wrap in several places to allow liquid to reach the sweetbreads during poaching.

7.   Poach in court bouillon (acidulated water with sliced carrots, onions, celery, bay leaves, peppercorns, and salt) for about 15 to 20 minutes, depending on the size of the roll. Remove from the heat and let cool in the liquid before removing.

8.   Place a light weight on top of the sweetbread roll to increase density. Keep refrigerated.

9.   To serve, cut the desired thickness from the roll, and remove the outside plastic wrap.

Medaglione di Animelle di Vitello alla Crema di Basilico
BROILED MÉDAILLONS OF VEAL SWEETBREADS WITH BASIL CREAM SAUCE

Yield: 6 servings

2 pounds	veal sweetbreads	1/2 cup	poultry glace (see chapter 7)
4 tablespoons	dried egg whites	1 to 2 tablespoons	prepared mustard
1 gallon	court bouillon	1 1/2 cups	heavy cream, reduced to 3/4 cup
1/2 ounce	butter		
3 tablespoons	small-diced scallions, white parts only	1/2 cup	melted butter
		2 cloves	garlic, minced
1 cup	dry vermouth	1/2 cup	dry, very fine breadcrumbs
1 cup	dry white wine		
2	chili peppers, chopped	3 tablespoons	chopped basil
		1 tablespoon	chopped parsley
2	bay leaves		

1.   Prepare the sweetbreads with the dried egg whites and poach in the court bouillon as outlined in the text immediately preceding this recipe.

2.   Heat the 1/2 ounce of butter in a 2-quart saucepan, and add the scallions. Cook over low heat for several minutes, then add the wines, chili peppers, and bay leaves. Reduce by half, and remove the bay leaves.

3.   Add the poultry *glace,* and reduce to a light coating consistency. Whisk in the mustard, and add the reduced cream.

(continued)

4. Cut the sweetbread roll into *médaillons,* and remove the plastic wrap. Place the *médaillons* on an ovenproof tray, and brush with the melted butter. Combine the garlic, breadcrumbs, and remaining butter, and sprinkle this mixture over the *médaillons.* Broil just long enough to form a light crust.

5. Add the basil and parsley to the sauce, and spoon onto heated serving plates. Arrange the broiled *médaillons* on the sauce (see color plate 42).

Fegato di Vitello con Mele e Mirtille Rosse
SAUTÉED CALF'S LIVER WITH APPLES AND CRANBERRIES

Yield: 6 servings

12	calf's liver slices, 2 ounces each	1/4 cup	cranberries, fresh or frozen
1 teaspoon	crushed juniper berries	1 1/2 cups	brown veal stock (see chapter 7)
1/2 teaspoon	ground black pepper	to taste	salt and cayenne pepper
1/2 cup	flour	2 ounces	butter
6 tablespoons	clarified butter (see chapter 1)	12	apple rings, cored and thickly sliced
1 tablespoon	shallots	12	bacon slices, fried crisp (optional)
1/2 cup	dry sherry (Manzanilla)	6	mint sprigs
1 cup	dry red wine		

1. Sprinkle the liver with the juniper berries and black pepper. Dredge lightly in the flour.

2. Heat the clarified butter in a large skillet, and sauté the calf's liver quickly, until medium-done. Remove from the pan, and keep warm.

3. Degrease the skillet, add the shallots, and reheat. Add the wines and half of the cranberries. Reduce almost completely.

4. Add the brown veal stock, and reduce to 1 cup. Add the salt and cayenne.

5. Strain the sauce through a fine-mesh sieve. Reheat, and add the remaining cranberries. Simmer for 1 minute, then remove from the heat.

6. Swirl in 1 1/2 ounces of butter carefully, so as not to break up the berries.

7. Sauté the apple rings in another skillet with the remaining butter until tender-crisp.

8. Overlap 2 sautéed liver slices on each hot serving plate. Spoon the sauce over the liver, and arrange the apple rings on top, along with the crisp bacon. Garnish with the mint sprigs.

Fegato di Vitello alla Veneziana

SAUTÉED CALF'S LIVER WITH CRISP ONIONS

This recipe fits beautifully with the contemporary style of cooking. Rather than being smothered and greasy, the onions in this recipe are crisp.

Yield: 6 servings

1 1/4 cups	olive oil	2 tablespoons	balsamic vinegar
1 1/2 pounds	onions, thinly sliced	1 cup	dry white wine
12	calf's liver slices, 2 1/2 ounces each	2 cups	brown veal stock (see chapter 7)
to taste	freshly ground black pepper	1 tablespoon	chopped marjoram
		1 tablespoon	chopped parsley
1/2 cup	flour	12	savoy cabbage leaves, blanched
2 tablespoons	lemon juice		

1. Heat the oil in a large skillet, and sauté the thinly sliced onions, stirring occasionally to ensure even browning. When brown and almost crisp, remove the onions with a slotted spoon to a sieve, and let the fat drain off completely. Place the onions on absorbent paper and keep near the oven to keep warm. Reserve the oil used to sauté the onions.

2. Season the sliced liver with black pepper, and dredge in the flour.

3. In the skillet used to sauté the onions, heat 6 tablespoons of the reserved oil, and sauté the calf's liver quickly on both sides until medium done. Remove from the pan and keep warm.

4. Completely degrease the pan, and deglaze with the lemon juice, balsamic vinegar, and white wine. Reduce almost completely.

5. Add the brown veal stock and reduce to 9 fluid ounces. Add the marjoram and parsley, and season with salt and black pepper.

6. Arrange 2 blanched savoy cabbage leaves on each heated serving plate. Set 2 slices of the cooked liver on the leaves, and coat with the sauce. Top with the crisp onions. Steamed cauliflower florets and broiled tomatoes go well with this dish.

— *Cervella di Vitello* —
CALF'S BRAIN

Calf's brain is a high-cholesterol food found almost exclusively on European menus. It is not popular in the United States.

The texture of the calf's brain is somewhat soft, almost creamy to the bite, but it firms up considerably when poached in acidulated court bouillon. If one wishes to poach it in this method, it is advantageous to use dried egg whites when putting the brain together in order to avoid waste and to finish with a firmer, more sliceable product.

The applications for calf's brain are endless. It can be sautéed in butter and garnished with compatible vegetables. Or it can be cut coarsely, and sautéed in butter with diced red onions and lightly beaten raw eggs. This is customarily highly seasoned and served like a *frittata*. Fresh chopped chives and herbs can also be added to this omelet, and it can be served on toast. Calf's brain can also be breaded, deep-fried, and served with lemons, or it can be poached, marinated in a vinegar dressing, and garnished with a medley of young vegetables.

Cervella di Vitello Dorata con Coulis di Prezzemolo
SAUTÉED CALF'S BRAIN WITH PARSLEY COULIS

Yield: 6 servings

2 pounds	calf's brain	to taste	nutmeg
3 to 4 tablespoons	dried egg white	6 tablespoons	chicken glace (see chapter 7)
1 gallon	court bouillon		
7 ounces	Italian parsley	1/2 cup	milk
1 ounce	chervil	1/2 cup	flour
2 ounces	spinach	6 tablespoons	clarified butter (see chapter 1)
1 ounce	butter		
1/2 ounce	shallots, finely diced	3/4 cup	hot cream
to taste	salt and freshly ground black pepper		

1.   Soak the calf's brain in cold water for 1 to 2 hours to remove the excess red pigment.

2.   Remove from the water, and carefully pull out all membranes from the crevices. Gently blot dry with a towel.

3.   Place the brains on a towel and sprinkle liberally with the dried egg white, being sure to get it into the crevices.

4.   Arrange the calf's brain on a large sheet of plastic wrap and sprinkle with more of the dried egg white. Wrap tightly into a thick, sausagelike roll, and twist at both ends. Press it against a flat surface, holding the twisted ends securely, until the mass inside the plastic tightens somewhat. When firm, secure the twisted ends with butcher's twine. Roll the brain in wrap again, until there are four or five layers of plastic around it. Tie it around the center with twine.

5.   Carefully puncture the wrap in several places to allow the liquids to reach the interior during poaching.

6.   Place the wrapped, punctured roll into simmering court bouillon, and cook *below* the simmering point for 15 to 20 minutes, depending on the thickness of the roll. Remove from the heat, but not from the liquid. Let cool in the poaching liquid.

7.   When cool, remove the rolled brains from the court bouillon, place in a suitable dish, and refrigerate.

8.   Pluck the leaves from the parsley, chervil, and spinach, and wash carefully. Blanch together in boiling water for 2 to 3 seconds, drain, and shock in cold water. Drain and press out the liquid. When somewhat dry, chop coarsely.

9.   Heat the ounce of butter in a noncorrosive saucepan, and sweat the shallots over low heat until soft. Add the parsley, chervil, and spinach, and reheat for 1 minute. Add salt, pepper, and nutmeg. Add the chicken *glace,* and bring to a boil. Remove from the heat, and puree until extremely smooth in a blender (not a food processor). Add more liquid if the *coulis* is too thick, and strain through a fine sieve. (Up to this point, the *coulis* may be prepared several days ahead of time. If this is the case, cool immediately, cover, and refrigerate.)

10.   Cut the brain roll into 12 slices; remove the plastic wrap.

11.   Dip each slice in the milk, and dredge in the flour. Sauté in the hot clarified butter until golden brown. Remove from the skillet and keep warm. Sprinkle with salt and pepper.

12.   Reheat the *coulis* if necessary, and add the hot cream. Adjust the seasonings. Spoon the parsley *coulis* on hot serving plates, and arrange 2 sautéed calf's brain slices neatly on top of each. Steamed potatoes and vegetables such as carrots, cauliflower, fennel, zucchini, green beans, and tomatoes go well with this dish.

— *Agnello e Capretto* —
LAMB AND KID

Traditionally, lamb and sheep have been available in Italy in three forms: milk-fed (suckling) baby lamb, or *abbacchio;* yearling lamb, or *agnello;* and mutton, or *castrato.* Milk-fed baby lamb, or house lamb, is almost impossible to find in the United States. The young animal has not been weaned (and has never seen a green pasture), which results in an almost whitish flesh. These lambs are generally sold whole or quartered and are most commonly eaten on religious and other festive occasions, such as Easter, when the animal is spit-roasted. The meat is as tender as chicken and excellent for roasting, sautéing, and deep-frying. The neck, breast, and shoulder parts are excellent braised. The meat does not keep well for long and should be processed and consumed as quickly as possible.

The yearling lamb plays an important part in classical cooking the world over. Yearling lamb is also a young animal that has not yet reached maturity. When six months old or younger, this lamb is commonly called spring lamb. The best parts are the loin, rack, and leg, which are excellent grilled, sautéed, and roasted. The more muscled parts, such as the shoulder and shank, are good stewed and braised.

Mutton, or adult sheep, is very tasty and easy to digest as long as the animal is not too old. The meat is darkish red and hardly distinguishable from the meat of the yearling except it is slightly tougher. Good-quality mutton is recognizable by a firm-textured white fat layer. Lesser-quality animals have a more oily, off-white fat covering. The tender parts of the mutton and mutton kidneys are best grilled; the tougher cuts are usually braised. Older animals are consumed quite heavily in parts of the Middle East and Asia.

Goats are raised primarily for dairy production because the meat of the mature animal has a very strong taste which many find unpleasant. The baby goat, or kid *(capretto),* is a culinary treat and should be treated like milk-fed baby lamb.

Abbacchio Farcito all'Arrabbiata
ROAST BABY LAMB STUFFED WITH RICE AND SAUSAGE

The roast baby lamb in this recipe may be left whole, with the head on, for a special presentation. Leaving the head on is also helpful in maintaining the animal's shape during roasting. When serving, begin slicing from the tail toward the head, then discard the head.

Yield: 10 to 12 servings

12 ounces	long-grain rice	1 pound	onions, diced
½ cup	olive oil	6 cloves	garlic, minced

1½ pounds	hot Italian sausage, cut into small pieces	2 tablespoons	olive oil
1 cup	pine nuts, lightly toasted	½ pound	onions, coarsely chopped
1 cup	grated fennel knob	¼ pound	celery, coarsely chopped
1 cup	grated pecorino cheese	¼ pound	carrots, coarsely chopped
2	egg yolks	4 cloves	garlic, coarsely chopped
1 tablespoon	crushed dried hot chili peppers	2 tablespoons	tomato paste
½ cup	chopped parsley	1	rosemary sprig
¼ cup	chopped sage	1	thyme sprig
¼ cup	chopped oregano	1	bay leaf
1	whole milk-fed baby lamb, 12 pounds	2 quarts	brown veal stock (see chapter 7)
to taste	salt and freshly ground black pepper		

1.   Cook the rice in 1 gallon of salted, boiling water for 10 minutes. Drain.

2.   Heat the ½ cup olive oil in a large skillet, and sauté the diced onions until lightly browned. Add the garlic and sausage, and continue to cook for a few more minutes. Add the pine nuts and grated fennel. Remove from the heat.

3.   In a suitable mixing bowl, combine the grated *pecorino* cheese, egg yolks, chili peppers, parsley, sage, and oregano with the cooked rice. Add the sausage mixture. Mix well and chill.

4.   Lay the lamb on its back, and carefully remove the rib bones with a knife starting from the ends and working toward the spine. Reserve the bones.

5.   Next, remove the spine, starting from the tail end and being very careful not to cut through the skin. Slowly loosen the spine and sever just below the neck, keeping the head intact. Reserve.

6.   Sever the lower foreshank bones above the joints, loosen the meat around the shank bones, and then twist them out. Reserve.

7.   Pull the boneless shanks completely into the cavity of the lamb. If necessary, cut away some of the meat from the leg and distribute evenly within the cavity as well. Remove the eyes.

8.   Fill the cavity with the cold rice stuffing, and sew up with heavy butcher's twine. Tie the twine loosely around the circumference of the body in two or three places as well to secure the stuffing further and prevent any bursting.

(continued)

9. Place the stuffed lamb on its belly on a small sheet pan, and set the sheet pan with the lamb in a larger roasting pan. Coat with a little oil, salt, and black pepper.

10. Place in a preheated 350°F oven, and roast for about 1½ to 2 hours, basting frequently or covering with oiled parchment paper during the latter stages of roasting. Remove from the oven and let rest for at least 15 minutes before removing the twine and carving.

11. Heat the 2 tablespoons of olive oil. Chop the lamb bones and any trimmings and brown in the oil with coarsely chopped onions, celery, carrots, and garlic. Add the tomato paste, and continue to brown until the paste starts to lose its bright red color. Add the rosemary and thyme sprigs, bay leaf, and brown stock, and simmer for 1½ to 2 hours. Strain. Continue to reduce if desired, being sure to skim away any fat and impurities that rise to the surface.

12. Carve a 1-inch-thick slice of roast lamb for each serving, and divide each in half. Overlap the 2 slices on a preheated plate. Spoon the sauce around the meat. A bouquet of freshly steamed vegetables goes well with this dish.

Abbacchio Impanati alla Tirolese
FRIED BABY LAMB, TYROLEAN STYLE

Breaded, deep-fried baby lamb is a specialty in Alto Adige, the Tyrolean region of Italy, during the Easter holidays. The breading locks in the juices and flavor and retains the overall succulence of the meat.

Whatever trends there are regarding the deep-frying of foods, it is still a most popular cooking method. From a nutritional point of view, it is perhaps better to consider the daily balance of foods ingested rather than pondering if it is a good idea to eat fried foods occasionally.

Yield: 6 servings

3 pounds	milk-fed baby lamb, cut into smaller pieces (approximately 3 pieces per serving)	3 cups	dry breadcrumbs, from stale Italian or French bread
to taste	salt and white pepper	to deep-fry	vegetable oil or shortening
2	eggs	2 bunches	Italian parsley, with large stems removed
½ cup	water	12	lemon wedges
1½ cups	flour		

1.   Season the lamb with the salt and pepper.

2.   Beat the eggs and water together to make an egg wash.

3.   Dredge each piece of lamb in the flour. Dip in the egg wash. Coat completely with the breadcrumbs.

4.   Deep-fry the pieces at 325° to 350°F until nicely browned and crisp, approximately 7 to 9 minutes. Remove to paper towels and drain.

5.   Deep-fry the parsley quickly at 350°F until crisp. The parsley should remain green and should not turn brown.

6.   Arrange the fried lamb in folded napkins with the fried parsley on top. Serve with the lemon wedges alongside.

Abbacchio alla Romana
PAN-FRIED BABY LAMB, ROMAN STYLE

This is a Roman specialty served at Easter time. One leg of these small creatures will serve about 4 people.

Yield: 6 servings

¾ cup	virgin olive oil	¼ cup	lemon juice
3 pounds	leg of milk-fed baby lamb, boned and cut into 2-ounce pieces	¼ cup	white vinegar
		½ teaspoon	freshly ground black pepper
6 cloves	garlic, minced	½ teaspoon	salt
4	salted anchovy fillets, boned and rinsed	2 tablespoons	chopped rosemary
		2 tablespoons	chopped mint

1.   Heat ¾ cup of olive oil in a large skillet, and pan-fry the lamb pieces over high heat until nicely browned. Reduce the heat, and continue to cook until tender.

2.   Puree the garlic, anchovies, lemon juice, vinegar, pepper, salt, rosemary, and mint in a blender, and add to the lamb. Remove from the heat, adjust the salt, and serve. Fresh green vegetables and rice go well with this dish.

Fricassea di Capretto con Carciofini e Funghi

FRICASSEE OF BABY GOAT WITH BABY ARTICHOKE HEARTS AND MUSHROOMS

The preparation of baby goat, or kid, is the same as for baby lamb *(abbacchio)*.

Yield: 6 servings

1 ounce	butter	1½ ounces	flour
1 tablespoon	lemon juice	1½ cups	dry white wine
¼ cup	water	3 cups	beef broth or water
pinch	salt and white pepper	1	bouquet garni of carrots, celery, and leeks (see chapter 1)
12	baby artichokes, quickly blanched (see chapter 12)	pinch	nutmeg
		2	egg yolks
12	pearl onions, quickly blanched	3 ounces	pecorino cheese, grated
12 ounces	mushrooms, cleaned and quartered	½ teaspoon	grated lemon rind
½ cup	clarified butter (see chapter 1)	½ to ¾ cup	heavy cream
		6	basil sprigs
6 ounces	onions, finely diced		
3 pounds	kid shoulder or breast, cut into 1-ounce pieces		

1.   Heat the butter, lemon juice, water, salt, and pepper in a 2-quart noncorrosive casserole. Add the blanched artichokes and pearl onions. Cover and cook slowly for 5 minutes. Add the cleaned mushrooms, and cook for an additional 2 to 3 minutes. Remove from the heat and cool. Strain and reserve the liquid for the stew. Hold the vegetables in a suitable covered dish.

2.   Heat the clarified butter in a heavy-bottomed 6-quart noncorrosive casserole. Add the onions, and cook until soft and translucent.

3.   Add the kid pieces, and smother over low heat for about 10 minutes (do not brown).

4.   Stir in the flour, and cook for several more minutes.

5.   Add the wine, broth (or water), and the reserved liquid from the vegetables, and bring to a simmer. Add the *bouquet garni,* nutmeg, and a pinch of salt and of pepper.

Cook, covered, over low heat for about 30 to 35 minutes, until the meat is tender but still somewhat firm. Discard the *bouquet garni* and add more liquid if the sauce seems too thick. Adjust the seasonings, and remove from the heat.

6.   Combine the egg yolks, *pecorino* cheese, grated lemon peel, and cream. Carefully mix into the stew. Do *not* bring to a boil again, or the sauce will curdle.

7.   Add the vegetables to the stew.

8.   Spoon the fricassee into shallow soup or dinner plates, and decorate each with basil sprig. Boiled rice goes well with this dish (see chapter 6).

Carre d'Agnello Arrosto all'Erbe al Sugo d'Aglio
ROAST HERBED RACK OF LAMB WITH GARLIC SAUCE

Yield: **6 servings**

1/4 cup	oil	1/2 cup	dry breadcrumbs, from Italian or French bread
1 pound	lean lamb trimmings		
4 ounces	onions, coarsely chopped	1/4 teaspoon	dried crushed hot red pepper
2 ounces	carrots, coarsely chopped	1/4 cup	chopped Italian parsley
2 ounces	celery, coarsely chopped	2 tablespoons	chopped rosemary
1	rosemary sprig	3 tablespoons	prepared mustard
1	thyme sprig	2 ounces	butter, melted
1	bay leaf	6 tablespoons	dry white wine
12 cloves	garlic, minced	1	egg
10	black peppercorns, crushed	1/2 teaspoon	salt
1 quart	brown veal stock (see chapter 7)	3 pounds	single rack of lamb, French trimmed

1.   Heat 2 tablespoons of oil in a 4-quart heavy-bottomed saucepan, and sear the lamb trimmings. Add the onions, carrots, and celery, and continue to sear until well browned.

2.   Add the rosemary, thyme, bay leaf, 6 minced garlic cloves, peppercorns, and the brown veal stock, and simmer for 1 hour over very low heat. Skim any fat and impurities that rise to the surface.

(continued)

3. Strain through cheesecloth or a very fine-mesh sieve.

4. Adjust the salt, and reduce to 1½ cups. Keep the sauce hot in a hot water bath.

5. Combine the breadcrumbs, hot pepper, remaining garlic, parsley, rosemary, mustard, melted butter, wine, egg, and salt.

6. Place the rack of lamb on a roasting rack, rub with the remaining oil, and roast in a preheated 500°F oven for about 12 minutes (time depends on size of rack). Cover exposed ribs with aluminum foil to prevent scorching. The lamb should be cooked rare.

7. Spread a thin layer of the herb mixture evenly over the roasted lamb. Place back in the hot oven, preferably near the top of the oven, and roast until the herb mixture is nicely browned.

8. Slice 1 rib portion at a time without disturbing the herb crust. Arrange 3 ribs on each heated serving plate. Spoon about ¼ cup of sauce around the meat.

Costolette d'Agnello Farcito alla Cacciatora

SPRING LAMB CHOPS STUFFED WITH PORCINI AND SUN-DRIED TOMATOES

Yield: 6 servings

3 tablespoons	oil	8 ounces	porcini, diced small
1 pound	lean lamb trimmings	¼ cup	coarsely grated fennel knob
4 ounces	onions, coarsely chopped	6	marinated sun-dried tomatoes, cut small (as purchased)
2 ounces	celery, coarsely chopped		
2 ounces	carrots, coarsely chopped	1 tablespoon	chopped rosemary
1	rosemary sprig	2 tablespoons	chopped parsley
1	bay leaf	½ teaspoon	freshly ground black pepper
10	black peppercorns, crushed	1 tablespoon	dry breadcrumbs
6 cloves	garlic, crushed	12	double lamb chops, bone in
1 quart	brown veal stock (see chapter 7)	3 tablespoons	dried egg white
1 ounce	pancetta, chopped	12	6- by 4-inch pieces pork caul, well rinsed and dried
¼ cup	finely diced onions		

| *1 cup* | *small diced tomatoes* | *1 tablespoon* | *butter* |
| *1 cup* | *small diced porcini* | | |

1.   Heat 2 tablespoons of oil in a heavy-bottomed 4-quart saucepan. Add the lamb trimmings and sear. Add the onions, celery, and carrots, and continue to sear until nicely browned.

2.   Add the rosemary, bay leaf, peppercorns, garlic, and the brown veal stock, and simmer over low heat for 1 hour. Skim any fat and impurities that rise to the surface while simmering. Strain through a fine-mesh sieve, and set aside ¼ cup of stock. Continue to reduce the remaining stock to 1½ cups. Keep hot in a hot water bath.

3.   Render the *pancetta* in a large skillet. Add the finely diced onions and diced *porcini*, and sauté quickly for 1 minute.

4.   Add the grated fennel, sun-dried tomatoes, rosemary, parsley, pepper, and reserved ¼ cup of lamb stock. Reduce completely. Remove the skillet from the heat, and mix in the breadcrumbs. Cool.

5.   Butterfly the lamb chops by slicing in half to the bone and spreading the two halves. Place between sheets of plastic wrap, and flatten both sides slightly with the flat side of a meat cleaver.

6.   Place 1 tablespoon of stuffing on one side of each butterflied chop. Sprinkle dried egg white near the edge of the other side. Fold the sides together and press the outer edges together.

7.   Spread the pork caul pieces on a worktable, and wrap each chop in a piece of caul, leaving the bone exposed. Refrigerate until ready to cook.

8.   Because of the caul, little additional fat is needed to sauté the chops. The fatty tissue of the caul will contract and maintain the lamb chop's shape. Heat 1 tablespoon of oil in a large skillet. Sauté the chops on both sides, turning once, until medium done; finish in the oven if more well-done chops are desired.

9.   In a skillet, sauté the tomatoes and *porcini* mushrooms in a little butter. Add to the sauce.

10.   Spoon the sauce onto each heated serving plate; arrange 2 chops over the sauce. Sautéed zucchini and potato *gnocchetti* go well with this dish.

Costate d'Agnello ai Funghi in Mille-Foglie con Salsa d'Aglio e Peperoni Rossi
LAMB CHOPS WITH MUSHROOMS IN PUFF PASTRY WITH GARLIC AND RED-PEPPER SAUCE

Yield: 6 servings

6	double lamb chops, bone in	2 tablespoons	chopped Italian parsley
2 tablespoons	oil	1 tablespoon	chopped rosemary
2 tablespoons	clarified butter (see chapter 1)	to taste	salt and freshly ground black pepper
1/4 cup	finely diced onions		
9 ounces	wild and domestic mushrooms, diced small	6	large, tender savoy cabbage leaves
6 tablespoons	dry white wine	6	puff pastry sheets, 5 by 6 by 1/8 inches
2 tablespoons	veal glace (see chapter 7)	1 ounce	milk
2	egg yolks	1 1/2 cups	garlic and red-pepper sauce (see chapter 7)
1 tablespoon	dry breadcrumbs		

1.   Cut away the extra rib bone on each lamb chop so that only one remains. Trim away all fat, and scrape the rib bone completely clean with a paring knife.

2.   Heat the oil in a large skillet, and sauté the lamb chops quickly on both sides. The lamb chop should be rare. Refrigerate under a light weight.

3.   Drain the oil from the skillet, and heat the clarified butter in it. Sauté the onions and mushrooms until lightly browned.

4.   Deglaze the skillet with the wine, and reduce completely. Add the veal *glace*, and continue to reduce until syrupy. Remove from the heat.

5.   Lightly beat 1 egg yolk and quickly stir it in. The yolk should bind the mixture, not scramble.

6.   Add the breadcrumbs, parsley, rosemary, salt, and pepper. Mix well, and cool.

7.   Blanch the savoy cabbage leaves in salted water for a few seconds. Remove with a spider, and shock in cold water. Drain and blot dry. Cut out the center rib of each leaf.

8.   Spread the mushroom mixture on each chop, and place a cabbage leaf on top. Wrap the leaf tightly around the chop, leaving the rib bone exposed. Cover each with a sheet of puff pastry. Lightly beat the remaining egg yolk with the milk to make an egg wash. Brush the edges of the dough with the egg wash to secure.

9. Wrap the dough around the chop so the seam will be underneath. Press the seam together (add more egg wash if necessary). Trim off any excess dough around the base of the rib bone: the bone should remain exposed.

10. Refrigerate for at least 2 hours before baking.

11. Wrap the exposed rib bones with aluminum foil to prevent scorching. Brush egg wash on the dough of each chop, and score with the tines of a dinner fork.

12. Bake in a preheated 350°F oven for about 12 to 15 minutes, until the dough is nicely browned. The meat should not be more than medium done.

13. Spoon ¼ cup of the garlic and red-pepper sauce on each heated serving plate. Cut the baked lamb chops in half lengthwise, exposing the inside flesh of the chops. Arrange neatly over the sauce. Steamed fresh vegetables go well with this dish (see color plate 43). No other starchy side dishes are necessary.

Costolette d'Agnello ai Peperoni Rossi in Salsa Piccante
SAUTÉED LAMB CHOPS WITH ROASTED RED PEPPERS AND PIQUANT SAUCE

Yield: 6 servings

5	roasted red peppers (see chapter 1)	6 tablespoons	veal glace (see chapter 7)
to taste	salt and freshly ground black pepper	2	hot chili peppers, chopped
¼ cup	olive oil	3	anchovy fillets, rinsed, blotted dry, and chopped
18	rib lamb chops, 2 ounces each, French trimmed		
		1 tablespoon	capers, rinsed
		18	black olives, cut into small strips
SAUCE:			
1 cup	thinly sliced scallions, white parts only	3 tablespoons	chopped oregano
		2 ounces	butter
6 cloves	garlic, minced	**GARNISH:**	
¾ cup	dry white wine	6	basil sprigs
6 tablespoons	balsamic vinegar		

(continued)

1.   Quarter and seed the roasted peppers, and remove most of the membrane inside. Sprinkle lightly with salt and pepper and keep warm.

2.   Heat the olive oil in a large skillet, and sauté the lamb chops until medium-done. Remove and keep warm. Degrease the pan.

3.   Add the scallions and garlic to the same skillet, and sauté for about 10 seconds.

4.   Deglaze the skillet with the wine, and reduce to ¼ cup.

5.   Add the balsamic vinegar and veal *glace,* and reduce to a light syrup.

6.   Add the chopped chili peppers, anchovies, capers, olives, and oregano. Swirl in the butter to create an emulsion just prior to serving.

7.   Arrange 3 roasted red-pepper quarters neatly in a semicircle on each heated serving plate. Put 1 lamb chop on each pepper piece, with the rib bones pointing outward. Spoon the sauce over each chop. Decorate the center of each plate with a basil sprig. Green string beans and small roasted potatoes go well with this dish.

Costolette d'Agnello al Forno, con Pomodori Freschi e Patate
SHOULDER LAMB CHOPS BAKED WITH TOMATOES AND POTATOES

Shoulder lamb chops are recommended for this dish because the meat found in this cut are more suitable for braising, as well as being more economical. Do not trim the chops too closely, leaving some of the fat intact to add flavor to the pan liquids. Mutton chops are particularly well suited for this dish because of their pronounced flavor. When using mutton, increase the cooking time accordingly.

This dish can be assembled in individual casseroles and baked as needed for à la carte service.

Yield: 6 servings

6 tablespoons	olive oil	3	hot chili peppers, chopped
12	shoulder lamb chops		
		9 ounces	green bell peppers, roasted, seeded, and cut into strips (see chapter 1)
½ teaspoon	freshly ground black pepper		
12 to 16 ounces	onions, sliced		
6 cloves	garlic, minced		

9	*ripe tomatoes, peeled, seeded, and cut into strips (see chapter 1)*	*1½ pounds*	*yellow potatoes, peeled and sliced ⅛ inch thick*
¼ cup	*chopped rosemary*	*3 to 4 cups*	*warm brown veal stock (see chapter 7)*
1 tablespoon	*chopped marjoram*	*⅓ cup*	*chopped Italian parsley*
2	*bay leaves*		
to taste	*salt and freshly ground black pepper*		

1. Heat the olive oil in a large skillet. Season the lamb chops with the pepper, and sear on both sides. Remove from the skillet, and arrange side by side in a 12- by 9-inch baking dish.

2. Sauté the onions in the same skillet until well browned. Add the garlic, peppers, tomatoes, rosemary, marjoram, bay leaves, salt, and pepper, and spoon this mixture over the chops.

3. Arrange the potato slices neatly over the top of the chops and tomato mixture. Pour the brown stock over the potatoes. Press the potatoes down a bit to ensure they are well covered with the sauce.

4. Place the dish in a preheated 350° to 375°F oven, and bake for about 30 to 40 minutes. The potatoes should be nicely browned and crisp on top when done.

5. Arrange some of the potato/tomato mixture neatly on each heated serving plate, with 2 of the chops nearby. Sprinkle with the chopped Italian parsley.

Garretti d'Agnello alla Giardiniera

LAMB SHANKS BRAISED IN WHITE WINE AND HERBS WITH GARDEN VEGETABLES

Yield: 6 servings

6	lamb shanks, 8 to 9 ounces each	1	marjoram sprig, chopped
½ cup	flour	1	bay leaf
¼ cup	olive oil	1 teaspoon	grated lemon peel
12 ounces	onions, finely diced	to taste	salt and freshly ground black pepper
6 cloves	garlic, minced		
2 ounces	prosciutto, diced small		
2 tablespoons	tomato paste	**GARNISH:**	
2 cups	dry white wine	1½ pounds	large, olive-shaped turned vegetables (carrots, white turnips, zucchini, potatoes)
2	hot chili peppers, chopped		
1½ cups	peeled, seeded, and chopped fresh tomatoes (see chapter 1)	12	tomato petals (see chapter 1)
		6	basil sprigs
3 cups	brown veal stock		
1	rosemary sprig, chopped		

1.   Cut the shank bones close to the meat on both ends. Dredge the shanks in the flour.

2.   Heat the olive oil in a 6-quart heavy-duty shallow braising pan, and sear the shanks on all sides. Remove from the casserole, and keep warm.

3.   Add the onions to the same casserole, and cook until lightly browned. Add garlic, *prosciutto,* and tomato paste, and continue to cook for several minutes.

4.   Deglaze the pan with the wine, and reduce to 1 cup. Stir in the chili peppers, tomatoes, brown stock, rosemary, marjoram, bay leaf, lemon peel, salt, and pepper. Simmer for several minutes.

5.   Add the seared lamb shanks to the sauce and cover. Braise very slowly for about 1¼ hours, until cooked to the desired doneness. When the meat is fork tender, remove it from the sauce, and keep warm.

6. Adjust the seasonings, and strain the sauce through a fine-mesh sieve. Continue to reduce the sauce if necessary to a light coating consistency. Return the shanks to the sauce, and keep hot.

7. Steam all the vegetables separately.

8. Place a lamb shank on each heated serving plate, and spoon the sauce over the meat. Arrange the vegetables, lightly buttered, in a nice color sequence, together with quickly heated tomato petals. Add a basil sprig.

Spezzatini d'Agnello alla Calabrese
LAMB STEW WITH EGGPLANT, TOMATOES, PEPPERS, AND OLIVES

Yield: 6 servings

3 pounds	boneless lamb shoulder or breast meat, cut into 1-ounce cubes	to taste	salt and freshly ground black pepper
1 ounce	flour	3 cups	beef broth or water
¾ cup	olive oil	**GARNISH:**	
12 ounces	onions, diced small	5 ounces	eggplant, peeled and cut into small strips
6 cloves	garlic, minced		
3	hot chili peppers, chopped	¼ cup	olive oil
3 ounces	green and red bell peppers, chopped	5 ounces	onions, sliced medium thick
3 tablespoons	tomato paste	5 ounces	green bell peppers, cut into small strips
3 ounces	eggplant, peeled and diced small	5 ounces	tomatoes, peeled, seeded, and cut into small strips (see chapter 1)
6	plum tomatoes, peeled, seeded, and chopped (see chapter 1)		
3	anchovy fillets, chopped	18	black olives, quartered
1	oregano sprig	to taste	salt and freshly ground black pepper
1	mint sprig	¼ cup	chopped parsley
1	bay leaf	2 tablespoons	chopped mint leaves

(continued)

1. Sprinkle the lamb cubes with the flour.

2. Heat ½ cup of olive oil in a shallow 6-quart heavy-duty braising pan. Sear the lamb cubes, a bit at a time, over moderate to high heat, and remove with a slotted spoon as they are browned. Keep warm.

3. Add the remaining oil to the same braising pan, and reheat.

4. Add the onions, and brown, stirring occasionally.

5. Add the garlic and the hot and sweet peppers, and continue to brown. Stir in the tomato paste, eggplant, and tomatoes. Smother for 5 minutes.

6. Add the anchovies, oregano, mint, bay leaf, salt, pepper, and broth (or water). Cook over low heat for 10 minutes.

7. Return the seared lamb cubes to the sauce and cover. Braise in a preheated 300°F oven or at the lowest heat level on the stove for 1¼ to 1½ hours, until the meat is cooked to the desired doneness. Remove from the heat, and discard the bay leaf.

8. Salt the eggplant strips for the garnish, and let rest for 10 minutes. Blot dry.

9. Heat a little olive oil in a large skillet, and sauté the onions, peppers, and eggplant; the vegetables should remain very crisp. Add the tomatoes, olives, salt, and pepper.

10. Spoon the lamb stew into heated shallow soup dishes or onto heated dinner plates, and arrange the garnish neatly on top of or around the stew. Sprinkle with the parsley and mint. Small macaroni go well with this dish.

Piccate d'Agnello con Salsa d'Aglio e Ginepro in Bacche
BATTER-FRIED LAMB MÉDAILLONS WITH GARLIC AND JUNIPER SAUCE

To prepare the brown lamb stock for this recipe, follow the recipe for brown veal stock in chapter 7, substituting lamb trimmings and bones for the veal.

Yield: 6 servings

18	lamb médaillons from loin or leg, 1¼ ounces each	2 or 3	eggs
		2 ounces	Parmesan, grated
		2 ounces	butter

4 ounces	onions, finely diced	1 teaspoon	arrowroot (optional)
4 cloves	garlic, finely minced	2 tablespoons	cold red wine (optional)
1 tablespoon	tomato paste	8 to 10 tablespoons	olive oil
1½ cups	dry red wine	2 tablespoons	chopped rosemary
1 quart	brown lamb stock	½ teaspoon	freshly ground black pepper
¼ teaspoon	grated lemon rind	½ cup	flour
1 teaspoon	finely ground juniper berries	¼ cup	finely chopped scallion tops
to taste	salt and freshly ground black pepper		

1. Flatten the lamb *médaillons* slightly between layers of plastic wrap, using the dull edge of a meat cleaver.

2. Combine the eggs and cheese thoroughly.

3. Heat the butter in a 2-quart saucepan, and add the onions. Brown slightly, stirring occasionally. Add the garlic and tomato paste. Continue to cook for several minutes.

4. Deglaze the pan with the 1½ cups of red wine, and reduce almost completely.

5. Add the brown lamb stock, and simmer over low heat until reduced to 3 cups. Skim any impurities that rise to the top while reducing.

6. Add the lemon rind, juniper berries, salt, and pepper.

7. If the sauce does not seem thick enough, dissolve the arrowroot in the wine, and mix into the sauce. Bring to a boil, remove from the heat, and keep warm in a hot water bath.

8. Heat the olive oil in a large skillet. Sprinkle the lamb with the rosemary and pepper.

9. Dredge the lamb in the flour, and dip in the egg/cheese mixture. Pan-fry until lightly browned on both sides. Do not overcook.

10. Spoon the garlic and juniper sauce onto heated serving plates, and sprinkle the scallions over the sauce. Neatly arrange 3 pieces of lamb on top of the sauce on each plate.

— *Maiale* —
PORK

Zampone

STUFFED PIG'S TROTTER

Although this traditional northern Italian specialty seems to have originated in Modena, it is the concept, rather than the particular method of preparation, that makes this dish so uniquely and recognizably Italian. The shoulder and trotter of a (preferably) young pig is first scalded and debristled, then carefully skinned, from the shoulder end to the first joint of the toe. The meat is then removed from inside the leg, and the skin is soaked in fresh water or brine for 24 hours. The skin is then blotted dry, stuffed with forcemeat made from the meat of the leg, and immediately sewn together with thin butcher's twine (making small holes in advance facilitates this process). The assembled *zampone* is then punctured with a clean needle and cooked in a strong meat broth just below the simmering point (170°F) until an internal temperature of 160°F is reached, which takes approximately 3 hours.

As always, there are variations in the preparation and method of cooking. Originally the meat intended for the farce was ground medium to fine. Afterward, the stuffed trotter was dried in a special cold smoker until the skin turned to a reddish brown color, then poached.

When curing the *zampone* farce, use ¼ teaspoon of curing salt for every 3 pounds of meat. Curing salt, which is commercially available, is composed of 94 percent salt and 6 percent sodium nitrate. The mixture is then dyed pink to avoid its accidental use as regular salt. Sodium nitrate has been found to be carcinogenic, and should be used sparingly. There is no adequate substitute for preservation at this time.

Zampone is most often served hot with legumes or fresh vegetables and polenta (see color plate 44).

Yield: 6 servings

1	whole, unskinned pork shoulder or foot, 4 to 6 pounds	⅛ teaspoon	ground juniper berries
1 pound	pork shoulder, jowl, and/or hock meat	½ teaspoon	chopped marjoram
		½ teaspoon	paprika
5 ounces	pork shoulder fat or fatback	pinch	nutmeg
1 teaspoon	salt	½ teaspoon	freshly ground black pepper
⅛ teaspoon	ground coriander	½ teaspoon	finely minced garlic

⅛ teaspoon	curing salt	½ cup	diced lean pork, ¼-inch cubes
1 ounce	crushed ice		
3 tablespoons	shelled pistachios	2 gallons	beef broth, for poaching (see chapter 3)
½ cup	diced smoked ox tongue, ¼-inch cubes		

1.   Scald a long pig's foot or shoulder. Remove any bristles with a knife or tweezers. Remove the bone and all meat, and soak the skin for 24 hours in cold water.

2.   Dice the pound of pork meat and the fat small. Keep everything, including the grinder attachments, refrigerated and covered.

3.   Place only the meat in a small stainless steel bowl. Thoroughly combine the salt, coriander, juniper, marjoram, paprika, nutmeg, pepper, garlic, and curing salt with the meat. Cover with plastic wrap, and cure overnight in the refrigerator.

4.   Partially freeze the cured meat. Grind it through the fine plate of a meat grinder. Grind the fat in a similar fashion, and combine it with the meat in the bowl. Set over ice, and work the ground fat and meat into a homogeneous mass with a wooden spoon or pestle. Add the crushed ice when mixing.

5.   Add the pistachios, ox tongue, and diced pork, and refrigerate.

6.   Remove the pig skin from the water and blot dry. Puncture the seam edges with small holes to aid in sewing up later.

7.   Stuff the skin completely with the cold forcemeat, being careful to avoid any air pockets. Do not overfill.

8.   Sew up the seams with thin butcher's twine, and prick the skin in several places to prevent swelling when cooking.

9.   Wrap the *zampone* tightly in cheesecloth to maintain a good shape and prevent splitting.

10.   Poach in the broth at 170°F for about 3 hours, until an internal temperature of 160°F is reached. (If desired, the *zampone* may be smoked prior to poaching.)

— *Porchetta* —
SUCKLING PIG

Suckling pigs are milk-fed piglets, which weigh about 10 to 12 pounds. In the United States, the smallest piglets available are usually 20 pounds or more. The important thing to remember when dealing with a larger pig is to increase the cooking time. Normally a suckling pig of up to 20 pounds needs about 12 minutes of roasting per pound. For larger piglets, allow 15 minutes per pound. If the animal is stuffed, allow an additional 5 minutes per pound.

When cooking a suckling pig it is important to plan how to serve it. The easiest method for formal service is to bone the pig before cooking, which results in less waste and less mess. It is important that the animal be crisp but not so crisp that neat slicing becomes impossible. Carving straight from the carcass is fine when the suckling pig is the main attraction at a picnic or other informal event.

In southern Europe, especially northern Italy, Austria, and the Balkan countries, it is customary to spit-roast a whole piglet for various occasions. These piglets are milk-fed, usually no heavier than 10 pounds, and less than 6 weeks old.

Porchetta Farcita Arrosta alla Bolzana
ROAST STUFFED SUCKLING PIG, BOLZANESE STYLE

Pork is a rather bland meat and needs strong herbs and spices. The following recipe is heavily flavored with caraway and garlic, both of which are greatly appreciated in central Europe. The simple but appropriate bread stuffing is very compatible with the rich piglet meat, and it also serves as the starch for the meal.

For this recipe, the piglet is completely boned and dressed in the classic *ballottine* fashion, with the head left on.

Yield: 12 to 14 servings

1	whole suckling piglet, 10-12 pounds	2 ounces	butter
		8 ounces	onions, diced
		1/2 cup	chopped parsley
		1/2 cup	milk
STUFFING:		2	eggs
20 ounces	stale Italian bread, in 1/4-inch cubes	to taste	salt and white pepper
1 ounce	flour	to taste	nutmeg

24 cloves	garlic, finely minced	3 ounces	carrots, diced small
4 tablespoons	caraway seeds	3 ounces	celery, diced small
1 tablespoon	freshly ground black pepper	4 to 5 cups	brown veal stock (see chapter 7)
3 tablespoons	salt	to taste	salt and freshly ground pepper
		to taste	marjoram
SAUCE:		to taste	bay leaves
2 tablespoons	oil		
6 ounces	onions, diced small		

1. Thoroughly clean the piglet, especially the ear cavities. Remove the eyes.

2. Lay the pig on its back, and carefully remove the rib bones, starting from the outer tips and working toward the spine. Reserve.

3. Remove the spine, starting from the tail end and being careful not to cut through the skin. Slowly loosen the spine and sever it below the neck, keeping the head intact. Reserve.

4. Sever the hind shank and foreshank bones above the joints, and loosen the meat around the bones. Then twist out the severed leg and foreshank bones. Reserve.

5. Pull the boneless leg meat and foreshank meat completely into the pig cavity.

6. Since most of the meat is now concentrated around the shoulder and leg area, it should be cut and distributed around the cavity of the piglet to ensure even cooking. Remove any small splinter bones.

7. Place the diced bread in a large mixing bowl, and add the flour.

8. Heat the butter and sauté the onions until lightly browned. Remove from the heat and add the parsley.

9. Mix the milk with the eggs, salt, pepper, and nutmeg.

10. Combine all ingredients for the stuffing, and mix well. Be careful not to crush the bread cubes.

11. Place the pig on its back on a tray, and fill the cavity with the stuffing. Shape the abdomen into a classic *ballottine*, and sew up with butcher's twine or secure with a large needle or skewer.

12. Mix the garlic, caraway seeds, pepper, and salt.

13. Puncture the skin of the piglet all over with a thin needle to release fat during cooking. Do *not* penetrate the cavity of the piglet with the needle.

(continued)

14.   Cover the tail and ears with aluminum foil to prevent burning.

15.   Put a sheet pan upside down in a roasting pan, and place the piglet on the pan.

16.   Roast in a preheated 350°F oven for 30 minutes. Rub the garlic/caraway mixture into the skin of the pig. Continue roasting for another 2½ hours, basting frequently. During the latter stages of roasting, cover the skin of the pig with oiled parchment paper to prevent the skin from drying out too much, which would make slicing difficult.

17.   Remove the sheet pan with the pig, and let rest for 10 minutes. (Since suckling pig is highly gelatinous, it is easier to remove the pig on the sheet pan than attempting to separate it from the roasting pan—that is why the sheet pan is used. Removing the pig from the sheet pan is far easier.)

18.   Chop the reserved piglet bones and any trimmings. Heat the oil in a shallow casserole, and brown the bones and trimmings. Add onion, carrots, and celery, and continue to sear until nicely browned. Add the drippings from the roasted piglet, the brown veal stock, and the salt, pepper, marjoram, and bay leaves. Simmer slowly for 1½ hours, and adjust the seasonings. Strain.

19.   Slice the roasted piglet and divide each slice in half. Arrange 2 halves on each heated serving plate, and spoon the sauce around them. Braised savoy or red cabbage, *caponatina* (see chapter 2), glazed fennel, or other vegetables go well with this dish.

Arista di Maiale alla Genovese con Salsa d'Aglio e Senape
ROAST PORK LOIN STUFFED WITH PESTO AND PORK FARCE WITH GARLIC MUSTARD SAUCE

To prepare the brown pork stock for this recipe, follow the instructions for brown veal stock in chapter 7, substituting the trimmings from the pork loin for the veal. Brown veal stock may be substituted for the pork stock.

Yield: 6 servings

3½ to 4 pounds	boneless pork loin	6 ounces	pork loin trimmings, with about 20 percent fat, diced small
2 tablespoons	chopped basil		
2 tablespoons	chopped parsley		
2 tablespoons	pine nuts, toasted	3 ounces	hot Italian sausage
3 cloves	garlic, crushed		
2 tablespoons	grated pecorino or Parmesan cheese	1 ounce	white breadcrumbs

2 tablespoons	ice water	5 ounces	onions, diced medium
1	egg yolk		
1/4 teaspoon	crushed hot red pepper	1 1/2 cups	dry white wine
		1	thyme sprig
2 tablespoons	dried egg white	1	bay leaf
8 ounces	pork caul, soaked in cold water and drained	to taste	freshly ground black pepper
		3 tablespoons	prepared mustard
		2 ounces	butter
SAUCE:		18 cloves	garlic (for garlic puree, see chapter 1)
3 cups	brown pork stock		
1 ounce	butter		

1.   Trim the pork loin, removing excess fat, skin, and the side flanks. Dice and reserve 6 ounces of lean trimmings for the farce, and use the rest for the pork stock.

2.   Butterfly the trimmed loin twice. First butterfly the top of the loin lengthwise, then repeat with the bottom part, to ensure a nice, flat, rectangular shape.

3.   Chop the basil, parsley, pine nuts, garlic, and cheese in a food processor. Spread this *pesto* evenly inside the butterflied loin.

4.   Grind the trimmings and fat through the medium plate of a meat grinder. Combine in a bowl with the Italian sausage, breadcrumbs, ice water, egg yolk, and hot pepper. Chill.

5.   Shape the farce into a thick sausage and place in the center of the loin, on top of the *pesto.*

6.   Sprinkle the dried egg white along the seam. Tie the loin every 2 inches with butcher's twine. Wrap completely in the caul.

7.   Roast the stuffed loin on a rack, seam side down, in a preheated 350°F oven for about 1 hour. Remove from the oven, and keep warm. Degrease the roasting pan, and deglaze the meat drippings with a bit of the brown pork stock.

8.   Heat the butter in a 2-quart saucepan, and lightly brown the onions. Add the wine, thyme, bay leaf, and pepper, and reduce to about 1/4 cup. Add the brown pork stock and pan drippings from the roast pork, and simmer slowly for 30 minutes. Strain the sauce through a fine-mesh sieve. If necessary, reduce further to the desired consistency. Mix a bit of the sauce with the mustard to prevent lumping. Add the mustard mixture to the saucepan, and whisk in the butter to create an emulsion. Add the roasted garlic cloves.

9.   Spoon the sauce onto each heated serving plate; include 3 whole cloves of garlic in each serving. Remove the butcher's twine from the roast pork, and slice the loin so as to have 2 slices per portion. Overlap these slices on the sauce.

Bollito di Maiale alle Verdure Fresche e Rafano Grattato
BOILED PORK SHOULDER WITH FRESH VEGETABLES AND GRATED HORSERADISH

Yield: 6 servings

3½ pounds	pork shoulder (not too fat)	6 ounces	carrots, cut in 2-inch julienne
3 quarts	water	6 ounces	fennel, cut in 2-inch julienne
2	bay leaves		
3	cloves	6 ounces	yellow turnips, cut in 2-inch julienne
15	black peppercorns, crushed	6 ounces	celeriac, cut in 2-inch julienne
10	juniper berries, crushed	1 cup	grated fresh horseradish
1	thyme sprig	¼ cup	finely chopped chives
1	rosemary sprig		
to taste	salt	¼ cup	chopped Italian parsley
6 tablespoons	white vinegar		
6 ounces	onions, cut in 2-inch julienne		

1. Tie the pork shoulder with butcher's twine to obtain a uniform shape, thus ensuring better portion control.

2. Bring the water to a boil in a 6-quart noncorrosive stock pot, and submerge the pork in it. Simmer slowly for 30 minutes.

3. Make a spice sachet of the bay leaves, cloves, peppercorns, juniper berries, thyme, and rosemary (see chapter 1). Add the sachet and salt to the pork, and continue to simmer for another 30 minutes, until tender but not overcooked.

4. Add the vinegar, and adjust the salt. (This dish can prepared ahead of time up to this point.)

5. Just before serving, add the onions, carrots, fennel, turnips, and celeriac, and simmer for a few minutes at the most. The vegetables should retain their crispness and color.

6. Remove and untie the pork shoulder. Cut to allow 2 slices per serving. Overlap 2 slices of pork on each heated serving plate. Arrange the vegetables neatly around the sliced meat. Spoon about 6 tablespoons of the cooking liquid over the meat on each plate, and then sprinkle generously with the grated horseradish. Sprinkle the chopped chives and parsley over the vegetables. Steamed or boiled new potatoes go well with this dish.

Spezzatino di Maiale con Peperonata
PORK STEW WITH PEPPERS, TOMATOES, AND ONIONS

Stewing is a cooking method generally reserved for tougher cuts containing more connective tissue. The meat is slowly cooked in a heavy-duty casserole with significantly less liquid than is used for braising. The moist heat gelatinizes the connective tissue and gives the meat a succulent flavor and texture.

Yield: 6 servings

¼ cup	olive oil	1 cup	water
3 pounds	lean pork shoulder, cut into thin strips	to taste	salt and freshly ground black pepper
2 ounces	pancetta, chopped		
1½ pounds	onions, diced medium	2 tablespoons	chopped marjoram
		2 tablespoons	chopped oregano
10 cloves	garlic, minced	4 tablespoons	chopped parsley
3	hot chili peppers, chopped	1 pound	red and green bell peppers, roasted and cut into strips (see chapter 1)
6 ounces	green and red bell peppers, chopped		
2 tablespoons	tomato paste	6 ounces	scallions, cut diagonally in 2-inch lengths
4	ripe tomatoes, peeled, seeded, and chopped (see chapter 1)	1 ounce	olive oil
2	bay leaves	to taste	salt and black pepper

1.   Heat the olive oil in a heavy-bottomed 6-quart casserole, and quickly sear the pork strips. Remove and keep warm.

2.   Add the *pancetta* to the casserole, and reheat.

3.   Lightly brown the onions in the rendered *pancetta*. Add the garlic, peppers, tomato paste, chopped tomatoes, and bay leaves. Simmer over low heat for 5 minutes.

4.   Add the seared pork strips, and as much water as necessary to maintain a fluid consistency—about 1 cup. Simmer very slowly for about 45 minutes, until the meat is cooked to the desired doneness.

5.   Add the salt and black pepper. Remove from the heat, and add the marjoram, oregano, and parsley. Remove the bay leaves.

(continued)

6. Sauté the peppers and scallions quickly just to heat in a bit of oil, and season with salt and pepper. Arrange the pork stew in individual casseroles or soup bowls or on heated plates, and top neatly with the peppers and scallions. Boiled rice goes well with this dish (see chapter 6).

Costolette di Maiale con Salsa di Mele e Cremazola
SAUTÉED PORK CHOPS WITH APPLES AND CREMAZOLA

Yield: 6 servings

6	lean pork chops, 6 to 7 ounces each	½ teaspoon	dried crushed hot red pepper
to taste	salt and freshly ground black pepper	6 tablespoons	grappa
		1 cup	dry vermouth
¼ cup	clarified butter (see chapter 1)	2 tablespoons	prepared mustard
6 ounces	red onions, cut in 2-inch julienne	2 cups	heavy cream, reduced to 1 cup
6 ounces	tart (Granny Smith) apples, cut in 2-inch julienne	3 tablespoons	Cremazola cheese, softened
6 ounces	red bell peppers, roasted, peeled, and cut in 2-inch julienne (see chapter 1)	6	mint sprigs

1. Season the pork chops with the salt and pepper. Heat the clarified butter in a large skillet, and cook the pork chops over moderate heat for about 2½ minutes on each side, turning once. Remove the chops from the skillet to a preheated dish. Place the dish in a 350°F oven for a few minutes.

2. Reheat the same skillet, and add the onions, apples, red peppers, dried hot pepper, and salt to taste. Cook over high heat for 20 seconds.

3. Remove the apple mixture to a suitable dish. Deglaze the pan with the grappa and vermouth. Reduce quickly to ¼ cup, and then mix in the prepared mustard.

4. Add the heated cream and softened Cremazola to the skillet, and adjust the seasonings. Return the apple mixture to the sauce.

5. Place a pork chop on each heated serving plate, and spoon the sauce neatly around it. Decorate with a sprig of fresh mint.

Filetto di Maiale Arrosto all'Arancia e Senape
ROAST PORK TENDERLOIN WITH ORANGE MUSTARD SAUCE

Yield: 6 servings

2	pork tenderloins, 1¼ pounds each	3 tablespoons	clarified butter (see chapter 1)
¼ cup	orange juice concentrate	2 tablespoons	finely diced shallots
		1½ cups	dry red wine
2 tablespoons	honey	2 cups	brown veal stock (see chapter 7)
¼ cup	prepared mustard		
¼ cup	brandy	3	hot chili peppers, thinly sliced
2	bay leaves		
1	rosemary sprig	to taste	salt
pinch	cayenne pepper	1 ounce	butter

1. Trim the pork tenderloins, remove any skin, and place in a small, deep pan.

2. Combine the orange juice concentrate, honey, mustard, brandy, bay leaves, rosemary, and cayenne, and pour over the pork. Keep the meat submerged in the marinade for several hours or overnight.

3. Remove the pork from the marinade, and blot dry. Reserve the marinade.

4. Heat the clarified butter in a skillet, and sear the pork on all sides. Place on a rack in a roasting pan, and roast in a preheated 350°F oven for about 10 minutes. Remove from the oven and keep warm.

5. Sweat the shallots in the skillet used for the pork, and deglaze with the red wine. Reduce to ¼ cup.

6. Add the brown veal stock, the chili peppers, and the salt, and reduce to 1 cup. Mix in the marinade, and bring to a simmer. Strain into a small saucepan. Reduce quickly to a light coating consistency. Remove from the heat, and whisk in the butter to achieve an emulsion.

7. Spoon the sauce onto heated serving plates. Slice the roast pork on the bias. Neatly overlap the slices on the sauce.

Filetto di Maiale Incrostato con Salsa d'Aglio e Pepe Verde

HERBED PORK TENDERLOIN WITH GARLIC AND GREEN-PEPPERCORN SAUCE

Yield: 6 servings

2	pork tenderloins, 1¼ pounds each	¼ cup	olive oil
		½ cup	diced red onions
1 ounce	olive oil	1 cup	dry red wine
to taste	salt and freshly ground black pepper	½ cup	roasted, peeled, seeded, and finely chopped red bell peppers (see chapter 1)
3 tablespoons	prepared mustard		
		½ cup	fresh tomatoes, peeled, seeded, and chopped (see chapter 1)
HERB COATING:			
¼ cup	chopped parsley		
2 tablespoons	chopped oregano		
½ cup	breadcrumbs, from Italian bread	1	chili pepper, chopped
½ cup	grated Parmesan cheese	1 cup	brown veal stock (see chapter 7)
1 teaspoon	grated lemon rind	1 tablespoon	green peppercorns
⅛ teaspoon	cayenne pepper	to taste	salt
		1 ounce	butter
SAUCE:			
18 cloves	garlic, unpeeled		

1. Trim the fat and cartilage from the pork.

2. Heat the oil in a skillet. Season the tenderloins with salt and pepper, and sear them on all sides over medium heat until approximately medium-done. Remove the tenderloins from the skillet, and spread the mustard all over them.

3. Combine the parsley, oregano, breadcrumbs, Parmesan, lemon rind, and cayenne. Roll the mustard-coated pork in this mixture. Be sure to apply a little pressure to ensure an even coating. Up to this point, this recipe can be prepared ahead of time. (If that is the case, keep the pork well chilled.)

4. Blanch the garlic cloves in boiling water for 3 minutes. Drain and peel.

5.   Heat the olive oil in a 2-quart saucepan, and cook the garlic cloves over low heat, being sure to turn them every so often. Do not brown the cloves. When soft, remove and reserve.

6.   Add the diced onion to the same oil, and cook over moderate heat until lightly browned. Add the wine, and reduce to ½ cup.

7.   Add the chopped peppers, tomatoes, and chili pepper to the wine reduction. Cook over low heat for about 10 minutes. Puree through the finest food mill or sieve.

8.   Return the puree to the saucepan, and add the brown veal stock and green peppercorns. Simmer, reducing to the desired consistency. Add the salt.

9.   Place the pork on a rack in a roasting pan, and roast in a preheated 375°F oven until nicely encrusted, about 15 to 20 minutes. Be sure to use the upper level in the oven to roast. Reduce the temperature to 350°F if the oven seems too hot.

10.   Whisk the butter into the sauce. Add the cooked garlic cloves.

11.   Pour some sauce onto each heated serving plate. Slice the tenderloins carefully on the bias. Overlap three slices on the sauce, placing 3 garlic cloves from the sauce on the meat.

Fettini di Maiale in Saor Alle Noci
PORK SCALLOPS IN SWEET-AND-SOUR ONION SAUCE WITH PINE NUTS

This delicious recipe plays on the delicate balance of sweet and sour on the palate. If more sweetness is desired, add brown sugar when sautéing the onions or reduce the amount of vinegar.

Yield: 6 servings

³/₄ cup	brown veal stock (see chapter 7)	to taste	salt and freshly ground black pepper
³/₄ cup	red wine	¹/₂ cup	flour
¹/₂ cup	red wine vinegar	³/₄ cup	virgin olive oil
¹/₂ cup	balsamic vinegar	2 pounds	onions, thinly sliced
3	bay leaves	¹/₂ cup	seedless raisins
3	whole cloves	¹/₂ cup	pine nuts, lightly toasted
1 teaspoon	mustard seeds		
to taste	salt	¹/₂ teaspoon	dried crushed hot red pepper
18	thin pork scallops, from tenderloin, 1¹/₂ ounces each		

1.   Combine the brown veal stock, wine, vinegars, bay leaves, cloves, mustard seeds, and salt in a noncorrosive pot. Bring to a simmer. Remove from the heat, and steep for 10 minutes. Strain, reserving the liquid.

2.   Season the pork scallops with salt and pepper, and dredge in the flour, shaking off any excess.

3.   Heat ¼ cup of olive oil in a large skillet, and sauté the pork scallops quickly, being sure to keep them slightly underdone. Remove from the pan and keep warm.

4.   Add the remaining oil to the skillet and reheat. Sauté the onions until they begin to brown, stirring constantly.

5.   Add 1¹/₂ cups of the infused liquid, the raisins, pine nuts, and crushed hot red pepper to the onions. Adjust the salt and pepper, and simmer a few minutes. Remove from the heat.

6.   Add the sautéed pork scallops to the onion sauce, and reheat. Do *not* boil.

7.   Overlap 3 pork scallops on each heated serving plate, and spoon the sauce over the meat.

Nodini di Maiale Saltate all'Origano

SAUTÉED PORK MÉDAILLONS WITH OREGANO SAUCE

Yield: 6 servings

6 tablespoons	clarified butter (see chapter 1)	¼ cup	chopped oregano
6 ounces	red onions, finely diced	18	lean pork médaillons, 1½ ounces each
6 cloves	garlic, finely minced	to taste	salt and freshly ground black pepper
2 cups	dry white wine		
½ cup	Marsala	2 ounces	butter
½ cup	meat glace (see chapter 7)		
1 to 2	chili peppers, chopped		
3	tomatoes, peeled, seeded, and diced small (see chapter 1)		

1.   Heat 2 tablespoons of clarified butter in a 1-quart saucepan, and sauté the onions until lightly browned. Add the garlic, and cook for 1 more minute.

2.   Deglaze the pan with the wines, and reduce to 1 cup.

3.   Add the meat *glace*, chili peppers, and diced tomatoes. Simmer slowly for several minutes, add the oregano, and salt to taste.

4.   Heat the remaining ¼ cup of clarified butter in a skillet, and sauté the pork *médaillons* quickly on both sides, turning once. Add salt and pepper to taste.

5.   Swirl the butter into the sauce to create an emulsion.

6.   Spoon the oregano sauce onto heated serving plates, and neatly overlap the pork *médaillons* on top of the sauce.

Portafoglia di Maiale con Salsa Boscaiola

STUFFED PORK CUTLETS WITH TOMATO-MUSHROOM SAUCE, WOODSMAN'S STYLE

Yield: 6 servings

6	pork cutlets, 6 ounces each (cut from the leg)	1	egg
6	thin cooked prosciutto slices, 2 by 3 inches	2 cups	water
		2 cups	dry breadcrumbs, from Italian bread
6	thin Fontina slices, 2 by 3 inches	to fry	oil
6	marinated sun-dried tomatoes (as purchased), sliced small	6	lemon wedges
		6	parsley sprigs
2	hot, red chili peppers chopped	2¼ cups	tomato-mushroom sauce, woodsman's style (see chapter 7)
1 cup	flour		

1.   Pound the pork cutlets between sheets of parchment paper or plastic wrap with the flat end of a meat mallet or cleaver so that the cutlet is approximately 6 by 6 inches.

2.   Place a slice of *prosciutto* on half of each cutlet, and top with a slice of Fontina. Top the Fontina with some sliced sun-dried tomatoes. Sprinkle with the chili peppers.

3.   Fold the empty half of each cutlet over the filled half, to make a purse. Pound the seams gently with the meat mallet to seal.

4.   Dredge the stuffed cutlets in flour. Lightly beat the egg and water to make an egg wash. Dip the floured cutlets in the egg wash. Dredge in the breadcrumbs.

5.   Pan- or deep-fry the cutlets in moderately hot oil on both sides for about 3 to 4 minutes, until the breading is nicely browned. Remove the cutlets from the pan, and drain on absorbent paper.

6.   Place each cutlet on a heated plate with a lemon wedge, and decorate with a sprig of parsley. Serve with the tomato-mushroom sauce.

— *Bue/Manzo* —
BEEF

Italy's most renowned beef comes from the Val di Chiana, which gives the celebrated Chianina cattle their name. These are one of the world's largest and leanest breeds of beef cattle, traditionally the source of the famous *Bistecca alla fiorentina,* which is a rib or T-bone steak grilled over a charcoal fire and then sprinkled with extra-virgin olive oil and served with a lemon half. Unfortunately, this famous breed of swampland cattle is becoming harder and harder to find in Italy.

Medaglione di Bue ai Funghi col Pesto con Salsa Pizzaiola
BEEF MÉDAILLONS AND MUSHROOMS FILLED WITH PESTO WITH PIZZA-STYLE TOMATO SAUCE

To obtain the beef marrow for this recipe, cut marrow bones in short sections and hold at room temperature. When the interior is soft, push the marrow out of the bone, pushing from the narrow end. Marrow bones can also be poached in broth, below the simmering point, for about 5 minutes. Remove the bones from the broth and cool to room temperature before pushing the marrow out. The marrow can be further loosened by running a long, thin knife along the inside of the bone. Always have marrow at or near room temperature when slicing, as cold marrow will crumble.

Yield: 6 servings

12	large mushroom caps	1/2 cup	grated Parmigiano Reggiano
2 tablespoons	olive oil	2 tablespoons	dried breadcrumbs
to taste	salt and freshly ground black pepper	12	médaillons of beef filet, 2 1/2 ounces each
1/4 cup	basil sauce, Genoese style— pesto (see chapter 7)	6 tablespoons	clarified butter (see chapter 1)
12	beef marrow slices from marrow bones, about 1/4-inch thick	2 1/4 cups	pizza-style tomato sauce (see chapter 7)

(continued)

1.   Brush the mushroom caps with the olive oil, and sprinkle with salt and pepper. Place them on a wire rack, and broil for 2 minutes.

2.   Arrange the mushroom caps in an ovenproof dish and fill the cavity of each with 1 teaspoon of *pesto,* and cover each with a slice of beef marrow. Mix the cheese with the breadcrumbs, and sprinkle over the marrow.

3.   Season the beef *médaillons.* Heat the clarified butter, and sauté the beef to the desired degree of doneness.

4.   Reheat the mushroom caps under the broiler, and set 1 on each sautéed *médaillon.* Spoon 3 ounces of pizza-style sauce on each heated plate, and arrange 2 beef médaillons neatly over the sauce. Serve immediately. Grilled radicchio and zucchini go well with this dish.

Medaglione di Bue alla Castellana
SAUTÉED BEEF MÉDAILLONS WITH ARTICHOKES AND TOMATOES

Yield: 6 servings

3	*artichokes, precooked (see chapter 12)*	*3 cloves*	*minced garlic*
6	*tomatoes, peeled and seeded (see chapter 1)*	*18*	*ripe olives, pitted and quartered*
12	*médaillons of beef tenderloin, 2½ ounces each*	*3*	*hot red chili peppers, thinly slice*
to taste	*salt and freshly ground black pepper*	*6 tablespoons*	*meat glace (see chapter 7)*
		¼ cup	*shredded basil*
½ to ¾ cup	*olive oil*	*¼ cup*	*shredded mint leaves*
3 ounces	*scallions, cut diagonally in 1½-inch lengths*		

1.   Cut the precooked artichokes into halves and then into small wedges. Cut the tomatoes into strips.

2. Season the beef *médaillons* with salt and pepper. Heat ¼ cup of olive oil, and sauté the beef to the desired degree of doneness. Remove from the pan, and keep warm.

3. Heat the remaining olive oil in the same skillet, and sauté the scallions, garlic, artichokes, and tomatoes quickly; keep crisp. Add the olives, chili peppers, and meat *glace*. Add salt and pepper to taste.

4. Arrange 2 sautéed *médaillons* on each heated serving plate. Arrange the vegetables neatly around the meat, and sprinkle the vegetables with the shredded basil and mint (see color plate 45).

Filetti di Bue Grigliati all'Essenza d'Aglio con Peperoni Arrosti Misti e Gorgonzola

GRILLED FILLETS OF BEEF WITH GARLIC, ASSORTED ROASTED PEPPERS, AND GORGONZOLA

Yield: 6 servings

2	red bell peppers, roasted and peeled (see chapter 1)	6 tablespoons	meat glace (see chapter 7)
2	yellow bell peppers, roasted and peeled (see chapter 1)	6	filet mignon steaks, 6 ounces each
		to taste	salt and freshly ground black pepper
2	green bell peppers, roasted and peeled (see chapter 1)		
		6 ounces	Gorgonzola, coarsely grated
4 ounces	butter	3 tablespoons	finely chopped chives
18 cloves	garlic, peeled		
3 tablespoons	finely diced shallots	18	scallions, trimmed, white parts only
2 cups	dry red wine		

1. Cut each roasted pepper into 6 wedges. Remove the seeds.

2. Heat 1 ounce of butter in a 1-quart saucepan, and add the garlic. Cover and cook for 10 minutes in a preheated 325°F oven. The garlic should become glossy but not brown. Add the shallots and wine to the garlic, and reduce to 6 tablespoons.

3. Add the meat *glace* and reheat.

(continued)

4.   Season the steaks with salt and pepper, and grill to the desired degree of doneness.

5.   Place a grilled steak in the center of each heated serving plate, and overlap the pepper wedges around it neatly. Sprinkle the Gorgonzola over the peppers, and place in a hot oven just long enough to heat.

6.   Whisk 3 ounces of butter into the garlic sauce to create an emulsion. Add the chopped chives.

7.   Spoon the garlic sauce over the grilled steaks, placing 3 cloves of garlic from the sauce on top of each. Sauté scallions in 1 tablespoon butter for just 30 seconds, and garnish with these as well. New potatoes go well with this dish.

Filleti di Bue alle Noci

BEEF MÉDAILLONS WITH WALNUT CREAM SAUCE

Yield: 6 servings

12	white bread slices	1½ cups	dry vermouth
6 tablespoons	clarified butter (see chapter 1)	1	bay leaf
		1 cup	walnuts, blanched and peeled
12	beef médaillons, 2½ ounces each	½ cup	meat glace (see chapter 7)
to taste	salt and freshly ground black pepper	1½ cups	heavy cream, reduced to ¾ cup
2 tablespoons	finely diced shallots		
¼ cup	brandy		

1.   Cut circles that are the same size as the *médaillons* from the white bread. Brush both sides of the bread circles with the clarified butter, and brown under a broiler or in a hot oven. Reserve.

2.   Heat the remaining clarified butter in a large skillet, season the beef with salt and pepper, and sauté on both sides to the desired degree of doneness. Remove from the pan and keep warm.

3.   Degrease the skillet, and add the shallots. Cook over moderate heat, add the brandy, and ignite.

4.   Add the vermouth, bay leaf, and walnuts, and reduce completely. Remove the bay leaf.

5. Add the meat *glace* and cream, and adjust the seasonings.

6. Arrange 2 bread disks on each heated serving plate, and top each with a *médaillon*. Spoon the walnut sauce over the meat. Steamed fennel hearts and sautéed diced tomatoes with fresh basil go well with this dish.

Cuori di Filetto di Bue alla Crema di Marsala
BEEF MÉDAILLONS WITH MOREL MARSALA SAUCE

Yield: 6 servings

12	white bread slices	¹/₂ cup	dry Marsala
4 ounces	clarified butter (see chapter 1)	1	bay leaf
6 ounces	fresh morels	6 tablespoons	meat glace (see chapter 7)
12	tournedos, 2¹/₂ ounces each	1 tablespoon	pickled green peppercorns
to taste	salt and freshly ground black pepper	1¹/₂ cups	heavy cream, reduced to ³/₄ cup
3 tablespoons	finely diced shallots	2 tablespoons	chopped parsley
1 cup	dry white wine	1 tablespoon	chopped rosemary

1. Cut circles that are the same size as the tournedos from the white bread. Brush both sides of the bread circles with melted butter, and brown under a broiler or in a hot oven. Reserve.

2. Clean the morels under cold running water to remove sand and grits. Blot dry with a towel, and cut off the ends of the stems. Cut the morels in half lengthwise.

3. Heat the remaining butter in a large skillet, season the tournedos with salt and pepper, and sauté to the desired degree of doneness. Remove from the pan and keep warm.

4. Add the shallots and morels to the same skillet, and sauté for several minutes. Add the wines and the bay leaf, and reduce almost completely.

5. Add the meat *glace* and green peppercorns, and stir in the cream. Adjust the seasonings, and add the parsley and rosemary.

6. Place 2 bread disks on each heated serving plate, and put a tournedos on each. Spoon the sauce over each tournedos. Steamed asparagus tips and glazed carrots go well with this dish.

Asticciole alla Calabrese

STUFFED BEEF KABOBS WITH MOZZARELLA AND SAUSAGE

Yield: 6 servings

1 cup	virgin olive oil	18	mozzarella sticks, 1 inch long
1 tablespoon	chopped oregano		
1 tablespoon	chopped rosemary	18	Italian bread slices, cut into 1- by 1-inch squares
1 teaspoon	freshly ground black pepper		
10 cloves	garlic, finely minced	18	bay leaves
18	beef tenderloin slices, 1 ounce each	18	hot Italian sausage pieces, 1 inch long

1.   Combine the olive oil, oregano, rosemary, pepper, and garlic, making a marinade.

2.   Brush each tenderloin slice with the marinade. Place 1 mozzarella stick in the center of each slice and roll up tightly.

3.   Brush each slice of bread with the marinade.

4.   Thread a piece of bread, bay leaf, sausage piece, and beef roulade on a long metal skewer; repeat. Continue threading in this order, repeating the sequence three times on each skewer.

5.   Brush the skewers with the marinade. Broil or grill to the desired degree of doneness. Boiled rice (see chapter 6) and *caponatina* (see chapter 1) go well with this dish.

Spezzatino di Filetto di Bue alle Verdure Fresche in Bordura di Riso

SAUTÉED BEEF STRIPS WITH FRESH VEGETABLES IN A RICE RING

Yield: 6 servings

30 ounces	beef tenderloin, well trimmed	2 ounces	scallions, cut diagonally in 2-inch lengths
10 tablespoons	olive oil		
2 ounces	red onions, sliced	8 cloves	garlic, minced

3	hot chili peppers, sliced in thin strips	*1 cup*	dry white wine
		1/2 cup	Marsala
1	green bell pepper, sliced in thin strips	*1/2 cup*	veal glace (see chapter 7)
1	red bell pepper, sliced in thin strips	*to taste*	salt and freshly ground black pepper
3 ounces	porcini, thickly sliced		
		3 tablespoons	prepared mustard
3 ounces	broccoli florets, cooked and shocked in cold water	*3 ounces*	butter
		1/4 cup	chopped parsley
		2 tablespoons	chopped marjoram
2 ounces	pea pods, with strings removed	*6 portions*	boiled rice (see chapter 6)
1 cup	sliced marinated sun-dried tomatoes (as purchased)	*6*	basil sprigs
		12	tomato petals (see chapter 1)

1. Cut the beef tenderloin with the grain into slices, then cut across the grain, making ¼ by 2½-inch strips.

2. Heat 6 tablespoons of olive oil in a large skillet, and quickly sauté the beef strips, a few at a time, until medium-rare. Remove with a slotted spoon to a small colander or sieve. Save all drippings for the sauce.

3. In the same pan, heat remaining 4 tablespoons (¼ cup) of oil, and sauté the onions, scallions, garlic, peppers, mushrooms, broccoli, pea pods, and tomatoes. Do not over-cook—the vegetables should remain crisp. Remove with a slotted spoon to a suitable dish, and reserve.

4. Deglaze the skillet with the wines. Add the veal *glace,* and reduce quickly to a light coating consistency. Add the meat and vegetable drippings, salt, and pepper. Whisk in the mustard and butter. Remove from the heat.

5. Combine the cooked beef and vegetables, and add to the hot sauce. Reheat, but do not allow to cook further. Mix in the parsley and marjoram.

6. To prepare a rice ring, spoon the cooked rice into a 1-cup capacity pan form, press it down with a tablespoon, and turn it out onto a heated plate. Repeat 6 times.

7. Arrange the beef/vegetable medley inside individual rice rings, and decorate with basil sprigs and heated tomato petals (see color plate 46).

Pasticcio di Manzo alla Primatura
BEEF POT PIE WITH FRESH VEGETABLES

To prepare the herbed puff pastry for this dish, follow the instructions for making puff pastry dough in chapter 14, but add 1 cup of chopped herbs (basil, parsley, rosemary, and marjoram) for every pound of butter.

Yield: 6 servings

6 tablespoons	olive oil	2 cups	brown veal stock (see chapter 7)
2¼ pounds	boned beef shank or shoulder, cut in 1-inch cubes	to taste	salt and freshly ground black pepper
1 pound	onions, diced		
6 cloves	garlic, minced	3 to 4 ounces	turnips
3 tablespoons	tomato paste	3 to 4 ounces	carrots
2 cups	dry red wine	3 to 4 ounces	potatoes
3	tomatoes, peeled, seeded, and chopped (see chapter 1)	3 to 4 ounces	pearl onions
		12	black olives, pitted
		12	green olives, pitted
3	hot red chili peppers, thinly sliced	1	cup water, salted
		1 ounce	butter
2	bay leaves	1½ pounds	herbed puff pastry dough
1 tablespoon	chopped marjoram	1	egg
1 teaspoon	chopped rosemary	1 fluid ounce	milk

1.   Heat the olive oil in a 6-quart heavy-duty braising pan, and sear the cubed beef a bit at a time on all sides. Remove the meat with a slotted spoon and keep warm.

2.   Reheat the oil, add the onions, and cook until lightly browned. Add the garlic and tomato paste, and continue to cook until the tomato paste starts to brown.

3.   Add the wine, tomatoes, chili peppers, bay leaves, marjoram, rosemary, and brown veal stock. Simmer for 5 minutes. Add salt and pepper.

4.   Add the seared meat cubes to the sauce, and cover. Cook over very low heat for about 2½ hours, or to preferred tenderness. Remove from the heat and cool.

5.   Use an oval-shaped scoop to shape the turnips, carrots, and potatoes into olive shapes. Steam these vegetables, plus the pearl onions and the olives, in the salted water with 1 ounce of butter. Cool. Add the liquid used for steaming to the meat filling.

6.   Use individual-size 12-ounce soufflé dishes (or similar crockery) for the pies. Fill each dish with 1 cup of the meat filling, and arrange the vegetables neatly on top.

7.   Roll out the herbed puff pastry dough to a ¼-inch thickness, and cut 6 circles, large enough to extend ½ inch over the edges of the dishes on all sides.

8.   Combine the egg and milk, and brush the edges of the dishes with this egg wash. Set a dough circle on top of each dish. Press the edges gently. If the dough extends more than ½ inch over the edges, trim.

9.   Brush the dough with egg wash, and refrigerate until ready to bake.

10.   Score the dough with the tines of a dinner fork to make a nice design. Brush again with egg wash. Using a ¼-inch round cutter or the plain tip of a pastry bag, make a hole in the center of the dough to vent steam during baking.

11.   Bake in a preheated 350°F oven for 20 to 25 minutes. Serve in folded napkins.

Braciolette di Bue Ripiene al Barolo

BEEF ROULADES BRAISED IN BAROLO

Yield: 6 servings

6	beef cutlets, cut from the cross rib, 8 ounces each	2	bay leaves
		1/4 cup	tomato paste
9 ounces	cotechino sausage	1 cup	fresh tomatoes, peeled, seeded, and chopped (see chapter 1)
2 tablespoons	prepared mustard		
1 teaspoon	freshly ground black pepper		
		2 cups	Barolo
1/4 cup	chopped parsley	to taste	salt and crushed hot red pepper
1 tablespoon	chopped rosemary		
1 tablespoon	chopped marjoram	2 cups	brown veal stock (see chapter 7)
6 tablespoons	olive oil		
3 tablespoons	flour		

GARNISH:

1/2 ounces	butter
12 ounces	chanterelles
2 tablespoons	chopped parsley
to taste	salt and dried crushed hot red pepper

SAUCE:

12 ounces	onions, diced
4 cloves	garlic, minced
4 ounces	carrots, thinly sliced
4 ounces	celery, thinly sliced
4 ounces	fennel stalks, thinly sliced

1.   Flatten the beef cutlets slightly. Cut the *cotechino* sausage into 6 pieces.

2.   Spread each cutlet with mustard, and sprinkle with the pepper, parsley, rosemary, and marjoram. Place a piece of the sausage in the center of each and roll up. Secure the seam with a toothpick.

3.   Heat the olive oil in a shallow casserole. Dredge the roulades in the flour, and brown over moderate heat on all sides. Remove from the casserole, and keep warm.

4.   Add the onions to the same casserole, and cook until they are nicely browned.

5.   Add the garlic, carrots, celery, and fennel, and cook over moderate heat for 5 minutes.

6.   Stir in the bay leaves, tomato paste, chopped tomatoes, wine, salt, and red pepper. Simmer an additional 5 minutes. Add the brown veal stock.

7.   Place the roulades back in the sauce, and cover. Braise over low heat for about 1¼ to 1½ hours or to the desired degree of doneness.

8.   Remove the toothpicks from the roulades, and strain the sauce through a sieve or a food mill. Adjust the seasonings and return the meat to the sauce. Keep warm. (The sauce can be reduced further if too thin.)

9.   Heat the butter, and sauté the chanterelles until thoroughly heated. Add the parsley, salt, and red pepper.

10.   Place each roulade on a heated serving plate, and coat generously with the sauce. Spoon the chanterelles on top. *Penne* or potato *gnocchi* go well with this dish.

Stufato di Manzo alla Romana
BEEF STEW, ROMAN STYLE

Any part of an animal that is continually exercised is bound to be tougher than other cuts, but at the same time more flavorful and succulent. These cuts are perfect for braising.

When braising, the meat is often seared before the liquid ingredients are added, but sometimes the meat is left unseared, which is called stewing.

Yield: 6 servings

3 pounds	*boned beef shank or shoulder, cut in 1-inch cubes*	*1 teaspoon*	*chopped lemon peel*
½ teaspoon	*freshly ground black pepper*	*6*	*sage leaves*
		1	*thyme sprig*
2 ounces	*flour*	*2*	*bay leaves*
10 tablespoons	*olive oil*	*to taste*	*salt and freshly ground black pepper*
1 pound	*onions, finely diced*		
6 cloves	*garlic, minced*	**GARNISH:**	
½ cup	*tomato paste*	*1 ounce*	*butter*
1 cup	*fresh tomatoes, peeled, seeded, and chopped (see chapter 1)*	*8 ounces*	*fennel knob, cut in fine strips and blanched*
2 cups	*dry red wine*	*8 ounces*	*green and red bell peppers, cut in fine strips*
2 cups	*brown veal stock (see chapter 7)*	*¼ cup*	*chopped parsley*
1	*bouquet garni with carrots, parsnips, and celery (see chapter 1)*		

1.   Season the meat cubes with the pepper, and sprinkle with the flour.

2.   Heat 6 tablespoons of oil in a shallow 4-quart casserole, and sear the meat cubes, a few at a time, on all sides. Remove with a slotted spoon.

3.   Add the remaining oil to the casserole, and sauté the onions until nicely browned. Add the garlic and tomato paste, and continue cooking until the tomato paste starts to brown.

4. Add the chopped tomatoes, wine, brown veal stock, *bouquet garni*, lemon peel, sage, thyme, bay leaves, salt, and pepper. Simmer for 10 minutes. Add the seared meat, cover, and cook over very low heat for about 1½ hours, or to the desired tenderness. Adjust the seasonings, and discard the bay leaves and *bouquet garni*.

5. Arrange the stew in preheated deep plates. Heat the butter and quickly sauté the fennel and peppers. Season to taste, and spoon over the stew. Sprinkle with the parsley.

Lingua di Bue Affumicata con Salsa di Rafano

SMOKED BEEF TONGUE WITH HORSERADISH SAUCE

Yield: 6 servings

2	smoked beef tongues	1 teaspoon	sugar
1 cup	double beef broth (see chapter 3)	½ teaspoon	salt
		to taste	white pepper
1½ cups	fresh white breadcrumbs, from Italian bread, no crusts	to taste	nutmeg
		1 cup	hot heavy cream
		⅓ cup	fresh grated horseradish
3 tablespoons	white vinegar		

1. Simmer the beef tongues in water to cover for about 2 hours, or until cooked to the desired tenderness.

2. Peel the skin from the tongues—it should now come off easily—and trim away any tough parts. Keep hot in the liquid.

3. Bring the double beef broth to a boil in a 1-quart noncorrosive saucepan.

4. Whisk in the breadcrumbs until completely smooth. The sauce should be thick. Add more breadcrumbs if too thin.

5. Stir in the vinegar, sugar, salt, pepper, and nutmeg, and simmer for 5 minutes. Add the hot cream, and adjust the seasonings. Add the grated horseradish. Cover the sauce and keep hot in a hot water bath.

6. Cut the trimmed beef tongue diagonally into oblong slices. Spoon the horseradish sauce generously onto heated plates, and overlap the tongue neatly over the sauce. Boiled or steamed new potatoes and a medley of steamed baby root vegetables or vegetables in the cabbage family go well with this dish.

Trippa di Bue alla Veneto

BRAISED BEEF TRIPE WITH TOMATOES AND GRAPPA

Yield: 6 servings

4½ to 5 pounds	beef tripe
¾ to 1 cup	olive oil with prosciutto trimmings
2 pounds	onions, sliced
10 cloves	garlic, minced
3 to 4	hot red chili peppers, chopped
¾ cup	tomato paste
2 pounds	fresh tomatoes, peeled, seeded, and chopped (see chapter 1)
3 cups	dry white wine
½ cup	balsamic vinegar
2	bay leaves
⅛ teaspoon	ground cloves
to taste	salt and freshly ground black pepper
¾ cup	grappa
2 tablespoons	chopped marjoram
2 tablespoons	chopped sage
2 tablespoons	chopped rosemary

GARNISH:

2 tablespoons	olive oil
2 ounces	scallions, white parts only, cut in 2-inch lengths
4 ounces	red bell peppers, cut in 2-inch strips
4 ounces	green bell peppers, cut in 2-inch strips
2 ounces	yellow bell peppers, cut in 2-inch strips
to taste	salt
⅓ cup	chopped Italian parsley

1. Wash the beef tripe, place in a 6-quart saucepan, and cover with water. Simmer for 10 minutes and drain. Shock the tripe in cold water and trim off any excess fat. Cut the trimmed tripe into large strips, approximately 2 by 4 inches.

2. Return the tripe strips to the saucepan, and fill with enough water to cover. Simmer the tripe slowly for 4 to 6 hours, or until it begins to soften.

3. Heat the oil with the *prosciutto* trimmings in a shallow 6-quart casserole. Add the onions and brown lightly. Stir in the garlic.

4. Add the chili peppers, tomato paste, chopped tomatoes, wine, balsamic vinegar, bay leaves, cloves, and salt and pepper to taste. Simmer for 30 minutes. Add a bit of the liquid from the simmering tripe as this mixture simmers.

5.   Add the tripe to the tomato sauce, and continue to simmer for another 2 hours, until the tripe reaches the desired tenderness. Add the liquid from the simmering of the tripe as needed.

6.   When the sauce has sufficiently reduced to a thick consistency, and the tripe is very soft, add the grappa, marjoram, sage, and rosemary, plus salt and pepper.

7.   Heat the 2 tablespoons of olive oil, and sauté the scallions and peppers quickly. The vegetables should remain very crisp. Season with salt.

8.   Arrange the tripe and sauce on hot serving plates, top with the scallions and peppers, and sprinkle with the chopped parsley. Neatly scooped polenta mush or boiled potatoes go well with this dish (see color plate 47).

POULTRY

Poultry includes a variety of domestic fowl. The following list defines the more common Italian terms for poultry.

Anatroccolo: Duckling.
Anitra or **Anatra:** Duck.
Cappone: A capon—a castrated rooster weighing up to 6 pounds, normally roasted.
Dindo: A turkey cock.
Faraona: A guinea fowl.
Gallina: An old hen, fowl, or soup/stew chicken.
Oca: Goose.
Pollastra: A young hen, usually 6 to 8 months old; also referred to as a roasting chicken.
Pollastro: A young cock, usually 3 to 4 months old; also referred to as a frying chicken.
Pollo: General term for chicken.
Pulcino: Baby chicken or *poussin;* a very young bird of a special breed weighing about 1 pound and slaughtered when 6 to 8 weeks old; also referred to as a spring chicken.
Tacchino: General term for turkey.

— *Pollo* —
CHICKEN

When purchasing chicken breasts, it is more economical in a commercial setting to buy the whole bird, using the remaining parts for other recipes and for stocks. The chicken breast recipes that follow all call for the breast with the last section of the wing bone intact (and Frenched), which makes a nicer presentation. If the breasts are purchased already filleted, this bone will be missing, but the recipes will not be affected.

Petti di Pollo Ripieni con Prosciutto e Porri in Salsa Crema all'Erbe

CHICKEN BREASTS STUFFED WITH PROSCIUTTO AND LEEKS IN HERB CREAM SAUCE

Yield: 6 servings

6	chicken breasts, 5 ounces each	to taste	salt and white pepper
6	leek whites, approximately 4 inches long	2 tablespoons	dried egg white
		2¼ cups	herb cream sauce (see chapter 7)
2 quarts	double chicken broth (see chapter 3)		
6	cooked prosciutto, thinly sliced, 2½ by 4 inches		

1.   Trim the chicken breasts, leaving the last section of wing bone intact. French the wing bone by slicing the meat from the base up toward the joint and then scraping this meat up toward the end of the bone. Carefully sever the bone just under the joint with the breast. Do not splinter the bone. Remove all the skin from the breasts.

2.   Butterfly the breasts lengthwise.

3.   Spread the breasts open between 2 sheets of plastic wrap and pound gently with a flat mallet from where the wing bone is attached outward.

4.   Blanch the cleaned leek whites in the double chicken broth for 2 minutes. Remove and blot dry with a towel. Retain the broth for poaching the breasts. Wrap the blanched leeks tightly in the cooked *prosciutto*.

5.   Place the wrapped leeks in the centers of the flattened breasts, and season with salt and pepper.

6.   Sprinkle the outer edges of the breasts with the dried egg white. Fold the narrow outer portion of each breast at the far end up over the leek, then roll each breast up tightly around the leek, forming a bananalike shape.

7.   Wrap the chicken rolls in at least 3 layers of plastic wrap. Refrigerate until ready to cook.

8.   Poach the breasts, still wrapped in plastic, in strong chicken broth for 7 to 8 minutes—keep the broth below the boiling point. It is also possible to steam the breast in a perforated insert or steaming basket over a double boiler for about 5 minutes.

9. Remove the plastic wrap from the breasts, and cut the rolls on the bias into 5 to 6 pieces. Neatly overlap the slices on heated serving plates. The leek/*prosciutto* interior should be visible, and the arrangement should resemble a fan, with the wing bone piece in place at the end. Spoon the herb cream sauce around the fanned breasts (see color plate 48).

Petti di Pollo Imbottiti alla Valdostana con Salsa di Pomodoro
CHICKEN BREASTS STUFFED WITH PROSCIUTTO AND FONTINA WITH TOMATO SAUCE

Yield: 6 servings

6	chicken breasts, 6 ounces each	*2*	eggs
		¼ cup	water
to taste	freshly ground black pepper	*2 cups*	extra-fine breadcrumbs, from Italian or French bread
6	cooked prosciutto, thinly sliced, 2 by 4 inches		
		to deep-fry	oil
6	Fontina sticks, 4-inch-long "fingers"	*12*	lemon wedges, trimmed and seeded
		6	parsley sprigs
3 tablespoons	chopped basil	*2¼ cups*	tomato sauce (see chapter 7)
3 tablespoons	dried egg white		
1 cup	all-purpose flour		

1. Trim the breasts, leaving the wing intact. Sever the wing bone at the first joint down from the breast without splintering. Remove the skin from the breast. Shave the attached wing bone clean of meat and tendons with a paring knife.

2. Butterfly the breasts lengthwise.

3. Spread the breasts open between 2 sheets of plastic wrap, and gently pound the meat with a flat mallet, working from the wing bone toward the narrow end. Season with the pepper.

4. Place the thin *prosciutto* slices on a worktable. Press the cheese fingers into the chopped basil and wrap tightly in the *prosciutto*.

5. Place a wrapped cheese finger in the center of each breast. Sprinkle the dried egg white along the edges of the meat. Fold the narrow tip of breast meat inside and over the cheese, then roll the breast into a bananalike shape. Refrigerate the breasts until *well chilled*, or semifrozen.

(continued)

6.   Dredge the chicken in the flour. Lightly beat the eggs with the water to make an egg wash. Dip the floured chicken in the egg wash and then into the breadcrumbs.

7.   Deep-fry the chicken in 350°F oil for 4 to 5 minutes. Place on absorbent paper to drain.

8.   Place a chicken roll on each heated serving plate, and garnish with the lemon wedges and parsley. Serve the tomato sauce separately alongside.

Petti di Pollo con Prosciutto e Mozzarella alla Salsa di Peperoni Rossi
CHICKEN BREASTS WITH PROSCIUTTO AND MOZZARELLA IN RED-PEPPER SAUCE

Yield: 6 servings

6	chicken breasts, 5 to 6 ounces each	1 cup	red and green bell peppers, roasted, seeded, and cut in fine julienne (see chapter 1)
¼ cup	clarified butter (see chapter 1)		
6 tablespoons	dry white wine	6	mozzarella slices, approximately 2½ by 5 inches
to taste	salt and freshly ground black pepper		
6	Fontina slices, approximately 2 by 5 inches	2¼ cups	sweet red-pepper sauce (see chapter 7)
2 ounces	cooked prosciutto, cut in fine julienne	6	basil sprigs

1.   Trim the chicken breasts, leaving the last wing bone intact. French this bone by severing the meat and tendons and scraping clean. Remove the skin from breasts.

2.   Heat the clarified butter in a skillet, and cook the chicken breasts over low heat, turning once. Keep undercooked—total cooking time should be about 6 minutes. (If the breasts are especially thick, finish the cooking in a preheated 325°F oven.)

3.   Remove the skillet from the heat, and pour the wine over the chicken. Let the breasts absorb the flavor, and then season with salt and pepper, but do not simmer.

4.   Place the breasts in an ovenproof dish, and place one slice of Fontina on each.

5. Top the Fontina with the julienne of *prosciutto* and the peppers.

6. Top with a slice of mozzarella. Heat in the oven just long enough to melt the cheeses.

7. Spoon the sweet red-pepper sauce on heated plates, and place the chicken over the sauce. Decorate with basil sprigs.

Filetti di Pollo alla Cacciatora
SAUTÉED CHICKEN CUTLETS, HUNTER'S STYLE

Yield: 6 servings

6	boneless, skinless chicken breasts, approximately 5 ounces each	3/4 cup	veal glace (see chapter 7)
to taste	salt and freshly ground black pepper	1/3 teaspoon	dried, crushed hot red pepper
		1/4 cup	chopped Italian parsley
1/4 cup	flour	1 tablespoon	chopped marjoram
10 tablespoons	olive oil	12 ounces	fresh porcini, thickly sliced
9 ounces	onions, cut into 2-inch strips	18 ounces	ripe tomatoes, peeled, seeded, and cut into strips (see chapter 1)
4 cloves	garlic, minced		
1 1/2 cups	dry white wine		

1. Cut the boneless breasts in half lengthwise, and place between sheets of plastic wrap. Gently flatten with a smooth mallet, and trim off any rough edges.

2. Season the cutlets with salt and pepper, and dredge lightly in the flour.

3. Heat 6 tablespoons of olive oil in a skillet, and sear the cutlets quickly on both sides. Remove from the pan before fully cooked.

4. Add the onions and garlic to the skillet, and sauté for 1 minute. Deglaze the pan with the wine, and reduce completely. Add the veal *glace,* hot red pepper, Italian parsley, marjoram, and salt to taste.

5. In another skillet, sauté the *porcini* in the remaining 4 tablespoons of oil for 1 minute. Add the tomatoes, reheat, and combine with the sauce. Adjust the seasonings.

(continued)

6.   Return the chicken to the sauce to absorb some flavor. Do not simmer again.

7.   Overlap 2 chicken cutlets on each heated serving plate, and spoon the sauce over the sides of the cutlets.

Battute di Pollo con Salsa alle Verdure
CHICKEN BREASTS WITH VEGETABLE SAUCE

Yield: 6 servings

6	chicken breasts, 6 ounces each	2¼ cups	vegetable sauce (see chapter 7)
to taste	salt and white pepper	18	tomato petals (see chapter 1)
½ cup	flour	2 tablespoons	melted butter
6 tablespoons	olive oil	6	basil sprigs
6 tablespoons	clarified butter (see chapter 1)		

1.   Remove the skin and wing bones from the chicken breasts, and butterfly. Trim the breasts into heart shapes.

2.   Place the chicken between sheets of plastic wrap, and pound gently with the flat end of a meat mallet or cleaver until about ¼ inch thick. Trim the side edges. Refrigerate, wrapped in the plastic.

3.   Remove the chicken from the plastic, and season with salt and white pepper. Dredge lightly in the flour, shaking off any excess.

4.   Heat the oil and butter in a very large skillet.

5.   Cook the chicken over moderate heat on both sides till just underdone.

6.   Spoon 6 tablespoons of the hot vegetable sauce onto each heated serving plate, and place a chicken breast on top of the sauce.

7.   Brush the tomato petals with a little butter and season to taste. Warm in a hot oven.

8.   Garnish by overlapping the petals in a fan shape and adding a basil sprig.

Pollo Grigliato alla Diavola con Cipolline Verde e Radicchio ai Ferri

DEVILED GRILLED CHICKEN WITH GRILLED SCALLIONS AND RADICCHIO

Yield: 6 servings

3	spring chickens, 2 pounds each	1/4 cup	finely diced shallots
		6 cloves	garlic, minced
MARINADE:		6 tablespoons	balsamic vinegar
1/4 cup	olive oil	1 cup	dry white wine
2 tablespoons	grappa	to taste	dried, crushed hot red pepper
2 tablespoons	dry white wine		
3 cloves	garlic, minced	6 tablespoons	poultry glace (see chapter 7)
1/2 teaspoon	dried, crushed hot red pepper	to taste	salt and freshly ground black pepper
30	scallions		
3 heads	radicchio, very firm	6	sage leaves, finely chopped
3/4 cup	extra-virgin olive oil		

1.   Halve the chickens, and remove all the bones except the wing bones. Cut each wing bone at the first joint from the breast without splintering the bone. Trim away the skin, fat, and tendons, and scrape the wing bone clean with a paring knife.

2.   Combine olive oil, grappa, wine, garlic, and hot pepper for the marinade, and coat the boned chicken halves thoroughly. Place in a suitable dish and cover.

3.   Clean the scallions, and trim to approximately 5 inches long, removing most of the green tops.

4.   Clean the radicchio. Discard any wilted outer leaves, and then split the heads lengthwise into quarters. Keep chilled.

5.   Heat 2 tablespoons of extra-virgin olive oil in a 1-quart saucepan, and cook the shallots and garlic for a few minutes. Add the balsamic vinegar, wine, and hot red peppers. Reduce to 6 tablespoons. Add the poultry *glace,* and adjust the seasonings. Remove from the heat.

6.   Place the chicken halves on a tray, skin up. Tuck the boneless legs under the tip of the breast, forming almost a rectangular shape.

7.   Arrange the tucked halves between a folding broiler rack, and grill on both sides for about 12 minutes total, basting occasionally with the marinade.

(continued)

8.   Season the scallions and radicchio with salt and pepper, let rest for 10 minutes, and brush with 6 tablespoons of extra-virgin olive oil.

9.   Grill the radicchio quarters on three sides until the leaves start to take on a bit of color. Remove. Grill the scallions quickly on one side only.

10.   Reheat the sauce, and stir in the remaining 4 tablespoons (¼ cup) of extra-virgin olive oil and the chopped sage.

11.   Arrange 2 quarters of grilled radicchio on each heated plate, and top with the grilled chicken. Spoon the sauce over the chicken, and garnish with the grilled scallions.

Pulcini Ripieni in Tecia agli Spugnole

BABY CHICKENS STUFFED WITH MORELS, BAKED IN EARTHENWARE

Pulcini are a special breed of young chicken weighing from 1 to 1½ pounds. Also referred to as Hamburg chickens or *poussin*, they are very lean, excellent for frying and sautéing. Boned and stuffed, they are often seared and finished in an earthenware dish with herbs and spices. A 1½-pound chicken will serve two when prepared in this fashion.

Yield: 6 servings

STUFFING:		
2½ cups	chicken broth (see chapter 3)	
¼ cup	barley	
¼ cup	clarified butter (see chapter 1)	
½ cup	diced chicken livers	
½ cup	diced onions	
3 cloves	garlic, minced	
¾ cup	small-diced celeriac	
¾ cup	small-diced fennel	
½ cup	small-diced mortadella	
¼ cup	chopped Italian parsley	
6	sage leaves, chopped	

1	egg, lightly beaten	
½ teaspoon	salt and freshly ground black pepper	
3	baby chickens (poussin) 1¼ to 1½ pounds each	
¼ cup	oil	
½ cup	coarsely chopped onions	
¼ cup	coarsely chopped celery	
¼ cup	coarsely chopped carrots	

3 cloves	garlic, crushed	5 cups	brown veal stock (see chapter 7)
½ cup	Marsala	to taste	salt and freshly ground black pepper
1 cup	dry white wine		
1	rosemary sprig	¼ cup	clarified butter (see chapter 1)
1	thyme sprig		
1	bay leaf	12	fresh morels, well cleaned
10	black peppercorns, crushed		
3	whole cloves		

1.   Heat the chicken broth in a 1-quart saucepan, and cook the barley in the broth over low heat for 1½ hours, until soft. Drain the liquid and reserve. Put the cooked barley in a mixing bowl.

2.   Heat ¼ cup of clarified butter in a skillet, and quickly sauté the chicken livers until medium-done. Remove with a slotted spoon, and add to the barley. Cool and chill.

3.   Add the ½ cup of onions, 3 cloves of garlic, and the diced celeriac and fennel to the same skillet and sauté for 1 minute. Deglaze the skillet with ½ cup of the reserved barley cooking liquid, and reduce completely. Add the *mortadella,* Italian parsley, and sage, and remove from the heat. Cool completely and chill.

4.   Combine all the well-chilled ingredients for the stuffing. Mix in the egg, salt, and pepper. Keep chilled until needed for stuffing the chicken.

5.   To prepare the chickens, glove-bone them according to the instructions given in the introduction on quail, in chapter 11, in which the bones are removed without cutting the skin. They are pulled from the neck cavity, leaving the bird wholly intact. Only the drumsticks are left in. Chop and reserve 1½ pounds of bones.

6.   Heat ¼ cup of oil in a skillet, and add the reserved chicken bones and any trimmings. Sear over high heat, and add the onions, celery, and carrots, continuing to brown. Add the garlic, and deglaze the skillet with the wines. Reduce by half. Add the rosemary, thyme, bay leaf, peppercorns, cloves, and brown veal stock, and transfer to a small saucepan. Simmer slowly for 1½ hours, and strain into a smaller pan. Continue to reduce to 2½ cups. Keep hot in a hot water bath.

7.   Stuff the baby chickens with the cold stuffing. Close the ends with skewers or toothpicks, and season with salt and pepper. Heat the clarified butter in a skillet, and sear the chickens on all sides over moderate heat. Place the birds in a preheated 375°F oven for about 5 minutes.

8.   Remove the chickens from the oven, and place in individual-size earthenware casseroles. The dish should be just large enough to hold the bird. Add 4 morels and ¾ cup of the reduced sauce to each dish.

(continued)

9.   Cover each dish with a tight-fitting lid, and bake in a preheated 350°F oven for about 20 to 25 minutes. (It is also possible to seal the lids with a water/flour paste. Mix just enough water with flour to form a thick paste, similar to pizza dough. Roll out into fairly thin, long strips and secure them around the lids.)

10.   Place each casserole on a neatly folded napkin, and open tableside before the guests (see color plate 49). (Crack the flour seal, if used, with a knife and remove before opening.)

Giambonette di Pollo Farcite alla Boscaiola
STUFFED CHICKEN LEGS WITH WILD MUSHROOM AND GARLIC SAUCE

Yield: 6 servings

STUFFING:		8 ounces	pork caul, rinsed, blotted dry, and cut into six 5- by 5-inch pieces
1 tablespoon	olive oil		
2 ounces	onions, finely diced		
3 cloves	garlic, minced		
1/4 cup	chopped parsley	**SAUCE:**	
1 tablespoon	chopped rosemary	1/4 cup	olive oil
9 ounces	boned pork shoulder, ground medium-fine	6 ounces	onions, finely diced
		6 cloves	garlic, minced
		12 ounces	wild mushrooms (such as porcini, or chanterelles)
3 tablespoons	fresh breadcrumbs		
1/4 teaspoon	freshly ground black pepper		
pinch	salt	1 cup	dry white wine
1	egg, beaten	6 to 10 tablespoons	meat glace (see chapter 7)
6	chicken legs, from 3-pound chickens		

½ teaspoon	dry, crushed hot red pepper	3 tablespoons	chopped parsley
1½ cups	ripe tomatoes, peeled, seeded, and diced (see chapter 1)	1 tablespoon	chopped oregano
		to taste	salt
		1½ ounces	butter

1.   Heat the tablespoon of oil, and sauté the 2 ounces of onions for the stuffing in it for 2 minutes. Add the garlic, parsley, and rosemary. Remove from the heat, cool, and chill.

2.   Combine the ground pork with the breadcrumbs, pepper, salt, and sautéed onions in a mixing bowl. Mix well, and add the beaten egg. Keep well-chilled.

3.   Bone the chicken legs by removing the drumstick bone without cutting into the skin. Remove the thigh bone as well. Fill the cavity with sufficient stuffing to give the legs a plump sausage or *ballottine* shape.

4.   Wrap each leg tightly in the pork caul, and secure with butcher's twine tied around the thigh. Refrigerate.

5.   Heat the ¼ cup of olive oil for the sauce in a large skillet, and sauté the onions, garlic, and mushrooms for 1 minute. Deglaze the skillet with the wine and reduce almost completely. Add the meat *glace,* hot red pepper, tomatoes, parsley, oregano, and salt. Stir in the butter.

6.   Place the stuffed legs, seam side down, on a wire rack. Place the rack on a sheet pan, and bake in a preheated 350° to 375°F oven for about 15 minutes, until well done.

7.   Remove the butcher's twine from the legs, and slice them on the bias in even slices. Overlap the slices neatly on heated serving plates. Spoon the sauce on one side of the slices (see color plate 50). Grilled polenta and braised fennel go well with this dish.

Giambonette di Pollo Aromaticie agli Spiedini con Salsa Crema alla Mostarda
STUFFED CHICKEN LEG KABOBS WITH MUSTARD CREAM SAUCE

Yield: 6 servings

4 ounces	pancetta, coarsely chopped	2 tablespoons	chopped oregano
3 cloves	garlic, minced	1/4 cup	dry bread crumbs
1/2 cup	minced red and green bell peppers	1	egg, lightly beaten
2	hot chili peppers, chopped	12	chicken legs, from 2 1/2-pound chickens
1/4 cup	chopped sun-dried, marinated tomatoes (as purchased)	to taste	salt and freshly ground black pepper
2 tablespoons	chopped parsley	2 1/4 cups	mustard cream sauce (see chapter 7)

1.   Render the *pancetta* in a hot skillet until crisp. Drain the fat, and add the garlic, peppers, and sun-dried tomatoes. Cook for 1 minute, and remove to a suitable bowl. Stir in the parsley, oregano, breadcrumbs, and egg. Cool.

2.   Bone the chicken legs by slitting completely down one side and removing the bones. Do not skin. Arrange the rectangular pieces of chicken on a worktable, skin side down. Season with salt and pepper.

3.   Spread the cooled filling on the meat and roll up tightly. Trim to make neat rolls.

4.   Cut each roll in half, and thread 4 pieces on each 8-inch skewer.

5.   Place on a sizzle platter or a metal platter for broiling, and broil until nicely browned and crisp. Drain on absorbent paper.

6.   Spoon mustard cream sauce onto heated serving plates, and slide the chicken pieces off the skewers onto the sauce.

Pollo alla Romana

CRISP-FRIED CHICKEN STRIPS, ROMAN STYLE

Yield: 6 servings

MARINADE:

1	egg
2 tablespoons	olive oil
2 tablespoons	lemon juice
3 cloves	garlic, minced
1/2 teaspoon	fresh ground black pepper
1/2 teaspoon	salt
2 1/2 pounds	boneless, skinless chicken breast, cut into finger-size strips
1 cup	flour
1 cup	olive oil

SAUCE:

12 ounces	pancetta, cut into strips
1/2 ounce	butter
6 ounces	onions, diced
3 cloves	garlic, minced
1/2 teaspoon	dried, crushed hot red peppers
1 cup	Marsala
1 cup	dry white wine
3/4 cup	poultry glace (see chapter 7)
3 ounces	fennel, cut in julienne
6 ounces	red bell peppers, roasted, seeded, and cut in julienne (see chapter 1)
6 ounces	green bell peppers, roasted, seeded, and cut in julienne (see chapter 1)
4	tomatoes, peeled and seeded, cut into small strips (see chapter 1)
to taste	salt and freshly ground black pepper
1/2 cup	chopped parsley
1 tablespoon	chopped sage

1.   Combine the egg, 2 tablespoons of olive oil, lemon juice, garlic, pepper, and salt in a suitable mixing bowl, and add the chicken strips. Marinate for several hours.

2.   Dredge the marinated chicken pieces in flour, shake off any excess flour, and spread out on a large tray so the pieces won't stick together.

3.   Heat the cup of olive oil, and pan-fry the chicken until crisp. Remove to absorbent paper and keep warm.

4.   Render the *pancetta* in a large skillet until slightly crisp. Remove with a slotted spoon to absorbent paper, and drain the fat from the skillet.

(continued)

5. Heat the butter in the same skillet, and sauté the onions and garlic for 1 minute. Add the hot red pepper and wines, and reduce to ¾ cup.

6. Add the poultry *glace* and fennel strips, and simmer for 3 minutes.

7. Add the peppers and tomatoes to the sauce, and adjust the seasonings.

8. Combine the fried chicken pieces and *pancetta* with sauce, and heat for a few minutes, until they absorb the sauce's flavor. Place on heated serving plates, and sprinkle generously with the parsley and sage. This dish is commonly served with a molded ring of white risotto (see chapter 6).

Petti di Pollo e Gamberi Peperonati

SAUTÉED CHICKEN AND SHRIMP WITH PEPPERS, TOMATOES, AND ONIONS

Yield: 6 servings

½ cup	olive oil	12 ounces	red and green bell peppers, roasted, seeded, and peeled, cut into 2-inch strips (see chapter 1)
18 ounces	boneless, skinless chicken breast, cut into small strips		
12 ounces	shrimp, peeled and deveined		
8 cloves	garlic, minced	12 ounces	ripe tomatoes, peeled, seeded, and cut into 2-inch strips (see chapter 1)
1 teaspoon	dried, crushed hot red pepper		
6 tablespoons	brandy		
2 tablespoons	tomato paste	to taste	salt
1 cup	dry white wine	¼ cup	chopped parsley
¾ cup	poultry glace (see chapter 7)	2 tablespoons	chopped basil
to taste	salt	2 tablespoons	chopped oregano

GARNISH:

4 to 6 tablespoons	olive oil
6 ounces	onions, coarsely sliced

1.   Heat ¼ cup of olive oil in a large skillet, and sauté the chicken strips for a few minutes, keeping underdone. Remove with a slotted spoon to a suitable dish and keep warm.

2.   To the same skillet, add ¼ cup of olive oil and sauté the shrimp for a few minutes, again keeping underdone. Remove with a slotted spoon and add to the chicken.

3.   Add the garlic and hot red pepper to the skillet, and heat but do not brown. Deglaze the skillet with the brandy, and ignite. Immediately mix in the tomato paste, and stir until smooth.

4.   Add the white wine, and reduce to ¼ cup. Stir in the poultry *glace* and add the salt. Add the chicken and shrimp to the sauce. Do not simmer but keep warm.

5.   In another skillet, heat the 4 to 6 tablespoons of olive oil, and sauté the onions quickly. Add the peppers, tomatoes, salt, parsley, basil, and oregano. Cook until just heated through, and combine with chicken and shrimp mixture. Adjust the seasonings. This dish can be served with a molded ring of risotto with wine and saffron (see chapter 6).

Fegatini di Pollo agli Spiedini con Risotto ai Porcini
CHICKEN-LIVER KABOBS AND RISOTTO WITH WILD PORCINI

Yield: 6 servings

18	whole chicken livers	4 cloves	garlic, minced
1 cup	buttermilk	1 cup	finely chopped scallions
3 tablespoons	prepared mustard		
1½ cups	very fine breadcrumbs from dry Italian bread	1 teaspoon	freshly ground black pepper
		36 slices	bacon, 4 inches long
½ cup	chopped parsley	6 portions	risotto with wild porcini (see chapter 6)
2 tablespoons	chopped marjoram		
1 teaspoon	grated lemon rind		

1.   Halve the chicken livers, remove all sinews, and rinse in cold water. Drain.

2.   In a suitable bowl, mix the buttermilk with the mustard and add the chicken livers. Make sure the livers are covered. Cover the bowl, and let the livers rest in the buttermilk for several hours.

(continued)

3. Combine the breadcrumbs, parsley, marjoram, lemon rind, garlic, scallions, and pepper in a small bowl.

4. Remove the livers from the buttermilk, and dip each in the breading mixture, using a dinner fork for easy handling. Place the breaded livers on a tray without handling.

5. Wrap each piece of liver in bacon, and place on 8-inch skewers, 6 per skewer.

6. Place on a sizzle platter or metal plate and broil until crisp and golden.

7. Slide the livers from the skewers onto heated serving plates, and serve with the risotto with wild *porcini*. The risotto may be molded in a 1-cup timbale and turned out onto each plate.

— *Tacchino/Dindo* —
TURKEY

Turkey is leaner than chicken, as well as higher in protein, and therefore tends to dry out more quickly if overcooked. Turkey can be prepared in almost any way imaginable, especially as a replacement for veal, which has recently become almost unaffordable to the average consumer. Owing to the size of a whole turkey, it is more practical to buy specific parts instead, which allows for better cost control and menu utilization. When sautéing turkey meat, it is preferable to use the breasts from very young birds and to leave the flesh slightly underdone.

Costolette di Tacchino Impanate alla Castellana
TURKEY CUTLETS FILLED WITH PROSCIUTTO, FONTINA, AND WHITE TRUFFLES

Yield: 6 servings

12	turkey cutlets, 3 ounces each	12	thin white-truffle slices
6	thin cooked prosciutto slices, 2 by 3 inches	6	thin Fontina slices, 2 by 3 inches

2 tablespoons	*dried egg white*	6 to 8 tablespoons	*olive oil*
¾ cup	*flour*	6 to 8 tablespoons	*clarified butter (see chapter 1)*
2	*eggs*		
¼ cup	*water*	*12*	*lemon wedges*
2 cups	*fine dry breadcrumbs, from Italian bread*	*6*	*parsley sprigs*

1. Pound the turkey cutlets between sheets of plastic wrap until very thin and about 4½ by 3 inches.

2. Arrange 1 slice of *prosciutto,* 2 truffle slices, and 1 slice of Fontina on each of 6 cutlets.

3. Sprinkle the edges of these cutlets with dried egg white, and then place a second cutlet on top. Press down along the edges to seal.

4. Dredge each cutlet in flour. Lightly beat the eggs and water to create an egg wash. Dip the cutlets in the egg wash, and coat with the breadcrumbs.

5. Heat the olive oil and clarified butter in a large skillet, and pan-fry the cutlets over medium to high heat, turning once.

6. Serve with the lemon wedges and parsley sprigs as a garnish.

Costolette di Tacchino alla Pizzaiola

TURKEY CUTLETS WITH MIXED PEPPERS, TOMATOES, AND MOZZARELLA

Yield: 6 servings

6	turkey cutlets, 5 to 6 ounces each	6 ounces	ripe tomatoes, peeled, seeded, and cut into small strips (see chapter 1)
to taste	salt and freshly ground black pepper		
½ cup	olive oil	2 tablespoons	chopped parsley
6 ounces	onions, diced	2 tablespoons	chopped basil
4 cloves	garlic, minced	½ cup	flour
2 to 3	hot chili peppers, finely sliced crosswise	6	Fontina slices, cut to the size of the cutlets
6 ounces	green bell peppers, roasted, seeded, and cut into fine strips (see chapter 1)	6	mozzarella slices, cut to the size of the cutlets
6 ounces	red bell peppers, roasted, seeded, and cut into fine strips (see chapter 1)	2¼ cups	pizza-style tomato sauce (see chapter 7)
		6	basil sprigs

1. Gently pound the turkey cutlets between sheets of plastic wrap. Do not thin too much. Season with salt and pepper.

2. Heat ¼ cup of olive oil in a large skillet, and quickly sauté the onions, garlic, and peppers. Add the tomatoes, parsley, basil, and salt and pepper to taste, and reheat. Adjust the seasonings, and remove from the heat to a suitable dish. Reserve and keep warm.

3. Heat the remaining ¼ cup of olive oil in another large skillet. Dredge the cutlets in the flour, shaking off any excess. Pan-fry the cutlets on both sides until medium-done, and remove to a sizzle platter or oven roasting tray.

4. Spoon a generous amount of the vegetables onto each cutlet. Cover with a slice of Fontina and a slice of mozzarella. Place in a hot oven just long enough to melt the cheeses completely.

5.   Spoon 6 tablespoons of hot tomato sauce on each heated serving plate, and top with turkey cutlet. Decorate with a basil sprig.

Piccate di Tacchino con Salsa al Pepe Verde
BATTER-FRIED TURKEY CUTLETS IN CREAM SAUCE WITH GREEN PEPPERCORNS

Yield: 6 servings

18	turkey cutlets, 1¼ ounces each	6 tablespoons	olive oil
to taste	salt and white pepper	6 tablespoons	clarified butter (see chapter 1)
½ cup	flour	2¼ cups	cream sauce with green peppercorns (see chapter 7)
2 or 3	eggs		
2 ounces	Parmesan, grated		

1.   Cut the turkey cutlets into uniform shapes.

2.   Place the cutlets between sheets of plastic wrap, and gently pound to thin a bit.

3.   Season the turkey, and dredge in the flour, shaking off any excess.

4.   Lightly beat the eggs and Parmesan together.

5.   Heat the olive oil and butter in a large skillet.

6.   Dip the turkey in the egg/cheese batter, and pan-fry quickly on both sides until slightly underdone. Drain on absorbent paper.

7.   Spoon 6 tablespoons of cream sauce with green peppercorns on each heated serving plate. Neatly top each with 3 pieces of turkey, slightly overlapping.

Spiedini di Tacchino alla Pancetta e Salvia con Ragù di Funghi Assortiti

TURKEY, BACON, AND SAGE KABOBS WITH MUSHROOM RAGOUT

Yield: 6 servings

36 ounces	boneless young turkey breast	12 ounces	cultivated mushrooms, cleaned and thickly sliced
12	sage leaves, chopped		
1/4 cup	chopped Italian parsley	6 ounces	onions, finely diced
		4 cloves	garlic, minced
1/2 teaspoon	freshly ground black pepper	1 1/2 cups	dry white wine
		3 1/2 cups	brown veal stock (see chapter 7)
36	bacon slices, 1 by 3 inches	2 ounces	butter, softened
		1 ounce	flour
		to taste	salt
SAUCE:		1/2 teaspoon	freshly ground black pepper
1/2 cup	clarified butter (see chapter 1)	1/4 cup	chopped Italian parsley
9 ounces	porcini, cleaned and thickly sliced		
9 ounces	chanterelles, cleaned and thickly sliced		

1.   Cut the turkey breast into thirty-six 1-inch cubes.

2.   Mix the sage, Italian parsley, and black pepper, and toss with the turkey cubes.

3.   Wrap each turkey cube in a slice of bacon. Thread 6 cubes on each 8-inch skewer.

4.   Heat 6 tablespoons of the clarified butter in a large skillet. Add all the mushrooms, and sauté until lightly browned. Remove to a suitable dish and keep warm.

5.   Add the remaining 2 tablespoons of clarified butter to the same skillet, and heat. Add the onions, and brown just a bit. Add the garlic.

6.   Deglaze the skillet with the white wine and reduce completely. Add the brown veal stock, and reduce to about 1½ cups. Combine the softened butter and flour into a paste, known as kneaded butter. Remove the sauce from the heat and quickly mix in the kneaded butter to thicken the sauce. Return the sauce to the heat, add the mushrooms, and simmer for a few minutes. Add salt, pepper, and Italian parsley.

7.   Place the skewers of turkey on a sizzle platter or oven roasting rack, and broil on both sides until slightly underdone.

8.   Slide the turkey kabobs from the skewers onto heated serving plates. Spoon the mushroom sauce alongside the turkey, near the rim of the plate.

Fricassea di Tacchino con Carciofini, Funghi, e Peperoni

TURKEY FRICASSEE WITH BABY ARTICHOKES, MUSHROOMS, AND PEPPERS

Yield: 6 servings

2 ounces	butter	12 ounces	mushrooms, thickly sliced
2½ ounces	flour	6 ounces	red bell peppers, roasted, peeled, seeded, and cut into short strips (see chapter 1)
3½ cups	hot chicken broth (see chapter 3)		
1½ cups	heavy cream, reduced to ¾ cup		
to taste	salt and white pepper	2 tablespoons	lemon juice
12	baby artichokes, trimmed (see chapter 13)	30 ounces	boneless young turkey breast, cut into small strips
¾ cup	clarified butter (see chapter 1)	18	black olives, pitted, quartered, and rinsed in water
6 ounces	red onions, cut into short strips		

1.   Heat the 2 ounces of butter in a 2-quart saucepan. Add 2½ ounces of the flour to make a roux. Cook, stirring constantly, over very low heat for 6 to 8 minutes. Cool.

2.   Add the hot chicken broth to the roux, and stir until smooth. Simmer over low heat for 30 minutes.

3.   Add the cream, and season with salt and pepper. Strain, cover, and keep warm.

4.   Blanch the baby artichokes in boiling, salted water for 5 minutes. Drain.

5.   Heat ¼ cup of clarified butter in a noncorrosive 3-quart casserole. Add the onions, artichokes, mushrooms, peppers, lemon juice, salt, and pepper, and cover. Stew slowly for about 5 minutes. Remove from the heat and drain in colander or sieve, reserving the cooking liquid. Strain this liquid, reduce to 2 tablespoons, and add to the cream sauce.

(continued)

6.   Heat the remaining ½ cup clarified butter in a large skillet, and quickly sauté the turkey strips until medium-done. Remove from the heat, drain off all fat, and add the black olives.

7.   Combine the cream sauce and cooked vegetables, and add to the turkey. Adjust the seasonings and reheat, but do not allow to simmer or boil. Boiled rice goes well with this dish; it can also be served in vol-au-vents (puff pastry cases).

Petto di Tacchino con Peperoni e Olive Nere

STIR-FRIED TURKEY WITH PEPPERS AND BLACK OLIVES

Yield: 6 servings

30 ounces	boneless turkey breast, cut into thin strips	6 ounces	green bell peppers, roasted, peeled, seeded, and cut into strips (see chapter 1)
to taste	salt and freshly ground black pepper		
		12 ounces	ripe tomatoes, peeled, seeded, and cut into strips (see chapter 1)
2 ounces	flour		
¾ cup	olive oil		
6 ounces	pancetta, cut into small strips	¾ cup	poultry glace (see chapter 7)
12 ounces	onions, sliced	18	ripe black olives, pitted and quartered
8 cloves	garlic, minced		
4	hot chili peppers, finely sliced crosswise	2 tablespoons	chopped parsley
		2 tablespoons	chopped oregano
12 ounces	mushrooms, thickly sliced	2 tablespoons	chopped basil
3 ounces	red bell peppers roasted, peeled, seeded, and cut into strips (see chapter 1)		

1.   Season the turkey strips with salt and pepper, and sprinkle with the flour.

2.   Heat the olive oil in a large skillet, and sauté the strips quickly until medium-done. Cook only a few strips at a time to retain maximum heat. Remove to a suitable dish.

3.   Add the *pancetta* to the same skillet, and cook until crisp. Remove with a slotted spoon and add to the turkey.

4.   Reheat the fat in the skillet, draining excess *pancetta* fat if necessary. Add the onions and garlic, and sauté for 1 minute. Add the chili peppers and mushrooms, and continue to cook over high heat for 1 more minute. Mix in the bell peppers and tomatoes.

5.   Add the poultry *glace,* olives, parsley, oregano, and basil. Reheat.

6.   Combine the cooked turkey with the vegetables and reheat, but do not let simmer. Adjust the seasonings. Boiled rice or risotto goes well with this dish (see chapter 6).

—— *Faraona* ——
GUINEA FOWL

Guinea fowl, originally from Africa, have been domesticated throughout Europe and North America. They are primarily gray with black and white speckles.

The guinea fowl was considered a prime specialty in Roman times, being sacrificed on occasion to the emperor Caligula in his self-appointed role as a god. When the empire began to decline, the guinea fowl vanished from Europe, only to be reintroduced by Portuguese explorers in the sixteenth century, who had come across this specialty once again in western Africa.

Guinea fowl should be treated like any other poultry. For roasting, a fowl of six to eight months or younger is ideal. The flesh of the older, adult birds tends to dry out when even slightly overcooked. Successful roasting of older birds can only be accomplished with frequent basting or by barding with bacon strips or the like. The breast of the young guinea hen is excellent for sautéing and should be handled in the same manner as the partridge or pheasant: by cooking over moderate heat until slightly underdone, and serving with a compatible reduction sauce and an appropriate garnish, such as wild mushrooms, sweet and/or hot peppers, a macédoine of fresh vegetables, whole roasted garlic or shallot cloves, tomatoes, olives, or the bird's own giblets.

Traditional in the northern areas of Italy is *faraona alla creta,* guinea fowl baked in clay. Several years ago I was treated to such a dish in Lucca. The trussed bird was heavily seasoned, then wrapped in fresh herbs and foil and completely encased in clay. The outside of the clay was beautifully decorated for an exquisite presentation. After having been baked in a hot oven for approximately 1½ hours, it was presented at the table, then placed to the side so that the waiter could delicately crack the clay with a special mallet. The hen was then carved and neatly arranged on hot plates, with a sauce served on the side.

The time allowed for baking guinea fowl depends, as always, on the age and condition of the bird. It is very easy to overcook these delicacies, so special care should be taken throughout the entire preparation process to ensure against overcooking.

Faraona Arrostita con Fichi e Melagrane in Salsa Vino Marsala

ROAST GUINEA FOWL WITH FIGS AND POMEGRANATES IN MARSALA SAUCE

Yield: 6 servings

3	young guinea hens, 2 to 2¼ pounds each	10	black peppercorns, crushed
1	pomegranate	1 quart	brown veal stock (see chapter 7)
12	fresh figs	1 teaspoon	arrowroot
1 cup	Marsala	2 tablespoons	minced green peppercorns
2 cups	dry red wine		
2	bay leaves	9	thin pancetta slices
1	rosemary sprig	2 ounces	butter, softened
¼ cup	olive oil	1 tablespoon	prepared mustard
4 ounces	onions, coarsely cut	2 tablespoons	honey
2 ounces	celeriac, coarsely cut	6	mint sprigs
2 ounces	carrots, coarsely cut		

1.   Trim the wing tips from the guinea hens. Chop, along with the necks and giblets, and reserve.

2.   Remove the thick skin from the pomegranate. Press the pulp in a sieve to produce ¼ cup (4 tablespoons) of juice. Reserve the juice and seeds.

3.   Plunge the figs into boiling water for 10 seconds. Shock immediately in cold water, and carefully peel when cool.

4.   Heat the Marsala and red wine in a small noncorrosive saucepan with the bay leaves and the rosemary sprig.

5.   Poach the peeled figs in the wines over low heat for about 3 minutes. Remove the pan from the heat, and allow the figs to cool in the wines. (This needs to be done well ahead of time.) Remove when cool, and strain the wine marinade; reserve both.

6.   Heat the olive oil in a 4-quart heavy-bottomed saucepan and add the chopped wing tips, necks, and giblets. Brown, add the coarsely chopped onions, celeriac, and carrots, and continue to brown. Add the peppercorns.

7.   Deglaze the pan with the reserved fig marinade, and reduce to ½ cup.

8.   Add the brown veal stock, and simmer slowly for 1 hour. Skim any fat and impurities that rise to the top while reducing. Strain through cheesecloth or a fine-mesh sieve into a smaller saucepan. Continue to reduce, to 2½ cups. Dissolve the arrowroot into 2 tablespoons of cold pomegranate juice, and add to the sauce to thicken. Bring sauce to a quick boil, and then keep hot in a hot water bath.

9.   Clean and truss the guinea hens with butcher's twine. Rub the minced green peppercorns into the skin, and place 3 strips of *pancetta* over each bird.

10.   Combine the butter, mustard, honey, and 2 tablespoons of pomegranate juice.

11.   Put the hens on a rack in a roasting pan, and roast in a preheated 450°F oven for 8 to 10 minutes. Remove the *pancetta,* and lower the heat to 375°F.

12.   Continue to roast the birds for 25 to 30 minutes, basting frequently with the honey mixture.

13.   Place the figs in the small saucepan, and reheat them in a bit of the sauce.

14.   Bone the guinea hens along the breastbone, leaving the short trimmed wing bone intact. Remove the thigh bones from the legs. If the fowl are still underdone, return them to the oven and roast for a bit longer.

15.   Spoon the sauce onto heated serving plates, and sprinkle pomegranate seeds over the sauce. Arrange 1 breast and 1 leg on each plate, and garnish with 2 heated figs and a mint sprig.

Petti di Faraona con Salsa di Canterelli
SAUTÉED BREASTS OF GUINEA HEN WITH CHANTERELLE SAUCE

Yield: 6 servings

4 ounces	pancetta, cut into thin strips	1½ cups	heavy cream, reduced to ¾ cup
6 tablespoons	clarified butter (see chapter 1)	6	guinea hen breasts
18 ounces	fresh chanterelles, cleaned and cut into large pieces	to taste	salt and freshly ground black pepper
¾ cup	onions, minced	⅓ cup	chopped Italian parsley
3 cloves	garlic, finely minced		
1½ cups	dry white wine		
¾ cup	poultry glace, prepared from guinea fowl trimmings (see chapter 7)		

1.   Render the *pancetta* in a large skillet until fairly crisp. Remove with a slotted spoon and reserve.

2.   Discard half the *pancetta* fat, and add 2 tablespoons of clarified butter to the skillet; reheat. Sauté the chanterelles for 3 minutes. Remove with a slotted spoon and reserve with the *pancetta*.

3.   Sauté the onions and garlic in the same skillet for several minutes, but do not brown.

4.   Deglaze the skillet with the white wine, and reduce completely.

5.   Add the poultry *glace*, and reduce to a coating consistency.

6.   Add the cream and reheat. Return the chanterelles and *pancetta* to the sauce and keep warm.

7.   Remove the skins from the guinea hen breasts. Trim the wing bones, and trim the base around the wing. Season with salt and pepper.

8.   Heat the remaining ¼ cup of clarified butter in a large skillet, and cook the breasts for about 2½ minutes on each side over moderate heat. They should remain under-cooked.

9. Cut the breasts on the bias, and arrange neatly in a fan shape on a heated plate. Spoon the sauce around the inner border of the breast meat where it is flush with the plate. Sprinkle the chopped Italian parsley over the chanterelles. Spinach *tagliolini* and sautéed tomatoes go well with this dish.

Petti di Faraona alla Panne e Uva in Grappa

BREASTS OF GUINEA FOWL IN BRANDIED CREAM SAUCE WITH GRAPES

Yield: 6 servings

6	guinea hen breasts, 5 to 6 ounces each	2 ounces	red onions, finely diced
¼ teaspoon	salt	½ cup	poultry glace (see chapter 7)
pinch	cayenne pepper		
6 tablespoons	grappa	pinch	salt and white pepper
9 fluid ounces	heavy cream		
6 ounces	white or yellow seedless grapes	6	mint sprigs
¼ cup	clarified butter (see chapter 1)		

1. Remove the skin from the breasts, leaving the wing bone intact. Trim the wing bone neatly around the base, and sever the wing at the first joint near the breast. Rub the ¼ teaspoon of salt and cayenne lightly into the flesh. Mix the grappa and cream, and pour over the breasts. There should be enough of this marinade to cover the breasts. Rest the breasts overnight in the marinade.

2. Plunge the grapes into boiling water for about 8 seconds, and then shock in ice water. Drain immediately and peel. Reserve.

3. Remove the breasts from the marinade and blot dry. Reserve the marinade.

4. Heat the clarified butter in a skillet, and cook the breasts for about 2 minutes per side over moderate heat. Remove and keep warm. The breasts should remain somewhat underdone.

5. Add the onions to the same skillet, and cook for several minutes without browning. Add half the grapes, and continue to cook over moderate heat for a few more minutes.

6. Add the poultry *glace* and reduce to a heavy coating consistency. Add the reserved marinade, and reduce further until smooth and velvety. Add the salt and white pepper.

(continued)

7. Strain the sauce through a fine-mesh sieve, being sure to press on the solids. Reheat, and add the remaining peeled grapes.

8. Spoon the sauce onto heated serving plates. Cut the breasts into four or five slices on the bias. Fan the slices neatly over the sauce, and garnish with a mint sprig.

Giambonette di Faraona Ripiene in Salsa alle Cipolle
STUFFED GUINEA FOWL LEGS BRAISED IN ONION SAUCE

Yield: 6 servings

12	guinea fowl legs, 4 ounces each	SAUCE:	
1 cup	stale Italian bread, very finely diced	2 ounces	butter
		9 ounces	onions, finely diced
1 ounce	butter	1/2 ounce	flour
1/4 cup	olive oil	1 1/2 cups	dry white wine
6 ounces	guinea fowl liver, diced small	2 cups	hot brown veal stock (see chapter 7)
2 ounces	pancetta, chopped		
3 ounces	onions, finely diced	1/4 teaspoon	dry, crushed hot red pepper
3 cloves	garlic, minced		
1/2 teaspoon	crushed juniper berries	1	small spice sachet of thyme and bay leaves (see chapter 1)
1/2 teaspoon	freshly ground black pepper		
		to taste	salt
2 tablespoons	chopped parsley	2 tablespoons	prepared mustard
1 tablespoon	chopped marjoram	2 tablespoons	dry white wine
1/3 teaspoon	salt		
1	egg		
1/4 cup	milk		
12 ounces	pork caul, well rinsed and blotted dry		

1.   Bone the legs by slitting down the length of the drumsticks, from the joint connecting them with the thighs. Loosen the meat around the thigh bone, and carefully pull the thigh meat back to the connecting joint. Cut carefully around the joint to loosen the meat, then pull the meat completely off.

2.   Sauté the diced bread in the butter until lightly browned. Place in a suitable mixing bowl.

3.   Heat the olive oil in a skillet, and quickly sauté the liver until medium-rare. Remove with a slotted spoon and add to the bread.

4.   Add the *pancetta* to the same skillet, and reheat. Sauté the onions until lightly browned, and add the garlic. Remove from the heat, and add the juniper berries, pepper, parsley, marjoram, and salt. Lightly beat the egg with the milk. Combine the bread/liver mixture, onions, and egg/milk mixture. Let rest for 30 minutes.

5.   Arrange the boned legs, skin side down, on a worktable. Fill each cavity with the stuffing, and secure with butcher's twine tied around the thigh section.

6.   Cut the caul into 5- by 5-inch squares, and wrap a leg in each square. Put them on a roasting rack, and place in a preheated 450°F oven for about 15 minutes.

7.   Heat the butter for the sauce in a shallow 4-quart braising pan, and add the onions. Sauté until light brown. Stir in the flour and cook over low heat for 5 minutes. Add the wine, brown veal stock, hot pepper, spice sachet, and salt. Simmer for 30 minutes.

8.   Add the legs to the sauce, and braise very slowly for 35 to 45 minutes, until tender. Remove the legs from the sauce. Remove the butcher's twine, and keep warm in a suitable covered dish.

9.   Strain the sauce through a fine-mesh sieve into a smaller pot, pressing on the solids to extract as much liquid as possible. Return to a simmer, and skim off any fat and impurities that rise to the surface. Dissolve the mustard in the wine, and stir into the sauce. Adjust the seasonings.

10.   Return the legs to the sauce to serve; or the sauce may be served separately alongside the stuffed legs.

Anatra/Anitra e Anatroccolo

Anatra/Anitra e Anatroccolo
DOMESTIC DUCK AND DUCKLING

Anatroccolo Arrosto in Salsa di Melacotogna e Ciliegia
ROAST DUCKLING WITH QUINCE AND CHERRY SAUCE

Yield: 6 servings

½ cup	water	1 tablespoon	salt
1½ cups	red wine	3 ounces	red onions, finely diced
¾ cup	orange juice		
1 tablespoon	grated orange peel	2 ounces	celeriac, finely diced
1½ ounces	sugar	1	quince, peeled, cored, and cut into thin slices
6 ounces	dark, sweet cherries, pitted (4 ounces for the sauce; 2 ounces for garnish)	2	bay leaves
		1 teaspoon	dry, crushed hot red pepper
3	ducklings, 3 pounds each	3 cups	brown duck or veal stock (see chapter 7)
2 tablespoons	green (Madagascar) peppercorns		

1.   Combine the water, red wine, orange juice, orange peel, and sugar in a noncorrosive small saucepan. Bring to a simmer, add the pitted cherries, and poach for about 3 minutes. Remove the cherries with a slotted spoon to a suitable dish, and cover. Reserve the poaching liquid.

2.   Clean the ducklings inside and out, and truss with butcher's twine to maintain their shape. Puncture the skin covering the fatty parts of the duck with a needle, to allow undesirable fat to escape during roasting.

3.   Crush the green peppercorns with the salt, and rub into the ducklings' skin.

4.   Put the ducklings on a rack in a suitable roasting pan, and roast in a preheated 375°F oven for about 45 minutes, until tender. Be sure to baste frequently. When done, remove the birds, and keep warm. Discard the fat from the roasting pan, but be careful to retain all meat drippings. Place the degreased pan on top of the stove.

5.   Add the red onions and celeriac to the roasting pan, and cook over medium heat for several minutes. Add the quince, and continue to cook for 5 minutes over low heat. Add 4 ounces of the poached cherries, bay leaves, and the hot pepper.

6.   Stir in 1½ cups of the cherry poaching liquid and the brown stock. Simmer slowly for about 30 minutes.

7.   Remove the bay leaves. Puree the sauce in a blender. Bring to a boil in a small saucepan pot, and reduce to a light coating consistency. Strain through a fine-mesh sieve, and keep warm in a hot water bath.

8.   Halve the ducklings lengthwise, and remove the breast and thigh bones. Leave the drumstick and wing bones intact.

9.   Place the boned ducklings, skin side up, on an ovenproof tray. Brush liberally with some of the quince and cherry sauce, and heat under the broiler until glazed and crisp. Reheat the remaining poached cherries. Arrange each duckling half on a heated plate. Spoon the sauce around the duckling, and garnish with the reheated poached cherries.

Anatroccolo Farcito al Marroni e Prugne Secche

ROAST DUCKLING STUFFED WITH CHESTNUTS AND PRUNES

Yield: 6 servings

3	*ducklings, 3 pounds each, drawn*	*¼ cup*	*milk*
3 ounces	*chestnuts*	*to taste*	*salt and freshly ground black pepper*
6 ounces	*smoked bacon, diced small*	*¼ cup*	*olive oil*
3 ounces	*onions, small diced*		
9	*prunes, pitted and sliced*	SAUCE:	
6 ounces	*stale Italian bread, diced small*	*4 ounces*	*onions, diced*
		2 ounces	*carrots, diced*
⅓ teaspoon	*black pepper*	*2 ounces*	*celery, diced*
⅓ teaspoon	*salt*	*5 cups*	*brown duck or veal stock (see chapter 7)*
pinch	*grated nutmeg*		
¼ cup	*chopped parsley*	*1*	*rosemary sprig*
1 tablespoon	*chopped rosemary*	*1*	*bay leaf*
1	*egg*	*10*	*black peppercorns, crushed*

(continued)

1. Clean the ducklings inside and out. Blot dry with a towel. Sever the wings at the first joint up from the breasts. Cut off any protruding neck bones, and reserve all trimmings and giblets for the sauce.

2. Make an incision on the flat side of the raw chestnuts, and roast on an ovenproof tray in a preheated 375°F oven until they start to crack open. Remove the shells and skins, and chop coarsely.

3. Render the bacon in a skillet, and add the onions. Cook over medium heat until soft.

4. Add the chopped chestnuts and sliced prunes, and heat thoroughly. Mix with the bread cubes in a suitable mixing bowl. Combine the pepper, salt, nutmeg, parsley, rosemary, egg, and milk, and pour into the bread mixture. Toss lightly to combine all ingredients. Let rest for 30 minutes.

5. Fill the cavities of the ducklings with the stuffing, and secure with butcher's twine. Rub salt and pepper into the skin before puncturing all over (especially the high-fat areas) with a needle to release excess fat during roasting. Then, rub the ducks with oil.

6. Place the duck trimmings in a roasting pan. Set the ducklings on a wire rack above the trimmings in the pan. Roast the birds in a preheated 375°F oven for about 45 minutes. Finish at 350°F for another 15 minutes, basting frequently throughout roasting. Occasionally stir the trimmings to prevent scorching. Remove the duckling from the pan, and keep warm.

7. Pour off all fat from the roasting pan, add the onions, carrots, and celery, and sear until brown. Deglaze the pan with the brown stock and add the rosemary, bay leaf, and peppercorns. Simmer for 30 to 40 minutes. Adjust the seasonings, and strain through cheesecloth or a fine-mesh sieve into a smaller saucepan. Reduce further if a thicker consistency is desired, and skim off any fat and impurities on the surface. Keep hot in a hot water bath.

8. Carve the breasts and legs from the duckling carcasses, and remove the thigh bones. Just before plating, put the duck pieces, skin side up, under a broiler to crisp the skin.

9. Split the carcasses to expose the stuffing, scoop out the stuffing, and arrange it neatly on heated serving plates. Neatly place 1 leg and 1 breast over the stuffing, and spoon the sauce around the pieces (not over the top).

Anatroccolo al Barolo con Cipolline e Porcini

DUCKLING BRAISED IN BAROLO WITH PEARL ONIONS AND PORCINI

Yield: 6 servings

3	ducklings, 3 pounds each	1 tablespoon	tomato paste
3 cups	Barolo	2 cups	brown duck or veal stock (see chapter 7)
1 teaspoon	freshly ground black pepper	½ cup	flour
1	rosemary sprig	2 tablespoons	clarified butter (see chapter 1)
1	thyme sprig		
2	bay leaves	12 ounces	smoked bacon, cut into small strips and blanched
4 cloves	garlic, minced		
1	onion, finely diced	12 ounces	fresh porcini, thickly sliced
10	juniper berries, crushed		
½ cup	olive oil	9 ounces	pearl onions, peeled and blanched
2 ounces	onions, diced small	⅓ cup	chopped Italian parsley
1 ounce	carrots, diced small		
1 ounce	celery, diced small		

1. Bone the ducklings, and remove the breasts. Sever the wings at the first joint up from the breast. Trim off excess fat, and remove the thigh bones, leaving the drumsticks in place. Reserve 1 pound of bones and trimmings.

2. Arrange the duck pieces in an earthenware dish, and combine the Barolo, pepper, rosemary, thyme, bay leaves, garlic, onion, and juniper berries. Pour over the duck pieces, and marinate overnight.

3. Chop the reserved duck bones. Heat ¼ cup of olive oil in a heavy-duty casserole. Sear the bones until well browned, and add small-diced onions, carrots, and celery. Continuing to brown, add the tomato paste and caramelize lightly. Deglaze the pan with the marinade from the duck, and reduce to 1½ cups. Add the brown stock, and simmer slowly until reduced to 3 cups. Season, strain, and keep warm.

4. Blot the duck pieces dry, and dredge in the flour. Heat ¼ cup of olive oil in a 4-quart heavy-duty casserole. Sear the duck pieces and remove all fat from the casserole. Add the sauce, cover, and braise over low heat for about 35 to 40 minutes, until tender. Remove the duck pieces, and reduce the sauce further if desired. Skim any fat and impurities from the surface. Strain the sauce, add to the duck, and keep warm.

(continued)

5.   Heat the clarified butter in a skillet, and sauté the blanched bacon strips until crisp. Remove with a slotted spoon. Drain most of the fat from the pan. Add the *porcini,* and sauté quickly. Remove and add to the bacon. Sauté the blanched pearl onions until lightly browned. Deglaze the pan with a bit of water, and cook for a few more minutes. Combine the bacon and *porcini* with the onions, and season.

6.   To serve, arrange 1 breast and 1 leg on each heated serving plate. Spoon the mushroom garnish and the sauce neatly over the top, and sprinkle with the chopped Italian parsley.

Petti d'Anitra con Salsa d'Arancio e Frangelico
SAUTÉED DUCK BREASTS WITH ORANGE FRANGELICO SAUCE

To make the brown duck stock for this recipe, follow the instructions for making brown veal stock in chapter 7, substituting duck bones and trimmings for the veal.

Yield: 6 servings

6	duck breasts from 4½- to 5-pound ducks	2	bay leaves
		2	whole cloves
to taste	salt and freshly ground black pepper	½ teaspoon	dried, crushed hot red pepper
		2 cups	dry red wine
to taste	juniper berries, crushed fine	3 cups	brown duck stock
1 tablespoon	sugar	1 tablespoon	prepared mustard
2½ ounces	butter	¼ cup	Frangelico
6 to 8 tablespoons	orange juice concentrate	to taste	salt
1 tablespoon	currant jelly	3 tablespoons	olive oil
1 tablespoon	small-diced shallots		

1.   Trim the duck breasts by severing the wings at the first joint from the breast. Scrape the remaining wing clean with a paring knife. Do not the remove the breast skin, but cut away excess fat and any skin that extends beyond the meat. Rub the breasts with salt, pepper, and juniper berries, and keep refrigerated until ready to cook.

2. Caramelize the sugar in a large skillet with ½ ounce of butter and the orange juice concentrate, currant jelly, shallots, bay leaves, cloves, hot pepper, and red wine. Reduce to ½ cup.

3. Add the brown duck stock, and continue to reduce to 1¾ cups. Stir in the mustard and Frangelico, and strain into a small saucepan. Season with salt, and keep warm.

4. Heat the olive oil in another skillet, and sauté the duck breasts, skin side down, until well browned. Turn, and finish in a preheated 350°F oven for about 4 to 6 minutes, or less if preferred medium-rare. Do not cook the meat well-done or it will be tough.

5. Reheat the sauce if necessary and whisk in the remaining 2 ounces of butter to create an emulsion. Spoon the sauce onto heated serving plates. Thinly slice the breasts on the bias, and overlap the slices in a neat fan arrangement over the sauce. An optional garnish might include orange sections briefly warmed in butter, plus mint sprigs.

Petti d'Anitra Saltati con Salsa di Mirtillo Rosso
SAUTÉED DUCK BREASTS WITH CRANBERRY SAUCE

To make the brown duck stock for this recipe, follow the instructions for making brown veal stock in chapter 7, substituting duck trimmings and bones for the veal.

Yield: 6 servings

6	duck breasts, from 4½- to 5-pound ducks	1 quart	brown duck stock
to taste	salt and freshly ground black pepper	4 to 5 ounces	fresh cranberries
3 ounces	red onion, minced	½ cup	orange juice
2 cups	dry red wine	1 tablespoon	grated orange peel
½ cup	Marsala	pinch	cayenne pepper
1	rosemary sprig	2 tablespoons	grappa
1	bay leaf	½ teaspoon	arrowroot (optional)
10	juniper berries, crushed	3 tablespoons	olive oil

(continued)

1. Trim the duck breasts by severing the wings at the first joint from the breast. Scrape the remaining wing bone clean with a paring knife. Leave the skin on the breast, but cut away excess fat and any skin that protrudes from the meat. Season with salt and pepper, and refrigerate until ready to cook.

2. Heat the onions and wines in a noncorrosive saucepan. Add the rosemary, bay leaf, and juniper berries, and reduce to ½ cup.

3. Add the brown duck stock, half the cranberries, orange juice, the grated orange peel, and the cayenne. Continue to simmer until reduced to 2½ to 3 cups. Adjust the seasonings.

4. Strain the sauce through a fine-mesh sieve into a smaller saucepan, pressing as much of the berries through the sieve as possible.

5. Add the remaining cranberries and grappa. Remove from the heat, and keep warm. Arrowroot can be used to thicken the sauce at this time if necessary—mix it with a bit of orange juice and stir into the sauce.

6. Heat the olive oil in a skillet, and sauté the duck breasts, skin side down, until well browned. Turn and finish in a preheated 350°F oven for about 4 to 6 minutes, or less if desired medium-rare. Do not overcook.

7. Spoon the sauce onto heated serving plates. Thinly slice the breasts on the bias. Overlap the slices in a neat fan arrangement over the sauce.

Salsiccia d'Anitra con Risotto ai Porcini e Pomodori Ripieni
ROAST DUCK SAUSAGE, RISOTTO WITH WILD PORCINI, AND STUFFED TOMATOES, SICILIAN STYLE

Yield: 6 servings

2	ducklings, 3 to 3½ pounds each	1 teaspoon	chopped marjoram
9 ounces	lean pork shoulder	½ teaspoon	dried, crushed hot red pepper
3 ounces	pork shoulder fat	pinch	grated nutmeg
1 cup	fresh white breadcrumbs	1 ounce	pistachios, peeled and coarsely chopped
¼ cup	heavy cream		
1	egg	2 tablespoons	dried egg white
1 teaspoon	salt	8 ounces	pork caul

| *6 portions* | *stuffed tomatoes, Sicilian style (see chapter 12)* | *6 portions* | *risotto with wild porcini (see chapter 6)* |

1. Completely bone the ducklings. Sever the wings at the first joint from the breast, and sever the drumsticks at the joint with the thigh. Make an incision through the skin along the backbone and carefully separate the meat from the carcass, working toward the breastbone. Do *not* cut any more of the skin. Remove the carcass. Lay the ducks, skin side down, on a worktable. Separate the thigh bones from the leg meat. Pull the leg meat inward, thus separating and removing the thigh bones. Do the same with the wing bones, leaving the flesh completely without bones.

2. Carefully remove the breast meat and most of the leg meat, again without breaking the skin. Dice the duck breast and leg meat small, and chill.

3. Dice the pork and pork fat small, and chill, separate from each other and from the duck meat.

4. Combine the breadcrumbs, heavy cream, and egg, making a panada. Chill.

5. Grind the chilled, diced pork twice through the medium blade of a meat grinder. Grind the pork fat once in the same way. Put the ground meat and fat into a mixing bowl, add the salt, and place in a freezer until well chilled, approximately 15 to 20 minutes.

6. Pound the ground pork and fat with a pestle or wooden spoon, and mix in the bread panada a bit at a time. Add the marjoram, hot pepper, and nutmeg, and finally the pistachios and diced duck meat. Keep this forcemeat well chilled until ready to use.

7. Lay the boneless ducks, skin side down, on a worktable, and spread the chilled forcemeat in the center (where the breasts once were). Sprinkle the dried egg white along the edges of the skins, and roll the ducks up loosely.

8. Secure each seam with a long bamboo skewer, and tie both ends of each sausage with butcher's twine.

9. Rinse the pork caul and blot dry. Wrap each duck sausage in a piece of the caul. Refrigerate until ready to cook.

10. Place the sausages on a rack in a small roasting pan, and roast in a preheated 350°F oven for 35 to 40 minutes. Remove and cool a bit. Place under the broiler to crisp the skin.

11. Remove the skewers and twine before slicing. Cut each sausage diagonally into 6 thick slices. Overlap 2 slices on each heated serving plate. Serve with stuffed tomatoes, Sicilian style, and risotto with wild *porcini*. If desired, a sauce may be prepared from the duck carcass and trimmings to accompany the sausages.

GAME BEASTS AND BIRDS

Furred and feathered game are found throughout Italy, depending on region and season. They are highly prized ingredients in Italian cuisine. Unlike game in the United States, that in Italy is readily available to the consumer in stores, open markets, and the like.

In the northern Alpine regions of the Valle d'Aosta and Alto Adige, a variety of furred animals, including the *capriolo* (roebuck), *cervo* (red deer), *daino* (fallow deer), and *camascio* (mountain goat), are hunted. *Piccioni* (pigeons), *anitre selvatice* (wild ducks), *pernici* (partridges), *quaglie* (quail), *beccaccea* (woodcock), *lepri* (hare), and *cinghiali* (wild boar) are plentiful in Tuscany, Umbria, and Marches.

With regard to game fowl, it has always been traditional to hang a wild bird for a prescribed period of time so that the volatile oils of the feathers supposedly have a chance to be absorbed by the flesh. The bird is hung whole, head down, for several days, depending on size. It is entirely possible that hanging game is simply a tradition carried over from the days before refrigeration, when a bird that had been killed several days earlier was stored in a cool larder to await consumption.

In any case, our society demands the freshest possible ingredients, and the hanging of fowl seems to have gone out of favor. This does not mean, however, that the well-aged wild birds I have prepared were not of exquisite quality and flavor. Therefore, I retain hanging procedures in the following recipes. I do this in part to emphasize the exceptional flavor that I have tasted in birds handled in the traditional fashion. A bird that arrives from the butcher sallow and shrunken is not a chef's favorite sight, but it is what we most often have to use, unfortunately.

— *Capriolo* — ROEBUCK

The meat of the different deer may be considered similar. That of younger animals is usually roasted or grilled and left unmarinated. Older animals are marinated to tenderize and bring out the flavor of the meat. Since the meat of deer is usually lean, interlarding or barding is common. Young meat is classically cooked underdone, the choice parts being the saddle, rack, and legs.

Noci di Capriolo in Salsa Crema di Ginepro con Castagne e Cipolline Glassate

NOISETTES OF VENISON IN JUNIPER CREAM SAUCE WITH GLAZED CHESTNUTS AND PEARL ONIONS

Yield: 6 servings

SAUCE:		GARNISH:	
1 ounce	pancetta, chopped	30	chestnuts
1 tablespoon	oil	³/₄ cup	Marsala
3 ounces	onions, finely diced	2 ounces	butter
1 ounce	carrots, thinly sliced	36	pearl onions, peeled
2 ounces	celery, thinly sliced	2 ounces	pancetta, diced small
3 cloves	garlic, minced		
15	juniper berries, crushed in blender	¹/₂ to ³/₄ cup	chicken broth (see chapter 3)
10	black peppercorns, crushed	to taste	salt and freshly ground black pepper
2	bay leaves		
1	rosemary sprig	¹/₄ cup	finely chopped chives
2 cups	dry white wine		
1 quart	brown game stock (see chapter 7)	6 tablespoons	clarified butter (see chapter 1)
¹/₄ cup	grappa	12	venison loin slices, 2¹/₂ ounces each
1 cup	heavy cream, reduced to ¹/₂ cup	to taste	salt and freshly ground black pepper
to taste	salt and freshly ground black pepper	6	juniper berries, crushed

1.   Render the ounce of *pancetta* with the oil in a heavy-duty casserole, and add the onions, carrots, celery, and garlic. Cook over moderate heat until lightly browned, and add the juniper berries, peppercorns, bay leaves, and rosemary.

2.   Deglaze the pan with the white wine, and reduce almost completely.

3.   Add the brown game stock, and reduce to 2¹/₂ cups. Add the grappa, and simmer for 5 minutes. Strain through a fine-mesh sieve, being sure to press the solids to extract as much liquid as possible.

4.   Reheat the sauce in a smaller pan, and add the cream. Add salt and pepper. Reduce further if a thicker sauce is desired. Keep warm.

5.   Make a slit in the flat side of each chestnut with a sharp paring knife. Place them on a metal tray, and roast in a hot oven for about 10 to 12 minutes, until they start to crack open. Peel while still hot. Reduce the Marsala in a skillet almost completely, and add the butter. Heat the chestnuts in the butter until well coated.

6.   Render the *pancetta* for the garnish in a small pan, and add peeled pearl onions. Cook over low heat for a few minutes, and add the chicken broth. Cover and smother the onions until the liquid is almost gone. Season with salt and pepper, and stir in the chopped chives.

7.   Heat the clarified butter in a large skillet. Season the venison slices with salt and pepper, and quickly sauté on both sides to the desired degree of doneness (remember, venison cooks quickly). The *noisettes* are best when cooked medium-rare.

8.   Spoon the sauce onto hot serving plates, and sprinkle with crushed juniper berries. Arrange 2 *noisettes* over the sauce on each plate, along with some glazed chestnuts and pearl onions (see color plate 51). Angel hair pasta with tiny broccoli florets goes well with this dish.

Medaglioni di Capriolo in Salsa d'Arancia e Mirtilli Rossi

VENISON MÉDAILLONS IN ORANGE SAUCE WITH CRANBERRIES

Yield: 6 servings

1 ounce	pancetta, chopped	3 ounces	fresh or frozen cranberries
½ cup	clarified butter (see chapter 1)	1 quart	brown game stock (see chapter 7)
2 ounces	red onions, finely diced	1 cup	fresh orange juice
2 ounces	celeriac, finely diced	to taste	salt and freshly ground black pepper
1 ounce	grated orange zest		
¼ cup	balsamic vinegar	1 teaspoon	arrowroot (optional)
2 cups	dry red wine	18	venison médaillons from loin, 1½ ounces each
3	whole cloves		
2	bay leaves	6	mint sprigs
2	hot red chili peppers, chopped		

1.   Heat the *pancetta* and 2 tablespoons of clarified butter in a heavy-bottomed 4-quart saucepan. Sauté the onions and celeriac until soft. Add the orange zest, and continue to cook for several minutes.

(continued)

2.   Add the balsamic vinegar, wine, cloves, bay leaves, and chili peppers, and reduce almost completely.

3.   Add 2 ounces of cranberries and the brown game stock, and reduce to 2 cups.

4.   Mix in the freshly squeezed orange juice, and simmer for about 10 minutes. Strain through a fine-mesh sieve into a smaller pan, pressing through as much of the solids as possible. Adjust the seasonings.

5.   If a thicker sauce is desired, dissolve the arrowroot in a little cold red wine, and stir into the hot sauce.

6.   Add the remaining cranberries to the sauce, and keep warm.

7.   Heat the remaining 6 tablespoons of clarified butter in a skillet, and sauté the venison *médaillons* quickly on both sides until medium-rare. Arrange 3 *médaillons* per serving on heated plates. Drain any grease from the skillet, and deglaze the pan with a little wine; strain into the sauce. Spoon the sauce around the venison, and decorate with the mint sprigs (see color plate 52). Braised fennel and carrots and potato croquettes (see chapter 12) or *penne* go well with this dish.

— *Coniglio* —
RABBIT

The term *coniglio* is used to refer to domestic rabbit. *Coniglio selvaggio*, or wild rabbit, is less fatty, has firmer meat, and is also considered tastier than the domestic variety. *Lepre* is the hare, a hardier breed that usually lives in more remote or mountainous areas.

Rabbit is perfect for roasting or sautéing, especially when very young, about 3 to 4 months old. Any rabbit or hare species can be used in the following recipes.

Coniglio alla Borghese

FILLETS OF RABBIT SAUTÉED IN BUTTER WITH WHITE WINE AND HERBS

Yield: 6 servings

3	*full rabbit saddles from 3-pound rabbits*	6 tablespoons *clarified butter (see chapter 1)*

to taste	salt and freshly ground black pepper	1	hot chili pepper, chopped
3 tablespoons	thinly sliced scallions, white parts only	6	sage leaves, thinly sliced (chiffonade)
		2 tablespoons	chopped Italian parsley
9 ounces	mushrooms, sliced	1½ ounces	butter
2 cups	dry white wine		
6 tablespoons	meat glace (see chapter 7)		

1.   Cut the loins from the saddles, for 6 single loins. Remove the skin completely.

2.   Heat the clarified butter in a large skillet. Season the rabbit with salt and pepper, and sear quickly on all sides over moderate to high heat. Remove the rabbit to an ovenproof pan, and place in a 400°F oven for no longer than 2 minutes. Remove from the oven to a suitable dish, and keep warm.

3.   Reheat the skillet, and add the scallions and mushrooms. Sauté until lightly browned. Remove the mushrooms with a slotted spoon.

4.   Deglaze the skillet with the white wine, and reduce to ¾ cup. Add the meat *glace,* and reheat.

5.   Return the cooked mushrooms to the skillet, and add the chili pepper, sage, and parsley. Stir in the butter, but do not continue heating the sauce.

6.   Thinly slice each rabbit loin on the bias and overlap in a neat fan arrangement on hot plates. Spoon the mushroom sauce alongside. White risotto (see chapter 6) and a medley of fresh green vegetables go well with this dish.

Sella di Coniglio Selvaggio Farcita di Cavolo Verde e Funghi con Salsa Marsala e Peperoni Rossi

ROAST SADDLE OF WILD RABBIT STUFFED WITH SAVOY CABBAGE AND MUSHROOMS IN MARSALA SAUCE WITH RED PEPPERS

Yield: 6 servings

6	savoy cabbage leaves	SAUCE:	
2 ounces	pancetta, diced	1/4 cup	olive oil
2 tablespoons	olive oil	4 ounces	onions, diced
3 ounces	onions, diced	2 ounces	celery, diced
9 ounces	mushrooms, assorted varieties, diced small	2 ounces	carrots, diced
to taste	salt and freshly ground black pepper	8	black peppercorns, crushed
		10	juniper berries, crushed
2 tablespoons	game or veal glace (see chapter 7)	1	rosemary sprig
2 ounces	mortadella, diced small	1	thyme sprig
		1	bay leaf
1	egg yolk, lightly beaten	1 quart	brown game or veal stock (see chapter 7)
2 tablespoons	fresh breadcrumbs	1 cup	Marsala
3 tablespoons	chopped Italian parsley	1 teaspoon	arrowroot
2 tablespoons	pine nuts, toasted	1/4 cup	roasted, seeded, and diced red bell peppers (see chapter 1)
2	full rabbit saddles, with racks, from 3-pound rabbits		
3 tablespoons	dried egg white	1 tablespoon	green peppercorns
8 ounces	pork caul		

1.   Blanch the cabbage leaves in salted, boiling water for about 1 to 2 minutes. Shock in cold water immediately. Drain and blot dry with a towel. Remove the ribs.

2.   Heat the *pancetta* and olive oil in a skillet, and sauté the onions and mushrooms over high heat until lightly browned. Add the salt and pepper, meat *glace*, and *mortadella*. Remove from the heat. Stir in the egg yolk, breadcrumbs, parsley, and pine nuts. Adjust the seasonings and cool completely.

3.   Bone the saddles. To do this, lay each saddle, skin side down, on a worktable, and carefully remove the ribs and loin bone, starting from the outer tips and working toward the spine. Separate the meat from the spine, starting slowly from one end, without cutting into the skin. The two loins should *not* be separated from each other, only from the bone and surrounding tissue. Remove all cartilage. Turn over and remove the membrane from the skin side of the boneless saddles. Reserve 1 pound of bones and trimmings.

4.   Place the boned saddles, skin side down, on the worktable. Place the cabbage leaves in the center of each, and spread the filling on leaves.

5.   Trim off any excess flaps from the loins, and sprinkle the inside edges of the remaining flaps with dried egg white. Fold the flaps over. Rinse and dry the caul, and wrap each stuffed saddle in a piece of it. Tie loosely with butcher's twine at 2-inch intervals to help maintain a uniform shape.

6.   Place the stuffed saddles on a rack in a roasting pan, and roast in a preheated 400°F oven for about 12 minutes. Rest for 5 minutes before slicing.

7.   Heat the oil for the sauce in a heavy-duty casserole, and add the reserved rabbit bones and trimmings. Brown in a 400°F oven. Add the onions, celery, and carrots. Continue to sear until the onions are well browned.

8.   Add the peppercorns, juniper berries, rosemary, thyme, bay leaf, and brown stock, and simmer very slowly for 1 hour. Add the Marsala, and cook another 15 minutes. Strain through a fine-mesh sieve into a smaller saucepan, and skim off all fat.

9.   Dissolve the arrowroot in a little cold wine, and stir into the sauce to thicken it.

10.   Add the diced red peppers and green peppercorns.

11.   Cut the saddles into 18 slices. Overlap 3 slices neatly on each hot serving plate and spoon the sauce around them. Steamed baby carrots and turned zucchini coated in butter and spinach *tagliolini* with grated Parmesan make excellent accompaniments to this dish (see color plate 53).

Cosciotti di Coniglio alla Cacciatora

RABBIT LEGS BRAISED IN WHITE WINE, TOMATOES, AND MUSHROOMS

Yield: 6 servings

4 to 6 tablespoons	olive oil	1	bay leaf
2 ounces	pancetta, chopped	1	rosemary sprig
6	rabbit legs from 3-pound rabbits	6	ripe tomatoes, peeled, seeded, and diced (see chapter 1)
6 ounces	onions, diced	12 ounces	wild mushrooms, thickly sliced
3 cloves	garlic, minced		
1	hot chili pepper, chopped	to taste	salt and freshly ground black pepper
2 cups	dry white wine	1 teaspoon	grated lemon rind
2 cups	brown game or veal stock (see chapter 7)	1/4 cup	chopped Italian parsley
1 ounce	dried porcini, reconstituted		

1. Heat the oil and *pancetta* in a heavy-duty casserole. Sear the rabbit legs over moderate heat on all sides, and remove to a suitable bowl. Keep warm.

2. Add the onions to the same casserole, and brown lightly.

3. Add the garlic and hot chili pepper, and cook for several minutes. Deglaze the pan with the wine, and reduce by two-thirds. Add the brown stock, and return to a simmer.

4. Return the rabbit legs to the casserole, and cover. Braise over low heat for 30 minutes.

5. Add the reconstituted *porcini* (without the water used for reconstituting), bay leaf, rosemary, and diced tomatoes, and continue to simmer slowly until the meat is almost tender. Add the mushrooms, salt and pepper, and grated lemon rind, and cook for 5 more minutes. Remove from the heat, and adjust the seasonings.

6. Sprinkle with the Italian parsley and serve (see color plate 54).

Salmi di Lepre con Pappardelle alla Toscana
HARE SALMI WITH PAPPARDELLE, TUSCAN STYLE

For this preparation, try to obtain a hare that is no older than 1 year. Older hare are less than ideal for cooking.

Yield: 6 servings

1	hare, approximately 4 pounds, completely dressed, with blood reserved (well chilled)	4 cloves	garlic, minced
		10	juniper berries, crushed
		10 to 15	black peppercorns, crushed
1 quart	dry red wine	to taste	salt
½ cup	flour	1 quart	brown game or veal stock (see chapter 7)
¾ cup	olive oil		
6 ounces	onions, finely sliced	¼ cup	grappa
3 ounces	celeriac, finely sliced	18 ounces	pappardelle (see chapter 5)
3 ounces	carrots, finely sliced		
2	rosemary sprigs	1 ounce	butter
1	thyme sprig	½ cup	grated Parmesan
3	bay leaves		

1.   Section the hare into 18 pieces, and marinate for several hours at room temperature in the red wine. When ready to cook, drain and reserve the wine. Pat the rabbit pieces dry with paper towels.

2.   Sprinkle the flour over the dry rabbit pieces.

3.   Heat the oil in a heavy-duty casserole, and sear the meat over moderate heat. Remove with a slotted spoon and keep warm.

4.   Add the onions to the same casserole, and brown. Add the celeriac and carrots, and continue to cook until lightly browned. Pour in the reserved wine, and add the rosemary, thyme, bay leaves, garlic, juniper berries, and peppercorns. Reduce a bit, and add the salt and brown stock.

5.   Place the seared hare pieces in the sauce, and cover. Braise very slowly for about 1 hour, until meat is very tender.

6.   Remove the meat from the sauce. Strain the sauce through a fine-mesh sieve, pressing some of the solids through the sieve. Reheat the sauce in a smaller pan, and skim off the fat. Add the grappa and adjust seasonings.

(continued)

7. Stir 6 tablespoons of the hare blood into the sauce. This thickens the sauce and adds flavor.

8. Return the rabbit pieces to the sauce, and keep warm. Do not overheat or boil the sauce, or the blood will curdle.

9. Cook the *pappardelle al dente,* drain, shock in cold water, and drain again. Toss with the butter and Parmesan.

10. Place 3 pieces of hare on each heated serving plate, and spoon a generous amount of sauce over the top. Spoon the *pappardelle* alongside.

— *Quaglia* —
QUAIL

There are over 100 species of quail in the world. Those of the Old World are migratory, whereas those of the New World are the bobwhite and crested quail. The American quail are somewhat larger than their European counterparts.

The quail's plumage is for the most part buff and mottled brown, barred and streaked with black, darker brown, and white. The bobwhite weighs, on the average, approximately 5 ounces. They are usually served in pairs as an entrée. When boned and stuffed, one bird may be sufficient.

Quail are excellent when split and grilled or oven- or spit-roasted. Today they are also commonly sautéed, or glove-boned, stuffed, and roasted or cooked *en cocotte* with wild mushrooms.

Italians have traditionally preferred their game birds well-done, but the rise of nuova cucina *(nouvelle cuisine)* has changed this to a great extent. Quail are simply better when kept slightly underdone. Cooking time depends on preparation method and bird size. If split and grilled over high heat, they take barely 3 minutes per side. Roasted at 500°F, they will need about 8 minutes, less if seared first. A boneless stuffed quail should not require more than 10 to 15 minutes. The commercial raising of quail has produced a bird that need not spend so much time in the oven, as these cooking times indicate.

Small birds such as quail are frequently glove-boned before being stuffed or encased in pastry. This is a rather arduous process with a bird with such delicate skin, but it is well worth the time in aesthetic appeal and portion control. With this method, the bones are removed from inside, starting at the neck end, and with the skin left intact. Only the drumstick bones remain.

To glove-bone, always trim the wing bones at the first joint from the breast. Using a very sharp, narrow-tipped paring knife, loosen the skin around the wing joints where they connect with the breast. Keeping the knife tip toward the carcass, probe patiently, using your fingers to help loosen the meat from the breastbone. Pull the boned meat back over the carcass as it is detached. Disconnect the thigh bones where they join the body and loosen skin from them as well. Next, loosen the skin from the rear end of the backbone. This is the most difficult part and should be done with considerable patience, especially where the skin adheres to the back. Remove any splinter bones (such as the wishbone), and place any dislodged pieces of meat in the bird's cavity. Straighten the skin and keep the boned bird chilled until ready to use. Save all carcass and trim pieces for sauces.

Quaglia Arrosta Ripiena al Sugo d'Aglio
STUFFED ROAST QUAIL WITH GARLIC SAUCE

Reserve the bones from glove-boning the quail in this recipe for use in the garlic sauce.

Yield: 6 servings

STUFFING:

¼ cup	clarified butter (see chapter 1)
3 ounces	quail and chicken livers, diced small
⅓ cup	sliced scallions
½ ounce	dried porcini, reconstituted and diced
2 tablespoons	brandy
2 tablespoons	meat or poultry glace (see chapter 7)
2 tablespoons	chopped parsley
1 tablespoon	chopped rosemary
1	hot chili pepper, chopped
1	egg yolk, lightly beaten
¾ cup	finely diced, toasted stale Italian bread

3 ounces	onions, diced small
10 cloves	garlic, sliced
1½ cups	dry white wine
½ cup	Marsala
1 quart	brown veal stock (see chapter 7)
to taste	chopped thyme
to taste	chopped rosemary
to taste	salt and freshly ground black pepper
6	quail, glove-boned (see introduction to this section)
12	spinach leaves
1½	dried egg white
8 ounces	pork caul
2 tablespoons	olive oil
1 ounce	butter

SAUCE:

¼ cup	olive oil

(continued)

1. Heat the clarified butter in a skillet, and sauté the livers quickly until medium-rare, about 10 seconds. Place in a small mixing bowl.

2. Sauté the scallions and reconstituted *porcini* in the same skillet for 1 minute. Add the brandy and meat *glace,* reduce by half, and remove from the heat. Stir in the parsley, rosemary, and chili pepper and cool. Add the livers, egg yolk, and toasted bread cubes. Allow to rest for 30 minutes.

3. Chop the quail bones reserved from glove-boning. Heat the olive oil for the sauce in a shallow heavy-duty casserole, and sear the chopped bones over high heat. Add the onions, and continue to sear until browned. Add the garlic and cook for several more minutes. Deglaze the pan with the wines, and reduce to ½ cup. Add the brown veal stock, thyme, and rosemary, and simmer slowly until reduced to 2½ cups. Adjust the seasonings, and strain through cheesecloth into a small saucepan. Keep warm.

4. Blanch the spinach leaves in boiling water for 1 second. Shock in cold water, drain, and blot dry.

5. Soak the caul, blot dry, and cut into six 4- by 5-inch pieces. Place on a tray lined with plastic wrap, and cover with plastic wrap.

6. To stuff the quail, place 2 spinach leaves neatly together (overlapping slightly), and wrap 1½ ounces of the stuffing in the pair of leaves. The size should be approximately the same as the bird's cavity. Sprinkle the stuffed spinach roll with the dried egg white, and slide into the quail's cavity. Do this for each quail.

7. Wrap each stuffed bird in a piece of caul, keeping the drumsticks close against the body. Secure loosely with 1 or 2 pieces of butcher's twine. Keep well chilled until ready to cook.

8. To roast, heat the 2 tablespoons of olive oil in a skillet, and sear the birds quickly on all sides over medium to high heat. Place on a roasting rack set on a sheet pan, and roast in a preheated 475° to 500°F oven for 8 minutes. Remove and let rest for a few minutes before slicing.

9. Swirl the ounce of butter into the warm garlic sauce.

10. Remove the butcher's twine from the quail, and cut 3 to 4 diagonal slices from each, starting at the neck end and working toward the legs, leaving about one-third of the body toward the back end—with the drumsticks—intact. Neatly overlap the slices from the legs outward. Spoon the sauce over the slices (see color plate 55). This dish is traditionally served with polenta or risotto (see chapter 6).

Quaglie Arroste alla Vignaiola con Risotto

ROAST QUAIL WITH BRANDIED GRAPES AND RISOTTO

Yield: 6 servings

12	quail, 4 to 5 ounces each	1 cup	dry white wine
		½ cup	muscatel
to taste	salt and freshly ground black pepper	1 quart	brown game stock (see chapter 7) or poultry broth (see chapter 3)
to taste	juniper berries, crushed		
		6	juniper berries, crushed
12	very thin smoked bacon slices, 4 inches long	10	black peppercorns, crushed
60	tart, seedless grapes	1	bay leaf
¼ cup	grappa	1 tablespoon	prepared mustard
¼ cup	olive oil	6 portions	white risotto (see chapter 6)
3 ounces	butter		
3 tablespoons	red onions, finely diced		

1.   Season the quail by rubbing the salt, pepper, and juniper berries into their skin. Bard with the smoked bacon strips, securing with butcher's twine.

2.   Plunge the grapes into boiling water for 8 seconds, and shock in ice water. Place in a small container with the grappa, and macerate until needed.

3.   Heat the olive oil in a large, heavy-bottomed skillet, and sear the quail quickly on all sides. Turn the birds breast side up in the skillet, and place it in a preheated 500°F oven. Roast for 6 minutes; the flesh should remain a bit underdone. Remove and keep warm.

4.   Degrease the skillet completely, being careful to retain the drippings.

5.   Heat 1 ounce of butter in the skillet, and sauté the onions until browned. Add half of the macerated grapes and grappa, and cook over high heat for a few minutes.

6.   Deglaze the pan with the wines, and reduce completely. Add the stock or broth, juniper berries, peppercorns, and bay leaf, and continue to reduce to about 2½ cups. Adjust the seasonings, and strain through a fine-mesh sieve into a small saucepan.

7.   Combine the remaining 2 ounces of butter and the mustard into a paste. Whisk into the sauce to create an emulsion.

(continued)

8.   Add the remaining grapes to the sauce.

9.   Bone the quail breasts, leaving the wing bones attached. Bone the legs as well, leaving just the drumsticks intact. If the legs appear to be too bloody, place them under the broiler for a few minutes.

10.   Mold the risotto in six 1¼-cup ring molds. Unmold each in the center of a heated serving plate. In the center, arrange 2 split semiboned breasts and 4 semiboned legs alternately, with all bones pointing out. The breasts should sit a bit on the legs to form something of a pyramid. Spoon the sauce over the quail, and serve.

Quaglie Grigliate alla Diavola
GRILLED DEVILED QUAIL

Yield: 6 servings

12	quail, 4 to 5 ounces each	3 cloves	garlic, finely minced
6 to 8 tablespoons	olive oil	2 tablespoons	chopped oregano
¼ cup	balsamic vinegar	3	hot red chili peppers, finely chopped
3 tablespoons	honey		
2 tablespoons	prepared mustard	⅓ teaspoon	salt

1.   Split the quail in half along the backbone without separating the two halves. Cut away the backbones, and fold in the wings.

2.   Combine the olive oil, vinegar, honey, mustard, garlic, oregano, chili peppers, and salt, mixing well to create an emulsion.

3.   Put the quail in a suitable noncorrosive pan, and brush each with the marinade. Pour the remaining marinade over the birds, and marinate for several hours.

4.   Place the quail, skin side up, on a metal sheet pan, and broil under the top broiler (salamander) for about 4 minutes on each side. Brush with the marinade during broiling. Halve the quail.

5.   Arrange 4 halves on each hot serving plate, with the drumsticks pointing toward the rim of the plate. Risotto with wine and saffron goes well with this dish (see chapter 6).

Quaglie Dorate ai Funghi Selvatici con Fonduta di Pomodoro
PAN-FRIED QUAIL STUFFED WITH WILD MUSHROOMS WITH TOMATO FONDUE

Yield: 6 servings

9	quail, 4 to 5 ounces each	2	egg yolks
to taste	salt and freshly ground black pepper	2 tablespoons	heavy cream
		1½ cups	flour
2 cups	olive oil	2	eggs
¼ cup	clarified butter (see chapter 1)	¼ cup	milk
		3 cups	dry breadcrumbs, from Italian or French bread
½ cup	onions, finely diced		
18 ounces	assorted wild mushrooms, very finely diced	2¼ cups	tomato fondue (see chapter 7)
¼ cup	chopped Italian parsley	12	lemon wedges
¼ cup	finely chopped chives	6	basil sprigs

1. Split the quail in half along their backs and remove all bones except the drumsticks. Season with salt and pepper.

2. Heat the olive oil in a skillet, and quickly sauté the quail, skin side down for just long enough to stiffen the skin somewhat. Blot dry immediately with paper towels, and refrigerate until well chilled. Reserve the oil.

3. Heat the clarified butter in a large skillet, and sauté the onions and mushrooms until lightly browned. Add salt and pepper to taste, the parsley, and the chives, and remove from the heat. Lightly beat the egg yolks with the cream, and combine with the mushrooms to bind. Chill completely.

4. Spread the inside of each quail half with the mushroom filling, and pat firmly into place. Refrigerate again until firm.

5. Dredge each stuffed quail half in the flour. Beat the eggs and milk together to make an egg wash. Dip the quail in the egg wash, and coat with the breadcrumbs. Place, unstacked, on a large tray.

6. Reheat the oil in a skillet, and pan-fry the quail on both sides until nicely browned. Drain on absorbent paper.

(continued)

7. Spoon the tomato fondue onto each hot serving plate, and arrange 3 quail halves over the sauce on each. (The sauce may also be served separately.) Garnish with the lemon wedges and basil sprigs.

Suprema di Quaglie Affogate alle Verdure Fresche

POACHED QUAIL BREASTS WITH FRESH VEGETABLES

Yield: 6 servings

12	quail, about 5 ounces each	3 ounces	white turnips, turned in olive shapes
¼ cup	olive oil		
3 ounces	red onions, sliced	9	pearl onions, peeled
2	cloves garlic, sliced	6	baby artichoke hearts
3 ounces	celeriac, sliced		
3 ounces	fennel, sliced	1 fluid ounce	lemon juice
1½ cups	dry white wine	12	savoy cabbage leaves, with ribs removed
2 quarts	chicken broth (see chapter 3)		
1	bay leaf	6 ounces	leeks, white parts only, well rinsed
10	black peppercorns, crushed	2 to 3 ounces	butter
½	thyme sprig	to taste	salt and freshly ground black pepper
½	tarragon sprig	12	tomato petals (see chapter 1)
pinch	grated nutmeg		
3 ounces	carrots, turned in olive shapes	6	basil sprigs

1. Remove the breasts from the quail, keeping the wing bones intact. Sever the wings at the first joint from the breast, and remove all the skin. Trim the breasts neatly, and scrape the attached wing bone clean.

2. Cut off the legs, and reserve for another use. Chop the carcass and giblets, and rinse quickly in water.

3. Heat the olive oil in a 4-quart stainless steel casserole, and add the chopped carcass pieces, red onions, garlic, celeriac, and fennel. Stew for a few minutes, deglaze the pan with the wine, and reduce to ½ cup. Add the chicken broth, bay leaf, peppercorns, thyme, tarragon, and nutmeg, and simmer for 1 hour. Skim off any impurities that rise to the surface while reducing. Strain through cheesecloth.

4. (If preparing the dish to order—*à la minute*—have all vegetables prepared and precooked.) Steam the carrots, turnips, and pearl onions until tender-crisp, using a bit of the broth for the steaming liquid. Shock in cold water.

5. Cook the artichoke hearts in lightly salted water with a little lemon juice until tender-crisp. Shock in cold water.

6. Blanch the cabbage leaves in lightly salted water for about 1 minute. Shock immediately in cold water, place on a towel, and cover with plastic wrap. Cut the leeks in ¼-inch diagonal slices.

7. Cut the artichoke hearts and onions in half.

8. Reheat the broth in a noncorrosive casserole, and add the leeks. Simmer for 1 minute, and remove the casserole from the heat. Add the quail breasts, and poach just below the simmering point until medium done, for about 4 minutes. Remove, and keep covered and warm.

9. Reheat the vegetables in the broth.

10. Place the warm cabbage leaves in the center of each hot serving plate. Cut each quail breast in half lengthwise, and arrange 4 breast pieces per serving in a semicircle over the cabbage. Point the wing bones toward the rim of the plate. Distribute the vegetables neatly inside the circle.

11. Whisk the butter into the broth to create an emulsion. Adjust the seasonings, and spoon the liquid over the quail breast pieces and vegetables.

12. Decorate each plate with 2 lightly heated tomato petals, with a basil sprig in between (see color plate 56).

—— *Piccione* ——
PIGEON OR SQUAB

There are many species of both domestic and wild pigeons. Domestic varieties evolved from the carrier and rock pigeons.

Among wild pigeons, the wood and ring doves are considered the best for cooking. Only young birds, four to six months old, should be used for roasting, grilling, or sautéing. Adult birds are used in salmis and forcemeats. Very old birds are suitable for flavoring sauces, stocks, and broths.

Roasting time for young pigeons, known in the United States as squab, is about 18 to 20 minutes at high heat.

Piccioni Grigliati alla Diavola
DEVILED GRILLED PIGEONS

Yield: 6 servings

6	young pigeons (squabs), each about 12 to 14 ounces, drawn	2 tablespoons	chopped parsley
		1/3 teaspoon	freshly ground black pepper
3 tablespoons	prepared mustard	2 cups	white breadcrumbs, soft
2 tablespoons	balsamic vinegar	5 fluid ounces	olive oil
2 cloves	garlic, minced	to taste	salt
3	sage leaves, chopped		
1 ounce	prosciutto, finely chopped		

1.   Split the squabs down their backs without separating the breasts. Remove the backbones, breastbones, and thigh bones. Sever the wings at the first joint from the breast. The only bones remaining should be the wing bones and drumsticks.

2.   Mix the mustard with the balsamic vinegar, and brush onto the birds, both inside and out.

3.   Combine the garlic, sage, *prosciutto*, parsley, pepper, and breadcrumbs. Dredge the birds in this mixture.

4.   Sprinkle the breaded squab liberally with the olive oil, and place them in a folding hand grill. Sprinkle with oil a second time, and broil under moderate heat on both sides. Continue to sprinkle with oil while broiling, and sprinkle with salt.

5.   Arrange the broiled squabs on hot serving plates. White beans, Tuscan style, and crisp potato cakes go well with this dish (see chapter 12).

Piccioncini ai Ferri al Crostone di Polenta con Salsa di Canterelli

GRILLED BABY PIGEONS ON POLENTA CANAPÉS WITH CHANTERELLE SAUCE

Use the bones and trimmings from the pigeons to prepare the brown game stock in this recipe. For instructions on preparing and pan-frying or grilling polenta, see chapter 6.

Yield: 6 servings

6	young pigeons (squabs) each about 12 to 14 ounces, drawn	2 ounces	onions, finely diced
		2 cloves	garlic, minced
		18 ounces	chanterelles, cleaned and quartered
1 tablespoon	chopped rosemary		
½ teaspoon	freshly ground black pepper	to taste	salt and freshly ground black pepper
6 tablespoons	olive oil		
1 quart	brown game stock (see chapter 7)	⅓ cup	chopped Italian parsley
6 portions	polenta (see chapter 6)	1 ounce	butter
¼ cup	clarified butter (see chapter 1)		

1.   Split the squabs down their backs without separating the breasts. Remove the breastbones and thigh bones. Sever the wings at the first joint from the breast. Trim the remaining wing bones and the drumsticks.

2.   Combine the rosemary, pepper, and olive oil, and brush onto the split, boned birds, inside and out. Keep the birds chilled.

(continued)

3.   Reduce the brown game stock to ¾ cup.

4.   Spread the polenta on a sheet pan in a ½-inch-thick layer. Cut it into 6 heart-shaped pieces just a bit smaller than the squabs.

5.   Place the squabs, skin side down, under a preheated broiler for 2 to 3 minutes. Turn the birds over, sprinkle lightly with salt, and grill for an additional 4 to 5 minutes. The birds must not be overcooked. Brush again with the remaining rosemary/oil mixture, and keep warm.

6.   Pan-fry or grill the polenta.

7.   Heat the clarified butter in a large skillet, and sauté the onions, garlic, and chanterelles for 3 minutes. Season with salt and pepper and add the reduced game stock. Reheat and reduce further if desired. Adjust the seasonings. Add the parsley and butter, and whisk thoroughly.

8.   Place a fried polenta heart on each hot serving plate, and place a grilled squab on top. Spoon the chanterelle sauce neatly along one side of the squab.

Piccioncini Saltati alla Provenzale
SAUTÉED BABY PIGEONS, PROVENÇAL STYLE

Breasts of poultry and game fowl have less connective tissue and are more tender than the leg meat and thus require less cooking time. In the following recipe, after the meat is removed from the pan, it is advisable to cook the legs a bit longer in a 350°F oven.

Yield: 6 servings

6	*young pigeons (squabs), each about 12 to 14 ounces*	1½ cups	*dry white wine*
		1½ pounds	*ripe tomatoes, peeled and seeded (see chapter 1)*
¾ cup	*olive oil*		
to taste	*salt and freshly ground black pepper*	½ teaspoon	*dried, crushed hot red pepper*
		18	*ripe olives, pitted and quartered*
12 cloves	*garlic, peeled*	¼ cup	*chopped parsley*
3 ounces	*onions, in 1½-inch slices*	2 tablespoons	*chopped oregano*

1.   Remove the breasts and legs from the pigeons. Remove the thigh bones, and sever the wings at the first joint from the breast. Trim the drumsticks at the joint end.

2.   Heat 6 tablespoons of olive oil in a large skillet, and sauté the breasts and legs on both sides over moderate heat. The meat should remain undercooked. Season with salt and pepper, remove to a suitable dish, and keep warm.

3.   Heat 6 tablespoons of olive oil in the same skillet. Cook the garlic cloves over low heat for 5 minutes without browning. Remove the garlic and reserve.

4.   Increase the temperature of the oil, and sauté the onions quickly. Deglaze the pan with the wine, and reduce to ¼ cup.

5.   Cut the tomatoes into 1½-inch strips. Add the tomatoes, hot pepper, and olives to the skillet. Season with salt and pepper, and cook for a few minutes. Remove from the heat, and add the parsley and oregano. Return the whole cloves of garlic to the skillet.

6.   Spoon the sauce onto each hot serving plate. Neatly arrange the pigeon breasts and legs alternately on the sauce, with the drumsticks and breastbones pointing upward, like a pyramid. Risotto and freshly steamed green vegetables go well with this dish.

— *Fagiano* —
PHEASANT

The word *pheasant* is derived from the Greek word *phasianos,* meaning "of the Phasis river" as it originally applied to a species that lived on this river (now known as the Rioni) in an area known as Colchis, east of the Black Sea. There are many species of pheasant, most of which originated in Asia. The green pheasant originally from Japan and the game pheasants originally from China to eastern Europe are the two most common species for culinary use. The game pheasant is now bred all over the world. It is commonly crossed with the Chinese ring-necked pheasant, and this is the variety most often encountered today. Such birds as the fabulous golden pheasant from central and western China and the silver pheasant from the Himalayas and Malaysia are rarely seen except in their native habitats.

A fresh pheasant should be hung at least 3 to 4 days with plumage intact to be truly appreciated. The ideal time to pluck the pheasant is actually as soon before deterioration begins as possible. Birds that are plucked at once do not develop the special aroma that comes from the meat absorbing the volatile oils from the feathers. This is said to greatly enhance the flavor and character of the flesh. Connoisseurs generally prefer the flavor of the hen over that of the cock pheasants.

For roasting, grilling, and sautéing, try to use the youngest birds obtainable. These can be distinguished by a pliable upper beak and soft keel bone (tip of breastbone). The spurs of younger birds are barely visible, becoming more prominent during the second year. In the third year, they are very distinct.

Pheasants are usually barded; interlarding is to be avoided. Roasting time is approximately 25 minutes in a hot oven. An average baby pheasant weighs around 1 pound whereas the older birds range from 2½ to 3½ pounds.

Fagiano Arrosto con Crauti al Vino Bianco

ROAST PHEASANT WITH SAUERKRAUT AND APPLES IN WHITE WINE

There are two schools of thought when it comes to roasting pheasants: some prefer to roast underdone, whereas others prefer them well-done. When cooked underdone (rare to medium-rare), the breast is always presented boneless, preferably sliced. The thighs are returned to the hot oven for an additional 5 to 8 minutes to be cooked until done, and they usually are served without the drumstick.

When roasted well-done, the style of presentation is optional.

Yield: 6 servings

3	pheasants, 2 to 2½ pounds each	1 cup	chicken broth (see chapter 3)
¼ cup	olive oil	10	juniper berries
to taste	salt and freshly ground black pepper	10	black peppercorns, crushed
to taste	juniper berries, crushed	2	bay leaves
		1	raw potato, peeled
6	bacon slices	2 ounces	onions, finely sliced
4 ounces	pancetta, chopped	2 ounces	carrots, finely sliced
4 ounces	onions, diced small	2 ounces	celery, finely sliced
9 ounces	tart apples, diced small	1 quart	brown game stock (see chapter 7)
1½ pounds	sauerkraut (rinsed and drained if held in brine)	1	bay leaf
		1	rosemary sprig
2 cups	dry white wine		

1.   Rinse the pheasants inside and out. Blot dry.

2.   Brush the birds with 2 tablespoons of olive oil. Rub the salt, pepper, and juniper berries into the skin. Wrap the pheasants in bacon, and secure with butcher's twine to help retain their shape.

3.   Render the *pancetta* with the remaining 2 tablespoons of olive oil in a 3-quart heavy-duty casserole (poultry fat may be used instead of olive oil). Add the diced onions, and cook until translucent.

4.   Stir in the apples, sauerkraut, wine, and broth. Prepare a spice sachet with the juniper berries, peppercorns, and bay leaves (see chapter 1), and add to the casserole. Bring to a simmer. Coarsely grate the raw potato directly into the mixture to help bind it. Simmer over low heat for 45 to 60 minutes. Add more wine or stock if the mixture becomes too dry.

5.   Place the pheasants, well spaced, on a rack in a roasting pan. Roast in a preheated 450°F oven for about 20 minutes (to roast underdone). Baste once or twice. Remove and let rest for a few minutes before cutting off the legs and returning them to the hot oven for an additional 5 to 8 minutes.

6.   Add the sliced onions, carrots, and celery to the drippings in the roasting pan. Cook until nicely browned. Deglaze the pan with brown game stock, add the bay leaf and rosemary, and reduce to 2 cups. Strain into a 1-quart sauce *bain-marie,* and skim any fat from the surface. Keep warm.

7.   Separate the drumstick parts from the legs, and bone the thighs. Put the thigh meat in the center of each heated serving plate. Sever the wings at the first joint from the breast. Remove the breasts and remaining wing bone from the carcasses. Cut each breast on the bias, and overlap neatly in a semicircular fan arrangement around the thighs. Remove the spice sachet from the sauerkraut mixture, and press the mixture into ½-cup timbale molds. Unmold onto each plate. Spoon the sauce around the sliced breasts. Potato *gnocchi* coated in herb butter go well with this dish.

Suprema di Fagiano in Salsa Crema di Porcini e Pepe Verde

SAUTÉED PHEASANT BREASTS IN PORCINI AND GREEN-PEPPERCORN CREAM SAUCE

Yield: 6 servings

6	pheasant breasts from 2½-pound birds (with wing bones attached)	6 ounces	porcini, cleaned and coarsely chopped
to taste	salt and freshly ground black pepper	½ cup	dry white wine
		6 tablespoons	game or veal glace (see chapter 7)
¼ cup	olive oil	1 teaspoon	green peppercorns, rinsed
2 ounces	clarified butter (see chapter 1)	2 cups	heavy cream, reduced to 1 cup
2 ounces	onions, minced	2 tablespoons	chopped chives

1.   Sever the wing bones at the first joint, then shave the attached wing bone clean with a paring knife. Season the pheasant breasts with salt and pepper. Heat the olive oil in a large skillet, and sauté the breasts quickly on both sides. Place in a preheated 350°F oven and roast for about 4 minutes. Remove and keep warm.

2.   Drain the oil from the skillet and heat the butter in it. Sauté the onions and *porcini* 1 minute. Add the wine, and reduce completely.

3.   Add the *glace,* green peppercorns, and cream. Bring to a simmer, and add the chopped chives.

4.   Thinly slice the breasts on the bias, and overlap neatly in a fan arrangement on heated serving plates. Spoon the sauce around the slices. A bouquet of steamed vegetables goes well with this dish (see color plate 57).

Fagianelle Grigliate con Burro alla Diavola
GRILLED BABY PHEASANTS WITH DEVILED BUTTER SAUCE

Yield: 6 servings

6	baby pheasants, 1 pound each	1 cup	dry white wine
¼ cup	olive oil	6 tablespoons	balsamic vinegar
to taste	salt and freshly ground black pepper	6 tablespoons	game glace (see chapter 7)
4 ounces	butter	3	hot chili peppers, seeded and chopped
2 ounces	onions, minced	2 tablespoons	prepared mustard
1 ounce	prosciutto, finely diced	6	sage leaves, coarsely chopped

1. Split the baby pheasants down their backs without separating the breasts. Remove the backbones, breastbones, and thigh bones. Sever the wings at the first joint from the breast, leaving the remaining wing bone attached. Trim the drumstick bones at the joint end.

2. Brush the pheasants with the olive oil and season with salt and pepper.

3. Heat 1 ounce of butter in a skillet, add the onions and *prosciutto,* and sauté for 1 minute.

4. Deglaze the skillet with the wine and balsamic vinegar, and reduce to 6 tablespoons (3 fluid ounces).

5. Add the game *glace,* and continue reducing to a light syrupy consistency. Add the hot chili peppers and prepared mustard. Keep warm.

6. Place the pheasants in an oiled folding hand grill. Sprinkle or brush the birds with a little more oil, and broil, cavity side up, for about 2½ minutes. Turn, brush again with oil, and broil, skin side up, for another 2½ minutes. Split the birds in half along the breasts. Arrange 2 halves on each heated serving plate.

7. Reheat the sauce if necessary. Cut the remaining 3 ounces of butter into small pieces, and whisk into the sauce to achieve an emulsion. Add the sage, and spoon the sauce over the pheasants (see color plate 58).

Beccaccino e Beccaccia
SNIPE AND WOODCOCK

These birds greatly resemble one another (the snipe being somewhat smaller), and both are considered choice among the migratory birds by game connoisseurs. The preferred species are the European jacksnipe and the American Wilson snipe. The snipe is more of a marshland bird, whereas the woodcock belongs to the sandpiper family and inhabits mostly forest regions. The Eurasian woodcock breeds all over Europe and in parts of Asia. The American woodcock is found east of the Great Lakes.

The main shared characteristic of these birds is their long narrow beaks, which are used to dig up worms and insects underground. The birds are at their plumpest in the fall and are therefore preferred fresh at this time.

Like most game birds, snipe and woodcock should be hung for a few days to develop the gamy taste and tenderness so much appreciated by connoisseurs. They should be hung, head down, with plumage intact, in a cool, well-ventilated space. Be careful to pluck before they begin to decompose.

European epicures are particularly fond of the entrails, or intestines, of these birds. They are chopped, sautéed quickly with shallots, herbs, or other aromatics, spread on canapés, and served together with the roasted or grilled bird. The chopped entrails are also added to sauces just before they are served. The entrails thicken sauces slightly, in addition to adding a gamier flavor. Though seldom available to the average consumer, entrails are included in the following recipes, as they are important in most regional dishes for which these game birds are readily available. There really is no substitute for them, but if you find a sauce to be thinner than desired, you can thicken it with arrowroot.

Both the snipe and the woodcock should be cooked underdone. When roasting the snipe, keep the head intact, but remove the lower part of the beak and the eyes. The larger woodcock needs about 12 to 15 minutes roasting time at high heat; the snipe, 9 to 11 minutes. Both birds should be barded with thinly sliced fatback or bacon. The preferred cooking methods are spit-roasting, grilling, and sautéing; they are also used in salmis.

Beccacce in Salmi al Barolo

SALMI OF WOODCOCKS WITH BAROLO

The woodcocks for this recipe should be hung for 2 to 3 days, plucked, and drawn. Reserve the giblets and intestines in a separate bowl.

Yield: 6 servings

6	*young woodcocks*	*18*	*fresh morels, well washed*
2 tablespoons	*olive oil*		
to taste	*salt and freshly ground black pepper*	*1 ounce*	*clarified butter (see chapter 1)*
		3 cups	*brown game or veal stock (see chapter 7)*
6	*thin pancetta slices*		
2 ounces	*clarified butter (see chapter 1)*	*6 to 10*	*juniper berries, crushed*
4 ounces	*onions, thinly sliced*		
2 ounces	*carrots, thinly sliced*	*10*	*black peppercorns, crushed*
2 ounces	*celery, thinly sliced*		
¼ cup	*grappa*	*2 ounces*	*butter*
2 cups	*Barolo*	*18*	*Italian bread slices, lightly buttered*
1	*rosemary sprig*		
1	*thyme sprig*	*⅓ cup*	*chopped Italian parsley*
1	*bay leaf*		

1. Rinse the birds inside and out, and blot dry.

2. Brush the woodcocks with the olive oil, and rub salt and pepper into the skins. Wrap each in a slice of *pancetta,* and secure with butcher's twine to maintain a uniform shape.

3. Start making the sauce. Heat the clarified butter in a shallow heavy-duty casserole, and cook the onions, carrots, celery, and reserved chopped giblets until lightly browned.

4. Add the grappa, and ignite. Deglaze the pan with the Barolo, and reduce completely. Add the rosemary, thyme, and bay leaf.

5. Place the birds on a rack in a roasting pan, and roast in a preheated 475° to 500°F oven for 8 to 12 minutes, cooked underdone. Remove from the oven, remove the *pancetta,* and reserve it for the sauce.

(continued)

6.   Remove the breasts and wings from the carcasses. Sever the wings at the first joint from the breast. Remove the legs from the carcasses, and remove the thigh bones, leaving the drumsticks intact. Put these pieces in individual-size *cocottes*. Reserve the carcasses for the sauce.

7.   Rinse the morels under cold running water to remove all sand and grit and blot dry. Sauté in clarified butter for 3 minutes. Moisten the morels with ¼ cup Barolo wine, and place 3 in each *cocotte*. Cover the *cocottes*, and keep warm in very low oven.

8.   Chop the carcasses, and add to the casserole along with the reserved *pancetta* and the brown stock. Reduce to 2½ cups. Add the juniper berries and peppercorns, and adjust the salt.

9.   Chop the reserved intestines to make ½ cup, add to the sauce, and remove it from the heat. Strain through a fine-mesh sieve into a small saucepan, pressing well to extract as many of the solids as possible. Reheat, but do *not* boil.

10.   Whisk in the butter to achieve emulsion.

11.   Grill or toast the buttered Italian bread.

12.   Pour the sauce over the roasted woodcock pieces in the *cocottes*. Sprinkle with the parsley, and place the *cocottes* in neatly folded napkins. Serve with the grilled or toasted bread slices arranged on the napkin.

Pasticcio di Beccaccia ai Funghi Assortiti

WOODCOCK PIE WITH ASSORTED WILD MUSHROOMS

The woodcocks for this recipe should be hung for 2 to 3 days, plucked, and drawn. Reserve the intestines, but discard the giblets.

Yield: 6 servings

6	young woodcocks	3 ounces	clarified butter (see chapter 1)
¼ cup	olive oil		
to taste	salt and freshly ground black pepper	8 ounces	onions, finely sliced
		2 ounces	carrots, finely sliced
		2 ounces	celery, finely sliced
6	thin pancetta slices	3 cloves	garlic, minced
12	romaine lettuce leaves	1 cup	dry red wine

10 cups	Madeira	1 cup	dry white wine
1 quart	brown game or veal stock (see chapter 7)	6 tablespoons	game or poultry glace (see chapter 7)
16	juniper berries, crushed	3	egg yolks
		3 tablespoons	chopped parsley
1	thyme sprig	3 tablespoons	chopped chives
1	rosemary sprig	2 tablespoons	chopped rosemary
1	bay leaf	1¾ pounds	puff pastry dough (see chapter 14)
2 tablespoons	green peppercorns		
3 ounces	onions, finely diced	2 tablespoons	water
18 ounces	assorted wild mushrooms, diced small	2 ounces	butter

1. Clean the birds inside and out, and blot dry.

2. Brush the birds with the olive oil, and rub salt and pepper into their skins. Wrap each in a slice of *pancetta*, and secure with butcher's twine to maintain a uniform shape.

3. Place the birds on a rack in a roasting pan, and roast in a preheated 500° to 550°F oven for 6 minutes. Remove from the oven and cool.

4. Untie the birds, remove the *pancetta*, and reserve it for the sauce. Remove the breasts from the carcass and skin. Remove the legs, severing the drumsticks and boning and skinning the thighs. Reserve the drumsticks and wings for the sauce.

5. Blanch the lettuce leaves for 1 to 2 seconds in lightly salted water. Shock immediately in cold water, and blot dry. Cut out the large central ribs, cover, and chill.

6. Heat 2 tablespoons of clarified butter in a large skillet, and brown the finely sliced onions, carrots, and celery. Chop the woodcock carcasses and bones into small pieces. Add the garlic, the chopped carcasses, and the reserved *pancetta* to the skillet, and sauté for several minutes.

7. Deglaze the pan with the red wine and Madeira, and reduce completely.

8. Add the brown stock, 10 crushed juniper berries, the thyme, rosemary sprig, and bay leaf. Reduce to about 2½ cups. Strain through a fine-mesh sieve into a small saucepan. Reheat, add the green peppercorns, and adjust the seasonings. Keep warm.

9. Heat the remaining ¼ cup of clarified butter in another large skillet. Add the diced onions and the mushrooms, and sauté for 1 minute.

10. Add the white wine, and reduce completely.

11. Add the *glace*, and reduce completely.

(continued)

12.   Chop enough of the reserved woodcock intestines to make ¼ cup. Add the wood-cock intestines, the remaining 6 crushed juniper berries, and salt and pepper to the skillet.

13.   Beat 2 egg yolks lightly. Remove the skillet from the heat. Stir in the parsley, chives, and rosemary. Stir the yolks in gradually, mixing briskly to avoid cooking them in the hot sauce. Chill the sauce completely.

14.   Roll the puff pastry dough out ⅛ inch thick. Cut 6 oval pieces, 3½ by 5 inches, and 6 oval pieces, 4½ by 6 inches. Place on a sheet pan, cover, and chill.

15.   Place the blanched lettuce leaves in pairs, side by side, overlapping slightly. Spoon equal amounts of the chilled mushroom filling evenly on each pair of leaves.

16.   Slice the woodcock breasts and thighs on the bias, and place over the stuffing (2 split breasts and 2 legs each), trying to restore something of the birds' original shape. Wrap completely in the lettuce.

17.   Put each packet in the center of a small puff pastry oval. Lightly beat the remaining egg yolk with the water to make an egg wash. Brush the edges of each small puff pastry oval with the egg wash, and cover with a larger puff pastry oval. Press the seams gently with the tines of a fork to seal. Add elegance to the presentation by cutting out various decorative shapes from the puff pastry scraps and attaching them to the tops of the pies with the egg wash.

18.   Wrap the pies in plastic wrap and chill in the refrigerator for at least 2 hours before baking.

19.   Remove the plastic from the pies, and place them on a sheet pan. Brush again with the egg wash. Bake in a preheated 350°F oven for about 15 minutes until nicely browned. Let rest for a few minutes.

20.   Whisk the butter into the sauce to achieve an emulsion.

21.   Place each pie on a heated serving plate and cut in half. Spread the two halves slightly apart to expose the interior. Serve the sauce in a sauceboat alongside. A bouquet of steamed green vegetables goes well with this dish.

Beccacce Saltate allo Spumante con Tartufi Neri

SAUTÉED WOODCOCK WITH SPUMANTE AND BLACK TRUFFLES

The woodcocks for this recipe should be hung for 2 to 3 days, plucked, and drawn. Reserve the intestines, but discard the giblets.

Yield: 6 servings

6	young woodcocks	¼ cup	grappa
6 tablespoons	olive oil	2 cups	dry spumante
1 teaspoon	freshly ground black pepper	1 quart	brown game or veal stock (see chapter 7)
1 teaspoon	freshly crushed juniper berries	1	rosemary sprig
2 ounces	red onions, finely diced	1	thyme sprig
2 ounces	celeriac, finely diced	1	bay leaf
2 cloves	garlic, minced	2 ounces	clarified butter (see chapter 1)
2	hot chili peppers, chopped	2 ounces	butter
1 ounce	black truffles	6 portions	spinach tagliolini (see chapter 5)

1.   Bone the breasts of the woodcocks, retaining the wings. Sever the wings at the first joint from the breast. Skin. Cut the legs from the carcasses, skin, and bone the thighs. Trim the drumstick bones at the joint end. Reserve the carcasses for the sauce.

2.   Mix 2 tablespoons of olive oil with the ground pepper and juniper berries. Rub this into the flesh of the bird parts. Place in a suitable dish, and chill until ready to cook.

3.   Chop the reserved carcasses into small pieces. Heat the remaining ¼ cup of olive oil in a shallow heavy-duty casserole, add the chopped bones, and sear over moderate to high heat until the bones start to brown. Add the onions and brown. Add the celeriac, garlic, and chili peppers, and continue to cook for several minutes.

4.   Peel and finely slice the truffles, reserving both the peelings and slices.

5.   Add the grappa to the bones and vegetables, and ignite. Deglaze the pan with the spumante. Add the truffle *peelings,* and reduce to ¼ cup.

6.   Add 3¾ cups of brown stock, the rosemary, thyme, and bay leaf, and reduce to 2½ cups. Skim any fats and impurities that rise to the surface while reducing.

(continued)

7.   Chop enough of the reserved woodcock intestines to make ¼ cup. Stir the chopped intestines into the sauce, and bring to a simmer. Strain through the finest-mesh sieve, pressing through as many solids as possible.

8.   Add the truffle *slices* to the sauce, and keep warm.

9.   Heat the clarified butter in a skillet. Place the woodcock pieces in the skillet, skin side down (that is, the side once covered by skin). Sauté over moderate heat for 1½ to 2 minutes and turn. Cover the skillet, and place in a preheated hot oven for 2 to 3 more minutes, keeping the birds undercooked. Remove and keep warm. Be careful not to overcook the woodcock, or it will dry out.

10.   Drain the fat from the skillet, and deglaze the pan with the reserved ¼ cup of brown stock. Simmer to dissolve the drippings, and strain into the sauce. Swirl the butter into the sauce to create an emulsion.

11.   Arrange the *tagliolini* in the center of each hot serving plate. Place the woodcock pieces neatly around the pasta, with wing tips and drumsticks pointing outward. Spoon the sauce over the woodcock.

Beccacce Arroste con Cavolo Verde Brasato
ROAST WOODCOCK WITH BRAISED SAVOY CABBAGE

The woodcocks for this recipe should be hung for 2 to 3 days, plucked, and drawn. Reserve the giblets, including the liver, and intestines.

Yield: 6 servings

6	young woodcocks	1 ounce	butter
½ teaspoon	freshly ground black pepper	1 quart	brown game or veal stock (see chapter 7)
½ teaspoon	freshly crushed juniper berries	1	thyme sprig
3 tablespoons	olive oil	1	sage sprig
6	thin pancetta slices	1	bay leaf
		10	black peppercorns, crushed
SAUCE:		1 teaspoon	arrowroot (optional)
8 ounces	onions, diced	2 tablespoons	cold beef broth (optional; see chapter 3)
2 ounces	carrots, diced		
2 ounces	celery, diced		

CANAPÉS:

1½ ounces	butter	2 tablespoons	fresh white breadcrumbs
2 ounces	onions, minced	18	fresh Italian bread slices, lightly buttered and toasted
½ cup	dry white wine		
½ cup	woodcock and chicken livers, finely diced		
		⅓ cup	grated Parmesan
6	sage leaves, chopped	6 portions	braised savoy cabbage (see chapter 12)
3 tablespoons	chopped parsley		
to taste	salt and cayenne pepper		
2	egg yolks, lightly beaten		

1. Clean the birds inside and out. Sever the wings at the first joint from the breast, and reserve for the sauce.

2. Rub the ground pepper and juniper berries into the skins of the woodcocks. Brush with the oil. Wrap each woodcock in a slice of *pancetta,* and secure with butcher's twine to maintain their shape.

3. Place on a rack in a roasting pan, and roast in a preheated 500°F oven for 8 to 12 minutes, keeping underdone. Remove the *pancetta* from the birds, chop it finely, and reserve for the canapés. Keep the birds warm.

4. Put the diced onions, carrots, celery, wing tips, wings, and giblets in the same roasting pan, and brown in 1 ounce of butter. Deglaze the pan with the brown stock, and add the thyme, sage, bay leaf, and peppercorns. Reduce to 2½ cups. Skim any fat and impurities that rise to the surface while reducing. Strain through a fine-mesh sieve into a small saucepan. If a thicker consistency is desired, dissolve the arrowroot in the cold beef broth, and mix into the simmering sauce. Keep warm.

5. Heat the butter for the canapés in a skillet, and sauté the onions until lightly browned. Add the wine, and reduce completely.

6. Chop enough woodcock intestines to make ¼ cup. Add the reserved *pancetta,* livers, intestines, sage, parsley, salt, and cayenne, and cook over high heat for a few minutes. Remove from the heat, and stir in the egg yolks. Add the breadcrumbs, and adjust the seasonings.

7. Puree this mixture in a food processor. Spread equal amounts on the toasted Italian bread. Sprinkle with the grated Parmesan.

8. Bone the breasts and thighs of the woodcocks, leaving only the drumsticks and remaining wing bones intact.

(continued)

9.   Put the braised cabbage in the center of each hot serving plate, and arrange the reheated woodcock pieces around the cabbage, with the drumsticks and wings pointing up.

10.   Place the canapés in a hot oven to reheat. Neatly arrange 3 on each plate. Serve the sauce separately. Fresh greens, such as watercress, arugula, or scallions, make an attractive garnish for this dish if desired.

— *Pernice* —
PARTRIDGE

Partridge is as popular a game bird as pheasant is. The most common and preferred species is the gray partridge, or chukar, which is generally found in open fields. A large horseshoe-shaped marking on the chest distinguishes this bird from others. The red-legged partridge is a somewhat larger species common in France. It has a red bill and legs with white cheeks and black bordering the throat. Whether any partridge is native to America is debatable. The bobwhite, actually a quail, is sometimes incorrectly called a partridge. In any case, we do have the ruffed grouse and the ptarmigan, which are native to this continent and similar, for culinary purposes, to the partridge.

As always, select young birds when roasting, grilling, and sautéing; these weigh about 14 to 16 ounces. Adult birds are delightful braised (in salmis) and in forcemeats. The oldest birds should be reserved for sauces, stocks, and broths. Like other game birds, partridges should be hung for several days to develop their gamy flavor. The roasting time for younger birds is approximately 18 to 20 minutes at high heat.

Pernice in Graticola Glassate con Purea di Susina all'Aceto Balsamico
BROILED PARTRIDGE GLAZED WITH PLUM PUREE AND BALSAMIC VINEGAR

Yield: 6 servings

6	young patridges, 14 ounces each	2 tablespoons	prepared mustard
8 ounces	plums, pitted and quartered	2 cloves	garlic, finely minced
¼ cup	balsamic vinegar	4 to 6 tablespoons	olive oil
		pinch	cayenne pepper

| 12 | *thin bacon slices, 5 to 6 inches long* | *to garnish* | *arugula sprigs* |
| *to garnish* | *fine sliced scallions* | | |

1.   Split the partridges along their backbones without separating the breasts. Remove the back, breast, and thigh bones. Sever the wings at the first joint from the breast. The remaining wing bones and drumsticks should be the only remaining bones.

2.   Puree the plums in a food mill, and combine with the vinegar, mustard, garlic, olive oil, and cayenne.

3.   Place the boned partridges in a suitable deep dish, and pour the plum marinade over them. Be sure to cover them thoroughly with the marinade. Marinate for 1 hour.

4.   Place the birds on a hot, oiled broiler or grilling rack, and grill or broil for 3 minutes per side. Remove the partridges from the rack, and place on a sizzle platter or metal tray. Arrange the sliced bacon on their tops, and brush generously with the marinade. Finish on the upper shelf of a very hot oven, roasting until the bacon becomes very crisp. Caramelization should occur quickly owing to the high sugar content of the marinade, but be careful not to overcook the partridges. Roasting boneless game fowl is a delicate proposition, and less cooking time is needed to prevent the meat from drying out.

5.   Serve the birds with the crisp bacon on top, sprinkled with the finely sliced scallions and garnished with arugula sprigs.

Pernice alla Piemontese
ROAST PARTRIDGE, PIEDMONT STYLE

This is a variation of the classic Piedmont recipe that calls for the boned partridge to be served on heart-shaped croutons with the sauce spooned over the top.

Yield: 6 servings

6	young partridges, 14 ounces each	¼ cup	brandy
6	thyme sprigs	1½ cups	dry white wine
6	bay leaves, cut in half	1 cup	brown game or veal stock (see chapter 7)
to taste	salt and freshly ground black pepper	pinch	cayenne pepper
		3	egg yolks
6	bacon slices	2 tablespoons	chopped parsley
2 ounces	clarified butter (see chapter 1)	1 tablespoon	chopped sage

1.   Clean the partridges inside and out with a dry towel. Distribute the thyme and bay leaves inside the cavities, and season both inside and out with salt and pepper. Wrap each in a bacon slice, and secure with butcher's twine.

2.   Heat the clarified butter in a skillet, and sear the birds on both sides. Place the birds in the skillet in a preheated 375°F oven, and roast for about 15 to 18 minutes.

3.   Remove the bacon strips, and drain all fat from the skillet. Pour the brandy over the birds, and ignite. Remove the partridges to a suitable dish, and keep warm.

4.   Deglaze the skillet with 1 cup of the wine, and reduce completely.

5.   Add the remaining wine and brown game stock, and bring to a simmer. Do not reduce further. Adjust the seasonings, and strain through cheesecloth. Cool. There should be 1½ cups of sauce.

6.   Remove the partridge breasts and legs from the carcasses, keeping the wing bones (trimmed at the first joint from the breast) and thigh bones intact.

7.   Combine the egg yolks with the sauce, and whisk in a double boiler until frothy, like *sabayon*. Add the parsley and sage.

8. Pour the sauce onto each hot serving plate, and arrange the boneless breasts and the legs neatly over the sauce. Celeriac flan and glazed carrots go well with this dish (see chapter 12).

— Anitra Selvatica/Anitra Germana —
WILD DUCK/MALLARD

The mallard is the best known of the wild ducks. It is the ancestor of most domestic ducks available today. In ancient Rome, duck was highly esteemed, but modern Italians do not favor duck as a specialty.

Wild ducks are well endowed with fat and therefore need no barding. They should be roasted in a hot oven for about 20 minutes, cooked underdone.

Ducks are fully grown at about four to five months. Very young birds are excellent for grilling, roasting, and sautéing. Adult birds should be braised and used for salmis and the like. Old ducks are tough and have a very strong odor, and so should not be used, even for sauces and stocks. An average mallard weighs 2½ pounds and serves two.

Anitra Germana Brasata in Barolo con Fichi e Ciliegie
BRAISED MALLARD IN BAROLO WITH FIGS AND CHERRIES

Yield: **6 servings**

12	green figs (slightly underripe)	4 ounces	onions, finely diced
30	large red cherries, pitted	2 ounces	celeriac, finely diced
		2 ounces	carrots, finely diced
3 cups	Barolo	2 cloves	garlic, minced
1 cup	orange juice	4	whole cloves
2	rosemary sprigs	pinch	cayenne pepper
2	bay leaves	to taste	salt
3	mallard ducks, 2½ pounds each	1 quart	brown game or veal stock (see chapter 7)
¼ cup	olive oil	1 teaspoon	arrowroot (optional)
2 ounces	smoked pancetta, chopped	1 ounce	Barolo (optional)

(continued)

1. Trim the stem ends from the figs and place, with the pitted cherries, in a suitable china dish. Add the Barolo, orange juice, rosemary, and bay leaves. Cover and macerate overnight.

2. Poach the fruit for 2 to 3 minutes in the marinade, and let cool in it.

3. Clean and truss the ducks.

4. Heat the olive oil in a large heavy-duty casserole, and sear the ducks on all sides.

5. Add the smoked *pancetta,* onions, celeriac, carrots, garlic, cloves, cayenne, and salt to the casserole, and place in a preheated 350°F oven for 15 minutes.

6. Pour off the wine mixture from the fruit, and add to the ducks. Cover, and braise at about 300°F for 15 minutes.

7. Add the brown stock, and continue to braise until the ducks are tender (check the thighs for doneness by touch, or puncturing with a skewer).

8. Remove the ducks to a suitable tray, and keep covered and warm.

9. Reduce the sauce on the stove to about 1 quart. Strain through a fine-mesh sieve into a smaller pot, pressing some of the solids through the sieve if possible. Reheat the sauce, skimming off any fat and impurities that rise to the surface.

10. If the sauce seems too thin, dissolve the arrowroot in a little cool wine, and stir into the sauce to thicken it.

11. Add the poached figs and cherries to the sauce.

12. Remove the breasts and legs from the ducks, and arrange on heated serving plates. Spoon the sauce on top, with the fruits neatly around the duck. Potato or semolina *gnocchi* go well with this dish.

VEGETABLES, LEGUMES, AND POTATOES

In the past decade or so, our perceptions of what contributes to a healthy diet have changed considerably. The trend toward lighter, more natural food preparations is a result of this awareness on the part of more educated consumers. Despite the improved standard of living in the second half of this century, faulty eating habits and chemically adulterated foods have taken their toll. It becomes more and more apparent that a true diet cannot be based on caloric intake alone, but must be planned with consideration of the natural and organic elements that sustain health. To do this, we must be aware of the composition of the raw foods we eat and understand how they are affected by the cooking methods to which they are subjected.

The important factors when cooking vegetables (including potatoes) and legumes are nutrition, flavor, color, and texture.

Nutrition: The preservation of nutrients should take precedence over all other factors when cooking. As we shall see, cooking to maintain flavor, color, and texture actually helps to retain nutrients as well.

Flavor: Proper cooking of vegetables means maintaining as much of the fresh flavor as possible. Here are several guidelines to consider: Steam vegetables whenever possible to avoid leaching of nutrients and flavor. Cook vegetables for the shortest possible amount of time. Tender leafy vegetables, such as spinach, can be quickly steamed (covered) without additional liquid, using their own natural moisture. This method is best when the vegetable is to be served immediately; otherwise, blanch these vegetables for only a few seconds, shock in cold water, and drain. To prevent loss of flavor, keep all blanched vegetables well chilled and covered until ready to reheat. Leafy vegetables can also be cooked in olive oil with aromatics.

Color: The most attractive visual characteristic of a properly cooked vegetable is its color. Understanding the factors that cause color change during cooking is important. The main pigments involved in vegetable coloring are green (chlorophylls), red (anthocyanins), yellow (carotenoids), and white (anthoxanthins).

When subjected to prolonged high temperatures, most vegetable pigments will break down, causing color change. Chlorophylls will become olive to brown in color with prolonged high heat. The pH (acidity) of the cooking liquid will also cause changes. Because acids adversely affect the green pigment, it is best to cook nonleafy green vegetables quickly, in large amounts of slightly salted water, which keeps the temperature high and acid levels low during the brief cooking time. They should be shocked in cold water immediately if not being served right away. On the other hand, leafy greens should be cooked quickly in small amounts of water and immediately shocked in cold water to prevent the leaching of nutrients. The color of red vegetables is enhanced by acids (such as lemon juice or vinegar), which actually intensify the red. But the red pigment is also extremely water-soluble, and so as little acidulated liquid as possible should be used. The yellow-white vegetables, such as cauliflower, parsnips, celeriac, turnips, and artichoke bottoms, will also benefit from slightly acidic conditions. It is important to realize that color loss in vegetable cookery most often indicates loss of nutrients as well.

Texture: Vegetables are made up primarily of cellulose and pectins and are very susceptible to texture change. Heat softens these materials, as does the presence of alkalines (such as baking soda). Alkalines especially promote vitamin loss and produce a very mushy texture (and so they should never be used to retain the green color that is affected by exposure to acids). Good vegetable texture not only assures us of good nutrition, but also aids in digestion.

Legumes are one of the world's most important sources of protein and have been an important part of the human diet since prehistoric times. To show the high esteem accorded these important foodstuffs, just examine the names of several famous Roman citizens: Favius got his name from the fava bean, whereas Cicero's name is derived from none other than the chick-pea. Such names as Lentulus (lentil) and Piso (pea) were not uncommon either.

With the exception of the soybean and the peanut, dried legumes are low in fat but high in proteins and carbohydrates. Legume proteins are low in some essential amino acids, which makes them an ideal complement for small amounts of animal proteins.

When cooking dried legumes, be careful not to oversoak them. This will leach vitamins and minerals and very often promote fermentation, which alters their nutritional qualities and can affect digestion. Soaking for 2 to 4 hours is usually sufficient. The table below gives some idea of the composition of various legumes.

LEGUME COMPOSITION (IN PERCENT)

	Water	Protein	Carbohydrates	Fat
Broad (fava) bean	12	25	58	1
Lima bean	10	20	64	2
Pinto bean	11	25	58	1
Lentil	11	25	60	1
Pea	12	24	60	1
Chick-pea	11	21	61	5

– Asparagi –

ASPARAGUS

Asparagus belongs to the lily family, whose members include garlic, leeks, and onions, and are low in calories and rich in vitamins A and C. The peak asparagus season runs from March to June, but today it is available year-round from countries in southern climes.

The most common varieties include the green asparagus, which owes its green color to growth in the sun, and the white variety, which is covered with heavy mulches that keep the sun's rays from reaching the stalk and developing its green pigments. Covering in this way adds to the expense of white asparagus but decreases its nutritional value.

Asparagus spears should be straight and firm, with a crisp stalk that snaps easily. Flowery or spread tips indicate older plants and should be avoided. To maintain the sweet flavor of asparagus, store unwashed with the stem ends wrapped in moist paper towels or plastic wrap. Keep refrigerated below 42°F.

When preparing to cook asparagus, cut or snap off and discard the woody ends. If very fresh, just peel the stem end of the stalk. Stalk thickness has no bearing on nutritional content, and when fresh, thick asparagus is every bit as tender as thin.

The cooking methods for asparagus should be simple. In fact, when very young, the vegetable is excellent raw, as in *bagna cauda* (see chapter 2). Otherwise, cook in very little salted water or steam *al dente*. It is easiest to cook spears of uniform length and thickness, to maintain a uniform texture. If the tips are to be used as a garnish, retain the stalks for soups, purees, timbales, and the like.

My personal preference is for asparagus served with melted butter. It may also be served with the ubiquitous hollandaise (see chapter 7), or combined with a little whipped cream and lemon juice, or a combination of the two blended with an herb coulis. Asparagus topped with fine Italian breadcrumbs and browned in a little butter is also excellent. Cold, it is good with a dressing of extra-virgin olive oil and lemon juice. It is important to examine with which other foods, if any, the asparagus will be served. As a side dish, it should never be loaded down with heavy sauces.

Barbabietole Glassate

GLAZED BEETS

Yield: 6 servings

1½ pounds	red beets, fresh	½	cinnamon stick
4 ounces	butter	½ cup	reduced beef stock (see chapter 3)
2 ounces	red onions, minced		
1 ounce	sugar	to taste	salt and freshly ground black pepper
6 tablespoons	lemon juice		
1	bay leaf		

(continued)

1. Peel the beets, and slice ¼ inch thick. Cut into ¼-inch sticks.

2. Heat half the butter in a 2-quart noncorrosive shallow pan. Add the onions and sugar, and cook over low heat until the onions are translucent.

3. Add 4 tablespoons of lemon juice, the bay leaf, cinnamon stick, and beef stock, and bring to a simmer.

4. Add the beets and cover. Simmer very slowly until the beets are pleasantly crisp. Remove the beets with a slotted spoon, and reduce the cooking liquid completely.

5. Mix in the remaining lemon juice, butter, and black pepper. Return the beets to the pan, and shake the pan until the beets are thoroughly glazed. Adjust the salt. The beets should be slightly tart.

Coste di Biete Stufate con Olio e Aglio
RIBS OF SWISS CHARD STEWED IN OIL AND GARLIC

Swiss chard is an important source of potassium and iron. It is most commonly prepared as two different vegetables. The spearlike stems are excellent stewed, stuffed, steamed, or even stir-fried in conjunction with other vegetables. Parboil the stems first for several minutes, depending on quality and freshness, then proceed as for fennel or celery. The leaves are like spinach but somewhat tougher and need a bit longer cooking time.

Yield: 6 servings

1½ pounds	swiss chard stems, cut into 3-inch lengths	2 ounces	onions, minced
		2	hot chili peppers, chopped
½ cup	olive oil	to taste	salt and freshly ground black pepper
6 cloves	garlic, minced		
2 ounces	carrots, minced	2 tablespoons	chopped basil
2 ounces	celery, minced	2 tablespoons	chopped parsley

1. Place the chard stems in a suitable noncorrosive pot with 1 pint of water and a little salt. Cover and cook until almost tender. Reserve the cooking liquid.

2. Heat the oil with the garlic in a very large skillet, and add the carrots, celery, onions, and chili peppers. Add the trimmings from the swiss chard stems, diced small, as well. Smother the vegetables for a few minutes.

3. Add ¾ cup of the reserved cooking liquid, arrange the chard stems over the vegetables, and season with salt and pepper. Cover and stew for 5 minutes. Add the basil and parsley just before serving.

4. Arrange the chard on heated plates with the other vegetables spooned over the top.

Bietole alla Pancetta Affumicata

SAUTÉED BEET TOPS WITH SMOKED BACON

Like most root tops, beet greens are high in nutrients and are low in calories. Use only young, tender greens for sautéeing, larger ones for stuffing or braising. The young greens need only a few minutes of cooking; therefore, it is advisable to cook them just before serving. They are excellent with boiled meats and roast pork.

Yield: 6 servings

1½ pounds	*beet tops, very fresh and young*	*¼ teaspoon*	*freshly ground black pepper*
2 ounces	*smoked bacon, finely diced*	*to taste*	*salt*
¼ cup	*olive oil or butter*	*2 tablespoons*	*water or broth*
2 cloves	*garlic, minced*	*2 tablespoons*	*fresh lemon juice*
2 ounces	*onions, diced small*		

1. Wash and coarsely shred the beet tops.

2. Render the bacon in the oil (or butter) in a large skillet.

3. Add the garlic and onions, and increase the temperature. Add the beet greens, pepper, and salt.

4. Stir the beet greens over high heat. Mix in the water or broth. Cover and stew until tender, about 3 minutes. Adjust the seasonings.

5. Just before serving, sprinkle the lemon juice over the beet tops.

Flan di Broccoli
BROCCOLI FLAN

As with most other flans, the tops and tender stems of the broccoli can be incorporated into this dish. Though attractive and easy to prepare, flans should never be served by themselves but, rather, in combination with other fresh vegetables of varying color and texture.

Yield: 12 servings

1 pound	*broccoli, very fresh*	*pinch*	*nutmeg*
½ ounce	*butter*	*⅓ teaspoon*	*freshly ground black pepper*
2 ounces	*leeks, white parts only, thinly sliced*	*½ teaspoon*	*salt*
¼ cup	*heavy cream*	*2 tablespoons*	*melted butter*
2	*eggs*		

1.   Cut any fibrous stem ends from the broccoli, and peel the stalks as much as possible. Cook the broccoli for 5 minutes in salted boiling water. Shock in cold water, drain, and cut into small pieces.

2.   Heat the butter in a small skillet, and cook the leeks over low heat until soft, about 5 minutes. Add the cream, and simmer for a couple of minutes. Remove and cool.

3.   Puree the broccoli, creamed leeks, eggs, nutmeg, pepper, and salt in a food processor for just a few seconds. Adjust the seasonings.

4.   Brush ½-cup metal or china timbale molds with the melted butter.

5.   Fill the molds three-quarters full with the broccoli puree, and refrigerate until ready to cook.

6.   Place the molds in a water bath, and cover with oiled parchment paper. Poach in a preheated 325°F oven until firm. Cool for several minutes, and unmold onto hot serving plates.

Carciofi/Carciofini
ARTICHOKES/BABY ARTICHOKES

Artichokes are one of the oldest foods known to man. They are indigenous to the Mediterranean and were esteemed by the ancient Romans. In Italy fresh-cooked artichokes are traditionally served as appetizers, as a vegetable, or in salads.

Before attempting to trim and prepare fresh artichokes, it is esssential to have fresh lemon juice on hand to stop the enzymatic browning that occurs almost immediately after the artichoke is cut. Professionals very often use a simple mixture of flour in water, stock, or court bouillon known as a *blanc* to retard this browning in artichokes, as well as for some other white vegetables.

The base of the artichoke is totally edible, as is the fleshy part of the petals (the artichoke is actually a flower). These are often eaten as finger foods, accompanied by melted butter, hollandaise sauce, garlic butter, or minted hot garlic oil for dipping. To eat in this way, dip the base of the petal in butter or sauce, squeeze the fleshy base between the teeth, and pull the petal tip outward to release the rich flesh into the mouth. Discard the remaining petal, which is inedible.

To prepare artichokes that are to be served as finger foods, remove the extreme outer leaves, which are often tough and wilted. Trim the remaining outer leaves with a scissors, and remove the choke with a melon scoop. (The stem of the artichoke, though usually trimmed away, is entirely edible and can be peeled with a potato peeler.)

Rub any cut parts immediately with lemon juice, and then place the artichokes in the *blanc*, which can be made by mixing 1 quart of water with ½ cup of flour. Place the artichokes in lightly salted acidulated water (using the juice of 1 lemon for every quart of water provides the proper amount of acid). Cook for about 15 minutes, until tender.

The artichoke bottom, or heart, is also edible as long as the hairy choke is first completely removed.

Artichokes can also be eaten with a knife and fork. In this case, the artichoke must be completely trimmed of all inedible portions before serving: the leaves are cut to the base, and the choke is removed. The cooking method is the same as for serving artichokes as a finger food.

The artichoke's cavity is often filled with a ragout; again, this method of preparation necessitates full trimming.

Very young artichokes *(carciofini)* need little trimming, as they are so tender that they can even be eaten raw—thinly sliced and tossed with lemon juice and olive oil.

Fondi di Carciofi
ARTICHOKE BOTTOMS WITH HERBS

Yield: 6 servings

9	artichokes, very fresh	to taste	salt
		1 tablespoon	chopped mint
3 ounces	butter	2 tablespoons	chopped parsley
3 ounces	onions, diced small	2 tablespoons	chopped basil
3 cloves	garlic, minced	¼ cup	grated Parmesan
2 tablespoons	fresh lemon juice		
1	hot chili pepper, chopped		

1.   Trim the artichokes carefully. Save and peel the stems.

2.   Blanch the trimmed artichokes and peeled stems in lightly salted acidulated water. Keep crisp. Shock in cold water, drain, and slice, not too thinly.

3.   Melt the butter in a suitable skillet, and sauté the onions, garlic, and sliced artichokes and stems without browning them. Add the lemon juice and hot chili peppers, cover, and stew for a few minutes. Do not overcook; the artichokes should not become too soft or mushy.

4.   Adjust the salt. Mix in the mint, parsley, and basil, and sprinkle the gralted Parmesan over the top.

Carciofini alla Giardiniera
BRAISED BABY ARTICHOKES WITH PANCETTA AND VEGETABLES

Yield: 6 servings

24	baby artichokes, very fresh	2 ounces	onions, diced small
		1 ounce	carrots, diced small
2 ounces	pancetta, diced small	1 ounce	fennel, diced small
		1 ounce	celeriac, diced small
¼ cup	olive oil		

3 cloves	*garlic, minced*	*to taste*	*salt and freshly ground black pepper*
1 cup	*peeled, seeded, and small-diced tomatoes (see chapter 1)*		
		2 tablespoons	*chopped parsley*
		2 tablespoons	*chopped basil*
2 tablespoons	*lemon juice*	*¼ cup*	*grated Parmesan*
¼ to ½ cup	*beef broth (see chapter 3)*		

1. Minimal trimming is required for these very young, fresh artichokes. Blanch them in lightly salted acidulated water for about 5 minutes. Shock in cold water, and drain.

2. Render the *pancetta* in the olive oil over moderate heat in a 3-quart stainless steel shallow casserole.

3. Add the onions, carrots, fennel, celeriac, and garlic, and smother for a few minutes. Add the blanched artichokes, tomatoes, lemon juice, and broth. Cover and cook over low heat for 5 minutes. Add salt and pepper.

4. Sprinkle with the chopped parsley and basil and grated Parmesan, and serve.

Carote Glassate

GLAZED CARROTS

All root vegetables, including carrots, parsnips, turnips, beets, and even pearl onions, are particularly well suited to glazing. Root vegetables retain their firm texture when exposed to heat, and their high sugar content facilitates the glazing process.

If the vegetables are very small, they need not be cut before cooking; just clean and trim them. Larger vegetables should be cut into smaller pieces, trimmed, turned, or sliced. In any case, the pieces should be of the same size to ensure even cooking—and so uniform texture—of the pieces.

Glazing itself can be accomplished in a number of ways. The vegetables can be precooked (parboiled) or raw before glazing. The glaze may include sugar and butter, various syrups, honey and butter, or just butter with finely diced onions and reduced (double) meat broth.

To prevent discoloration, red and white vegetables should be sprinkled with citric acid (such as lemon or orange juice) before cooking.

(continued)

Yield: 6 servings

18 ounces	miniature (baby) carrots	to taste	salt and white pepper
4 ounces	butter	2 tablespoons	chopped parsley
2 ounces	onions, minced		
½ cup	double chicken broth (see chapter 3) or white veal stock (see chapter 7)		

1.   Pare the carrots, and trim the green tops to ½ inch. If very fresh, they may be scraped instead of peeled.

2.   Melt 2 ounces of the butter in a noncorrosive shallow pan, and add the onions. Cook over low heat until translucent.

3.   Add the carrots, reduced broth or stock, and salt and pepper. Cover, and cook over low heat for 5 to 8 minutes, depending on size. Uncover, and reduce the liquid completely.

4.   Remove the pan from the stove, mix in the remaining butter, and shake until the carrots are completely glazed.

5.   Sprinkle with the chopped parsley and serve.

Purea di Castagna
CHESTNUT PUREE

Chestnut puree may be used as a vegetable or as a garnish. It is most often served with game. When stuffed into an apple casing and poached in wine and lemon juice, it makes a classic garnish for any game dish.

Yield: 6 servings

1½ pounds	chestnuts	3 ounces	celeriac, diced small
2 cups	white veal stock (see chapter 7)	1 ounce	butter

3/4 cup	*hot heavy cream*
to taste	*salt and cayenne or white pepper*

1. Make an incision on the flat side of each chestnut with a paring knife. Deep-fry them in hot fat, or place on a baking sheet with a little water and roast in a preheated 400°F oven for about 10 minutes. Peel and skin the chestnuts while still somewhat hot. Let cool.

2. Place the chestnuts and the veal stock in a noncorrosive 2-quart saucepan, and add the celeriac. Cover, and cook until the chestnuts are very soft.

3. Puree the mixture through a food mill or with a food processor, and return to the pan. Stir in the butter and cream, and whisk until smooth. Add salt and pepper.

Cetrioli Glassati

GLAZED CUCUMBERS

Although the cucumber is not a root vegetable, it lends itself well to glazing. Cook quickly, being careful not to overcook. To reduce the white veal stock for this recipe, follow the procedure used to make double beef broth in chapter 3.

Very slender cucumbers, about 12 to 16 inches long, are marketed in the United States as European cucumbers. These cucumbers are very firm and have few seeds. They are usually individually wrapped, and more expensive than their "American" counterparts.

Yield: 6 servings

2 pounds	*European cucumbers, peeled*	*to taste*	*salt*
3 ounces	*butter*	*2 tablespoons*	*chopped chives*
1 tablespoon	*green peppercorns*		
2 cups	*white veal stock, reduced to 4 ounces (see chapter 7)*		

1. Peel the cucumbers, and halve lengthwise. Remove the seeds and slice across into 1/4-inch-thick pieces.

(continued)

2.   Melt 2 ounces of the butter in a large, noncorrosive skillet, and add the peppercorns.

3.   Add the sliced cucumbers, and cook for 1 minute over high heat.

4.   Add the reduced veal stock, and cook over high heat to reduce the liquid to a coating consistency. Add salt.

5.   Mix in the remaining ounce of butter, and shake the pan to glaze the cucumbers thoroughly. Sprinkle with the chopped chives just before serving.

Cipolle Ripiene ai Funghi e Verdure

MUSHROOM-STUFFED BAKED ONIONS WITH VEGETABLES

Yield: 6 servings

12	yellow onions, approximately 3 ounces each	1	egg, lightly beaten
		2 tablespoons	dry breadcrumbs
2 ounces	smoked bacon, diced small	¼ cup	chopped parsley
		2 tablespoons	chopped oregano
2 tablespoons	olive oil	2 ounces	butter
4 cloves	garlic, minced	6 ounces	carrots, cut in julienne
9 ounces	porcini or domestic mushrooms, diced small	4 ounces	celeriac, cut in julienne
2 tablespoons	meat glace (see chapter 7)	½ cup	beef broth (see chapter 3)
to taste	salt and freshly ground black pepper	3 tablespoons	grated Parmesan

1.   Peel the onions, and blanch in lightly salted water for about 8 to 10 minutes. Drain and cool.

2.   Cut the tops off the onions, and remove the center portion of each with a melon scoop. Carefully trim away the root end.

3.   Dice the scooped onion centers (about 3 ounces), and reserve.

4.   Render the smoked bacon in the oil in a large skillet. Sauté the diced onions, garlic, and mushrooms until the mushrooms start to brown.

5.   Add the meat *glace,* and remove from the heat. Add salt and pepper.

6.   Stir in the egg, breadcrumbs, and half of the parsley and oregano. Adjust the seasonings, and cool.

7.   Fill the onion cavities with the stuffing.

8.   Melt the butter in a suitable baking dish, and add the carrots and celeriac. Stir over medium heat for a few minutes. Add the beef broth, and season to taste.

9.   Place the stuffed onions over the vegetables, and bake in a preheated 350°F oven for 10 minutes. Be sure to baste the onions occasionally.

10.   Sprinkle the Parmesan over the onions, and bake for another 5 to 10 minutes. Remove from the oven.

11.   Spoon the vegetables around the onions, and sprinkle with the remaining parsley and oregano.

Cipolline Verde alla Griglia
GRILLED SCALLIONS

Yield: 6 servings

30	*scallions*
6 tablespoons	*olive oil*
to taste	*salt and freshly ground black pepper*

1.   Trim the green tops and roots from the scallions, and discard.

2.   Moisten the scallion whites with the olive oil, sprinkle with salt and pepper, and grill quickly for about 1 minute on both sides. Serve immediately.

Fagioli/Fagiolini

BEANS/FRENCH GREEN BEANS OR HARICOTS VERTS

Beans are divided into two categories for culinary purposes. There are the edible-pod beans (or snap or string beans), such as flat Romano, or Italian pole, beans, Kentucky Wonder pole beans, and Blue Lake bush beans. Wax, or yellow, beans and Chinese yardlong, or asparagus, beans, as well as *haricots verts,* also are in this category. Different are the shell beans, of which only the seeds (or beans) themselves are used, with the pods being discarded. These include the Italian *fava,* or broad, bean (a new-comer to America); the red spotted cranberry, or *borlotto,* bean; the lima bean; the chick-pea, or *garbanzo;* the French *flageolet;* the Mexican pinto; and the common Great Northern and kidney beans. Although most people are familiar with dried shell beans, many varieties can also be cooked fresh.

Fagiolini, known in the United States as French green beans, or by their French name, *haricots verts,* are the highest-priced edible-pod bean. Do not confuse this variety of beans with French-cut beans, which refers to diagonally sliced snap beans. *Fagiolini* are actually indigenous to the New World and were not introduced to Europe until the sixteenth century. They have a more vibrant taste than snap beans do, and are crunchy rather than fleshy. They must be picked when very young to remain tender, and so they are smaller than snap beans.

Many bean varieties have been hybridized so that they are now practically stringless, although a few still must have their strings removed before cooking.

Fagioli alla Toscana

WHITE BEANS, TUSCAN STYLE

For excellent quality, select garden-fresh beans, and do not shell until ready to prepare.

These beans are excellent with lamb dishes.

Yield: 6 servings

2 cups	hot beef broth (see chapter 3)	to taste	salt and freshly ground black pepper
30 ounces	freshly shelled white beans		
5 fluid ounces	olive oil	1/4 cup	chopped parsley
6 cloves	garlic, minced	6	sage leaves, chopped
6 ounces	onions, finely diced		
2	hot chili peppers, chopped		

1.   Bring the beef broth to a simmer, and add the shelled beans. Cook slowly for 10 minutes, and drain, reserving a bit of the broth.

2.   Heat the olive oil in a 2-quart shallow saucepan, and add the garlic and onions. Cook until the onions become translucent.

3.   Add chili peppers, salt, pepper, cooked beans, and the reserved broth, and stew for about 10 more minutes. Remove from the heat when the beans are tender but not mushy or too soft.

4.   Stir in the parsley and sage just before serving.

Fagiolini con Aglio e Parmigiano
FRENCH GREEN BEANS WITH GARLIC AND PARMESAN

Yield: 6 servings

18 ounces	*French green beans (haricots verts)*	*3 tablespoons*	*grated Parmesan*
¹/₄ cup	*olive oil*	*6*	*basil leaves, chopped*
2 ounces	*onions, finely diced*		
2 cloves	*garlic, minced*		
to taste	*salt and freshly ground black pepper*		

1.   French green beans need practically no trimming. Just clean and cut off the stem ends.

2.   Steam the beans for just 2 minutes, keeping them *al dente*.

3.   Heat the olive oil in a skillet, and cook the onions and garlic until translucent. Add the beans, and shake the skillet to mix thoroughly. Remove from the heat.

4.   Toss with the grated Parmesan and basil, and serve immediately.

Finocchi Brasati con Macedonia di Verdure
BRAISED FENNEL WITH A MACÉDOINE OF VEGETABLES

Fennel has always been a favorite vegetable throughout the Mediterranean. Known sometimes as Florence fennel, it is usually available in the United States from fall to spring. The plant grows somewhat like celery but with a soft dill-like fern extending to the top of the plant. The bottom part is bulblike with curved layers and has a deliciously mild licorice or anise flavor. When fresh and young, the bulbs are often sectioned and included in raw vegetable dishes, such as *bagna cauda* (see chapter 2).

Yield: 6 servings

2	fennel	2 tablespoons	water
4 ounces	butter	3 ounces	zucchini, with skin, diced small
1 ounce	onions, very finely diced	3 ounces	leeks, white parts only, diced small
6 tablespoons	chicken broth (see chapter 3)	12	tomato petals (see chapter 1)
to taste	salt and white pepper	2 tablespoons	melted butter
3 ounces	carrots, diced small	¼ cup	chopped parsley
3 ounces	celeriac, diced small	6	basil sprigs

1.   Remove most of the stalk ends from each fennel, leaving just an inch or two of stem with a small amount of fern in the middle.

2.   Cut a small slice across the bottom of each fennel so that the stalks can be carefully separated from the bulb. Select 6 of the shovel-shaped stalks, separate them, trim them neatly into a uniform shape, and set aside. Dice 3 ounces of the remaining fennel and reserve.

3.   Blanch the selected stalks for 2 minutes in lightly salted water.

4.   Heat 2 ounces of butter in a large shallow skillet, and smother the onions in it. Add the chicken broth and salt and pepper, and place the blanched fennel stalks over the onions. Baste with the liquid and cover. Braise for 5 minutes over moderate heat, until slightly underdone.

5.   Melt the remaining 2 ounces of butter in another skillet, and add the carrots, reserved diced fennel, celeriac, and water. Cover and cook over low heat for 5 minutes. Add the zucchini, leeks, and salt and pepper, and continue to cook for another 2 minutes. Remove from the heat.

6. Brush the tomato petals with the melted butter, and place in the oven until just heated through.

7. Set a fennel stalk to one side of each heated serving plate. Spoon the vegetable macédoine into, and spilling over from, the fennel stalk, like a horn of plenty. Sprinkle with the chopped parsley, and decorate with 2 tomato petals and basil sprig.

Flan di Finocchi

FENNEL FLAN

Yield: **8 servings**

1 pound	*fennel, bulb only, peeled*	*to taste*	*nutmeg*
1 ounce	*butter*	*¼ cup*	*heavy cream*
½ cup	*chicken broth (see chapter 3)*	*2*	*eggs*
to taste	*salt and cayenne pepper*	*2 tablespoons*	*melted butter*

1. Use only the tender part of the fennel, being sure to remove the tough outer stalks. Cut the tender stalks into thin slices. Heat the butter in a shallow pan. Add the fennel slices and chicken broth, and cook until the fennel is slightly underdone and the liquid is reduced completely.

2. Add the salt, pepper, nutmeg, and cream, and simmer for an additional minute. Cool.

3. Puree in a food processor or, preferably, a blender, adding the eggs during the last few seconds of pureeing. Adjust the seasonings.

4. Brush eight ½-cup molds with the melted butter.

5. Fill the molds three-quarters full with the fennel puree. Refrigerate until ready to cook.

6. Place the molds in a hot water bath, and cover with oiled parchment paper or foil. Poach in a preheated 325°F oven until firm. Turn out from the mold, and cool for several minutes before serving.

Finocchi alla Griglia

GRILLED FENNEL

Yield: 6 servings

3	large, fresh fennel	1/4 teaspoon	salt
6 tablespoons	olive oil	2 tablespoons	chopped mint leaves
3 tablespoons	lemon juice	2 tablespoons	chopped parsley
2 cloves	garlic, finely minced		
1/4 teaspoon	freshly ground black pepper		

1. Cut most of the stem parts from the fennel, and halve the remaining bulbs lengthwise. Cook in lightly salted water for about 5 to 8 minutes, until cooked *al dente*. Remove to a colander, and cool.

2. Cut the major part of the core from the fennel when cool, being very careful not to separate the bulbs. Place the bulbs in a suitable dish.

3. Combine the olive oil, lemon juice, garlic, pepper, salt, mint, and parsley, and pour over the fennel bulb pieces. Rub the marinade into the fennel, and marinate at least 30 minutes, or until ready to grill.

4. Grill on both sides until nicely marked with brown, brushing with the marinade while grilling.

Funghi in Graticola all'Erbe

BROILED MUSHROOM CAPS WITH GARLIC AND HERBS

This recipe uses standard cultivated mushrooms. But Italy is blessed with an abundant variety of wild mushrooms, *porcini* and *cantarelli* (cèpes and chanterelles) being perhaps the most appreciated and accessible.

The white truffle *(tartufo bianco)* has a strong earthy flavor with a hint of garlic and is found in the forests of the Langhe region, south of Alba. When used as a garnish for hot dishes, white truffles are added at the very end and never cooked. They are most often sliced very thin or shaved over risottos, egg dishes, fondues, polenta, *carpaccio*, or *insalata con tartufi*.

The black truffle *(tartufo nero)* of Norcia and Spoleto is peeled or left unpeeled and precooked for about 8 to 10 minutes. They are then used in various marinades and served with pasta, risotto, omelets, or canapés. These truffles were already prized by the ancient Romans and their predecessors.

Yield: 6 servings

24	large mushroom caps, very white and fresh, 1 ounce each	8 cloves	garlic, finely minced
		1/4 cup	chopped parsley
		2 tablespoons	chopped oregano
		1/4 teaspoon	freshly ground black pepper
MARINADE:		1/4 teaspoon	salt
2 tablespoons	olive oil	2 tablespoons	lemon juice
1/3 teaspoon	freshly ground black pepper	1/2 cup	dry Italian breadcrumbs
1/3 teaspoon	salt		
2 cloves	garlic, finely minced	1 bunch	arugula, cleaned
2 tablespoons	lemon juice		

STUFFING:

6 ounces	butter, softened

1.   Cut the stems out of the mushrooms near the base—do not twist out. Wipe the mushroom caps clean with a dry towel.

2.   Combine the olive oil, pepper, salt, garlic, and lemon juice for the marinade in a suitable bowl.

3.   Add the mushroom caps to the marinade, and let steep for 30 minutes.

4.   Place the softened butter in a small mixing bowl, and incorporate the garlic, parsley, oregano, pepper, salt, lemon juice, and breadcrumbs, being sure to add the breadcrumbs in last.

5.   Place the mushrooms, stem side down, on a sizzle platter or metal tray, and broil about 2 minutes. Turn the mushroom over, fill the cavities with a small spoonful of the stuffing, and broil until nicely browned.

6.   Serve 4 caps per serving on a bed of the arugula.

Lenticchie con Pancetta Affumicata
LENTILS WITH SMOKED BACON

Lentils are an excellent accompaniment for boiled beef, smoked ox tongue, and roast lamb or duck.

Yield: 6 servings

8 ounces	dried lentils	1	bay leaf
4 ounces	slab bacon, diced	1	medium-sized raw potato
2 tablespoons	olive oil		
3 ounces	onions, diced	to taste	salt
3 cloves	garlic, crushed	3 tablespoons	balsamic vinegar
2½ cups	beef broth (see chapter 3)	2 tablespoons	chopped marjoram
		2 tablespoons	chopped parsley
¼ teaspoon	freshly ground black pepper		

1. Soak the lentils in cold water for 1 hour.

2. Render the bacon in the olive oil in a 2-quart saucepan. Add the onions and garlic, and cook over moderate heat for 2 minutes. Add the beef broth and drained lentils. Simmer over low heat for 15 minutes. Add the pepper and bay leaf.

3. Peel the potato, and grate coarsely into the lentils. Continue to simmer for about 30 minutes over low heat. The lentils should not be allowed to become mushy. If the mixture becomes too thick, add more broth.

4. Add the salt, balsamic vinegar, marjoram, and parsley, and remove from the heat. Discard the bay leaf, and serve.

Rotolini di Melanzane alla Siciliana
EGGPLANT ROULADES, SICILIAN STYLE

Yield: 6 servings

12	peeled eggplant slices, 3½ inches in diameter by ⅛ inch thick	12	black olives, pitted and chopped
to taste	salt and freshly ground black pepper	3	hot chili peppers, chopped
		3	anchovy fillets, chopped
½ cup	flour	2 tablespoons	pine nuts, toasted
2	eggs, lightly beaten	¼ cup	grated Parmesan
2 tablespoons	milk	¼ cup	fresh white breadcrumbs
1 cup	olive oil	¼ teaspoon	salt
2 ounces	onions, finely diced	2 tablespoons	chopped parsley
2 to 3 cloves	garlic, minced	2 tablespoons	chopped mint leaves
2 ounces	green bell pepper, finely diced	9 fluid ounces	hot tomato sauce (see chapter 7)
2 ounces	red bell pepper, finely diced	12	mozzarella strips 1 by 3½ inches
2 ounces	celery, finely diced		

1.   Season the eggplant slices with salt and pepper, and dredge in the flour. Combine three-quarters of the lightly beaten eggs with the milk. Dip the eggplant in this mixture. Heat ¾ cup of olive oil, and pan-fry the eggplant until nicely browned. Drain on absorbent paper.

2.   Heat the remaining ¼ cup of olive oil in a skillet, and sauté the onions, garlic, bell peppers, and celery quickly, keeping undercooked. Place in a suitable bowl.

3.   Add the olives, chili peppers, anchovies, pine nuts, Parmesan, breadcrumbs, salt, parsley, mint, and the remaining quarter of the lightly beaten eggs.

4.   Spoon this mixture onto the sautéed eggplant slices, and roll the slices up tightly.

5.   Pour the hot tomato sauce into a small shallow baking dish, and arrange the eggplant rolls, well spaced and seam side down, on top of the sauce. Top with the mozzarella strips, and bake in a preheated 400°F oven for about 8 minutes, just enough to heat the roulades thoroughly and melt the cheese.

6.   Spoon the sauce onto each heated serving plate, and top each with 2 eggplant roulades.

Melanzane alla Griglia

GRILLED EGGPLANT

Yield: 6 servings

2 pounds	eggplant, very fresh and firm
1 teaspoon	salt
½ cup	olive oil
3 tablespoons	lemon juice
3 cloves	garlic, finely minced
3 tablespoons	chopped oregano

1. Slice the unpeeled eggplant crosswise into ¼-inch-thick rounds. Sprinkle with the salt, and let rest for 30 minutes to drain the juices. Blot the pieces dry with a towel.

2. Arrange the eggplant slices on a suitable tray. Combine the olive oil, lemon juice, garlic, and oregano, and brush the eggplant slices on both sides with this mixture. Cook each side on a hot grill for 1 minute, and serve immediately.

Melanzane Farcite Provenzale

EGGPLANT STUFFED WITH GARLIC, MUSHROOMS, AND PROSCIUTTO

Yield: 6 servings

3	small Italian or Japanese eggplant	4 tablespoons	fresh white breadcrumbs
6 tablespoons	olive oil	1½ ounces	prosciutto, finely chopped
3 ounces	onions, finely diced		
4 cloves	garlic, minced	2 tablespoons	chopped parsley
4 ounces	mushrooms, diced small	2 tablespoons	chopped oregano
		to taste	salt
3	anchovy fillets, chopped	3 tablespoons	grated Parmesan
3	hot chili peppers, chopped		

1. Halve each eggplant lengthwise.

2. Heat the olive oil in a skillet, and sauté the eggplant halves, skin side up, until nicely browned. Remove from the pan, scoop out some of the pulp, and chop.

3. Sauté the onions, garlic, and mushrooms in the same skillet until lightly browned. Remove the pan from the heat, and add the anchovies, hot peppers, 3 tablespoons of breadcrumbs, the *prosciutto,* chopped eggplant pulp, parsley, and oregano. Mix well. Add the salt.

4. Stuff the eggplant halves. Combine the remaining tablespoon of breadcrumbs with the Parmesan, and sprinkle on the stuffing. Bake in a preheated 350°F oven for 10 to 15 minutes.

Peperoni, Melanzane, e Pomodori all'Acchiughe
SAUTÉED PEPPERS, EGGPLANT, AND TOMATOES WITH ANCHOVIES

Yield: 6 servings

6 ounces	green bell peppers	4 cloves	garlic, minced
6 ounces	red bell peppers	3	anchovy fillets, chopped
12 ounces	Italian or Japanese eggplant	to taste	salt and freshly ground black pepper
½ tablespoon	salt		
3	tomatoes, peeled and seeded (see chapter 1)	2 tablespoons	chopped parsley
		2 tablespoons	chopped basil
6 tablespoons	olive oil	¼ cup	grated Parmesan
3 ounces	onions, sliced		

1. Try to peel as much skin as possible from the peppers with a sharp vegetable peeler. (Do not roast them to peel, as they must remain somewhat crisp.) Halve the peppers, and remove the seeds and most of the spongy flesh. Cut into about ⅛-inch strips.

2. Peel the eggplant, and cut crosswise into ¼-inch thick slices. Cut the slices into ¼-inch sticks. Place the eggplant in a suitable dish, mix with the ½ tablespoon of salt, and let rest for 10 minutes. Press out as much liquid as possible.

3. Slice the tomatoes into ⅛-inch strips.

4. Heat the olive oil in a large skillet. Sauté the onions, peppers, garlic, and eggplant, keeping all undercooked and somewhat crisp.

(continued)

5.   Add the tomatoes, anchovies, salt, and pepper, and reheat.

6.   Remove from the heat, and stir in the parsley, basil, and grated Parmesan. Serve immediately.

Peperoni e Pomodori alla Parmigiana
SAUTÉED PEPPERS AND TOMATOES WITH PARMESAN

Yield: 6 servings

6 ounces	green bell peppers	3	hot chili peppers, finely sliced
6 ounces	red bell peppers	to taste	salt
6 ounces	yellow bell peppers	¼ cup	chopped parsley
3	tomatoes, peeled and seeded (see chapter 1)	2 tablespoons	chopped basil
		2 tablespoons	chopped oregano
6 to 8 tablespoons	olive oil	¼ cup	Parmesan, fresh grated
3 ounces	onions, sliced		
3 to 4 cloves	garlic, minced		

1.   Try to peel as much of the skin as possible from the bell peppers with a sharp vegetable peeler. (Do not roast the peppers to peel, as they should remain somewhat crisp.) Halve the peppers, and remove the seeds and most of the spongy flesh. Slice into ⅛-inch strips.

2.   Slice the tomatoes into ⅛-inch strips.

3.   Heat the olive oil in a large skillet, and sauté the onions, garlic, and bell peppers for 1 minute.

4.   Add the chili peppers and tomatoes, and reheat.

5.   Add salt, and stir in the parsley, basil, oregano, and grated Parmesan. Serve immediately.

Pomodori Ripieni alla Siciliana

STUFFED TOMATOES, SICILIAN STYLE

Yield: 6 servings

6	*ripe tomatoes, peeled (see chapter 1)*	*¼ cup*	*breadcrumbs*
		to taste	*salt*
6 tablespoons	*olive oil*	*to taste*	*dried, crushed hot red pepper*
3 ounces	*onions, finely diced*	*2 tablespoons*	*chopped oregano*
4 cloves	*garlic, minced*	*6 tablespoons*	*grated Parmesan*
1 tablespoon	*capers, chopped*	*6*	*anchovy fillets (oil-packed)*
3 ounces	*green bell peppers, finely diced*		
12	*black olives, pitted and chopped*		

1. Cut off the tops of the peeled tomatoes, and remove most of the interior meat with a melon scoop, shaking out the seeds and juice.

2. Heat the olive oil in a skillet, and sauté the onions and garlic for 1 minute. Add the capers, peppers, and olives, and cook for 2 minutes. Place the mixture in a suitable bowl.

3. Add the breadcrumbs, salt, hot pepper, oregano, and ¼ cup of Parmesan.

4. Brush the tomato shells inside and out with olive oil, and fill with the breadcrumb mixture, mounding the stuffing up over the edges of the tomatoes. Curve an anchovy fillet around the top of the stuffing, and sprinkle with the remaining 2 tablespoons of Parmesan.

5. Bake the tomatoes in a preheated 350°F oven until they are thoroughly heated and the cheese is melted. Serve immediately.

Radicchio Arrosto

GRILLED RADICCHIO

Yield: 6 servings

3 heads	radicchio, cleaned
1 teaspoon	salt
1/3 teaspoon	freshly ground black pepper
6 tablespoons	olive oil
1/4 cup	lemon juice

1.   Split the radicchio heads lengthwise in 4 parts, and sprinkle with the salt and pepper. Brush with the olive oil, and let rest for 10 minutes.

2.   Grill the oiled radicchio on both sides for about 1 minute, brushing with the oil from time to time. Be careful not to overcook or burn it. Remove the radicchio from heat, sprinkle with the lemon juice, and serve immediately.

Flan di Sedano Rapa

CELERIAC FLAN

Yield: 12 servings

1 quart	water	1 tablespoon	fresh lemon juice
1/2 cup	flour	5 tablespoons	heavy cream
1 1/2 pounds	celeriac, firm and not too woody	pinch	white pepper
1 ounce	butter	pinch	nutmeg
2 ounces	leeks, white parts only, thinly sliced	to taste	salt
		2	eggs
6 tablespoons	chicken broth (see chapter 3)	2 tablespoons	melted butter

1.   Prepare a *blanc* by combining the water and flour. This mixture will keep the celeriac from discoloring.

2.   Brush the celeriac under cold running water to remove any sand and grit. Peel completely, slice, and cut into small strips. Put the celeriac strips immediately into the *blanc,* and stir occasionally.

3.   Heat the butter in a shallow 2-quart noncorrosive pan, and add the leeks. Smother for a couple of minutes, until soft.

4.   Drain the celeriac in a colander, being sure to rinse away any flour residue. Add the celeriac to the leeks, along with the chicken broth and lemon juice. Cover and cook over low heat until soft. Reduce the liquid completely.

5.   Add the cream, pepper, nutmeg, and salt, and simmer for 2 minutes. Remove from the heat, and cool.

6.   Puree in a blender or food processor with the eggs.

7.   Brush twelve ½-cup molds with the melted butter. Fill each three-quarters full with the celeriac puree. Refrigerate until ready to cook.

8.   Place the molds in a hot water bath (in sheet or hotel pan), and cover with oiled parchment paper or foil. Poach in a preheated 325°F oven until firm. Cool for several minutes before unmolding to serve.

Cuori di Sedani Brasati con Burro e Parmigiana
CELERY HEARTS BRAISED IN BUTTER WITH PARMESAN

Celery has been appreciated throughout the Mediterranean for thousands of years. In ancient days it was considered more a medicine than a food. It contains a fair amount of vitamins A, B, and C, as well as many minerals.

Celery was cultivated (perhaps first) in Italy centuries ago and has been an important foodstuff there ever since. First used more to add flavor than as the centerpiece of a recipe, it eventually became an important ingredient on menus throughout Europe.

Aside from the celeriac *(sedano rapa),* there are basically two types of celery available in the United States. Pascal celery has light to dark green stalks, whereas Golden celery has bleached, white stalks. The Pascal type is preferred, having a more pronounced flavor and fewer strings.

Good-quality celery is characterized by the snaplike crispness of the stalks and a firm, plump heart, which is an absolute necessity for braised celery as well as for quality relishes.

(continued)

Yield: 6 servings

3 heads	Pascal celery with plump hearts	1 cup	hot white veal stock, strong (see chapter 7)
3 ounces	butter	to taste	salt and white pepper
6 ounces	onions, thinly sliced	½ cup	grated Parmesan
6 ounces	carrots, cut in julienne	¼ cup	chopped Italian parsley
2 cloves	garlic, minced		

1.   Cut the heads of celery crosswise to reveal heart portions, about 4 inches long. Remove the outer stalks; if fibrous, peel off any strings with a vegetable peeler. Halve the celery hearts lengthwise.

2.   Steam the celery hearts for 5 minutes.

3.   Melt the butter in a suitable shallow braising pan, and smother the onions, carrots, and garlic for a few minutes.

4.   Place the celery hearts, flat side down, over the vegetables, and add the hot veal stock, salt, and pepper.

5.   Cover with oiled parchment paper or foil, and put in a preheated 325°F oven. Braise for about 15 to 20 minutes, basting occasionally.

6.   When tender, turn the hearts over, sprinkle with the grated Parmesan, and continue cooking, uncovered, for 5 minutes.

7.   Arrange the celery on a bed of the vegetables, sprinkle with the parsley, and serve.

Spinaci con Prosciutto

SAUTÉED SPINACH AND PROSCIUTTO

This dish must be served immediately if the spinach is to retain its vitamins. If allowed to sit after cooking, the vitamins will simply leach out into the vegetable's own liquid.

Yield: 6 servings

1¾ pounds	fresh spinach leaves, stems removed	6 tablespoons	olive oil
		3 cloves	garlic, minced

3 ounces	onions, finely diced	1/4 cup	grated Parmesan
1 ounce	prosciutto, finely shredded		
to taste	salt and freshly ground black pepper		

1.   Wash the spinach leaves several times in deep, cold water, and drain.

2.   Heat the olive oil in a large, deep skillet, and add the garlic and onions. Cook over moderate heat until the onions are translucent and soft. Do not brown.

3.   Add the *prosciutto* and spinach to the skillet, and season with salt and pepper. Stir-fry the spinach over high heat for 2 minutes. Remove from the heat, sprinkle with the grated Parmesan, and serve immediately.

Verza Brasata con Carote

BRAISED SAVOY CABBAGE WITH CARROTS

Yield: 6 servings

1 head	savoy cabbage	1 cup	chicken broth (see chapter 3)
2 ounces	butter		
1/4 cup	olive oil	to taste	salt and white pepper
3 ounces	onions, finely diced	1/4 cup	chopped parsley
6 ounces	carrots, cut in julienne		

1.   Remove the core from the cabbage head. Blanch the cabbage in boiling, salted water for 8 to 10 minutes, until almost cooked. Poke the center with a skewer to test for doneness; it should pierce the head without resistance. Shock in cold water, and drain.

2.   Heat the butter and olive oil in a shallow pan, add the onions, and smother over moderate heat. Add the carrots and chicken broth, cover, and bring to a simmer. Let cook for about 1 minute, then remove from the heat.

3.   Remove the outer leaves from the cabbage, and cut the head into 12 uniform wedges, about 1½ ounces each. Shape the sections neatly, and place on top of the carrots. Baste the cabbage with the cooking liquid, and season with salt and pepper. Cover with oiled parchment paper, and braise in a 350°F oven for 10 minutes.

(continued)

4. Arrange 2 cabbage sections on each serving plate, spoon the carrots over them, and sprinkle with the chopped parsley.

Verza Brasata con Pancetta

BRAISED SAVOY CABBAGE WITH PANCETTA

Yield: 6 servings

1 head	*savoy cabbage, about 3 pounds*	*18*	*scallions, cut diagonally into 1½-inch lengths*
6 ounces	*carrots, cut in julienne*	*6 cloves*	*garlic, minced*
1 cup	*beef broth (see chapter 3)*	*1 tablespoon*	*caraway seeds*
		⅓ teaspoon	*freshly ground black pepper*
3 ounces	*pancetta, cut into strips*	*½ teaspoon*	*salt*
2 ounces	*butter*		

1. Discard the tough outer leaves from the head of cabbage. Divide it into 4 equal-sized wedges, and remove the core sections from them. Slice each wedge across into thin strips.

2. Cook the carrot julienne in the beef broth for 1 to 2 minutes. Strain the broth, and reserve both the carrots and broth.

3. Heat a skillet, and render the *pancetta* in the butter. Add the scallions, garlic, cabbage, caraway seeds, pepper, and salt. Sauté but do not brown.

4. Return the carrots to the skillet, and add ½ cup of the beef broth. Cover, and cook over high heat for a few minutes. Keep the cabbage somewhat undercooked.

5. Adjust the seasonings, and serve immediately.

Fiori di Zucchina Ripieni con Ricotta

ZUCCHINI BLOSSOMS STUFFED WITH RICOTTA

Yield: 6 servings

18	zucchini blossoms	5 ounces	onions, finely diced
9 ounces	ricotta	2 cloves	garlic, minced
3 ounces	Parmesan, grated	1	hot chili pepper, chopped
1/2 teaspoon	freshly ground black pepper	3 to 4	tomatoes, peeled, seeded, and diced (see chapter 1)
1/2 teaspoon	salt		
pinch	nutmeg	to taste	salt and freshly ground black pepper
1/2 cup	fresh white breadcrumbs		
2	egg yolks	6	basil leaves, finely shredded (chiffonade)
2 tablespoons	chopped parsley		
2 tablespoons	chopped basil		
5 fluid ounces	olive oil		

1. Trim the stem ends of the zucchini blossoms, and gently open the flowers to remove the pistils and any bugs that may be within. The easiest way to remove the pistils is to use a melon scoop. Bugs are more easily removed by blowing. Place the flowers in cold, salted water for 5 minutes, and then rinse with cold water again. Place the blossoms on paper towels to drain, and hold in the paper towel until needed.

2. Combine the ricotta, Parmesan, pepper, salt, nutmeg, breadcrumbs, egg yolks, parsley, and basil, and chill until needed.

3. Heat 3 fluid ounces of olive oil in a large shallow baking dish or casserole, add the onions and garlic, and cook until translucent. Add the chili pepper, tomatoes, and salt and pepper to taste, and cook over low heat for about 5 minutes.

4. Put the ricotta filling in a pastry bag with a plain tip, and carefully stuff the flowers. Lightly press the petals against the filling inside.

5. Arrange the stuffed blossoms in the casserole over the sauce, and brush each with the remaining olive oil. Season with salt and pepper to taste, and cover with foil. Bake in a preheated 375°F oven for 5 minutes. Reduce the oven temperature to 325°F, and continue to bake until the petals are soft, about 10 more minutes. Sprinkle the shredded basil over the sauce, and serve.

Zucchini Trifolati

SAUTÉED SLICED ZUCCHINI WITH OLIVE OIL, GARLIC, AND OREGANO

Yield: 6 servings

1½ pounds	small, firm zucchini	to taste	salt
3 cloves	garlic, minced	2 tablespoons	chopped parsley
¼ teaspoons	freshly ground black pepper	2 tablespoons	chopped oregano
6 tablespoons	olive oil	¼ cup	grated Parmesan

1.   Cut the zucchini crosswise into ⅛-inch rounds. Mix with the garlic and black pepper.

2.   Heat the olive oil in a large skillet, and add the zucchini. Brown the slices on one side without disturbing at all, turn them over, and continue to cook over very high heat until lightly browned on the other side as well. The zucchini should remain very crisp; the whole cooking procedure should not take more than 2 minutes.

3.   Adjust the seasonings, and remove from the heat. Stir in the parsley, oregano, and cheese, and serve immediately.

Patate al Pomodoro e Basilico

POTATOES WITH TOMATOES AND BASIL

Yield: 6 servings

1½ pounds	peeled potatoes	3	tomatoes, peeled, seeded, and diced small (see chapter 1)
6 tablespoons	olive oil		
3 ounces	onions, medium diced		
3 cloves	garlic, minced	to taste	salt
3	hot red chili peppers, chopped	2 tablespoons	chopped parsley
		2 tablespoons	chopped basil

1.   Using a melon baller, scoop the potatoes into small balls (known as *parisienne*).

2.   Heat the olive oil in a large skillet, add the onions, and brown lightly. Add the garlic and potatoes, and cook until they begin to brown.

3.   Add the chili peppers, tomatoes, and salt, and cook, uncovered, until the potatoes are soft but not mushy. Stir in the parsley and basil, and serve.

Crocchette di Patate

POTATO CROQUETTES

These may be accented by filling with grated Fontina or mozzarella cheese and served as appetizers.

Yield: 6 servings

18	*peeled Idaho russet potatoes*	*1 cup*	*flour*
3	*egg yolks*	*1*	*egg*
½ ounce	*butter, softened*	*¼ cup*	*milk or water*
pinch	*white pepper*	*1½ cup*	*dry breadcrumbs from Italian bread*
pinch	*nutmeg*	*to deep-fry*	*oil*
⅓ teaspoon	*salt*		

1.   Cut the peeled potatoes into large pieces, and place in a 2-quart pot with cold water to cover. Simmer slowly until soft (pierce with a fork to test for softness).

2.   Drain the potatoes in a colander, and return to the pot. Dry them completely in a 300°F oven. This is important, as the recipe works best when the potatoes are completely dry and hot before the eggs are added. Have a potato ricer and a warmed mixing bowl ready to use when the potatoes come out of the oven.

3.   When the potatoes are completely dry, remove from the oven. Rice them quickly in the warm mixing bowl, and immediately add the egg yolks. Stir the yolks in quickly to stiffen the mixture. (If the mixture seems loose, the potatoes were wet and luke-warm.)

(continued)

4. Mix in the butter, pepper, nutmeg, and salt.

5. Shape the mixture into 1½-ounce cylindrical logs. (Other shapes are possible and acceptable.)

6. Dredge the potato logs in the flour. Whisk the egg with the milk to make an egg wash. Dip the potato logs in the egg wash, and then coat with the breadcrumbs. Reshape on a table if necessary. Deep-fry until golden brown.

—— *Variazioni* ——
VARIATIONS

Fritatelle di patate (**Crisp potato cakes**): Prepare the potato croquette mixture (no breading). Sprinkle the work surface with cornstarch. Shape the mixture into cylinders about 6 inches long and 2 inches in diameter. Cut each cylinder into 12 slices, about ½ inch each. Flatten each slice with a metal spatula into a round patty. Pan-fry the patties in hot oil, flipping once, until lightly browned on both sides.

Fritatelle di patate con prosciutto e prezzemolo (**Crisp potato cakes with** *prosciutto* **and parsley**): Prepare the potato croquette mixture (no breading). Add 1 ounce of chopped *prosciutto* and ½ cup of chopped parsley. Shape and fry as for plain crisp potato cakes.

Teglia di Patate Gratinata
POTATOES AU GRATIN

Yield: 6 servings

1½ pounds	potatoes, peeled yellow	4 ounces	Parmesan, finely grated
2½ cups	milk	3 tablespoons	dry breadcrumbs
to taste	white pepper	2 ounces	butter
pinch	nutmeg		
4 ounces	mozzarella, coarsely grated		

1. Slice the potatoes into ⅛-inch-thick rounds.

2. Heat the milk in a shallow 3-quart saucepan.

3. Add the potatoes, pepper, and nutmeg, and simmer over low heat until the potatoes are almost soft, stirring occasionally, but not vigorously enough to break up the potatoes. (The starch released by the potatoes in cooking should be enough to give the sauce a creamy consistency.) Remove from the heat.

4.   Mix in half of the cheese, and adjust the pepper and nutmeg.

5.   Spoon the mixture into a greased ovenproof baking dish or into individual-size au gratin dishes.

6.   Combine the remaining cheeses with the breadcrumbs, and sprinkle over the potatoes. Dot with the butter.

7.   Bake on the top rack of a 500°F oven until nicely crusted.

Patate all'Anna

POTATOES ANNA

This is a contemporary version of potatoes Anna, suitable for any type of service. Try to select elongated potatoes, and trim them into cylindrical shapes before slicing.

Yield: 6 servings

1 1/2 pounds	*peeled potatoes*
1/4 cup	*melted butter*
to taste	*salt and freshly ground black pepper*

1.   Cut the potatoes into uniform ⅛-inch-thick slices. Wash quickly in cold water, and blot dry with a paper towel.

2.   Lightly oil six 9- by 9-inch sheets of parchment paper, and place on a metal sheet pan.

3.   Overlap the potato slices in a semicircle on the papers (the size of the semicircles should coordinate with the serving plates).

4.   Brush the potato slices with the melted butter, and season with salt and pepper.

5.   Place the sheet pan on the lowest rack of a preheated 375°F oven, and bake for about 8 to 10 minutes, until the bottoms of the sliced potatoes are brown and crisp.

6.   Invert each parchment paper with both hands onto a serving table.

SALADS

Our health depends on how we digest, assimilate, and eliminate. Our diet is determined by an instinctive demand from our bodies to receive the nutrients necessary for sustaining life. Years ago I was greatly influenced along these lines while reading Jethro Kloss's *Back to Eden*. Kloss's premise is essentially this: adulterated foods have led us unsuspectingly away from a proper nutritional balance in our diets. Certainly one of the most common causes of disease is incorrect eating habits. For too long we have violated our systems by the overuse and overconsumption of refined and adulterated foods. The elements that fuel the human body must be bountifully supplied by the proper intake of natural foods. The foods supplying us with these nutrients should be given proper respect and attention, even by today's medical establishment. With this attention, it would be easier for us to reject the advice often heard regarding the intake of manufactured vitamins, fast diet schemes, and the like.

The raw leafy vegetables so common in salads are especially worthy of attention because they supply the body with minerals such as iron, sulfur, fluorine, chlorine, and sodium. Fresh fruits are high in natural acids that aid the body in the elimination of various toxins. As more diners have become aware of the healthful nature of salads, they have become a focal point on the well-constructed menu. Americans have become quite imaginative with salads, and one finds anything crisp and colorful included in them. This would seem to be in accordance with healthy eating were it not for the vast amounts of rich dressing often accompanying these salads. In addition, these dressings disguise the natural flavor of the salad itself, actually overpowering its taste. In Italy's finer restaurants, it is most common for a salad to be served only with cruets of oil and vinegar or lemon juice. The dressing is made by customers to suit their individual tastes (to be sure, one must order the salad *non condita*—not dressed.)

Salads are served as appetizers, as a separate course, or as a main course. Appetizer salads are part of the antipastos. They are made up of different components, which may include raw and marinated vegetables, seafoods, meats, or pasta. Salads served as a course are *contorni*. Main-course salads are *piatti freddi* and may include an array of cold roast meats, poultry, game, seafood, and pasta with compatible garnishes. Special fruit salads are included with *frutta* and are usually served with dessert.

There are absolutely no rules concerning the combination of salad ingredients. The greens for the salad, however, must be crisp to the bite and well cleaned of dirt and sand. If tomatoes are used, they should be sun-ripened and peeled (see chapter 1).

Cucumbers should be seeded; mushrooms, cleaned and stemmed; and carrots and celeriac, finely shredded or cut in julienne. The textures and sizes of all vegetables must be complementary.

The most common greens used in salads are listed below.

Arugula: Also known as rocket, arugula has green leaves shaped like oak leaves. It has a very pungent radishlike flavor. Arugula is expensive.

Belgian endive: Also known as witloof chicory or French endive, belgian endive is a type of chicory with a tight, firm spear of leaves that are white with pale yellow edges.

Beet tops: The aboveground portion of the root vegetables, beet tops are used in salads as well as cooked. Only the young, tender leaves should be used for salads.

Chicory: Chicory is a family of salad greens that includes endive, belgian endive, escarole, and radicchio. In the United States, the green known as chicory or curly chicory is actually endive. It has narrow leaves, with curly green outer leaves and off-white crunchy ribs.

Dandelion greens: Often considered to be annoying weeds, the long, toothed, narrow leaves of dandelions are excellent in salads. If harvested wild, use the tender leaves that appear in the spring, before the flowers go to seed. Mature plants should be cooked.

Escarole: Also known as broadleaf endive, escarole is a type of chicory with flat, spreading, slightly wrinkled green leaves and off-white, crunchy ribs. Escarole is somewhat bitter and tough.

Field salad: Also known as corn salad, lamb's lettuce, or *mâche,* field salad is very tender and sweet but easily damaged. The commercially grown varieties are very expensive. It can be found growing wild in early spring along brooks.

Lettuce: Lettuce is available in many shapes and colors. Leaf lettuce is an open, loosely branched variety that does not form a head. Its leaves are smooth and elongated. Butterhead lettuce forms loose heads of pliable leaves that are sweet and tender. Boston and Bibb lettuces are butterheads. The best-quality leaves are in the heart of the head. Crisphead lettuces form tight heads of crisp, brittle leaves; the ubiquitous iceberg is a crisphead lettuce. Cos lettuce, or romaine, forms loose oblong heads of sweet, crisp green leaves with long, stiff, off-white ribs.

Radicchio: A type of chicory, American-grown radicchio is usually firm-headed with purple-red cuplike leaves and off-white ribs. It is also grown in northeastern Italy.

Spinach: A popular cooked vegetable, raw spinach is also a wonderful salad green. Use only the very young, tender leaves for salads.

Watercress: Watercress has small green leaves that have a very sharp, pungent flavor. Use only very fresh commercially grown or wild young spring plants.

To clean salad greens:

1. Wash in deep, cold water, and remove.
2. Drain in colander, or use salad spinner to shake out the water completely.
3. Do not stack greens in container. Avoid bruising.
4. Depending on the type of salad to be prepared, determine to what size the leaves should be trimmed. Small-leaved greens, such as arugula, watercress, field salad, dandelion tops, beet tops, and belgian endive, should be left whole.

If salad is dressed in the kitchen, toss it very carefully in the dressing. The leaves must not be bruised or wilt, or they will absorb the oil from the dressing. Toss with salad dressing at the last possible moment, and arrange loosely on salad plates or in bowls.

CONDIMENTS FOR ITALIAN SALADS

Extra-virgin olive oil is the most important condiment for a genuine Italian salad. As it is obtained from the first pressing of the olive, all its natural fruitiness makes it very agreeable to the palate. It cannot be replaced by any other oil, olive or vegetable.

The choicest vinegars for Italian salad dressing are red wine and balsamic vinegars. White wine and cider vinegars are less commonly used. Red wine vinegar is more frequently used for mixed green, tomato, and various legume salads. Balsamic vinegar is usually used in combination with red wine vinegar—just a few drops will enhance any dressing.

Citrus juices, especially lemon juice, are mainly used for seafood salads or special salads such as those containing mushrooms, artichokes, and various root vegetables. Occasionally lemon juice is combined with vinegar, though this is seldom the case. From a nutritional standpoint, citrus juices are most beneficial, as they are rich in vitamin C.

An unlimited number of ingredients can be used to enhance a salad. Cayenne pepper is often used in place of black pepper because *Capsicum* peppers help to stimulate digestion. Also used are mustard, anchovy paste, finely minced garlic, capers, grated fresh horseradish, minced scallions, oregano, basil, parsley, and grated Parmesan.

In Italian cooking today, there is less propensity toward emulsion dressings, for example, cream cheese, thickened french, or mayonnaise dressings. They are mainly prepared for appetizer salads.

TOMATOES

Some Italian cookbook authors have remarked that Americans are not accustomed to the very firm, sometimes even underripe tomatoes encountered in Italian salads. It is important to realize that vine-ripened tomatoes, much as in this country, are not available year-round in all parts of Italy. Since quality varies with season, sometimes a hard, somewhat bitter tomato will indeed be found. But this is in no way the norm. Italians, who understand the tomato perhaps better than anyone, realize that it is a fruit and that raw, unripe fruit is digestible only with great difficulty by the human system. A fresh tomato picked at the peak of ripeness is not only firm but has the optimal balance of sweet and acid flavors. This is the characteristic of the tomato that Italians have come to cherish and that makes the fruit such a delightful accompaniment to fresh greens.

Insalata Mista
ITALIAN TOSSED SALAD

Yield: 6 servings

¹⁄₃ head	romaine lettuce	3 tablespoons	red wine vinegar
¹⁄₃ head	curly chicory	2 tablespoons	balsamic vinegar
¹⁄₂ head	radicchio	2 cloves	garlic, minced
1	cucumber	2	anchovy fillets, minced
12 ounces	tomatoes, peeled and seeded (see chapter 1)	¹⁄₂ teaspoon	freshly ground black pepper
6 ounces	red onions	¹⁄₂ teaspoon	salt
6	red radishes	1 tablespoon	chopped parsley
1 bunch	arugula	1 tablespoon	chopped oregano
		2 tablespoons	grated Parmesan

DRESSING:

7 tablespoons   extra-virgin olive oil

1.   Wash the romaine, chicory, and radicchio, and drain thoroughly. Tear into smaller pieces.

2.   Peel and cut the cucumber in half lengthwise, cut out the seeds with a melon scoop, and then slice crosswise.

3.   Slice the peeled and seeded tomatoes, onions, and radishes.

4.   Combine the romaine, chicory, radicchio, cucumbers, tomatoes, onions, and radishes in a deep salad bowl. Wash and drain the arugula, tear into smaller pieces, and add. If the leaves are small, leave them whole.

5.   Mix all the ingredients for the dressing, and adjust the seasonings.

6.   Toss the vegetables in the dressing just before serving, or serve the dressing on the side.

Funghi e Spinaci all'Olio e Limone

MUSHROOM AND SPINACH SALAD WITH OLIVE OIL AND LEMON JUICE

Yield: 6 servings

12 ounces	spinach leaves, young, tender, and smooth	to taste	salt and freshly ground black pepper
12 ounces	mushrooms, very fresh	1/4 cup	thinly sliced scallions
5 tablespoons	extra-virgin olive oil	2 ounces	pancetta, diced small and fried crisp
2 tablespoons	freshly squeezed lemon juice	1/2 cup	grated Parmesan
1 clove	garlic, minced		

1.   Trim the stems from the spinach, and wash thoroughly in several deep sinkfuls of cold water. Drain completely and tear into small pieces.

2.   Clean the stem ends and caps of the mushrooms with a towel, and slice thinly.

3.   Combine the olive oil, lemon juice, garlic, salt and pepper, and scallions, and carefully toss with the mushrooms and spinach.

4.   Arrange the dressed salad in a suitable dish, and sprinkle the top with the fried *pancetta* and Parmesan cheese.

Insalata di Pomodori, Cipolle, e Basilico
TOMATO SALAD WITH RED ONIONS AND BASIL

Yield: 6 servings

1 bunch	arugula, washed and stemmed	6 tablespoons	red wine vinegar
6	ripe tomatoes, peeled (see chapter 1)	to taste	salt and freshly ground black pepper
2	red onions	12	basil leaves, coarsely chopped

DRESSING:

1 cup	extra-virgin olive oil

1.   This salad is prepared in individual portions. Place a few arugula leaves on each chilled salad plate.

2.   Slice each tomato horizontally into 5 slices. Thinly slice each red onion horizontally into 15 slices. Arrange 5 tomato slices and 5 onion slices alternately over the arugula on each plate.

3.   Combine the ingredients for the dressing, and adjust the seasonings. Spoon over the tomatoes and onions.

Insalata di Carciofi, Finocchi, e Cipolle Crude
RAW ARTICHOKE, FENNEL, AND ONION SALAD

This salad is made just before serving to prevent discoloration of the artichokes.

Yield: 6 servings

DRESSING:

1 cup	extra-virgin olive oil	2	hot red chili peppers, chopped
7 tablespoons	freshly squeezed lemon juice	2 cloves	garlic, minced

3 tablespoons	grated Parmesan	2	red onions
to taste	salt and freshly ground black pepper	3	artichokes, very fresh
		1 bunch	arugula, cleaned and stemmed
2	fennel knobs		

1. Combine the dressing ingredients in a stainless steel bowl.

2. Remove the outer stalk from the fennel knobs. Halve the knobs lengthwise, and remove the cores. Cut crosswise into half-rings that are as thin as possible (paper thin).

3. Halve the onions, and cut into thin strips.

4. Trim all inedible parts from the artichokes, including the outside leaves and the choke. The bottom are the only really useful part. Cut these paper thin, and add to the dressing immediately to prevent discoloration.

5. Place arugula leaves on a chilled plate, and arrange the sliced fennel, onions, and artichokes on top. Spoon the dressing over the vegetables.

Insalata di Radicchio con Pancetta
RADICCHIO WITH HOT BACON-VINEGAR DRESSING

This is a typical northern Italian/southern Austrian dish. It is most often made with romaine lettuce or some other sturdy, textured leaf lettuce.

Yield: 6 servings

1½ pounds	radicchio with very firm, fresh leaves	6 tablespoons	red wine vinegar
6 ounces	bacon, coarsely chopped	½ cup	grated Parmesan
to taste	salt and freshly ground black pepper	½ cup	thinly sliced scallions

1. Wash and drain the radicchio, and tear into smaller pieces.

(continued)

2.   Heat the bacon in a skillet, and render carefully until it just begins to color. Do not brown.

3.   Place the radicchio pieces in a deep salad bowl, and season with salt and pepper. Remove the bacon from the heat, and drain half the fat. Pour the vinegar into the bacon, and heat to a strong simmer. Quickly add the radicchio. Sprinkle with the Parmesan and scallions, and serve immediately.

Insalata di Cetrioli

CUCUMBER SALAD

Cucumbers taste most refreshing when ice cold and prepared just before serving. They are very compatible with potatoes, field salad *(mâche)*, radishes, and horseradish. The European cucumbers used in this recipe are practically seedless. The dressing may be very plain or can include yogurt and chopped mint leaves, seasoned with cayenne pepper and lemon juice.

Yield: 6 servings

2 pounds	*European cucumbers*	*1 clove*	*garlic, finely minced*
1 head	*Boston lettuce*	*3 tablespoons*	*white wine vinegar*
⅓ teaspoon	*salt*	*¼ cup*	*extra-virgin olive oil*
⅓ teaspoon	*freshly ground black pepper*	*¼ cup*	*finely chopped chives*
2 ounces	*red onions, in very thin 1½-inch slices*		

1.   Peel the cucumbers and slice them very thinly into a salad bowl (use a mandoline if available).

2.   Clean the lettuce, and drain well.

3.   Combine the salt, pepper, onions, garlic, vinegar, and olive oil, and toss well with the sliced cucumbers. Keep well chilled.

4.   Serve the cucumber salad on beds of Boston lettuce, sprinkled with the chives.

Insalata di Porri e Spinaci Mimosa

MARINATED LEEKS ON SPINACH BEDS, MIMOSA STYLE

Yield: 6 servings

12	small leeks	1 clove	garlic, minced
8 ounces	spinach leaves, tender, smooth, and stemmed	1/3 teaspoon	freshly ground black pepper
3/4 cup	clear beef broth (see chapter 3)	to taste	salt
3	tomatoes, peeled and seeded (see chapter 1)	2	hard-cooked eggs, finely chopped
6 tablespoons	freshly squeezed lemon juice	6	black olives, pitted and finely sliced
6 tablespoons	extra-virgin olive oil	9	basil leaves, very finely shredded (chiffonade)
1 teaspoon	prepared mustard		

1. Remove the roots and green tops from the leeks. Wash and trim the remaining whites to be approximately 3 to 3½ inches long.

2. Wash the spinach well, and drain.

3. Bring the beef broth to a simmer in a noncorrosive pan, and poach the leeks in the broth, covered, for about 2 minutes; the leeks should be cooked *al dente*. Remove from the heat, and cool. Drain, reserving the broth.

4. Cut the tomatoes into fine strips.

5. Strain the cooled broth into a small mixing bowl. Combine the lemon juice, olive oil, mustard, garlic, pepper, and salt with the broth, and adjust the seasonings.

6. Place the spinach leaves on each chilled salad plate. Top with 2 poached leeks sliced in half lengthwise.

7. Spoon the tomato strips over the leeks. Sprinkle with the chopped eggs, sliced olives, and shredded basil. Spoon about 3 tablespoons dressing over each serving.

Insalata Capricciosa con Verdure Cotte e Crude
COOKED AND RAW VEGETABLES IN OIL AND VINEGAR

Yield: 6 servings

6 tablespoons	extra-virgin olive oil	1 ounce	fennel, finely sliced
2 tablespoons	white wine vinegar	1 ounce	red onions, finely sliced
2 tablespoons	lemon juice		
1 clove	garlic, minced	1½ ounces	tart apples, cut in julienne
1 to 2	hot red chili peppers, chopped	1 ounce	mortadella, cut in fine julienne
2	anchovy fillets, chopped	1 bunch	red leaf lettuce, cleaned and drained
to taste	salt		
1 ounce	carrots, cut in julienne	12	tomato petals (see chapter 1)
1 ounce	celeriac, cut in julienne	1 bunch	arugula

1. Combine the olive oil, vinegar, lemon juice, garlic, chili peppers, anchovies, and salt in a noncorrosive salad bowl.

2. Steam the carrots and celeriac for 1 minute, until *al dente*. Toss with the dressing along with the fennel, onions, apples, and *mortadella*.

3. Arrange the lettuce leaves on chilled plates, and spoon the dressed salad in the center of each. Garnish each with 2 tomato petals and arugula sprigs.

Asparagi con Coulis di Pomodori Piccante
ASPARAGUS WITH SPICY TOMATO DRESSING

Yield: 6 servings

1½ pounds	fresh, thin green asparagus spears	4 cloves	garlic, peeled
1 bunch	leaf lettuce	2	ripe tomatoes, peeled and seeded (see chapter 1)
¾ cup	extra-virgin olive oil		

¼ cup	diced red onions	to taste	salt and freshly ground black pepper
1	hot chili pepper, chopped		
¼ cup	freshly squeezed lemon juice	½ cup	thinly sliced scallions
3 tablespoons	balsamic vinegar		

1. If the asparagus is very fresh, cut away the tough stem ends and peel only the toward the ends of the spears. Occasionally, asparagus is too mature when cut, or is stored too long; the tougher spears need to be peeled close to the tops. Tie the spears into 2-inch bunches, and cook in salted water for 1 to 2 minutes. Shock in ice water, drain on towels, and chill.

2. Clean the lettuce, and drain.

3. Heat 2 tablespoons of olive oil in a small skillet, and cook the garlic cloves until lightly browned. Remove from the heat.

4. Cut the peeled tomatoes into small pieces.

5. Place the garlic, tomatoes, remaining olive oil, onions, chili peppers, lemon juice, vinegar, salt, and pepper in a blender, and puree until smooth. Adjust the seasonings, pour into a glass or china dish, cover, and refrigerate.

6. Arrange the lettuce leaves on chilled salad plates, and top each neatly with 3 ounces of asparagus. Spoon the tomato dressing over the stem ends of the asparagus. Sprinkle the dressing with the thinly sliced scallions.

Sedano Rapa all'Olio e Limone
CELERIAC IN OIL AND LEMON JUICE

This is an excellent salad to serve with roast veal or game foul. When properly stored and refrigerated, it should keep for several weeks. Serve it on a bed of radicchio or arugula. The salad should be made at least 1 day ahead of time.

Celeriac is not in its prime during the hot summer months, and even when good-quality celeriac is available, it is not inexpensive. Select firm knobs that seem heavy for their size. Lightweight knobs will have soft, dehydrated interiors.

Yield: 6 servings

2	*celeriac, no stalks*	½ ounce	*sugar*
		⅓ teaspoon	*salt*
DRESSING:		1	*bay leaf*
2 cups	*water*	pinch	*white pepper*
6 tablespoons	*freshly squeezed lemon juice*	½ cup	*finely diced onions*
		6 tablespoons	*extra-virgin olive oil*
2 tablespoons	*white vinegar*		

1.   Clean and lightly scrub the celeriac under running water.

2.   Combine all the dressing ingredients except the olive oil in a 2- to 3-quart stainless steel saucepan.

3.   Peel the celeriac completely, and cut into wedges, then cut crosswise into ⅛-inch slices. Rinse in cold water, and add to the dressing. Cook over low heat until *al dente*. Remove from the heat, adjust the seasonings, and cool completely.

4.   Add the olive oil, and store, well-covered, in the refrigerator. Allow the salad to marinate in the dressing for at least 1 day before serving.

Insalata di Barbabietole e Cipolle
RED-BEET SALAD WITH ONIONS

Yield: 6 servings

2 pounds	small red beets	1	bay leaf
		⅓ teaspoon	freshly ground black pepper
DRESSING:		to taste	salt
1 cup	water	6 ounces	onions, sliced into 1½-inch strips
6 tablespoons	white or cider vinegar	6 tablespoons	extra-virgin olive oil
1½ ounces	sugar		
1 teaspoon	caraway seeds		

1. Scrub the beets well with a brush. Boil them in slightly acidulated water until the skins slide off easily. Peel while still hot, and cut into medium slices.

2. Combine all the dressing ingredients except the onions and olive oil in a noncorrosive 2-quart saucepan, and simmer slowly for about 5 minutes. Adjust the seasonings and sugar.

3. Add the onions, and cook for an additional 5 minutes. Remove from the heat, and cool completely.

4. Add the olive oil to the dressing, and combine dressing with the sliced beets.

5. Chill, well covered, in glass or china jars.

Insalata di Patate con Pancetta Affumicata
POTATO SALAD WITH BACON

This recipe comes from the Alto Adige region of northern Italy and has a typical Tyrolean-Austrian character. Peeled and seeded cucumbers or thinly sliced tart apples are excellent additions to this salad. In the early spring, young field salad *(mâche)* or dandelion greens can be cut up and added to this salad with wonderful results.

Yield: 6 servings

2 pounds	small yellow potatoes	1 tablespoon	prepared mustard
4 ounces	smoked bacon, cut into short, thin strips	1/3 teaspoon	freshly ground black pepper
		1/2 teaspoon	salt
4 ounces	onions, finely diced	2 tablespoons	finely chopped chives
6 tablespoons	extra-virgin olive oil		
1/4 cup	white vinegar		
1/2 cup	beef broth (see chapter 3)		

1.   Wash the potatoes, and cover with cold water in a saucepan. Simmer the potatoes slowly until almost cooked through. Drain, and peel the potatoes while hot. Slice thin while still warm into a suitable mixing bowl.

2.   Sauté the bacon strips until fairly crisp but not brown. Drain off most of the grease.

3.   Combine the onions, olive oil, vinegar, beef broth, mustard, pepper, and salt. Add the bacon, with the remaining bacon grease. Adjust the seasonings.

4.   Combine the dressing with the potatoes, and keep warm.

5.   Serve in a suitable dish, preferably on a bed of crisp lettuce, arugula, or field salad, sprinkled with the chives.

DESSERTS

— *Dolci Freddi* —
COLD DESSERTS

Gelati

ICE CREAMS

Gelato is generally made in the same way as egg-based ice cream; in this recipe, the milk-fat content of the *gelato* is lower because milk is used instead of cream. For even lower-calorie versions, dry milk solids are used instead of milk, and the eggs are either used more sparingly or eliminated altogether. The amount of sugar, however, remains the same (14 to 15 percent) to ensure a smooth and even freeze.

The *gelato* can be flavored as desired. Possibilities include finely chopped nuts; strong coffee, coffee extracts, or instant coffee granules dissolved in a very small amount of water; fruit puree; or praline paste. If a sweet flavoring, such as a very sweet fruit puree, is used to flavor the *gelato,* reduce the sugar in the recipe accordingly.

Yield: 3 quarts

1 quart	milk or nonfat milk	6 to 8	eggs
8 ounces	sugar	to taste	vanilla extract or other flavoring

(continued)

1. Bring the milk and half of the sugar to a boil.

2. Mix the remaining sugar and the eggs well by hand.

3. Whisk a portion of the hot sweetened milk into the sugar/egg mixture. Now reverse the process, and slowly combine the sugar/egg mixture with the remaining hot sweetened milk.

4. Heat this mixture until it has a smooth coating consistency and naps a spoon.

5. Cool the sauce over an ice bath to below room temperature.

6. Stir in the vanilla or other flavoring.

7. Churn and freeze the mixture in an ice-cream machine to the desired consistency.

Gelato di Panna alla Vaniglia
VANILLA ICE CREAM

No stabilizers are used in this recipe, so it can only be stored for about 3 days before excessive crystallization occurs. When this happens, the ice cream can be thawed (or melted gently) and refrozen. Any flavoring can be added to this basic recipe, but be careful not to use a heavy hand when flavoring.

For proper freezing consistency, try to keep the sugar amount at 8 ounces per 1 quart of liquid. Too much sugar will result in a mushy product; too little, and you will have a rock. The easiest way to test for this proper balance is to float a raw egg in the mixture. If the part of the egg that floats above the mixture is the size of a dime, then the balance is good. If less egg shows, increase the sugar. If too much egg appears, increase the liquid. It is advisable to be very sure of just how much sugar you are adding at any time and to consider the sweetness of any flavorings you add. Remember that such flavorings as semisweet chocolate contain high levels of sugar. When using chocolate, try using a mixture of semisweet and sweet chocolate to give the desired result.

Yield: 6½ pints

1 quart	milk
1 pint	heavy cream
8 ounces	sugar
8	egg yolks
to taste	vanilla or other flavoring

1.   Combine the milk, cream, and half of the sugar in a heavy-bottomed, noncorrosive saucepan, and bring to a boil. If using a vanilla bean to flavor the ice cream, split it and add it to the milk.

2.   Combine the remaining sugar and egg yolks in a suitable mixing bowl, and whisk well by hand.

3.   Pour a little of the hot sweetened milk and cream into the yolk mixture, whisking vigorously.

4.   Stir the yolk mixture into the remaining hot sweetened milk and cream, and heat until the mixture has light coating consistency or naps a spoon.

5.   Place the sauce in an ice bath, and stir to cool below room temperature.

6.   Add the desired flavoring.

7.   Churn and freeze the mixture in an ice-cream machine until the desired consistency is achieved. Store, well covered, below −10°F in clean containers.

Gelato allo Yogurt
FROZEN YOGURT

Yield: 1 quart

14 ounces	low-fat yogurt
2½ ounces	confectioners' sugar
¼ cup	lemon juice
to taste	flavoring

1.   Whisk the yogurt, sugar, and lemon juice together in a stainless steel mixing bowl.

2.   Add the flavoring.

3.   Churn and freeze in an ice-cream machine.

Soufflé Dolce al Gelato
FROZEN SOUFFLÉS

Frozen soufflés can be prepared ahead of time and stored in a freezer for several weeks until needed. Prepare the molds in which to freeze them ahead of time, as follows:

1. Use a regular earthenware or porcelain soufflé dish, about 2 inches deep.
2. Cut a strip of parchment paper or heavy aluminum foil about 4 inches wide and a bit longer than the circumference of the mold. Tape the two ends of the strip together, so that the resulting collar fits tightly around the soufflé dish. This collar will surround the soufflé mixture and hold it in place until frozen.
3. Brush the outside of the mold with melted butter, and slip the collar over the mold, so that it extends 2 to 3 inches above the mold. The melted butter keeps the collar in place.

Soufflé Dolce al Frangelico
FROZEN SOUFFLÉ WITH HAZELNUT LIQUEUR

Yield: 8 servings

4	eggs
2	egg yolks
6 ounces	granulated sugar
2 cups	heavy cream
¼ cup	Frangelico
to garnish	sweetened cocoa powder or finely crushed macaroons

1.   Prepare eight ½-cup soufflé dishes. Place the eggs, egg yolks, and sugar in a 6-quart mixing bowl over a hot water bath, and beat until the mixture reaches a temperature of 115°F.

2.   Remove from the heat, and continue beating until thick and below room temperature.

3.   Fold in the Frangelico.

4.   Whip the heavy cream to soft peaks and fold into the mixture.

5.   Pour the mixture into the prepared soufflé molds, filling almost to the tops of the collars. Freeze for at least 3 hours before serving.

6.   Remove the collars by dipping the molds into hot water for an instant to melt the butter.

7.   Dust the tops of the soufflés with sweetened cocoa powder or sprinkle with finely crushed macaroons (see color plate 59).

Variazione

VARIATION

Soufflé dolce all'arancia (**Frozen orange soufflé**): Follow the recipe for the frozen soufflé with hazelnut liqueur, but substitute Grand Marnier, Curaçao, or Cointreau for the Frangelico. Instead of freezing in a soufflé mold, the mixture may be frozen in scooped-out orange shells.

Sorbetti

SORBETS

The French word *sorbet* and the Italian *sorbetto* both stem from the Arabic word *sharbah*. These flavorful frozen fruit desserts were probably first introduced to Europe by the Arabs, although they were being made in China and India long before. Some think Marco Polo may have brought the production techniques for *sorbets* to Italy on his return from the Orient. In any case, *sorbets* were common long before ice cream, which was not introduced until the seventeenth century. True *sorbets* do not contain any dairy products. They are therefore different from sherbets, which do contain milk products. In the United States, *sorbets* are sometimes called ices or water ices.

As in ice-cream production, the sugar balance of *sorbets* is the most important consideration. With too little sugar, the mixture will be rock hard; too much, and the product will never harden. Egg whites can be added to stabilize the mixture and to produce high overrun levels (this refers to the amount of expansion during freezing: ideal is an overrun of 100 percent, which means 1 pint of mixture will freeze into 2 pints of sorbet). When preparing the mixture, aim for a hydrometer reading of 16 degrees Baumé or use the easier raw egg technique described for vanilla ice cream.

To flavor *sorbets*, purees of raspberries, strawberries, cranberries, red currants, cherries, kiwi, passion fruit, rhubarb, canteloupes, apples, peaches, or apricots all work well. The fruit should be pureed in a blender with a little sugar and lemon juice. Alternative flavoring, such as liqueurs, can be added to the basic recipe as well.

(continued)

Yield: 2½ pints

1 pint	warm water
6 ounces	granulated sugar
6 tablespoons	lemon juice
½	egg white
¼ cup	liqueur (optional)

When using fruit purees, follow the recipe below:

1 pint	warm water
4 ounces	granulated sugar
to taste	fruit puree

1.   Combine all ingredients. Check the density level with a hydrometer or an egg. Freeze in a *sorbet* machine.

Granite

GRANITE

Granite are similar to *sorbets,* but rather than being frozen in machines, they are frozen in a freezer and broken up occasionally to produce a pleasant, grainy mass. Less sugar is used in *granite* than in *sorbets*. They should have a density of 14 degrees Baumé or less on a hydrometer. The tip of a raw egg immersed in the fruit juice mixture should barely touch the surface.

Granite are typically laced with white wine, spumante, or liqueur to taste. They are usually served between banquet courses but are excellent as a refresher anytime.

Yield: 12 portions

2 cups	citrus fruit juices
1 cup	water
1 cup	dry spumante or dry white wine
3½ ounces	sugar

1.   Combine all the ingredients, and pour into a shallow stainless steel container.

2.   Place in the freezer. When the liquids around the sides of the container begin to freeze, agitate the mixture to break it up into small, uniform crystals.

——— Coppe Gelati ———
ICE-CREAM SUNDAES

Sundaes are ice creams of different flavors and colors served together in fancy silver or glass parfait goblets. Sundaes can be garnished and presented in a wide variety of ways, which is why they are so attractive. Garnishes can include macaroons, meringues, assorted nuts, diced fresh or candied fruits, liqueur-laced berries, and chocolate or caramel sauce, to name just a few. Very often these desserts are topped with an additional whipped-cream garnish, chocolate shavings or ornaments, candied violets, or pieces of fresh fruit. The following are only a few ideas for ice-cream sundaes.

Coppa al cappuccino (**Vanilla and chocolate ice-cream sundae with** *espresso* **and chocolate shavings**): Fill a goblet with 1 round scoop of vanilla and of chocolate ice cream. Pour 6 tablespoons of iced espresso or mocha over the scoops. Decorate the top with vanilla whipped cream and chocolate shavings or ornaments. Serve with ladyfingers.

Tutti Frutti (**Vanilla and strawberry ice-cream sundae with mixed fruit and berries**): Mash 3 tablespoons of fresh raspberries with a small amount of sugar. Place in the bottom of a goblet. Top with 1 scoop of vanilla and of strawberry ice cream. Spoon 3 tablespoons of diced fresh fruit and berries that have been macerated in Kirsch over the scoops. Decorate with a fresh fan-cut strawberry and mint leaves.

Coppa con pesca (**Vanilla ice-cream sundae with fresh peaches**): Make sure the peach used here is very ripe; if not, poach it before preparing the sundae. Dice half of a fresh peach small. Place the diced peaches in the bottom of a goblet with 2 tablespoons of apricot brandy. Top with 1 scoop of vanilla ice cream. Crumble 3 macaroons over the ice cream. Cover the macaroons with another scoop of vanilla ice cream. Place half of a ripe, peeled peach on top. Spoon 2 tablespoons of raspberry puree around the peach half, and decorate with vanilla whipped cream and chopped pistachios.

Cassata alla Siciliana

SICILIAN BOMBE WITH CANDIED FRUITS AND NUTS

Yield: 12 servings

2½ pints	vanilla ice cream (see recipe earlier in this chapter)	1 pint	heavy cream
		1	egg white
2 pints	chocolate ice cream (see recipe earlier in this chapter)	3 ounces	confectioners' sugar
		3 ounces	semisweet chocolate, coarsely grated
3 ounces	candied fruits, finely diced	1 ounce	toasted almonds, finely chopped
2 tablespoons	maraschino or Kirsch		

1.   Line a 4-quart round bombe mold with the vanilla ice cream. Use a curved spatula to ensure even coating. Freeze until firm.

2.   Spread a layer of chocolate ice cream over the vanilla ice cream, and freeze.

3.   Macerate the candied fruits in the maraschino or Kirsch for 1 hour.

4.   Whip 1 cup of cream until fairly stiff.

5.   Beat the egg white to stiff peaks, add 2 ounces of sugar, and beat for another 15 seconds.

6.   Fold the beaten egg white into the whipped cream. Fold the candied fruits, chocolate, and almonds into this mousse mixture.

7.   Fill the center of the ice-cream-lined mold to the top with the mousse mixture. Cover with plastic wrap, freeze for at least 4 to 6 hours.

8.   To unmold, dip the mold quickly into hot water and then turn the bombe onto a cold tray. Return to the freezer immediately, and keep frozen until ready to serve.

9.   Whip the remaining cup of cream with the remaining ounce of sugar. Cut the bombe into serving portions, and decorate with the whipped cream. A fresh fruit sauce can also be used as a garnish if desired.

Cassata Napoletana

NEAPOLITAN BOMBE

Yield: 12 large servings

3 pints	*softened vanilla ice cream (see recipe earlier in this chapter)*
2 pints	*softened chocolate ice cream (see recipe earlier in this chapter)*
1 pint	*softened strawberry ice cream (see recipe earlier in this chapter)*
1	*7-inch layer basic sponge cake (see recipe later in this chapter)*

1. Lightly oil a bombe mold or stainless steel bowl that is approximately 4 inches deep and 7 inches in diameter. Place it in the freezer for at least 1 hour.

2. Line the mold with a 1-inch layer of softened vanilla ice cream using a curved spatula. Freeze for an hour, or until hard. Spread the vanilla ice cream with a layer of chocolate ice cream, and freeze until hard. Fill the remaining cavity with strawberry ice cream, and freeze.

3. Place a ½-inch-thick layer of sponge cake on top of the ice cream. Cover with plastic wrap, and freeze for at least 4 to 5 hours.

4. To unmold, dip the mold quickly into hot water. Turn the bombe out onto a cold platter, and refreeze immediately. The bombe may be garnished with whipped cream, macaroons, chocolate ornaments, or strawberry puree if desired (see color plate 60).

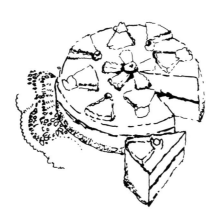

Semi-Freddo Meringato con Salsa al Cioccolata
ICE-CREAM MERINGUE CAKE WITH CHOCOLATE SAUCE

Yield: 16 servings

8	egg whites (from large eggs)	1½ pints	softened chocolate ice cream (see recipe earlier in this chapter)
2 cups	granulated sugar		
1 teaspoon	instant coffee granules	½ cup	finely chopped pistachios
½ cup	confectioners' sugar	1 cup	dried cake crumbs
1½ pints	softened vanilla ice cream (see recipe earlier in this chapter)	1 cup	heavy cream
		1 tablespoon	confectioners' sugar
		1 quart	chocolate sauce (see recipe later in the chapter)
1½ pints	softened strawberry ice cream (see recipe earlier in this chapter)		

1.   On each of 2 sheets of parchment paper, draw a circle that is 10 inches in diameter.

2.   Beat the egg whites with the granulated sugar in a large mixing bowl in a double boiler until the mixture reaches a temperature of 110° to 115°F. Remove from the heat, and continue to beat with an electric mixer until very stiff and at room temperature.

3.   Combine the instant coffee granules with the confectioners' sugar, and fold gently into the meringue by hand.

4.   Using a pastry bag with a plain tip, pipe the meringue in a continuous spiral to fill the circles drawn on the parchment paper. The meringue should be about ½ inch high.

5.   Bake the meringue circles in a preheated 225°F oven until completely dry, for about 2 hours. Cool.

6.   Place 1 cooled meringue circle on the bottom of a springform pan.

7.   Spread the softened vanilla ice cream in an even layer over the meringue, and freeze for 1 hour. Spread the strawberry ice cream in an even layer over the vanilla ice cream, and freeze for 1 hour.

8.   Spread the chocolate ice cream in an even layer over the strawberry ice cream. Place the second meringue circle over the chocolate ice cream, and press gently. Place a flat tray on this meringue circle and top with a light weight. Freeze in this way for an additional 4 to 6 hours.

9.   Combine the chopped pistachios and cake crumbs. Unhinge the mold, and sprinkle the sides of the cake with the pistachio/crumb mixture. Freeze until ready to serve.

10.   If the cake is too hard to slice, thaw it in the refrigerator for 10 minutes. Whip the cream, then fold in the sugar.

11.   Spoon ¼ cup of the chocolate sauce onto each chilled serving plate, and place a wedge of meringue cake on the sauce. Decorate with the whipped cream.

Pan di Spagna

BASIC SPONGE CAKE

Yield: 2 10-inch cakes

12	*eggs*
12 ounces	*granulated sugar*
10 ounces	*cake flour*
2 ounces	*cornstarch*
½ cup	*melted butter*

1.   Beat the eggs and sugar over a hot water bath until 110°F.

2.   Remove from the heat, and continue to beat at high speed until thick and at room temperature.

3.   Sift the flour and cornstarch together several times, and fold into the egg/sugar mixture with a spatula. Gently stir in the melted butter.

4.   Pour the batter into buttered and floured 10-inch cake pans, and bake in a preheated 350°F oven for about 25 minutes. Cool.

Pan di Spagna alla Cioccolata
CHOCOLATE SPONGE CAKE

Yield: 2 10-inch cakes

12	eggs
12 ounces	granulated sugar
9 ounces	cake flour
2 ounces	cornstarch
2 ounces	cocoa powder
1 teaspoon	baking soda
¼ cup	melted butter

1.   Beat the eggs and sugar over a hot water bath until 110°F.

2.   Remove from the heat, and continue to beat at high speed until thick and at room temperature.

3.   Sift the flour, cornstarch, cocoa powder, and baking soda together several times, and fold into the egg/sugar mixture with a spatula. Gently stir in the melted butter.

4.   Pour the batter into buttered and floured 10-inch cake pans, and bake in a preheated 350°F oven for about 25 minutes. Cool.

Pasta Sfoglia
PUFF PASTRY DOUGH

Because of the large amount of butter required for this dough a high-quality flour should be used. I recommend a good hard flour from winter wheat such as bread flour.

Yield: 2½ pounds of dough

1 teaspoon	salt
1 cup	very cold water
1 pound	unsalted butter
1 pound	bread flour

1.   Dissolve the salt in the water.

2.   Soften 2 ounces of butter in a mixing bowl, and add 14 ounces of the bread flour and the water. Work into a very smooth-textured dough. Remove from the bowl, and shape into a ball. Cover with a damp towel and refrigerate for about 1 hour.

3.   Work the remaining 14 ounces of butter and remaining 2 ounces of flour quickly into a smooth paste. Form the butter into a flat square about 2 inches thick.

4.   Take the rested dough from the refrigerator. With a knife cut a cross shape about halfway through the dough ball. Roll the dough out into a cross shape, leaving the center of the cross much thicker.

5.   Place the butter square in the center of the dough, and fold the four flaps over it.

6.   Roll out this dough envelope into a long rectangle about 1 inch thick. The dough should be three times as long as it is wide.

7.   Fold the dough into thirds, like a letter. The procedure of rolling the dough and folding it into thirds is called giving the dough a simple turn. Cover the dough with a damp cloth, and refrigerate for 30 minutes.

8.   Give the dough 4 more simple turns, being sure to rest the dough in the refrigerator for 30 minutes between each. Cover with a damp cloth or plastic wrap until ready to use. The dough can be stored, wrapped, in the refrigerator for 3 to 4 days.

9.   An alternative way of preparing the dough is to roll out the dough into a rectangle rather than a cross, and dot with the 14 ounces of butter on two-thirds of the rectangle. Fold the unbuttered third over half of the buttered portion, and the remaining buttered third over that (again, like a letter). Press the sides to seal. Proceed as above, giving the dough 4 more simple turns, resting between turns.

Pasta Brioscia

BRIOCHE DOUGH

Yield: 2½ pounds of dough

¾ ounces	*yeast*	*½ teaspoon*	*salt*
¼ cup	*lukewarm milk*	*5 to 6*	*eggs*
20 ounces	*bread flour*	*10 to 12 ounces*	*softened butter*
2 ounces	*sugar*		

(continued)

1.   Dissolve the yeast in the lukewarm milk, and stir in about 4 ounces of the flour, just enough to make a very soft dough. Place this in the bottom of a mixing bowl, and cover entirely with the remaining flour. Let rise in a warm place for about 1½ hours.

2.   Add the sugar, salt, and eggs, and mix with an electric mixer until the dough becomes elastic and no longer sticks to the sides of the bowl or the mixing paddle.

3.   Add the softened butter and mix until well incorporated. Do *not* overmix. Place the dough in a warm space, and let rise until almost tripled in volume.

4.   Remove the dough from the mixing bowl, and place, covered, in the refrigerator to cool. It is best to let the dough rest overnight in the refrigerator before using because of its high butter content.

Pasta Frolla I
BASIC PIE DOUGH

Yield: 3 pounds of dough

pinch	*salt*
pinch	*sugar*
1 cup	*cold water*
1½ pounds	*all-purpose flour*
1 pound	*shortening*

1.   Dissolve the salt and sugar in the water.

2.   Sift the flour into a suitable mixing bowl.

3.   Add the shortening to the flour and cut it with a pastry blender. Then work the shortening in with both hands until the mixture consists of uniform pea-sized crumbs.

4.   Add the cold water all at once to the dough, and mix gently but quickly. Do not overmix.

5.   Refrigerate, covered, until ready to use.

Pasta Frolla II
SWEETENED TART DOUGH

Yield: 2 pounds of dough

18 ounces	all-purpose flour
9 ounces	butter
3 ounces	sugar
3	egg yolks, lightly beaten
pinch	salt
to taste	vanilla, grated lemon rind, or other flavoring

1.   Sift the flour into a mixing bowl.

2.   Add the butter to the flour and cut it with a pastry blender. Then work the butter in with both hands until the mixture consists of uniform pea-sized crumbs.

3.   Add the sugar, egg yolks, salt, and flavoring, and mix into the dough gently but quickly. Do not overmix.

4.   Cover the dough and refrigerate until ready to use.

Crema Pasticceria
BASIC PASTRY CREAM

Yield: 3½ cups

2 cups	milk	2 ounces	butter
½	vanilla bean		
4 ounces	granulated sugar	**FOR USE AS A FILLING:**	
1½ ounces	cornstarch	½ ounce	gelatin
2	eggs	6 tablespoons	water
2	egg yolks	½ cup	heavy cream

(continued)

1.   Scald the milk with the vanilla bean. Stir often to prevent the milk from burning.

2.   Combine the sugar and cornstarch in a stainless steel mixing bowl. Whisk in the eggs and egg yolks.

3.   When the milk is heated, remove the vanilla bean, and stir the milk into the egg mixture. Whisk vigorously in a double boiler until thick.

4.   Remove from the heat, and stir in the butter. Pour the cream into a small bowl. If the pastry cream is to be used as a filling, go to step 5. If not, cover the plastic wrap and cool. Stir occasionally while cooling.

5.   If the pastry cream is to be used to fill puff pastry, éclairs, or sponge cake, dissolve the gelatin in the water. Stir into the pastry cream while it is still hot. Then stir the cream over an ice bath to cool. Whip the cream to soft peaks, and fold gently into the pastry cream. Fill the pastries with the cream immediately.

------- *Bavarese* -------
BAVARIAN CREAMS

In order for a bavarian cream to have the proper consistency, the ingredients must be in exactly the right proportions. For every pint of vanilla sauce and flavoring, there must be an equal amount (1 pint) of heavy cream whipped to soft peaks. Also needed is ½ ounce of gelatin that has bloomed in ½ cup of water.

The amount of fruit puree to be used must combine with the vanilla sauce to equal 1 pint total. If the fruit is highly acid, cook it for several minutes before adding the gelatin, or the protein in the gelatin will be broken down by the acids.

Any dry flavoring ingredients, such as walnuts or pistachios, should be finely chopped and folded in immediately after the whipped cream.

Bavarese alla Vaniglia con Purea di Lamponi
VANILLA BAVARIAN CREAM WITH RASPBERRY PUREE

Yield: 8 servings

½ ounce	gelatin	2 cups	heavy cream
½ cup	tepid water		
2 cups	vanilla sauce (see recipe later in this chapter)	**GARNISH:**	
		1½ cups	vanilla-flavored whipped cream

to garnish	chocolate ornaments (optional; see instructions later in this chapter)	¹/₄ cup	smooth apricot jelly
		2 cups	raspberry puree (see recipe later in this chapter)
8	macaroons (see recipe later in this chapter)		

1. Combine the gelatin with the water, and let bloom. Combine with the vanilla sauce in a suitable bowl.

2. Place the sauce in an ice bath, and stir until it starts to thicken.

3. Whip the cream to soft peaks, and gently fold into the sauce.

4. Pour immediately into molds before the bavarian sets. Refrigerate for at least 3 hours.

5. To unmold, dip the molds in hot water, and carefully turn the bavarians out onto chilled serving plates. Decorate each with a rosette of vanilla-flavored whipped cream and a chocolate ornament (optional). Make another rosette of whipped cream on the plate near the unmolded bavarian, and top with a fresh macaroon. Pipe a border of smooth apricot jam on the plate, and fill the center with raspberry puree. The apricot jam will keep the puree in the design (see color plate 61).

Bavarese alle Fragole con Purea di Lamponi

STRAWBERRY BAVARIAN CREAM WITH RASPBERRY PUREE

Yield: 8 servings

1¹/₂ cups	vanilla sauce (see recipe later in this chapter)	to taste	chocolate ornaments (optional; instructions later in this chapter)
¹/₂ cup	strawberry puree (see recipe later in this chapter)	8	ladyfingers (see recipe later in this chapter)
¹/₂ ounce	gelatin	2 cups	raspberry puree (see recipe later in this chapter)
¹/₂ cup	tepid water		
2 cups	heavy cream		

GARNISH:

1¹/₂ cups	vanilla-flavored whipped cream

(continued)

1.   Combine the vanilla sauce and strawberry puree at room temperature.

2.   Combine the gelatin with the water; let bloom. Add to the strawberry/vanilla sauce mixture.

3.   Place the mixture in an ice bath, and stir until it starts to thicken.

4.   Whip the cream to soft peaks, and gently fold into the mixture.

5.   Pour immediately into metal timbales or molds, and refrigerate for at least 3 hours.

6.   To unmold, dip the timbales in hot water, and carefully turn the bavarians out onto chilled serving plates. Decorate with vanilla-flavored whipped cream and chocolate ornaments if desired. Serve with a ladyfinger on the side. Spoon the raspberry puree around each timbale.

Bavarese alla Cioccolata con Fonduta di Cioccolata
CHOCOLATE BAVARIAN CREAM WITH CHOCOLATE FONDUE

Yield: 8 servings

1 1/2 cups	*warm vanilla sauce (see recipe later in this chapter)*	1 cup	*chocolate-flavored whipped cream*
1/2 cup	*melted semisweet chocolate*	to taste	*chocolate ornaments (optional; see instructions later in this chapter)*
1/2 ounce	*gelatin*	8	*Florentine cookies (see recipe later in this chapter)*
1/2 cup	*tepid water, to bloom gelatin*		
2 cups	*heavy cream*	1 1/2 cups	*chocolate fondue (see recipe later in this chapter)*

GARNISH:

1/2 cup	*dry chocolate sponge cake crumbs*

1.   Combine the warm vanilla sauce and melted chocolate in a 3-quart mixing bowl.

2.   Combine the gelatin with the water; let bloom. Add to the chocolate/vanilla sauce mixture.

3. Place the mixture in an ice bath, and stir until it starts to thicken.

4. Whip the cream to soft peaks, and gently fold into the mixture.

5. Pour immediately into metal timbales or cake molds, and refrigerate for at least 3 hours.

6. To unmold, dip the timbales in hot water, and turn the bavarians out onto chilled serving plates. Sift the dry cake crumbs gently over the top. Decorate with chocolate-flavored whipped cream and chocolate ornaments if desired. Place a Florentine cookie next to each bavarian. Spoon the cold chocolate fondue around the bavarians (see color plate 62).

Bavarese Tricolori con Purea di Lamponi e Ribes
CHOCOLATE, VANILLA, AND STRAWBERRY BAVARIAN CREAMS WITH RASPBERRY AND RED-CURRANT PUREE

Yield: 8 servings

1. This dessert simply consists of a presentation of the three previous bavarian creams. Pour each of the bavarian cream mixtures into 2-inch circular timbale molds, and refrigerate for at least 3 hours.

2. To unmold, dip the timbales in hot water, and carefully turn one of each flavor onto each chilled serving plate. Cut each in half.

3. Arrange neatly in a fan shape, and decorate with a chocolate ornament and a Florentine cookie (see color plate 63).

4. Serve with any fruit puree.

Bavarese allo Yogurt con Fragole

YOGURT BAVARIAN WITH FRESH STRAWBERRIES

Any seasonal fruit may be substituted here. If the fruit has a high acid content, it should be quickly cooked before adding the gelatin.

Yield: 6 servings

2 cups	fresh strawberries	2 tablespoons	maraschino liqueur
1/2 ounce	confectioners' sugar	3 to 4 ounces	sugar
2 tablespoons	brandy	2 cups	plain yogurt
1/2 ounce	gelatin	1 cup	strawberry puree (see recipe later in this chapter)
1/2 cup	tepid water		
1 cup	heavy cream	6	mint sprigs
4 tablespoons	freshly squeezed orange juice		
2 tablespoons	freshly squeezed lemon juice		

1.   Clean, stem, and quarter the strawberries. Combine with the sugar and brandy, and macerate for 30 minutes.

2.   Stir the gelatin into the water, and let bloom for 10 minutes.

3.   Whip the cream to soft peaks.

4.   Heat the gelatin and water in a 2-quart stainless steel bowl over a warm water bath until the gelatin is completely melted. Add the citrus juices, maraschino, and sugar. Cool slightly, add the yogurt, and then gently fold in the whipped cream.

5.   Spoon the macerated strawberries into parfait or sundae glasses.

6.   Fill the glasses three-quarters full with the yogurt cream, and refrigerate until set.

7.   Spoon 2½ tablespoons of strawberry puree on top of each sundae. Garnish with a dollop of whipped cream (optional) and the mint leaves.

Bordure di Riso con Pere Cotte e Purea di Lamponi

RICE PUDDING RINGS WITH POACHED PEARS AND RASPBERRY PUREE

Yield: 12 servings

RICE PUDDING:

1 cup	water
3¹/₃ ounces	rice
1 teaspoon	butter
3 cups	hot milk
1¹/₂ ounces	sugar
¹/₂ teaspoon	grated lemon zest
to taste	vanilla extract
1 teaspoon	gelatin
¹/₄ cup	tepid water
2	egg yolks
³/₄ cup	heavy cream

PEAR GARNISH:

12	small Bosc pears

1 cup	dry white wine
2 quarts	water
8 to 10 ounces	sugar
1	cinnamon stick
4	whole cloves
³/₄ cup	freshly squeezed lemon juice
1¹/₂ cups	raspberry puree (see recipe later in this chapter)
1 tablespoon	confectioners' sugar
³/₄ cup	fresh cream
12	mint leaves

1. Bring 1 cup of water to a boil in a noncorrosive saucepan. Add the rice, and cook, uncovered, for about 5 minutes. Drain.

2. Add the butter and hot milk, and simmer, covered, over low heat or in a preheated 300°F oven for 30 minutes. Add the sugar, lemon zest, and vanilla, and cook for another 10 minutes. Remove from the oven or stove.

3. Soak the gelatin in the tepid water for 5 to 10 minutes, to bloom.

4. Mix the egg yolks with 2 tablespoons of cream.

5. Fold the gelatin into the rice, followed by the egg yolks. The rice should be hot enough to achieve an emulsion but not so hot as to coagulate the eggs.

6. Cool completely, stirring occasionally. Whip the remaining 5 fluid ounces of cream to soft peaks and gently fold into the cooled rice.

7. Pour immediately into prepared ¹/₄-cup ring molds that have been rinsed in cold water. Cover the filled molds with plastic wrap, and cool. When cool, refrigerate until ready to serve.

(continued)

8. Peel the pears, leaving the stems intact, and submerge immediately in acidulated water. Combine the wine, water, sugar, cinnamon, cloves, and lemon juice in a deep stainless steel half hotel pan. Bring to a simmer, add the pears, and poach gently until soft, about 8 to 15 minutes depending on the ripeness of the pears. Cool the pears in the liquid.

9. Cut off the stem ends of the pears about one-quarter of the way down, and scoop out the centers of the bottoms with a melon baller. Wrap the pear pieces with plastic wrap, and chill until ready to serve.

10. Dip the rice molds quickly in hot water, and unmold carefully onto chilled serving plates. Fill the pear cavities with raspberry puree, replace the tops, and set in the center of the rice rings.

11. Combine the confectioners' sugar with the ¾ cup of cream to firm peaks, and decorate the dessert with this whipped cream and the mint leaves.

Torta di Ricotta Siciliana con Purea di Lamponi
SICILIAN CHEESECAKE WITH RASPBERRY PUREE

Yield: **12 servings**

⅓ cup	finely chopped candied fruits	3	eggs, separated
¼ cup	white maraschino liqueur	1 teaspoon	cinnamon
		1 teaspoon	grated lemon zest
1 cup	apricot puree (see recipe later in this chapter)	1¾ pounds	ricotta, finely pureed
		¾ cup	heavy cream
1	10-inch sponge cake (see recipe earlier in this chapter)	3½ ounces	baking (bitter) chocolate, coarsely grated
5½ ounces	sugar	½ cups	finely chopped hazelnuts
2 tablespoons	freshly squeezed lemon juice		
6 tablespoons	water	1½ cups	raspberry puree (see recipe later in this chapter)
pinch	cream of tartar		

1.   Macerate the candied fruits in the maraschino for 30 minutes.

2.   Spread the bottom of a springform pan with half the apricot puree.

3.   Cut the sponge cake into 2 even layers. Place the top layer upside down in springform pan on top of the puree.

4.   Combine 4 ounces of sugar, the lemon juice, and the water in a clean stainless steel saucepan, and bring to a boil. Add the cream of tartar, and boil until syrupy, about 230°F.

5.   Lightly beat the egg yolks in a suitable bowl, and slowly whisk in the sugar syrup until light and creamy. Add the cinnamon and lemon zest, and fold in the ricotta.

6.   Beat the egg whites to soft peaks. Add the remaining 1½ ounces of sugar, and continue to beat until stiff.

7.   Whip the cream to soft peaks.

8.   Gently fold the egg whites into the ricotta mixture, followed by the whipped cream.

9.   Fold in the grated chocolate, hazelnuts, and drained macerated candied fruits.

10.   Pour the mixture over the sponge layer in the springform pan. Top with the second sponge layer, pressing it gently onto the cheese mixture. Spread the remaining apricot puree over the second sponge layer.

11.   Cover completely with plastic wrap and place in the freezer until needed.

12.   Before serving, place the cheesecake in the refrigerator to soften. Slice the cake, and serve with raspberry puree spooned around each slice. Decorate with neatly sliced fresh fruits if desired.

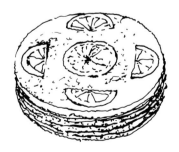

Tirami-Su

COFFEE SPONGE CAKE WITH MASCARPONE CREAM

Meaning literally "pick-me-up," this dessert was created about twenty years ago by the owner of El Toula, a restaurant in Treviso. *Tirami-Su* has gained worldwide popularity in a very short time and, like most other famous recipes, has already spawned numerous variations.

To make the vanilla-flavored confectioners' sugar, store the sugar in a closed container with a vanilla bean.

Yield: 12 servings

4 or 5	egg yolks	2	sponge cake sheets, about 7 by 9 by ½ inches (see recipe earlier in this chapter)
3 ounces	vanilla-flavored confectioners' sugar		
2 tablespoons	rum		
10 ounces	Mascarpone	1 pint	strong coffee (espresso or mocha)
2	egg whites		
2 ounces	granulated sugar	2 ounces	cocoa powder
¾ cup	heavy cream		

1. Beat the egg yolks with the confectioners' sugar until thick. Add the rum.

2. Whisk the Mascarpone until smooth, and fold into the egg yolk mixture.

3. Whip the egg whites with the granulated sugar until very stiff. In another bowl, whip the cream to soft peaks.

4. Fold the stiff egg whites gently into the yolk/Mascarpone mixture, followed by the whipped cream.

5. Place the sponge cake sheets on a suitable pan, and brush 1 with the strong coffee.

6. Spread half the Mascarpone cream evenly over each of the sponge cake layers. Place the coffee-soaked layer over the other layer. Spread the rest of the Mascarpone cream on top.

7. Sprinkle with the cocoa powder, and refrigerate for 3 to 6 hours before serving.

8. Cut into even-sized portions to serve. *Tirami-Su* can also be constructed in individual-size molds.)

Zuccotto

CHOCOLATE SPONGE CAKE FILLED WITH CHOCOLATE WHIPPED CREAM AND NUTS

Yield: 10 to 12 servings

1	basic sponge cake (see recipe earlier in this chapter)	1½ ounces	hazelnuts, finely chopped
3 tablespoons	Amaretto	1½ ounces	almonds, toasted and finely chopped
3 tablespoons	Grand Marnier	2 ounces	candied fruits, chopped
1½ pints	heavy cream		
3½ ounces	confectioners' sugar, sifted	1 ounce	cocoa powder
3½ ounces	semisweet chocolate, coarsely grated		

1. Slice the sponge cake into 3½-inch-thick layers, and then cut one layer into narrow triangular wedges. Reserve the rest of the sponge cake for another use.

2. Line a round bombe mold or stainless steel 3-quart mixing bowl with plastic wrap.

3. Combine the Amaretto and Grand Marnier and brush the sponge cake lightly with the liqueurs. Line the inside of the mold or bowl with the dampened sponge triangles, with the points meeting at the center and the broad ends extending toward the rim of the mold.

4. Whip the cream to soft peaks, and gently fold in the confectioners' sugar, chocolate, hazelnuts, and almonds. Divide this mixture into 2 bowls. Add the candied fruits to the first bowl, and fill the sponge-lined mold with this. Cover with another layer of sponge layer circle of suitable diameter to seal. Cover with plastic wrap, and place a light weight on top. Refrigerate overnight.

5. Unmold, and remove the plastic wrap. Coat the entire cake evenly and smoothly with the reserved chocolate whipped cream.

6. Dust with cocoa powder, and cut into uniform wedges. Decorate further with vanilla whipped cream and chocolate shavings if desired.

Torta allo Zabaione di Cioccolata

CHOCOLATE SABAYON CAKE

The following recipe is extremely rich, but for chocolate lovers it is unmatched. Prepare the chocolate sponge cake for this recipe a day ahead of time.

Yield: 16 servings

1	chocolate sponge cake (see recipe earlier in this chapter)	4 ounces	sugar
		4 ounces	Marsala
		4 teaspoons	gelatin
1 cup	water	1/2 cup	tepid water
2 ounces	sugar	1³/₄ cups	heavy cream
2 tablespoons	freshly squeezed orange juice	4 ounces	semisweet chocolate, melted
2 tablespoons	freshly squeezed lemon juice		

CHOCOLATE SABAYON FILLING:

CHOCOLATE WHIPPED CREAM:

		4 ounces	semisweet chocolate
6	egg yolks	2 cups	heavy cream

1.   Slice 2 very thin layers from the sponge cake for this recipe. Freeze the rest for another use.

2.   Boil the cup of water in a stainless steel saucepan. Add the sugar and citrus juices, and cook and stir for a few minutes. Cool.

3.   Sprinkle both layers of the sponge cake generously with the cooled sugar syrup. Place 1 layer into a 10-inch cake pan.

4.   Beat the egg yolks, sugar, and Marsala in a 4-quart stainless steel bowl over a hot water bath until the mixture reaches 110°F. Remove from the heat, and continue to whip until fluffy and at room temperature. Dissolve the gelatin in the tepid water. Whip the cream to soft peaks. Add the gelatin and melted chocolate to the egg yolk mixture. Fold in the whipped cream.

5.   Pour the *sabayon* filling onto the sponge layer in the cake pan, and cover with the second sponge layer. Cover with plastic wrap, and refrigerate for at least 3 hours.

6.   To unmold, dip the cake pan quickly in hot water and turn out onto a suitable chilled tray. Refrigerate again.

7. Melt the 4 ounces of semisweet chocolate in a 2-quart stainless steel bowl over a hot water bath. Whip the heavy cream in a 4-quart mixing bowl to soft peaks. Add half of the whipped cream to the chocolate, and mix until smooth. Gently fold in the remaining whipped cream.

8. Spread the top and sides of the cake neatly and evenly with the chocolate whipped cream. Using a pastry bag and tip, make 16 chocolate rosettes from the remaining chocolate whipped cream evenly spaced along the top edge of the cake. Decorate with chocolate ornaments if desired (see color plate 64).

Torta di Albicocche

APRICOT CAKE

This recipe is unique in its simplicity and yet is extremely versatile. It does not dry out as easily as sponge cake does, and because oil is used as the fat, less work is required to prepare it. To make the vanilla sugar for the recipe, store a vanilla bean in a closed container of sugar for several days.

Yield: 16 servings

4	eggs	pinch	salt
8 ounces	sugar	7 tablespoons	oil
1 tablespoon	vanilla sugar	7 tablespoons	cold water
9 ounces	flour	16	very ripe apricots
1 teaspoon	baking powder	2 tablespoons	confectioners' sugar
1 teaspoon	grated lemon zest		

1. Whisk the eggs with the sugars in a stainless steel mixing bowl until thick and foamy.

2. Combine the flour, baking powder, lemon zest, and salt, and fold into the egg mixture.

3. Very gently fold in the oil and water.

4. Brush a 10-inch springform pan generously with melted butter and dust with flour.

5. Pour the cake batter into the pan. Halve the apricots, and arrange neatly, cut side up, on top of the batter.

(continued)

6.   Bake in a preheated 350° to 360°F oven for 45 minutes. Cool completely.

7.   Before unhinging the pan, make sure the cake is not sticking to its sides. If it is, slide a thin knife between the cake and the pan. Unmold. Dust with confectioners' sugar before serving.

Crostate di Frutte Fresche

FRESH FRUIT TARTLETS

For fruit pies or tartlets, either the basic pie dough or sweetened tart dough receipe can be used.

Select only perfectly ripe, unblemished fruits or berries. Stone fruits should be peeled, sliced, and arranged in an overlapping fan or spiral shape over the top of the pastry cream for individual tartlets, and overlapped in a continuous pattern for larger tarts and pies. If fresh berries are available, they may be interchanged with the fruit wedges.

For the glaze, select fruit jelly compatible in color and flavor with the fresh fruit in the tart. For light-colored tarts, apricot, quince, or apple jelly is ideal. Black-currant, red-currant, or strawberry jelly works well with dark fruits or berries. Melt the preserves before using, and strain them through a fine-mesh sieve.

All the components for this recipe, except for the pastry cream and fresh fruit, can be prepared well in advance.

Yield: 12 servings

1 pound	*sweetened tart dough (see recipe earlier in this chapter)*
2½ cups	*basic pastry cream (see recipe earlier in this chapter)*
1 pound	*fresh fruit and berries*
1 cup	*melted, strained fruit jelly*

1.   Roll the tart dough out about ⅛ inch thick, and cut into circles slightly larger than the circumference of the tartlet molds, or about 3½ inches in diameter.

2.   Press the circles gently into the tartlet molds, so that the molds are completely lined with the dough. Cut away any dough that extends over the rims of the molds.

3.   Prick the dough with a fork, and place another well-greased mold of the same size on top of the dough. Fill the second mold with dried beans or peas, and refrigerate for 2 hours.

4.   Place the tartlets on a preheated sheet pan in a preheated 375°F oven, and bake for 8 minutes. Lower the temperature to 325°F, and bake for another 6 to 8 minutes. If the shells are still too pale, remove the second shell with the beans, and return the uncovered shells to the oven until nicely browned. Let cool.

5.   Fill the tartlet shells with the pastry cream.

6.   Arrange the fruit or berries neatly over the pastry cream.

7.   Gently brush the heated fruit jelly on the fruit. Chill, and serve.

Mousse alla Cioccolata

CHOCOLATE MOUSSE

Any compatible liqueur can be added to flavor this mousse, such as Frangelico, Sambuca, Grand Marnier, Kirsch, or maraschino.

Yield: 6 to 8 servings

3	*egg yolks*
2 tablespoons	*Marsala*
2 tablespoons	*brandy*
4 to 5 ounces	*semisweet chocolate, melted*
1 cup	*heavy cream*
3	*egg whites*
1 ounce	*sugar*
to garnish	*whipped cream*
to garnish	*chocolate shavings*

1.   Combine the egg yolks, Marsala, and brandy in a 3-quart stainless steel mixing bowl. Whip over a hot water bath until thick and creamy. Remove from the heat.

2.   Stir in the melted chocolate.

(continued)

3.   Whip the cream to soft peaks.

4.   Beat the egg whites with the sugar until stiff.

5.   Gently fold the whipped cream into the chocolate mixture. Fold in the egg whites. All ingredients should be completely combined.

6.   Spoon into suitable serving dishes, and refrigerate until well chilled and set, about 2 hours.

7.   Decorate with a rosette of whipped cream and chocolate shavings. Serve with wafers or ladyfingers if desired.

Zabaione al Cioccolato in Tazzette con Fonduta alla Cioccolata
CHOCOLATE SABAYON TIMBALES WITH CHOCOLATE FONDUE

Yield: 6 servings

3	egg yolks	1 ½ cups	chocolate fondue, cold, (see recipe later in this chapter)
1 ounce	sugar		
¼ cup	Marsala		
2 tablespoons	maraschino liqueur	1 ½ cups	vanilla-flavored whipped cream
2 teaspoons	gelatin		
¼ cup	water	6	Florentine cookies (see recipe later in this chapter
3 ounces	semisweet chocolate, melted		
7 fluid ounces	heavy cream, whipped to soft peaks	as desired	chocolate ornaments (see instructions later in this chapter)
1 cup	dry chocolate sponge cake crumbs		

1.   Beat the egg yolks, sugar, Marsala, and maraschino together in a 2-quart stainless steel mixing bowl over a hot water bath until the mixture reaches 110°F. Remove from the heat, and continue to beat until cold and fluffy.

2.   Dissolve the gelatin in the water, and add to the yolk mixture.

3.   Add the melted chocolate. Whip the cream to soft peaks, and gently fold into the *sabayon*.

4.   Fill six 4-ounce metal timbale molds with the mixture, and refrigerate for 3 hours.

5.   To unmold, dip the molds into hot water, and carefully turn over onto chilled serving plates. Coat the sides with the chocolate cake crumbs.

6.   Spoon ¼ cup of chocolate fondue near each timbale, and decorate with the vanilla whipped cream and a Florentine cookie. If desired, add chocolate ornaments to garnish (see color plate 65).

Bomba di Marzipane
MARZIPAN BOMBE

To prepare this three-layered cream bombe, all components should be prepared ahead of time and be handy during assembly.

Save the remaining layers of the vanilla and chocolate sponge cakes for another purpose (they freeze fairly well). The sweet cherries may also be cooked in advance if kept refrigerated.

The marzipan (almond paste) is best if purchased already made and then combined with the pistachio paste. If desired, the pale green color of the pistachio paste may be augmented with a bit of a green food coloring.

To prepare the vanilla sugar, store a vanilla bean with the sugar in a closed container for several days.

Yield: 16 servings

36	sweet cherries, pitted	2 ounces	semisweet chocolate, melted
¼ cup	freshly squeezed lemon juice	2 ounces	vanilla sugar
4 ounces	sugar	1	10-inch layer of vanilla sponge cake (see recipe earlier in this chapter)
¾ cup	dry red wine		
2 tablespoons	maraschino liqueur		
2 tablespoons	Kirsch	1	10-inch layer of chocolate sponge cake (see recipe earlier in this chapter)
3 ounces	stemmed fresh strawberries		
1 cup	water		
2 tablespoons	freshly squeezed orange juice	4 ounces	confectioners' sugar
		1 pound	marzipan
3 cups	heavy cream	2 to 3 ounces	pistachio paste

(continued)

1. Place the pitted cherries, 2 tablespoons of lemon juice, 2 ounces of sugar, and red wine in a stainless steel saucepan or enameled casserole. Bring to a simmer, cover, and cook over low heat for about 5 to 8 minutes. Remove to a suitable smaller container, and cool. Strain off the liquid, and add the maraschino and Kirsch to the cherries. Refrigerate until ready to use.

2. Puree the strawberries, and let rest in a fine-mesh sieve to remove excess liquid. Reserve both the fruit and liquid.

3. Boil the cup of water in a stainless steel saucepan. Add the remaining 2 ounces of sugar, the remaining 2 tablespoons of lemon juice, and the orange juice, and cook and stir for a few minutes. Cool this sugar syrup.

4. Whip the cream to soft peaks. Divide the cream equally into three 2-quart mixing bowls. Mix the melted chocolate into the cream in the first bowl and chill. In the second, combine the cream with the strawberry puree. Beat the cream further until stiff. In the third, beat in the vanilla sugar and chill.

5. Cut two ¼-inch-thick layers of both sponge cakes.

6. Place 1 chocolate sponge layer in a 10-inch cake pan. Brush lightly with the sugar syrup. Spread a very thin layer of the chocolate whipped cream over this layer. Using a pastry bag with a plain tip, pipe a large dot of the chocolate whipped cream in the middle of the cream-coated chocolate sponge, pipe a circle about 1 to 2 inches out from this dot, and pipe a circle around the outer edge of the layer.

7. Place the macerated cherries between the whipped cream circles.

8. Top with a layer of vanilla sponge cake, and again brush with sugar syrup. Spread with a thin layer of vanilla whipped cream.

9. Place a second layer of chocolate sponge over the vanilla whipped cream, and press the edges gently to begin the shaping of the bombe. Brush with the sugar syrup.

10. Mound the strawberry whipped cream on the chocolate sponge, creating a classic bombe shape with a metal spatula.

11. Place the last layer of vanilla sponge over the strawberry cream, and again press gently around the edges to create a bombe shape. Brush with sugar syrup, and refrigerate for 1 hour.

12. Dust a worktable with the confectioners' sugar, and work the marzipan and pistachio paste together. Add green food coloring if desired. The marzipan should not stick to the work surface; add more sugar if needed.

13. Spread more confectioners' sugar on the worktable, and roll out the paste with a plain rolling pin. When the sheet is even and large enough to cover the surface of the bombe, roll it once more with a patterned rolling pin to give it a decorative pattern.

14. Cover the bombe with the marzipan sheet, carefully pressing to eliminate air spaces and to avoid wrinkles.

15. Trim the edges of the marzipan (save the trimmings for another use).

16. Decorate with tempered chocolate ornaments (see instruction later in this chapter) or with any decorative garnish as desired (see color plate 66).

Cannoli alla Siciliana

SICILIAN CREAM HORNS

Yield: 12 cream horns

6 ounces	flour	1 ounce	semisweet chocolate, coarsely grated
1 tablespoon	sugar		
½ teaspoon	instant coffee granules	½ cup	chopped candied orange peel (see recipe later in this chapter)
1 teaspoon	cocoa powder		
1 ounce	shortening or lard		
1	egg, lightly beaten	to taste	vanilla extract
½ cup	Marsala	6 tablespoons	heavy cream (optional)
pinch	salt		
1¼ pounds	ricotta, very fresh	to deep-fry	oil
3½ ounces	confectioners' sugar	¼ cup	chopped pistachios

1. Combine the flour, sugar, coffee, and cocoa powder in a mixing bowl, and work in the shortening with the fingers until the mixture resembles crumbs.

2. Add half of the egg, the Marsala, and the salt, and knead into a smooth dough. Let rest for 30 minutes.

3. Puree the ricotta in food processor, and transfer to a mixing bowl. Whisk in the confectioners' sugar, chocolate, candied orange peel, and vanilla extract. If desired, whip the cream to soft peaks and gently fold into the mixture.

4. With the palms of your hands, press the dough into a finger-thick layer. Cut into 12 pieces.

(continued)

5.   With a rolling pin, roll out each piece into a ¹⁄₁₆-inch-thick, 3½-inch-wide oval. Wrap each oval very loosely around a *cannoli* tube. Overlap the ends, brush with the remaining beaten egg, and pinch promptly to seal.

6.   Deep-fry the shells a few at a time in 350° to 375°F oil until very crisp and nicely browned. Place on absorbent paper to drain and cool.

7.   Remove the shells from the tubes before completely cool.

8.   Pipe the ricotta filling into the shells from both ends, using a pastry bag with a large plain tip.

9.   Dip the ends in the chopped pistachios, and dust with confectioners' sugar.

Savoiardi

LADYFINGERS

Yield: 40 to 50 ladyfingers

6	egg yolks
6 ounces	sugar
2 tablespoons	freshly squeezed lemon juice
6	egg whites
6 ounces	cake flour, well sifted
to dust	sugar

1.   Whisk the egg yolks with half the sugar until thick. Add the lemon juice.

2.   Beat the egg whites with the remaining sugar until stiff, and fold into the egg yolk mixture.

3.   Fold in the flour very gently.

4.   Fit a pastry bag with a plain tip. Cover a sheet pan with parchment paper that has been folded lengthwise in quarters. Pipe the mixture using the folds as a guideline for uniform length: pipe straight from fold to fold, or at an angle for longer ladyfingers.

5.   Sprinkle lightly and evenly with sugar, and bake in a preheated 400°F oven, with another sheet pan underneath to prevent scorching, until pale brown (see color plate 67).

Amaretti

MACAROONS

Yield: 60 macaroons

8 ounces	almond paste
8 ounces	sugar
3 to 4	egg whites

1.   Combine all ingredients into a smooth paste. The mixture should be stiff enough so that it will not run.

2.   Using a pastry bag with a plain tip, pipe the mixture onto a parchment-covered sheet pan in quarter-sized dots. Sprinkle with sugar, and bake in a preheated 350°F oven, with another sheet pan underneath to prevent scorching, until nicely browned (see color plate 67).

Biscotti alla Fiorentina

FLORENTINE COOKIES

Yield: 50 cookies

2½ ounces	butter, softened	6 ounces	candied fruits, finely diced
8 ounces	confectioners' sugar		
½ cup	heavy cream	2 ounces	bread flour
6 ounces	hazelnuts, finely ground	1 cup	melted semisweet chocolate

1.   Cream the butter and sugar in a stainless steel mixing bowl. Whisk in the heavy cream. Add the hazelnuts and candied fruits, and stir in the flour.

2.   Drop the batter with a spoon, or pipe using a pastry bag with a plain tip, onto a greased sheet pan. The drops should be quarter-sized. Leave plenty of space between each drop, as they expand quite a bit.

3.   Bake in a preheated 400°F oven until the edges start to brown.

(continued)

4.   Remove the cookies from the pan with a flexible spatula, and cool on a wire rack.

5.   Brush the bottoms with the melted, tempered chocolate (the chocolate should be approximately 86°F when brushed). Cool until the chocolate hardens (if tempered correctly, this should be in a matter of minutes). Store airtight in a cool place until needed. See color plate 67 for presentation.

Scorzette d'Arancia Candite
CANDIED ORANGE PEEL

Candied orange peel is used in the same way as candied fruits, as well as for garnishing desserts and ice creams. If the oranges are fresh and the peels firm, use a sharp vegetable peeler to cut off the peels, without the white pith underneath. (This colored peel is called the zest.)

Yield: 4 to 5 cups

1 pound	orange zest, cut into ¼-inch strips
10 ounces	sugar
1¼ cups	water

1.   Soak the strips of zest for 4 days in cold water in a noncorrosive container, changing the water daily.

2.   Drain, and cook the orange zest in fresh water for 10 minutes. Drain again.

3.   Combine the sugar and water in a stainless steel saucepan, and bring to a simmer (this syrup may be flavored to taste with an appropriate liqueur if desired). Add the orange strips, and cook until the liquid becomes syrupy.

4.   Drain off the syrup, and roll the orange strips in granulated (or crystal) sugar while still warm. Place the candied strips on a noncorrosive tray, and let them dry for about 3 days.

5.   Store the candied orange peels in a glass or metal container with a tight-fitting lid in a dry place until needed.

Fonduta di Cioccolata
CHOCOLATE FONDUE

Yield: 3 cups

2 cups	heavy cream
8 ounces	semisweet chocolate, coarsely grated

1.   Heat the heavy cream to a boil, and add the chocolate. Remove from the heat, and stir until smooth. If desired, the fondue can be flavored to taste with brandy or liqueur. Serve hot or cold.

Salsa di Cioccolata
CHOCOLATE SAUCE

This sauce is excellent hot or cold.

Yield: 2 cups

4 ounces	sugar
5 fluid ounces	water
5 ounces	baking chocolate, grated
1 ounce	cocoa powder (unsweetened)
5 fluid ounces	heavy cream

1.   Boil the sugar with the water in a very clean 1-quart stainless steel saucepan for several minutes.

2.   Reduce the heat, add the grated chocolate and cocoa powder, and bring to a simmer, stirring until well combined.

3.   Add the cream, and remove from the heat.

4.   Use immediately, or chill.

Salsa di Caramella

CARAMEL SAUCE

Caramel syrups and sauces are used mainly for ice creams and puddings.

Yield: 2 cups

3 ounces	sweet butter
8 to 10 ounces	sugar
1½ cups	heavy cream
2	egg yolks
to taste	vanilla extract, or any liqueur

1.   Melt the butter with the sugar in a stainless steel skillet. Cook over moderate heat until lightly caramelized, stirring continuously with a clean wooden spoon.

2.   Add the cream, and simmer slowly until completely dissolved in the caramel sauce. Cool.

3.   Place the sauce in a blender (not a food processor), and add the egg yolks and flavoring. Blend until velvety and smooth. Store in a tightly covered glass container. The sauce should keep for at least 1 week in clean, well-chilled containers.

Sciroppa di Lamponi

RASPBERRY SYRUP

For this recipe, select only the freshest unblemished berries, picked on a sunny day, preferably in the late afternoon. Crush the berries to release their juices in a glass or ceramic bowl to which a little sugar has been added. Do *not* use an aluminum bowl.

Let the berries steep in the sugar and their own juices, at room temperature, for at least 2 days, or until a raft clearly forms on the top. This indicates that the pulp has risen and that the desired juices have settled underneath. Line a stainless steel china cap with moistened cheesecloth, and pour in the fruit. Do not agitate or stir. Let the juices drain freely through the cloth into a clean glass or ceramic container. This may take a while, so it is best to just cover the china cap with plastic wrap and let it sit until drained dry.

This technique can be used for almost any fruit syrup, including currants, gooseberries, cranberries, blueberries, and strawberries. If using cranberries, red currants, or gooseberries, more sugar may have to be used to compensate for the greater acidity of the berries.

If the syrup is intended to last a year or more, sterilize all glass jars or bottles in which they will be stored, together with their seals and lids. Do this by boiling them for 20 minutes in water just before filling with the finished syrup. Remove the sterilized containers from the water with clean metal tongs and drain. Fill immediately with hot syrup up to ½ inch from the top, and cover the mouth of the jar with a small piece of plastic wrap. Seal tightly with a screw lid. Cool the bottles on a vented rack, and store in a dark place. These syrups can be used for glazes and can even be used for jellies if gelatin or pectin is added to the reheated syrups.

Yield: 2 cups

6 tablespoons	water
2 tablespoons	freshly squeezed lemon juice
1½ cups	sugar
1½ cups	freshly strained raspberry juice

1.   Bring the water and lemon juice to a boil in a 3-quart stainless steel saucepan. Add the sugar, and boil until the mixture has a heavy syrupy consistency, or a liquid temperature of 245°F.

2.   Add the raspberry juice to the cooked sugar, and cook rapidly for about 5 minutes. Skim off any impurities that rise to the top. Pour the syrup into a hot, clean glass or ceramic container.

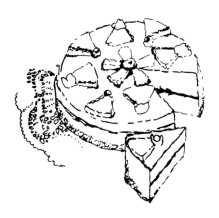

Composta di Susine

PLUM COMPOTE

Cooking brings out a remarkable aroma in plums. Aside from their high nutritional value, plums are perhaps the most versatile fruit in the kitchen.

For this recipe, select very ripe, small Italian plums or other dark, oval varieties. The skin should not be removed, as it adds color and flavor to the compote. If peeling is for some reason necessary, plunge the fruit (not too many at a time) into boiling water for about 30 seconds, and shock in cold water. The skins should slide off easily.

As with other acid fruits, never use utensils made of anything but stainless steel or some other noncorrosive material for plums. If storing for prolonged periods of time, package in sterilized jars as for fruit syrups (see the preceding recipe).

Yield: 2 cups

1 pound	ripe Italian plums
2 ounces	sugar
1 tablespoon	freshly squeezed lemon juice
1/2	cinnamon stick
1/2 teaspoon	grated lemon zest

1.   Wash the plums, remove the pits, and quarter.

2.   In an enameled or stainless steel pot, melt the sugar with the lemon juice. Add the plum quarters, cinnamon, and grated lemon zest. Cook over moderate heat for about 10 minutes. Remove from the heat. The hot compote can be served with a variety of desserts, such as pancakes, steamed puddings, sweet *gnocchi,* or fritters or it can be stored in sterilized jars for future use.

Purea di Lamponi

RASPBERRY PUREE

Yield: 1¼ cups

12 ounces	fresh, ripe raspberries, cleaned
3 ounces	confectioners' sugar
¼ cup	raspberry liqueur

1.   Crush the raspberries with the sugar in a glass or ceramic bowl. Add the raspberry liqueur, and let steep for 15 minutes.

2.   Puree through the fine blade of a stainless steel food mill. Keep refrigerated in a suitable glass jar with a tight-fitting cover.

Purea di Lamponi e Ribes Rosse

RASPBERRY AND RED-CURRANT PUREE

Yield: 1¼ cups

8 ounces	fresh, ripe raspberries, cleaned
4 ounces	fresh red currants, cleaned and stemmed
4 ounces	confectioners' sugar
¼ cup	crème de cassis

1.   Crush the raspberries and currants with the sugar and crème de cassis, and let steep in a glass or ceramic bowl for 15 minutes.

2.   Puree through the fine blade of a stainless steel food mill. Keep refrigerated in a suitable glass jar with a tight-fitting cover.

Purea di Fragole

STRAWBERRY PUREE

Yield: 1¼ cups

12 ounces	fresh, ripe strawberries
1½ ounces	confectioners' sugar
1 tablespoon	Grand Marnier
1 tablespoon	freshly squeezed lemon juice

1.   Stem the strawberries, and cut into smaller pieces. Wash quickly in fresh water, and drain.

2.   Combine the strawberries, confectioners' sugar, Grand Marnier, and lemon juice, and steep together for 10 minutes.

3.   Puree through the fine blade of a stainless steel food mill into a glass jar. Cover with a tight-fitting cover, and store refrigerated.

Purea di Albicocche

APRICOT PUREE

Yield: 1¾ to 2 cups

½ cup	light corn syrup
1 pound	very ripe apricots
1 teaspoon	grated orange zest
2 tablespoons	white maraschino liqueur

1. Heat the syrup in a 2-quart stainless steel saucepan.

2. Remove the pits from the apricots, and cut into smaller pieces. Add to the syrup with the grated orange zest, and cook for about 5 minutes. Skim any impurities that rise to the top.

3. Puree through the fine blade of a stainless steel food mill, and add the white maraschino. Cool completely. Keep refrigerated in a suitable glass jar with a tight-fitting cover.

—— *Ornamenti di Cioccolata* ——
CHOCOLATE ORNAMENTS

To make chocolate ornaments that have a shiny, attractive appearance, the chocolate must be heated and tempered. Chocolate that is heated but not tempered will not harden properly and will look dull. To temper chocolate for molding:

1. Put finely chopped semisweet chocolate in a stainless steel mixing bowl, and melt slowly over a warm double boiler. Be very careful to prevent steam and water from coming into contact with the chocolate as it melts. If any water comes into contact with the chocolate, it will cause the cocoa butter in the chocolate to seize, making it grainy and unusable for molding. When three-quarters of the chocolate is melted, remove the mixing bowl from the heat, and continue to stir until the chocolate is entirely smooth.

2. Add solid pieces of chocolate to the melted chocolate (the amount depends on the quantity of chocolate you have melted), until the temperature of the chocolate is 90° to 92°F. Experienced chefs can monitor temperature by checking with the fingers or by bringing some of the chocolate up to the lower lip. When the temperature is 86°F, remove any unmelted chocolate, and use immediately.

To make solid geometric ornaments, the chocolate can be thinly spread onto parchment paper. When sufficiently hard, cut into the desired shapes. For delicate piped ornaments, make a paper cone from an elongated triangular piece of parchment paper, fill with the chocolate, and cut off the tip of the cone. Pipe the desired figures onto parchment paper or directly on the item to be decorated. To remove the ornaments from the paper, gently peel the chocolate away. This is most easily done on or near the edge of a table. Store the ornaments at room temperature if they are not to be used immediately.

— *Dolci caldi* —
HOT DESSERTS

Crema Inglese
VANILLA SAUCE

Vanilla sauce, sometimes called by its French name, *crème anglaise,* is the basis for countless other preparations, including pastry cream (with starch added), bavarians (with gelatin and whipped cream), custards (baked), and ice cream (frozen). The sauce can be flavored with fruit purees, ground nuts, chocolate, or liqueur. Common flavorings include Frangelico, Grand Marnier, maple syrup, raspberry puree, mocha, hazelnuts, or milk chocolate.

Yield: 3 cups

1 pint	*milk, light cream, or heavy cream*
1	*vanilla bean*
4 ounces	*sugar*
6 to 8	*egg yolks*

1.   Scald the milk with the vanilla bean and half of the sugar. Remove the bean.

2.   In another bowl, combine the remaining sugar with the egg yolks.

3.   Add a bit of the hot sweetened milk to the egg yolk mixture, then add the yolk mixture to the remaining hot sweetened milk. Whisk over a hot water bath until the cream lightly coats a spoon.

4.   Strain through a fine-mesh sieve.

Crema alla Cioccolata

CHOCOLATE CREAM SAUCE

Use light cream to prepare the vanilla sauce for this recipe.

Yield: 2 cups

4 ounces	*semisweet chocolate, melted*
1½ cups	*hot vanilla sauce (see preceding recipe)*
2 tablespoons	*Frangelico*

1.   Mix the melted chocolate into the hot vanilla sauce. Flavor with the Frangelico (or use ½ teaspoon of dry instant coffee). Serve with hot puddings or pastry.

Zabaione

ZABAGLIONE

Zabaglione, also called by its French name, *sabayon,* is made by cooking egg yolks, sugar, and wine together. Marsala wine is most commonly used, but any sweet wine, such as sherry, port, or Madeira, can be substituted. If dry white wine is used, flavor with an additional liquor, such as Kirsch or rum. Zabaglione is basically just a vanilla sauce that has wine rather than milk in it.

The formulas for zabaglione vary from source to source. It can be flavored in a number of different ways. Champagne may be used as the liquid, melted chocolate,

(continued)

whipped cream, and gelatin may be incorporated, and the cream can be combined with layers of sponge cake to make a zabaglione torte. Zabaglione can be served alone, with cookies, or with fresh fruit. It can also be used as a base for frozen *sabayon*.

Yield: 6 to 8 servings

1 cup	Marsala
1 cup	sugar (less if the wine is very sweet)
1 cup	egg yolks (approximately 10)

1.   Whisk together the sugar and egg yolks. Stir in the wine.

2.   Whisk the mixture constantly over a simmering double boiler until thick and foamy. Do not overcook yolks. Try to incorporate as much air during the whisking as possible.

Frutte Fresche allo Zabaione, Glassate
FRESH FRUIT GLAZED WITH ZABAGLIONE

Yield: 6 servings

2	ripe peaches	4 tablespoons	sugar
2	oranges	1/4 cup	raspberry liqueur
6	figs	1/4 cup	dry white wine
2 cups	fresh berries (such as strawberries, raspberries, blueberries)	1 teaspoon	grated lemon and orange zest
		to taste	vanilla extract
1/2 cup	heavy cream	6	mint sprigs
3	egg yolks		

1.   Peel the peaches and oranges. Remove the pits from the peaches, and slice into sections. Remove the membranes from the orange sections, and quarter the figs. Clean the berries. Larger berries, such as strawberries, should be halved.

2.   Arrange the berries in the center of a deep ovenproof serving plate or suitable shallow dish. Arrange the peaches, oranges, and figs in an attractive pattern around the berries. (This may all be prepared ahead of time.) Cover and chill.

3.   Whip the cream to soft peaks.

4.   Combine the egg yolks, sugar, raspberry liqueur, wine, citrus zests, and vanilla in a 2-quart stainless steel bowl. Whisk over a double broiler until thick and creamy. Fold in the whipped cream, and pour over the fruit. Glaze immediately under a salamander (top broiler) until lightly browned. Garnish with the mint leaves. If desired, fruit *sorbet* can be scooped on top, or ladyfingers can be served alongside (see recipes earlier in this chapter).

Pere Cotte al Mascarpone

POACHED PEARS FILLED WITH MASCARPONE IN FRUIT ZABAGLIONE

Yield: 6 servings

1½ cups	dry white wine	1½ ounces	confectioners' sugar
1½ cups	orange juice	2 tablespoons	brandy
¼ cup	lemon juice	3	egg yolks
½	cinnamon stick	1 teaspoon	finely grated orange zest
½	vanilla bean		
1½ ounces	sugar	6	macaroons, crushed (see recipe earlier in this chapter)
6	Bartlett or Bosc pears		
12 ounces	Mascarpone	6	mint sprigs

1.   Combine the white wine, orange juice, lemon juice, cinnamon stick, vanilla bean, and sugar in a small enameled or stainless steel bowl. Bring to a boil.

2.   Peel the pears, and halve lengthwise. Scoop out the cores, with the seeds, using a melon scoop. Poach the pear halves in the wine mixture until tender. Remove with a slotted spoon to a suitable plate. Cover and keep warm.

3.   Reduce the poaching liquid to 1 cup. Remove the cinnamon stick and vanilla bean.

4.   Combine the Mascarpone with the confectioners' sugar and brandy.

5.   Combine the egg yolks with 1 cup of the reduced poaching liquid and the grated orange zest. Whisk in a double boiler until thick and creamy.

6.   Spoon the zabaglione onto each heated serving plate, and place 2 pear halves, cut sides up, on the sauce. Fill the pear halves with the Mascarpone mixture, and top with the crushed macaroons. Decorate with mint sprigs.

Composta di Frutte con Gelato

WARM BERRY COMPOTE WITH VANILLA ICE CREAM

This dessert should be prepared just before serving to keep the berries as fresh as possible.

Yield: 6 servings

¼ cup	water	1 cup	black raspberries
¼ cup	orange juice	1½ cups	halved strawberries
2 tablespoons	lemon juice	2 ounces	butter
3 to 4 ounces	sugar	1½ pint	vanilla ice cream (see recipe earlier in this chapter)
1 cup	pitted cherries		
1 cup	blueberries	6	mint sprigs
1 cup	red raspberries		

1.   Combine the water, citrus juices, and sugar in a large stainless steel or enameled saucepan. Let simmer for a few minutes.

2.   Add the pitted cherries, and cook for 5 minutes.

3.   Add blueberries, raspberries, and strawberries, and bring to a simmer. Remove immediately from the heat.

4.   Cut the butter into small pieces, and gently swirl into the compote to create an emulsion.

5.   Serve immediately in deep plates with a large scoop of vanilla ice cream in the center of each. Garnish with a mint sprig.

Crespelle

SWEET CRÊPES

When deciding on a crêpe batter, it is important to consider how the crêpe is to be used, as different batters will produce different textures and consistencies. A fresh crêpe that is to be filled with preserves or creams should be more tender, and therefore more melted butter and less egg is added to the batter. On the other hand, crêpes intended for table service or topping with sauces should be stronger and less absorbent.

Yield: 12 to 16 crêpes

4 ounces	all-purpose flour	to taste	vanilla extract
1 1/2 cups	milk	pinch	salt
3	eggs	1/2 cup	clarified butter (see chapter 1)
1 tablespoon	melted butter		
1/2 tablespoon	sugar		
1/2 teaspoon	finely grated lemon zest		

1.   Combine the flour and half of the milk in a mixing bowl. Whisk to a smooth paste. Add the remaining milk, eggs, melted butter, sugar, lemon zest, vanilla, and salt. Let the batter rest for 1 hour.

2.   Heat the clarified butter in a 7-inch crêpe pan until very hot. Pour about 2 table-spoons of the batter into the center of the pan. Tilt the skillet quickly in a circular fashion to distribute the batter thinly and evenly over the entire bottom of the pan. Cook until lightly brown on both sides, turning once.

3.   If intended for later use, place the crêpes on a parchment-lined tray. Stack when cooled, and cover. See color plate **68** for presentation.

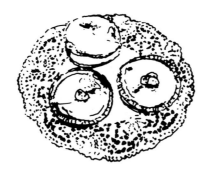

Crespelle di Ricotta con Crema Inglese

CRÊPES FILLED WITH RICOTTA CUSTARD IN VANILLA SAUCE

Yield: 6 servings

1½ ounces	raisins	1 ounce	sugar
2 tablespoons	maraschino liqueur	12	thin sweet crêpes (see preceding recipe)
3 ounces	sweet butter		
1 ounce	confectioners' sugar		
3	egg yolks	¼ cup	melted butter
1 teaspoon	grated lemon zest	2¼ cups	hot vanilla sauce (see recipe earlier in this chapter)
to taste	vanilla extract		
9 ounces	ricotta, finely pureed	to dust	confectioners' sugar
3	egg whites		

1.   Combine the raisins with the maraschino, and macerate for 30 minutes.

2.   Cream the butter, confectioners' sugar, and egg yolks together gradually. Add the lemon zest, vanilla, and ricotta.

3.   Beat the egg whites to soft peaks, and add the sugar. Continue to beat until stiff. Fold the whites gently into the ricotta mixture, and add the macerated raisins.

4.   Spoon the ricotta mixture onto the crêpes. Fold over ½ inch of the crêpe on both sides. Then roll around the filling.

5.   Place the crêpes on a buttered ovenproof serving dish, and brush with the melted butter. Heat in a preheated 350°F oven for about 7 to 9 minutes. Do not overheat, or the ricotta will swell and seep out.

6.   Spoon the vanilla sauce around the crêpes, and dust with confectioners' sugar. Serve immediately.

Crespelle con Frutte Fresche al Galliano
CRÊPES WITH FRESH FRUIT IN GALLIANO

Seedless grapes, canteloupe, pears, apricots, peaches, strawberries, and raspberries are just some of the fruits that go well in this dessert.

Yield: 6 servings

2 ounces	sugar	2 cups	diced fresh fruit and berries
4 ounces	butter		
¼ cup	Galliano	18	small strawberries
6 tablespoons	orange juice	6	mint sprigs
12	sweet crêpes (see recipe earlier in this chapter)	2 cups	ice cream, 1 cup of each flavor (optional; see recipe earlier in this chapter)
¾ cup	basic pastry cream (see recipe earlier in this chapter)		

1. Melt the sugar in a bimetal copper *sauteuse*. Add the butter, and when it has completely melted, add the Galliano. Ignite the liqueur, and deglaze the pan with the orange juice. Stir until completely dissolved.

2. Dip each crêpe in the sauce, and fill with 2 tablespoons of the pastry cream. Add the mixed fruit, and fold. Place 2 filled crêpes on each serving plate, and top with some of the Galliano sauce. Garnish with small strawberry sections and mint sprigs (see color plate 68). Two balls of different ice creams can be scooped alongside the crêpes if desired.

Gnocchetti di Patate di Papaneri con Composta di Susine,
Purea di Lamponi e Ribes Rosse

SMALL POTATO GNOCCHI IN BUTTERED POPPY SEEDS WITH PLUM COMPOTE AND RASPBERRY AND RED-CURRANT PUREE

The key to making *gnocchi* is to have the cooked potatoes as dry as possible. For additional information, see chapter 6.

Yield: 6 servings

20	mature yellow or russet potatoes (do not *use* new potatoes)	9 fluid ounces	plum compote (see recipe earlier in this chapter)
5 ounces	bread flour	9 fluid ounces	raspberry and red-currant puree (see recipe earlier in this chapter)
2	egg yolks		
7 ounces	butter	6	mint sprigs
1½ ounces	semolina flour	to garnish	fresh raspberries
1 teaspoon	grated lemon zest	2 ounces	confectioners' sugar
pinch	salt		
2 ounces	poppy seeds, coarsely ground		

1.   Cook the unpeeled potatoes in boiling water until tender.

2.   Peel the potatoes, and puree immediately with a ricer. Cool.

3.   Stir in the flour, egg yolks, 1 ounce of butter, semolina, lemon zest, and salt. Knead the dough quickly, adding more flour if it seems too soft. The dough should be firm yet pliable.

4.   Roll the dough into finger-width logs, and cut crosswise into 1-inch pieces. Roll each piece on a flour-dusted board with your palm into a small pointed oval. These are the *gnocchetti.*

5.   Cook the *gnocchetti* in plenty of lightly salted boiling water for about 4 to 5 minutes. Remove them as they rise to the surface with a spider or slotted spoon. Drain in a small shallow colander.

6.   Heat the remaining 6 ounces of butter with the poppy seeds in a large skillet. Add the *gnocchetti,* and shake the pan gently until they are thoroughly coated with the poppy seeds.

7.   Arrange 2 neat piles of *gnocchetti* on opposite sides of each hot serving plate. Spoon some plum compote on one side of the plate between the *gnocchetti*, and spoon the raspberry and red-currant puree on the other (see color plate 69). Garnish with mint sprigs and raspberries, dust with the confectioners' sugar, and serve immediately.

Gnocchetti di Patate con Briciole Burrose, Purea di Albicocche e Lamponi

SMALL POTATO GNOCCHI IN BUTTERED BREADCRUMBS WITH APRICOT AND RASPBERRY PUREES

To make the *gnocchetti*, follow the procedure used in the preceding recipe (steps 1 through 5).

Yield: 6 servings

9 ounces	butter	¾ cup	raspberry puree (see recipe earlier in this chapter)
3 ounces	dry, very fine, unseasoned breadcrumbs		
		6	mint sprigs
6 portions	gnocchetti	to garnish	fresh berries
¾ cup	apricot puree (see recipe earlier in this chapter)	2 ounces	confectioners' sugar

1.   Melt the butter in a large skillet until it is clear, and add the breadcrumbs. Toast until lightly browned.

2.   Add the *gnocchetti* to the skillet, and gently shake until they are thoroughly coated with the breadcrumbs.

3.   Neatly arrange 2 piles of *gnocchetti* on opposite sides of each hot serving plate. Spoon the apricot puree on one side between the *gnocchetti*, and the raspberry puree on the other. Garnish with the mint sprigs and fresh berries, and dust with the confectioners' sugar.

Canederli di Patate con Susine alla Tirolese
POTATO DUMPLINGS FILLED WITH PLUMS, TYROLEAN STYLE

To prepare the dumpling, follow steps 1 through 3 in the first *gnocchetti* recipe.

Yield: 6 servings

12	ripe Italian or Stanley plums
6 portions	gnocchetti dough
12	sugar cubes
9 ounces	butter
6 ounces	dry, very fine unseasoned breadcrumbs
2 ounces	confectioners' sugar

1.   Make an incision in the plums just large enough to remove the pits; do *not* cut in half. Remove and discard the pits, and set the plums aside.

2.   Shape the dough on a flour-dusted board into a cylindrical roll about 2 inches in diameter. Cut crosswise into 12 even slices.

3.   Place 1 cube of sugar in the cavity of each whole plum. Encase each plum in a slice of dough. Gently shape each into a ball with your palms. Dust with flour.

4.   Heat a generous amount of lightly salted water in a large shallow casserole, and gently simmer the dumplings for about 15 minutes with the pan half-covered. Do not let the water boil rapidly.

5.   Melt the butter in a large skillet, and add the breadcrumbs. Toast the breadcrumbs until lightly browned and remove from the heat.

6.   Remove the dumplings from the water with a spider or slotted spoon, draining in the spoon for a few seconds. Roll each dumpling in the toasted breadcrumbs.

7.   Arrange 2 dumplings on each heated serving plate. Dust with the confectioners' sugar, and serve immediately. The sugar cubes inside the plums should be completely melted when the dumplings are cut (see color plate 70).

Frittelle di Mele alla Tirolese, con Sciroppo di Lamponi
APPLE FRITTERS, TYROLEAN STYLE, WITH RASPBERRY SYRUP

To make the vanilla sugar for this recipe, place a vanilla bean in a closed container with the sugar for several days.

Yield: 6 servings

4 ounces	flour	1 ounce	vanilla sugar
pinch	salt	2 tablespoons	apricot brandy
1/2 ounce	sugar	1 teaspoon	cinnamon
1/2 ounce	yeast	2 tablespoons	lemon juice
1 teaspoon	grated lemon zest	to deep-fry	oil
1	egg	1 1/2 cups	raspberry syrup (see recipe earlier in this chapter)
1/2 cup	lukewarm milk		
3	Granny Smith apples	2 tablespoons	confectioners' sugar

1.   Combine the flour, salt, sugar, yeast, lemon zest, egg, and milk, and whisk until smooth. Let the batter rest for 30 minutes.

2.   Peel and core the apples. Cut into 12 ¼-inch rings. Place in a small bowl.

3.   Combine the vanilla sugar, apricot brandy, cinnamon, and lemon juice, and pour over the apple slices. Steep for at least 5 minutes.

4.   Dip each apple ring in the batter, and deep-fry in preheated 350° to 375°F oil until golden brown. Drain on absorbent paper.

5.   Spoon some raspberry syrup onto each heated serving plate, and arrange 2 apple rings on each plate over the syrup. Dust with the confectioners' sugar.

Frittelle di Polenta con Composta di Susine
POLENTA FRITTERS WITH PLUM COMPOTE

Yield: 6 to 8 servings

1³/₄ cups	water	¹/₄ cup	water
3 ounces	medium-grain yellow cornmeal	¹/₂ cup	dry, fine breadcrumbs
pinch	salt	¹/₄ cup	finely chopped walnuts
1 ounce	sugar	to deep-fry	oil
¹/₂ teaspoon	finely grated lemon zest	2 cups	plum compote (see recipe earlier in this chapter)
to taste	vanilla extract		
2	egg yolks	2 tablespoons	confectioners' sugar
6 tablespoons	heavy cream	6	mint leaves
1 ounce	butter, softened	to garnish	fresh berries (optional)
¹/₂ cup	flour		
1	egg		

1.   Bring the water to a boil in an enameled or bimetal copper pot. Whisk in the cornmeal quickly, to prevent lumping. Add a pinch of salt, and cook over low heat, stirring frequently, for about 30 minutes. Remove from the heat, and stir in the sugar, lemon zest, and vanilla.

2.   Combine the egg yolks and cream, and mix into the polenta while it is still hot, then mix in the softened butter.

3.   Spread the polenta in a ¹/₂-inch-thick layer on an oiled tray. Cover with plastic, and refrigerate until firm.

4.   Cut the chilled polenta into any desired shape.

5.   Dredge the polenta pieces in the flour. Lightly beat the egg and water to make an egg wash. Combine the breadcrumbs and chopped walnuts. Dip the floured polenta pieces in the egg wash. Coat completely with the breadcrumb/nut mixture.

6.   Deep-fry the breaded polenta until golden brown. Serve with the heated plum compote (any fruit puree also goes well with these fritters). Dust with the confectioners' sugar and decorate with mint leaves and berries if desired.

Pasta di Strudel

STRUDEL DOUGH

Strudels are common in the northeastern part of Italy where Austrian and eastern influences are most strongly felt. *Phyllo* dough is a staple for savory and sweet food preparations throughout the Middle East and southeastern Europe. It was probably introduced into Hungary and the Balkan region by the Ottoman Turks around the sixteenth century.

Essential to this type of dough is its elasticity or stretchability. If properly prepared, the dough can be stretched as thin as parchment paper or even plastic wrap—almost transparent—without tearing.

To achieve this desirable effect, some important factors must be taken into consideration:

- Work in a draft-free area when pulling the dough. Drafts will cause the dough to become too brittle to handle.
- The type of flour used must contain gluten, which provides the dough with its essential elasticity. Given this requirement, a good bread flour is the ideal choice. However, all-purpose flour can produce a decent phyllo dough.
- Before the actual stretching of the dough is begun, be sure to remove all jewelry, rings, and watches, which can easily tear the dough. Long fingernails may do the same if you are not careful.
- Always have plenty of melted butter and a brush on hand.

The only ingredients needed for a basic strudel dough are bread flour, warm water, and a little oil. There are, as with any specialty, variations of this formula in every region that produces the dough. Some recipes include eggs or vary the amount of oil. Some chefs will add a little vinegar, hoping that the acid will denature the protein, rendering the finished product more tender and crisp.

Yield: 1½ pounds (for 24 servings)

1 pound	bread flour
8½ fluid ounces	tepid water
3 tablespoons	olive oil
pinch	salt
1 teaspoon	olive oil
⅓ cup	melted butter

1. Combine the flour, water, oil, and salt. Knead together for 10 minutes until smooth and satiny in appearance. Brush with oil, cover, and rest for 1 hour.

(continued)

2.   Cover the work surface with a clean tablecloth that has been dusted with flour.

3.   Depending on the size of the dough sheet required, cut the dough in half for a smaller sheet and keep the rest of the dough covered.

4.   Start by rolling out the dough just a bit. Then begin pulling the dough very carefully with the fingertips, without tearing it. It is best to have two people pull from opposite sides, grasping the outer edges gently, to prevent the center from becoming too thin in the beginning. The final stretched sheet should be almost transparent.

5.   Once the dough is completely stretched, brush the whole surface immediately with melted butter to prevent it from drying out and cracking.

6.   Arrange the desired filling (see recipes that follow) over the stretched dough, leaving about 2 inches at the top end of the sheet free of the filling so that the strudel can be sealed.

7.   Hold the tablecloth at the end toward you with both hands, and lift it evenly. The strudel should actually roll itself. Brush the portion free of filling at the top with more melted butter to seal.

8.   Place the strudel, seam side down, on a greased baking sheet, and brush generously with more melted butter. Bake in a preheated 350°F oven. The baking time depends on the type and size of the strudel.

Strudel di Mele

APPLE STRUDEL

Yield: 6 to 8 servings

30 ounces	*Granny Smith apples*	*1 teaspoon*	*grated lemon zest*
		¾ cup	*melted butter*
1 teaspoon	*cinnamon*	*3 to 4 ounces*	*breadcrumbs*
1 to 2 ounces	*sugar (adjust depending on the tartness of the apples)*	*1 recipe*	*strudel dough (see preceding recipe)*
		2 tablespoons	*confectioners' sugar*
1 ounce	*raisins*		

1.   Peel, core, and quarter the apples; slice very thinly. Combine in a mixing bowl with the cinnamon, sugar, raisins, and lemon zest.

2.   Heat ½ cup of melted butter in a skillet until it is clear, add the breadcrumbs, and toast until nicely browned with a nutty aroma.

3.   Pull the strudel dough into a 16- by 16-inch sheet, as explained in the previous recipe. Brush the entire surface with melted butter.

4.   Sprinkle the surface with two-thirds of the toasted breadcrumbs, leaving 2 inches at the top free. Combine the remaining breadcrumbs with the apples.

5.   Arrange the apple mixture over the breadcrumbs.

6.   Lift the tablecloth to roll the dough; seal the edge of the strudel with melted butter. Place, seam side down, on a greased baking sheet, and brush with more melted butter. Bake in a preheated 350°F oven for about 35 minutes. Let the strudel rest for 10 minutes before slicing. Dust with confectioners' sugar and serve.

—— *Variazioni* ——
VARIATIONS

Strudel di ciliege (**Cherry strudel**): Follow the recipe for apple strudel, but replace the apples with pitted, halved, dark sweet cherries mixed with 2 tablespoons of lemon juice. The sugar may not be necessary if the cherries are very sweet. Summer fruit are usually very rich in sugars and liquids. This sometimes necessitates adjusting the sugar content and/or draining some of the excess liquid from the fruit to avoid making a soggy strudel.

Strudel di uva (**Grape strudel**): Follow the recipe for apple strudel, but replace the apples with seedless, halved grapes (preferably sour).

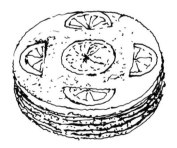

Budino alla Cioccolata con Crema Inglese
STEAMED CHOCOLATE PUDDING WITH VANILLA SAUCE

Yield: 6 to 8 servings

2½ ounces	sweet butter, softened	1 ounce	flour
2 ounces	confectioners' sugar	1 ounce	fresh breadcrumbs or soft cake crumbs
4	egg yolks		
2 ounces	semisweet chocolate, melted and cooled	1½ cups	vanilla sauce (see recipe earlier in this chapter)
4	egg whites		
1 ounce	sugar		
1 ounce	hazelnuts, finely chopped or grated		

1. Cream the softened sweet butter with 1½ ounces of confectioners' sugar. Beat in the egg yolks until thick and foamy.

2. Add the melted, cooled chocolate, and continue to beat.

3. Beat the egg whites and ounce of sugar to soft peaks.

4. Gently fold the beaten egg whites into the egg yolk mixture. Fold in the nuts, flour, and breadcrumbs. Do *not* overwork.

5. Brush individual-size timbales or similar straight-sided 6-ounce metal molds with melted butter and dust with flour. Fill each mold with the pudding to ¼ inch from the rim.

6. Set the molds in a gently simmering water bath. Space them well—using a deep hotel pan for the hot water bath is best.

7. Cover the hotel pan (not each mold) with foil, and steam the puddings over low heat for about 12 minutes. The pudding will rise up above the mold and then recede somewhat.

8. Remove the puddings from the pan, and let rest for a few minutes. Then turn out onto heated serving plates. Dust with the remaining confectioners' sugar, and spoon the vanilla sauce around the puddings.

Glossary

abbacchio: Suckling baby lamb, not yet weaned.

acidulated water: Water that is seasoned with either acetic or citric acid (vinegar or lemon juice), primarily used for poaching artichokes, calf's brains, sweetbreads, etc.

agnello: Lamb.

agnolotti: Ravioli-like pasta, either square or round, from Piedmont, Lombardy, and Tuscany.

agrodolce: Sweet-and-sour.

Alba: A town in Piedmont known for its white truffles.

al dente: Literally "to the tooth"; cooking pasta so as to retain a slight chewiness.

alice: Anchovy.

alla bava: With melted cheese.

all'onda: Literally "wavy"; the creamy texture of well-made risotto.

amatricana: A tomato-based sauce originally from the small town of Amatrice in Latium, with bacon, red peppers, garlic, wine, and Pecorino Romano cheese, usually served with pasta.

anatra: Duck.

anatroccolo: Duckling.

anitra: Duck.

anitra germana: Mallard duck.

antipasto: Literally "before pasta"; an appetizer.

arista: An ancient term for oven. Also refers to a spit-roasted loin of pork.

au gratin: Literally "browned on top"; usually a dish topped with a sauce of grated cheese, breadcrumbs, and bits of butter, then baked in a hot oven or top broiler until a light crust forms on top.

baccalà: Salt cod.

bagna cauda: A hot garlic, anchovy, olive oil, butter, and herb dip from Piedmont, usually accompanied by raw vegetables.

ballottine: A piece of meat, poultry, or game which is boned, stuffed, then usually formed into a cylinder shape before cooking, and served either hot or cold.

bain-marie: A double boiler for preparing and storing delicate sauces.

bard: Wrapping lean meat with sliced fatback or saltpork before cooking to protect meat and retard dryness as a result of exposure to high temperatures.

battuto: Uncooked *pancetta* with garlic, onions, and finely chopped herbs. When cooked, it becomes *soffrito*.

ben cotto: Well cooked; well-done.

bigoli: Venetian term for pasta made from fine buckwheat or whole-wheat flour.

blind baking: Preparing a pre-baked pie or tart shell. Before filling, the pastry shell is lined with parchment or foil and filled with legumes or grains, then baked. Filling is then added and baking is completed.

bombe: A conical or spherical mold usually for frozen desserts.

borlotto: Cranberry bean; a speckled, light brown bean.

bottargo: A Venetian specialty consisting of sun-dried and thinly sliced gray mullet roe, seasoned with virgin olive oil, pepper, and lemon juice.

braciola: A chop, flank steak, or rib chop from veal, pork, or lamb.

braise: A method of cooking usually reserved for less tender vegetables or cuts of meat. In the case of meat, the item is seared, then simmered in a small amount of liquid while tightly covered.

brasato: Braised.

broccoli di rape: Winter broccoli tops.

brunoise: A small dice cut, about ⅛-inch cube, usually for vegetables.

budelli: Pork intestines.

busecca: Tripe stew, Milanese style.

butterfly: Splitting in half without separating. Used for cutlets, chicken breasts, fish fillets, shrimp, etc.

calamaretti: Baby squid.

calamari: Squid, cuttlefish.

calzone: A stuffed pizza that is a Neapolitan specialty.

canestrelli del mare: Bay scallops.

canterelli: Chanterelle mushrooms.

capesante: Venetian term for scallops.

caponata: A southern Italian dish of marinated eggplant and vegetables.

cappone: Capon; a castrated rooster weighing up to six pounds.

capretto: Baby goat, kid.

caramelize: To heat sugars to the point of caramelization. Foods containing sugar (onions, for example) are usually sautéed in hot fat until brown.

carciofo: Artichoke.

cassata: A Sicilian cheesecake *or* an ice cream bombe.

castradina: Mutton.

cervella di vitello: Calf's brain.

chiffonade: A garnish of raw greens (sorrel, basil, lettuce, etc.) cut into fine strips. Usually used for soups or salads.

china cap: A cone-shaped strainer or sieve.

cinghiale: Wild boar.

cocotte: A small round or oval earthenware and ovenproof china dish. Dishes cooked individually in such a container are referred to as "en cocotte."

coda di bue: Oxtail.

colapasta: Colander.

condition: Treatment for omelet and roasting pans to prevent sticking. Initially, an omelet pan is filled with 1 teaspoon of coarse salt which is then heated and rubbed vigorously into the pan's surface. This is thoroughly removed, and a small amount of oil is added to the pan, heated again for several minutes, and then removed with a paper towel. A roasting pan is simply preheated with the oil at 300°F for about 20 to 30 minutes.

cotechino: Large pork sausage, usually boiled and served hot, from Modena.

cotoletta: Cutlet, chop.

coulis: A concentrated liquid or puree derived from cooked game, poultry, shellfish, vegetables, or fruits.

crauti: Sauerkraut.

cremini: Edible wild mushrooms.

crocchetta: Croquette.

crosta: Crust.

crostino: Crouton.

crostona: A large piece of bread fried crisp in oil.

crouton: Stale white bread which has been cut into various shapes and sautéed or fried in fat.

degrease: To skim off the fat which collects at the top of simmering stocks, soups, and sauces. Can also refer to the removal of excess fat from a sauté or roasting pan before saucemaking.

dindo: A turkey cock.

emulsion: Blend of two incompatible liquids, such as oil and vinegar, into a solution. Also, an egg yolk and melted butter combined into a Hollandaise sauce.

fagioli: Shelled beans.

fagiolini: French green beans, *haricots verts.*

faraona: Guinea fowl.

Farce: Meat, poultry, seafood, etc. ground (and usually seasoned) for stuffing.

fegatino: Small liver, chicken liver.

fegato di vitello: Calf's liver.

fegato d'oca: Goose liver.

fonduta: Fondue, melted cheese.

forcemeat: Finely ground meat, game, poultry, or seafood which has been rubbed through a sieve and seasoned.

formaggio: Cheese.

fragola: Strawberry.

fragoline: Wild strawberries.

frattaglie: Animal's entrails, giblets.

Frenched: In the "French style"; a method of trimming where a bone is left intact but completely trimmed of meat and cartilage. Commonly used for chicken breasts, lamb racks, etc.

frittata: Italian omelet.

frittella: Fritter.

fritto misto: Mixed fried seafood, meats, or vegetables.

frutta secca: Dried fruit.

fumet: Highly concentrated and flavored fish or game broth.

fungo, funghi: Mushroom, mushrooms.

galantine: Boned poultry stuffed with forcemeat, pressed into a symmetrical shape, and poached in a seasoned and highly concentrated and flavored chicken broth. Usually served cold.

gallina: Old fowl, stewing chicken.

gamberello: Small shrimp.

gamberetto: Tiny shrimp.

gambero: Medium to large shrimp.

gambero di fiume: Freshwater crayfish.

gamberone: Very large shrimp, prawn.

gelato: Ice cream.

gelato di tutti frutti: Ice cream with different fruit and candied fruits.

genovese: Genoa style.

giardiniera: Literally "gardener's style"; with garden-fresh vegetables.

giuliana: Julienne cut.

glace: A concentrated meat, game, poultry, fish, or seafood broth reduced to a syrupy consistency and used for the preparation of reduction sauces, and for adding potency to sauces and soups.

gnocchetti: Small gnocchi.

gnocco, gnocchi: A special regional type of dumpling, usually prepared from potatoes.

granite: Flavored crushed ices.

gratella: Grilled.

guanciale: Literally "pillow"; a special type of hog fat (bacon) of central Italy.

hotel pan: Stainless steel pan used in steam tables.

infusion: Liquid obtained by steeping herbs, flowers, spices, etc. in a heated liquid. The infused liquid is strained and used for soups, sauces, etc.

interlard: To insert small strips of fatback into lean cuts of meat.

insalata: Salad.

involtino: Roulade.

julienne: Fine strips cut from meat or vegetables usually from $\frac{1}{16}$ to $\frac{1}{8}$ inch thick and from 2 to $2\frac{1}{2}$ inches long.

latte di pesce: Fish milt from the male reproductive gland.

legare: Bind, thicken with a liaison.

lepre: Hare.

liaison: A binding agent that gives body to a liquid or sauce. The most common liaison is a mixture of egg yolks and cream, but may include animal blood or pure starches like arrowroot, tapioca, etc. The latter are first dissolved in a small amount of cold water before being incorporated into a hot sauce or broth.

limone: Lemon.

macèdoine: A mixture of a small diced raw or cooked fruit or vegetables.

macedonia di frutta: Diced fresh fruit for salads or cocktails.

macerate: In general, soaking foods in marinades or liqueurs; usually refers to fruit which is soaked in sugar and liqueur.

mandolino: Vegetable cutter, mandoline.

mangiatutto: Snow pea.

mantecato: Stirred or churned.

mascarpone: Italian sweet cream, or sweet cream cheese.

matterello: Rolling pin.

medaglione: Médaillon, scallop of meat.

médaillon: Food cut into small rounds or ovals. Usually applied to sliced lobster tail, venison loin, or veal, pork, or beef tenderloin.

melanzana: Eggplant.

mezzaluna: A half-moon-shaped blade with handles on either end, used for chopping nuts and vegetables.

mortaio: Mortar.

moscardino: Small member of the squid family.

mostarda: Mustard.

nape, naper: To mask or coat; to cover with a sauce.

nodini: Small cuts of meat from the loin.

noisette: A hazelnut. Also refers to a small round cut from the loin of veal, lamb, or venison, which is slightly thicker than a médaillon. Roasted potatoes shaped like nuts can also be referred to as *noisettes.*

oca: Goose.

olio: Oil.

padella, in: Fried in a frying pan.

paiolo: Untinned copper pot for cooking polenta.

panada: A farinaceous preparation used to bind forcemeats, vegetable terrines, etc. Examples are white bread soaked in milk, choux paste, cooked rice or potatoes, etc.

pancetta: Italian unsmoked bacon, a prime ingredient in *soffrito* and a flavor enhancer for sauces, soups, and many other dishes.

pancetta affumicata: Smoked *pancetta,* mainly produced in Alto Adige.

pancetta coppata: A heavily spiced, cured, unsmoked, rolled bacon.

pancetta fresca: Fresh, uncured bacon.

pancetta stesa: Cured slab bacon.

panna montata: Whipped cream.

papa nero, seme di: Poppy seed.

pappardella: A broad egg noodle; a Tuscan specialty often prepared with rabbit.

passa brodo: Soup strainer.

passatelli: A mixture of breadcrumbs, eggs, and cheese pressed through a ricer, boiled, and used as a garnish for broths.

passa verdure: Food mill.

pasticcio: Pie.

pastone: Flour and water dough, used to seal *cocotte* and ramekin covers.

pavese: Pavia style.

pecora: Ewe.

pecorino: Cheese made from ewe's milk.

peperoncini: Small hot or mild chili peppers.

pescheria: Fishmonger.

pesto: A sauce made of crushed basil, nuts, cheese, garlic, and oil.

piccata: Small, thin slices of meat.

piccolo: Small.

piede di maiale: Pig's foot.

pignoli: Pine nuts.

polipetto: Baby octopus.

polipo: Octopus (or small squid).

pollastra: A young hen, usually six to eight months old; also known as a roasting chicken.

pollastro: A young cock, usually three to four months old; also known as a frying chicken.

pollo: Chicken.

porcino, porcini: Cèpe, cèpes; edible mushrooms of the boletus family.

prosciugato: Dried up.

prosciutto cotto: Cooked ham.

prosciutto crudo: Air-dried, cured ham.

pulcino: Poussin, a Hamburg or baby chicken, six to eight weeks old.

pullman bread: White sandwich bread.

rafano: Horseradish.

ragout: Literally "to restore taste"; a dish with various ingredients lending flavor to each other as a result of cooking, usually a meat or fish stew with uniform pieces.

ravanello: Radish.

reduce: To simmer or boil liquid down to a desired consistency or volume.

rognone di vitello: Veal kidney.

rondeau: A heavy two-handled pot used for stewing, braising, sauce-making, etc.

rotella taglia pasta: Pasta cutter.

roux: A mixture of fat and flour, cooked to a white, blond, or brown tone, used for thickening sauces or soups.

salsiccia: Sausage.

saltimbocca: Literally, "jump into the mouth"; a sautéed veal cutlet (*scaloppina*) with fresh sage and *prosciutto.*

sambuca: Anise-flavored liqueur.

sangue, al: Bloody, extra rare.

sanguinante: Bleeding, rare.

saor: Venetian sweet-and-sour marinade for fried fish.

sauté, sauter: A quick cooking process; browning rapidly in a small amount of hot fat over high heat. (A skinless chicken breast is sautéed over moderate heat.)

sauteuse: Shallow frying pan with sloping sides and a single handle for sautéing.

sautoir: Shallow frying pan with straight sides for sautéing.

scald: To dip in boiling water, or blanch quickly. Also, heating milk to just below the boiling point.

sedano: Celery.

sedano rapa: Celeriac.

semi-freddo: Parfait, frozen soufflé, ice-cream cake.

setaccio: Sieve.

sformato: Soufflé, or firm steamed pudding.

smother: Slow, covered stewing in a small amount of fat or liquid.

soffritto: Literally, "pan-fried"; cooked *pancetta,* garlic, onions, and finely chopped herbs.

sorbetto: Sorbet, water ice.

spider: A metal, coarse- or fine-meshed skimmer with a long handle.

spugnole: Morels.

spumone: Ice-cream bombe with nuts and berries.

stagione: In season.

stampino di ravioli: Ravioli press.

stracciatella: A Roman broth thickened with beaten egg, semolina, and grated Parmesan.

strutto: Lard.

sugna piccante: A spread prepared from peppers cooked in pork lard, a specialty of Basilicata.

suprême: Literally, the "best part" of a product, often refers to a chicken breast.

sweat: To partially cook over low heat without browning.

tacchino: Turkey.

tagliate: Minced.

taglio: Cut.

tajarin: A narrow egg noodle produced in Piedmont.

tartufo: Truffle.

tiepido: Lukewarm.

timbale: From *thabal,* Arabic for drum; a small, flat-topped conical mold.

timballo: Timbale.

tirami-su: Literally, "pick-me-up"; a famous Venetian sweet cake of coffee-soaked sponge cake with rich Mascarpone cream.

tonnato: With tuna sauce.

trifolato: Thin slices of food that are usually sautéed in olive oil and garlic.

trofie: Special Ligurian potato *gnocchi* served with *pesto.*

turn: To sculpt or shape vegetables with a paring knife.

velouté: Literally, "velvety, smooth"; a rich white sauce made from chicken, veal, or fish stock thickened with a blond roux, or a classic soup with the above as its base.

vincisgrassi: A corruption of the name Windischgrätz, an Austrian field marshal whose cook invented a rich lasagne dish with livers, sweetbreads, sausage, and truffles.

zabaglione, zabaione: A dessert in which egg yolks, flavored with sugar and Marsala (or other spirits), are beaten over simmering water until frothy; *sabayon*.

zafferano: Saffron.

zampone: Stuffed pig's trotter.

zest: The grated rind of citrus fruits used for flavoring.

Index